Nathaniel Bowditch and the Power of Numbers

TAMARA PLAKINS THORNTON

Nathaniel Bowditch and the Power of Numbers

How a Nineteenth-Century Man of Business, Science, and the Sea Changed American Life

The University of North Carolina Press *Chapel Hill*

This book was published with the assistance of the Anniversary
Fund of the University of North Carolina Press.

The paper in this book meets the guidelines for permanence
and durability of the Committee on Production Guidelines for
Book Longevity of the Council on Library Resources.

The University of North Carolina Press has been a member of the
Green Press Initiative since 2003.

Cover illustration: Charles Osgood, *Nathaniel Bowditch*, 1835.
© 2006 Peabody Essex Museum. Photo by Mark Sexton.

Library of Congress Cataloging-in-Publication Data
Thornton, Tamara Plakins, 1957– author.
Nathaniel Bowditch and the power of numbers : how a nineteenth-century man of
business, science, and the sea changed American life / Tamara Plakins Thornton.
    pages cm
Includes bibliographical references and index.
ISBN 978-1-4696-2693-2 (cloth : alk. paper)—ISBN 978-1-4696-2694-9 (ebook)
1. Bowditch, Nathaniel, 1773–1838. 2. Astronomers—United States—Biography.
3. Mathematicians—United States—Biography.
4. Industrial organization—United States—History. I. Title.
QB36.B7T55 2016
510.92—dc23
[B]
2015032057

For my daughters, Lydia Sarah and Dora Jane,
And my sisters, Naomi and Ava.

And in memory of my mother,
Edith Sarah Fischgrund Plakins
(February 25, 1920–February 25, 2010).
You have never left us.

Contents

Illustrations

Acknowledgments

Just before he died, Bowditch had all his personal letters burned, though likely hoping that he would be remembered for his contributions to scholarship, he spared his scientific correspondence. Thanks to the many repositories that have kept letters he sent and the papers of institutions with which he was associated, Bowditch could not consign the entire record of his life to the flames. My first debts are therefore to the uniformly helpful librarians and archivists at these repositories: the American Philosophical Society; the Andover-Harvard Theological Library, Harvard Divinity School; the Archives of the Massachusetts General Hospital; the Baker Library, Harvard Business School; the Boston Athenaeum; the Boston Public Library; the Carl A. Kroch Library, Division of Rare and Manuscript Collections, Cornell University; the Countway Library of Medicine, Harvard Medical School; the Harvard University Archives; the Historical Society of Pennsylvania; the Knox College Library, Special Collections and Archives; the Massachusetts Historical Society; the Massachusetts State Archives; the National Library of Scotland; the Phillips Library, Peabody Essex Museum; the Rauner Special Collections Library, Dartmouth College; the Rhode Island Historical Society; the Royal Irish Academy; the Royal Society of London; and the State Library of Massachusetts. I owe a particular debt of gratitude to Irene Axelrod and Kathy Flynn at the Phillips Library; Kimberly Reynolds at the Boston Public Library; and the Massachusetts Historical Society, which supported my work with an Andrew W. Mellon research fellowship. I am grateful as well to Nate and Susan Bowditch, who generously shared with me Bowditch's apprentice diary from their personal collection. At my own institution, the State University of New York, Buffalo, the Interlibrary Loan Office, led by the ever helpful Ann Bouvier, has been invaluable. Thanks go as well to the *Journal of the Early Republic* and the *New England Quarterly* for permission to incorporate materials published in early versions in those journals.

My university has also supported my research, with grants from the history department's Lockwood Fund and with a fellowship at the College of Arts and Sciences' Humanities Institute. The latter presented me with time to focus on writing, with a community of fellow scholars, and with its public lecture series and its sponsorship of a Science Studies Reading Group, genuinely useful forums to present my work. I owe a debt of gratitude as well to my departmental colleagues who have lent their support and assistance in many ways, especially James Bono, Susan Cahn, David Gerber, Erik Seeman, and Liana Vardi. Gail Radford deserves special thanks for the expert historian's eye she lent to the manuscript as it neared completion.

My colleagues in the profession have shaped this project, pointing me toward works of scholarship, sharing their own work, offering feedback to my conference presentations and written drafts, and helping me think about the shape of a biographical project. Much of this interchange can in some way be traced back to my second professional home, the Society for Historians of the Early American Republic, an organization that welcomed me as a graduate student and has ever maintained an unusually hospitable and convivial academic culture. My thanks go to Ed Balleisen, Hannah Farber, Paul Gilje, Myra Glenn, Josh Lauer, Sharon Ann Murphy, Rich Newman, Mary Beth Norton, Craig Robertson, Caitlin Rosenthal, Amy Dru Stanley, Joe Torre, and Rachel Van. My colleagues of many years, Jim Stewart, Chris Clark, Richard John, and Randy Roth, have offered me their powerful intellectual insights and their steadfast friendship. I am ever grateful for both. Randy Roth and Daniel Vickers provided me with enormously discerning evaluations of the entire manuscript, and I have tried to do justice to the issues they raised. Allison Sweeney also reviewed the entire manuscript, and her pitch-perfect editorial guidance helped me strike the right tone and express myself with greater clarity. And Chuck Grench offered me pointed, truly invaluable advice along with his support of the project.

Given the nature of the some of the subject matter, I also sought the help of three quantitative scientists. My cousin Yuval Filmus evaluated the content of Bowditch's mathematical papers. It is always good to have a mathematician in the family, especially one whose talents and loyalties go well beyond mathematics. My dear friend Tony Auerbach argued with me over what it means to be a scientist. I listened, though I am sure we will argue again. And Harvard physicist George Brandenburg generously shared with me his own work on Bowditch the navigator, vetted my presentation of Bowditch's science, and in a particularly thought-provoking exchange reflected on the scientist's aesthetic appreciation of the universe. I am so sorry that he died before I could meet him in person.

My completion of this project casts my memory back to the many teachers to whom I owe so much. My remarkable fifth-grade teacher, Barbara

Livingston, and my equally remarkable high school history teacher, Howard Preston, introduced me to intellectual labor as a realm of curiosity, adventure, and meaning. In college, I was inspired by both the professors and the graduate students in the history of science department. It has been my privilege to cite two of them in this book: Lorraine Daston, whose contributions in Erwin Hiebert's class made a powerful impression on me my freshman year, and Joan Richards, my sophomore tutor who had us reading Henri Poincaré with gusto. In my junior year, Professor Hiebert generously met with me weekly to discuss the *Bridgewater Treatises* that had so captured my fancy, and in my senior year, Shirley Roe shepherded me through my undergraduate thesis. And I will forever be in the debt of my graduate school mentor, David Brion Davis, whose greatness is matched by his kindness.

Several of my family and friends commented on early drafts of this book, sometimes setting me straight on reaching an audience outside of academe. My mother-in-law, Barbara J. Thornton, is no longer here to see her name in print, but she knew she would be among those I would thank. I hope I was able to convey to her the many things for which I owe her my gratitude, not the least of which is the example of intellectual energy and ethical commitment she set for us all. Thank you also to Wendy Hunter, Naomi Plakins, Ava Plakins, Arthur Ziller, and above all, my husband, Jonathan. I owe them, and other friends and family, for far more than their direct help with this book. They have never failed to share my joy in the work of scholarship and to add the joy of being in their company. I have also been sustained by the gifts of friendship and music I receive from the community of our Irish session in Buffalo. A special toast to Jim Dywinski, and a parting glass to Kathy Strachan Englert and Jim Warde.

I dedicated my first book to my husband, Jonathan, with love and devotion. That will never change. I add now the constancy and harmony we sing of—and with—when we sing "Roseville Fair." This new book is in part dedicated to four women—my sisters, Naomi and Ava, and my daughters, Lydia and Dora Jane—more precious to me than I can express. I am ever grateful for their presence in my life.

My parents did not live to see this book completed. Both were characters on a grand scale; it is as impossible to evoke as to forget them. Still, I can thank them. My father, H. Gregory Plakins, M.D., set an example of a person whose deep respect for his work ("a noble profession") meant that he never thought but to honor the highest standards of skill, dedication, and integrity. He recognized and admired those efforts in others, including his daughters, son-in-law, and granddaughters. I am grateful to him for my own commitment to my work as a historian.

But if I have any insight into the past and those who peopled it, it is because of my mother, Edith Sarah Fischgrund Plakins. A person of moral profundity and gay irreverence, she possessed the deepest soul and the lightest heart I will ever encounter. From her, I learned about infinity.

Introduction

In his own day, Nathaniel Bowditch needed no introduction. From the dawn of the nineteenth century to his death in 1838, he was America's foremost astronomer and mathematician. Thomas Jefferson praised him as a "meteor of the hemisphere" in which he lived. James Madison paid homage to his "distinguished genius." His countrymen compared him to Benjamin Franklin and even Isaac Newton, and his name became synonymous with brilliance, not unlike Einstein's is today. Even the juvenile readers of the *Youth's Gazette* could be expected to understand just how difficult a calculation must be that "would have puzzled Mr. Bowditch himself."[1] In fact, Bowditch did make a lasting impact as a man of science, but not in the ways we might assume. The work for which he is best remembered, his *New American Practical Navigator* of 1802, soon became the standard how-to guide for America's commercial and naval vessels, but though it was filled with tables of calculated figures, there was nothing cutting-edge about its contents. His purely scientific publications lacked originality and enduring significance. But when he brought his mathematician's sensibility to America's business, academic, and cultural institutions, he transformed the world of practical affairs. Insistent on order and exactitude, he instituted new systems to organize information and manage office work. Stirred by the unerring regularity of the physical universe, he put forward a vision of the corporation as a clockwork mechanism. If we want to understand the origins of that touchstone of modern life, that cornerstone of modern capitalism—the impersonal bureaucracy—then we must look to Bowditch. He will point us to the role of quantitative science in transforming American life.

Impersonal procedures and institutions are so much a part of our lives that it is hard to recognize that people used to go about their affairs in a different way. Yet something as simple as a printed blank form was long a rarity. Ship's logs mixed nautical information with personal commentary. Loan requests were little more than handwritten letters—if they were written down at all. Institutional record keeping varied with the predilections of the compilers. Enter Bowditch. In Salem, Massachusetts, he distributed printed logbook forms to his fellow ship's officers. In Boston, he insisted his company's potential borrowers fill out printed mortgage applications. In

Cambridge, horrified that the minutes of the Harvard Corporation meetings consisted of "detached scraps," he took steps to standardize and depersonalize the clerical task.[2] Impersonal systems—filing systems, cataloging systems, data collection and entry systems—captured his imagination. Figures did too: paginated records, numbered mortgage loans, museum accession numbers. But the mathematician as executive meant more than a set of office procedures. Bowditch represented corporate bylaws as tantamount to the laws of physics, unbreakable and universal, unaffected by the idiosyncrasies of personal relationships. No, you cannot deposit a check that won't be backed by cash until tomorrow, even if you are one of Boston's wealthiest men. No, you cannot unilaterally decide to waive a needy student's tuition, even if you are Harvard's president. Institutions must run with the same rule-bound regularity as the universe itself. Every corporation, whether a business enterprise, a gentlemen's library, or a college, was a miniature solar system.

In the early nineteenth century, few Americans had the knowledge and reputation to reshape practical affairs according to a mathematically inspired commitment to system and number. It may be hard to imagine in our STEM-smitten society, but even Harvard did not require so much as a basic competence in arithmetic for admission, nor did its faculty pursue original research. Yet Bowditch mastered and then did his best to keep up with a developing body of European mathematical and astronomical scholarship almost entirely unknown to his countrymen. Amazingly, he was entirely self-taught. Between 1804 and 1818 he published essays on topics ranging from comets to pendulums, but his crowning achievement came at the end of his life, between 1829 and 1838: his multivolume translation and annotation of Pierre-Simon Laplace's *Mécanique Céleste*, the Newtonian era's magisterial synthesis of the workings of the solar system. Many admired it. Few read it. His *New American Practical Navigator*, on the other hand, brought him fame—it appears in *Moby-Dick*, and even now editions continue to be printed—but Bowditch considered it merely a *"practical manual,"* offering nothing like the lifelong inspiration he found in Laplace.[3]

Bowditch did not start out to become a man of science, nor was scholarship ever his exclusive focus. After an apprenticeship in a waterfront business and five trading voyages to Europe, the Indian Ocean, and Asia, he settled down in 1804 at the age of thirty-one to head two business enterprises. He first ran a marine insurance company in Salem. Then in 1823 he moved to Boston to run a corporation specializing in trusts and investments. There his long-standing approach to practical affairs developed into something closer to an ideological vision. Working at the center of several institutions with immense economic, social, and cultural power, he exerted his influence at a transformational time and in a transformational place. Even as he ran the largest financial institution in New England, he reformed the administration of Harvard's affairs and set the city's literary and scientific institutions on a similar track toward Laplacian system.

Many recent scholars have associated the emergence of impersonal institutions and the rage for quantification with either a particularly rationalized form of capitalism or the exertion of state control. In the plantation account book, the mercantile credit score, and even the fungible farm mortgage, the abstractions of system and number made profit-seeking practices appear to be natural, agentless operations. Meanwhile, it is argued, government bureaucratic practices and social statistics transformed citizens into subjects of state power.[4] The connections with economic and political agendas undoubtedly exist, but Bowditch's work suggests that the origins of impersonal institutions and their quantifying ways lie, at least in part, outside of a straightforward urge to maximize profits and exert control. It was quantitative science that provided the impulse, model, and working practices for the institutions Bowditch managed. He applied this approach to business and nonbusiness corporations alike. And while the state issued the charters, creating clockwork mechanisms was not on its agenda.

None of this should be taken to mean that the operation of those institutions was ideologically neutral, unrelated to the social realities of their time and place. That would be accepting uncritically the message projected by the image of the mathematician, ostensibly objective as a matter of temperament and intellectual practice, running these operations. No, Massachusetts elites had their own reasons to embrace a Laplacian approach to practical affairs, even if their interest in mathematics stopped with bookkeeping. These reasons were as much ideological as economic but nonetheless critical to their sense of individual well-being and their interests as a class. They found Bowditch's predilection for order and certainty a reassuring counterpoint to the social chaos and economic instability of the antebellum era. Even more important, in the face of competing interests, social conflict, and political opposition—for elites experienced both internal fissures and external hostility—Bowditch's institutions suggested impartiality in the way that only impersonal mechanisms run by a mathematician could. Clockwork corporations promoted the notion that their ways were as natural, immutable, and removed from human concerns as the solar system itself. Their operations were to be understood as the product of mechanically executed rules, not individual or class interest. And since all such corporations, whether an investment firm or a university, were making the same ideological point, all had value for the circles they served.

Though he created impersonal institutions on the model of the Laplacean solar system, the world Bowditch grew up in was anything but impersonal. It would have to be made that way. In his youth during the 1780s and 1790s, links of kinship and friendship sliced through strata of wealth, power, and prestige, creating dense webs of patronage and allegiance. It was precisely such personal ties that afforded Bowditch a path to fame and fortune. Steeped in this intimate world, Bowditch was nonetheless no small-minded provincial. As a man of commerce, Bowditch placed a high value on a cosmopolitan perspective. Merchants believed their uniquely broad outlook on the world gave them a certain authority in human affairs, especially in contrast with those of their countrymen who, they imagined, never glanced up from the furrow they ploughed. What is more, as a man of learning Bowditch sought citizenship in the international Republic of Letters, an imagined community of scholarly inquiry that transcended national, religious, and ideological boundaries. As he voyaged into the Indian and Pacific Oceans to trade goods and across the Atlantic to exchange knowledge, Bowditch's frame of reference was at once as small as a New England town and as vast as the globe.

In adulthood, Bowditch joined the same kind of patrician circles that had once lent him a helping hand. Personal ties continued to be the key to opportunity in these circles, just as they had in his youth, even, we should note, as elite institutions evolved into impersonal mechanisms. That wrinkle warns against oversimplifying the narrative of historical transformation into a tidy before-and-after tale. After all, in Bowditch's youth many Salemites ventured from their close-knit community to conduct business with strangers in faraway places. And in Bowditch's prime elite Bostonians operated in a world of overlapping personal bonds that structured their livelihoods, leisure activities, civic commitments, and social lives. Still, much had changed. Though personal ties continued to matter, they were folded into a network of ostensibly impersonal corporations. And these ties were horizontal ones of privilege, linking members of the top stratum, not vertical ones of patronage that sliced through the social pyramid.

Bowditch's rise in the world had been made possible by just such patronage, but being assisted by the elite had never been the same as being accepted into it. A personal world is not the same as an inclusive one. Even when he became a prominent business executive and scholar of some repute, there were those who questioned whether Bowditch possessed the je ne sais quoi of a true gentleman. If Harvard would not have taught him much math, it would have given him the classical learning that passed for social polish among New England patricians. It might have given him a better sense of how a mercantile aristocracy acted with what they termed "delicacy" in social relations even as they maintained a heavy hand in generating profits. In a nation with no titled classes, officially committed to egalitarianism, membership in a social elite involved the subtlest of distinctions.

Bowditch the voyager, Bowditch the navigator, Bowditch the businessman, Bowditch the institutional reorganizer, Bowditch the gentleman—in the end, he was always Bowditch the mathematician. As an "inquisitive" youth, wrote an early mentor, he "found too much of opinion" in literature, but when he turned to mathematics, "he found from *the power of numbers*," at last, "something sure." Here is the essential key to Bowditch. His love for mathematical order and certainty colored his perspective on all human affairs. It also defined his temperament. Moral gray areas did not exist for him; right and wrong could no more be confused with each other than plus and minus. Stoked by moral self-assurance, he vented his temper in calling out what he perceived as incompetence, venality, or injustice. His tactlessness sometimes alienated his associates, but in many ways his mathematical temperament was congruent with his age. In the decades after the Revolution, partisan allegiances polarized the nation, and Bowditch's black-and-white take on public affairs was hardly out of place. Toward the end of his life his mathematician's perspective overlapped with the Victorian penchant for bisecting the world into opposing categories—right and wrong, civilized and savage, human and animal. His reduction of moral questions to mathematical certainties took on the appearance of virtue. "All who knew him," wrote a close friend, "would as soon have thought of the sun's turning back in its course as of his deviating from the straight line of integrity and truth."[5] Above all, his enthrallment with the precision and certainty of numbers shaped his impulse to systematize the institutions under his control. The result was a model for organizational conduct that had far-reaching implications for American capitalism and American life more broadly.

Mind you, Bowditch was no automaton. He was, as one contemporary stated, "a *live* man." He expressed deep love for his wife, children, and close friends. His letters sparkle with wry humor. Many commented on his characteristic inclination for rubbing his hands in glee, jumping out of his chair with excitement, and giggling with delight. When Lafayette visited Boston,

Bowditch could not resist quitting the steps of the Bank of the United States to run and shout with the celebratory crowd. Horsewhip in hand, he participated in the nineteenth-century equivalent of drag racing through Boston's streets. When his son mingled with French scientists in Paris, Bowditch was not above asking for gossip on their personal lives. He enjoyed two glasses of wine twice a day, an amount he referred to, in a masterpiece of mathematical wit and ambiguity, as his "certain quantity."[6]

But if Bowditch was more than the sum total of his mathematical talents, his course in life was surely defined by their interaction with his times. Had he been born much earlier, his abilities might have led him to navigation or amateur astronomy. Had he been born much later, he might have found a place in the professional infrastructure of universities, observatories, and scientific societies that emerged only after his death. In either case, he would probably be remembered as a skilled calculator but not an original thinker. As it was, his mathematical mind found the opportunity to make a lasting impact. As business corporations powered the rapidly growing New England economy, and the region's charitable and educational corporations bolstered the cultural power of its urban elites, Bowditch's predilection for creating impersonal systems found its uses beyond the world of science. He was indeed the practical navigator, setting a course for a transformed America.

BEFORE WE BEGIN, a word on terminology: the terms "science" and "scientist," "business" and "businessman" would for the most part not have been used in Bowditch's day. "Natural philosophy" and "natural philosopher," "practical affairs," and "man of affairs" or "merchant" are probably the closest analogs, but even here there are problems. What we call science, for example, was divided between natural philosophy (roughly, the physical sciences and mathematics) and natural history (roughly, the life sciences and geology). We limit the use of the term "scientist" to a credentialed individual seeking to generate original knowledge, but in the absence of a science professionalized in the modern sense of the term, these kinds of qualifications did not apply. And where we limit the use of the term "merchant" to one engaged in commerce, Bowditch's contemporaries stretched that term to include men engaged in banking, insurance, real estate, and manufacturing. Nevertheless, to avoid confusion, I make use of both nineteenth-century and contemporary sets of terms.

CHAPTER ONE

Born into Salem

The week Bowditch was born, in March 1773, the front page of Salem's *Essex Gazette* carried the proceedings of a town meeting in Boston—the Revolution was already brewing—but inside the paper the news was mainly from abroad. Readers learned about the "East India business" in Parliament, fires in Paris and Rome, the failure of two banking houses in Amsterdam, the opening of a 300,000-volume library in Vienna, and the sighting of a southern continent by French naval vessels in the Indian Ocean. Even the advertisements spoke of a wider world. Monsieur de Viart informed his "Friends and the Public" that he would soon be opening his dancing school for the season. Someone asked for the return of a stolen copy of Samuel Richardson's novel *Clarissa*, promising "no Questions will be asked." And among the items offered for sale were salt from Cádiz and oil from Florence, Fayal wine and Jamaican rum, Russian duck and Irish linen, and "a large Assortment of English and India GOODS."[1]

Bowditch's seaport birthplace faced the outside world. From Salem vessels voyaged to ports along the North American coast, to the islands of the Caribbean, and even across the ocean to the British Isles, southern Europe, and the wine islands of the South Atlantic. By the eve of the Revolution it was second only to Boston as a New England port. Its 110 vessels employed about 900 men at sea, roughly three-quarters of the town's men between the ages of fifteen and forty-five, while many on shore made a living off the seafaring economy in the town's cooperages and ropewalks, chandleries and counting houses, wharfs and warehouses. And the wealth generated by the fisheries and deepwater commerce spun off other enterprises, from craftsmen catering to the carriage trade to teachers offering night classes in navigation.[2]

Like their town, the Salemites of Bowditch's day were neither isolated nor provincial. In Bowditch's youth his townsmen could catch a glimpse of zebra skins in a merchant's store, pay to see a live elephant, even encounter a native of Madras on the streets.[3] The wealthy and educated among them imported books, fashions, and furnishings from abroad, but cosmopolitan awareness, if not gentility, extended beyond the elite. After all, a good portion of Salem's men had voyaged to places hundreds, even thousands,

Balthasar Friedrich Leizelt, "Vuë de Salem. Salem – eine stadt in Engelländischen America," 177–. Hand-colored etching. The harbor as it would have appeared during Bowditch's childhood, busy with shipping and related maritime activities. Prints and Photographs Division, Library of Congress.

of miles away.[4] Still, if Salem on the eve of the Revolution was a surprisingly global entrepôt, it was also a New England village. Its maritime population looked outward, but also inward to the community shared by 5,000 or so inhabitants, packed into 700 dwellings and shops covering about 300 acres. It was a small world. As Salemites walked the fifty streets and alleys of their town, they must have recognized almost every face. Marriage ties going back decades linked individuals in tight webs of kinship, but even those who somehow escaped the family tree were familiar, encountered in multiple contexts. Crammed together on a neck of land between the North and South Rivers, Salemites turned almost exclusively to each other to conduct most of life's business. There were enemies and outcasts in Salem but few strangers.[5]

Like most of New England in the eighteenth century, the town was a relatively homogeneous place. Almost everybody was white and Protestant and had descended from English families that had settled the town over a century earlier. Whether or not their ancestors had emigrated for explicitly religious reasons, almost all were steeped in Puritan traditions, like the shunning of Christmas as a "popish" holiday and the belief in civic responsibility for the communal welfare. A small minority did not fit this profile. The provincial census of 1776 recorded 173 African Americans, enslaved and free, living in Salem, about 3 percent of the population. There were also sprinklings of French Catholic refugees from Acadia in Nova Scotia and a scattering of recent immigrants from France, Germany, and Ireland.[6]

As elsewhere in the colonies gentlemen and ladies stood apart from the common people. For William Pynchon, a prosperous and well-connected lawyer, the split was between what he termed "people of property" and the "rabble." John Adams experienced that social divide firsthand. He spent an evening at Pynchon's house "very agreeably," drinking punch and wine and smoking pipes of tobacco in the company of other gentlemen. But outside, it was "Popes and bonfires," wrote Adams, referring to the popular, anti-Catholic style of commemorating Guy Fawkes Day, "and a swarm of tumultuous people attending them." There were many who fell somewhere between such genteel circles and the "tumultuous people," of course, respectable artisans, tradesmen, and shipmasters, but all understood that this was a ranked society. Everywhere hierarchy was the reality. In households, men held the authority of masters over wives, children, apprentices, servants, and slaves. At sea, ordinary sailors deferred to the mate, who in turn deferred to the shipmaster.[7]

Still, to describe Salem in 1773 as a place divided by class would be misleading. More important in structuring the lives of all Salem's residents were the lines of patronage and loyalty, personal obligation and dependency that connected people of many ranks, cutting through strata of wealth and status. In this society, individuals were defined above all by their relationships with others. Nathaniel entered this world as a member of the long-settled Bowditch family, but also as an Ingersoll, a Gardner, and a Turner, and to a lesser but real extent, as one linked to the families with whom *those* families had marriage ties. There were other kinds of ties that involved the granting of favor and the obligations of loyalty. What were termed "friends," people with wealth and influence who acted as patrons to those below them, used their money and connections in what amounted to a secular act of grace.[8]

Nathaniel Bowditch is remembered as a citizen of the world. His *New American Practical Navigator* instructed men in how to range far and wide. His work as a mathematician launched him into the international Republic of Letters. But as a child, then an apprentice, and finally as a young man, Bowditch felt the influence of family and social relationships formed over decades in Salem. Events played an important role in his early life too. He was, after all, born on the eve of a revolution and a war. Even so, it was his ties to others in the community and to generations past that structured his experiences and his possibilities. They provided him with an entrée into commerce, navigation, and mathematical scholarship, the worlds of numbers.

NATHANIEL'S PARENTS, HABAKKUK Bowditch and Mary Ingersoll, were married in 1765. The groom had just returned from a four-month trading voyage to Barbados, commanding the forty-ton schooner *Swan*. In taking to the sea he was following in the footsteps of his father and grandfather, as did his three brothers. Mary's father had also been a shipmaster, like generations of Ingersoll men before him. Despite the similarities in background, the two families were actually following different social trajectories. Mary Ingersoll had been brought up amidst the telltale marks of a certain level of gentility—a tea table, chinaware, "Delph glass and yellow ware," a looking glass, a clock, and "sundry pictures"—but her family never approached the level of wealth or distinction achieved by Bowditch forebears in the first half of the eighteenth century.[9] Bowditch success had come with profits in trade and marriages into the highly ranked, well-connected Gardner and Turner clans. Nathaniel's grandmother, Mary Turner Bowditch, had grown up in a mansion (later made famous as the model for Nathaniel Hawthorne's *House of the Seven Gables*) that was the scene of elegant entertainments, complete with fine porcelain, silver, and glass—and three slaves to do the work. It was all part of the gentry's new focus on the display of taste and refinement—wit and polish for men, and for women the polite "accomplishments" of music, French, and needlework. As a young girl, Mary Turner had been sent to Boston for just such a finishing.[10] Had her husband, Ebenezer, maintained that level of wealth and status, their son Habakkuk might never have married the more modestly placed Mary Ingersoll. But by midcentury Ebenezer Bowditch was in serious debt, and by the time he died in 1768 he owed more than he was worth. Probate documents designated him as "gent/shopkeeper": the "shopkeeper" a snapshot of a downhill trajectory but the "gent" an indication of the staying power of family social status in this era.[11]

Early in their married life Habakkuk's seafaring career was typical of Salem's prerevolutionary shipmasters: voyages to the West Indies in vessels laden with manufactured goods, produce, fish, lumber, and barrel staves for the islands' plantations and their enslaved laborers, returning with sugar and molasses. For Mary the long voyages meant caring for a growing family on her own. For Habakkuk they meant facing a variety of dangers and decisions. At sea, winter winds ripped sails, broke masts, and blew vessels off course, and in summer vessels ran the risk of being becalmed. Whatever season, ships leaked, and sailors pumped. Once in the islands, the shipmaster turned merchant, with the responsibility of disposing of his freight and acquiring a return cargo on favorable terms. Before leaving Salem, captains like Bowditch met with those who had invested in the outbound cargo to discuss where the vessel should head, what prices the goods should bring, what commodities should be bought, and at what price. But it was understood that the captain must be given leeway to make decisions on the spot. Usually conditions demanded that he sail from island to island looking for the most favorable markets. Yet nobody liked to linger in the Caribbean—the possibility of succumbing to a tropical fever was too great.[12]

With an eye to just such risks, Habakkuk joined the Salem Marine Society in 1767. Its main purpose was to offer relief to shipmasters fallen on hard times and, even more ominously, to their widows. Membership was limited to men who actually commanded vessels. Mere owners did not face the same risks, and common seamen may have lacked the wherewithal to make the required monetary contributions into the common "box" used for assistance. Probably more critical was the esprit de corps these shipmasters shared, a common identity and pride born of years of experience, the achievement of considerable skill, and the autonomy and authority that came with command. Consider all that went into the term "shipmaster." These were men who kept the title "Captain" for life—and beyond. The gravestone of Mary's father, Nathaniel Ingersoll, was chiseled with the title, as Habakkuk's would also be.[13]

In 1773 more immediate dangers awaited the Bowditch family: first a smallpox epidemic and then the sometimes violent fallout of anti-imperial resistance. By the time Nathaniel was two years old, all-out war had come to Massachusetts. The town did not start off as a hotbed of Patriot sentiment. Salemites must have had "an opiate administerd [sic] to them," wrote Samuel Adams a few months before Nathaniel's birth. In 1774, Governor-General Thomas Gage believed he was escaping the white heat of anti-British agitation when he moved the provincial capital from Boston to Salem, but by this time the town's anti-imperial factions, led by merchants like Richard Derby, were gaining the upper hand. When Gage ordered the arrest of the Patriot Committee of Correspondence, Derby insisted that even if bail were set at "the ninetieth part of a farthing," he would not pay. Hundreds, perhaps thousands of men pledged to rescue the committeemen, and after Gage left town somebody set fire to the store belonging to the man who had conducted the arrests. In February 1775, when Gage ordered troops into Salem to seize hidden ordnance, townspeople pulled up the drawbridge to prevent their pursuit of the weapons across the North River. Some sat atop the upraised bridge "like hens at roost," hurling epithets at the redcoats. The cannon got away.[14]

Less than two months later another military mission to confiscate weapons, this one to Lexington and Concord, ended in mass casualties. Independence was well over a year away, but violence was here to stay, and with it terror. Families like the Bowditches took note. On June 17 Salemites saw a "most prodigious smoke" rising from the direction of Boston. It proved to be the terrible result of the Battle of Bunker Hill. "The destruction of Charlestown by fire (for it is all burnt down)," wrote Salem physician Edward Holyoke, has "struck our People at Salem with such a panic, that those who before thought our Town perfectly safe, now are all for removing off." Then, in early October a British admiral ordered the HMS *Canceaux* "to destroy and lay waste" the coastal towns of Massachusetts, calling for "the most vigorous Efforts to burn the Towns, and destroy the Shipping in the Harbours." Only a few days later, the HMS *Nautilus* fired its guns at a church spire in nearby Beverly; from across the harbor 200 hastily assembled Salemites responded with cannon. Later that same month the news of the near total destruction of Falmouth (now Portland), Maine, reached Salem. "We are yet in Salem but how soon we may be drove out I know not," wrote Elizabeth Smith. "We are in daily expectation of a Fleet which is sent out to distroy and burn all the seaports towns [*sic*]."[15]

Once all-out war came the conditions of everyday life quickly deteriorated. Traders and fishing craft dared not venture out, and the entire maritime economy crashed. Many in the maritime workforce signed on to naval vessels and privateers and then were captured or killed. With vessels unable to venture in, and virtually no farming activity in the port towns, basic supplies ran low. "Salem people quarrel for bread at the bakers," reported William Pynchon in the spring of 1777. By autumn, the Commonwealth was providing grain to Salem's poor. "We crawl about and exist," wrote Pynchon, "but cannot be said truly to live.[16]

Sometime during this season of fear and want, probably in the fall of 1775, when Nathaniel was two and a half years old, the Bowditch family moved three miles inland to the neighboring village of Danvers. They were hardly alone in their flight. In 1773 the town's population numbered 6,000; by 1776 only 3,800 remained. The village lay far enough from the coast to be safe from bombardment but still offered ready access to Salem by river. The Ingersolls had roots in Danvers, and the family may still have had relations there. The Bowditches did not return to Salem until early 1779.[17] Nine people occupied the small dwelling: Habakkuk and Mary, Habakkuk's mother—a lifetime away from the Turner mansion of her youth—and six children, of which Nathaniel was the fourth. As an adult Nathaniel recalled the Bowditches as "a family of love." A favorite memory, perhaps because it seemed to anticipate his career in astronomy, featured his mother holding him up to the window in her arms, sharing a view of the new moon. Many years later he often took his own children to see the cottage, and as they rode by he would point out the window.[18]

In fact, Nathaniel seems to have been something of a favorite among his parents and siblings. "My mother loved idolised & worshipped me," he told his daughter on his deathbed, "my Father put me upon a pinnacle my brothers & sisters loved me dearly, they all smiled upon me, they would do anything for me." He was especially fond of his older sister Elizabeth and of his younger brother William, a young man noted for his "distinguished piety," "good information," and considerable mathematical talent and knowledge.[19] If Nathaniel was indeed the family pet, it may be because from an early age it was clear he was unusually bright. "Learning came natural to him," recalled one woman from Danvers, "and his mother used to say that he would make something or nothing." His first teacher, a woman who ran a dame school across the village crossroads from the Bowditch cottage, took notice of the three-year-old. "He was the best scholar she ever had," the teacher's niece reported. "He learnt amazing fast, for his mind was fully given to it. He did not seem like other children; he seemed better."[20]

Even in Danvers, though, there was no escaping the impact of war. These were lean years for the Bowditch family. Some days the family sat down to meals of little else than potatoes.[21] The break with Britain also affected something of particular concern to Nathaniel's mother: the ability to raise her children in the Church of England. Mary's Anglican faith had long distinguished her from her neighbors. Most Salemites were either orthodox Congregationalists, emphasizing sin, depravity, and the awful power of the Divinity as revealed in Scripture, or what would later be termed Unitarians, who focused instead on the human capacity for benevolence and self-improvement and a God whose beneficence was clearly legible in the Book of Nature. Habakkuk was a Unitarian, but Mary saw to it that her oldest children were baptized at St. Peter's Anglican Church in Salem. When the Revolution forced the church to shut its doors, Mary did her best to continue raising her children in this tradition. Along with her love of truth, affection for family, and faithful discharge of her duties, she was remembered above all for her piety. To be sure, in this era just about any "good" woman was characterized in these generic terms, as if women's narrowly proscribed roles both defined them sufficiently and limited the differentiation of their personalities, but Mary may in fact have gone beyond the usual level of religious devotion. It took some gumption to stick to the Church of England in Puritan Massachusetts, let alone Revolutionary New England.[22]

Wartime brought a special hardship to the Bowditch family, for at some point after the summer of 1775 Habakkuk went to sea, was captured by the British, and was held as a prisoner in Halifax, Nova Scotia.[23] There conditions for the POWs were atrocious. "Herrings salted in Casks will best convey some idea of the situation of the prisoners," wrote one British official. "Deaths are extremely frequent." Men who had been held in Halifax recalled the "barbarous Manner" in which they had been treated: smallpox victims who were "almost rotten with the disorder," sick men housed "indiscriminately with the well," "scanty allowances" of "tainted, dirty, mouldy" food, the prevalence of scurvy and "gaol distemper," and heat so intense that even the guards "often fainted away" during their two-hour shifts.[24] By 1777 Habakkuk had managed to escape, pleading his "most necessitous and distressed circumstances and Situation" to a sympathetic sea captain (a distant Ingersoll relative originally from Salem), but upon his return to Danvers he was not able to put his family on solid economic ground.[25]

It was the Ingersoll men who picked Habakkuk up and put their brother-in-law back on track for prosperity. In their era personal relationships defined both identity and opportunity. Mary's brothers had been involved in wartime privateering since 1776, as commanders, officers, crew members, owners, and bonders. Sometime in early 1779 the Bowditches returned to Salem, most likely so that Habakkuk could be brought in on what had proven to be a very lucrative enterprise.[26] There is no evidence that Habakkuk ever sailed in a privateer, but the account books of a Salem auctioneer document his related activities. As "agents for the privateer brig 'Monmouth'" in 1779, "Capt. Jonathan Ingersoll and Capt. Bowditch" sold off an "East India packet" and various goods to Salem merchant Elias Hasket Derby, Richard's son, for over £8,000. A year later "Capt. H. Bowditch" profited from the sale of a sloop captured by a privateer commanded by Samuel Ingersoll. Habakkuk's fortunes went up and down, but at war's end he could point to modest but substantial holdings in a dwelling, warehouse, wharf, vessels, and trade goods.[27]

When Habakkuk Bowditch married Mary Ingersoll in 1765, he must have felt that his family connections were more valuable than hers. His father had married into the powerful Turner family, and his grandfather into the equally influential Gardner family. Key Bowditch relations held major royal appointments, including Nathaniel's great-uncles Joseph Bowditch, clerk of the Essex County courts, and John Turner, who sat on His Majesty's Provincial Council. But the Revolution elevated some families while depressing others. In their drive to create an exclusive clan on the model of British aristocrats, imperial officials like Bowditch and Turner had intermarried within their tight circle and eschewed maritime trade as coarse. Their hold on social and economic power relied on the single thread of imperial connections, and with the Revolution that thread snapped. Meanwhile, the Ingersoll siblings were connected to wealthy and powerful families with Patriot credentials. Hannah Ingersoll had married a cousin of Timothy Pickering, a leader of the Revolution in Salem and eventually adjutant general and then quartermaster of the Continental Army. Even more important connections were provided by Jonathan Ingersoll, whose marriage to Mary Hodges connected him to Boardmans, Ropeses, Ornes, Silsbees, and above all, the biggest players in the new Salem political order and maritime economy, the Crowninshields and Derbys.[28] In time Nathaniel's future would be shaped by these wider connections, but meanwhile the Ingersoll bond pulled Habakkuk and his family out of whatever financial squeeze they had found themselves in Danvers.

Once the war ended, though, Habakkuk entered a downward spiral from which he never recovered. Tax records reveal a steep decline from 1784; within five years he was propertyless. His wife died in 1783, when Nathaniel was ten, and two years later his mother. Mary Turner Bowditch had advanced her son money before, and though she left him some family property, Habakkuk soon sold it off, and she was no longer around to use her own inheritance to tide him over here and there. In 1789 the Salem Marine Society voted "that the Treasurer should pay out of the Box unto Capt. Habakkuk Bowditch the sum of forty shillings lawful money he being under necessitous circumstances." A year later, hoping for a patronage job in the U.S. Customs Service, he asked his fellow marine society members to "Speak to the officers of the revenue for any Small place for me." Where kinship left off, perhaps "friendship" could pick up. But the customs job never materialized, and Habakkuk received the society's charity for the rest of his life, a small supplement to a scanty living as a cooper. When he died in 1798 his meager possessions totaled little over $100 in value, mostly the fish hogsheads he had made with his own hands. His debts ran well over his paltry assets, and his estate was declared insolvent.[29]

Many factors contributed to Habakkuk's fate. Privateering opportunities ended with the war. By then he was too old to return to the sea, especially if imprisonment in Halifax had broken his health. Perhaps his captivity had been so harrowing as to knock the wind out him forever. He had endured the death of his wife, his mother, a daughter, and a son. In the end he took to drink. "Habb. Bowditch had a paralytic stroke for which he has been preparing himself by many years of intemperance," wrote his minister William Bentley in 1798 after the fatal event.[30]

Habakkuk's downfall made a lasting impression on his son. "It was the misery of the last years of our grandfather's life," wrote Nathaniel's own son William, "which, no doubt, led father to express to us the wish that he himself might not live too long."[31] What did it mean to live "too long" in Salem at the end of the eighteenth century? We have no evidence that Habakkuk suffered through chronic illness. He seems to have been struck down at once by a stroke. To be sure, he was widowed in his forties, and lost two children in his fifties. Poverty he certainly endured in his last years. Perhaps, if he was a drinker, he felt some degree of humiliation at the loss of public esteem. But we cannot be certain that such humiliation was his lot. The charity dispensed by the Salem Marine Society was an act of brethren who well understood that even the best of shipmasters could themselves be mastered by the seafaring life.

Habakkuk's greatest misery stemmed from his sense of failure. It was not so much that he was poor and obscure as that he was not born to be such. He had "outlived those prospects of usefulness and happiness," wrote his grandson, "which, upon his entrance into life, seemed to be within his reach." He was, after all, a Bowditch—and a Turner, and a Gardner, and all the other families into which these families had married. No one in eighteenth-century Salem was an isolated individual, bound to rise or fall according to his own talents and efforts. William Bentley transmitted just this sense of embeddedness when, in his records of parish deaths, he summarized Habakkuk's earthly existence: "Habbaccuc Bowditch, Capt. Apoplexy, 61. Eighteen years married. He has left three sons and two daughters. His mother daughter of Col. Turner. He left a very worthy family."[32]

SOMETIME IN 1783 ten-year-old Nathaniel left Master Watson's school, where he had been a pupil for three years, and went to work for his father in the coopering business. At age twelve he started as an apprentice clerk at Ropes and Hodges, a ship chandlery in Salem. Until he reached the age of majority (twenty-one), in 1794, Nathaniel lived in his master's house and worked in a waterfront shop that outfitted ocean-going vessels with everything from ship's nails to cooking pots. Here he would learn the ways of maritime business, selling wares, and keeping the books. It was the basis of a long and successful career in trade and finance.[33]

John Ropes and Jonathan Hodges were brothers-in-law. Theirs was a business arrangement typical of an era when individual entrepreneurs and family partnerships, rather than corporations, dominated the economy.[34] They were also related to Nathaniel. Jonathan Ingersoll, the boy's maternal uncle, had married Hodges's sister Mary in 1775. In deciding what to do with his son, Habakkuk must have once more looked to the resources his wife's family provided him. Even when Ropes and Hodges dissolved their partnership "by mutual consent" in 1789, sixteen-year-old Nathaniel continued working for family, for the successor business was run by Samuel Curwen Ward, and in 1790 Ward married Jane Ropes, sister of both John Ropes and Elizabeth Ropes Hodges. A family relationship to the chandlery partners was no guarantee of good treatment, but it seems that Nathaniel was lucky. Ropes was recalled for his "kind, gentle, and generous manners and spirit," while Hodges was remembered for his charity. John Ropes's second wife, Hannah, played a particularly important role in the motherless boy's life. Treating him with "kindness and affection," he recalled, she "attended to many little matters by which his comfort was thus much promoted." Her conduct had been "always that of a mother whose affection never knew any interruption or abatement."[35]

Nathaniel's everyday life as an apprentice took place in this family setting. In a diary he kept at the age of sixteen, he often referred to his master's family as his own: "Mr Wellcome Arnot & Lady came to Town, keep at our House," "Ch[urch] Society at our house," and "dined at Br^o Joseph's," the last likely a reference to Jonathan Hodges's sibling. There are glimpses as well of domestic tasks, as when Nathaniel "put bacon in [the] Chimney," and "made Soup." And there was a good deal of socializing: "drank tea at Mrs Prince's," "dined at David Green's with Capt Francis & Lady &c, &c," "went to pay the wedding visit to Mrs Maryat." He even attended the elegant evening dances offered at the town's assembly room, including one where George Washington was the guest of honor. If Nathaniel participated in the rites of this genteel social life, it was largely because as a Bowditch he was connected to families worthy of respect and not a little notice. Even the "best" families had their share of poorer relatives, and those relatives partook of the standing that came with their kin connections. Lines of favor and obligation reached down through the ranks of Salem society.[36]

For the young Bowditch apprenticeship did not mean drudgery. When the 820-ton *Massachusetts*, soon to sail for China, was launched from a shipyard south of Boston, Nathaniel was there. He attended a Wednesday evening performance of "the Oratorio, or, Concert of Sacred Music" in Boston. He even accompanied a Salem acquaintance on a weeks-long journey to Connecticut and Rhode Island. It was not just significant events that found him absent from the chandlery. "Fine day," wrote Nathaniel on an April Thursday. "Went to Moore hill." On an early September Tuesday, he "went to Whitings a fishing."[37] But Nathaniel was no "idle 'prentice." There was as yet no rigid division between working and nonworking hours or strict time discipline in the workplace. Later in life he would become a stickler for punctuality, but he grew up in an era before timekeeping devices were widespread enough to change the pace of life and work. In 1786 William Bentley noted that Salem's school convened at one because at that time, "Public notice is given through the town of the hour, & as there are few clocks & watches in the Town in families, there can be no other certain time of collecting."[38]

Nathaniel worked along Salem's busy waterfront, at the foot of Neptune Street, adjacent to Union Wharf.[39] The chandlery carried almost everything required to maintain and repair vessels, provision a crew, and otherwise carry on the business of an ocean voyage. In a record of merchant and shipowner Elias Hasket Derby's account with Ward's chandlery, penned by Nathaniel, we find all manner of goods. There were tools: hammers, handsaws, chisels, axes, sail needles, gimlets, ship scrapers, cooper's vices, tar brushes and scrub brushes, caulking irons, and marking irons. We find several colors of paint, bits and pieces of hardware, and specialized kinds of rope. For the cook there were iron pots and frying pans, coffee pots and coffee mills, fire steel, bellows and cord wood, a "Cooks axe," and bushels of corn and beans. Chandleries also carried materials for record keeping and correspondence, everything from logbooks to sealing wax. Sophisticated nautical instruments would have been sold by a skilled craftsman specializing in their fabrication, but log lines and hour glasses for calculating a ship's speed were available, as were compasses and speaking trumpets to communicate with passing vessels. There were fish hooks to supplement the dull diet of salted meat and dried peas, and there was brimstone to fumigate the vessel of vermin and disease.[40]

Much of Nathaniel's work was paperwork, especially important because businesses in this era depended so routinely on dealing in noncash payment and extending credit. In his multiple transactions with Ward in the spring and summer of 1791, Derby put something toward the account at the end of May, when he paid with half a chest of tea, but the account was settled with a cash payment in August. Such record keeping called for accuracy in totaling pounds, shillings, and pence—despite the Revolution, this was still the currency of record—a tidy hand, and careful attention to the particulars of multiple small transactions. Calculation of any sort had long been Nathaniel's forte, and his penmanship more than passed muster. As for attention to detail, one anecdote suggests that he acquired his later methodical business habits the hard way. In that story, a customer purchased a pair of hinges, but when he returned a few days later to pay for them—note what we would consider the lackadaisical attitude toward prompt payment—there was no sign of the transaction in the chandlery's books. Anxious to return to his work on a mathematical problem, Nathaniel had put off the task and then forgotten it altogether. "From that day on," the moral lesson ran, "he made it an invariable rule to finish every matter of business which he began, before undertaking any thing else."[41] If the story is true, it shows not so much a disorganized mind as one that had yet to learn how to pursue two distinct lines of intellectual effort, a challenge he soon mastered and put into his practice his entire life.

Keeping business records is not just a matter of temperament and application, of course. It is also a practice that requires training. Early in 1784 Nathaniel began to study bookkeeping. His teacher, Michael Walsh, instructed his pupils by having them copy large chunks of Daniel Dowling's *Complete System of Italian Book-keeping* into notebooks, a standard pedagogical technique in this era when books could be expensive or unavailable altogether. Bowditch's notebook was a homemade affair. It consisted of leaves of paper, hand ruled to resemble a ledger, and sewn together with a brown paper cover. On the cover we see a young boy's pride—"Nathaniel Bowditch his book & pen"—and a glimpse of his new situation—"Mrs. Ropes."[42] Inside the notebook, though, it was all business. Pupils copied the classic trio of bookkeeping documents. First came waste books, or daily records of transactions. The cardinal rule governing their use was that transactions had to be entered as they occurred, the rule Bowditch had not yet internalized when he neglected to note the purchase of hinges. Then came journals, in which the daily records of the waste book were organized into debits and credits; and finally ledgers, which grouped into separate accounts the debit and credit records for each person with whom the merchant dealt and each branch of trade in which he engaged. The point was not to analyze the profitability of an enterprise—this was eighteenth-century bookkeeping, not modern cost accounting—but to keep track of myriad transactions with many individuals in multiple ventures.

Still, these transcriptions taught more than record keeping, for the model documents recreated the complex dealings of a hypothetical merchant based in Dublin. This imaginary Irishman bought goods from home and abroad, shipped goods on his own vessels, consigned goods to others, invested in yet other shipping, contracted for marine insurance, loaned money, drew on his own accounts in London and Paris, and entered into partnership with others to form a joint stock company. He traded in everything from tea to tallow, hides to hops, barrels of beef to barrels of claret. He bartered, paid cash, and dealt in the bewildering variety of bills and notes that spelled credit transactions in the eighteenth century. He worked with local shopkeepers, masters of vessels, and foreign sales agents. His trade embraced ports in England, France, Spain, and Italy. More than an introduction to bookkeeping, then, the *Complete System* introduced boys like Nathaniel to the entire world of international commerce. They would then be ready for entrance into a merchant's counting house or some other kind of mercantile enterprise, if not in the same sense as Dowling's Dublin merchant, whose first waste book entry recorded £2,000 "from my Father in ready Money and Bankers Notes to begin the World."[43]

Nathaniel learned how to keep the books, but most of the stories of his days in the chandlery focus on his work with the slate. It was the pure operations of numbers, not their uses in commerce, which captured his imagination. He "always kept a slate by his side," wrote his son, "and, when not occupied by the duties of the shop, he was busied with his favorite pursuit of arithmetic." In the summertime, when the top part of the shop door was open to catch an ocean breeze, the apprentice "was frequently seen by the neighbors ciphering, while his slate rested upon the half-door of the shop." "Every moment that he could snatch from the counter," wrote one of his eulogists, "was given to the slate." One customer was said to remark to his wife that "I never go into that shop but I see that boy ciphering and figuring away on his slate, as if his very life depended upon it." Nathaniel spurned "the intrusions of frivolity," "selfish indulgences," and "artificial excitements," all to study numbers.[44]

Of course we know that Nathaniel was not a dull boy in the least. This was the same apprentice who "went to Whitings a fishing." In his teens he joined a young men's debating society and took up the flute. And though he later claimed to have never seen the launch of a vessel, and doubted "that such a sight, or any thing like it, should be able to draw him away from his books," his apprentice diary records his miles-long journey to see the launch of the *Massachusetts*.[45] Still, throw out the all-work-and-no-play

Nathaniel and you still have a boy with a precocious interest in and ability for numbers. Even before he became an apprentice, anxious to go beyond what his older brother had taught him of mathematics, he begged his schoolmaster to teach him more. Eventually Master Watson gave him an arithmetic problem, one the teacher assumed was above the beginner's abilities (allegedly to serve him right), and when Nathaniel solved it Watson accused him of cheating, an "indignity and act of injustice" that persisted as a "bitter, almost vindictive" memory for decades. Later, when he was fourteen, Nathaniel's younger brother told him there was "a mode of ciphering by means of letters." Stumped, and consumed with curiosity, he begged to see the book. "The boy did not sleep that night," wrote his son, so "delighted" was he to learn the secret of algebra. The title page of the notebook he used to record his discovery reads "NATHl BOWDITCH HIS Book//Augt 23d 1788//I began to learn Algebra, on the 1st of August 1787." In it, he copied hundreds of pages on everything from quadratic equations to logarithms.[46]

For a boy destined to become one of the early republic's outstanding mathematicians, Bowditch's years as a chandlery clerk might seem like the wrong kind of apprenticeship. Shouldn't he have been groomed for college and a career in science? But when we consider the world of mathematical knowledge and practice as it existed in late eighteenth-century America, we will see that the Ropes and Hodges apprenticeship made sense after all. Little in that world resembled our own, not the nature of universities, not the kinds of people engaged in scientific pursuits and the types of knowledge they pursued, not the sorts of people with mathematical knowledge, not the kinds and purposes of that knowledge.

In the Salem of the 1780s, college could mean only one place: Harvard. Not until 1800 would a Salemite graduate from a different institution. But Harvard then was not what it is now. In Bowditch's youth it focused on educating boys for the learned professions: the ministry, law, and medicine. What the professions held in common, what made them learned in the sense of that era, was their grounding in a thorough knowledge of Latin and Greek. Only the classics, it was widely held, could discipline the mind, cultivate the faculties, and impart the intellectual authority and social polish required of clergymen, lawyers, physicians, and statesmen. Accordingly, the school Salem supported to prepare boys for Harvard was called the Grammar School, referring to instruction in Latin grammar. It did not teach mathematics. Why would it? Not until 1803 did Harvard require so much as a basic competence in arithmetic for admission.[47]

Once a student enrolled at Harvard, the focus remained on the classics. In 1727 mathematics and science had received a boost when merchant Thomas Hollis endowed a chair in these fields, but still there was no advanced mathematical curriculum. Isaac Greenwood, the first Hollis professor, taught his classes with his *Arithmetick Vulgar and Decimal*, subjects we now cover in elementary school. His successor, John Winthrop, was a serious scholar, publishing in the most prestigious scientific journal of the English-speaking world, the *Philosophical Transactions* of the Royal Society in London, and winning election as a fellow of that society. Winthrop brought much of this sophistication into the classroom, even teaching fluxions, the term Isaac Newton gave to the method of calculus he had developed, but it was not to last. By the 1780s, when Samuel Williams and then Samuel Webber took over, underclassmen studied arithmetic and geometry, and seniors algebra; calculus largely disappeared. At the turn of the nineteenth century, recalled a graduate of that era, the textbook in use began with "numeration" and went no farther than elementary spherical astronomy, but "nine tenths of every class had broken down in quadratic equations." So it is no surprise that in 1802 the Harvard-educated members of Boston's elite Society for the Study of Natural Philosophy realized that if they were to pursue their common interest, they needed to brush up their knowledge of fractions and to begin the study of algebra.[48] It was possible to receive advanced mathematical training at Harvard in Bowditch's day, but it was hardly an obvious reason to attend that institution.

Nor did Harvard's Hollis professors provide a model for an academic career in mathematics. Winthrop, Williams, and Webber followed their graduation from Harvard with ordination in the ministry. The fact is that in eighteenth-century America there was no such thing as a professional mathematician or scientist, at least not in the modern sense. That is, there were no individuals who pursued scholarly research into these fields—or any other, for that matter—as their primary occupation. There was no Isaac Newton, no Edmund Halley, no Nevil Maskelyne, Britain's Astronomer Royal. Harvard's Hollis professor was there to teach, and not even to teach mathematics and science as ends in themselves but only to instill an appreciation of the perfection and beneficence of God's handiwork.[49]

To the extent that postrevolutionary Americans were aware of professional mathematicians and natural philosophers, they understood that such men were to be found in the Old World, at its universities or, better yet, its lavishly funded, often government-supported scientific societies and

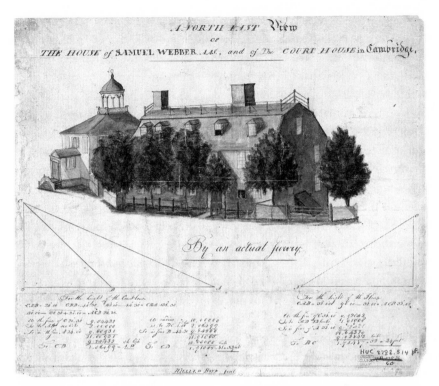

William Boyd, "A North East View of the House of Samuel Webber, A.A.S., and of the Court House in Cambridge, by an Actual Survey," Harvard mathematical thesis, 1796. Executed by a Harvard senior, the perspective drawing attests to the elementary nature of most mathematical instruction at the college in this era. HUC 8782.514 (60), Harvard University Archives.

observatories. In Bowditch's youth, any Salemite who read the local newspaper would have caught glimpses of this world. The notices of mathematicians were fleeting, a quick mention of a study of magnetism "handled in a mathematical and masterly manner by Mr. Euler," a brief notice of the death of "Mons. d'Alembert . . . one of the ablest, if not the first mathematicians of the age." The real superstars were the astronomers. Nathaniel may well have read that the "celebrated Herschel" had finished his forty-foot reflecting telescope, that "our great astronomer, Mr. Herschel, has lately discovered three volcanos [*sic*] in the moon," and that this discovery was "the subject of praise in every learned society in Europe." We must wonder if the fourteen-year-old apprentice came across the account of William Herschel as a "very extraordinary self-taught philosopher" who had started off as a "fifer on Coxheath" and ended up a "great favourite at court."[50]

If not professionals in the European sense of the term, there were nonetheless learned gentlemen who took an interest in things mathematical and scientific. These were well-educated amateurs, usually college-trained clergymen, physicians, and lawyers, with here and there a man of leisure, including wealthy planters and an occasional merchant. For such men a polite interest in all branches of study went along with their status as gentlemen and their desire to be included in a cosmopolitan, transatlantic world of learning, what contemporaries referred to as the Republic of Letters. As conceptualized, this global republic encompassed learning in all its branches and transcended national boundaries and ideological and religious differences. It was celebrated as a zone of free inquiry and communication, realized through the exchange of ideas in learned societies, learned publications, and written correspondence among its members. At least theoretically, the Republic of Letters transcended class boundaries as well—merit alone was to matter—but in practice the level of learning required to establish one's merit tended to require some degree of social station. Hence citizens of the republic tended to be gentlemen.[51]

In America Thomas Jefferson is an obvious example of this kind of person, but Bowditch's Salem furnished its own such men. Physician Edward Holyoke (Harvard '46) kept daily weather records, observed celestial phenomena with his telescope, published medical papers, and corresponded with English chemist Joseph Priestley. The Reverend John Prince (Harvard '76), the "philosophical mechanician," turned the skills acquired as a pewterer's apprentice to fabricate microscopes and air pumps. The Reverend William Bentley (Harvard '77) mastered more than a dozen languages and assembled a 4,000-volume library from around the globe. He was the rare, perhaps unique American who could write in his diary that he had sent his "Dolland [telescope] to Sheik Ahmet," a correspondent in Yemen.[52]

We should note that their brand of gentlemanly science required little in the way of quantitative skill, and that was just as well, given their limited mathematical training. Today we are used to thinking of science and mathematics as going hand in hand, but science was structured and pursued differently then. The branch known as natural history, which encompassed living things and their physical environments, was largely a matter of observation. Here Americans might establish themselves with some authority, for they could exploit the geographic specificity of the phenomena under study, in their case, New World plants, animals, and rocks. Natural philosophy, comprising mathematics, physics, and astronomy, presented other opportunities based on a New World location. Observations of celestial phenomena like eclipses and comets vary from place to place, as do weather phenomena, so astronomical and meteorological observers from all corners of the globe have something unique to report. The role of experimentation in natural philosophy likewise opened up some space for Americans. Benjamin Franklin's experimental work on the nature of electricity won him recognition in Europe, culminating in his election as a fellow of the Royal Society. But it was not quantitative. As an adult Franklin had taught himself arithmetic and geometry, but he had gone no further. He read Newton's *Opticks*, which stressed observation and experimentation, but not the work on which Newton's fame rested, the mathematically challenging *Principia*. He would not have been able to understand it.[53] Bowditch could see no one in his corner of the world who exemplified a link between mathematical talents and the gentlemanly world of science.

Much more obvious models for a boy with unusual mathematical ability were those individuals belonging to the now extinct category of mathematical practitioners. These men, who were not college educated, functioned as jacks of all mathematical trades. They took on a variety of tasks that demanded advanced mathematical knowledge: surveying, mapmaking, and navigation; the publication of almanacs, along with the requisite astronomical calculations; and instruction in mathematical techniques, including trigonometry, gauging (the technique of calculating the volumes of barrels), and dialing (used to generate accurate sundial faces). Many also fabricated what were then termed "mathematical instruments"—such practical tools of the trade as nautical and surveying instruments—and so-called philosophical apparatus, a category that included telescopes, microscopes, barometers, and air pumps, as well as such demonstration devices as orreries and planetaria. Some also made clocks.[54]

In Bowditch's America, the most famous of these practitioners was the self-taught David Rittenhouse of Philadelphia.[55] Closer to home was Boston's Osgood Carleton, who, from the late 1780s, offered instruction in a range of mathematical subjects, prepared maps, drew up boundary lines, published an almanac and an arithmetic textbook, and offered public lectures on astronomy. Salem did not have anyone near the stature of Rittenhouse, or even Carleton, but it did have a nautical and surveying instrument maker named Daniel King who taught mathematics and used an electrostatic machine to demonstrate the "wonderful and surprizing Operations in Electricity."[56]

To Americans of the late eighteenth century, mathematics was simply not the stuff of a learned career. It might be linked with a craft, as with Daniel

King. Above all, it was a vocational skill most commonly associated with commerce. Before arithmetic was linked to reading and writing in the three R's of nineteenth-century America, it was linked with penmanship and bookkeeping as the core triad of mercantile training. Mathematical knowledge beyond arithmetic was called for mainly by those seeking instruction in navigation and surveying. The people who taught an advanced mathematical curriculum in Bowditch's youth were not Harvard professors but private instructors offering specialized courses, often at night. In 1772, for example, Salemite Charles Shimmin proposed to teach "Writing, Arithmetic, Book-keeping, Square and Cube-Root, with their Use, Algebra, Geometry, Conic-Sections, Trigonometry, Rectilinear, logarithmically, instrumentally, &c. Navigation ditto, Surveying by various Methods and different Instruments, Guaging [*sic*], Dialling [*sic*], Projection of the Sphere (in plane), Geography, the Use of the Globes, Perspective, Spherical Trigonometry, Astronomy, Fluxions, &c."[57]

From the perspective of the 1780s, then, it made the most sense for Nathaniel to pursue a career in commerce and navigation, where his skill with numbers would be put to its most common uses. At Ropes and Hodges, and from his lessons in bookkeeping, he would learn the ins and outs of commerce, and many a boy moved from this kind of apprenticeship to a career at sea. Meanwhile, he began to study navigation with Samuel Smith, no ordinary old salt. Smith had once been in the Royal Navy, likely as a sailing master, where he would have taught navigation to midshipmen. William Bentley recalled him as not just "the best master [of navigation] that ever I knew," but also a man with "a great fondness for mathematical studies." In fact, navigation was all about mathematics. Using the kinds of precision instruments made by the likes of Daniel King, navigators made terrestrial and celestial observations and then processed these observations using advanced mathematical skills—plane and spherical geometry, plane and spherical trigonometry, and logarithms—to calculate geographical positions on land and sea. Even Nathaniel's lessons in astronomy were purely mathematical; there was no discussion of stars or heavenly bodies or the solar system. "My boy, you have a taste for these things," Smith is said to have told Nathaniel. "Keep on studying, and you will be a great man yet."[58]

Nathaniel's three navigation notebooks were made by hand.[59] The bindings were hand sewn and had no proper covers, yet they were sources of pride and objects of care. "Navigation and Astronomy," reads the cover of the first notebook, "owned/By/Nathaniel Bowditch of Salem In County of Essex & State of the/Massachusetts Bay/New England/November the eighth one thousand Seven hundred & Eighty Six." An ink flourish punctuates the title. Already we see signs of his punctilious approach to organizing information and his patience, even his pleasure, in processing large quantities of numbers. The almost 400 pages are paginated, and Bowditch has created a table of contents. There is a prefatory list of "Characters used in This Book." Included also are copies of several tables used for nautical calculations, with painstaking transcriptions of hundreds of digits. He was thirteen years old and already taken with numbers and systems.

Bowditch's notebook also reveals his awareness of the gentlemanly science practiced by Harvard professors and their ilk. He recorded observations made by "President Willard" and "Professor Sewall" and those made on the transit of Mercury "by President Willard & Mr Caleb Gannett at Cambridge at presidents house." During the same period that he studied navigation he also undertook his study of algebra. Some of the material, such as on logarithms, overlapped, but algebraic equations belonged more to the academic world of President Willard than the maritime world of Mr. Samuel Smith. Though he may not have realized it yet, his future lay in both worlds. For now, though, he could have only the vaguest conception that mathematics existed apart from its practical applications. So as he was studying navigation, he was also learning surveying.[60]

With this vocational instruction, Bowditch moved closer to the ranks of mathematical practitioners. He fabricated a sun dial, a barometer, and a Gunter's quadrant, an instrument used by navigators to measure the angles of celestial objects. None of these survive, but what does is an almanac he produced in 1789.[61] To prepare it Nathaniel had calculated the dates and times of the solar and lunar eclipses that would take place in 1790, along with the year's sunrises and sunsets, phases of the moon, and tidal movements. But it was not all mathematics. In the monthly tables he included several saint's days, along with Candlemas and Whitsun, days that in Puritan New England only Episcopalians recognized. Though he would soon join William Bentley's Unitarian meetinghouse, Nathaniel was apparently still hewing to his mother's Anglicanism.[62] He also incorporated dates significant in the new republic's patriotic calendar, giving particular emphasis to New England. Alongside Washington's birthday and Independence Day came the battles of Lexington and Bunker Hill, the closing of Boston's port, the destruction of the tea in Boston harbor, the discovery of Cape Cod, and the founding of Harvard. But Salemites were as cosmopolitan as they were provincial. The almanac informs us when Boston burned but also when Lisbon shook in a great earthquake, when John Calvin was born but also when "Mahomet" died. We see also his awareness of the larger world of science: the birth of Copernicus and the death of Newton, and two more recent events covered in the Salem newspapers: the hot-air balloon crossing of the English Channel and Herschel's discovery of a new planet.[63]

Bowditch was soon asked to put his new knowledge to work. Jonathan Hodges tapped him to divide an irregularly shaped field he owned with another man into two parts of equal areas. Although the apprentice accomplished the task "with the most minute accuracy," the co-owner was wary of being cheated and hired a practicing surveyor to make his own division. Nathaniel was "indignant at the suspicions entertained in regard to his own result" and "could not help feeling a malicious pleasure when he found that the gentleman alluded to received for his half part several square feet less than he was entitled to."[64] The story is not unlike the one about the schoolmaster who accused him of cheating. It displays the same moral indignation, touchy sense of personal honor, ill will disguised as righteousness, and even pettiness, all of which we will see many times again. But it is an even better illustration of Nathaniel's utter confidence in his mathematical abilities. The surveyor's results did not lead him to question his own, only to gloat over the unfavorable consequences they held for the man who had questioned his ability and integrity. Mathematical and moral certitude went hand in hand. It was an equation Bowditch would make all his life.

IN HIS LATE TEENS, Bowditch "threw music aside for mathematics," forsaking the flute.[65] He had long been cyphering and calculating, of course, but now his mathematical knowledge ascended to a new level and assumed a new place in his life. Earlier he had picked up mathematical skills the same way other Salem boys headed for counting houses or merchant vessels did, through evening lessons and instruction manuals. All this was vocational learning. But now he was to gain access to a world of scholarship that would change his life. Books were the key.

The apprentice clerk was living in the Nathaniel Ropes house, and as a learned judge and a colonial gentleman, Ropes had accumulated a significant library. Bowditch sampled some of the library's literature and poetry, but the one work that consumed his interest was *Chamber's Cyclopedia*, a multivolume "universal dictionary of arts and sciences," a product of the Enlightenment confidence in the ability of humankind to systematize all knowledge and of educated men to grasp the entire range of learning. He "read through the whole of" it "without omitting an article" and copied all the mathematical entries into a notebook.[66] In the summer of 1788 Nathaniel gained a second introduction to the world of learned mathematics and science. Nathan Read, a young Harvard graduate, discovered that Nathaniel was spending Sunday evenings at his apothecary shop in the company of Read's shop assistant, Bowditch's former schoolmate. Nathaniel was not socializing; he was reading the apothecary's books. "On perceiving his insatiable thirst for knowledge," Read recalled, "I offered him the loan of any books in my possession, & I particularly recommended to him Simson's Euclid, Enfield's Institutes of Natural Philosophy & Ferguson's Astronomy." These were not original works of scholarship, only texts used to teach these subjects to gentlemen with no previous training, but Bowditch was "highly delighted" with them. He soon "made himself master of the Mathematical, Philosophical & Astronomical books" in the collection.[67]

So far, Bowditch's entrée into the world of mathematics and natural philosophy had been fortunate, but not fortuitous. He had the connections with which to parlay his interest and skill into access. Nathaniel Ropes's well-stocked library was open to him because he was a respectable member of the family. Family may have also played a role in Read's decision to extend a helping hand, for he was soon to marry the granddaughter of Joseph Bowditch, Habakkuk's Tory uncle. But then came an element of genuine serendipity. By sheer luck, a magnificent collection of over 200 volumes of advanced science and mathematics ended up in Salem. What was originally the private library of an Irish chemist was auctioned off in nearby Beverly as part of a cargo seized by a Patriot privateer. It was bought by a consortium of college-educated clergymen and physicians, including Salem's John Prince and Edward Holyoke, for the bargain price of £858, or about $435. Soon after, they established the Philosophical Library, with membership available only to those who purchased an expensive share and whose applications were approved unanimously by current members. Bowditch did not have that kind of capital, but he did have the right friends.[68]

In 1791 Nathan Read, admitted to membership the year before, suggested to John Prince that Bowditch be granted free access to the library. He met with a receptive audience. Prince had his own scientific pursuits, and he had once been an apprentice himself, so he took a special interest in the boy. So too did another recently admitted member, William Bentley. Years earlier Bentley had baptized Nathaniel's three younger siblings, and Habakkuk had just formally become a member of his East Society. But Bentley, polymath and gossip, would not have missed a boy with unusual mathematical abilities and interests under any circumstances. "Dr. Bentley used never to pass the store," wrote Bowditch's son of the chandlery, "without stepping in, to talk with his young friend." The son of a Boston carpenter, Bentley had been able to realize his own intellectual ambitions only through the patronage of his wealthy maternal grandfather. Perhaps he saw a kindred spirit in the young clerk. At any rate, by the time he was eighteen Bowditch had "secured to himself the gratuitous and invaluable assistance of the two ablest instructors whom the town then contained," Prince and Bentley. Along with Read, he could count them as "among his warmest friends and patrons." So when the proposal came before the library's proprietors, he was in.[69]

The collection must have come as a revelation to the talented young man. Unlike Read's library of textbooks for mathematically unsophisticated audiences, this library contained works by active scholars written for other active scholars. The original collection consisted almost entirely of the serial publications issued by the most important learned societies of Europe, including Britain's Royal Society, France's L'Académie Royale des Sciences, and Berlin's Preußische Akademie der Wissenschaften. Almost as soon as they established the library, its members began to add to its collection, sometimes by donating books, in other cases by purchasing them from London. By the time Bowditch was granted access, the collection included treatises by such major figures as Isaac Newton, Joseph Priestley, and Johann and Jacob Bernoulli. Bowditch borrowed the volumes and copied anything that had to do with mathematics, over 2,000 pages of material, into twenty-one notebooks.[70]

Once Bowditch saw what the world of European mathematics and natural philosophy was all about, he realized that he would have to learn Latin, the universal language of Western scholarship. Many works in the Philosophical Library, including Newton's *Principia*, were in Latin. So too was a copy of Euclid's *Elements* his brother-in-law gave him as a present around the same time.[71] Meanwhile, courtesy of William Bentley, Bowditch got his own copy of the *Principia* as a permanent loan.[72] Bowditch first requested assistance with Latin from some local college graduates, but they were stumped by the specialized scientific vocabulary. Then, as Bentley explained, Bowditch "soon comprehended the nature of a technical language, and how distinct it might be from the general language, especially when accommodated to modern sciences." Mastering Newton, in other words, was not the same as mastering Cicero. Still, some help was needed. Bentley himself stepped forward. So too did Frederick Jordy, a newly arrived German fleeing the Haitian Revolution who was giving Bentley lessons in his native language. Then, when Bowditch observed that much of the latest mathematical research was coming out of France, he turned to Jordy for French lessons.

At first Bowditch butchered the pronunciation—he insisted he only wanted to learn to read the language—but he eventually learned to speak it as well. As it turned out, that dual fluency would serve him well in his dual life as a man of global commerce and cosmopolitan learning.[73]

THE EARLY REPUBLIC is known as a time during which ordinary people experienced a new desire and ability to acquire knowledge. In the wake of the Revolution, many Americans felt that rank should proceed from merit, not inherited position or social connection, an outlook that encouraged self-improvement and upward mobility through self-education. Literacy rates rose dramatically, reaching nearly universal levels in New England. Even as the imports of books and periodicals from England continued, American printing presses produced a flood of print, and not just more print but new genres of print—novels, magazines, and self-instructors catering to ambitious young men on the make. Peddlers combed the countryside with packs full of books, and townsfolk turned to bookstores and lending libraries.[74] Salem was no exception. In 1789 Salem printer John Dabney advertised hundreds of volumes for sale or loan at his new bookstore at affordable prices. In the colonial period only a man like Nathaniel Ropes had access to such a collection, but after the Revolution ordinary Salemites wanted in. Even as an apprentice Bowditch could have come up with the few pence it took to borrow John Ward's *Young Mathematician's Guide; Being a Plain and Easy Introduction to the Mathematicks* or John Theophilus Desaguliers's *Mathematical Elements of Natural Philosophy*, a popularization of Newtonian science.[75]

We might place Bowditch among this burgeoning group of postrevolutionary self-improvers—certainly he had the desire to educate himself—but there are key differences. Bowditch's self-education entailed the kind of sponsorship that recalled an older order of social connections more than an emerging one of individual merit. John Dabney would take the money of any self-motivated striver, but gaining access to the *Philosophical Transactions* required a personal entrée. As long as he sought only what contemporaries celebrated as "useful" knowledge, Nathaniel did not need this network of contacts. Michael Walsh would teach him bookkeeping, Samuel Smith would teach him navigation, and John Dabney would loan him the *Young Mathematician's Guide*. Even less practical knowledge could be considered useful if it imparted information and social polish used to advance in the world. Desaguliers's explication of Newton might be useful in this way, but not Newton's *Philosophiæ Naturalis Principia Mathematica*. No, Bowditch's self-education in the Philosophical Library's collections was not undertaken in the classic postrevolutionary spirit of self-advancement. He was no longer seeking mathematical skills with vocational utility. Instead, the library opened his eyes to the production of original mathematical knowledge, revealing a world of scholarship that barely existed in America and could not be the realistic object of practical ambition. But to a mathematical creature like Nathaniel Bowditch it was irresistible.

Long after Bowditch had become famous, William Bentley described his young protégé's attraction to mathematics. Nathaniel had been an "inquisitive" youth, he wrote, and "not possessing the means for a public education, he directed himself by the best helps he could find." Here we can imagine Nathaniel in Ropes's library. He "attended to belles letters," wrote Bentley, "but found too much of opinion to be able to satisfy himself of the sure principles by which the questions could be determined." Then "in his researches he found from *the power of numbers*, in his first lessons, something sure."[76]

Bowditch was not the only one to be drawn to mathematics for the certainty it offered. "In a cloudy state of existence," George Washington wrote in 1788, "where so many things appear precarious to the bewildered research, it is here"—in "the science of figures"—"that rational faculties find a firm foundation to rest upon." Jefferson was drawn to numbers for the same reason: they were a welcome contrast to the ambivalence and ambiguity that marked his life. The certainty of Newtonian science rubbed off on all quantitative practice, such that Daniel Dowling described even bookkeeping as a "Science, whose Principles are so simple and solid, whose Conclusions are so certain and evident," that "the very Speculation is no less pleasing than the Practice is profitable." But nothing could beat the original referent. Mathematics "is valued for its extensive usefulness," wrote Colin MacLaurin in his *Fluxions*, one of the Philosophical Library's books, "but has been most admired for its evidence; mathematical demonstration being such as has been always supposed to put an end to dispute, leaving no place for doubt or cavil." The mathematical vision of predictability and certitude was aesthetic or even spiritual in nature. Dowling used the word "pleasing"; MacLaurin, the word "sublime."[77] It was a vision that enthralled Bowditch for his entire life and that would drive his transformation of American institutions.

CHAPTER TWO

Parts Unknown

Until he reached the age of majority, Nathaniel Bowditch had never traveled farther than Connecticut and had never been to sea. Then in January 1795 he set sail on the ship *Henry*, serving as the vessel's clerk in its year-long voyage to the Indian Ocean and back. Over the next six years he would make four voyages that took him to Spain and Portugal, the Philippines, Indonesia, and Réunion, an island east of Madagascar. One day he had seen nothing beyond coastal New England; the next he was on his way halfway around the world to see places he had only heard or read about and people he could only imagine. He responded with the mix of provincialism and cosmopolitanism typical of port city dwellers in an age of sail, but his job was not to observe but to transact business. In Salem, as in other trading communities on both sides of the Atlantic, business affairs had long been conducted largely among known quantities, but after the Revolution the commercial environment was changing rapidly. Perpetually concerned with who could be trusted, especially when distances were great and information scarce, merchants traditionally sought to do business with members of their families, friends, or those whose integrity had been vouched for by reliable associates. Even commerce with the town's long-standing foreign markets—primarily the West Indies, with some transatlantic ports—put Salem merchants and captains in contact with familiar agents. Bowditch's voyages epitomize a new kind of commercial enterprise undertaken in the postrevolutionary era, one that meant making deals with men who were not just unknown but also different, strangers in every sense.[1]

Major political events, both at home and abroad, forced the transformation in Salem's commercial strategies.[2] The first such challenge was posed by national independence. Whatever the shortcomings of the imperial system, it had guaranteed Americans ready access to the British West Indies, the mainstay of their foreign commerce. Now, as citizens of the United States, they were no longer welcome to trade in Britain's colonial ports. They would have to adjust to pursuing maritime trade as outsiders to the world's great commercial empires. They called on non-British markets in the Caribbean and opened trade with Baltic and Mediterranean ports. No longer bound to respect the East India Company's monopoly on British trade with the

East, they also explored new trade routes beyond the familiar confines of the Atlantic basin. Boston specialized in the China trade, rounding Cape Horn to bring back fabulously valuable cargoes of tea. Salem took another tack. Its leading merchant families—the Derbys, Crowninshields, Grays, and Silsbees—saw their opportunities in the Indian Ocean basin, and they sent their vessels around the Cape of Good Hope.

Then came a second challenge. Between 1793 and 1815 Britain and France were engaged in almost constant warfare, not just in Europe but around the globe. As neutrals, Americans were theoretically free to sail the world's oceans, but the legal distinction did not always hold in practice. British and French warships and armed privateers from both sides boarded American merchant vessels. If convinced the Americans were operating as neutral carriers, they would allow the vessel to continue on its way, but if they believed the Americans were trading with the enemy, or that the crew consisted of enemy nationals, they might seize the vessel and its cargo and capture its crew. Even more alarming from the sailors' perspective, American seamen suspected of being British by birth could be impressed into service in the Royal Navy. Still, as with the challenges presented by the Revolution, new political conditions presented opportunities. British and French trading vessels, and those of their European allies, took to the seas at their peril. At any rate, the warring powers were having a hard time maintaining any sort of merchant marine, because tens of thousands of their sailors found themselves conscripted into their navies. Into this vacuum stepped American traders, none more enthusiastically than those from Salem. Though not immune from search and seizure, Americans were still in the most advantageous position to transport cargoes around the globe, from far-flung colonial possessions in the Atlantic, Indian, and Pacific Oceans to America and Europe. Even for the common sailor the risk of impressment might be worth it, because the maritime labor shortage had raised seamen's wages to an unprecedented level.[3]

This period, between about 1785 and 1807, is often termed Salem's maritime Golden Age, and it was indeed an age of spectacular commercial expansion. Between 1784 and 1810 the town's registered ship tonnage, the measure of a merchant vessel's carrying capacity, increased over fourfold. In 1784 there were two wharves in Salem harbor; twenty years later there were thirty. Between 1791 and 1801 over 1,500 vessels entered Salem from foreign ports, and they paid duties amounting to almost $3 million. In the following decade 1,758 vessels entered, and their duties came to over $7 million.[4] Streets lined with newly built, elegant houses spoke of the influx of wealth. If only for a generation, Salem emerged as a truly global city. For all the growth, though, the basic structure of Salem society and tenor of daily interactions remained the same. It was still a town of elites, commoners, and the "rabble," bound together in a complex web of personal connections.

THE KEY TO Bowditch's appointment as the *Henry*'s clerk was the *Henry*'s owner, Elias Hasket Derby. Derby had inherited a small fortune from his father, the patriot merchant Richard Derby, but he had made his own fortune in wartime privateering and postrevolutionary trade with the West Indies, Europe, and Asia. Ultimately he focused on commerce with the Indian Ocean: coffee from Mauritius, then known as the Île de France, and the nearby island of Réunion, earlier called the Île de Bourbon; sugar from Manila; pepper from Sumatra; and textiles from India. That trade routinely turned profits of 100 percent. "Wealth with full tide flows in upon that successful man," wrote William Bentley. By the time he died in 1799, Derby was worth a million dollars, perhaps the first American to leave that kind of money.[5]

It is useless to wonder when Bowditch first attracted Derby's notice, for at no time in the boy's life did the two not have *some* connection. Let us count the ways. They were distantly related by marriage: Derby's mother, like Nathaniel's aunt by marriage, was a Hodges. Derby bought a piece of property from Habakkuk. He purchased ship's goods from Samuel Curwen Ward's chandlery and must have looked over the accounts and receipts penned by the apprentice clerk. In the compressed world of maritime Salem, where Ward's chandlery lay a quick saunter along the harbor from Derby's waterfront home, and hard by the wharves where Derby ships anchored, it is hard to imagine that the merchant never set foot in the shop. Then there was Derby's connection to Nathaniel's maternal uncle. Jonathan Ingersoll had captained privateers and trading vessels for Derby, and in 1785 he returned from Cape Town with intelligence that the French were allowing foreign vessels to trade freely from the Île de France, a rarity in a region dominated by European monopolies. That island soon became the pivot point in Derby's far-flung Indian Ocean trading empire. By the time Bowditch completed his apprenticeship, Derby could draw a direct line from his wealth to Bowditch's uncle.[6]

Most immediately, in the summer of 1794, a long-time Derby captain named John Gibaut hired Bowditch, who had just come into his majority, to assist him in conducting a survey of Salem. Almost certainly it was Bentley, Gibaut's instructor at Harvard and a longtime friend of the Gibaut family, who recommended the young mathematical whiz for the job.[7] Years later, when Bentley and Bowditch were not on speaking terms, the Salem minister insisted that his sometime protégé claimed far too much credit for the survey, that it was Gibaut who "gave every angle, directed every calculation, & actually made every projection." But toward the end of his life, when bygones were bygones, Bentley clarified that while Gibaut took the observations, Bowditch did the calculations. "His enquiries had been directed to every combination of numbers," he wrote, "and while he left the projections to his friend, he was the oracle of every thing that figures could report to the company."[8] Bowditch was paid twenty-seven pounds for his work, but the real payoff was the invitation to sail with Gibaut. After a quarrel, Derby replaced Gibaut with Henry Prince, but he decided to keep Bowditch on. "From this moment," it was said, Derby "was the determined friend and patron of Mr. Bowditch."[9]

By the 1790s it was not unusual to tap a young man with no nautical experience for a position of responsibility at sea. In the colonial era skill in seamanship and navigation had been the paramount qualifications for such an opportunity, and Salemites like Habakkuk Bowditch worked their way up from common seaman to mate to master. Now, in the postwar world, the ability to conduct business in an unprecedentedly global, complex, and uncertain environment became essential. Many voyages had multiple legs, and trading ventures often involved novel commodities, unknown middlemen with different customs and laws, and foreign languages. Markets were global, competition fierce, and the risks as prodigious as the potential rewards. Under such circumstances business experience could loom as large as traditional nautical skills. The new position of supercargo, the vessel's business agent outside the chain of maritime command, arose as an adaptation to these new realities.[10]

Bowditch was in fact advancing in the mercantile world in a way typical of the era. Young men tapped for mobility in maritime trade often came from families related to their patrons. Whether the sons of merchant princes, shipmasters, shopkeepers, or craftsmen, they got their start with business experience, not the acquisition of nautical skill. First came a portside apprenticeship as a clerk, perhaps in a merchant's counting house, perhaps in a waterfront business like Ropes and Hodges. Then came a shipboard stint as a captain's clerk—Nathaniel's *Henry* post—tending to the paperwork, assisting in conducting business in port, perhaps taking a turn as a hand at sea. A promotion to supercargo or, with training in navigation, to a mateship might follow. Either position might lead to a captaincy. Eventually

came a return to dry land, to pursue commerce as a so-called sedentary
merchant. Some captains still came up the old-fashioned way, the nautical
route "through the hawse-hole," but Bowditch's commercial route "through
the cabin window" was more common.[11] He came with the usual personal
connections, bookkeeping experience, and familiarity with maritime commerce, along with a few extras: knowledge of navigation, skill with numbers,
and a working knowledge of French and even some Spanish. All these would
serve him well.

The ship *Henry* was built for Derby in 1791. It measured eighty-five feet
in length—a little less than the distance between home plate and first base
on a baseball field—and twenty-five in width. We use the word "ship" as a
general term, but in the age of sail the term was more specific, denoting a
three-masted, square-rigged vessel. In the mid-eighteenth century Salemites
had pursued the Atlantic trade mainly with double-masted schooners and
brigantines, some 100 tons or more, but these farther flung voyages required
even larger brigs, or the yet larger ships. At 190 tons—the tonnage measured
carrying capacity, not weight—the *Henry* was a bit smaller than many other
Derby vessels but not essentially different from other American vessels trading in the Indian Ocean. It was certainly smaller than the massive Indiamen
of the European trading monopolies, which routinely exceeded a thousand
tons, but American merchants preferred the smaller vessels. In the unpredictable and risk-laden world of global commerce, spreading investments
out in this manner provided more flexibility to capitalize on unexpected
opportunities while minimizing the chances of losing everything.[12]

The *Henry* carried thirteen men to the Indian Ocean and back, under
the command of Captain Henry Prince. Like Bowditch, Prince had been
apprenticed to a cooper and did not go to sea until he turned twenty-one.[13]
Within three years he had risen to the rank of shipmaster, but it was one
thing to assume command of a schooner bound for the West Indies and
quite another to take a ship halfway around the world. To become one of
these elite captains, a young man usually had the kind of personal connections enjoyed by Elias Hasket Derby Jr.—captain of a voyage to the Île de
France at the age of twenty-two—or, for that matter, Nathaniel Bowditch.
What Prince did have was the cutting-edge technique in celestial navigation
known as "working lunars," a skill necessary for the new voyages into the
remote Pacific and Indian Oceans. Woe to the vessel that was not captained
by men with these skills. In 1790 the *Massachusetts*, the very vessel Bowditch
had seen launched in his apprentice days, lost its way in the Indian Ocean
because, its second mate would later claim, no officer on board knew how

to work lunars.[14] Bowditch had learned this technique from Samuel Smith and used it on the *Henry* voyage. John Batton, the *Henry*'s mate, could work lunars too, but if we are to believe Bowditch, his work could not be trusted. Mr. Batton's celestial observations were "not very accurately taken," he wrote in his log, adding "selon sa coutume," that is, as is his habit. But it was not the only habit Bowditch took exception to—always in French—for Batton got drunk almost every day and made little attempt to hide his compromised state from the sailors.[15]

As for the *Henry*'s crew of ten, the common seamen referred to in the parlance of the day as "the People," they were mainly local youths in their teens and twenties who would either move up to mate or master, later retiring to the land, or die at sea. Salemite Joseph Beadle was nineteen during the *Henry* voyage and later rose to become a shipmaster and then merchant. Fellow townsman Isaac Downes never made it past seaman in the United States Navy and was killed off the shores of Tripoli in 1804. Sixteen-year-old Ned Hulen, Batton's nephew, had many maritime adventures ahead of him: impressment in the British navy when in India, command of commercial vessels sailing to Europe and the Caribbean, privateering service during the War of 1812, and after all that, death off nearby Cape Cod, "supposed to have been washed overboard."[16] Their fate is a reminder that, regardless of the degree of risk undertaken by merchants, it was the men at sea who faced the greatest perils.

Taking to the open ocean for the first time, bound for the other side of the globe, was a voyage into the unknown. "I found the terrors of it far less than what I had an idea of," Bowditch remarked in his private log one day out. A shark he caught "caused no more terror than the sight of a cod would," he wrote a few weeks later. "So much travelers are inclind [*sic*] to magnify objects from hearsay I had understood a terrible idea of it." Months out, recording a heavy sea, he commented that it "no way equals the descriptions of them as given by voyagers."[17] He had been apprehensive.

Nothing signified the transformative nature of the deep-sea experience more than the set of rituals sailors conducted to initiate those "crossing the line" for the first time. Old Neptune himself, a sailor dressed up in outlandish costume, presided over the ceremony, which almost always involved some variation of a choice between a dunking in seawater and a "fine" in the form of a round of liquor for the crew. As the *Henry* neared the Tropic of Cancer, Bowditch at first resolved not to participate at all, perhaps sensing that his status and dignity were at stake, but he was won over by "the artfull & pleasing manner in which the Seamen informd me that it was necessary to provide some refreshment for the 'Old Man.'" The sailors had bypassed a dunking and gone straight to the more dignified fine. When the Henry later crossed the Equator, Bowditch again got off easy, subject only to a dousing, not a "shave" with some kind of filth and a rusty hoop. The crew had approached Bowditch with just enough deference to make him feel that his superior status would not be compromised, and by treating the sailors Bowditch reinforced that status, since that kind of largesse was part of the noblesse oblige approach of the eighteenth century. Such notions were losing currency in postrevolutionary America, but if they persisted anywhere, it was on a large trading vessel, where the separation between a ship's officers and its crew could be profound.[18]

If the sea was strange, land would be even more so. In May the *Henry* dropped anchor in Saint-Denis, a commercial entrepôt on the Île de Bourbon 430 miles east of Madagascar, 120 west of Derby's Indian Ocean trading hub, the Île de France. The vast majority of the island's population was made up not of French colonials but of African slaves working coffee plantations. In 1795 Bourbon was in a state of political upheaval. From thousands of miles away the French Revolution had arrived. The island itself had been renamed two years earlier—Bourbon would no longer do with the Bourbons themselves guillotined—and the new name, Réunion, celebrated the uniting of revolutionaries from the trading port of Marseilles with the National Guard in Paris.[19]

Bowditch sometimes tried to assimilate the strangeness of Réunion by using the familiar as his frame of reference. He often noted, for example, how the island either physically resembled or differed from the United States: the vegetable gardens (peas, onions, and carrots "as in America"), the water system (piped in from the mountains, "no wells as in America"), and the domestic architecture (floors of local wood "on which they rub wax as the women in America do on their furniture").[20] But other aspects of life on the island clashed more profoundly with what he knew and believed. For one, the island was Roman Catholic. There were no Catholic churches in Massachusetts in Bowditch's youth, and Protestant New Englanders had long regarded Catholicism as corrupt at best, a dangerous evil at worst. Anxious to see for himself, he went into the town's church only a day after the *Henry* dropped anchor. There he saw paintings of the crucified Jesus and the martyred Saint Denis, along with figures of Jesus, Mary, and Joseph. "I asked one of the Frenchmen what the Statue of Joseph was," he wrote, and "he told me it was the patron of Cuckolds." On a later visit, he noted a black woman "crossing herself & kissing the ground & repeating what she did not understand." He soon "tired of their superstitious worship."[21]

Edouard Auguste Nousveaux, "Vue de Saint Denis, Ile Bourbon." Pl. 229 in Jules-Sébastien-César Dumont d'Urville, *Voyage de la corvette l'Astrolabe. Atlas Historique.* [Paris]: Tastu, [1833]. Lithograph. With his sailor's eye, Bowditch described the harbor's treacherous onshore swells. With his mathematical eye, he noted that "all the streets run in a strait line from the shore & cross one another at right angles." National Library of Australia. Rex Nan Kivell Collection, NK3340.

Even more disturbing was his encounter with slavery. Here Bowditch's attitudes were complex. A court decision in 1783 had banned slavery in Massachusetts, but Bowditch must have remembered the days when Salemites, including his relatives, had owned slaves, and he grew up in a town where freed African Americans did not enjoy any kind of equality. He had his own prejudices. When Monsieur Desommes, the wharfinger, invited the *Henry's* officers to dine, Bowditch "hardly knew what reply to make," because he had taken Desommes for a mulatto. Only when he learned that the wharfinger's appearance was "very deceiving"—Desommes was in fact "of a good family in France"—did he accept the invitation. But if he did not subscribe to racial equality, neither could he abide slavery. Already on the voyage to the Indian Ocean, the sight of a Liverpool slaver had filled him with moral loathing. "God grant that that detestable traffic which she pursued may soon cease," he had written, "& that the tawny sons of Afric [*sic*] may be permitted quietly to enjoy the blessings of Liberty in their native Country."[22]

The aspect of slavery that Bowditch found most objectionable was less its physical cruelties, though he noted the floggings, and more the deprivation of the liberty that seemed to be the right of all human beings, even those that might not be equal to whites. Remarking on "the unhappy wretches" who tried to escape back to their native Madagascar, he wrote that they "generally perish in trying to regain that liberty they are so unjustly deprived of." He was disgusted by the French colonial attempts to keep the French Revolution a whites-only affair. "They receivd the decree of the National convention for liberating the blacks," he wrote, "but tho' they were fond of liberty themselves they would not suffer others to have it when it clashd with their interest." The local printer had withheld distribution of the *Rights of Man*, he reported, "for fear of the slaves, some of which have been put into prison for preaching too freely." Somehow, though, the revolutionary ideology had leaked out. Three slaves had been imprisoned for "saying they had as good a right to be free as the whites," and between twenty and thirty Mauritian slaves had stowed away on French naval vessels, "intending to fight to help give that liberty to others which they had no hopes of enjoying themselves." They were sent ashore and jailed. "While in prison," reported Bowditch, "they kept singing always the Marsall hymn"—that is, "La Marseillaise."[23]

Bowditch was not there as a social commentator, of course. He was busy attending to the *Henry*'s business: the requisite meeting with local officials and the payment of duties; the unloading of cargo into boats manned by enslaved workers and its transfer into government warehouses; the sale of the motley goods, everything from brandy to butter; and finally, the purchase and loading of a return cargo of coffee and indigo. Commission merchants, middlemen who provided a variety of commercial services to vessels, were a must. Prince engaged Felix Vergoz, Heriard & Company, and one Monsieur Amalitre. These were the men the Americans would have to trust.[24]

Because he could speak passable French, Bowditch spent a good deal of time with these merchants, especially Vergoz, frequently dining at his house, mixing with his family and friends, and even staying overnight at the merchant's residence. He also socialized with government officials and their wives. To some extent the ways of the French community were reassuringly familiar. Commercial practices ran along the usual lines. Though as remote as could be, Saint-Denis had the traces of European intellectual life: a printing press, though both paper and type were in desperately short supply; a botanical garden, though "much neglected"; and even an observatory—a hole in the roof of the assembly building with a meridian line running through it—though it too was in disrepair. But it did not take long for Bowditch to perceive the French colonials as shockingly different from the people he had grown up with. Above all, he was scandalized by their sexual mores. In America, he explained to his hosts, nobody thought twice about leaving women alone with their suitors until midnight, a fact the French found a matter of "great astonishment," given the suspicions that surrounded a French woman left alone with a man for so much as an hour. "They laugh at us for our primness," Bowditch noted, while "we blush for their indelicacy." Nothing seemed to make the colonials blush. Madame Vergoz openly alluded to her pregnancy. Madame Chauvillon, the wife of a high government official, flirted with a local merchant by telling him she had dreamt she was by pregnant by him, whereupon he responded, "'Madame it remains with you alone to make your dream a reality.'" Madame Bruno, the wife of another colonial official, "had criminal correspondence with a black man" and then divorced her husband and absconded for Mauritius.[25]

Bowditch's shock and disgust came to a head when he accompanied Monsieur Bonnefoy, a French passenger on the *Henry*, to the house of Madame Dupon, the mistress of a high colonial official. In America, Bowditch wrote, Bonnefoy's demeanor had been "modest & so conformable to the American Character," but no sooner was he in Réunion than the Frenchman literally exposed himself as a "worn out old rake." Bonnefoy had gotten drunk and, "like Noah of old" in the same condition, uncovered "what modesty bids conceal," thereby displaying "the marks of his vices." Ostensibly Bowditch was referring discreetly to the visible evidence of a sexually transmitted disease. Worse yet, Bonnefoy's medical condition was such "that all he can do is to speak of things which he is unable to perform, which makes him like the company of the most abandoned women with whom he can converse without restraint." One such comment made Bowditch literally blush. Laughing, Bonnefoy pointed to the reddened cheeks of the "petit garcon" and suggested that Bowditch had not yet lost his virginity. Madame Dupon examined Bowditch intently, asked him his age, and when he replied twenty (he was in fact twenty-one), said that it was absolutely impossible to keep one's virginity at that age. "I could not help regarding her with pity," he reflected, though he also could not help but regard her "very handsome" figure.[26]

What did it mean to do business with such people? Though in many ways recognizable to a Yankee, could they really be trusted? A rumor that several American vessels had arrived was being propagated to drive up export coffee prices. Some of the coffee brought on board was not fit for sale. Arbitrators came on board the next day and pronounced it no good, and the coffee was sent back ashore.[27] Questionable dealings were part and parcel of trade among Americans too, of course, but conducting business with relatives, townsmen, and people of long-standing reputation reduced risks. On Réunion, people might not be what they at first seemed to be. A lady proved to be a hussy. A gentleman proved to be a rake. And a broker like Vergoz? Could he in fact be trusted? In this remote setting, contact with known quantities took on special significance. Prince exchanged political, military, and commercial intelligence with Captain Silsbee, another Derby captain, then at Mauritius. In Saint-Denis the small band of Derby shipmasters, officers, and supercargoes socialized at the tavern and dined aboard one another's vessels. Salemites were not beyond reproach—Bowditch disapproved of Silsbee's decision to turn two black stowaways over to the colonial authorities for punishment—but at least you knew what you were getting.[28]

The process of selling, buying, and loading cargoes seemed interminable. Prince had estimated it would take six weeks or two months to complete their business, but instead it took almost five months. When coffee supplies dried up, the *Henry* was forced to sail to other ports on the island looking for more. "Would to god it was for America," Bowditch commented in his journal in late July, but it was not until the end of September that he could write, "All business being finished on shore at 10 oclock we weighed anchor & got underway for America." It was a largely uneventful passage. The sailors were kept occupied painting the ship. On the 25th of December, Bowditch wrote that "this day is the one celebrated by the Romish & other churches as the anniversary of the Birth of Jesus Christ" but more properly commemorated as the anniversary of the American victory over British troops at Trenton. He had made the transition from his mother's Anglicanism to Bentley's Unitarianism. On the 26th the *Henry* caught sight of a vessel with its colors flying upside down as a distress signal. It was the *Polly*, sixty days out of Plymouth, England, and bound for Boston, driven off course by a gale and dangerously short of provisions. The *Polly*'s supercargo came on board with coal and potatoes and left with beef and bread. Finally, on the morning of 11 January 1796, the *Henry* "came to anchor in Salem Harbor being 12 months exactly from the time of leaving Salem to our return."[29]

BOWDITCH DID NOT STAY LONG. In late March he set sail on Derby's 321-ton ship *Astrea*, this time for Manila, a port only recently opened to Western trade by its Spanish rulers and as yet only a stopover point for a few American vessels engaged in the China trade. Once more, Henry Prince was the captain, but now Bowditch sailed as supercargo. Bowditch's first trading voyage had exposed him to many of the perils entailed in maritime ventures, but in this respect his second voyage was to be even more instructive. The route to the Philippines would take the *Astrea* around the Cape of Good Hope and then continue on through largely uncharted waters. Trade with Manila was another unknown. Derby did not know what there was to buy in the Philippines and could only guess that wine and brandy, a mainstay of American commercial cargoes, would find a market there. So the *Astrea* would first make a stop in Portugal and Madeira. As for who would help them conduct business in Manila, Bowditch would have to figure this out once he got there, but the city's mix of Spanish colonials, native Filipinos, and Chinese and Malay merchants loomed as even stranger than the French creoles of Saint-Denis.[30]

The voyage across the Atlantic was unremarkable, but the journey from Madeira to Manila began inauspiciously. A month out a sailor named Samuel Bier began to exhibit "marks of insanity arising from religious melancholy." Bier had entered Prince's cabin, fallen on his knees, and begged for forgiveness. Over the next few days Bier was intermittently "disordered" and then suddenly "grew quite outrageous secreting 2 or 3 knives & by his actions seemed inclined to attack the people." The knives were taken from him, but "soon after he jumped overboard." With full sail and a strong wind, it proved impossible to get a rescue boat out before he drowned. Bowditch tried to make sense of the suicide. Bier had been a local man, a neighbor, settled with a wife and child, and to all appearances "harmless" and "inoffensive." In Bowditch's time, "religious melancholy" was perceived as a form of insanity, but it was a form of madness that took on its particular character from the ambient religious culture of the era. It was the logical extreme of a commonly held, theologically based belief in human depravity, one that could create an unbearable sense of sinfulness.[31] Unitarians like Bowditch focused on the possibilities for individual self-improvement and social benevolence rather than human wickedness. He could not comprehend the "religious gloom" that had taken hold of Samuel Bier.

As the *Astrea* approached Indonesia the vessel entered barely charted seas full of dangers. Near Java the ocean itself took on an air of eerie mystery, for everywhere the water had the color of milk. Bowditch drew up a bucket and could detect nothing in it by candlelight, but in the dark it glowed brightly. Off the coast of Sumatra they saw snakes in the water eight feet long and drifting trees they took at first to be prows, vessels favored by Malay pirates. The ship squeezed through the notoriously narrow and shallow strait between Sumatra and Java and then threaded its way through a maze of islands into the Pacific. Ever fearful of running aground, soundings were taken at frequent intervals, but who could proceed with confidence when the measurements did not agree with published charts and the depths varied tremendously within short distances? They encountered other Western vessels with frightening stories. One reported that two sailors had fallen overboard in a gale. Another reported widespread disease. "Very sickly at Batavia," wrote Bowditch, "seven American masters having died." It must have come as a relief when the *Astrea* entered Manila Bay.[32]

The Philippines was a new trading destination for American merchants, and as supercargo it was Bowditch's responsibility to bring back relevant commercial information. His lengthy Manila Harbour Journal covered such topics as the depth of the harbor and the schedule of tides, harbor regulations and the duties on goods, the prices of ship's provisions, and the local systems of money, weights, and measures. He discussed the types, grades of quality, calendar of availability, and method of procurement of local commodities. And because it was impossible to separate narrowly commercial information from a description of the society in which that trade took place—who lived there? what customs shaped their trading practices? how should one approach them?—much of the journal reads like an ethnography.[33]

Derby had taken a risk on bringing wines to the Filipino market, and it proved to be a bad choice. In Réunion anything and everything imported by American vessels found a ready sale, so focused were the island's planters on producing nothing but hugely profitable coffee.[34] But over a month into their Manila stay, Bowditch was still reporting that the "chief part of our wine still continues on hand." Native Filipinos did not drink wine, and two vessels of the Royal Company of the Philippines had recently saturated what market for wine there was. How could you make a profit off its sale anyway, when the poorest madeira sold for nearly as much as the best? As for spirits, their sale was forbidden by the government, "so that we had to enter 6 casks of NE Rum as Brandy." (Bowditch ultimately recommended that spirits be sold in small barrels, rather than the larger casks, so they could be passed off as produce. The ruse does not seem to have disturbed his profound sense of personal integrity.) The Madeiran brandy sold among Manila's Europeans, but there were hardly any of those. Even the hats the Americans had brought sold slowly. Local tastes favored a finer product with broader brims. About the only thing Bowditch had luck with was, of all things, compasses. He sold wooden ones for eight dollars apiece and brass ones for ten, netting a 300 percent profit. "Vessels ought never to bring any thing to Manilla [*sic*] but Dollars"—precious metal currency—he grumbled.[35]

In this alien territory a middleman was a must, noted Bowditch, but here too there were risks. Because Spain had only recently allowed in foreign traders, there was no mercantile community in Manila with men of long-standing reputations for probity. If anything, remote locales attracted men who had some reason to leave their pasts behind. Already in Madeira Bowditch had been warned to be on the lookout for shady dealings in the Philippines. There he had heard that a French broker had been among those Manila merchants who had fleeced an English trader, so that the captain "was obliged [*sic*] to return home with an empty vessel." Forewarned, reported Bowditch, we were "shy of engaging too deeply with any man." In Manila, a Portuguese and several Englishmen looked to act as brokers for the *Astrea*, but, commented Bowditch, "there is not one who has been settled there any considerable time but what has some blur on his character." A later American arrival engaged one middleman who, Bowditch reported, "is a man by all account of an Infamous character." A Swedish captain had made the mistake of not personally inspecting and weighing the indigo he purchased, entrusting the tasks instead to a "black fellow" notorious for accepting bribes from sellers in exchange for overrating the quality of their goods.[36]

Bowditch engaged the services of the lone American in the city, a Philadelphian named John Stuart Kerr. He acted as their interpreter—Bowditch's elementary Spanish was, by his own admission, insufficient—guided them through the requisite interactions with the local authorities and merchants, and rented them a warehouse and the use of his own house. But Bowditch never did quite trust him. Though Kerr had "appeared in all his conduct to behave perfectly to our satisfaction," wrote Bowditch after the *Astrea* had departed for Salem, "stories are reported to his disadvantage." All in all, Bowditch was forced to conclude that anyone trading in Manila "ought to be well on his guard."[37]

What made the situation in Manila even more unnerving were the mores of the government officials and merchants with whom business had to be transacted. Given his Yankee prejudices, Bowditch had probably not been surprised to discover sexual immorality among the French colonials in Réunion, but he brought an even more scathing perspective to the Spaniards of Manila. English-speaking Protestants had long associated Spain with cruelty and intolerance and regarded Mediterranean populations in general as lazy. The Catholic Church, bad enough in a place like France, could only reach a low point in such a barbaric and backward society as Spain. Now Bowditch subjected Manila's Spanish colonials to predictable criticism. He noted their "dronish disposition," described the locals' veneration of Mary and the saints as little more than paganism, blamed the clergy for banning the importation of any books that contradicted Catholicism, and noted with disgust the unmarked grave of an English sea captain dumped unceremoniously as a heretic in little more than a "stinky mud puddle."[38]

As a Yankee Bowditch was predisposed to this kind of condemnation, but as a supercargo he leveled an even more pointed criticism at the commercial environment he found in Manila. Efficient business enterprise, he was convinced, was incompatible with Roman Catholicism. Spanish colonials were indolent and unproductive. They drank chocolate for breakfast(!), dined at noon, and then slept till three. "Very little business can be transacted" during their siesta, he reported, and none whatsoever during the myriad saints' days. Earlier in Lisbon he had noted the same problem: "About 120 days in the year are set apart for the worship of their saints," and on these days, as on Sundays, the custom house was closed. Given Bowditch's penchant for mathematical precision and his stake in astronomical order, nothing testified more pointedly to Catholic backwardness than the fact that Manila's calendar was one day behind. "It has often been proposed to alter this manner of computation," wrote Bowditch, "but the Clergy not being fond of innovations are averse to it."[39]

Most of the people living in Manila were not Spanish at all but Filipino natives, Malays, and Chinese. Intriguingly, Bowditch regarded these groups more favorably than he did the Spaniards. As we have seen, he was not immune to racial prejudice, but he had no frame of reference for Asians as he did for people of African descent, and in an era before scientists purported to establish a biological basis for a racial hierarchy, it was still possible to approach unknown peoples with some degree of openness. So he admired the Filipinos as "very ingeneous [sic]" craftsmen and approached Malays much as one would any familiar maritime power. They had a king, a naval fleet of "cruisers . . . known to attack vessels even in Manilla [sic] Bay," and armed merchant ships commanded by captains and carrying many merchants, "having each his own adventure," that is, trading on his own. But it was the Chinese with whom business had to be conducted, because they controlled trade in what turned out to be Manila's winning commodity, sugar. Here too he turned out to be surprisingly relativistic in his judgments. Listening to a Chinese singing, he admitted that the man's voice "was so little harmonious that if I had met him in the street I should have thought he had been crying," but he added, "I dare say they thought it excellent." He noted with respect the large vessels Chinese merchants used in their operations. Their odd shape rendered the junks useless in headwinds, he wrote, but their holds were "divided into different apartments so that if one part leaks, it will not damage the goods in the other."[40]

Gaspard Duche-de-Vancy, "Vue de Cavite dans la Baie de Manille." Pl. 41 in Jean-François de Galaup, *Atlas du voyage de La Pérouse*. Paris: L'Imprimerie de la République, 1797. Courtesy of the Rare Book & Manuscript Library, University of Illinois at Urbana-Champaign. The French artist portrayed the local residents as stylized Europeans, except for the Chinese man, a member of the mercantile community that also intrigued Bowditch.

The clearest sign of Bowditch's attitude was his fascination with the Chinese system of mathematical notation and computation. He figured out their method of designating numbers with characters by watching a Chinese merchant weighing pepper and recording amounts. He found out the names of their numbers, how they notated numbers above 100, and how they added up columns of numbers. And he transcribed all this information, Chinese characters and all, into his journal. He noted their use of the abacus and commented that "long practice has renderd [*sic*] this method so familiar to them that they can perform any simple arithmetical operation nearly as quick as any European." Bowditch bought one, practiced, and remarked that he could do any addition problem on it almost as fast as with Western methods. This was Bowditch the supercargo recognizing a fellow merchant's proficiency with the arithmetic required for commerce. But this was also Bowditch the mathematician expressing admiration for a system of computation that was new to him—the ultimate sign of respect.[41]

It is possible to conclude from Bowditch's journal that Manila's Westerners, whether European brokers or Spanish officials, were less trustworthy and capable than its Asians. He held a similarly low opinion of the European sea captains he met in port. The English captains lived "in stile rowling about in their Coaches." The Swedish captain—the one who should have been attending to his indigo purchases—had "coaches ten horses & twenty odd servants," not to mention "a miss (who has 50 dols per month)." By contrast, Bowditch shared his bed only with Prince (unremarkable in those days), and the two made "use of what is called here the Coach of Saint Francis viz shoe leather."[42] Entrusted as they were with making profits for the *Astrea's* owners and investors, it would have been irresponsible to live in luxury. It could only add to Bowditch's reputation as a trustworthy business agent to have it known that he had pinched pennies in Manila, a fact anyone who read Bowditch's account—written for the benefit of the vessel's owners—would discover.

From this perspective, the real villain of Bowditch's journal was not the loose-living, loose-dealing Swedish shipmaster but an American, one Captain Doble of the newly arrived *Three Sisters*. The vessel's Captain Cathcart had died during the voyage, and Doble, the mate, had assumed command. While all that was in order, Doble's behavior was anything but. "I never saw a man so much above himself," wrote Bowditch. Doble claimed to be part owner of the ship and to have always been its captain. In town he kept a coach and "a six oared barge with an awning to it," and when he hosted a "grand feast" on his ship he invited "every Englishman in the place," but not Captain Prince. With his characteristic penchant for righteous disdain, Bowditch had not so much as "saluted him in the street." The behavior was not just reprehensible; it drew Bowditch's suspicion, for a man acting the role of another—Doble even wore Cathcart's clothes—and imitating European shipmasters was essentially an impostor. Doble had taken twice as long to reach Manila as he should have, Bowditch noted, because he had chosen a "very odd" route from Mauritius to the Philippines. He had not requested the *Astrea* to bring back letters to his ship's owners, a standard form of cooperation among Western vessels, surely a sign that he wanted to keep them in the dark.[43]

The *Astrea* left Manila harbor in early December, two months after its arrival. Having bought a Spanish grammar in Manila and filled its flyleafs with vocabulary, Bowditch practiced his schoolboy Spanish in his log: "Hoy hacia buen tiempo, viento fresco. Tenia mucho pescador area el fragata." In February the ship sprang a leak, and the sailors were put to the pump, a task repeated every fifteen minutes for over three months. In late May the *Astrea* sailed into Salem harbor carrying 750,000 pounds of sugar, almost 64,000 pounds of pepper, and almost 30,000 pounds of indigo. The duties amounted to more than $24,000. Bentley recorded that he had seen "Capt.

Prince, lately from Manila, who has made the greatest voyage from this Port, tho' not the greatest in proportion to the Stock, but upon the actual advance of the Cargo, for Mr. Derby."[44] The supercargo had done well by his patron.

BOWDITCH UNDERTOOK TWO further voyages with Henry Prince in the *Astrea*—in 1798–99 to Spain and in 1799–1800 to Batavia (present-day Jakarta) and Manila. Each taught him more about the risks of global maritime commerce. A crossing to Cádiz and Alicante might seem nothing compared with the dangerous passages into the Indian and Pacific Oceans, but in 1798 the United States was newly involved in an undeclared war with France, one more development in America's squeezed position as a neutral carrier in a period of European warfare. French warships and privateers, along with their Spanish allies, were seizing American merchant vessels on the high seas. "The loss of several Vessels belonging to this Town, captured by the French . . . in Spanish ports, has given a serious alarm to our Merchants," commented Bentley.[45]

The story of Bowditch's third voyage reads like something out of a classic boy's adventure novel. Heading into the Atlantic, Prince kept a sharp eye, ready to evade any sail spied in the distance and to run out the guns if necessary. "Privateers very thick in the gut"—the Strait of Gibraltar—wrote Bowditch in his log. Off Cádiz on the Atlantic coast the British Royal Navy provided a protective escort, but Spanish gunboats appeared, and the rival warships exchanged fire. Once in port, the news was mixed. Though there would be no trouble selling the *Astrea*'s cargo, prices were dropping. More critically, the return cargo—the wines of southern Spain so in demand in New England and the Indian Ocean islands—was not to be had. The *Astrea* would have to go elsewhere for these: to Alicante, on the southern coast of Spain—through the strait.[46]

In the run for Alicante, the *Astrea* joined an American convoy taking cover with the British fleet, but forced to wait up for a slow-sailing vessel, the *Astrea* soon lost sight of the Royal Navy. The next morning Prince spied "a small sail a roaring for the ship." Taking it for a "frinch [*sic*] privateer," he ordered a shot to be fired, whereupon it immediately hoisted the Spanish colors. Two days later, when the *Astrea* entered the strait, ten French privateers appeared but did not approach them.[47] On the following day, a suspicious sail once more sighted, Prince got the crew ready for action. Years later, he recalled assigning Bowditch the job of passing powder from the cabin up to the deck above. Stepping below, Prince recounted, "there sat Mr. Bowditch at the cabin table, with his slate and pencil in hand, and with the cartridges by his side." Prince burst into laughter and asked his super-cargo, "Well, Mr. Bowditch, can you be making your will now?" Bowditch, now distracted from the calculations that had so thoroughly absorbed his attention, replied with a smile in the affirmative.[48]

In Alicante the warfare was conducted between rival merchants—they were "at swords points," wrote Prince—competing for the *Astrea*'s business. Again, it was necessary to be on guard. As soon as a vessel anchored, noted Prince with disgust, one merchant would send a boat to inquire after its business and, "with the greatest pretensions of friend ship [*sic*]," invite those responsible for the cargo to his house. Once they arrived, his wife would insist so strongly on their overindulging at her table that either "one must a front [*sic*] her or kill him self [*sic*] with eating." But all this hospitality "is only to answer their own end," reflected Prince on the merchant's merce-nary motives, as was often the case "with a stranger," no matter how "polite" he appeared.[49]

Once the cargo was assembled, the *Astrea* headed for the Atlantic, again in company with other American vessels, altogether ninety-eight guns strong. Obliged to tow a slow-sailing compatriot, the convoy made slow progress. Some of the vessels decided to take their own chances, so as the *Astrea* approached the strait it looked as if it might have to make the pas-sage on its own. Captain Clements of the *Sultan* planned to seek shelter in Gibraltar, and Prince bid him farewell, but Clements changed his mind and stayed with the *Astrea* as it passed through. One by one, the vessels now took their leave of the convoy. The last to go was the *Sultan*, "the only one that any dependance [*sic*] could be put in," commented Prince. For several days the ships exchanged a show of lights at night, but as the distance between the two vessels increased, there soon came "no answer." Wrote Bowditch in his log: "We are all alone."[50]

Bowditch and Prince anchored in Salem in April 1799, but by the end of July they readied for the sea once again. The *Astrea* was now owned by merchant Thomas Amory of Boston, and with the transfer of the vessel to Boston Harbor there came a new problem. It proved difficult to gather a full crew and to keep those that already signed on. In Habakkuk's day Salem vessels carried small numbers of local men, often acquaintances if not relatives. In this new era of trade beyond the Capes, vessels were bigger and crews larger and much less likely to be local. Bonds of kinship, friend-ship, and trust could no longer be relied upon, and with upward mobility for ordinary seamen increasingly rare, they had less motivation to establish a good reputation. Though the *Astrea* was hauled off into the harbor to "keep the people from running away," explained Bowditch in a letter to his cousin Mary Ingersoll, one "Salem lad" and a "Boston scoundrel" deserted. The Salem lad returned on his own, but Bowditch and Amory were forced to chase the Boston scoundrel through Charlestown and Cambridge and back to Charlestown again, where they finally caught him. Meanwhile, two other sailors had gotten away altogether.[51]

As finally assembled, the crew was, as Bowditch characterized them, "a curious set." Among them could be found "Tinkers, Tailors, Barbers, Country Schoolmasters, one old Greenwich Pensioner, a few Negroes, Mullatoes [sic], Spaniards &c&c&c," but, he averred, they "will do well enough when properly disciplined." It was probably in light of this motley crew that Amory asked Bowditch to remain on the *Astrea* once the money to be invested in the return cargo had been brought aboard. Bowditch had little desire to bunk ashore anyway. I have "but few acquaintances in Boston," he wrote, "& have no particular business on shore." He enclosed sixty-five dollars with the letter, asked Mary to give it to her "Pa to put with the other money left with him," and bid "adieu for a few months."[52]

The voyage entailed by now familiar dangers and setbacks. Heading for Batavia, the *Astrea* encountered "an English Guineaman" that desired to verify the *Astrea*'s neutrality. Their surgeon came aboard, Bowditch wrote of the detested slaver, "and after examining our papers and acting in a manner becoming a guineaman, they made sail." Once in Batavia they could not obtain a full cargo of coffee, so they quickly left that notoriously fever-ridden city and continued on to Manila. Again the *Astrea* threaded its way through the region's seemingly interminable number of islands. "Our patience," wrote Bowditch in his log, is "nearly exhausted." After several weeks in Manila, their cargo complete, the *Astrea* set sail for Salem. They encountered a Nantucket vessel, whose captain reported that "it was very sickly in Batavia" and "that he had buried his supercargo." Next they were boarded by a British privateer but "treated politely." In its almost fourteen months at sea, the *Astrea* had escaped capture, shipwreck, and disease, but only a week from home Samuel Cook, "a black died of the scurvy in his stomach." Then two days later, "at 2 AM Thomas Gardner (a black man) being upon the cross jack yard missed his hold & fell upon the mizzen chains, which we suppose killed him instantaneously as his hat was seen floating upon the water, he being sunk." A few days later an item appeared in the *Salem Gazette*: "Tuesday arrived at Boston, ship Astrea, Captain Prince, 177 days from Manilla [sic]. Left no Americans." There was no mention of Cook or Gardner.[53]

Bowditch's four voyages secured him a place among Salem's solidly prosperous and socially prominent citizens. The officers of a merchant vessel, though paid wages, profited far more from the privilege of trading on their own, and Bowditch had done well. The Salem tax records assessed Bowditch's wealth at a mere $100 in 1795 but $1,100 in 1796. After his first return from Manila, Bowditch's wealth came to some $4,500, and after his second, $6,400. As an up-and-coming Derby supercargo, he had no problem purchasing his own share in Salem's Philosophical Library.[54]

He was now also marriageable. In March 1798, one day before his twenty-fifth birthday and shortly before his third voyage, he wed eighteen-year-old Elizabeth Boardman, a distant cousin connected on their mothers' Hodges sides. This being Salem, Elizabeth's father was not without connection to Nathaniel's family either. Years earlier Francis Boardman had sailed as mate under Thomas Bowditch, another distant cousin. The marriage was an advantageous match. Boardman had died in Port-au-Prince, leaving a substantial estate. He had been a rough-edged man, but having grown wealthy from the West Indian trade, he had sought to make it into the local gentry by acquiring a little polish. In 1782 he bought a lot on Salem Common, hired the carriage-trade architect Samuel McIntyre, and spent over £2,500 building an elegant house of considerable distinction. Elizabeth was raised in an atmosphere of provincial gentility, one that included a conscious display of refinement. But the polish was thinly applied, at least on Francis. Bentley described Boardman as "fond of shew." Unlike lawyer Nathaniel Ropes, Boardman had no gentleman's library, only a "Bible and sundry books" worth a few dozen shillings.[55]

Elizabeth and Nathaniel lived together a scant few months. She died of what was then called scrofula, a form of tuberculosis, while he was in Cádiz.[56] In 1800 he remarried, this time to his first cousin Mary Ingersoll. She was eighteen, "a tall country girl with rosy cheeks and 'great red arms,'" he a prematurely gray man of twenty-seven, short, slight, altogether a "person under the common size."[57] It was not unusual for first cousins to marry, and given the Ingersoll family's role in young Bowditch's life—from their kinship connections with the Hodgeses, Ropeses, Boardmans, and Derbys to the helping hand Jonathan Ingersoll held out to Habakkuk during the Revolution—Nathaniel must have looked forward to forging yet another bond with his maternal relatives. Once again, the female line would prove critical to a Bowditch's success. In many ways, Jonathan looked out for Nathaniel as Habakkuk never had. "His friendly offices to me on many occasions are such as I shall always keep in remembrance," Bowditch wrote

Mary in 1803. From Ingersoll's point of view, Nathaniel made a good match for his daughter. If he figured on his widowed nephew inheriting something from his first bride, he miscalculated, for Bowditch had concluded that, given the brevity of the marriage, it was only right to return the Boardman property to her family. But Bowditch was a successful Derby supercargo, and given the way Salem business worked, his mercantile reputation and connections were capital enough.[58]

Like Elizabeth Boardman—also her cousin—Mary had been brought up with the ambitions to gentility attendant upon moderate wealth. A list of items stolen from the Ingersoll household in 1793 gives us a picture of what those ambitions translated into: a silver tankard, spoons, sugar tongs, cream pot, pepper and two pairs of salts, a silver watch, a gold ring, forty gold beads, and "several broken Gold Buttons." Mary was given a genteel education. Her teachers were Mehitable Higginson and her unmarried daughter of the same name, former Tory exiles who put aside their Loyalist past and parlayed their reputations as "among the best and most truly refined women of that day in New England" to open a school that catered to the children of the local gentry.[59] She studied arithmetic, not the logarithms and trigonometry of navigational instruction but the currencies, weights, and measures of an elementary education appropriate even for girls in a seaport town.[60] Like many young ladies of this era, Mary kept a commonplace book, an individualized compilation of prose and poetry pieces regarded as a tool of mental and moral self-improvement and a token of gentility. Her son later complained that many of the items were "unpleasantly of a 'romantic' type," too many "laments of swains or damsels for their 'wrecked hopes.'" But in Mary's youth a taste for this kind of literature spoke of what was termed "sensibility," an exquisite sensitivity to physical, emotional, and aesthetic stimuli that testified to the superior delicacy of the men and women who possessed it. It was what separated ladies and gentlemen from the boorish masses.[61]

Much is lost to the past, of course, but Mary was not remembered as a notable intellect. Judging by her letters, Mary's primary concerns were with family affairs, social news, and fashion. We knew her as "usually very sweet and bright," her son wrote decades later, "but far from literary in her tastes and in her influence over us." She was raised in a sea captain's family with aspirations to gentility, but not one in which intellectual accomplishments were the order of the day and polished conversation the norm. As a newly married woman, she must have caught wind of the feminist rumblings in Salem when, according to a shocked newspaper contributor, a number of young Salem women formed societies dedicated to "what they *stile* the '*rights of women*.'" But her views were more in concert with the Reverend Thomas Barnard, who condemned the "fancied . . . 'Rights of Women'" in a sermon to the Salem Female Charitable Society, an "approved" organization to which she belonged.[62]

Bowditch was happy with Mary as she was. What he considered her feminine foibles were a matter of affectionate humor to him. "How often you have laughed at me for altering my opinion of Persons in a short time, & for trivial things," she wrote him early in their marriage, and one can sense his amused and indulgent attitude toward feminine flightiness. In their over thirty years of marriage he often expressed his love with tenderness. Tucked in her travel diary of 1813 are several dried flowers, "pluck'd by my husband." Close to a quarter century after their wedding Nathaniel sent a letter to "My dear, very dear Mary" professing his "unceasing love" for her, "my dearest of all earthly friends."[63] There was a wider world out there, of eastern lands and modern women, but in 1800 Bowditch sought a safe harbor in Salem and Mary Ingersoll.

BOWDITCH'S VOYAGES INTO THE Atlantic, Indian, and Pacific Oceans introduced him to the perils of maritime trade as no chandlery clerkship could. The *Henry* and *Astrea* faced age-old maritime hazards of stormy seas, uncharted waters, hostile vessels, and foreign fevers. There were commercial hazards too, the long-standing one of unpredictable markets now even more perilous given the newly global scale of trade. Who could one trust in these untried ports? The places were strange. Their inhabitants were strangers. These new voyages took American traders like Bowditch outside of their networks of relations, long-standing acquaintances, and individuals with reputations vouched for by people whose word could be relied upon. As in Salem, business in Saint-Denis and Manila was conducted face to face, but unlike in Salem, you could never be sure if the person you were dealing with had one face or two. Decades later Bowditch's commercial instincts would still have him differentiating between those he knew and those he did not, even as he designed institutions that (ostensibly) operated according to a principle of impersonality.

Amid this mercantile drama of peril and suspicion Bowditch had found an oasis of sorts on his trading voyage to Cádiz, when he made the acquaintance of the Count Louis-Charles-François Mallevault, "a Gentleman from Martinico." Mallevault owned large plantations in the Caribbean, had commanded a French frigate in Martinique, and in that capacity supported the cause of a Bourbon counterrevolution in 1795. By the time Bowditch encountered him, he was a post-captain in the Spanish navy. Whatever the implications of befriending a French slave owner, aristocrat, royalist, and French-allied naval officer, Bowditch was no doubt most interested in where this friendship led, namely, to a visit to Cádiz's newly opened astronomical observatory.[64] If the observatory building, an elegant two-story edifice fronted by columns and topped with the telltale dome, impressed Bowditch, he did not record those feelings. Instead, he noted only that "we were shown all the instruments they had mounted," most made in England, adding: "These were not any of them very new." He struck up a lively exchange with Don Cosmo de Churruca, a sometime Spanish naval commander and, more to the point, a man who had undertaken astronomical observations and calculations during recent scientific expeditions to Spanish America. Here was a fellow citizen of the Republic of Letters, a polity ruled by amity and cooperation, not rivalry and mistrust. "I promised to send him, on my arrival in America, the works of Holyoke, on Meteorology," wrote Bowditch. "I gave him my method of working a lunar observation, which he was to print at the end of the Nautical Almanac."[65]

Less than a year later, in September 1799, a notice appeared in the *Newburyport Herald* advising readers that a new book, "Moore's New Practical Navigator Improved," was hot off the press. Moore's volume was nothing new—the Englishman's maritime reference book had already gone through twelve editions—but the "improved" portions were another matter. The title page gave further details: "The *first* American, from the *thirteenth* English edition of John Hamilton Moore, improved by the introduction of several new tables, and by large additions to the former tables, and revised and corrected by a skilful mathematician and navigator." The preface identified just who this "skilful" man might be. It was "Mr. *Nathaniel Bowditch, of Salem, Fellow of the American Academy of Arts and Sciences,* whose acknowledged talents, both as a Theoretical and Practical Navigator, reflect high honor on the nautical character of his country."[66] Bowditch had been up to more than sailing the globe.

CHAPTER THREE

The *Navigator*

In 1802 printer Edmund M. Blunt of Newburyport, a maritime center just the other side of Cape Ann, published Bowditch's *New American Practical Navigator*. Within a few decades, "Bowditch," as the book soon came to be called, became a nautical best seller. In accounting for its popularity, many have pointed to its classically Yankee focus on useful knowledge. I have "carefully avoided all *scientific parade*," Bowditch later wrote a European astronomer of his book, and "have written the entire work according to the method of instruction used in our country, where we prefer in these matters, practice to theory." Just that contrast between the Old World and the New was drawn by *Moby-Dick*'s Ishmael when he warned Nantucket shipowners against hiring any lad "given to unseasonable meditativeness . . . who offers to ship with the Phædon"—a German philosopher's reflection on immortality—"instead of Bowditch in his head."[1]

Ostensibly the *Navigator* made it possible for any man with enough ambition and three dollars in his pocket to track the open ocean.[2] The book's key innovation in this respect was its easy-to-use method of taking and working a lunar observation, the advanced technique for determining longitude used by Prince and Bowditch in their East Indies voyages. No anecdote made this point more emphatically than one first published by the German astronomer Baron Franz Xaver von Zach in 1821 and subsequently recounted in many American newspapers, magazines, and biographical accounts. The story takes place in 1817, when the baron visited *Cleopatra's Barge*, a Salem pleasure yacht then anchored in Genoa, Italy. When Zach expressed surprise to find extensive knowledge of celestial navigation on board an American vessel, its navigator replied that even the ship's cook could calculate longitude and pointed to "a Negro in the after part of the vessel, with a white apron round his waist, a fowl in one hand, and a carving knife in the other." Summoned to prove the claim, the "colored navigator" fetched his Bowditch and proceeded to do just that.[3]

So there we have it: the *Navigator* was a groundbreaking book. Unprecedentedly practical and accessible, it quickly displaced the dusty tomes of Europe to become the "seaman's Bible."[4] But in fact, as Bowditch would have been the first to say, the *Navigator* was not the first practical navigation manual. Nor was most of it new. The book was a revised and expanded version of an older text, Englishman John Hamilton Moore's *New Practical Navigator*, which also targeted an audience of active seamen and also included a method of obtaining longitude by lunar observations. Still, this should not take away from the significance of Bowditch's book. The *Navigator* was immensely valuable, and within a decade or two it had solidified its hold on the American market. It appealed to its readers' patriotism and, above all, made its mark because of the unprecedented reliability of its navigational tables. You could stake your life on Bowditch's numbers. Many did. They returned home safely. It was Bowditch's exactitude, not his intellectual originality or democratic instincts, that established the value and popularity of his *Navigator*.

Once again, it came down to the power of numbers, this time the power of the numbers Bowditch himself had generated. At sea and back in Salem, he had recalculated the thousands of values found in Moore's tables and corrected thousands of errors. For all his mastery of European developments in mathematics and the physical sciences, his own work would often take the form of something much less conceptual or cutting edge—computation. As a young man he had developed a reputation for lightning-fast feats of mental arithmetic, a skill his countrymen marveled at as the emblem of an extraordinary intellect. With the *Navigator*, it was the sheer quantity of calculations that boggled the mind. Many educated Europeans regarded that kind of task not as superhuman but as other-than-human, the repetitive labor of a drone or a machine—certainly not that of a genius. But for Bowditch computation brought the delights of certainty and abstraction, the keys to his lifelong intellectual commitments and practical work. Nor was the European perspective shared by New England's premier institutions of learning. They chose instead to honor the exceptional mathematical talent in their midst. By 1802, the self-taught supercargo had become Nathaniel Bowditch, A.M., F.A.A.S., an honorary Harvard graduate and a fellow of the American Academy of Arts and Sciences.

LONG BEFORE THE *Navigator* was published, Bowditch was known in Salem as a young man of considerable mathematical skill and knowledge. On his voyages around the world that reputation grew. Some anecdotes testified to the intensity of his focus on mathematical pursuits, like the one with the *Astrea* under imminent attack in 1798, Bowditch below decks ready to pass gunpowder above, all the while "figuring away" with "slate and pencil." Other shipboard tales depicted Bowditch as almost constantly engrossed in his studies, pausing only for meals or to take observations, catch a nap, or pace the deck. When observed "walking rapidly, and apparently deep in thought," it was "well understood, by all on board, that he was not to be disturbed, as we supposed he was solving some difficult problem, and when he darted below, the conclusion was, that he had got the idea." Sometimes "when the idea came to him, he would actually run to the cabin, and his countenance would give the expression, that he had found a prize."[5]

A second kind of anecdote described Bowditch's growing fame as a computational whiz kid, capable of solving mind-bending mathematical puzzles in feats of mental arithmetic. The earliest such story takes place in 1796 in Boston. On that occasion, the story ran, Elias Hasket Derby was at the theater with a self-styled "professor of mathematics" from England, who commented that he had yet to find anyone in the United States who was competent in his field. "I have a question," the Englishman said, "which I have proposed to several persons here who are reputed the most knowing, and they cannot solve it." Recalling that Henry Prince had described Bowditch as "the greatest calculator in America," Derby pointed to Bowditch in an opposite box and suggested that there sat an American well up to the task. That night a messenger delivered the problem to Bowditch. The Salemite accepted the challenge and produced the correct answer the following morning. He was ready with a return challenge, a problem that had "puzzled me once a good while before I could make it out"—a boast masked in modesty. He never received a reply. The implication, of course, was that Bowditch had stumped the arrogant Englishman.[6]

Such challenges had been in vogue in England since at least the beginning of the eighteenth century, when a translation of Jacques Ozanam's *Recreations Mathematical and Physical* posed many such "Delightful Problems" and the *Ladies' Diary* turned away from recipes to focus on such puzzles submitted and solved by its readers, many of them men. By the Revolution American almanacs, magazines, and newspapers had followed suit, so such trials of computational skill were familiar to Bowditch and his countrymen.[7] Prince in particular enjoyed putting forward his junior officer as a kind of mathematical pit bull. "During these voyages," commented one of Bowditch's eulogists, "numerous occasions occurred of making known, in foreign countries, his extraordinary mathematical powers; to the astonishment of all who were witnesses to the rapidity of his calculations and the accuracy of his results." On Madeira Prince bragged to an American shipmaster that his supercargo was "a great calculator," and the two laid a wager on it. The skeptical captain presented Bowditch with a difficult mathematical problem, and "the great sum, which had puzzled the brains of the gentleman and all his friends at home, for a whole winter, was done in a few minutes." On that same voyage, Bowditch and Prince attended a dinner at the home of merchant John Pintard, the American consul in Madeira. Having heard of Bowditch's legendary computational feats, Mrs. Pintard decided to test his skill with a difficult problem. Bowditch admitted the problem would not be an easy one, but laying down his knife and fork, he squeezed the tips of his fingers together for two minutes and produced the correct answer. John Pintard's head clerk, "esteemed a very skilful [*sic*] accountant," was astonished. He had been working on the problem himself, and "taking his long calculation out of his pocket," averred: "There is not a man in this island that can do it in two hours; if there is, I will suffer death!"[8]

In Bowditch's youth this kind of computational skill held enormous significance, for human intelligence itself was conceptualized as the ability to take apart and recombine ideas and sensations by means of what are fundamentally arithmetical operations. Nothing therefore testified to mental power more definitively than astounding feats of mental arithmetic. Stories of such wizardry figured in contemporary biographical accounts of the most renowned mathematicians. Now that Bowditch had made a name for himself with these kinds of virtuoso performances, he became someone to take seriously as a man not just of mathematical learning but also of recognized mathematical accomplishments. He began to rub shoulders with formally educated gentlemen on terms of equality. By the fall of 1797 he had developed just such a friendship with Theophilus Parsons, a distinguished Newburyport lawyer with his own substantial reputation as a mathematical savant. They exchanged letters on the fine points of Newtonian astronomy. Parsons, it was later said, "distinguished" the young man "by his particular friendship and most flattering attentions" on many occasions. Bowditch's election in 1799 to the American Academy of Arts and Sciences, Boston's answer to Philadelphia's American Philosophical Society and the French Académie des Sciences, was probably one of these attentions. With admission to the American Academy Bowditch joined many of the most learned men of the region, almost all Harvard graduates, along with such honorary members as David Rittenhouse and British Astronomer Royal Nevil Maskelyne.[9]

Meanwhile, just back from Alicante in 1797, Bowditch was approached by another man seeking his mathematical skill, printer Edmund M. Blunt. Blunt had heard of Bowditch "by means of a mutual friend," perhaps his fellow Newburyporter Parsons, but he wasn't interested in carrying on a learned correspondence. He was having major success with his *American Coast Pilot*, a revised version of the book American mariners used to navigate America's coastal waters, and now he wanted to issue a revised version of the book they relied on to navigate the open ocean. That book was John Hamilton Moore's *New Practical Navigator*, first published in London in 1772, now in its twelfth edition.[10] To be clear, Bowditch's *Navigator* still lay five years away. All that Blunt contemplated now was a modified Moore marketed as an American edition. There was no need to worry about stealing Moore's work. By necessity in a book largely consisting of tables of numbers, Moore had himself incorporated material from earlier authors. More to the point, it would be decades before American publishers would be subject to an international copyright agreement.[11]

Moore's book was a hefty tome. It contained lessons in geometry, logarithms, and trigonometry; instructions in seamanship; directions for surveying harbors; a glossary of nautical terms; a model log kept from England to the Canary Islands; even a study guide for the examination required of officers in the Royal Navy and East India service. Most of the volume, though, was taken up with instructions and information related to determining one's position at sea. Here was the cutting-edge technique of "working lunars" that qualified a man like Henry Prince to take a vessel into the Indian Ocean. Given its significance to Moore's *Navigator*—and to Bowditch's—we need to understand just what this technique involved, what made it so revolutionary, and why it proved vital to America's newly global trade.

Mariners had been using celestial navigation for centuries.[12] In the eighteenth century, sea captains crossing the Atlantic had specialized knowledge and instruments to chart a course to the other side. Making observations of the sun with their quadrants and using a bit of trigonometry, they could quite easily determine their latitude. It was longitude that was the problem. Traditionally, Atlantic captains estimated their longitudinal position by means of dead reckoning, that is, by approximating their vessels' locations from the distances traveled and the courses steered, allowing for such factors as tides and currents. This method also required instruments—the log, line, and glass for distance and compasses for direction—and specialized knowledge of the oceans, but it yielded nothing more than a good guess. Living with this imprecision, many Atlantic captains simply sailed northward or southward along the coast to the latitude of their final destination, then sailed due east or west until dead reckoning and the sighting of land birds and floating vegetation suggested the coast was near and it was time to take soundings.

Bouncing from one side to the other of the Atlantic basin might have worked for Salem vessels making runs to Europe, but the voyages beyond Cape Horn and the Cape of Good Hope required the ability to determine longitude with accuracy. By the middle of the eighteenth century that goal was achievable, at least theoretically. In fact, there were now two methods of determining longitude with precision. Both depended on the fact that it takes twenty-four hours for the earth to rotate 360 degrees around its axis, so four minutes of time corresponds to one degree of longitude. Both involved determining the time at sea and comparing it with the simultaneous time at a position of established longitude, and then converting the difference in times into the difference in distances. We tend to remember the first method—the use of a newly invented, extraordinarily exact timepiece known as the chronometer—because this was the method that triumphed by the middle third of the nineteenth century. But while chronometers were easy to use, they were also very expensive and in Bowditch's day were therefore used almost exclusively by royal naval vessels and the well-bankrolled vessels of Europe's East India companies.

The second, so-called lunar method turned the sky itself into a timepiece. Using this method, the celestial navigator tracked the movement of the moon against the background of other heavenly bodies, so that the moon was in effect a clock hand and the sun, planets, and stars were the "hours" on the clock face. The first step in "working lunars" involved using a sextant to measure the distance between the moon and either the sun, a planet, or a star. Even assuming a clear sky, that was easier said than done. "When a ship is close hauled to the wind, with a large sea, or when sailing before the wind, and rolling considerably," wrote Bowditch with understatement, "it is difficult to measure the distance of the objects." The shipboard time of the observation (itself regulated by a separate series of observations and calculations) would then be compared with the time when this same measurement was predicted for the reference longitude, in this case Greenwich, England. The difference in times could then yield the difference in space. But even apart from the mistakes introduced by human error and heavy seas, there were inherent inaccuracies in these sextant measurements, because light bends as it enters the atmosphere and because lunar observations, measured as angles, are made from the surface, not the center, of the earth. To correct for those inaccuracies required mathematical manipulation. So the final step in reading the celestial clock for position at sea was a complex series of trigonometric and logarithmic calculations.[13]

Those who practiced advanced celestial navigation were of a different kind than those who determined their positions with dead reckoning, and not just because they could find their way across the ocean. When, in the middle of the eighteenth century, Bowditch's uncle Ebenezer studied navigation, he never went beyond trigonometry, but he did learn how "to find how many Signs & Degrees of the Zodiack the Moon is Departed from the Sun Since her last Conjunction with him." For him the skies still existed as a realm of mythic powers and semihuman presences. Not so this new breed. For them, the sky was a source of data they could rely on and manipulate with advanced mathematics into vital knowledge. If we want to locate Bowditch's formative experiences with a clockwork mechanism, the ultimate referent of regularity, certainty, and predictability, we need only look up at the sky.[14]

Moore's *Navigator* was the indispensable book for these new sorts of mariners. It contained instructions for taking astronomical observations, along with pages and pages of tables necessary for mathematically converting those observations into global positions. Navigators had to rely on the accuracy of those tables, and here is where Moore was beginning to fail them. In 1791, when Thomas Jefferson was looking to get hold of a copy, he stipulated a 1781 edition, noting that "the later edns. are so incorrect as to be worth nothing."[15] Blunt turned to "several Gentlemen of the first mathematical and nautical talents in our country" to revise Moore. Though mathematically skilled, Theophilus Parsons contributed material that made the volume more useful, not more accurate: essays on marine insurance and commercial paper. But the others attended to the numbers. Nathaniel's brother William contributed a particularly fussy correction of a computational technique. Like Nathaniel, he seems to have been a stickler for accuracy and detail. Nicolas Pike, with a Harvard master's degree, and author of a popular arithmetic book, contributed a table. Originally Pike was to be the lead editor, but it was Bowditch who ultimately emerged as the true luminary of the revisions. The title page of the 1799 work did not stipulate just who was the "skilful [*sic*] mathematician and navigator" that had "corrected" Moore, but Blunt's preface made it clear that man was Bowditch.[16]

Of the changes and additions Bowditch had made, two stand out as of particular importance. The first was his particular technique for working lunars that he had developed on his very first voyage. "This day thought of a method of making a Lunar observation," he had written in his log on the journey home from Réunion, "which to me is new & in some respects I think it preferable to any method hitherto published." He then detailed the advantages: "No more than 4 places of figures need be taken in the Logarithms"; "shorter than any method I ever saw published"; and "the corrections are always to be applied in the same manner." What he meant by that last remark was that, unlike other existing methods of working lunars, where the results of the numerous calculations were sometimes subtracted and sometimes added to produce the final number, Bowditch's method stipulated that the quantities were always added, so there was less room for confusion and error. Other methods then in use either required the use of logarithms to only four (instead of the usual six) places *or* called for corrections to be always added. Bowditch's had both benefits. It must have been this method that he passed to Don Cosmo de Churruca on his visit to the observatory at Cádiz.[17]

Blunt noted the new lunar method in his preface to the 1799 edition, but he gave it the same single-sentence treatment he gave to the other modifications. If anything got attention, it was the second of Bowditch's major contributions, his correction of almost 500 errors. Most of these involved erroneous numerical entries in the all-important navigational tables. One error in particular was singled out. In his tables of the sun's declination, a particularly crucial set of figures navigators relied on to determine latitude, Moore had erred in counting 1800 as a leap year. In fact, a parliamentary act amending the calendar in 1751 had designated 1800 a so-called centurial rather than a bissextile, or leap, year. That blunder rendered Moore's "present edition useless after Feb 28 1800," Bowditch had written Pike. The tables are "erroneous & ought not to be published." In his preface Blunt too noted that "Mr. MOORE, by reckoning the year 1800 as a leap year, has caused an error at times of 23' in the declination."[18]

With the second American edition, issued in 1800, again with Bowditch's assistance, Blunt amplified his criticism of Moore. While he had no desire "to depreciate the scientific reputation of Mr. Moore," he wrote, the "encreasing [*sic*] incorrectness of Moore's later Editions . . . has so mutilated that very excellent treatise, that, in its present English dress, it cannot fail of proving an erroneous, and perhaps a fatal guide to the deluded Mariner." Indeed, the latest London edition was even worse than the last one. Whether it was Moore's fault or that of his printer—consider the nightmare of typesetting and proofreading all those digits—the new volume had "been sent into the world with new impurities of its own, more dangerous than those it was heir to."[19]

Blunt knew he was onto something in producing a more error-free manual. Suppose he could subject it to a truly thorough cleaning? The second American edition was already under way when Blunt sought out Bowditch in Boston, where the supercargo was to sail the next day with Henry Prince to Batavia. "If you had not corrected the declination," Blunt was supposed to have said, referring to the leap year error, "I should have lost the whole of the last edition." He asked Bowditch to undertake a thorough examination of Moore's entire work during his voyage and gave him a copy to mark up with corrections. Bowditch agreed. Over the next months, he crossed out phrases, paragraphs, and even whole pages, inserted new explanatory notes and, above all, made numerous corrections in the tables. Prince noted that on the homeward passage he passed by Bowditch at work in his cabin and remarked, "'Well, sir, you seem to put a great many black marks on Johnny Moore.' 'Yes,' replied Mr. Bowditch, 'and well I may, for he deserves it; his book is nothing but a tissue of errors from beginning to end.'" Prince then suggested that Bowditch might better write a whole new book than continue "to mend that old thing," whereupon Bowditch, smiling, replied, "I find so many errors that I intend to take out the work in my own name."[20]

And so he did. In 1802 his name appeared on the title page as the author, and Blunt published it as the first edition of the *New American Practical Navigator*. In his preface, Bowditch did have some praise for Moore. Unlike older treatises on navigation, which took a theoretical approach to the topic, the London manual had included "only such matter as might be useful to the mere practical navigator" and combined that material with the appropriate tables. But while "the principle of its construction" was sound enough, "the execution of the work" was another matter. In particular, Moore's leap year error had been "fatal to several vessels." This was the same error Blunt had alluded to as "perhaps a fatal guide," but with Bowditch there was no "perhaps." Mathematics gave certainty, and with mathematical certainty came moral certainty—and outrage. Moore's error amounted to "a very criminal inattention," Bowditch wrote. It had been "the cause of losing two vessels to the northward of Turk's Island, and bringing others into serious difficulties." Now that Moore was off the title page, Blunt too became more, well, blunt. "While tendering his thanks to such as have assisted in the establishment of the work," he wrote in the prefatory advertisement, "it would be highly criminal to omit those due to *John Hamilton Moore*; . . . as his late editions have been so erroneous that no person would hazard his interest, much less his life, in navigating his vessel by the rules there laid down."[21]

Bowditch's presentation of what set his work apart from that of Moore focused almost entirely on this and other numerical errors. Not only had Moore made his own mistakes, he wrote in his preface, but he had unthinkingly copied the mistakes of others, including those made by no less august a personage than British Astronomer Royal Nevil Maskelyne. All told,

		1 HOUR.							
M.	S.	Log ½ela Time.	LogMid Time.	Logarith Rising.	M.	S.	Log ½ela Time.	LogMid Time.	Logarith Rising.
0	0	0.58700	4.71403	3.53243	10	0	0.52186	4.77917	3.66542
	10	0.58583	4.71520	3.53482		10	0.52086	4.78017	3.66747
	20	0.58465	4.71638	3.53721		20	0.51986	4.78117	3.66952
	30	0.58348	4.71755	3.53959		30	0.51886	4.78217	3.67156
	40	0.58232	4.71871	3.54197		40	0.51787	4.78316	3.67359
	50	0.58115	4.71988	3.54434		50	0.51688	4.78415	3.67562
1	0	0.57999	4.72104	3.54670	11	0	0.51589	4.78514	3.67765
	10	0.57884	4.72219	3.54905		10	0.51491	4.78612	3.67967
	20	0.57768	4.72335	3.55140		20	0.51393	4.78710	3.68168
	30	0.57653	4.72450	3.55375		30	0.51294	4.78809	3.68369
	40	0.57539	4.72564	3.55608		40	0.51197	4.78906	3.68570
	50	0.57424	4.72679	3.55841		50	0.51099	4.79004	3.68770
2	0	0.57310	4.72793	3.56074	12	0	0.51002	4.79101	3.68969
	10	0.57196	4.72907	3.56306		10	0.50905	4.79198	3.69169
	20	0.57083	4.73020	3.56537		20	0.50808	4.79295	3.69367
	30	0.56970	4.73133	3.56767		30	0.50711	4.79392	3.69566
	40	0.56857	4.73246	3.56997		40	0.50615	4.79488	3.69763
	50	0.56745	4.73358	3.57226		50	0.50519	4.79584	3.69961
3	0	0.56633	4.73470	3.57455	13	0	0.50423	4.79680	3.70158
	10	0.56521	4.73582	3.57683		10	0.50327	4.79776	3.70354
	20	0.56409	4.73694	3.57910		20	0.50232	4.79871	3.70550
	30	0.56298	4.73805	3.58137		30	0.50137	4.79966	3.70745
	40	0.56187	4.73916	3.58363		40	0.50042	4.80061	3.70940
	50	0.56076	4.74027	3.58589		50	0.49947	4.80156	3.71135
4	0	0.55966	4.74137	3.58814	14	0	0.49852	4.80251	3.71329
	10	0.55856	4.74247	3.59038		10	0.49758	4.80345	3.71523
	20	0.55747	4.74356	3.59262		20	0.49664	4.80439	3.71716
	30	0.55637	4.74466	3.59486		30	0.49570	4.80533	3.71909
	40	0.55528	4.74575	3.59708		40	0.49477	4.80626	3.72101
	50	0.55419	4.74684	3.59930		50	0.49383	4.80720	3.72293
5	0	0.55311	4.74792	3.60152	15	0	0.49290	4.80813	3.72485
	10	0.55203	4.74900	3.60373		10	0.49197	4.80906	3.72676
	20	0.55095	4.75008	3.60593		20	0.49104	4.80999	3.72867
	30	0.54987	4.75116	3.60813		30	0.49012	4.81091	3.73057
	40	0.54880	4.75223	3.61032		40	0.48920	4.81183	3.73247
	50	0.54773	4.75330	3.61251		50	0.48828	4.81275	3.73436
6	0	0.54666	4.75437	3.61469	16	0	0.48736	4.81367	3.73625
	10	0.54559	4.75544	3.61686		10	0.48644	4.81459	3.73813
	20	0.54453	4.75650	3.61903		20	0.48553	4.81550	3.74001
	30	0.54347	4.75756	3.62120		30	0.48462	4.81641	3.74189
	40	0.54242	4.75861	3.62336		40	0.48371	4.81732	3.74376
	50	0.54136	4.75967	3.62551		50	0.48280	4.81823	3.74563
7	0	0.54031	4.76072	3.62766	17	0	0.48189	4.81914	3.74750
	10	0.53926	4.76177	3.62980		10	0.48099	4.82004	3.74936
	20	0.53822	4.76281	3.63194		20	0.48009	4.82094	3.75121
	30	0.53718	4.76385	3.63407		30	0.47919	4.82184	3.75307
	40	0.53614	4.76489	3.63620		40	0.47829	4.82274	3.75491
	50	0.53510	4.76593	3.63832		50	0.47740	4.82363	3.75676
8	0	0.53406	4.76697	3.64043	18	0	0.47650	4.82453	3.75860
	10	0.53303	4.76800	3.64254		10	0.47561	4.82542	3.76043
	20	0.53200	4.76903	3.64465		20	0.47473	4.82630	3.76227
	30	0.53098	4.77005	3.64675		30	0.47384	4.82719	3.76409
	40	0.52995	4.77108	3.64885		40	0.47295	4.82808	3.76592
	50	0.52893	4.77210	3.65094		50	0.47207	4.82896	3.76774
9	0	0.52791	4.77312	3.65302	19	0	0.47119	4.82984	3.76955
	10	0.52690	4.77413	3.65510		10	0.47031	4.83072	3.77137
	20	0.52589	4.77514	3.65717		20	0.46944	4.83159	3.77318
	30	0.52487	4.77616	3.65924		30	0.46856	4.83247	3.77498
	40	0.52387	4.77716	3.66131		40	0.46769	4.83334	3.77678
	50	0.52286	4.77817	3.66337		50	0.46682	4.83421	3.77858

Nathaniel Bowditch, "Table XXI: For Finding the Latitude by Two Altitudes of the Sun." In Bowditch, *New American Practical Navigator*. Newburyport, Mass.: Edmund Blunt, 1802. Most of the volume's hundreds of pages were filled with hundreds of numbers, each the product of a series of (re)calculations. Division of Rare and Manuscript Collections, Cornell University Library.

Bowditch counted some 8,000 errors in Moore and over 2,000 in Maskelyne. He proceeded methodically from table to table, all twenty-nine of
them, detailing the corrections he had made. His irritation with mathematical error seeps through the dry prose. Of table VII he commented: "There is
not a single number in Moore's table that agrees with that published in this
work." Of table XIX he wrote peevishly: "I have discovered no less than nine
hundred thirty errors in this table, which only contains four pages." Only at
the end of his seven-page preface did Bowditch address the new prose material he had introduced into his manual, and then in only two paragraphs.
Much of this material, he wrote, was "taken from useful publications."[22] In
an age before international copyright agreements, neither piracy nor plagia-
rism was an issue. Authority, not originality, was required. And Bowditch's
authority came from his numbers.

In fact, though, Bowditch's method of working lunars was original—
almost. In his preface he took pains to establish his authorship of it, not to
tout the method as a revolutionary discovery—he knew many alternative
methods existed—but to make clear that he had not copied it from anyone else. He invented the method in 1795, he explained, and then taught it
to several others the following year, but in 1797, he acknowledged, Joseph
de Mendoza y Rios, a Spanish mathematician, had published "a method
somewhat similar" in the Royal Society of London's *Philosophical Transactions*. That journal, and the scientific circles in which Mendoza y Rios
traveled, carried with them an authority that Bowditch and his provincial
contacts did not.[23] Bowditch had been scooped. No doubt the Spaniard's
work had eluded him. It took time, after all, for the *Philosophical Transactions*
to arrive in Salem, and he was often away at sea. Already in 1799, believing
(mistakenly) his lunar method was about to be published in the American
Academy's *Memoirs*, Bowditch recognized the need to establish priority. He
had asked his old benefactor, academy member Nathan Read, to make certain his article appeared with a note, indicating his invention of the method
in 1795 and its presentation to the American Academy in 1797. But with the
publication of the *Memoirs* indefinitely delayed, Bowditch could not make
his claim of priority until the publication of his *Navigator*, a full five years
after Mendoza y Rios's method had appeared in print.[24]

Just what, then, lay behind the success of Bowditch's *Navigator*? It was not
the first truly practical book of its kind. That honor belonged to Moore, as
both Blunt and Bowditch readily acknowledged. It did not pioneer *the* lunar
method of calculating longitude at sea. Many such methods had been in use
for decades, and they continued to be used even after Bowditch published

his. Nor was Bowditch's method a breeze, in contrast to all previous ones. The heavy lifting of making the lunar method into a practical reality had occurred years earlier, when Maskelyne published tables of precomputed values in his *Nautical Almanac* and his *Requisite Tables*. Those texts first made it possible to simplify the task from at least four hours of calculations, requiring comprehension of mathematical principles, to a half hour's work of retrieving the appropriate numbers from tables and plugging them into a rote formula.[25] Even so, like other versions, Bowditch's first required calculations preparatory to taking lunar observations. Then the observations themselves had to be taken, a task requiring skill in the use of the sextant. Finally, those observations had to be run through a series of computations involving familiarity with trigonometry and logarithms.

One could argue that Bowditch's work proved successful because it opened up the world of navigation to a broader, humbly educated audience by providing the ABCs of nautical mathematics.[26] The very first sentence of Bowditch's *Navigator* departed from Moore in this manner: "Many persons who have acquired considerable skill in common Arithmetic," wrote Bowditch, "are however unacquainted with the method of calculating by decimals, which is of great use in navigation." Bowditch presented fuller instruction in geometry, trigonometry, and logarithms than had Moore. His text was clearer and better organized. He provided a list of abbreviations and symbols at the beginning of the text, instead of midway through the presentation of geometry, as had Moore. But the differences should not be exaggerated. Both authors included practical examples of mathematical problems, and neither made the acquisition of nautical mathematics a simple enterprise. There was nothing easy, for example, about understanding the rules for solving all the possible types of problems in right-angle and oblique-angle trigonometry, even if Bowditch had collected them all into two text-thick tables.[27]

But if not the very first practical guide, if not a revolutionary breakthrough, if not an automatic self-instructor, the *Navigator* was nonetheless enormously useful, clear, and comprehensive. It also had several unique virtues. Unlike Moore's volume, it offered much material useful to sea captains as they engaged in trade. These included a lesson in calculating compound interest using logarithms; coverage of marine insurance, bills of exchange, commercial contracts, and the laws governing shipowners, shipmasters, factors, and agents; and examples of properly executed mercantile forms and captain's accounts. Such advanced commercial knowledge was becoming increasingly vital as American trading vessels moved outside of the familiar coastal and transatlantic routes of the colonial era.[28]

Even more critical, the *Navigator's* pointedly American perspective mag-
nified the book's usefulness. Bowditch listed the latitudes and longitudes
of over 100 more places along the American coastline than had Moore. Its
exemplar of a ship's log detailed a voyage from Boston to Madeira instead
of London to Tenerife. Bowditch eliminated the fawning dedication to
the Lord High Commissioners of the Admiralty and the model examination given to prospective officers in the Royal Navy and the East India
service. But apart from the relevance the book offered to American users,
its American provenance appealed to their nationalism. Salem's East India
Marine Society endorsed the *Navigator* "as being a genuine American production." After Blunt sold the rights to publish the *Navigator* in England for
a whopping 200 guineas, one American newspaper reported the copyright
sale price in capital letters, while others printed the London edition preface "that the public may be informed of the high reputation of the 'NEW
AMERICAN PRACTICAL NAVIGATOR' in England." Some reports even
claimed—inaccurately—that the purchasers of the English copyright were
none other than Moore's publishers, as if they had finally wised up and bid
good riddance to their countryman in favor of Mr. Bowditch of Salem.[29]

Though nationalism played an important role in the *Navigator's* success, it was above all the book's unprecedented accuracy that accounted
for its popularity. Ultimately what mattered most was the reliability of the
numbers. The lives of men and the safety of cargoes were at stake. In its
endorsement of the book, the East India Marine Society praised Bowditch's
"improved . . . methods of calculation" and his addition of latitudes and
longitudes for places along American coast "hitherto very inaccurately
ascertained," but item number one was his correction of "many thousand
errors, existing in the best European works of the kind."[30] Who would have
guessed that Moore, the author of the most popular navigation manual in
the English-speaking world, could not be trusted? Who would ever have
dreamed of questioning the numbers provided by Nevil Maskelyne, a tow-
ering figure in the world of astronomy and navigation? Bowditch, of course.
He knew that numbers held no power unless they were accurate.

Accuracy depended as much on typesetting and proofreading as on
the generation of the correct numbers in the first place. For that reason,
Bowditch stuck with Blunt for thirty-five years, producing another eight
continually revised and expanded editions. As Bowditch had commented
to Nicolas Pike in 1798, Blunt was "determined to publish the work as correct as possible." His faith did not waver. In a letter to Bowditch regarding
the upcoming 1817 edition, Blunt promised that the volume "shall be very

handsome and perfectly correct." Bowditch later responded, "I presume it will have the usual marks of your accuracy in printing." Though Blunt was not an easy man to get along with—quick to anger, litigious—and there were more than a few testy moments between the two men, both realized that in their shared commitment to exactitude they were a good match.[31]

FOR ALL ITS VIRTUES, Bowditch's *Navigator* was not without its critics. Scarcely had the book appeared when a writer for London's *Monthly Magazine* cited the book as evidence that European culture transplanted to America invariably degenerates, for what was it but a purloined copy of Moore's *Navigator*? An American obtains a copy of a "most esteemed British publication" and then "puts it to the press, puffs it in the newspapers, entreats the partiality of his brethren to the new American work, in exclusion of the British, and palms a very inferior edition upon them, at more than double the price!" "Jealousy," sputtered the Boston rebuttal. Everyone knew the imperfections of Moore. It was left to Bowditch to "correct its innumerable errors, alter its arrangement, and in fact, from a huge mass of words, figures and hieroglyphics, jumbled together, to produce a correct, methodical and scientific work." Bowditch's *Navigator*, the Boston writer claimed, "has contributed more to the literary reputation of America" than any other recent American work. It stood as a rebuttal to the Old World's perception that Americans were either too boorishly commercial to appreciate and encourage what was broadly termed "literature" or too primitive to produce it. But any *real* gentleman, we can imagine the British critic responding, would know that literature did not encompass a how-to book for the merchant marine.[32]

A second salvo was fired by George Baron, an English-born teacher of mathematics and navigation living in New York.[33] The tone of his critique is made clear from the title of a pamphlet he published in 1803: *Exhibition of the Genuine Principles of Common Navigation, with a Complete Refutation of the False and Spurious Principles Ignorantly Imposed on the Public in the "New American Practical Navigator."* In it, he described Bowditch as "unacquainted with the Mathematical principles of the subject" and an "ignoramus" foisting his "contemptible book" upon a credulous public.[34] Baron was not to be taken seriously. He was one of those characters who needed to put some miles between the source of and the market for his credentials. He claimed to have been associated with England's military academy at Woolwich but was more likely a self-taught village schoolmaster. He had recently been fired from a teaching post at West Point for "improprieties" that involved accusations of mutiny, theft, infidelity, and even murder. He was also more than a little delusional. He claimed to be writing his own manual that would allow a seaman to determine his position at sea "without the least calculation whatever."[35] No such work ever appeared—how could it?

It would have been wisest to ignore Baron's charges, and Bowditch made no public move to discredit him, though behind the scenes he attempted to blackball Baron's recent submission to the *Memoirs* of the American Academy.[36] But Edmund Blunt was an excitable man, soon to be known as the man who hurled an iron skillet at an engraver in his employ. (The engraver took revenge by memorializing the incident in a satirical cartoon that soon appeared on custom-designed chamber pots.)[37] In the pages of his *Newburyport Herald*, Blunt denounced Baron as "a quack mathematician." In New York's *Mercantile Advertiser*, he offered "FIVE HUNDERD DOLLARS REWARD" to Baron if he could prove to the satisfaction of an "impartial Mathematician" that Bowditch's book was truly based on "false principles." Baron accepted the challenge and called for "any Mathematician to meet me publicly," but that seems to have been the end of the matter.[38]

A far more serious critique appeared in a rival navigation text published in London in 1804. Its author, Scotsman Andrew Mackay, though not a university graduate, had received an honorary L.L.D. from Aberdeen's Marischal College, was elected a fellow of the Royal Society of Edinburgh, taught mathematics, astronomy, and navigation in Aberdeen and London, and published a *Theory and Practice of Finding the Longitude at Sea*. In the preface to his *Complete Navigator*, Mackay stated that while Bowditch's work "pretended to be very correct," in fact it contained "many errors and contradictions." He detailed a few of those mistakes and then concluded that it would be "a tedious task to enumerate the errors contained in the above-mentioned book." Mackay's American publisher soon picked up on the critique, noting that "*pretensions* to accuracy are, indeed, more numerous than real *attentions* to that subject." Perhaps just to rub it in, he advertised the newly published work on the front page of the *Newburyport Herald*, hard by an advertisement for Bowditch's *Navigator*, placed by a bookseller located "in Blunt's building."[39]

The problem was that Mackay was correct. These errors did exist, but only in the English edition Blunt had sold to a London editor. Either that editor, or his printer, or perhaps both, introduced the errors Mackay quite rightly detected. Bowditch must have found the whole situation galling. He could only address the mix-up in the preface to the second edition of his *Navigator*, published by Blunt in 1807. It was a tour de force of postured humility and equanimity. Bowditch began by addressing the issue of errors obliquely, simply stating the steps taken to ensure accuracy in calculation and typesetting. Perhaps to avoid any appearance of arrogant self-regard, he no longer totaled Nevil Maskelyne's mistakes to over 2,000 and instead reported that his tables agreed with those published by the Astronomer Royal "excepting a small alteration," or "nearly," or differing but "a little." By the time he got to the latitudes and longitudes of world ports, he claimed only to be presenting a table "*at least* as complete and accurate as any extant," adding, "it is so difficult to obtain perfect accuracy in a table depending solely on observations, that no one ever published was perhaps entirely free from error." And simply as "proof of this assertion"—payback was of course out of the question—he enumerated some examples from three works: Maskelyne's *Requisite Tables*; J. W. Norie's *Epitome of Practical Navigation*, a new English contender; and Mackay's *Complete Navigator*. Now he was ready to literally turn the tables on Mackay. "The remark made by Doctor Mackay in the preface of his work," he concluded, "that 'the case of the seaman who has to trust to such tables . . . is truly lamentable,' might in many instances apply with equal justness to his own table." Only then did Bowditch address Mackay's charges directly. The London edition had indeed contained mistakes, he conceded, but not a single error mentioned by Mackay had appeared in the Newburyport imprint.[40]

Quite suddenly at the beginning of the nineteenth century, American mariners had to choose among rival practical navigation manuals. Where once there had been only one truly practical manual in the English language, Moore's *Navigator*, now there were four: Moore, Bowditch (1802), Mackay (1804), and Norie (1805). Competition took the form of a war in which the battleground was accuracy. Bowditch had taken on Moore over the issue of errors. Mackay had taken on Bowditch over the same matter. And Norie, without naming names, simply stated that, as an instructor of navigation, he "frequently had occasion to lament that most of the existing works on Practical Navigation, and particularly some that have been very generally circulated, are extremely erroneous." Up and down the American coast, booksellers advertised the competing manuals. Bowditch's competitors were at their strongest south of New England, but by the 1820s, though Norie dominated elsewhere in the English-speaking world, Bowditch had won out in America, and nautical authorities could assume Bowditch's *Navigator* as a universal presence on board American vessels.[41] "If the ship cannot be saved," read the *Kedge-Anchor; or Young Sailors' Assistant*, "the passengers and crew are the first objects, with some fresh water and biscuit; a compass, quadrant and Bowditch." And sure enough, when in 1820 the Nantucket whaler *Essex* was wrecked by a whale, a story that soon seized the imagination of Herman Melville, its survivors salvaged what its first mate later called "the probable instruments of our salvation"—compasses, quadrants, and Bowditch.[42]

In part, Bowditch achieved supremacy in the United States because Moore and Mackay died, new editions of their books soon ceased, and no American edition of Norie was ever issued. Meanwhile, Bowditch and Blunt continued to issue new editions every few years, adding new information, improved methods, additional tables, and the longitudes and latitudes of yet more places. Bowditch's attachment to numbers, even apart from the accuracy they generated, can be seen in his sluggish acceptance of the rival technique of finding longitude, the chronometer. That method required no tables and only the simplest of calculations. Bowditch first included a section titled "To find the Longitude by a perfect time-keeper, or chronometer" in the 1821 edition. Still he insisted that while "it is wonderful to observe how accurately some of these chronometers perform their office," ultimately they could only be "useful in a short run." In "a long voyage," he explained, "implicit confidence cannot be placed in an instrument of such a delicate construction, and liable to so many accidents." By 1826, he directly acknowledged the growing use of chronometers as the result of rapidly falling prices and increasing reliability, and responded by expanding the section on chronometers while detailing their shortcomings. Too many things might throw a chronometer off—firing guns on board, a sudden jarring, bad watch oil—and so, as he had in 1821, he provided instructions on how to reset the chronometer at sea to true time—by using lunar observations. By the 1833 edition, Bowditch had not changed his tune, but on its final page, Blunt advertised "CHRONOMETERS," "now considered as an indispensable addition to the sextant," for sale at his nautical bookstore.[43]

WE SHOULD PAUSE and reflect on just what was involved in producing the *Navigator*, because it tells us something fundamental about Bowditch's skill as a mathematician, his very personality, and his place in the contemporary world of mathematics. The main selling point of his book, its accuracy, derived from his calculation of thousands upon thousands of numerical values found in its many tables. The calculations were, of course, *recalculations*. Others had done them before, mathematical assistants known since the seventeenth century as "computers," though no single individual ever undertook as many as Bowditch did. When we look at what these computers did, and who they were, we begin to see why.

In Britain, Maskelyne had been hiring computers since 1765 to produce the annual *Nautical Almanac*.[44] This publication, the companion to navigational manuals like Moore's and Bowditch's, was a compilation of ephemerides, tables of celestial positions needed to calculate longitude at sea. Each ephemeris provided a month's worth of values, calculated and tabulated at three-hour intervals, totaling up to 1,365 values for each month. Each tabular entry called for locating as many as a dozen values in other tables and performing perhaps fourteen arithmetical operations on seven- or eight-figure numbers. Some of the computers, working in pairs, performed identical computations. Others served as "comparators," comparing the calculators' ideally identical results to catch errors. All did their work at home on a piece-work basis, with Maskelyne's handwritten instructions and preprinted blank tables, and the results were transmitted back and forth by post. Meanwhile, at the Royal Observatory in Greenwich, Maskelyne hired a live-in assistant who took astronomical observations and performed related calculations. Here too the computational duties, performed six days a week, were taxing.

To undertake these labors, Maskelyne did not hire men like himself, university graduates with international reputations for their scientific work and a host of publications and learned society memberships. Instead, he hired individuals who could do the computations but may or may not have been fully conversant with the theoretical science and mathematics that lay behind the numbers. Most were country schoolmasters, clergymen, and surveyors. Often something in their background prevented their ability to get further education, or to rise in the world even if they did. Israel Lyons was a Jew, for whom the required profession of Christian belief ruled out an Oxford or Cambridge degree. Others came from too far down in Britain's social hierarchy. As for Mary Edwards, the only woman of thirty-five computers Maskelyne employed, well, need more be said? Stamina figured at least as much as education in qualifying them as computers. A Greenwich assistant must possess "a good constitution to enable him to apply several hours in the day to calculation," stipulated Maskelyne, as well as be "sober & diligent, & able to bear confinement." The *Almanac* computers were not full-time employees, but their work was much the same, so that Greenwich computer Thomas Evans's descriptions of his labors probably held for them all: "Nothing can exceed the tediousness and *ennui* of the life the assistant leads in this place," he wrote in 1810. "He spends, days, weeks, and months in the same long wearisome computations."[45]

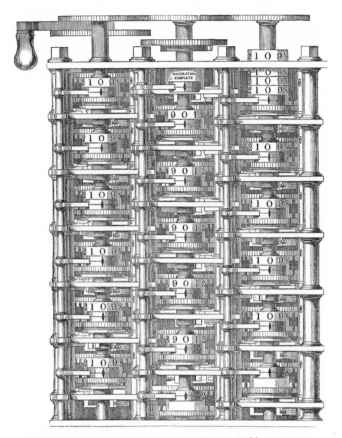

"Difference Engine No. 1," 1833. In Henry Prevost Babbage,
*Babbage's Calculating Engines: Being a Collection of Papers Relating
to Them, Their History and Construction.* London: E. and F. N.
Spon, 1889. Babbage designed the mechanism to replace human
computers (like Bowditch) in the production of nautical tables,
on the assumption that humans could not perform such laborious
calculations without error. Division of Rare and Manuscript
Collections, Cornell University Library.

Was it even possible for the human mind to engage in such drudgery
and produce accurate results? Writing in 1824, Englishman Francis Baily
pointed to "the impossibility of confining the attention of the computers
to the dull and tedious repetition of many thousand consecutive additions
and subtractions." Having undertaken just this kind of work, his countryman Charles Babbage concluded that human computers must invariably
make errors. "I wish to God these calculations had been executed by steam,"
he reportedly exclaimed, and he went on to invent a machine, considered

the first mechanical computer, to calculate and print mathematical values for just such tables, including the kinds of nautical tables Bowditch had recalculated. Baily had the highest of hopes for this "substitution . . . of the unvarying action of machinery for this laborious yet uncertain operation of the mind."[46]

But for Bowditch such work was anything but mechanical drudgery. He delighted in it. Working as an eighteenth-century human computer, he aspired to the "unvarying" accuracy of the mechanical computers of the nineteenth (or twenty-first) century. He found pleasure and fulfillment in this superhuman, perhaps inhuman, machinelike undertaking, one Babbage later characterized (in a letter to Bowditch) as a task "from which all human agents would shrink in hopeless despair." Enjoyable in itself, it led to the further delight of finding errors in others' work. We find Bowditch as a teenager copying Daniel Fenning's *Algebraist's Companion* and correcting the author's demonstration of a geometrical theorem in a margin note. In his late twenties Bowditch sent a letter to Samuel Webber, Harvard's Hollis Professor of Natural Philosophy, reporting an error in Newton's *Principia*. The story may have gotten garbled—Bowditch may have been aiming much lower, at James Winthrop's mathematically misguided essay in the American Academy's *Memoirs*—but in either case, it was Bowditch the calculator-critic at work.[47]

It is not surprising, then, that even before Blunt approached him with a request to revise all of Moore, Bowditch was scouring that manual for mistakes. The practical benefits of correcting errors were obvious, but for Bowditch there was a satisfaction in a correct number that went beyond utility, just as there was pleasure in computation that a chronometer could never provide. In his first labors on Moore's *Navigator*, he had not bothered correcting errors that were too insignificant to make a practical difference at sea, settling instead for "sufficient exactness," but when he published his own work he could not resist aiming for absolute accuracy. "Most of the errors in Maskelyne's collection," he wrote of some 2,000 mistakes, "were in the last decimal place, and the corrections in many instances would but little affect the result of any nautical calculation." Nevertheless, he added, since "most of these tables are useful on other occasions, where great accuracy is required, it will not be deemed a useless improvement to have corrected so great a number of small errors."[48]

Perhaps, but then he would have had to argue as much. Many in this era regarded mathematics as a pursuit for pedants, constricting the mind into a narrow fixation with pinpoint precision. Bowditch might have also wanted to avoid the lingering stereotype of the mathematician with his head in the clouds. Jonathan Swift's *Gulliver's Travels* had satirized just such characters in depicting the floating island of Laputa, a circular isle populated by distracted mathematicians who ate food cut in the shape of "mathematical figures" but whose houses were built with not a single right angle "from the contempt they bear to *practical geometry*, which they despise as vulgar and mechanic." Many of Bowditch's countrymen looked askance at theoretical science as smacking too much of aristocratic leisure. Science and mathematics could win a place at the republican table only if they were clearly useful.[49]

However he might justify his labors, it was not utility that powered Bowditch's passion for recalculating the values in the *Navigator*'s tables. He was drawn by the pages and pages of numbers themselves. Consider that they replaced dead reckoning, when mariners found answers to where they might be in the quality of the sand at the ocean's bottom, the color of the water, the type of bird flying overhead, even the smell of an approaching shore. The lunar method took the mariner out of this focus on the particular and the material into the universal and abstract, the sublime world of pure numbers. It was fitting that these numbers appeared in print, the medium that, by contrast with handwriting, was associated with the impersonal. Numbers meant not just abstraction but also certainty, and here too Bowditch experienced a kind of aesthetic appreciation, even a spiritual quest that emanated from the core of his personality. Eventually that quest shaped his design of impersonal institutions, but in the realm of pure computation it meant that Bowditch would find equal pleasure in generating accurate numbers and identifying erroneous ones.

Benjamin Peirce, later Bowditch's mathematical protégé and a sophisticated and accomplished mathematician in his own right, grasped this aspect of his mentor's disposition. In his evaluation of Bowditch's scientific career, Peirce divided astronomers into three types: the practical astronomers (the "lowest class") like Herschel, who observe the heavens; the theoreticians (the "noblest of astronomers") like Copernicus, Kepler, Galileo, and Newton; and the critics, those who occupy "the judicial bench of astronomy." Bowditch, Peirce wrote, was of this third type, able to detect the errors and omissions in others' work.[50] That sort of scientific temperament, we may reflect, draws equally on the pleasure felt in mathematical certainty and the irritation experienced with inaccuracy. That was Bowditch to a tee, a man at once rigidly confident in his own correctness and peeved by others' shortcomings, mathematical and otherwise.

Critiquing the scientific work of others was a difficult balancing act. On the one hand, criticism was inherent to the workings of the Republic of

Letters, working in tandem with dissemination to advance toward scientific truth. Years later, when a novice college instructor politely pointed out an error in Bowditch's work, Bowditch took no offense and was in fact moved that his work had reached "the outer verge of civilization." On the other hand, within the intimate Boston/Cambridge/Cape Ann community of learned gentlemen, social considerations demanded finesse. On this score, Bowditch failed miserably. In 1799, for example, he had submitted a scathing critique of a mathematical essay by James Winthrop that had appeared in the American Academy's *Memoirs*, looking for it to be published in that same journal. Though accurate, it could hardly be allowed to appear in print. Winthrop was a Harvard graduate, a founding member of the academy, altogether a pillar of Boston's social and cultural elite. To be sure, Harvard professor and academy officer Samuel Webber wrote Bowditch, published errors must be subject to published refutations, but it was important to consider one's approach in doing so. Though "preferring truth to every other consideration" (including the unspoken consideration of social delicacy), he continued, Bowditch might "perhaps think it expedient, upon reconsideration, if not to cancel, at least materially to alter" some of the criticisms and leave others out altogether. No need to go on at length about it. Best to let the embarrassing moment pass as quickly as possible.[51]

Bowditch never really learned this social lesson, especially outside the realm of mathematics. In future years he would be taken to task for what many considered unnecessarily candid exposés of others' shortcomings. On the other hand, where there was genuine respect he was quite capable of tact. In 1802, for example, he responded to an essay published by David Rittenhouse in the *Transactions* of the American Philosophical Society that claimed to present an original demonstration of a theorem. Bowditch pointed out that "it was only a simple corollary of a much more general proposition published by Newton . . . and by many other authors, . . . some of which were published near a century ago." But Rittenhouse and the society merited his intellectual respect, and Bowditch was accordingly deferential. "Accept this, Sir," he wrote the society's secretary, "from a young man (an American) who without any education except such as could be procured by himself during the few hours spared from a busy employment, hopes that if this trifle does not meet with approbation, it will be excused from the consideration of the difficulties the writer laboured under in pursuing his studies."[52]

Three years later Bowditch was so bold as to point out mistakes made by the French mathematician Sylvestre François Lacroix in his text on integral calculus, filling the three-volume work's margins with corrections. He tempered his critique with a display of fawning obsequiousness. Having read the work "with great attention, profit & pleasure," he wrote Lacroix, "I discovered several small typographical faults, which though trifling in themselves, I thought might be useful if you were about publishing another edition of your work & from its great merit I had no doubt that would be the case." Bowditch then laid on a second dose of flattery—"you must accept them [the corrections] as the offering of a young man & one of your scholars as the homage of his respect for the instructions he has received from your works"—followed by humility: "You must excuse any faults in these notes, as it is very probable I may have noticed for erroneous places which are in fact correct."[53] It was not like Bowditch to suspect himself of having made mathematical errors, but he recognized that he was a nobody from America and Lacroix a deservedly famous man.

Bowditch's mathematical skill won him recognition among New England's men of letters. As we have seen, in 1799 he was elected to Boston's American Academy of Arts and Sciences. An even bigger prize awaited after the publication of the *Navigator*, when Harvard conferred an honorary master's degree on him in 1802. The multiple links between Harvard and the American Academy suggest any number of ways Bowditch's name might have come up for consideration. Harvard's president, Joseph Willard, also served as vice president of the academy. Samuel Webber, Harvard's Hollis professor, was also one of the academy's counselors. Every single one of the six fellows of the Harvard Corporation, the leading governing board, belonged to the academy, and three of them assumed posts in its governance.

Bowditch's degree was announced and conferred at the college's commencement ceremony. In these years, this was very much a public affair, since the state contributed to its coffers and played a prominent role in its management. Newspapers throughout New England announced the order of proceedings—the speeches and poems delivered by specially honored graduates in English, Latin, and Greek—and later reported on the event, listing the names of all those granted degrees. The ceremony itself was accompanied by public pomp. In 1802 the Boston Dragoons escorted the governor to the Cambridge campus. There, a wide variety of officials, alumni, and curious locals joined the proceedings. Bowditch "always spoke of this as one of the proudest days of his life," his son recalled, and although he would receive many more distinctions, both in America and abroad, "he recurred to this with the greatest pleasure."[54] It is not that the degree somehow certified that he had received advanced mathematical training; as we have seen, a Harvard education neither emphasized nor guaranteed that kind of instruction. The 1802 commencement was proof enough of that fact. Bowditch had long ago surpassed the level of expertise represented by the "Pieces in Algebra, Perspective and Astronomy" presented at the ceremony, like the thesis presented by Asa Mitchell titled "Algebraic Solutions of Problems" or by Alexander Townshend, "Perspective View of Massachusetts Hall."[55] But he now had the same credential as his fellow gentlemen of science, men like Edward Holyoke, Nathan Read, William Bentley, John Prince, and Theophilus Parsons, and it must have boosted his sense of self-assurance in the learned circles in which he participated.

But in the wider world of scholarship Bowditch's status was much less secure. Over the course of his lifetime, understandings of what it meant to have mathematical talent underwent a sea change. Recall that when Bowditch first showed his skill at calculating—working away on his slate, solving mathematical conundrums for dumbstruck audiences, finding errors in Moore and Maskelyne—such abilities were understood as the very essence of intelligence. Then, as historian of science Lorraine Daston has written, "astonishing feats of mental arithmetic were soon to become the province of the idiot savant and the sideshow attraction"—ouch!—"no longer the first augury of profound mathematical gifts." By the early nineteenth century, new ideas of "genius" as a creative power arising from some mysterious essence and irreducible to rules replaced notions of mental ability as essentially computational in nature.[56]

We can see the Romantic movement at work here, with its temperamental and tragic poets and composers—and scientists. Mathematicians in particular, at least the true geniuses among them, were seen as driven to eccentricity or even madness by their distinctive occupational hazard, their removal from physical reality into a realm of pure abstraction. Bowditch, the Yankee supercargo, could not have been a worse fit for this emerging stereotype, and his mathematical labors never strayed far from the sea, the earth, and the stars. We can also see the industrial revolution at work in these changing conceptions of mathematical work. "Calculation took on the dull, patient associations of repetitive and ill-paid bodily labor," writes Daston. It now "ranked as the lowest of the mental faculties." Just such labor was Bowditch's delight. When he published the *Navigator*, Americans were primed to interpret his correction of 8,000 errors as evidence of astounding mental powers. But thereafter, the world, outside America anyway, was less and less likely to make the same judgment.[57]

Perhaps Bowditch himself knew as much. As his learned friend John Pickering recalled, the *Navigator* was not one to which Bowditch "himself attached any importance in respect to his scientific reputation, or in any other view than as a *practical manual*; the first excellence of which is, the greatest possible accuracy."[58] The work of establishing that kind of reputation still lay in Bowditch's future. So too did his application of mathematical order and certainty to the world of practical affairs, the realm in which his mathematical powers would prove the most influential.

CHAPTER FOUR

Gentleman Actuary

When he returned from his fourth trading voyage in 1800, Bowditch became the forty-ninth member of Salem's newly established East India Marine Society. The EIMS was far more exclusive than the Salem Marine Society, the one that had assisted Habakkuk when he had fallen on hard times, for it restricted its membership to masters and supercargoes of vessels that had "actually navigated the Seas near or beyond the Cape of Good Hope, or round Cape Horn." These men constituted Salem's maritime elite. Their camaraderie was based in common experiences at sea and in foreign lands and a pride in their superior technical skills and cosmopolitan knowledge. Nothing testified to that camaraderie more than their annual feasts, when members shared "an elegant dinner" and drank "appropriate toasts." And nothing testified to their cosmopolitan identity more than the processions that preceded the dinners, when members marched through town wearing "the dresses of the Eastern nations" and carrying "curiosities" from "those remote nations and islands."[1]

EIMS members shared a global perspective, but they were also enmeshed in a web of local ties. In this respect, the EIMS typified the town in which it was established. Salemites, like other Americans from port cities—but unlike their mostly rural countrymen—were used to toggling back and forth between global and local perspectives, between their planet and their neighborhood. EIMS members exchanged information on how to ply strange waters and conduct business with strange peoples, but they also mingled regularly over brandy and Spanish cigars. They knew each other intimately. Among Bowditch's fellow members were his uncle and father-in-law Jonathan Ingersoll, his former masters John Ropes and Jonathan Hodges, Henry Prince and John Gibaut, and others like Dudley Leavitt Pickman and Thomas Wren Ward who were close personal friends. If Greenwich was their reference point at sea, Salem was the prime meridian of their lives on land.

So though his *Navigator* brought him an ever-expanding reputation in America, and his work in science would receive some recognition abroad, it was here, in Salem, that Bowditch had to establish his place in society. He had long been poised to realize the social potential of his kinship connections and intellectual accomplishments, but they had never guaranteed

Michele Felice Corné, East India Marine Society sign, 1803. The shipmasters and supercargoes of the society shared a cosmopolitan identity derived from their voyages into the Pacific and Indian Oceans. © 2006 Peabody Essex Museum. Photo by Mark Sexton.

he would leave the humbler past of Habakkuk's cooperage behind him. It was his success as a Derby supercargo and his membership in the American Academy of Arts and Sciences that first raised his standing. His marriage into the Ingersoll clan reinforced his family connections, and his Harvard degree added heft to his reputation as a man of letters. Bowditch indulged his new social and cultural prominence; he carried a green silk umbrella and stocked his scientific library with European imprints.[2] The couple soon took their places among the town's most favored circles. They joined such exclusive organizations as the Salem Athenaeum, the successor to the Philosophical Library, and the Salem Female Charitable Society, and their religious and political affiliations classed them with others of their status. They lived in fashionable neighborhoods, educated their sons for a Harvard education, and socialized with men of learning, men of affairs, and women of celebrated intellect.

The cornerstone of the Bowditches' place in society was Nathaniel's leadership of a marine insurance company. It was something quite new in Salem, in fact in America: a business corporation. Much of elite life took place in incorporated institutions—the First Church, the Town of Salem, the Athenaeum, the EIMS, to name just those in Bowditch's life—but given their novelty and purpose, profit-making corporations might seem to be altogether different. Even with the official legislative charter and bylaws, though, Bowditch's insurance company operated much like everything else in town always had, with the informality and flexibility that comes with conducting business among a small community of familiar players. Personal relationships continued to constitute the basis of business affairs, and Bowditch was not shaking things up, at least not yet. Still, we catch a glimpse of what would later become his trademark approach to practical affairs—impersonal systems, standardization, regularity—in his work with the East India Marine Society. The EIMS was onto more than it knew when it appointed Bowditch to "methodize" its members' logbooks.

LIKE MANY A supercargo made good, Bowditch settled down and looked for a way to make money on dry land. His first approach, again a typical one, was to partner with other investors in overseas trading voyages. Along with Henry Prince, he was among five men with financial interests in the cargo of the *Recovery*, the first ship to return to Salem from Mocha, Yemen, with coffee. Not every speculation went well. In 1800 he invested in a vessel that was seized by the French. In 1802 he lost half his money in another venture. That same year the lure of a new commercial opportunity moved him to undertake a fifth voyage, hoping to realize the fabulous profits from the newly opened pepper trade with Sumatra. In November the 266-ton ship *Putnam* set sail for the Pacific, "Sixteen Kegs and One Box of Dollars" totaling $40,000 in its hold, with Bowditch as its captain.[3]

Bowditch had never been a shipmaster, and according to Henry Prince, while highly skilled at navigation, he "knew but little of what is called *seamanship*," that is, the actual handling of a vessel. Whether to circumvent his alleged lack of skill or, as his son claimed, to make more time for his studies, Bowditch struck a deal with his officers. He would navigate the *Putnam*, and they would sail it. As an experienced supercargo, he did know how to proceed once the *Putnam* arrived in Sumatra—with caution, given that business had to be conducted with the island's natives and there was no broker in sight. To Mary, he described the Sumatrans "to be as honest as the generality of people in other countries," but in his "Remarks on the N.W. Coast of Sumatra," written for his fellow merchants, he described a testier relationship. Still, the real difficulty lay in the competition among Americans, for they proved willing to offer a higher price—or "a handsome present"—to corner the limited supply of pepper. Unable to assemble a full cargo, the *Putnam* headed for Réunion. There they loaded up 260 bags of coffee, took on provisions, and set sail for home.[4]

By far the most renowned aspect of this voyage came to be the supposed circumstances of his Christmas night return to Salem, when Bowditch, to the utter amazement of his townsmen, sailed fearlessly into Salem harbor in a blinding snowstorm solely on the strength of his calculations. One element of this story is certainly true. A *Salem Register* item dated 26 December reported, "Arrived last evening, ship Putnam, Capt. Nathaniel Bowditch, from Sumatra, and the Isle of France." But we have reason to doubt the more dramatic elements. Edward Holyoke recorded rain that night, and Bowditch's logs mention nothing more dramatic than a clearing fog. Bowditch's eulogists did not include the alleged feat in their lengthy biographical accounts. It was his sons who first related the anecdote, with more than a touch of a father's tall tale about it: the "fierce gusts of wind," the fleeting glimpse of a lighthouse confirming the calculations, the "old tars" amazed by their captain, the anxious wife's recognition of the "quick knocking" on the door. "The story of his arrival home used to make me thrill as a boy as I listened to it," recalled Henry decades later.[5] A virtuoso navigational performance? Probably not.

The Sumatran voyage was Bowditch's last. He was now thirty, time to become a sedentary merchant once and for all. The *Putnam* venture had further increased his wealth, and Mary wanted him home, out of harm's way. Only a year earlier, her seventeen-year-old brother Henry had died in Batavia, on board the *Margaret*. "Try and think this will be your last voyage," read the letter from her he received in Sumatra. "I should think no sacrifice too great to make to enable you to tarry on shore for what is life when deprived of our nearest friends." In his response, he was not shy about expressing his love, with perhaps even a touch of the erotic. Say "to yourself for me every thing dictated by the tenderest & most ardent affection," he urged. And then, "Again my Mary I repeat that you must say for me (what in person I cannot say for myself) everything dictated by the purest & most ardent affection."[6]

A few months after his return, Bowditch spent much of the summer of 1804 surveying the harbors of Salem and nearby Marblehead, Beverly, and Manchester. He intended to complete the Salem survey of 1794, which had depicted the harbor itself in only the broadest of strokes, but he soon found that even this sketchy delineation was inaccurate. John Gibaut and William Bentley had produced this schematic harbor survey, but time had been short and the instruments poor, Bowditch explained tactfully, and the baseline for determining the distances of the harbor islands from shore had been too short. In the interest of discretion, he kept silent on just who had set the baseline, but of course it had not been Bowditch. The harbor survey would have to be done from scratch. Even with the help of assistants, the work extended into the next two summers, finally culminating in 1806 in a meticulously engraved chart and accompanying sailing directions printed by Edmund Blunt. "When we consider how very minute Mr. B. has been in the work before us," read Boston's *Monthly Anthology* of the work, "we cannot believe there is a single omission of importance to navigators." Bowditch had even included some shoals and ledges "that were hardly known to our best Pilots, . . . most of which were so little known, that names had not been given to them." It was typical of Bowditch to exceed the degree of accuracy that might actually be required for practical purposes.[7]

The survey was useful, but it did not point the way to a permanent livelihood. Though he might have continued on the usual path of investing in vessels and cargos, Bowditch was about to take up a new way of making a living he would follow for the rest of his life. In December 1804 the directors of the Essex Fire and Marine Insurance Company (EFM) appointed Bowditch president at an annual salary of $1,200. The vote was seven to one. Son Henry pointed to an unnamed EFM director, "a sturdy and sensible old sea-captain," as his father's inside track to the position. Bowditch had translated a Spanish document for him, without charge no less, and the ship-master was so impressed with Bowditch's cleverness and generosity that he "immediately used all his influence in promoting the election of his young friend."[8] Bowditch had no prior experience in marine insurance, unless including Parsons's essay on the topic in the *Navigator* or buying a policy on the *Putnam* from the Salem Marine Insurance Company are to count. Nor was he a Harvard-educated shipowner and merchant, like Jacob Ashton, president of Salem Marine, or alternate candidate Willard Peele, who had garnered the single dissenting vote.[9] So why did he get the position?

There was no obvious set of qualifications for the EFM post for the simple reason that insurance companies—indeed, financial institutions of any kind—were relatively new entities in the United States. The first American bank was established only in 1781, the first in Massachusetts in 1784, and the first in Salem, the Essex Bank, in 1799. Fire and marine insurance had been available even before the Revolution, but not from profit-making corporations. So-called fire mutuals, such as the one founded by Benjamin Franklin in Philadelphia, operated as mutual aid societies. As for marine insurance, ad hoc groups of individuals underwrote these policies, spreading the risks and profits among themselves. The first successful insurance company in America, the Insurance Company of North America, was not established until 1792, in Philadelphia. In the Bay State, the pioneer was Massachusetts Fire and Marine, some three years later. Ashton's Salem Marine Insurance Company was the first in Bowditch's home town, established in 1800. Corporate charters granted by state legislatures authorized the operation of all these enterprises. Stockholders contributed the capital and shared the profits in the form of company dividends, while corporate directors set policy and elected a president to manage affairs.[10]

Not only were banks and insurance companies new to the new republic; so too were business corporations of all kinds. In the eighteenth century, and well into the nineteenth, most businesses activity was conducted by individuals, partnerships, or informal associations of men banded together for the duration of a particular enterprise. There were no general incorporation laws; each required a special act of the state legislature. In line with the era's understanding of the purpose of corporations, which had heretofore been limited to such entities as towns, churches, and colleges, legislatures issued charters to only those bodies that could somehow establish themselves as contributing to the general welfare, usually by undertaking projects that served public ends but were beyond the means of government. Bridges, turnpikes, banks, and fire and marine insurance companies met these legislative criteria, since they encouraged urban development and commerce, thereby stimulating overall economic growth. But the privileges and powers invested in business corporations, and their associations with monopolies and aristocracies, could arouse popular suspicion and resentment. EFM does not seem to have excited these sentiments, but Bowditch would have his hands full with them later in his business career.[11]

When he assumed the EFM presidency, then, Bowditch was assuming control of a new kind of entity, and there were no preexisting set of qualifications set in stone. He had to attend to two distinct kinds of activities: investing the capital and underwriting risks. Marine insurance companies existed at least as much for the former as the latter, but in terms of the company executive's time and skill, the investment end of insurance work was relatively simple. In the case of EFM, the corporate charter stipulated that the capital could be invested only in "the funded debt of the United States, or of this Commonwealth, or in the stock of the United States bank, or of some incorporated bank in this Commonwealth." Bowditch had few decisions to make.[12] A far more complex responsibility was to assess the risk associated with each voyage to set an appropriate premium, or to deny insurance altogether, and to evaluate applications for loans in which vessels and their cargoes acted as collateral. These tasks took some quantitative skill, but far less than Bowditch possessed. What he could bring to the position, unlike Harvard graduates Ashton and Peele, was actual experience at sea. He had literally written the book on it. He understood the hazards relevant to particular voyages, from pirates to privateers, unreliable charts to shifting shoals. And as both a retired shipmaster and an EIMS officer familiar with its collection of members' logs, he was in a favored position to assess a captain's skill and judgment.[13]

Bowditch was socially familiar with many of the company's stockholders, directors, and customers, and that mattered too. As a corporation EFM may have been a modern form of economic enterprise, but in its day-to-day operations it operated according to long-established rules of business conduct oriented around personal relationships. Merchants dealt largely with other merchants, sea captains, and supercargoes known to them, many related to them by blood or marriage, some by friendship, and others by well-worn rivalry. Even when business dealings prompted suspicion or rancor, the men involved had engaged in personal (if tense) relationships and might resolve their conflict to avoid diminished reputations. If such relationships had long functioned as the foundation of trust in commercial affairs, given the new global scale of trade, with its unknown commercial players and incomplete information, they were now even more critical. Transacting business in the context of social equality, personal familiarity, and individual relationships, even corporations like EFM conducted themselves in a manner that to us today seems almost unbusinesslike. In the company's records, for example, we find a letter from Bowditch to his brother-in-law quoting him an insurance premium rate and passing on Mary's orders for household furnishings.[14]

Or take the issue of paying insurance premiums. The shipowners and merchants who insured vessels and their cargoes were used to paying premiums in notes—essentially IOUs—and to regarding payment due dates as flexible. Defaulting on an obligation was out of the question, of course, but if a merchant found payment on a particular date inconvenient, he might request a postponement and then pay compound interest for the extended period. In 1810 Boston merchants James and Thomas H. Perkins made just such a request of EFM. The affirmative reply came quickly, with the addendum: "As I expect to be in Boston in a few days, [I] shall defer the adjustment till I have the pleasure of seeing you." The company could hardly have responded differently to the Perkins brothers' request; Thomas was an EFM stockholder and director. Both brothers had shown particular "kindness" to Bowditch's father-in-law Jonathan Ingersoll during a rough patch and employed Mary's brother in Canton.[15]

It is critical to understand such practices as something other than the corrupt use of pecuniary or personal leverage. Such "insider" practices might be proscribed today, but in Bowditch's time they were standard operating procedure. Even more, servicing the financial needs of a small coterie of men—not just including but *especially* stockholders and directors—was the openly acknowledged raison d'être for the establishment of financial institutions in this era. Who better to trust, and to serve, than men of one's acquaintance? What is more, in a small community of economic actors, where business relationships stretched over years, it was understood that mutuality and forbearance ultimately best served the goal of making long-term profits. If I do a favor for you today, you will do one for me tomorrow. Pressing for payment when payment cannot be made will be fruitless. Better to wait and get something later. Under these circumstances, punctual payment could mean nothing more than timely notice of the inconvenience or impossibility of paying on the due date.[16]

Refusing such requests was therefore a tricky business. In 1811 Bowditch explained to merchant Israel Thorndike that, due to recent marine insurance losses and an upcoming dividend, he needed payment on two premiums, now four months overdue. He had sent a notice to Thorndike three weeks earlier, Bowditch noted, tactfully (and disingenuously) suggesting that Thorndike had probably not received it. Thorndike quickly paid up but asked Bowditch if he could hold off on cashing the check. "If it is possible to keep back the check till the 15th June I will do it with pleasure," answered Bowditch. Again, it would have been difficult to respond otherwise. Thorndike was an enormously wealthy Beverly merchant with multiple, long-standing ties to Salem's mercantile community. He was one of the movers and shakers behind the Essex Bridge linking Beverly with Salem and the Salem Turnpike connecting Salem with Boston. He collaborated on land deals with Salemite William Prescott, an EFM stockholder and the company's legal advocate. And he was a major Federalist leader, the political party with which the EFM directors allied.[17] To the president and directors of EFM, men like Thorndike were not mere customers but fellow participants in a social, economic, and political enterprise.

Given this broader definition of the interests EFM represented, it is not surprising that marine insurance companies tended to cooperate with one another. Marine risks had traditionally been shared by multiple underwriters, so it was nothing new for those seeking insurance to shop around their proposal with several companies. But cooperation extended well beyond the sharing of risk to the sharing of strategic information. Boston merchant Thomas C. Amory informed Salem Marine Insurance Company's Jacob Ashton of the legal response to an insurance claim taken by Boston's underwriters and asked him to pass the information along to Bowditch, "as he probably will be desirous of acting in concert with you." Acting on inside information ("communicated to me by a very influential Director"), merchant Dudley Pickman reported to Bowditch, his close friend, that several Boston insurance companies had met "to compare their ideas of premiums, not to bind themselves at all, but merely to find something of what each thought." It was not quite price fixing, but nor was it free market competition.[18] The insurance directors would probably not have thought of what they were doing as collusion any more than they would have seen anything inappropriate in conducting business with one of their own.

In Salem the physical embodiment of this interknit mercantile community was Essex Street, just as in Boston it was State Street; in New York, Wall Street; and in Philadelphia, Chestnut Street. Here were the insurance offices, banks, securities brokers, and, at one point, the U.S. Customs Office. Here too were the post office, the printing office of the *Salem Gazette*, the Sun Tavern, and the Essex Coffeehouse, where merchants might pick up the commodity that defined mercantile identity on both sides of the Atlantic: information. To make informed decisions, merchants needed to stay on top of world events, business intelligence, and gossip about individual commercial players. All this was available on Essex Street. At their counting houses and insurance offices, men of business kept libraries of relevant publications. At EFM, for example, Bowditch ordered works on marine insurance and subscribed to numerous newspapers. But much important information still traveled by personal letter or word of mouth. "Hearing some bustle one afternoon, in the street," wrote an English visitor to Salem in 1807, "I went to the window and beheld a principal officer of Massachusetts (appointed by the United States), who, seated in a one horse-chair, had stopped before the door of one of the marine insurance-offices, to relate the news." To evaluate insurance risks, Bowditch kept his ear to the ground. During the War of 1812, for example, he maintained an extensive "News Book" in which he recorded military and maritime intelligence acquired from newspapers, letters, and conversations with mariners, maritime passengers, overland travelers, and stagecoach drivers.[19]

As a business district, Essex Street was also a male preserve. When brothers-in-law Horace Story and John Forrester met there to settle a particularly acrimonious business dispute, a fight broke out in the middle of the street. Story "lifted his cane," wrote one Salemite, "struck Mr. Forrester across the head, beat him from the Insurance Office to the opposite side of the street, finally threw him down, broke his own cane and took another." At that, she reported, "they were parted by Dr. Bowditch." It was hardly a proper place for ladies, and not just because of the potential for fisticuffs. "To pass the insurance offices was like running a gauntlet," recalled Marianne Silsbee of what she termed "the Essex Street review." The "gentlemen swarmed out to the sidewalk to stand in judgment during at least an hour, and woe unto the luckless dame or damsel whose demeanor and costume did not suit their fancy." It was "an ordeal," she continued, especially because "now and then some uncivil commentator, after a steady stare, would insinuate that the pretty girls walked that way to be 'seen of men.'"[20] It is hard to imagine Bowditch acting in such a manner, but EFM employed three secretaries over the course of his tenure, all young, unmarried, and potentially uncivil.[21]

The densely packed, bustling, chattering streetscape of Essex Street reflected an underlying reality: the interconnectedness of all its institutions. The boards of Salem's banks, insurance companies, and turnpike and bridge companies constituted an interlocking directorate, and the same people could be found politicking and socializing together off-hours. Small wonder that the Salem Marine Insurance Company and the Salem Bank shared a building; that the cashier of the Essex Bank also served as treasurer of one of the bridge corporations; that the stockholders of that bank held meetings at the EFM offices; that the treasurer of the Salem Turnpike Corporation distributed dividends at the same location; that the East India Marine Society museum was located above the Salem Marine Insurance Company office; or that the Salem Athenaeum held meetings at the Essex Bank and established its library above the EFM office.[22] Essex Street had its factions, both personal and political, but through interconnected family, social, business, and political associations, it constituted a recognizable community, made up of multiply overlapping casts of characters. A stroll down Essex Street was a stroll through this world.

Bowditch achieved great success as president of EFM. The corporation's directors soon raised his salary, and the year after they reelected him to head their concern.[23] He developed a reputation for his skill and integrity, but there was nothing groundbreaking in the manner in which he conducted company affairs. That would come later, with his move to a far more influential financial corporation in Boston in the 1820s. Even in the early years of the nineteenth century, though, we can see the first signs of what would become his trademark innovations. He introduced them in his capacity as an officer of an institution a short stroll from the EFM insurance office, the East India Marine Society.

One of the primary goals of the society was to collect nautical and commercial intelligence for dissemination among its members. Its earliest bylaws directed members to submit their logbooks, along with a record of any important or unusual observations. That move was part of a larger trend in the trading community to see an advantage in sharing and even publicizing at least some information—as in the printed "price currents" for sale in port cities on both sides of the Atlantic—rather than keeping it all proprietary. Like merchants, Salem's shipmasters and supercargoes understood that it was better to settle for a smaller piece of the commercial action than to fall victim to the perils—shipwreck, above all—of monopolizing information. Then too the sharing of intelligence, because it ultimately benefitted the entire maritime community, countered the image of the EIMS as a socially exclusive club. "The object of this society is not a mere ostentatious parade," noted the *Salem Gazette*, referring to their spectacular annual processions, "but the promotion of nautical and commercial knowledge, which the journals and observations deposited in the library by the member[s] on their return from distant voyages fully testify." Nevertheless, the very language of the EIMS provision, requiring members "in all cases" to turn over their logs "without any excuse whatever," suggests sluggishness, even resistance. Turning over one's log could be a delicate affair. In recording weather conditions, courses, seamanship decisions, astronomical observations, and navigational calculations, logs documented potential errors of skill and judgment. They also often contained material that was irrelevant, or even private, such as Bowditch's remarks regarding the *Henry*'s drunken mate.[24]

Bowditch was at the forefront of efforts to circumvent this resistance. In 1801 he was one of three men charged with preparing "blank forms & printed directions to be furnished Members going abroad, for the purpose of collecting nautical information & procuring natural curiosities." The forms included preruled columns with printed headings for the various categories of nautical data. Separate pages at the end were reserved for such commercially valuable information as weights, measures, currencies, imports and exports, business practices, and "whatever is singular in the manners, customs, dress, ornaments &c. of any people." Once submitted, the next step was to make logbooks available to members. The 1800 bylaws had directed a committee to review such materials and the secretary to make extracts from them, but nothing was done until 1804, when the members instructed "Capt. Nathl Bowditch to make extracts from the Journals, and to arrange & methodize the same." As Inspector of Journals, a post he held almost continuously until 1820, Bowditch reviewed the journals, bound them in groups of ten, and provided an index with highly detailed annotations for each volume.[25]

The contents of the six volumes constitute a rich legacy of nautical and commercial information, but we should pay attention to their form as well. In Bowditch's time the systematic, standardized recording of information, epitomized by the use of printed blank forms, was rare. Consider the nautical world. In Britain, the East India Company used printed marine journal forms by the late 1700s, but the Royal Navy would not adopt them until early the next century, *after* the EIMS did. By the 1780s a few stores catering to the maritime trade began to sell blank "seaman's journals," with preprinted columns for observations, but they began to catch on only after 1800. It was little different in business affairs. Invoices and receipts accumulated by EFM are handwritten notes on variously sized scraps of paper. Only those issued for payment of newspaper subscriptions are printed. No surprise there— newspaper printers *would* stand out for their use of printed forms. Powers of attorney? Again handwritten, and on different sizes of paper, though for legal reasons the wording was standardized. Applications for marine insurance? More like personal letters, though the policies themselves were executed on printed forms. In fact, most documents we think of as "all business" still bore a personal touch. Bookkeeping ledgers, for example, were hand ruled and often included records of both business and personal expenditures of the owner. At the turn of the nineteenth century the use of blank forms was limited largely to the government in its interactions with citizens: seaman's certificates, bills of lading, tax receipts, military requisitions. But even the U.S. census did not distribute uniform printed forms until 1830, while most passport applications consisted of personal letters into the 1840s, with a uniform printed application form the rule only at the end of the century.[26]

Bowditch was drawn to blank forms at an early date, and would be over and over again in the decades to come. The implications of their use are not trivial. In contrast to individually generated writings, printed blank forms systematized the gathering of information and standardized the information collected, depersonalizing the entire process. British Astronomer Royal Nevil Maskelyne had distributed such forms to his computers, but all printed forms turned their users into computers, in the eighteenth-century sense of the term—that is, mechanical recorders of data.[27] Bowditch's work for the EIMS may be one of the first times we see him drawn to designing standardized and impersonal information systems, but it would not be the last.

Once elected EIMS president in 1820, Bowditch found a second target for his instinct to "methodize and arrange" the society's vast holdings of artifacts. First would come a thorough survey of the objects, followed by an updated catalog. He found the collection itself "in a perishing situation," moth-eaten, deteriorated, with "many articles (sometimes of entirely differ-ent forms & natures) . . . crowded together in the same cabinet." It was nearly impossible to figure out what was what. "None of the shells and minerals were classed and hardly any of them numbered," he wrote. "Many important articles were not entered upon the Catalogue, and roughly half the curiosities in the museum were without any marks by which they could be identified in the old catalogue." That catalog was nothing more than an inventory chron-ologically ordered by date of acquisition, similar to a clerk's raw waste book entries before, according to classic bookkeeping practice, they have been reorganized under ledger headings. The first job was to group and num-ber the objects according to the category in which they belonged. "New numbers have been painted upon most of the articles," he reported, "and it is proposed to label as many of them as will admit of conveniently." Then a new catalog was issued, listing thousands of numbered artifacts clus-tered by category of artifact, beginning with thirty-eight war clubs. Finally Bowditch recommended that "to provide greater regularity and accuracy in the entries on the Catalogue and in the arrangement of the articles which may hereafter be presented to the society," a superintendent of the museum be appointed.[28]

Regularity, uniformity, method: allegiance to these values had guided Bowditch in his work on the *Navigator* and would enter into his work in business affairs most forcefully in the 1820s and 1830s. During his Salem years we see them in his indexed logbook volumes, blank forms, accession numbers, and catalogs. They are the marks of the Enlightenment mathema-tician on practical affairs. With celestial navigation the shipmaster relied on the regular movements of the heavens, abstracted into tables of numbers, to locate his position with certainty. In Salem the EIMS's blank forms turned personal narratives into impersonal tables, while its museum classification scheme allowed one to locate a numbered artifact with equal certainty. Such practices would become a signature feature of Bowditch-directed institu-tions, with an impact that extended well beyond Salem's maritime elite.

BOWDITCH'S LEADERSHIP IN Salem's commercial community positioned him advantageously for entry into Salem's social elite, but by itself it did not guarantee full acceptance. Social distinction was a tricky thing in republican America. In Britain making one's money in active trade would disqualify a man from gentry status. Not so in America, where hereditary titles did not exist and where wealth meant full immersion in business affairs. Still, there was a sense that *mere* wealth was compatible with boorish materialism, so along with economic credentials there were social and cultural credentials to be considered. A classical education was one such testimonial to refinement, one that Bowditch, even with his knowledge of scientific Latin and his honorary Harvard degree, lacked. There were those in early nineteenth-century Salem, as there would be all his life, for whom that deficiency was critical. "The little Mr. Bowditch [is] puffed up by the flattery of his mathematical studies & destitute of every degree of literature, or manners," wrote Bentley in his diary in 1804. But, as we shall see, Bentley had other reasons to be peeved with Bowditch, and for the most part Salemites accepted Bowditch's participation in the Republic of Letters as clear proof of literary distinction. He was a critical member of the American Academy of Arts and Sciences. In 1810 he was a leader in establishing the Salem Athenaeum, a private library that merged the Philosophical Library with the even older Salem Social Library. (Its bylaws included a blank form for certifying membership.) His role in the Athenaeum spelled social as well as intellectual prominence, because the library's corporate charter allowed for only 100 shareholder members.[29]

A life of gentility also meant living in appropriate surroundings. In the early days of their marriage the Bowditches rented a "large, neat, well finished three story Dwelling-House" on Market Street, located between the residence of a wealthy sea captain and the Essex Bank. It was built for two families, a living arrangement common among the well-to-do in that era. Increasingly, though, the wealthy were opting to live away from the sources of their wealth, the harbor and the town's commercial district, and apart from the town's middling and poorer sorts. So in the middle of 1805 the Bowditches moved to an elegant, three-story brick dwelling on Chestnut Street in the newly fashionable west end of town. Across the broad avenue sat Hamilton Hall, the social headquarters of the town's smart set, or at least that portion affiliated with the Federalist Party. Both buildings were the work of Samuel McIntyre, a local woodcarver and architect known for his skilled craftsmanship and tasteful, au courant design. This house too was a double; each side of the hip-roofed box, typical of the so-called Federalist style, had its own entrance and interior staircase. The other half was occupied by their cousin, and Nathaniel's erstwhile master, Jonathan Hodges. Hodges had lost whatever fortune he had when his son failed in business, but he had been rescued—as Salemites with connections tended to be— and made the clerk of the Salem Bank, the secretary of the Salem Marine Insurance Company (whose president was married to Hodges's daughter), and the Treasurer of the Town.[30]

In 1811 the Bowditches bought their own house on Essex Street for just over $4,800, about three times Nathaniel's annual salary. It was yet another three-story Federalist box, though this one was built of wood. Mary decorated it with an eye to gentility, ordering "50 yds carpeting (plaid, red & yellow), best kind," and more in "Fruit Baskets of an oval or round form." The garden followed the same rules of refined taste. It featured box-lined alleys, beds, and a pear tree. The house was ample, and the Bowditches employed domestics to maintain it, but it was no mansion, nor did the family live like merchant princes. They didn't have that kind of wealth, and the Bowditches did not choose to spend what money they had on a higher degree of high-style display. Instead Bowditch was intent on building his scientific library, and that meant buying expensive publications from abroad.[31]

In raising their seven children—five boys and two girls born between 1805 and 1823—the Bowditches had all the usual genteel expectations. For the boys—Nat, Jonathan (always called by his middle name, Ingersoll), Henry, Charles, and William—that meant a Harvard education. The first step was private tutoring, followed by Salem Private Grammar School.[32] Bowditch took a special interest in his sons' mathematical progress. "Nat continues to do very well at school," Mary wrote a family friend, and "his master thinks he will succeed equally as well in his Cyphering as in other things he has undertaken, which you will readily believe pleases his Father *a little.*" Bowditch even undertook some of the instruction himself—Nat started in on the *Navigator* at the age of eleven—and he bribed his boys with gifts and money to attend to their arithmetic and French. But with Harvard in their futures—or so Bowditch hoped—he attended to their classical educations as well. A somewhat overanxious parent, perhaps living vicariously through his sons, he went so far as to study Greek to help them prepare for the college entrance examination.[33] His boys would get the classical polish he never did.

Bowditch's social circles partook of this same polish. Not all of his friends were learned; Dudley Pickman was an East Indies merchant plain and simple, recalled as "an absolute genius in financial affairs."[34] But most were. He engaged in astronomical observation cum socializing with some of the town's most distinguished physicians, for example. On one such occasion Bowditch invited Daniel Oliver and Reuben Mussey, along with Mussey's new bride, to his home. With the Dr. and Mrs. absorbed at Bowditch's telescope, Oliver invited Bowditch to use the telescope at his bachelor quarters, a setting Bowditch described as quite "as inaccessible to the company of ladies as a monastery would be." To tease him, Bowditch suggested they all go.

"The Home in Essex Street, Salem, Mass." In Vincent Y. Bowditch, *Life and
Correspondence of Henry Ingersoll Bowditch*. Boston: Houghton, Mifflin, 1902.
Constructed of wood rather than brick, the Bowditches' house was more
modest than the homes of Salem's wealthiest merchants but was decorated
with an eye to gentility. Author's collection.

"The poor Doctor's nerves were violently troubled," Bowditch reported
gleefully, especially when the Musseys, who were in on the joke, brushed
aside Oliver's excuses of "dirty rooms" and "no accommodations." Oliver
remained at the Bowditches until Dr. Mussey "safely deposited his lady," and
then the three men went to Oliver's for "a beautiful view of one of the finest
objects in the heavens, Saturn with his rings & Satellites."[35]

Bowditch's closest friendships were also with those of a scholarly bent.
Daniel White was a bookish Harvard graduate who found what he called the

"chicanery and drudgery" of a legal practice incompatible with his "scholarly tastes and habits." Later in life he eagerly accepted a judgeship, married Eliza Orne Wetmore, a wealthy widow and close friend of the Bowditches, and set up a handsome library in the Salem mansion that now belonged to him.[36] Bowditch's distant cousin Henry Pickering, though a merchant who had not attended Harvard, was nonetheless familiar with Latin, Greek, and French literature. "Delicate and refined in his deportment," with "a highly cultivated and tasteful mind," he was also an art collector, "a connoisseur in statuary," and, after he failed in business, even "something of a poet."[37] Bowditch's most intimate friend was John Pickering, Henry's brother. Remembered as "a youth of a rather retiring and studious nature," at Harvard Pickering excelled in classical learning but equally so in mathematics, even writing a thesis (in Latin) on fluxions, the Newtonian form of calculus. After years abroad in Lisbon and London, he opened a law practice in Salem, but like Bowditch he gave equal time to scholarly pursuits. It was claimed that "he was more or less familiar with twenty-two languages," and his philological publications ranged from an ancient Greek–English dictionary to an essay on American Indian languages. Salemites regarded Bowditch and Pickering as "the two scientific and literacy ornaments" of their town, each in their own orbit but sharing "an insatiable thirst for knowledge." In Pickering Bowditch found his true intellectual soulmate. "They were the counterpart of one another," son Henry reflected, Bowditch in science and Pickering in literature, "bound each to each by the warmest friendship of mutual respect."[38]

One more friend should be mentioned, another learned sort but not another Harvard graduate. Caroline Plummer was a bluestocking. She had been Mary's childhood friend, and Nathaniel came to know her early on. The three were on intimate terms; Plummer even lived in the Bowditch household for several years. Everything about her upbringing had encouraged her to cultivate her mind. Her father was a Harvard graduate and physician with literary and scientific interests, known for his satirical wit. Her mother, the daughter of a minister and a woman known for quoting English poetry, was said to possess an "ability to entertain intellectual company" nothing short of "remarkable." As if these factors were not enough, as a child Plummer had been a frequent visitor to the home of feminist Judith Sargent Murray. Not surprisingly, she grew up to become, as one Salemite remembered her, "eminently distinguished by her intellectual gifts and graces, and her powers of conversation," her "wit and humor," and her impressive "literary attainments." It was said that Bowditch was a "constant" and "affectionate" friend to her, that she in turn "dearly loved" him, and that "no one better understood her whole character, or held it in higher esteem."[39]

Besides maintaining deep friendships, the Bowditches participated at the entertainments frequented by elite society. "We are all dissipation in Salem," Mary wrote a friend in 1814. "Parties every evening." At one such, Mary had danced till one in the morning and had altogether "a brilliant time." That party had been quickly followed by two more; then Mary herself began to prepare feverishly for "her party (or 'sweep')."[40] A more detailed portrait of a party attended by the Bowditches comes from the pen of another participant, Marianne Silsbee. It was a typical evening party of the time, she wrote, attended by between thirty and fifty people, with invitations hand delivered by the host family's domestics or children. The festivities began at about seven, but most of the men did not appear until eight thirty or nine, when they arrived straight from their work. York Morris, "the stout colored waiter," served tea, coffee, and cake to the first round of guests. The gentleman latecomers arrived in time for a second round, this time "whips and creams, Madeira and Sangaree," Iberian wines of the kind Bowditch had once bought and sold. The women sat in a circle and the men circulated within it, engaging in conversation, occasionally taking a free seat. "Keen wit, good-natured argument, and sound sense never flagged," recalled Silsbee. "Men liked to visit, and took a laudable pride in making themselves as delightful as possible." Prominent in her memory were John Pickering "polished in manner, courteous of address"; his brother Henry, "refined in taste even to fastidiousness, poetic in nature"; and Daniel White, "so desirable a companion" because he "devoted the leisure hours of his professional life to . . . reading and study." And then there was Bowditch, "with a charming simplicity equaled only by his great learning."[41]

What are we to make of that reference to simplicity? A subtle and condescending allusion to Bowditch's lack of classical education? Probably not. Almost everyone who described Bowditch tried to capture that same quality and presented it as one of his greatest virtues. Son Nat wrote that in social situations his father responded alternately with "the utmost cordiality of friendship" and "almost the wild hilarity of childhood." One family friend recalled how Bowditch would "jump up and rub his face and head and caper around the room" when he had solved a mathematical problem, and then would grab Mary "as she was sewing and taking both hands make her dance around the room with him, both laughing as if they would die." Daniel White recalled his friend's "natural simplicity, frankness and affability" and his "unconsciousness and artless simplicity." He "took no care to disguise appearances," White wrote, "and he certainly never assumed any." In his eulogy, Alexander Young stressed the "perfect naturalness" of Bowditch's character, noting that "in conversation, he had the simplicity and playfulness and unaffected manners of a child."[42]

Henry Sargent (1770–1845), *The Tea Party*, ca. 1824. Oil on canvas. 163.51 × 133.03 cm (64 3/8 × 52 3/8 in.). Salem's genteel evening socials resembled the one depicted here, though during at least one such event attended by the Bowditches, guests were served drinks stronger than tea. Museum of Fine Arts, Boston. Gift of Mrs. Horatio Appleton Lamb in memory of Mr. and Mrs. Winthrop Sargent, 19.12. Photograph © 2016 Museum of Fine Arts, Boston.

In Europe great mathematicians had often been characterized as childlike in their simplicity. That trait allegedly allowed them to grasp truths about nature that others could not. But by the 1820s that image was passé, replaced by the mathematician driven to madness by his total immersion in the abstract world of numbers. Such ideas may have been floating around Salem, but as we have seen with the changing reputation of computational virtuosi, Salemites were not especially up-to-date on such matters. Still, if Bowditch's "charming simplicity" drew praise, it was more likely because it contrasted so powerfully with the lurking image of the scholar as abstruse and pomp-ous. Learnedness was one thing, but arrogant stuffiness was another. Young's assertion of Bowditch's artlessness was immediately preceded by his com-ment that Bowditch "had no pedantry of any kind. Never did I meet with a scientific or literary man so entirely devoid of all cant and pretension."[43]

The praise for Bowditch's personal bearing must also be placed in the context of his contemporaries' disdain for what they termed "artifice" or "fashion." Even the most polished of Americans looked askance at the high gloss of the European aristocracy, a veneer they believed hid a deeper moral and social corruption. That contempt may explain why some of those who knew the Bowditches best insisted that they "had no taste for large par-ties of pleasure," though they clearly did, but were instead "*old fashioned folks.*"[44] Much better to cultivate the refined but simple and sincere manners appropriate to a republican gentry and to allow the unfettered expression of humankind's natural sociability and benevolence. If Bowditch's "wild hilarity" broke the usual conventions of social intercourse, elite Salemites were ready to view it as charmingly natural. "An instantaneous spring of hearty glee, or mental delight," wrote Daniel White, "would sometimes, notwithstanding his natural and delicate sense of decorum, set all rules of etiquet [*sic*] at defiance, and exhibit itself in the same open and joyous manner, whether he were at the fireside of a friend, or at the Governor's Council Board." He "laughed heartily, and rubbed his hands, and jumped up, when an observation was made that greatly pleased him," commented Alexander Young, "because it was natural for him to do so, and he had never been schooled into the conventional proprieties of artificial life, nor been accustomed to conceal or stifle any of the innocent impulses of his nature."[45] Traces of status consciousness can be detected in both these observations— Bowditch had a "natural" but not a "schooled" sense of decorum—but in combination with his equally "natural" talents, this trait came in for praise. Bowditch, on the other hand, may have felt insecure about his less than gen-teel upbringing, just as he may have felt insecure about his lack of a Harvard education. If he genuinely did not enjoy balls and parties, it may well have been because of this self-consciousness.

MEMBERSHIP IN SALEM'S elite involved making decisions about religion and politics. Sometime in the late 1790s Bowditch moved from his mother's Episcopal faith to his father's Unitarianism, joining William Bentley's East Society. Most elite Salemites belonged to other congregations, but these were Unitarian too. There was no other choice for the town's upper crust. Bowditch's move was not mere social climbing; he was sincerely drawn to the denomination for its perspective on affairs human and divine. He had a firm belief in the Creator but did not worry too much about the details of theology. He regarded Jesus as the greatest teacher of mankind but saw no reason to insist on any other characterization. The Bible was authoritative to be sure, but he "preferred to rest its authority" on its ability to purify and inspire rather than on its (presumed) divine origins. Unitarianism also appealed to him as an Enlightenment scientist. He did not consider a belief in miracles as essential to Christianity. Far better evidence of the existence and beneficence of the Deity existed in the Book of Nature, universally legible through the human power of reason. When he encountered the absence of advanced laboratory apparatus and up-to-date scientific works at Yale, a contrast to Harvard's assets, he chalked it up to the college's orthodox Congregationalism. "The high calvinistic [sic] religion is all that is taught here," he reflected in New Haven, "& to that every thing must bow."[46]

Mary, on the other hand, had been raised as an Episcopalian. Once married, she worshipped at her husband's choice of congregations, but that did not prevent her from holding different ideas. "She was much more Orthodoxically inclined in her views than father was," reflected son William. The family celebrated Christmas, still anathema to Salem Unitarians. And Mary would not permit the children to go outside and play on the Christian Sabbath. In deference to her wishes, and promoted by his own not-so-secret desires, Bowditch kept his older sons quiet on Sunday mornings after religious services by having them work on arithmetic problems. Outdoor play was out of the question, but not other outlets for rambunctiousness. In the afternoons, recalled Henry, "we were allowed to have grand frolics in a back chamber," occasionally pelting each other with the heaps of rose leaves collected for Mary's rose water.[47]

If not as observant as his wife, though, Bowditch was equally moralistic. Convinced that the flute had led him into bad company when he was young, he forbid his children to study music. When Henry followed a marching band up the street, Bowditch shot him a "scornful look." When Henry whistled, Bowditch would "launch poetry" at him, saying "He whistled as he went, for want of thought." He rewarded good behavior—and made a point about thrift—by distributing "promissory notes," homemade cardboard coins marked with the likes of "H.I.B.//I cent//good." Less didactic, and more treasured, were the constellations he inked on the arm of the praiseworthy child—the Little or the Great Bear, the North Star, the Belt of Orion. The "mark of supreme love and commendation," Henry wrote, "was an *infinitely small* dot on the ends of noses," so small that only those "initiated in family secrets could recognize it." These were strict but loving parents. "Kiss my dear little children for me and give them a father's blessing," Nathaniel wrote Mary in 1808 from western Massachusetts. "Kiss the dear boys twenty times for me," Mary wrote her husband in 1811 from New Hampshire.[48]

In 1804 Bowditch quit Bentley's parish and bought a pew in the Unitarian meetinghouse of another of his early mentors, the Reverend John Prince. Bowditch "has attempted to sacrifice me to party by deserting my meeting house because he cannot approve my friendship to the present administration," fumed Bentley. He was correct. The differences between the two parishes were purely political and social. Bentley was an outspoken Jeffersonian Republican whose meetinghouse drew in many sailors and craftsmen. Prince, like Bowditch, was a Federalist, and his pews were filled by the wealthy and learned.[49] Not all members of Salem's elite were Federalists, but most were, with the Derbys standing at the head of the Federalists and the Crowninshields at the head of the Republicans. There was no middle ground.

It would be hard to overstate the partisan animosity that existed in this era, not just in Salem but in America as a whole. At its heart were two competing visions of the promise of America and the threats to its future. Federalists hoped America would become a great commercial empire along the lines of Great Britain. Jeffersonians believed that commercial might necessarily entailed moral corruption; better to maintain national virtue as an agricultural republic. Federalists feared democracy above all, believing voters should elect their betters, men of substance who alone had the understanding of what was good for America and the disinterestedness to pursue that good. Jeffersonians, on the other hand, regarded royal tyranny as the greatest threat to America. The French Revolution heightened these mutual fears. Once the so-called Reign of Terror took hold in 1793 and radical Jacobins sent French aristocrats to the guillotine, Federalists saw their worst nightmare of mob rule realized. To them Jeffersonians were nothing other than American Jacobins, bent on destroying the political and social order. From the Jeffersonian point of view, Federalists were nothing but "Anglomen," plotting to destroy the republic and replace it with oppressive monarchical rule.[50]

Salemites split along these same lines, but within the community of 10,000 souls ideological divisions became all too concrete. Federalists drilled with the Salem Artillery, Republicans with the Salem Cadets. Derby Wharf squared off against Crowninshield Wharf. Well-heeled Federalists moved to the new and tony west side of town. Republicans lived on the east side. Federalists read the *Salem Gazette* and Republicans the *Salem Register*. "The presses smoak," wrote Bentley, "& conversation has the constant tang of politics." Members of the two parties patronized different banks and held dances in different halls. ("The Jacobines [*sic*] are entirely excluded" from the "Federal assembly," Mary wrote Nathaniel in 1802.) Perhaps no day revealed the rift in Salem society like the Fourth of July, marked for twenty years with rival celebrations—parallel speeches, parades, toasts, songs, dinners, and fireworks.[51]

It was impossible not to choose sides, but Bowditch had always sought absolute certitude, whether mathematical or ideological. He committed himself wholeheartedly to the Federalist cause. His first foray into politics was disastrous, because he chose to make his debut in one of the very few places in which it was understood that partisanship could have no place: the East India Marine Society. Bowditch had censored the celebratory toasts submitted in preparation for the EIMS's 1802 annual dinner, pruning some, cutting out others altogether, lending a Federalist cast to their content. Bentley was furious and reported that "the Offended have required a publication of the Toasts for the public judgment & threaten a meeting on the subject. The Society will undoubtedly be injuried [*sic*]." Within days an article appeared in the Republican *Salem Register*. It named no names but printed the full list of unexpurgated toasts. It was a public relations nightmare for the EIMS, and its members hurried to adopt a bylaw stating that "politics shall not on any occasion be introduced into the Society." Bowditch was enraged. He no more liked being scolded by his fellow mariners than by Master Watson. "The results of these votes being declared," read the EIMS minutes, "the Secretary, Nathaniel Bowditch, resigned his office."[52]

Stung, but not put off from politics, Bowditch turned to more openly partisan affairs. In 1802 he ran for school committee, as politicized an election as any.[53] At a party meeting in 1804 he was chosen to be one of forty men in Salem's first ward charged with rounding up voters and distributing premarked Federalist ballots in the upcoming election. It was probably in connection with this task that, according to one of his sons, Bowditch "once assisted in carrying an invalid upon his bed to the polls to vote." That same year he was one of three men nominated by the Federalists for state representative. They lost, but Bowditch was hardly done with politics, for politics was hardly done with Salem.[54] Foreign policy moves implemented under Republican administrations hit the town hard. Jefferson's 1807 trade embargo crippled the town's economy. After the embargo was lifted in 1809, Madison threatened retaliation against Britain or France should either interfere with American shipping. The next step would be war. The question was with whom. Under Madison the drumbeat in 1812 sounded most loudly for war with Britain, much to the horror of Salem's "Anglomen" Federalists.

It was in this politically heated atmosphere that elections for state officials took place in Salem that April. There was no agreement on exactly what happened on voting day, but we do know that voters recently disqualified by Salem's Federalist selectmen blocked the ballot box until those town officials agreed to review their cases later in the day; that about an hour before the polls were set to close, they once more approached the selectmen; and that the selectmen, who later claimed they had been stormed and were in fear for their own safety and that of the ballots, called in the sheriff, who read the riot act and closed the polls prematurely. Several men were tried for rioting, and Bowditch was called to testify. He was probably one of the Federalist allies the selectmen had called in to act as a guard and would therefore have been an eyewitness to the melee. After the men were found guilty, the Federalist *Salem Gazette* hailed the impartiality of the justice system, but Bentley could see only a kangaroo court that had convicted the men "as in the Witchcraft." As for Bowditch, Bentley wrote: "For this affair N. Bowditch was the principal witness, a man of great mathematical labour, but not so well known for other enquiries."[55]

In mid-June a sharply divided Senate approved Madison's call for a declaration of war in a vote of nineteen to thirteen. Of New England's ten senators, eight had voted against it. When the news reached Salem, Bowditch was horrified. The following morning he attended a town meeting called in response to "the gloomy and desperate state of our public affairs." From that meeting came a committee assigned with drafting a memorial to Congress "praying that the People may yet be saved from an unjust and ruinous War with Great Britain." Bowditch was one of nine men appointed to the committee. By that afternoon they had their document. It admitted that Britain had interfered with America's rights as a neutral trader but claimed that France had done so first. "Your Memorialists are unable to perceive the justice of selecting Great-Britain as their enemy," they wrote. In other words, we were fighting the wrong country. What could result but "immense losses" to shipping, the capture of sailors, an alliance with France no better than enslavement, and disunion and desolation at home?[56]

For two days after he heard that war had been declared, Henry wrote many years later, Bowditch was too despondent even to turn to his studies. Then on the third day he woke up, went into the parlor, and told his wife this would not do. He was not going to think about it anymore, and he was going to go back to his mathematics. In fact, Bowditch was neither so passive nor so philosophical. While he continued to pursue his scholarship during the war, he did not keep his distance from political events. A month after the Salem town meeting, he attended the county-wide, anti-war Essex Convention as one of Salem's thirteen delegates. The delegates unanimously adopted resolutions that predicted economic ruin and condemned the likely alliance with France, a government "stamped with despotism and perfidy" and "now in the blood-stained hands of a monster whose falsehood, injustice, cruelty, ambition, and tyranny have not in any period of the world been surpassed." Then, according to Henry, sometime during the war Jonathan Ingersoll gave Bowditch a cane loaded with lead "as a weapon of defense from political opponents of that day."[57]

Unable to affect the course of events, Bowditch responded with his sardonic sense of humor. Returning from a visit to a friend in Portland, the Bowditches found themselves in Kittery, Maine, when Madison, in line with common wartime practice, declared a national day of "*Public Humiliation & Prayer*," humiliation in this sense meaning humility before God. Bowditch took it as an opportunity for political wit. The day "being that selected by our President for a day of humiliation for all who had been instrumental in stirring up this war," he wrote, "we concluded that we had nothing to do with it & that it was best to proceed to Portsmouth." Mary's travel diary recorded her own form of irreverence: "fast day," followed by "just made a dinner upon Lamb & charming apple pie." Back in Salem the distant war dampened the vigor of daily life. "We have so little to do in these days of non-intercourse, embargo & war," wrote Bowditch in February 1814, "that to keep ourselves from the horrors of '*Ennui*' (a wicked little word) we have with one assent begun to visit each other *furiously*."[58]

But by the spring of 1814, as the war came closer, the time for humor had passed. In April the USS *Constitution* was chased into Marblehead. In June the British burned an American vessel at Beverly. Guards were posted at Salem Neck. "We may now consider our State invaded," Bentley wrote in

July. By mid-September the news of the burning of Washington had reached Salem, and there were rumors of an imminent attack. Full-scale panic ensued. "Alarm of the intended invasion of Salem has been brought up from Halifax," wrote Bentley, "& it has made great shaking." The townspeople sought safety for their goods and their persons, much as they had during the Revolution. Bentley described the town as "nearly depopulated," its inhabitants "tumbling over [one] another to get out." Then followed "parading & deserting the settlement," next, "our Artillery on the Common" and "alarm at midnight." It may well have been at this time that Bowditch drilled with an old flintlock gun. But the invasion never came, and by the middle of the next month Bentley could write, "Our friends from the Country begin to return."[59]

The Bowditches were not entirely immune to what Nathaniel called "the *moving fever*." The "disorder" had "raged with great violence in Salem," he wrote in mid-October, but "most of our family had a slight attack." It "seized upon some of my *moveables*," he added, "& 'carried off' most of my library and astronomical instruments & a few trunks of the most valuable of our effects." Most of the prominent Republican families had "*scampered off*," he noted with amusement and contempt, adding "the Federalists generally 'stick by the stuff.'" Mary Bowditch was less flippant. "The moving off from here was incessant for a week or two," she wrote. "Every one now is talking of purchasing a Farm," she continued, and "even Mr. B. is among the number of wishing he had one."[60] Perhaps the "slight attack" had not been so slight after all.

BY THE TIME the War of 1812 had come to a close, Bowditch had established himself as a core member of Salem's gentry. He participated fully in the interlocking affairs of its mercantile, intellectual, social, religious, and political life. Given his family background, his Derby maritime credentials, and the moderate wealth he had accumulated, the door had been open to him to join the gentry, but his entry was not automatic. The inner circle required fine manners and conversation alternately witty and substantive. A Harvard degree was not an absolute prerequisite. Dudley Pickman didn't have one, nor did Henry Pickering. But their fathers and brothers did, unlike Nathaniel's and Mary's kinsmen. Elite Salemites were charmed by Bowditch's artlessness, but they looked for polish as well. Still, they could see he had exceptional talent. Learnedness, if not inborn gentility, would be his calling card.

To gain acceptance into this stratum, Bowditch also had to share certain core beliefs and attitudes. Like almost all elite Salemites, he was a Unitarian, and with them, he eschewed the bad news of sin for the good news of self-improvement. In politics one had to choose sides, and with it one's brand of gentry. Bowditch embraced the role of Federalist officeholder, delegate, and henchman. Yet his deepest commitments were shaped by neither religion nor politics. He never made the public declaration of belief necessary for full church membership. His spiritual impulses were stirred most deeply by nature's order, not divine grace. Even at his most politically involved, he was loath to mix party feeling with science, and when in the last twenty years of his life he withdrew from political controversy, he turned to what he himself termed his "peaceful mathematics."[61] The source of his identity and focus of loyalty was neither the fellowship of Christianity nor the Federalist Party but the Republic of Letters, a community that knows no faith, no party, and no nation.

CHAPTER FIVE

Celestial Events

Soon after he assumed the helm of Essex Fire and Marine Insurance Company (EFM) in 1806, Bowditch was faced with a new career possibility: he was offered Harvard's Hollis Professorship of Mathematics and Natural Philosophy. Theophilus Parsons, a newly elected fellow of the Harvard Corporation, had engineered the offer, once more showing Bowditch his "particular friendship and most flattering attentions." In academe, as elsewhere, personal networks continued to be key. Though "sensible of the great honour," Bowditch turned the offer down. John Pickering thought his friend's "chief objection" was the salary—at $1,400 a year, too low to woo him away from his better paid post in Salem—but money was not the only or even the primary factor that shaped his decision.[1]

In his letter to the college, Bowditch expressed his hope that "some one better qualified than myself" might be selected. His wording may simply reflect the ritual humility called for by genteel etiquette. It is hard to imagine, after all, that Bowditch did not feel competent to teach mathematics and natural philosophy to a bunch of teenage boys. But he had other reasons to feel uncertain about joining the college faculty. He "had a certain hesitation in his mode of speaking," a problem in the classroom. Far more significant was his lack of a Harvard education. Though "by far the ablest astronomical mathematician in this country & equal to any in Europe," wrote Bostonian Henry Dearborn in a letter to Thomas Jefferson, Bowditch had turned down the offer because "not having received a Collegiate education, he did not think himself adequate." More precisely, he did not have the classical learning that formed the core of the college curriculum and conferred social status and authority in this era. William Bentley certainly thought along these lines. "The Professorship of Mathematics has been offered to a self taught youth of this town, who has had no education or knowledge but in practical mathematics," he sniped. Of course, Bentley *would* be jaundiced, but he was not the only one thinking the same thing. At that same year's Harvard commencement, Bowditch found himself seated between two strangers who, leaning forward, discussed the likelihood of his accepting the post. One replied "that he rather thought not, since Mr. Bowditch would probably be afraid of 'singing small on classic ground.'" The story, relayed many years later, could only have come from Bowditch's mouth. The gossips were onto something.[2]

Then too, Bowditch enjoyed his insurance work. "Any writing except on mercantile business or mathematical subjects is a task to me," he once commented, indicating that both had their appeal. There was in fact no need for Bowditch to choose between the two, for his position at EFM actually furthered his scholarly pursuits. It offered a salary, an escape from the hustle and risk of commercial investments, and the financial security and emotional equanimity to pursue scholarship.[3] It also afforded him what he termed "considerable time" for "those studies which have been the delight of my leisure hours." Up at six, he had three hours to himself until his EFM duties began. "Before nine o'clock in the morning," he often stated, "I learned all my mathematics." Even at the office, "whenever a moment of leisure recurred, he was busily occupied in science." One son wrote that "it is very certain that he was not all the time, during office hours, actually engaged in business, but he was constantly liable to interruption." One begins to get the impression that the business came as an interruption to science, rather than the other way around. Bowditch was in no way derelict in his duties, but in this era of flexibility and intimacy in business affairs his work was not confined to what we think of as the business day. One January night in 1819, for example, the company's secretary knocked on the door of the Bowditch home on business, though there was no emergency; neither he nor Bowditch gave the evening intrusion a second thought. By the same token, he could snatch a few hours reading at the office.[4]

The Harvard offer must have been gratifying, but Bowditch had a good thing going in Salem. In 1818 Bowditch would turn down Jefferson's offer of a similar chair at the University of Virginia and in 1820 secretary of war John C. Calhoun's offer of a West Point post.[5] He had long ago made up his mind on what best suited his goals, and teaching teenagers played no part in that plan. He was looking to be acknowledged as a proper man of science, a full-fledged member of the Republic of Letters, not the provincial author of a merely vocational manual. Judging by his achievements—a spate of articles in the *Memoirs of the American Academy of Arts and Sciences*, a second Harvard degree in 1816, and honorary memberships in several British learned societies in 1818—he achieved that aim.

But there was more to the recognition of his talents than pure merit. Influential friends played a role—again. So too did Bowditch's use of print: press coverage of his work with eclipses, comets, and meteors; battles with his critics carried on in newspapers and magazines in which he came out the winner; and, most subtle, the employment of the American

Academy's *Memoirs* to expose the errors in European scientific publications. What is more, Bowditch himself understood that what recognition he had in Europe was not due to an original, or even truly significant, contribution to knowledge. That could occur only much later, once he completed the project he undertook in these years, the translation and annotation of Pierre-Simon Laplace's magisterial *Mécanique Céleste*. Bowditch's work on this chef d'oeuvre of the era's greatest mathematical astronomer would be the major intellectual labor of his lifetime, and it abounded with possibilities and problems alike. The *Mécanique Céleste* illuminated the workings of the heavens like no other work before it, all in a mathematical language incomprehensible to most of the English-speaking scientific community. It was recognized as a work of genius, and of ideological danger. Bowditch saw past these sources of difficulty and conflict to the heart of what had long inspired him, the sublimity of mathematics.

THE REPUBLIC OF Letters was connected by just that—letters. So in 1805 Bowditch sent his lunar method to French mathematician Sylvestre Lacroix, receiving a polite and gratifying reply the following year. Lacroix had shown the method to Jean-Baptiste Delambre, then director of the Paris Observatory and editor of the annual *Connaissance des Temps*, the French equivalent of the *Nautical Almanac*. Delambre had "examined it attentively" and included it in the latest volume of his almanac. "I think you will be pleased with the article," Lacroix wrote, adding to his distant correspondent "should you come across it." Perhaps. Though Delambre allowed that Bowditch's formulas had been constructed "with great skill" and that the prescribed calculations were indeed easy, he regarded the series of computations as "really very long for a correction that is most often of such minor importance." Then too, the method allowed for a "petite inexactitude"—Bowditch himself, Delambre indicated, admitted that the method yielded only an approximation—which in at least some cases could be significant.[6] Ireland's Royal Astronomer took note of the *Connaissance* coverage. So too did German astronomer Baron Franz Xaver von Zach, though it was only to wonder why Delambre had regarded Bowditch's method "as worth the trouble to give a long-winded description of the procedure," since many similar—and better—methods were already out there.[7] It was hardly a perfect debut on the international stage, but it was something to have a leading light of the French scientific establishment acknowledge the mathematical skill of a scientific unknown.

Still, Bowditch would have to do more to develop a reputation as something other than an unusually clever provincial engaged in lower-order, practical pursuits. His contributions to the *Analyst*, an American publication devoted to mathematical puzzles, were not the answer. As we have seen, that kind of virtuoso performance may have continued to impress Americans, but it had gone out of style as a sign of mathematical talent in Europe.[8] His contributions to the American Academy's *Memoirs* more closely fit the model of professional scholarship. The article generally considered today to be his most original, for example, analyzed the motion of a pendulum suspended from two points. But the *Memoirs* reached only a small audience of learned New Englanders. The pendulum motions Bowditch described are today known as Lissajous—not Bowditch—curves, though Bowditch was investigating them even before the Frenchman was born.[9] But there was one opening for an American. Much as Europeans took an interest in American observations of New World biological and geological specimens—information available *only* across the Atlantic—so did they take note of astronomical observations dependent on the location of the observer. Bowditch's publications on the solar eclipses, comets, and meteors that visited American skies in the early nineteenth century had the potential to draw European attention that his pendulum analysis did not.

Let us begin with solar eclipses. Bowditch's procedures for observing them were in many ways laughably provincial. On a Monday morning in 1806, for example, he put aside his office duties, seated himself in his garden, and observed the sky through a theodolite, an attachment to a surveying instrument—he had not been able to obtain a more powerful telescope. Yet his goals were more ambitious than Europeans anticipated from an American. "European Astronomers will expect to receive from this country a sufficient number of observations to determine this point of the lunar theory to the utmost accuracy," he wrote, referring to the technique of calculating the latitude of the moon from eclipse observations. But he wanted to compile those observations himself and, even more impressive, to do his own calculations. Europeans might expect Americans to undertake no more than the practical work of observation and leave the intellectual labor to their mathematical betters, but Bowditch knew he was up to both tasks.[10]

His work with the comets of 1807 and 1811 was even more ambitious. With them, he once again went beyond observation to calculation, but also to what he believed was a form of mathematical analysis that was cutting edge in the world of European science. Having observed the comets over the course of months as they moved across the Salem sky, he then used "the elegant method of La Place" to calculate the elements of their orbits and project their past and future trajectories. Now he was no mere computational whiz, the winner of a ten-dollar prize for "an ingenious solution" in the pages of the *Analyst*. This achievement called for a familiarity with recent theoretical developments in the physical sciences and deftness with the most current analytical techniques. Americans were impressed. Bowditch's calculations are "by far the most scientific account of this new visitor's path that I have seen," wrote the distinguished New York physician and professor Samuel L. Mitchill to a Bostonian in 1811. It is "eminently creditable to your friend, thus to have pioneered his way, among the astronomers of our country."[11]

When a mathematics teacher from Richmond, Virginia, challenged Bowditch's conclusions, the resulting newspaper controversy only helped to distinguish Bowditch as a scientific practitioner of a different order than could be found elsewhere in America. Bowditch's work, contended John Wood, "only proves the uncertainty of all calculation with respect to Comets." Bowditch never could tolerate incompetence, but Wood provoked him at an even deeper level, for the Virginian was challenging not just *his* mathematics but the very power of mathematics. When Wood doubted that the comet could not be as far from the earth as Bowditch had calculated because its tail was so bright, for example, the Virginian had done so "without making the least calculation on the subject." When he stated that it would take many more observations over a longer period of time before even approximate calculations of the comet's trajectory could be made, he did not understand that the regularity of the universe made precise predictions based on a sophisticated, mathematical understanding of celestial mechanics entirely possible. Bowditch was soon vindicated. Johann Karl Burckhardt of the French Academy (and the German translator of Laplace's *Mécanique Céleste*) had published his own elements of the comet, reported the *Essex Register*, and they agreed "very nearly" with those "calculated by Mr. Bowditch, of this town."[12]

Wood was an easy target for Bowditch's rebuttal. Not unlike the *Navigator* critic George Baron, he was an immigrant of dubious academic provenance and abilities trying to pass himself off as the real thing.[13] As the nation's press picked up on Bowditch's calculations and Burckhardt's indirect endorsement of them, Bowditch achieved a national reputation as something other than the author of the *Navigator* for the first time. That recognition had taken some trial and error on Bowditch's part. When he first published his work on eclipses and comets, in the first decade of the century, he had made the mistake of publishing either anonymously or in a limited-circulation gentlemen's periodical like Boston's *Monthly Anthology*. Waiting to publish in the American Academy's *Memoirs* was also a poor plan because that periodical came out only intermittently, and delays could be substantial. Meanwhile, others more forthcoming about their identity grabbed newspaper headlines, even though their contributions were less ambitious—observations only, no calculations—and less accurate. But by the time the second comet appeared in the sky, in 1811, Bowditch knew enough to publish his work in the popular press under his own name and then wait for other papers to pick up and spread the story.[14]

Bowditch's reputation in scientific circles spread beyond New England. In 1809 the American Philosophical Society elected him a member. The Connecticut Academy of Arts and Sciences followed in 1813, and the Literary and Philosophical Society of New York two years later. Meanwhile, Harvard continued to recognize the accomplishments of this self-educated man of letters. In 1815 it drafted him into an unsuccessful effort to build what would have been the first astronomical observatory in America. In 1816 it made Bowditch an honorary doctor of laws. From here on his publications announced him to the world as "Nathaniel Bowditch, LL.D." Mr. Bowditch had become Dr. Bowditch.[15]

But an enhanced reputation in America was not the big prize, and Bowditch knew it. In 1810 he sent a copy of his recent *Memoirs* articles to London's Royal Society. The society noted receipt of the articles in its *Philosophical Transactions*, but that was it. German periodicals picked up on Bowditch's eclipse and comet data, but again there was no broader notice.[16] Europeans would take American observations as raw material for their own calculations but would otherwise ignore American work in astronomy. Bowditch's use of Laplacean theory to calculate comet trajectories might convince Americans he ranked with European savants, but Europeans knew better. In calculating the elements of the 1811 comet, wrote Baron Bernhard August von Lindenau in the *Zeitschrift für Astronomie*, Bowditch had proceeded with "a, we would almost like to say too great expenditure of industry and trouble," for he had used Laplace's method, the "most painstaking" of all. That he had relied on this method "shows that our new advances in comet theory have not yet made headway in the knowledge of the new continent."[17] Bowditch was skilled but behind the times, out of the loop.

Where Bowditch could make his mark was with meteors. Only recently had scientists begun to puzzle over their nature and source. With multiple theories vying with each other, alternately suggesting terrestrial, lunar, and extraterrestrial origins, there was a place for new contributions, even from the New World. So when on the morning of 14 December 1807 a meteor streaked across New England skies, it portended a lucky break for Bowditch's international standing. He set out to gather reliable observations of the event and then convert them into astronomical measurements that would, with more than a little calculating, yield the meteor's height, direction, velocity, and magnitude. This task required ingenuity, for of course none of the observers had viewed the meteor through the lens of a mathematical instrument. He found one published set of observations reported by a Connecticut judge, a second penned by a Vermont "Esquire," and a third provided by John Pickering's learned aunt, "a very intelligent lady" who had watched the meteor "with great attention" as it traced a line from her barn to a neighboring dwelling. Bowditch used trigonometry, a novel use, he later claimed, of this form of mathematical manipulation, to make his calculations but was hesitant to move beyond empirical conclusions. "We have not yet sufficient data for a well grounded theory of their nature of origin," he wrote of meteors, but given the magnitude of the meteor's mass—perhaps as much as 6 million tons, he estimated—it seemed unlikely that it had formed in the earth's atmosphere or was spewed forth from a terrestrial or a lunar volcano. Nor did the uniformity of recovered meteor fragments, suggesting a common origin, "altogether agree with the supposition that such bodies are satellites of the earth." By process of elimination, Bowditch was suggesting that meteors originate in outer space. It was a rare, indeed uncharacteristic, use of his computational skill to hypothesize about the nature of physical reality.[18]

Bowditch's foray into informed speculation paid off in a way that his careful computations never did. He sent his article to London's well-regarded *Journal of Natural Philosophy, Chemistry and the Arts*, and in 1811 it appeared in that journal's pages. The breakthrough came in 1816 when the *Zeitschrift für Astronomie* detailed the contents of the American Academy's recent volume, most of which Bowditch had authored. This was the same journal issue that critiqued Bowditch's comet calculations as methodologically obsolete, but its editor gave star treatment to the meteor article, translating excerpts and commenting on its conclusions. Bowditch's essay is "an interesting work," wrote Lindenau, "for the results from it very much speak for the opinion, that in that puzzling mass we glimpse something belonging to the planet world." In France, François Arago and Joseph Louis Gay-Lussac, both close associates of Laplace, quickly picked up the *Zeitschrift*'s coverage in their own journal, *Annales de Chimie et de Physique*. Thereafter, many European treatments of meteors referred to Bowditch's work, especially after he published an analysis of another meteor sighted in 1819.[19]

Learned Americans traveling in Europe discovered that their countryman had made his mark abroad. When studying in Göttingen in 1817, Harvard graduate Joseph Cogswell visited Heinrich Olbers and proudly reported to a friend at home that the German astronomer knew of Bowditch. Almost twenty years later one of Bowditch's learned friends visited the cometologist Johann Franz Encke in Berlin and found that he too was familiar with the American. He "said he had known all about you" from the *Zeitschrift*, wrote Bowditch's friend, and ever since he had never met an American without inquiring about the astronomer from Massachusetts. Still, for the most part Europeans saw Bowditch as a reliable observer and a supremely patient and accurate calculator, not an innovative scientist. Ernst Chladni, a pioneer in meteor research, described him as an "industrious collector and calculator." Lindenau praised Bowditch's eclipse calculations for their sheer quantity and the extreme care with which they were executed and listed him among those international experts providing reliable calculations of geographic locations.[20] Americans had their place as data gatherers, especially if, like Bowditch, they could be counted on to process the data accurately. True international recognition continued to elude him.

WHEN HE BOARDED the *Putnam* in 1802, Bowditch brought with him a small library of European scientific works. Edmund Blunt had imported the volumes for him as payment for the *Navigator*. The centerpiece of the collection was Pierre-Simon Laplace's *Mécanique Céleste*, an advanced mathematical treatment of the workings of the solar system. With the help of the other books he carried with him, Bowditch was determined to master it. He could not have then known that his work with the first four volumes of the *Mécanique Céleste*, published between 1799 and 1805, would occupy the remainder of his years, or that he would come to regard it as his major contribution to science. From 1803, on the *Putnam*'s return to Salem, to 1806 he made copious notes on the volumes, explaining and elaborating upon the original text. Then between 1814 and 1817 he translated the original into English. Much later his translation and commentary appeared in print, having remained in manuscript for years, and only after Bowditch reworked his annotations.[21]

In focusing on the *Mécanique Céleste* Bowditch made an informed choice. It would be hard to overstate the esteem, even awe, with which European men of science regarded Laplace's master work. Typical of the praise were the remarks offered in 1810 by the Scottish mathematician John Playfair in the

Edinburgh Review, a periodical that was required reading for learned English speakers on both sides of the Atlantic. The *Mécanique Céleste*, wrote Playfair, "marks, undoubtedly, the highest point to which man has yet ascended in the scale of intellectual attainment." Newton established the "great edifice," he continued, and Laplace completed it. Today's historians of science agree that if Laplace was something less than a transformative intellectual force, he was nonetheless the "arch-codifier of the astronomical sciences" in his era and ultimately "among the most influential scientists in all history."[22]

The "genius" of the *Mécanique Céleste* lay in two interrelated achievements. First, making use of decades of observational data and, even more important, major advances in mathematical techniques of analysis, Laplace accounted for every astronomical phenomenon in the solar system in terms of a single principle, universal gravitation. He thereby vastly expanded the explanatory power of Newtonian science. Second, in so doing he demonstrated that the solar system was a perfect mechanism that never needed correction. Newton had not done so—in fact, he had not wanted to. Newton, his contemporaries, and later scientists working within his paradigm had noted apparent irregularities when they looked at astronomical observations over the centuries. Saturn was slowing down. Jupiter was speeding up. So too was the moon. At this rate, it would one day crash into the earth. And these were just the most dramatic of the many so-called "secular inequalities."[23] For Newton such trends proved the continuing need for a divine presence in the universe, for only He could make the necessary adjustments to keep everything going. The equally devout Leibniz scoffed at that view—surely God would not create an imperfect universe—but he did not resolve the system's irregularities.

Building on the work of others, Laplace established that the solar system was self-correcting and therefore permanently stable. It was a hugely complex analysis, one that involved calculating the simultaneous effects of gravity among multiple celestial bodies, applying the latest developments in calculus, and developing a new science of probability with its signature tool of statistical inference. With these mathematical tools Laplace demonstrated that the force of gravity accounted for all secular inequalities; these apparent irregularities were nothing other than regular oscillations around unchanging values. For example, Saturn was slowing down to be sure, but in the past it had been speeding up in a precisely opposite manner, and it would do so again—all in a mathematically regular and predictable fashion. What is more, Saturn's deceleration exactly balanced Jupiter's acceleration, and every 900 years or so the pattern would reverse.

As a tour de force of mathematical analysis, Laplace's achievement was astonishing, but for many its broader religious implications were at least as awe-inspiring. Though his celestial mechanics made no room for Newton's divine tinkerer, his self-correcting solar system could point to God as its creator. For some it went further, offering clear evidence of the heavens' divine creation and God's special care to give us a perfect solar system. Playfair signed on to this view. Since natural law allows for the possibility of a planetary system that is *not* self-regulating, he argued, our system is self-regulating only because of its *particular* arrangement of celestial bodies. "No one will be so absurd as to argue" that this arrangement "is the work of chance," he continued. It must therefore be "the work of design, or of intention, conducted by wisdom and foresight of the most perfect kind." Contemplating this "sublime picture," he concluded with a flourish: "Our system is thus secured against natural decay; order and regularity preserved in the midst of so many disturbing causes;—and anarchy and misrule eternally proscribed."[24]

We can well understand why Playfair, writing in the wake of the French Revolution and in the midst of war with Napoleon, was drawn to a vision proscribing "anarchy and misrule," but it was not just Britons who found Laplace's celestial mechanics inspiring. Harvard natural philosophy professor John Farrar marveled at the workings of the solar system, "without noise, without interference, and without errour," all "according to a law the most simple and the most perfectly adapted to the order and perpetuity of the whole system." Laplace "has established the stability of the universe," wrote an essayist for Philadelphia's *American Quarterly Review*. He has demonstrated "that the same supreme wisdom whence the creation emanated, has left its everlasting impress upon it, and rendered all disorder or confusion impossible."[25] Disorder and confusion stalked Boston and Philadelphia as it did Edinburgh, whether in the form of partisan strife, religious controversy, economic crises, or, at least for Federalists, social upheaval. Could it be that these disturbances, like those of heavenly bodies, would in time correct themselves? It was a comforting thought at a time when many Europeans predicted and Americans feared the headlong rush of the youthful republic into chaos and self-destruction.

Bowditch too found the Laplacean vision captivating. He certainly had his fears about the stability of the republic, especially when Jefferson and Madison occupied the White House. And the notion that God created a perfect world for us fitted the optimistic, rational Unitarianism he had learned in William Bentley's pews. No doubt he subscribed to the endlessly quoted sentiment that "an undevout astronomer is mad," a phrase that headlined an almanac he owned as a teenager. Yet as inspired as he was by Laplace's universe, his enthrallment did not depend on the fact of its stability. Unlike Playfair, and unlike most nonscientists who focused on the religious implications of a stable universe, Bowditch's understanding of the universe made room for change. To be sure, he wrote in 1825, Laplace has demonstrated that "if the *mutual attractions of the bodies composing the solar system upon each other only are noticed, that this system will be stable.*" "But," he added, "there may be other causes, which would destroy this stability." He thought it "probable," for example, that celestial bodies might encounter resistance from light, slowing them down. It was also possible that as the sun emitted light over time, it would gradually lose matter, and therefore its attractive force. The workings of the solar system would change accordingly.[26]

In incorporating the notion of change into his celestial mechanics, Bowditch was not straying as far from Laplace as might at first appear. Intrigued by William Herschel's ideas on the nebulae of deep space, Laplace had speculated that the solar system had condensed out of the sun's primeval atmosphere. But whereas Herschel theorized that the physical universe evolves continuously, Laplace insisted that once it had reached its present form the solar system had become as static as it was stable. Bowditch saw no reason to insist that change had stopped or that it had been limited to our solar system. "There are many proofs, that great changes take place in the bodies of matter composing the material universe," he wrote, adding that "Herschel noted this in some of the nebulae." Stars have come and gone, he continued. The earth's surface has changed over time. None of this was cause for alarm. It was evidence not of instability but only of change, change as regular and predictable as Laplace's planetary motions. "Wherever the attention is directed," Bowditch concluded, "changes of place and form are perceived, with new combinations of matter, and it is natural to suppose the whole solar system will obey this general law."[27]

Bowditch's "Remarks on the Usual Demonstration of the Permanency of the Solar System," published in 1818, gives us further insight into his stance on the critical issue of stability. Using an equation to analyze the motions of Jupiter, Saturn, and Uranus, Bowditch began, Laplace had concluded that these planets' orbits "will never vary much from a circular form" and "may be considered as perfectly stable, in respect to the eccentricities, which will oscillate about the mean values, from which they will vary but very little." Bowditch agreed. What he did not agree with was Laplace's deduction that this equation would demonstrate the same thing for *all* planets. In the case of Mercury, Venus, Earth, and Mars, he continued, the same equation could be satisfied assuming an "extremely elliptical, parabolic, or even hyperbolic" orbit, and he then went on to demonstrate that point mathematically. Laplace's equation, in other words, was "not sufficient for a complete demonstration of this permanency, though it may render it highly probable by considerations of analogy."[28]

It was easy to conclude that Bowditch was questioning the much vaunted stability of the solar system. That was certainly Thomas Jefferson's interpretation, and it upset him. "I had supposed Delaplace [*sic*] beyond correction," he wrote Bowditch after reading the essay. "Most of all I was fond of believing in the solidity of his demonstrations that the variations in the motions of the planets are secular" and therefore "regular so as to secure the permanency of form in their orbits." He freely admitted to the spiritual sustenance those demonstrations had given him. "It was comfortable to believe that the system does not involve within itself the principles of its own destruction," wrote Jefferson, "but will await the same fiat of wisdom & power which brought it into being."[29] But Jefferson was wrong. Bowditch was not arguing for the instability of the solar system. His focus was not on the solar system at all. It was on the math. Laplace had waved his mathematical wand over one secular inequality after another. Poof! They disappeared, leaving behind a deeper regularity. But Laplace did not do the calculations for the smaller planets. Bowditch fully expected that the smaller ones' orbits would be just like of those of the bigger ones, but the mathematics Laplace was using could not establish that as a fact.[30]

Bowditch approached Laplace as a mathematician, focusing on the adequacy and scope of the mathematical reasoning rather than the physical reality subjected to mathematical analysis. It was a subtle difference that Jefferson could not grasp, but it was critical to Bowditch's outlook. The Laplacean solar system provided him with a physical model of order and regularity he would transfer to human interactions, an influence that became especially clear in his later work in Boston's financial and learned institutions. But when focused on the *Mécanique Céleste* he was more deeply drawn to Laplace's mathematical wizardry than to what that wizardry revealed about the nature of our universe. He had long taken for granted that the heavens reflected the beneficence of God, but religion did not hold his attention for long. Then too, since the middle of the eighteenth century most learned men simply assumed the regularity of the solar system, though they did not yet have the evidence or the math to back it up. Show me something I don't already know, we can imagine Bowditch thinking. Stun me. And in the unprecedented power of his mathematical analysis, Laplace did just that. It was not the power of God Laplace made Bowditch feel, but the power of numbers. That force had always exerted the strongest hold on his imagination. The *Mécanique Céleste* provided him with intellectual sustenance for decades, and he turned to it again and again, much as devout Puritans had once turned to their Bibles. "I began the translation from mere curiosity," he wrote in 1818, "& continued for my own gratification & improvement, finding that I should by doing it become better acquainted with that immortal work."[31] God was immortal. The solar system was immortal. Old news. But so too was the *Mécanique Céleste*. Now *that* stirred Bowditch's soul.

BOWDITCH'S WORK WITH Laplace's masterpiece was a labor of translation and learned commentary. Though he might point out a few errors here or there, nowhere did he engage Laplace to advance scholarship with original results. And yet, given who he was and where and when he lived—a self-taught New England Federalist—Bowditch's project called for real boldness. Let us begin with the intellectual challenge he faced. He had overcome his ignorance before, teaching himself the science, mathematics, and languages he needed to pull even with the current state of knowledge in natural philosophy, at least as it was represented in Salem's Philosophical Library. But the *Mécanique Céleste* posed yet another obstacle. Laplace wrote in a mathematical language unknown to Bowditch, as it was to most learned men in the English-speaking world: Leibnizian calculus. Once again, he would have to teach himself what he needed to know.[32]

Since the time of Newton, mathematical approaches to the study of natural philosophy had followed two different trajectories. Newton had developed a technique known as fluxions, a form of calculus that persisted in Britain and America. In Germany, Gottfried Leibniz had developed a different form of calculus, and it was this tradition that dominated the Continent. Building on contributions made by the Swiss Leonhard Euler and the Frenchmen Joseph-Louis Lagrange, Alexis Clairaut, and Jean d'Alembert, Laplace further developed Leibnizian mathematics into a set of tools that enabled an astonishingly productive and comprehensive analysis of celestial mechanics. The so-called algebraic method of the Continent even *looked* different from Newton's "geometric" method—not a diagram to be seen but instead strings of unfamiliar symbols. Continental mathematicians had so completely transformed calculus, wrote John Playfair in 1808, that a well-educated Briton "may yet find himself stopped at the first page of the works of Euler or D'Alembert . . . from want of knowing the principles and

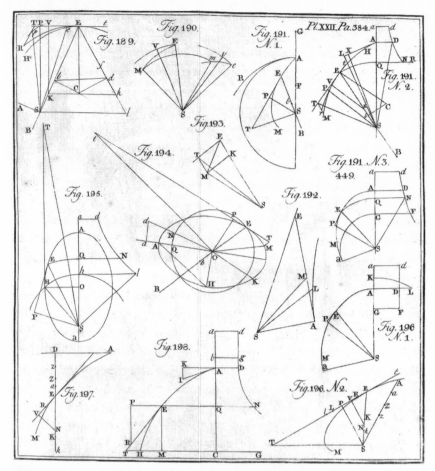

Colin MacLaurin, *A Treatise of Fluxions*. Edinburgh: T. W. and T. Ruddimans, 1742, Book 1, Plate XXII. Newton's fluxions: geometrical figures. Division of Rare and Manuscript Collections, Cornell University Library.

the methods which they take for granted as known to every mathematical reader." As for the even more difficult *Mécanique Céleste*, Playfair estimated the number of men in Britain who could read it "with any tolerable facility" as perhaps a dozen.[33]

If most of Britain's scientific establishment would have been stumped by Laplace, what chance had a self-taught insurance man from Salem, Massachusetts? By the 1810s, though, there were signs of change on both sides of the Atlantic. At Cambridge University a group of young students, including Charles Babbage, the future pioneer of mechanical computers, and John Herschel, the son of William, were promoting the use of continental

$$o = x \cdot \left(\frac{dU'}{dx'}\right) + y \cdot \left(\frac{dU'}{dy'}\right) + z \cdot \left(\frac{dU'}{dz'}\right);$$

$$x' \cdot \left(\frac{dU}{dx}\right) + y' \cdot \left(\frac{dU}{dy}\right) + z' \cdot \left(\frac{dU}{dz}\right) = \frac{\mu}{r^3} \cdot \left\{ x \cdot \left(\frac{dU''}{dx'}\right) + y \cdot \left(\frac{dU''}{dy'}\right) + z \cdot \left(\frac{dU''}{dz'}\right) \right\}$$

$$x' \cdot \left(\frac{dU'}{dx}\right) + y' \cdot \left(\frac{dU'}{dy}\right) + z' \cdot \left(\frac{dU'}{dz}\right) = \frac{\mu}{r^3} \cdot \left\{ x \cdot \left(\frac{dU'''}{dx'}\right) + y \cdot \left(\frac{dU'''}{dy'}\right) + z \cdot \left(\frac{dU'''}{dz'}\right) \right\} \quad ; (I')$$

$$x' \cdot \left(\frac{dU''}{dx}\right) + y' \cdot \left(\frac{dU''}{dy}\right) + z' \cdot \left(\frac{dU''}{dz}\right) = \frac{\mu}{r^3} \cdot \left\{ x \cdot \left(\frac{dU'''}{dx'}\right) + y \cdot \left(\frac{dU'''}{dy'}\right) + z \cdot \left(\frac{dU'''}{dz'}\right) \right\}$$

&c.

MÉCAN. CÉL. *Tome I.*   X

Pierre Simon Laplace, *Traité de Mécanique Céleste*. Paris: J .B. M. Duprat, 1799, 1:161. Laplace's differential calculus: numbers and symbols. Library of the State University of New York, Buffalo.

mathematics.[34] Meanwhile, Bowditch had absorbed the new techniques and notation and subscribed to their superiority. In 1818 he published a critique of a British mathematician's work in the American Academy's *Memoirs*, tracing the errors to the Briton's reluctance to adopt the new methods. "The mistake here noticed in Dr. Stewart's tracts may be attributed wholly to the use of the *geometrical* method of investigation," he wrote. "In fact there are very few questions in the higher branches of Physical Astronomy where the ancient geometry can be used with much advantage." Within half a dozen years John Farrar banished the "ancient geometry" from the Harvard curriculum when he translated, published, and introduced Étienne Bézout's *First Principles of the Differential and Integral Calculus*. Still, when Bowditch first read the *Mécanique Céleste* all this lay in the future. Ultimately his published translation and commentary would cater to, as he would write in his preface, those with "a strong and decided taste for mathematical studies" who "have been unable to prepare themselves for this study, by a previous course of reading, in those modern publications, which contain the many important discoveries in analysis, made since the time of Newton."[35] It was an audience he knew intimately; he had once been a member of it.

Mathematics was not the only impediment Bowditch had to confront. In Federalist circles, as in politically and socially conservative circles in Britain, French science was associated with ideological peril and irreligion, as much for its dangerously visionary abstraction from real-world realities—physical geometry and social hierarchy, to name two—as for its more direct association with the French Revolution and Napoleonic rule.[36] A sharp-eyed reader of American newspapers would have picked Laplace out as Napoleon's interior minister and president of the French Senate, one of those guilty of having "betrayed their king" and "denied their God." But in criticizing Laplace, Britons and Americans pointed to the content of the Frenchman's science more than the details of his biography, and they censured him more as an atheist than as a revolutionary. Both his nebular hypothesis of the origins of the solar system and his pioneering work in the new field of probability left God out of the picture. The deepest source of mistrust, though, lay elsewhere, in Laplace's vision of an eternally self-regulating system.[37] And here we run into an apparent paradox: didn't the English-speaking world eagerly embrace this vision as one bespeaking a perfect God who created a perfect world? Well, yes. But men and women of this era saw in Laplacean science what they chose to see. An eternally self-regulating solar system could also be interpreted as one that required *no* God, after all, and it was suspicious that Laplace never made the expected foray into pious reflection in his work.[38]

Detesting public shows of piety, Bowditch likewise kept his religious sentiments to himself. Nor did he ever publicly distance himself from the alleged religious implications of French science, even if he did privately acknowledge Laplace's "atheistical notions." His articles on astronomy for the *North American Review*'s gentlemanly but general audience provided the perfect opportunity for the kind of pious digression expected of scientists, but he demurred. His overview of "Modern Astronomy," for example, opened with "the science of Astronomy offers to our contemplation . . ."— one waits here for "the handiwork of God" but instead gets "some of the most powerful efforts of the human mind." The *human* mind? When he turned to national styles of astronomy, he noted only that the British excelled at practical observations and instrument making, while the French and Germans had advanced mathematical analysis and astronomical theory. And when he discussed d'Alembert, Laplace's mentor and a major figure in the Federalist pantheon of French infidels, it was from a most un-Federalist perspective. "The boldness of his attacks on the most commonly received opinions in religion and government," he wrote, "raised up against him numerous enemies, who, by their incessant attacks, embittered his life," so that he sought refuge in his "peaceful geometry." It was not d'Alembert's views but the boldness of their expression that landed him in hot water, apparently unfairly. Just who does that sound like? If we recall that Bowditch described his own turn away from political conflict as a retirement into his "peaceful mathematics," we have our answer.[39]

If Bowditch did not dissociate himself from religious radicalism by touting his own Christian faith or condemning French science and scientists as atheistic, it was because as a citizen of the Republic of Letters he knew that in this "nation," creed, country, and religion were not supposed to matter. He knew, for example, that the Royal Society of London had elected Laplace to foreign membership and the Paris Academy had conferred a parallel honor on Royal Society president Joseph Banks.[40] Bowditch's perspective was therefore not unusual among learned men, but it was unusual for learned New Englanders. Consider Boston's American Academy of Arts and Sciences. Between its founding in 1781 and 1787, with hard feelings from the Revolution lingering, the academy elected ten French foreign members but only two British. Next it was France, now associated with Jacobins and the "monster" Napoleon, who came in for Federalist suspicion. Accordingly, between 1788 and 1815 twenty-four of the new foreign members were British and only four were French. Only after the war would the American Academy move in a more cosmopolitan direction, when under Bowditch's leadership it elected six Britons, seven men working in Paris (including Laplace), and an equal number from German-speaking countries, along with one Swede.[41]

Committed to the ideal of the Republic of Letters, Bowditch took a jaundiced view of any attempt to corrupt the content of science with an ideological agenda. Though a confirmed patriot, he did not exclude nationalism from those corrupting influences. It was this conviction that figured in his public stand against a proposal submitted to Congress in 1810 by William Lambert, an obscure government clerk and amateur astronomer. Lambert suggested that the United States establish a new prime meridian, the "zero" point from which longitude is measured, at the nation's capital, thereby rejecting the Greenwich meridian as a "vestige of subjection" to Great Britain. The congressional committee was favorably disposed to the nationalist project and recommended further observations and calculations with the eventual goal of establishing a Washington meridian.[42]

Though nobody asked for his opinion, Bowditch gave it anyway, publishing an anonymous, scathing review of Lambert's proposal in Boston's *Monthly Anthology*. As a practical matter, he argued, it was useful for British and American mariners to exchange information based on a common reference. We should regard Greenwich as the prime meridian agreed upon by all English speakers, he continued, just as French speakers agree upon Paris, and Spanish speakers upon Cádiz. Highlighting the multiple prime meridians actually weakened Bowditch's argument; if other powers insisted on their own, surely the United States should as well. Instead Bowditch condemned Lambert's assertion that American use of the Greenwich meridian was demeaning as "an example of the introduction of national prejudices in matters of science, which cannot be too much reprobated." Perhaps, he insinuated, Lambert's motives were ultimately self-interested.

He suspected the clerk sought to head a national observatory needed to establish Washington's precise longitude.[43]

As disgusted as Bowditch was by Lambert's motivations, he was even more by Lambert's ineptitude. He systematically dismantled the amateur's work, enumerating "needless repetitions and palpable mistakes, evincing a great want of knowledge in the principles of the calculations." It was hardly an even match, and Bowditch, as was his habit with incompetence and venality, did not hold back. He pointed out many examples of Lambert's ignorance and error and reserved a particular disdain for his "affectation of correctness," calculating values to impossible and mathematically meaningless degrees of accuracy. Enraged, Lambert published a rebuttal that accused Bowditch of "*twistical* cunning, under the disguise of affected moderation," the one nail Lambert hit on the head. He challenged Bowditch to find just one actual error in his calculations. In a witheringly condescending tone, and mustering European authorities with devastating overkill, Bowditch published six.[44]

Countering his opponent's assertion that he was biased by "local and political prejudices," Bowditch had insisted it was Lambert who was making the meridian "a question of party politicks," something that could not "be more improper and unworthy [of] a man of *real* science." Yet Lambert had a point. Bowditch was no secret monarchist, but he held certain biases that he himself did not recognize. As a man of letters he was committed to objectivity in scientific matters, but as a New England Federalist he perceived Greenwich as the "objective" choice. Bowditch may not have known Lambert was a political appointee, but he did know he was a Virginian. (The Jeffersonian *Essex Register* understood the politics when, in anticipation of the 1811 eclipse, it designated Lambert—not Bowditch—as "the first rank among our Mathematicians.")[45] He also knew that the nation's capital had moved from Philadelphia to Washington as the result of a political concession to southern lawmakers. It is probably no accident that, with the exception of George Baron, the Americans with whom Bowditch became embroiled in scientific controversies were southerners: William Lambert, Virginian John Wood, and in the 1820s a navigation teacher from South Carolina and a mathematics professor from the same state.[46]

Still, though not immune to provincial bias, Bowditch was unusual among New England's learned men in the extent to which he ignored ideological divisions within the American scientific community. He maintained and even cultivated scientific interchange across religious and political divides. He corresponded with the Reverend Jedidiah Morse, for example, an orthodox Calvinist staunchly opposed to Unitarianism. And consider his vexed friendship with William Bentley. The common thread in his repeated attempts to hold out an olive branch was always a shared commitment to learning: he gave Bentley his Salem harbor chart; they conversed about his comet and meteor calculations; he loaned him mathematical books. Then too, when he published his request for eclipse observations in the *Salem Gazette*, he included instructions for "the Southern States," clearly anticipating—and hoping for—reprinting in southern newspapers.[47]

If it was remarkable that, in the thick of the partisan rancor leading up to the War of 1812, Bowditch discussed comets with Jeffersonian stalwart Henry A. S. Dearborn, it was surely even more extraordinary that he asked Dearborn to send his printed comet calculations to the ultimate Jeffersonian, Thomas Jefferson himself. If Jefferson had made observations of the recent eclipse, or knew of any, the New England astronomer politely requested, might he provide him with that information? It was a request addressed not so much to the former president of the United States as to the current president of the American Philosophical Society. Jefferson forwarded his data along with thanks to Bowditch as one of America's "philosophical citizens." He too understood the code of the Republic of Letters.[48] Both men consciously rose above the partisan fray. In 1815 Bowditch sent Jefferson some of his recent publications. "I am happy indeed to find that this most sublime of all sciences is so eminently cultivated by you," Jefferson wrote Bowditch, "and that our Rittenhouse was not the only meteor of the hemisphere in which he lived."[49] Three years later, it was Jefferson himself who tried, unsuccessfully, to lure Bowditch to the University of Virginia.[50] Science made for strange bedfellows.

IN JANUARY 1818 the *Boston Daily Advertiser* proudly announced that "the Hon. Mr. Bowditch, of Salem" had completed a translation of Laplace's *Mécanique Céleste*, adding to it "many important notes and illustrations." This was a great triumph for Bowditch—"few men could be found competent to the task," even in England—but it was a test for America. "It remains to be seen whether there is science enough in this country," read the article, "to encourage the publication of this splendid work." Such tomes were costly to print, and their readership was limited. But the *Advertiser* hoped that Bowditch's translation would be published, both for the stimulus it would provide to mathematics in America and for "the honour that such a publication will reflect upon" the United States. "It is creditable to us, that one of our distinguished scholars should, from the pure love of literature, have devoted himself to the accomplishment of so difficult a task," the article stated, "but it will be still more creditable, if it shall be proved that we have students enough devoted to these abstruse inquiries, to call for the publication of the work." In a private letter regarding Bowditch, German-trained Harvard professor Edward Everett was more blunt: "I am impatient for the time when his translation . . . will be given to the world. This will be something to boast of."[51]

Nationalist feelings were at a high pitch after the War of 1812. Americans felt they had come of age in the theater of the world. But in the realm of culture and learning there was a problem: a dearth of poets, writers, artists, and scientists universally acknowledged as worthy of the world's admiration. After the Revolution many Americans believed that liberty would unleash the latent talents of Americans, leading to an explosion of creative accomplishment, but so far no such eruption had transpired. Europeans were hardly surprised. Americans were too boorish, too materialistic to generate or appreciate art, literature, and science. That perspective was the unstated context for the Boston *Advertiser*'s boast that Bowditch had undertaken the work for the "pure love" of scholarship and its concern there might not be an audience for it.[52]

Bowditch was in a position to refute such views, but only if he could be induced to do so and only if his name and work were widely known. One man in particular took on this dual task, English émigré Benjamin Vaughan. In 1797 Vaughan had brought his 12,000-volume library, second only to Harvard's in New England, to his estate in Hallowell, Maine, where he pursued his interests in gentleman farming and science. He soon became a member of the American Academy of Arts and Sciences. Its low standing—apart from sporadic publication of its journal, it had not been up to much—was a thorn in his side. It is "asleep, perhaps in the sleep of death," he lamented in a letter to Bowditch in the summer of 1817. Whatever its name might gesture toward, it was the palest shadow of the famous academies in Paris, Berlin, and St. Petersburg, and it could not even be compared with its American rivals. "I rejoice in the character you give of the Academies of Philadelphia and New York," Everett wrote to a friend that same year. "One or two charitable gentlemen keep just enough soul in ours, to prevent the dry bones from falling apart; but they rattle sadly."[53]

Vaughan looked to Bowditch's "imprimis" to establish the American Academy as the "chief mover" in New England science, but he was also interested in promoting the international scientific reputation of his new country as a whole. For this larger task he had another, nastier idea. He suggested

Bowditch "exhibit some of the errors & deficiencies of our friends in Europe on mathematical subjects," although "with a gentleness and propriety which will add to the force & extent of the lesson." Vaughan was convinced that this kind of attack on the greats of European science would be more effective "than minor new discoveries originating here." The idea was to make the targets of criticism "more modest in their carriage towards us" and to show all Europe that it had better start paying attention to America. "Pray, my good sir," Vaughan asked, giving vent to his exasperation, "when is Europe to begin to think us out of our non-age, or rather out of that state of non-entity in which we have so long remained; unless by observing some signs of scientific existence in us, exhibited in overt acts?"[54]

If any American had experience correcting the mathematical work of European authorities, it was Bowditch. He had corrected the errors in Moore's *Navigator*, which in turn meant correcting the work of British Astronomer Royal Nevil Maskelyne. He had informed Zach of errors in his tables and drawn Lacroix's attention to mistakes in that savant's treatise. His 1809 *Memoirs* article pointed out an error in Laplace's calculation of the shape of the earth. So in 1818 Bowditch took up Vaughan's suggestion. Of the eleven articles he published in that year's volume of the *Memoirs*, seven found fault with European works. One was boldly titled "On a Mistake which exists in the Solar Tables of Mayer, Lalande, and Zach." Another endorsed a computational method forwarded by physicist Jean-Baptiste Biot but pointed out how it could be simplified. Other articles pointed out errors in the work of French luminary Siméon Denis Poisson, and even Laplace. Another critiqued a method of computing a particular astronomical value that had been endorsed by several prominent European mathematicians. One took on Newton himself. Without alluding to Vaughan's strategy, Bowditch alerted him to the upcoming volume. "We have several astronomical and physical papers, which will vie with any thing that has been published in this country," he wrote. "We shall get out the best number that has been printed in this country. This will add to the respectability of the Academy and have a tendency to unite the forces of its members."[55]

Meanwhile, Vaughan was at the center of a group pursuing another related goal, bringing Bowditch to the attention of the world. As we have seen, some Europeans were aware of Bowditch's lunar method and his publications on eclipses, comets, and meteors. But it was hit or miss. "We do not take any pains to send abroad what we publish," complained Everett in 1817. Lindenau, the *Zeitschrift* editor, had translated Bowditch's meteor article from the only copy available on the continent, continued Everett, the one "my brother had brought in his trunk to Holland, and I in mine to Germany, two years before." In Russia, John Quincy Adams gave a copy to an astronomer at the St. Petersburg Academy in 1811, and he in turn sent extracts of Bowditch's celestial observations to colleagues in Germany.[56] But something more was needed than this haphazard exposure—some serious recognition. That would take concerted action. Bowditch's "friends," as they were described in many a letter, knew just what that meant: getting Bowditch elected an honorary foreign member of Britain's most acclaimed scientific societies.

Benjamin Vaughan played a pivotal role in the initiative. His brother John in Philadelphia was secretary of the American Philosophical Society, and his brother William in London was a mover and a shaker in the Royal Society. "Application has been made to Sir Joseph Banks," wrote John Vaughan to Edward Everett in April 1817, referring to the Royal Society president, "in favor of Mr. Bowditch of Salem, whose friends have solicited for him the honors of the Royal Society." William presented Banks with testimonials gathered in Bowditch's favor. "Sir Joseph was pleased to express himself very warmly as to his [Bowditch's] character & reputation," he recollected, "& said that he was a fit person to be proposed for that honour, that he would himself sign the memorial which he seldom did, & procure the names of some of the council." And so Banks did, recruiting Charles Babbage and John Herschel as additional signatories. Banks had carried the suggested election through "with much Zeal and Energy," reported William Vaughan to Bowditch. "He had been no stranger to your Philosophical pursuits." Benjamin pointed out that "your French companions in honor on this occasion," giants of Continental mathematics and astronomy, "increase the respectability attending your own election."[57] Meanwhile, William Vaughan recalled, "the same measures were taken for his admission to the Edinburg[h] & Dublin societies, & with like success." Bowditch has been "highly recommended by some of the first names in America," wrote Scottish mathematician Dugald Stewart to his colleague Thomas Thompson, and they, along with John Playfair, soon nominated him to Edinburgh's Royal Society. The Royal Irish Academy followed a year later, prodded by the London society's clerk, "a Nautical Character" impressed by the *Navigator,* and perhaps by his society's reception of a copy of the American Academy's *Memoirs.*[58]

The prestige of these honors can hardly be overstated. London's Royal Society in particular was the gold standard of scientific accomplishment in the English-speaking world. Isaac Newton had served as its president. Its *Transactions* figured prominently in Bowditch's first exposure to the world of scientific learning. Few Americans had been honored with membership in the Royal Society, Benjamin Franklin and David Rittenhouse among them, and when they were, Europeans took notice. One scholarly journal published in Germany singled out "Dr. Bowditch, the astronomer" as the rare American whose "deep learning" had won him that much deserved recognition. In his *Correspondance Astronomique*, Zach described Bowditch as "the first and until now the only great geometer in America" and noted his British memberships. Bowditch himself was deeply gratified by what he termed the "highly flattering mark of distinction from these illustrious societies." It "may appear vain in me to show you these things," he remarked to a visitor to whom he showed off his membership diplomas, "but I am sure you will like to see them."[59]

No one liked to see them more than the American public. "We learn with pleasure," read newspapers in Salem, Boston, and New York, "that the Royal Society of London, at their annual meeting this spring, paid a tribute to American genius." The *Essex Register* noted that "the persons who were admitted at the same time, are of the highest reputation in Europe, and it is in itself a high honour to have received the particular attention of Sir Joseph Banks on the occasion." Even better, "the Great Herschell [*sic*]" himself had backed the election, "besides other persons who are high in literary fame." A Washington paper reprinted an excerpt from "an English gentleman" that provided the gratifying details.[60]

Leave it to Bowditch to detect the fly in the ointment. "This flattering mark of attention from that Respectable Society," he wrote of his Edinburgh honor, "would be more satisfactory if I could feel conscious that I had deserved it by any of my publications." He was right, of course. Neither the *Navigator* nor his *Memoirs* articles put him in the same class with that year's crop of French fellows. The Royal Society recognized the difference. The election certificate for mineralogist René Just Haüy, for example, praised his "ingenious discoveries and elaborate researches," while Bowditch's merely described him as "worthy of the Honour he solicits and likely to become a useful and valuable member."[61] If anything Bowditch had done merited the British honors, it was his Laplace translation and annotation, but that was not yet in print, nor was it likely to be anytime soon.

In some measure the cause of the publication delay was money. Issuing a multivolume work, filled with mathematical symbols requiring specialized printing skills, was an expensive affair. Learned Americans recognized as much and called on their compatriots to do their patriotic duty. It is "a matter of serious consideration to wealthy men, to the state governments, and to our universities," read the Federalist *Port-Folio*, "whether a general effort ought not to be made to enrich the literary reputation of North America by opening so valuable a vein of treasure to the English public." John Adams and the *Analyst's* mathematician-editor Robert Adrain were among those offering to subscribe to the treatise. The American Academy offered to pay for its publication "for the honor of the country, and for the cause of science." But Bowditch steadfastly refused all offers. He maintained that it would be unfair to ask either individual subscribers or institutions to pay for a set of books that few could understand. Benjamin Vaughan was exasperated with Bowditch's decision. "If you have contributed a portion of your *life* to this object, as one of public utility," he wrote Bowditch, "I do not see why you should be scrupulous in permitting others to employ some of their *money* in the same enterprize. They will have *their* gratification not only as regards *you*, but as regards science & the credit of their country; & doubtless ought to be indulged." Begging him to reconsider, he chided Bowditch for blocking "a public benefit for a private scruple; which so many good men before you have disregarded."[62]

Bowditch was unmoved. With so few potential readers, he responded, the money would be better spent on other objects, like finally building an observatory in America. In fact, he was at least as concerned with compromising his own position by being "under pecuniary obligations to others" as placing unfair monetary demands on others. "He did not wish any one [*sic*] to feel compelled, or to be induced to subscribe for it," explained his son, "lest he should have it in his power to say, 'I patronized Mr. Bowditch by buying his book, which I cannot read.'"[63] In other words, allowing others to pay for the *Mécanique Céleste* would give them social leverage over him. Better to wait.

There was a second reason for the delay. He thought it quite possible that Laplace would revise his own work based on subsequent "improvements" in mathematical demonstrations and calculations. Once Laplace died in 1827 this logic was no longer valid.[64] But there was at least one other motivation, probably the critical one: Bowditch could see that his commentary required more revision. While the translation took place between 1814 and 1817, the annotations were written as he read the volumes, between 1803 and 1806. Once Bowditch completed the translation, he realized that these early annotations were insufficient. "The advance of science," wrote Bowditch's sons, required extensive revisions of and additions to the original manuscript.[65] Bowditch encountered this "advance" not long after he finished the translation, for it was only then that Bowditch discovered a body of work of which he had been largely unaware, German mathematics and astronomy.

Much as France displaced Britain on the cutting-edge of quantitative science, so too did German-speaking scientists represent the next wave of intellectual innovation.[66] Bowditch was not entirely unaware of German developments. In a 1797 index to his commonplace books, two scientists from the German-speaking world made an appearance.[67] But he did not read German, and only in the 1810s did he become aware of the centrality of German scientific activity. In 1818 John Farrar sent him a copy of Lindenau's *Zeitschrift*, the one that had recently promoted his meteor essay as theoretically intriguing—and his comet essay as methodologically obsolete. To Zach, the editor of the *Correspondance Astronomique*, Bowditch tried to explain away his outdated mathematical approach to comets as deliberate, undertaken only as a scientific lark. "I made many unnecessary calculations," he wrote in a letter published in Zach's journal, "as you will see in my memoir, but it was amusing for me to see how close I could get to the real elements with observations made with a simple Borda reflecting circle," that is, a relatively primitive instrument. Perhaps we should forgive Bowditch for this, shall we say, inventive account, and for the wounded pride that prompted him to add that he "had the satisfaction to find" his results "accorded perfectly with those made by the best European astronomers."[68]

If he were ever to be taken seriously by the people who mattered, he would have to get up to speed with German science. The first step would have to be getting hold of German books and periodicals, and in this era that meant having someone on the spot to do the job for you. In 1818 he met the future historian George Bancroft, then a young Harvard graduate about to further his studies in Göttingen, and entrusted him with a list of German scientific works and a quantity of gold. Bancroft attended to the matter and then transmitted the names of additional works recommended by Carl Friedrich Gauss, Göttingen's celebrated professor of astronomy. Bowditch soon sent the young student thirty dollars to acquire those titles, but he had to watch his money. "I would like very much to own a complete set of Bodes Astronomische Jahrbucher [*sic*]," he wrote, "but have lately imported the Transactions of the Petersburg Royal Society & other expensive works & feel inclined for a little time to be *quite prudent* in the way of books, but I should regret very much to lose an opportunity of buying that work *cheap*, as it may sometimes happen at public sale &c."[69]

Meanwhile he was learning German. Over the winter of 1819–20 he devoted two hours a day to teaching himself the language, sufficient, he claimed, to read mathematical works "with tolerable facility." It was a revelation. The new German works he had received "engaged very much my attention," he wrote a German acquaintance who had sent him a copy of one such publication. He had read an account of Olbers's treatise on comets several years earlier "but had never read the original excellent work."[70] It was a prime example of the progress in comet science referred to by Lindenau as unknown to the New World.

In 1820 Bowditch published a review of Olbers's treatise and of a work by Gauss in Boston's *North American Review*. The goal of his essay, he began, was not to discuss the substance of these books but instead "to call the attention of the astronomers and mathematicians of our country to some of the improvements in the science, which have been for some time in common use in Germany, but which are hardly known here." Olbers's work, he pointed out, had been published over twenty years ago, and Gauss's, over ten. His criticism was not aimed so much at his countrymen as at the British scientific establishment, which he argued also ignored German mathematics. Perhaps Bowditch blamed it for his own embarrassing gaps in knowledge. At any rate, his enthusiasm for German science seemed to have few limits. He pointed out that Britain had awarded part of the Longitude Prize to a German astronomer, that twelve of the thirteen new planets and satellites discovered in the last thirty years were discovered by persons born in Germany, and that the great William Herschel, though he lived in England, was born in Hanover. Yet he ended his essay by admitting that "we cannot allow ourselves to pass over the most distinguished name" of all, that of Laplace. His *Mécanique Céleste*, he concluded, "place[s] this immortal man far above any of his contemporaries in the walks of science."[71]

The magazine's editor pointed out "what the delicacy of our learned correspondent led him to omit," namely, that the essay's author had annotated and translated Laplace, but clearly publication of that work was on Bowditch's mind.[72] He was realizing just how much he needed to absorb the work coming out of Germany in order to provide full and accurate commentary on the *Mécanique Céleste*. He had thought that Laplace might revise his work in light of James Ivory's contributions, for example, yet at least on the subject of comets Ivory's work was just a restatement of work Olbers had published years earlier. How could he fill in the gaps of Laplace's argumentation, trace the provenance of his ideas, and detect what was truly original if he knew so little about German mathematics and astronomy? Before his magnum opus could be published, he would once more have to teach himself what he needed to know. At the same time, he would learn new lessons about Salem's institutions when he turned his critical eye to the town's business affairs.

CHAPTER SIX

The Prudent Man

In 1820 Englishman Adam Hodgson came to Salem. "It is a singular little town of astonishing wealth," he wrote, "and formerly had 60 or 70 ships in the East India trade." The town's mercantile community impressed him as startlingly cosmopolitan. "I never met with merchants more intelligent on commercial subjects than at Salem," he reported, "or in more close connection with the most remote foreign markets." Nor were they concerned only with business affairs. "They have much leisure," he wrote, "good literary institutions, and the few whom I saw were very well informed on general topics." It was a flattering portrait, but a single word—the "formerly" used to describe the Indies trade—could only have confirmed Salemites' growing sense that their town's glory days were fast fading.[1]

After the War of 1812 America's maritime commerce began to concentrate in larger coastal cities, and elites in these larger centers began to shift some of their economic resources out of global commerce and into manufacturing. In New England Boston wealth established textile mills in Waltham, Lowell, and Lawrence, Massachusetts; Nashua and Manchester, New Hampshire; and Saco, Maine. Meanwhile, in Salem it was not until 1826 that prominent Salemites so much as established a committee "to enquire into the practicability and expediency of establishing manufactures," and the town's first big factory did not open until 1847.[2] A second trend boded ill for the entire New England region. As the American population expanded westward, so too did markets. Cities with access to the interior, like New York with its links to the Erie Canal, emerged as the economic winners.

As a port focused on ocean-borne commerce, and a secondary one at that, Salem could not keep pace. In 1790 it had been the seventh largest town in America, with a population of about 8,000, somewhat less than half that of Boston. By 1830, Salem dropped to fourteenth place, its population of about 14,000 now less than a quarter of that of the Massachusetts capital. At the beginning of the century Boston had two banks and Salem one. Thirty years later, Boston's eighteen banks were capitalized at close to $13 million, and Salem's six banks at less than $2 million.[3] As it fell behind, Salem's less opulent way of life seemed to mark it as a social and cultural backwater, in contrast to what Hodgson described as Boston's "liberality, intelligence, and cultivation" and "English taste and habits," which, though "rather expensive and luxurious," gave the city "an agreeable '*Je ne sais quoi*'" found nowhere else in America.[4] The trend was clear: Boston was the center of economic dynamism and cultural polish in New England. And Salem? Salem? Ah yes, the town that *formerly* could claim such distinctions.

Boston's gain was Salem's loss. Already after the Revolution many prominent Essex County merchant families, most notably the Lowells, Jacksons, Cabots, and Lees, had moved to the capital. On the eve of the next war a few wealthy Salemites joined them, including the Essex Fire and Marine Insurance (EFM) attorney William Prescott and merchant Thomas Wren Ward. By the 1820s many more Salemites were giving in to the gravitational force of what Oliver Wendell Holmes would soon call "the Hub of the Solar System."[5] "I have removed to this city [Boston], where the advantages of pursuing my professional business are much greater than they were in Salem," John Pickering explained to German savant Alexander von Humboldt. "Boston is also the centre of our Northern literature, and is only three miles (English) from our University of Cambridge."[6]

By 1823 Bowditch would pursue the same dual advantages of Boston, but even before then he was increasingly drawn into the city's social circles and their cultural, political, philanthropic, and business concerns. At the same time he found himself ever more deeply involved in the affairs of the Salem elite, especially their business affairs. As the EFM actuary he had long been a key player, insuring vessels and cargoes and directing capital into investments in federal and state debt and Massachusetts bank shares. Then in the late 1810s he directed his energies more directly into Salem's banking sector, when the Essex Bank, tightly associated with EFM, ran into fatal trouble. More critical for his future—and the nation's—was his leadership of a new kind of financial enterprise, the trust.

In this new financial sector triumvirate—marine insurance, banking, and trusts—Bowditch cooperated with a new bipartisan coalition of movers and shakers, for the old divisions no longer correlated to the economic realities of postwar New England. Salem attorney Joseph Story, for example, had been a Jeffersonian, but after the war he and Bowditch were fellow incorporators of a new bank, and even earlier he had served as the legal champion of the controversial financial mechanism that Bowditch administered, the trust. From regional and national stages that eclipsed fading Salem, both were to promote changes—Bowditch as a Boston financier, Story as a Supreme Court justice and Harvard law professor—that served urban elites well, but their understanding of elite interests derived from their Salem years. They also shared a desire to rationalize and systematize the world of affairs, again, Story dealing with the legal rules governing economic activity, and Bowditch in business. Such mathematical values had long guided Bowditch in his various endeavors, but in the late 1810s and early 1820s a range of "irregularities"—frauds parading as gentlemen, criminals pardoned for their misdeeds, corporate operations revealed as slipshod—may have primed him to regularize business affairs as never before.

IN JULY 1817, when James Monroe visited Salem, Bowditch was appointed one of ten men, half of them Federalist and half Republican, on the local Committee of Arrangements. Privately Bowditch retained a droll detachment from the proceedings. "Do you know that we have all become federalists, all republicans?" he wrote Eliza Orne Wetmore, a longtime family friend, echoing Jefferson's 1801 inaugural address, "and that we shall 'tender the homage of our highest respect & consideration' to the President, on his visit to this town"? Dropping a French phrase, he explained with wry bemusement, that "at a time like the present where federalists & democrats, orthodox & heterodox, and all other '*ists*' & *ox's* join in '*une grande expression*' of love for '*le plus grand chef de la nation Americaine*,' it is impossible to give full vent to our feelings without mixing a little bad French with some worse English."[7]

Monroe and his entourage were welcomed into Salem with an artillery salute, the ringing of bells, and an official party that included Bowditch. The president joined a formal procession into town to the "gratulating [*sic*] shouts of thousands." Salemites marched in company with other members of the corporate bodies to which they belonged: town and state officials, judges, army and navy officers, local military companies, attorneys, physicians, clergymen, school masters, the East India Marine Society, the Salem Marine Society, the "Officers of Insurance Companies and Banks," and the selectmen and Committee of Arrangements. Shopkeepers, craftsmen, sailors, and laborers were relegated to the crowds that lined the streets. Ladies held back from the public display and watched from their windows. The celebrations went on for days and involved speeches, a military review, fireworks, a formal dinner, an elegant musical soiree "with a brilliant assemblage of ladies and gentlemen," and visits to the town's fort, the East India Marine Society Museum, the Athenaeum, and the newly built almshouse. There was "a most sumptuous and elegant" breakfast at Israel Thorndike's "mansion house," evening entertainments bringing together "the taste and fashion of the town," and private visits to several individuals. Among these select few, reported the Republican *Essex Register*, was "the Hon. NATHANIEL

BOWDITCH, the first Mathematician in our country." So did Salem's "Jacobins" and "Anglo-men" enter this new "Era of Good Feelings."[8]

Political considerations played a role in this rapprochement. Monroe's national tour was designed to ground support for the new president in a nonpartisan nationalism, while New England Federalists, dogged by their opposition to the war and flirtation with secession, were anxious to redeem themselves and regain political strength. But just as critical, in an era of economic and demographic change, was that the prewar partisan divisions no longer made sense. Among Salem's commercial elite, new alignments formed around common economic interests. The shift from commerce to industry, and from overseas to domestic inland markets, threatened Federalist and Republican merchants equally, and it would be smarter to confront them in concert. So as he greeted Monroe at the entrance to Salem, merchant Benjamin Pickman took the occasion to express the hope that the new administration would give "every due encouragement" to maritime commerce. It was an indirect statement of opposition to tariffs on foreign manufactured goods, a policy that protected America's infant textile industries to the detriment of America's importers of Indian cottons. In a masterpiece of ambiguity, Monroe replied that commercial interests should indeed "meet with every encouragement which was consistent with a due regard to the other great interests of the country."[9]

The tariff issue was just one of the issues around which Salem's prominent families coalesced to promote their common interests. In their unity on this matter they differed from Boston, where commercial and manufacturing interests squared off until, by the early 1830s, they had consolidated their economic interests to the point where political consensus was once again possible.[10] But if elites of the two cities differed on how best to generate wealth, they were united on another, longer-term set of concerns: how to preserve that wealth over time, how to mobilize it for future economic enterprises, and how to keep at bay the public mistrust it could generate. Here too party differences were irrelevant. As he had in preparing for Monroe's visit, Bowditch now found himself working on financial matters in tandem with men who were former adversaries. He did so first as a pioneer in the field of trusts and then in his rescue of one of Salem's most respected financial institutions.

Bowditch's first experience with trusts came in 1817, the year of Monroe's visit. On Christmas Day 1816 merchant Charles Henry Orne died at the age of twenty-eight, a childless widower with considerable inherited wealth. The following year Orne's siblings—including the Bowditches' friend and cousin by marriage Eliza—established a fund in memory of their brother to be used to support the ministers of Salem's First Church. It was set up as a trust; designated individuals, the trustees, were the legal owners of the property and would have the sole responsibility for administering it in the interests of the beneficiaries. Bowditch was one of the three trustees. Such legal and financial arrangements are common today, sometimes to benefit charitable or nonprofit institutions like the First Church, in other cases to benefit an individual's heirs. Trusts were not unknown in Massachusetts— Benjamin Franklin had established one for the benefit of Boston, for example—but nor were they common. In Franklin's day, and even when the Orne Fund was devised, the legal infrastructure necessary for the enforcement of trusts did not yet exist in the Commonwealth.[11]

The law lagged behind practice because trusts were politically controversial.[12] They require a particular form of legal authority known as equity jurisdiction, theoretically concerned with providing relief from the harsh application of the law through remedies not otherwise provided by the courts. In Britain the King had granted equity powers to a special branch of the judicial system known as the court in chancery. To most postrevolutionary Americans, equity jurisdiction and chancery courts were everything they did not want. They regarded them as instruments of entrenched monarchical and ecclesiastical power. The people, in the form of the legislature, should have control over matters, not judges unchecked by popular will. Chancery court proceedings also had a much deserved reputation for being costly, interminable, arcane, arbitrary, and inscrutable, offering "equity" only to those with the most money and patience. (Several decades later, in its wicked presentation of *Jarndyce v. Jarndyce*, Charles Dickens's *Bleak House* would indict chancery courts on just these grounds.) So when Massachusetts citizens drew up their state constitution in 1780, they explicitly reserved equity powers to the legislature. Anyone seeking an equitable remedy—and that would include the establishment of a trust—would have to petition the state legislature to do so.

The elite families of the Commonwealth did not want the people's representatives butting in on their private affairs. Already in 1808 their representative, the learned attorney Joseph Story, had tried to get the legislature to grant equity powers to the judiciary. Story was a Jeffersonian Republican. He had set up his legal practice under the wing of the Republican Crowninshield family, helped draw up the incorporation papers for a Republican-affiliated bank and insurance company in town, and even engaged in "fisty cuffs" with one of the Federalist Derbys. His championing of the chancery cause tells us a good deal about politics and power in this era. In part it was an early sign of the political transformation that would have William Bentley cursing him as an apostate from the Republican cause, but Story's primary allegiance had always been not to party but to commercial elites. So even in 1808, smack in the midst of the Embargo, cross-party economic cooperation was possible whenever, as with the equity issue, all moneyed families, Federalist and Republican, stood to gain.[13]

Why exactly was this issue of such importance to them? Trusts offered many advantages. They were private arrangements; provisions could remain secret. More important, they would allow families to keep wealth intact as it passed from generation to generation, since beneficiaries received the earnings the principle generated, not the principle itself. With a private trust descendants would live in style but could not squander the family fortune. With a public trust earnings would fund the charitable and cultural institutions that would represent these families' leading role in society, affording them a kind of "soft" power to go along with their "hard" economic power. Meanwhile, the pools of capital created by trusts could be invested in further wealth-generating enterprises—real estate, trading voyages, banks, insurance companies, turnpikes, canals, railroads, and factories. A modest provision, the Orne trust was only an early indicator of the central role trusts would soon play in the lives of Boston's leading families under Bowditch's guiding hand.

In selling the legislature on his bill, Story did not represent the issue in this light. Instead, he insisted that Massachusetts could institute a form of chancery courts freed from the admitted weaknesses of their British antecedents. Such courts could be "administered upon determinate principles" to prevent them from acting in a seemingly arbitrary manner and to promote "exactness and regularity" in this branch of law. Commitment to such principles was typical of the "scientific reform" of law in the early republic, a movement in which Theophilus Parsons, Story's ally—and Bowditch's mathematical correspondent—played the leading role in Massachusetts. The absence of uniform and predictable arrangements, Story argued further, could spell disaster. On the one hand, there would be no way to compel trustees to act in the interest of the beneficiaries. On the other, the dead hand of the past would have a permanent death grip on "our most valuable estates." Heirs would fritter away "our surplus wealth" on "specious or mistaken charities," to "the impoverishment of friends, and the injury of the poor and deserving."[14]

In 1808 the legislature wasn't biting and the bill was defeated, but the setback was temporary. When a bill to add equity powers in the matter of trusts to the jurisdiction of the state's existing courts was introduced in 1817 it faced opposition. Critics pointed to the "chaos," the "bottomless pit," and the "expense, uncertainty and eternity" that was the English Chancery and characterized equity courts as the tools of "nabobs," a "mere deposit of rich men's power, over their more destitute antagonists" where the man with "a *long purse*" invariably held the advantage. Advocates countered that English Chancery decisions had "been reduced to order and methodical arrangement" and that the bill had the strong support of "gentlemen distinguished for their legal science." In early 1818 the bill was signed into law.[15]

The Orne Fund was established just as the General Court, Massachusetts's state legislature, took up the new legislation. It was quickly followed by a second that took effect upon the death in July 1817 of merchant Simon Forrester, the man William Bentley identified as "the richest man in Salem." This trust amounted to half a million dollars, and unlike the Orne Fund, it was set up not for charitable purposes but to support Forrester's female heirs. He left his money to be controlled by three men who were not family members, with Bowditch at the head, because he did not fully trust his sons to look after his wife and daughters. Bentley described son Thomas Forrester as "dissipated," while John Pickering alluded mysteriously to an "infirmity which has been the source of much unhappiness to his [Thomas's] relatives and friends." Son John lived opulently but was in fact deeply in debt, and he was known for a violent temper to boot. (He was the man who in 1822 would provoke the Essex Street scuffle in which Bowditch intervened.) Simon Forrester also had reason to be suspicious of his sons-in-law, for it was rumored that they had married only to gain access to Simon's wealth. As a widow, Rachel Forrester could retain control over her money, but any property Simon's married daughters inherited became the property of their husbands, unless explicitly stipulated otherwise in a legally binding document.[16]

Bowditch had experience managing money for women, including widow Eliza Orne Wetmore and the unmarried Caroline Plummer, and the Forrester trust functioned as Simon had hoped it would. Under terms of the will, Simon's wife and daughters received the income generated by his estate but had no control over or ownership of the property that constituted the estate itself. Neither they nor their brothers, sons, or husbands could sell it, bequeath it—or squander it. Instead, led by Bowditch, the trustees kept the Forrester fortune intact, even as the earnings derived from their investments provided for the Forrester women. They moved large sums out of London deposits and Louisiana speculations into corporate investments closer to home: stock in the Bank of the United States and a variety of Massachusetts banks and insurance companies, local turnpike and textile mill shares, and loans to the cities of Boston and Worcester.[17]

The Forrester trust stands out not just because it took advantage of a new legal environment but also because Bowditch and his cotrustees carried out their responsibilities in a manner sharply departing from contemporary practice. Many private trustees in this era did not bother to invest family property; left idle, the property generated no income. Meanwhile, the Forrester trustees were busy managing assets. Trustees of some other trusts treated the funds as their personal assets, to be mixed with and managed accordingly. At its worst such an approach meant the plundering of the estate, but at any rate it meant that fiduciary responsibility to the beneficiaries played no role in financial decisions. By contrast, Bowditch and his cotrustees strictly separated their personal finances from Forrester funds. It was a rare trustee who kept an adequate accounting of how he managed trust moneys, but the Forrester trustees produced annual accountings of the funds and kept meticulous records. In the early 1830s, bemoaning the slipshod state of many trust accounts, one legal authority in New York recommended that "printed forms" should "be appended to every order appointing a trustee" in response to "the extreme ignorance of some trustees etc. in stating their accounts." Fifteen years earlier, in one of his first acts as a Forrester trustee, Bowditch placed an order with a Salem stationer for just such forms.[18]

Bowditch benefited from his position as trustee. In 1818 he reported that he received $3,000 a year from the Forrester trust, twice his EFM salary.[19] But there is a much bigger picture here. First, in directing half a million dollars into the region's financial, transportation, and manufacturing corporations, the trust reinforced the economic power of the state's urban elites, much as the Orne trust reinforced its cultural influence. And second, these steps were taken by what were essentially professional money managers, not the wealth holders themselves. The process of preserving and investing wealth was becoming a matter of technical expertise, the operation of a legal mechanism, removed from the personal proclivities of the beneficiaries. These characteristics of the trust would become more overt and far more powerful in Bowditch's later business career, when the scale and impact of trust and investment operations under his control dwarfed the Forrester fortune.

Eventually, "Boston trustee" became a generic term with no geographic referent, and the wide influence of the Commonwealth it suggests was very real. The Supreme Judicial Court of Massachusetts issued a decision in 1830 critical for the future of trusts nationwide. In *Harvard College v. Amory*, the trust beneficiaries sued the trustees, arguing the trustees had taken unacceptable risks by investing in manufacturing and insurance stocks, inherently subject to wildly fluctuating values. But the judge ruled that trustees were not liable for the consequences of their bad decisions. "All that can be required of a trustee to invest," wrote Judge Samuel Putnam in language that has guided the practice of trusteeship ever since, "is, that he shall conduct himself faithfully and exercise a sound discretion. He is to observe how men of prudence, discretion and intelligence manage their own affairs, not in regard to speculation but in regard to the permanent disposition of their funds." The so-called Prudent Man Rule established a standard of fiduciary care while freeing up trustees to act unencumbered by beneficiaries. Perhaps the defendant, Bostonian Francis Amory, was Judge Putnam's model of prudence. But perhaps Putnam, a lawyer from Salem, had Bowditch in mind.[20]

Certainly Bowditch's reputation for prudence figured in his role in another of Salem's business affairs, this one a scandal. In the summer of 1818 the cashier and the chief clerk of the Essex Bank absconded to parts unknown, carrying with them tens of thousands of dollars of the Federalist bank's assets. Eventually, Bowditch would be one of the three prudent men to take over the bank's affairs in the wake of the debacle, but that still lay in the future. Meanwhile, the theft was a huge embarrassment to the bank's directors, among whom were some of the most prominent men in town, including business connections and personal friends of Bowditch. Efforts were made to hush up the dirty business. The local newspapers, Federalist and Republican, revealed nothing. A vaguely worded notice of a stockholders' meeting "to act upon such business as may be laid before them" appeared in the *Salem Gazette* under the name of a new cashier, attorney Benjamin R. Nichols. The *Essex Register* reported the appointment of Nichols in place of William Shepard Gray, "removed." Only out-of-town newspapers dared to break what Bentley termed "the dishonourable silence." The cashier and clerk had "eloped" with the money, it was reported in New York, and the bank's authorities were counting what was left in the vault to figure out just how much had been stolen. In November, when the *Essex Register* reported that a grand jury had indicted the two men, it added that "we announce this part of the Law history of the event, to remove any apprehension that there was a disposition to wink at crime, or to prevent justice," but it named no names.[21]

The two men got away with it: "Shepard Gray and James King the greatest Thieves that ever lived arrived in Canada," reported Benjamin Pickman in his diary.[22] Bentley went so far as to suggest that the Essex Bank directors engaged in secret negotiations with the fugitives, allowing them to remain beyond the law. He may have been right. Too many important people had been taken in by Gray and King for them to want to see the thieves publicly condemned. It could only reflect poorly on their own powers of judgment, starting with Pickman, who had entertained Gray in his own home just a few months earlier. Though the son of a house painter, Gray was by all appearances a thoroughly respectable and prosperous man. He had invested in local commerce and real estate, participated in Federalist politics, and served as treasurer of the Athenaeum. He had built a "superb house" in town, commented Bentley, and had "passed with many as rich." Over seventy years after the event, Bowditch's son remembered the shock that "came upon us all, boys and old men alike," that "the dignified and apparently immaculate Shepard Gray" had plundered the bank.[23] As for the chief clerk, King too was an active investor and politico, and he achieved special distinction as captain of the Federalist-affiliated Salem Light Infantry, where he was known for providing "generous libations" at the unit's annual parades. Worse, he was the son of James King, one of the Essex Bank's directors and its original cashier.[24]

Starting in the early nineteenth century, the specter of the con artist haunted the American scene, provoking anxieties that ultimately referred back to the changing tenor of everyday life and business affairs. Confidence men and fraudsters took root in the urban and frontier worlds of strangers. Counterfeiters trucked in the suspiciously abstract representation of value that was paper money. Even apart from such developments, the reality of migration and travel had long meant that individuals would encounter strangers, at least in port cities, whose appearances might be deceiving. What did Bowditch really know about a man like John Stuart Kerr, the Philadelphia merchant who had somehow washed up in Manila? How surprised could he have been when Frederick Jordy, the Rhinelander escaping from the Haitian Revolution who had taught him French, turned out to be a "vile" cheat?[25] Bowditch's scientific antagonists, George Baron and John Wood, were the intellectual equivalents of such characters—fresh off the boat, dubious pasts jettisoned, mathematical pretenders.

But the Essex Bank thieves and their crime were of a different type. They did not practice the sleight-of-hand associated with fraudulent paper. They stole gold doubloons. More important, they were anything but strangers, and as such, the implications of their crime went beyond embarrassing those who had placed confidence in them. It raised questions about the way Salemites customarily conducted business. As we have seen with EFM, the town's commercial affairs operated in the context of well-worn relationships, prompting flexibility and informality, and ostensibly mutual trust. Gray's and King's betrayal of that trust had the potential to cast doubt on long-established patterns of business conduct. Much was at stake, then, in how the directors responded to the plundering of the Essex Bank. They needed to establish the trustworthiness not so much of this particular institution—that was a lost cause—as of the cadre of merchants who had backed it, financial institutions in general, and the Salem way of conducting affairs.

What to do next? A lawsuit was in the works, filed by the heirs of a depositor whose barrel of Spanish gold worth over $50,000 had been stolen. Infighting broke out among the bank's directors. That summer the state legislature passed a law closing down the bank's operations and giving it three years to settle its affairs. Three administrators were appointed to settle accounts, Bowditch among them. He knew the bank well, for EFM deposited money in its vault, purchased its stock, and rented office space from it. The two financial institutions seem to have constituted one of those bank–insurance office twin stars so common in this era. Bowditch also knew Shepard Gray. Not only was Gray a childhood schoolmate and the apothecary's apprentice who introduced him to Nathan Read and his scientific library, but he also was EFM's first clerk and a stockholder.[26]

For the next three years the three men oversaw the affairs of the bank. Of greatest concern was making good on the bank's obligations, among which were the banknotes it had issued. That task took on a special urgency because just as the theft became public knowledge the nation plunged into the Panic of 1819. Banks suspended the exchange of paper for gold; many went under altogether. New England was largely spared a wholesale banking collapse, but New Englanders could hardly have avoided the national debates that often scapegoated banks and paper money as causes of the panic. Local events made the task of reestablishing trust even more difficult. First, there was the robbery of Salem's Merchants Bank bills from a mail coach, and then the counterfeiting of the nearby Gloucester Bank's notes. William Bentley knew what conclusions to draw: "We see the general character of Banks through the United States."[27]

From the end of 1819 until the bank expired permanently in June 1822, the bank administrators worked against this suspicion, calling on those holding the Essex Bank's bills to present them for payment.[28] We cannot be certain that they were offering 100 cents on the dollar, but that may have been a prime reason the Commercial Bank was established in February 1819. It was the institution to which holders of Essex Bank notes were directed.

Bowditch was one of its sixteen incorporators, along with a number of other Federalist stalwarts. But the prewar days of partisan banking were over. Benjamin W. Crowninshield, whose family name was synonymous with Salem's Jeffersonian elite, was also an incorporator, as was Joseph Story, two of his brothers-in-law, and two directors of the Republican-affiliated Merchants Bank he had helped establish in 1811.[29] The common interests of Federalist and Republican merchants were rapidly rendering older political stances obsolete, making new economic partnerships logical and desirable.

The Commercial Bank may have made good on its predecessors' paper money, but there was also the matter of that barrel of gold. Stockholder Benjamin Foster had left the doubloons with the bank as a "special deposit" to be held for safekeeping, much like property left today in a safe deposit box, except that the bank did not charge for the service. The presiding judge characterized the practice as having "originated in a willingness to accommodate members of the corporation with a place for their treasures." In other words, it was an informal arrangement and personal favor of the sort that these early corporations routinely granted. Foster's lawyers, John Pickering and Daniel Webster, focused on just this kind of looseness in business procedures in making a case for the bank's negligence. The false entries the cashier and clerk recorded in the bank's ledgers could be chalked up to dishonesty, but lax bookkeeping seemed endemic to the bank's operations. Until 1814, for example, no written records of transactions involving the receipt or dispersal of special deposits had been kept, and even then the directors never did ask for an accounting. As for the operation as a whole, by the time Gray and King absconded, the bank's books had not been posted for two and a half years. There was a provision for oversight, an annual inspection conducted by the stockholders, but apparently no one had noticed anything amiss. Ultimately the bank got off the legal hook, but the disclosure of its daily operations exposed the way some of the most prominent and respected men in Salem conducted business, and it painted a sobering picture.[30]

It was in fact the county's second such disclosure in recent years. In 1816 the financial mismanagement of Newburyport's Federalist-affiliated Union Marine and Fire Insurance Company in its dealings with a Maine bank had prompted a court-ordered audit of the company's books. Two of Bowditch's closest friends, Dudley Pickman and John Pickering, were among the three auditors. No criminal activity was alleged, but as with the Essex Bank case, a loose-dealing employee, in this case the company secretary, William Woart, was allowed to operate unchecked by the directors for years. The auditors' printed report was a tale of unlocked chests, unsecured keys, unrecorded money transfers, indiscriminate mixing of the Newburyport and Maine moneys, and commingling of the secretary's private papers and bank holdings with company documents and accounts. It was Woart himself who first discovered "a perplexity in the accounts"—thousands in missing monies—but though he reported the problem to the directors and "expressed a strong wish that they would examine the Books," no such examination was conducted. Later, when the annual statements presented to the stockholders and the directors did not match, the directors expressed some "uneasiness," but Woart's verbal reply that, "if there was any deficiency, he should hold himself responsible and expect to make it good" was good enough for them. Given "the very loose and confused situation" of the books, the "many omissions and mis-entries which they must contain," and "the obscurity in which all the Hallowell [Maine] Funds are involved," the auditors found themselves able to give no better than an estimate of how much money was missing.[31]

We cannot know for certain what lessons Bowditch took from these revelations. As we have seen, Bowditch accommodated his customers' desires in the usual style of personal service and institutional flexibility. The kind of favor granted Benjamin Foster would not have been out of place at EFM. When it came to office operations, though, Bowditch ran a tighter ship than did these other institutions. They set a particularly low standard, of course, but some degree of operational laxity was commonplace. In 1805, for example, following the death of its president—and, presumably, an encounter with the records he left behind—the directors of the Boston Marine Insurance Company passed a set of resolutions calling for tidier bookkeeping: monthly written accounts, the systematic recording of marine losses in a book designated for that purpose, the regular annual closing of the books, the availability of the books for the directors' examination, and, so "that the utmost regularity should pervade the affairs of the Company," a "distinct record . . . of the most trivial disbursements."[32] Bowditch, on the other hand, issued annual statements of profit and loss to the stockholders, though the corporate charter required such statements only every three years. He also had long employed outside examiners to review the office accounts and make certain they squared with the office books. Intriguingly, only in 1819, in the thick of the Essex Bank scandal, was a receipt issued for the examiners' cumulative sixteen years of services. Perhaps with an eye to the kind of unwelcome exposure garnered by the Essex Bank and Union Marine and Fire, he recognized the need to leave a paper trail of his careful management. Or perhaps he began to question even his own office habits as insufficiently stringent.[33] Certainly, when in 1823 he assumed command of a Boston financial corporation, he would introduce office procedures that amazed contemporaries for their rigor.

Meanwhile, his personal business gave Bowditch reason to wonder if Shepard Gray and James King were the only scoundrels parading as gentlemen. After Edmund Blunt quit Newburyport for New York in 1810, the publication of a third edition of the *Navigator*, along with the copyright, was taken up by a man named Edward Little. Though not a printer, Little seemed like a more than solid bet for the enterprise. He was a Dartmouth graduate, a lawyer who had studied with Theophilus Parsons, thrice elected to represent the town in the state legislature, and one of the founders of the Newburyport Athenaeum. Then only weeks after the third edition was ready for sale, in 1811 fire raced through Newburyport, obliterating most of the town's business district. "Edwd. Little has lost his large brick store with all its contents," Bowditch wrote Caroline Plummer. "The whole edition of the Navigator is burnt up." Little already owed Bowditch $860, and that plus his share of the expected profits from the third edition came to about $1,600 or $1,700.[34] Herein lay the seeds of the quarrel between the two, one that also pulled in Blunt and that stretched from 1817 until at least 1819.[35]

In their correspondence with Bowditch, Little and Blunt pointed the finger at each other. He would happily pay Bowditch, wrote Little, except that the promissory note he had received from Blunt was payable only in the "somewhat distant" future, and rumor had it that Blunt was "in some difficulty again himself." Not so, replied Blunt. He had paid Little for Bowditch's share of the profits, but Little had pocketed it for himself. Little chided Blunt for his "molasses history" of payment. Blunt described Little as "a most consummate villain." Little insisted he had never intended to defraud his creditors, though he may have taken steps that *appeared* wrong or imprudent. "I can truly say," he wrote Bowditch, "that I suffer as much from not being paid what is due me, from others, as you suppose you may suffer by me." Bowditch was not to be mollified. "Little has never paid me," he wrote Blunt, "but has offered me your notes which I refused to receive because you said they were fraudulently obtained." As to Little's offer of his father's land in Maine by way of payment, "I would not give 5 cents for 1000 acres to be obliged to hold them." Replied Blunt, "You may say what you please of rogues, but in all the transactions between Little and myself I find but one instance where he has not charged more than paid and credited less than received."[36]

Edward Little was not a fast-talking stranger who suddenly appeared on the Newburyport docks but a pillar of the town's Federalist elite. It had to have been disturbing to discover that he was a rogue. In fact, he was an even greater villain than either Bowditch or Blunt imagined, for it seems likely that he was the man responsible for burning down Newburyport. Three months before the disaster, a barn adjacent to his house had mysteriously gone up in flames. The Great Fire itself originated in a stable adjacent to a building he owned, the same he had advertised two years earlier as a "well built *Fire proof Brick Building*." Four years later, in 1815, he lost the contents of his business in Portland, Maine, "the third time," the newspaper noted, "Mr. Little has severely suffered by fire." Twenty-five years later, his carpet factory in Lewiston, Maine, burned down. It is hard to escape the impression that Little was a serial arsonist. Worse yet, in 1827 he was indicted in Portland for rape. He did not deny the charge, only claiming "a great provocation on the part of the woman," and the judge dismissed the case.[37] Bowditch knew none of this, of course, but in the year of the Essex Bank theft, encountering yet another two-faced North Shore gentleman was distressing enough.

THE YEARS IMMEDIATELY following the war saw Bowditch achieve major recognition, both at home and abroad, as a man of business and a man of science. But in these same years troubles seemed to come as often as honors, until both were finally overshadowed by family tragedy. First, in the spring of 1818 Mary became seriously ill. "From your letter," wrote Jonathan Ingersoll to Bowditch, "we find our affectionate daughter is confin'd with her Old Complaint with a depression of Spirits; but that the doctors think She will recover." It is not clear what was ailing Mary. Had the "Old Complaint" brought on a change in mood or was it itself a change in mood? Was it a bout of the tuberculosis that would eventually claim her? Clearly Mary and her family apprehended it as serious, even fatal. By late summer, though, Ingersoll was celebrating his daughter's "most miraculis [*sic*] recovery," prematurely as it turned out, for over the next winter she lost ground once more. Yet by the following December her friend Eliza could write that Mary "is so well this winter she goes about as much as any body," adding as evidence that "she was at Mrs. G. Tucker's ball, & danced three dances without being fatigued at all."[38]

All through Mary's health crisis the Bowditches had another problem to deal with: the conduct of their son Nat, now at Harvard. They had been overanxious to begin with. When Nat entered college in the fall of 1818 his parents fretted over his schoolwork. Mary critiqued his penmanship and spelling. Nathaniel sent him problems in right-angle spherical trigonometry. "Do them as soon as you can," he wrote. He soon urged his son to study

German, no doubt in light of his own recent acquisition of the language, recommending a private tutor on top of daily private study to promote what he termed "accuracy."[39]

Mary and Nathaniel worried about Nat's personal conduct even more than his academic performance, and with good reason. At thirteen he was the youngest in his class, nicknamed "Little Bowditch." Colleges in this era were the sites of periodic collective disruptions fueled by unruly teenagers. Sure enough, within months of his arrival the campus erupted in the so-called Rebellion of 1818. What started as a dining hall food fight turned into a rowdy student rally and ended only with the mass expulsion of the sophomore class. The Bowditches watched with anxiety, hoping that the events would prove "a useful lesson" for Nat. On a stage from Cambridge, Bowditch saw firsthand just what kind of boys might corrupt his son when a number of expelled sophomores began to insult the college dean, until Bowditch could hold his tongue no more. He told them that he might have respected their remarks if they had "indicated strength of mind or body, or that they had an immortal soul," he reported, "but when the whole difficulty arose from their putting themselves upon a level with mischievous monkeys or baboons, in breaking their plates, glasses &c., it was too contemptible."[40]

It was not long before Nat got into trouble. In April 1819 he was caught setting fire to an outhouse in Harvard Yard. Though horrified, Mary made every excuse in the book for her son. Nat had set the fire, but then almost immediately tried to extinguish it. Only a few square inches of the "necessary" were destroyed. "Older boys" had done the same thing many times; they just hadn't been caught. He had fallen in with "vile associates." It was probably only as a courtesy to one of their overseers that the college, as Bowditch wrote, "merely sent him home for my management," on the understanding that Nat could return in the fall if he attained what Mary termed "a sufficient degree of manly deportment," a tall order for a fourteen-year-old. "The anxiety and grief it has occasioned his good Father & myself . . . you may pass years & perhaps all your life my dear without passing through so unpleasant a scene," Mary wrote her cousin. Even Nat's brothers "feel disgraced more than you would conceive it possible."[41]

Despite parental admonitions to steer clear of drink and "*idle* boys," Nat got into trouble again. This time he was caught throwing "a Cannon Ball several times from an upper window of one of the Colleges on the step of the door . . . accompanied with deliberate insult to a College Officer." The other student involved was suspended, while Nat was only reprimanded for what was characterized as his "subordinate role" in the offense. ("A *Junior* was engaged and caught in the same scrape," wrote one student in his diary, "but owing to his *father's* fame his conduct was unnoticed.") Before much longer, Nat was fined two dollars for "disorderly & disrespectful conduct at a Lecture" and then "spoken to by the President for his different acts of contumely and disorder, & warned of his danger." In a letter to Bowditch, Harvard professor Edward Everett included a word to the wise: "P.S. Yr Son is inclined to be rebellious, and a word of admonition from You would be highly in Season."[42]

As they responded to their son's transgressions, the Bowditches mixed straightforward instructions and admonitions with more subtle emotional manipulation. Nathaniel tended to favor the former; Mary, the latter. Yet neither held back on their tenderness, perhaps the father even less so. "God bless you my dear child," Bowditch wrote Nat. That mix of authority, guilt, and love was precisely what contemporary experts on child-rearing matters advised as the "modern," improved alternative to corporal punishment. The idea was to act on children's souls rather than their bodies, so that they would internalize the lessons of self-restraint and moral behavior. For the most part it worked with Nat. He felt appropriately wretched, to the point that only the encouraging words of Henry Pickering, who told him that "a simply foolish act" had "*not utterly degraded* him," "lifted him up out of the distress."[43] And ultimately he knew how to redeem himself. In his senior year the sixteen-year-old completed a mathematical thesis. The precise mathematical projection of the earth and the sun and the tables of calculations executed in a polished hand must have pleased Nathaniel and Mary alike.[44]

All this was a minor vexation compared with the tragedy that befell the family midway through Nat's college career. "It is with the greatest sorrow my dear son that I inform you of the *death* of your dear brother Charles," Bowditch wrote Nat. Though seemingly collected in his thoughts, enough to relay precise instructions—"ask leave of absence from the College," "bring all your best clothes with you"—Bowditch was in fact distracted. "Tell Caroline [Plummer] this & that Mary is as well as can be expected," he wrote, forgetting the usual "Aunt Caddy" and "Mother" in writing his teenage son. "Charley," an affectionate boy described as "the pleasantest little fellow . . . ever," may have died of what was then termed throat distemper, that is, diphtheria, or possibly of scarlet fever.[45] Whatever it was had run through the entire Bowditch household, from Bowditch himself "to the girls in the kitchen." There does not seem to have been a general epidemic of either disease, but childhood illness and childhood death were ever-present realities in this era. What must Salemites have thought when their eyes traveled down the newspaper column from "The Hon. Dr. Bowditch has been elected Fellow of the Irish Academy of Arts and Sciences" to the terse death notice just inches below: "In this town, Master Charles Ingersoll Bowditch, son of Dr. Nathaniel Bowditch, aged 10 years."[46]

A week after Charles' death, Nat carried his father's letter to Caroline Plummer, now living in Cambridge. "We had a most private funeral," Bowditch wrote. "Hardly any of the relations & no strangers attended as I . . . gave out word that it would be pleasant for us to have none but our nearest relatives attend." Mary, he commented, "bears her loss with wonderful firmness & is tolerably well this morning." But clearly it was not just Mary's loss. "I buried him as an *infant* in a carriage," wrote Bowditch, the dual images of the new-born Charles and the dead child pulling him back into himself—*I buried him*—and his private grief. Carved on the boy's gravestone are an urn and a weeping willow, gentle symbols of sorrow that replaced the death's heads of an earlier era found in this same, ancient cemetery. But one wonders how much comfort they offered. Sometime after Charley died, Bowditch found the boy's notebook of Bible verses and wrote above one entry: "The last lesson of Charles I. Bowditch repeated a fortnight before his death 7 Feb 1820." The lesson itself must have cut Bowditch to the quick, for Charley had copied lines from Proverbs reading "Hear ye children, the instruction of a father, and attend to know understanding," and "For I was my father's son, tender, and only beloved in the sight of my mother."[47] Surely he was as beloved in the sight of his father.

AFTER THE WAR Bowditch emerged as a pillar of Salem's elite. He was everywhere important men could be found: the Essex Street banks and insurance companies, the Athenaeum and the East India Marine Society, the First Church, the Committee of Arrangements for President Monroe's visit. Yet increasingly Bowditch's affairs took him away from Salem and into contact with Boston's interlocking, overlapping elite circles of learning, politics, philanthropy, and business. Prominent Bostonians first sought to claim him as a cultural ornament to their region if not their city, but they soon discovered that he was very much a practical man, knowledgeable in the ways of modern finance, and they could well use him.

Bowditch's association with the learned men of Boston and Cambridge dated to the end of the last century, when he first became a member of the American Academy of Arts and Sciences. Now he became a much more central figure. As one of the academy's ten counselors and a member of its publications and membership committees, he forged working relationships with German-trained academics Joseph Cogswell and Edward Everett, Harvard's Hollis professor, John Farrar, and the college's president, John Thornton Kirkland. In 1810 he was elected a Harvard overseer. When first offered the appointment he had made tactful inquiries "relative to the *indispensable* duties of the office," and only after he had been assured that these were minimal—the real power lay with the much smaller Harvard Corporation—did he accept. Working with Farrar and Federalist lawyer John Lowell, he gave the observatory proposal one more (again unsuccessful) push, holding forth on the subject in the *North American Review* to drum up support among prominent Bostonians.[48] That article, one of three on scientific topics he wrote for the periodical, was another sign of his growing stature in the capital's cultural community, for the *Review* was a kind of in-house journal for the Boston elite. Established in 1815, the magazine published polished essays on literature, the arts, politics, education, reform, philosophy, history, law, economics, and science that implied a broadly educated and enlightened readership, thereby showcasing the intellectual and aesthetic sophistication of the Boston/Cambridge community.[49] The *Review* added a cultural dimension to the social and economic standing of the elite. Bowditch was a showpiece.

At the same time, Bowditch gained entry into Boston's elite political circles, serving as a member of the governor's executive council between 1815 and 1817. Some of the duties were ceremonial. The council appeared as a body at Independence Day orations, for example, and rode in procession to the annual Harvard commencement. But there were also frequent deliberations in Boston. Bowditch aimed to fulfill his responsibilities conscientiously, but it would have been impossible for him to attend the over 150 meetings held during the two years in which he served. As it was, he missed less than a third of them, an impressive record when one considers the distance to be traveled and the press of insurance business.[50] That he could leave his EFM post so regularly gives us further insight into the flexibility that position afforded him to pursue mathematics. It also illuminates the understanding shared by the Salem and Boston elites that it was their ostensibly disinterested obligation to exercise political leadership. If EFM directors and stockholders did not object to Bowditch's frequent absences, it was because they regarded a position on the council as the correct expression of a gentleman's civic duty and opportunity to influence public affairs.

Bowditch did not play a major role on the council. He dealt with routine matters, such as the granting of state pensions and the appointment of a pilot in one of Maine's treacherous bays.[51] Perhaps the only area in which he made an impression, if not an impact, was criminal justice. One of the council's duties was to review applications for criminal pardons and remission of prison sentences, and on these matters Bowditch held an idiosyncratic perspective. "Upon more than one trying occasion," wrote his son, "he gave his vote and exerted his influence in support of the law, and refused to screen from its penalties the murderer and other criminals who had deliberately violated its provisions without any palliating circumstances." Not so his fellow counselors, who seemed to respond not so much with sympathy for criminals as with recognition of the social position of their advocates. Counterfeiter Charles Robinson's "relatives and friends are respectable," read the council minutes, and in response to a petition signed by "a number of respectable persons," a pardon was recommended. James Sevoy, who had bashed in a man's skull with an iron crane, was released after his second appeal to the council, once it had received petitions from clergymen, physicians, and "other respectable inhabitants" of Wiscasset, Maine.[52]

The counselors' inclination to grant pardons and remissions in these cases only mirrored the way Massachusetts elites conducted affairs of all kinds. They placed a disproportionate weight on the authority of "respectable persons." Perhaps more to the point, they regarded even the exertion of state power as a matter of personal relationships. Bowditch was not a cruel man, and he ran EFM in a manner ever mindful of the interconnectedness of the parties involved, but he also believed deeply in rule-bound regularity. It reigned in the heavens—it should order the affairs of men. "He considered that a capricious exercise of even the prerogative of mercy," explained Nat, "would, in effect, convert a government of law into a government of men."[53] The universe, he knew from Laplace, was anything but capricious in its operations. Massachusetts should be no different.

So when a twenty-six-year-old sailor was found guilty of murdering a confectioner's apprentice in a tavern quarrel, Bowditch did not blink at the death sentence handed down, even as many prominent Bostonians called for a pardon. As one of three counselors appointed to consider the convicted man's petition for mercy, he resisted "the strong and urgent appeals . . . made by many excellent and benevolent citizens, among whom were some of his own personal friends." Bowditch was not entirely alone in insisting on the unvarying operations of the law. One newspaper essayist argued that "no man ought to wish such a pardon unless he would wish it in every other *like case*," while another stated that for the laws to be "*uniformly* administered" they must not "vary in their operations according to the weight and influence of the relations, and friends, or voluntary advocates of the persons under sentence." As it turned out, the petition was rejected, for reasons we do not know, and the sailor was hanged.[54] But nobody had been more consistent in demanding consistency than the Laplacean mathematician from Salem.

Bowditch's frequent service on the council gave him the opportunity to move more regularly in Boston circles. While in the city he stayed at a fashionable boardinghouse that catered to a distinguished clientele, sampled the city's cultural offerings, and socialized. On one January evening in 1816, for example, he went to hear a performance of Handel's *Messiah*. Also in the audience was Josiah Quincy, a former Federalist congressman, currently state senator, and soon to be Boston mayor, and his family. When Mrs. Quincy asked her husband who was the "remarkable man" standing in the aisle—it was "the shape of his head" that had drawn her attention—Josiah confirmed that "to be sure *he is very remarkable*" and identified him as the author of the *Navigator*, the translator of Laplace, and "a favorite friend of mine." Mrs. Quincy soon invited Bowditch to visit her. It was, commented Quincy's daughter, "the beginning of an important and life long friendship" between the two families.[55]

Bowditch likely knew Quincy through Federalist circles, but given the interlocking nature of Boston's political, social, economic, and cultural elites, that was not their only connection. Quincy was one of the trustees of the newly incorporated Massachusetts General Hospital, and in 1816 he and other trustees consulted Bowditch on the means to raise funds for the as yet unbuilt institution. To finance its operations the legislature had granted the hospital the right to sell annuities on lives, a financial instrument as yet untried in America, which guaranteed an investor a series of annual sums for the remainder of his or her life. The viability, not to mention profitability, of such schemes depended on the accuracy of the predictions of life span, but all such existing actuarial calculations were based on English statistics. Quincy was on a committee that recommended consulting "with Mr. Bowditch of Salem" to see if these actuarial tables would need to be altered for local conditions. By 1817 Bowditch sat on an annuities committee that included some of Boston's most powerful men, among them Josiah Quincy and Ebenezer Francis, an enormously wealthy merchant originally from Essex County. Also among their number were two others sought out for their particular expertise: Francis Cabot Lowell, brother of John, best known for his textile mills in Waltham and Lowell but regarded as a mathematical talent in his own day; and Peter Chardon Brooks, president of the Boston Marine Insurance Company, with whom Bowditch had a long-standing business relationship.[56]

The committee recommended against pursuing an annuities scheme for the time being, although as we shall see, it was not the last of the idea.[57] Meanwhile, Bowditch joined nine other prominent Salemites, including John Pickering, Dudley Pickman, and Joseph Story, in soliciting donations from members of their community for the hospital. Bostonians had already contributed "ONE HUNDRED and SEVEN THOUSAND dollars." Would Salemites open their purses sufficiently to merit capital letters? Implicit in their work was an acceptance of Boston's superiority, at least as a medical center, since they were not arguing that Salem establish its own rival institution. By early 1817 the *Salem Gazette* was proudly reprinting an item from a Boston paper that reported over $9,000 in donations from Salem.[58] Salem's citizens seem to have acquitted themselves with sufficient honor, but their activity on behalf of a Boston institution was a silent admission of their own town's rapidly waning status.

By the early 1820s Bowditch's connections with the Boston elite had become ever denser and ever more vital to the family's prosperity. Now he was being pulled into the orbit of their manufacturing interests and profiting from it. In 1820 a cadre of industrial investors, the so-called Boston Associates, called on Bowditch for his expert opinion in a court case, hoping he could establish that their patent on a textile machinery invention had been granted legitimately and had been infringed by several former mill employees. The invention in question was the double speeder, a spinning mechanism that required advanced calculations to guide its highly complex motions. Francis Cabot Lowell, the mathematically talented merchant with whom Bowditch had earlier collaborated on the annuities question, had supplied these calculations, and it was now up to Bowditch to testify on their novelty. If lots of people could come up with them, then they could no more be patented than the solution to two plus two. It was Bowditch's view that the calculations were beyond the abilities of all but a very few, so few in fact that he could not help commenting to Boston Associate Patrick T. Jackson "that there were some corrections introduced that he had not supposed any man in America familiar with but himself." The manufacturers won. Bowditch's opinions must have aided their case, though Benjamin Gorham's and Daniel Webster's legal talents and Joseph Story's presence on the bench no doubt also helped.[59]

A year later the Boston Associates turned their sights on East Chelmsford, Massachusetts, now renamed Lowell, for an even more extensive mill complex on the Merrimack River. When the Merrimack Manufacturing Company incorporated in 1822, its articles stipulated who had a right to become a shareholder. Patrick T. Jackson and Nathan Appleton purchased the lion's share of company stock, but within days the original subscribers voted to offer a few individuals the opportunity to purchase Merrimack shares. That select list included the Boston Associates' legal advocates Daniel Webster and Benjamin Gorham, and Nathaniel Bowditch.[60] The point is not that there had been some quid pro quo for Bowditch's favorable testimony. No doubt the suggestion would have horrified him. But having been raised in a society in which one's connections—whether through blood, marriage, or professional or social proximity—shaped one's economic possibilities, it must have seemed natural that he would now be in on this new business enterprise. As with EFM or the Essex Bank, the form was novel—the business corporation—but the assumptions about how business was conducted were old.

It may well have been this intensification of Bowditch's business contacts with the Boston elite that prompted the offer that finally tempted him away from Salem. The Massachusetts General Hospital group that had consulted Bowditch on the matter of annuities had never entirely given up on funding the hospital, and they would soon turn to him for leadership. In 1818 they had obtained a corporate charter for the Massachusetts Hospital Life Insurance Company (MHL), which authorized the entity to offer life insurance, annuities, and other services "in which the casualties of life and interest of money are principally involved." For several years the MHL existed only on paper; potential shareholders were wary of investing in an entity that by law dedicated a portion of the profits to the hospital. Then in early 1823 the Life Office, as MHL came to be known, came to life. The profit-sharing arrangement was modified to guarantee at least 6 percent to shareholders and the MHL suddenly became an attractive investment.[61]

Four men took the lead in getting the institution off the ground: Ebenezer Francis, John Lowell, William Prescott, and Josiah Quincy.[62] All knew Bowditch well, and in multiple ways that encompassed the interlocking networks of business, politics, learning, philanthropy, and society in Boston and Salem, but it was probably Francis that spearheaded the drive to involve Bowditch. In early February Bowditch's name was added to the elite list of individuals authorized to purchase company stock. In early March he was authorized to invest in another new enterprise headed by Francis, the Commercial Insurance Company. Sometime in the interim Bowditch had received a formal job offer as head of both the MHL and the Commercial, with salaries of $2,500 and $2,000, respectively. At the time Bowditch's salary at EFM was $1,500, but he turned the Boston offer down anyway. The Life Office responded by upping the combined salary to $5,000. Nat later wrote that his father recognized that further refusals would result only in sweetened offers and would therefore be "mere extortion." Believing he was now "obeying a call of duty," Bowditch accepted the offer, "though with great reluctance."[63]

Bowditch had turned down other offers before. Harvard had come calling in 1806 and he had said no. In 1818 Thomas Jefferson had tried to woo him to a similar post at the University of Virginia and he had again declined. His responsibility for the Forrester trust, he had explained to Jefferson, "upon principles of honour cannot be resigned but with my life." Then too, he was attached to Salem; his townsmen had long offered him "many civilities" that "endeared" him to the place where he had been born. Mary's health was delicate, and she did not want to leave the friends in Salem who had been so attentive to her during her illness. And then there was money. Jefferson had offered him a salary of $2,000 plus a house, and Bowditch noted that the income from his service as trustee alone amounted to over $3,000 a year, with "considerable time" left over to pursue mathematics.[64]

But the Life Office offer was altogether different. It paid extraordinarily well while allowing Bowditch to maintain his lucrative trust responsibilities and even to increase his income from these activities. "You can get as many *estates* to settle as you please," wrote Ingersoll to his father, quoting Boston merchant Thomas Wren Ward, to whom the teenager was then apprenticed. "You would have *Plenty* of *Money*," emphasized Ingersoll with double underlines. The size of the salary tempted Bowditch for another reason. "As you before observed," wrote Ingersoll, "it is flattering to one's vanity to be thought so much of." Then too there was reason to think that, as with the EFM post, this one would afford Bowditch leisure for his scientific pursuits. "You will have as much time if not more time than you have now," wrote Ingersoll, "because as before I told you the offices are *closed* at 2 o'clock."[65]

No doubt the Bowditches were reluctant to leave family and friends in Salem, but some were already gone. Their lifelong friend Eliza Orne Wetmore White had died in 1821. Others had moved away: Caroline Plummer to live with her brother in Cambridge; Mary's brother Nathaniel to Brookline; and Mary's father to a farm in Windsor, Vermont.[66] Perhaps it was time for the Bowditches to give in to the pull of Boston. They would still be able to maintain their social contacts in Salem while joining new circles in the state capital. "You will have many friends to converse with," promised Ingersoll. Boston offered the Bowditch daughters a better choice of marriage partners and the Bowditch sons better professional opportunities. Ingersoll was already following a mercantile career path in the capital under the tutelage of a Salem transplant. After Nat graduated in 1822 he had started a legal apprenticeship in the Salem office of Benjamin Nichols, Bowditch's associate in the affairs of the Essex and Commercial banks and a distant relative. But Nichols himself was on the verge of reestablishing himself in Boston. Even more important, Bowditch was ambitious for his son, looking for him to become, as Nat's memoirist would later write, "eminent as an advocate in the courts." Surely Boston offered a better stage for Nat, as it would for all his sons.[67] All in all, the MHL post provided both an exit from a slowly dying town and a triumphant entry into the thriving center of New England's economy, elite social circles, and cultural scene.

Perhaps there is one more factor that nudged Bowditch to accept the Boston position. He had first married at the age of twenty-five. In March 1823, during the very week he received the Life Office's second offer, he turned fifty. It may seem foolish to wonder if the roundness of that quantity did not somehow play some part in Bowditch's decision, but it would probably be more foolish to underestimate the power of numbers in his life.

ON 8 AUGUST 1823 a "large company" of Salem's "most respectable Merchants" and "gentlemen of the learned professions," along with distinguished out-of-town guests, gathered in Hamilton Hall for a "sumptuous and elegant" farewell dinner. All told about eighty or ninety attended. A dozen toasts submitted before the occasion were followed by over forty "volunteer" toasts. Some extolled the guest of honor. Both Harvard president John Kirkland and Hollis professor John Farrar sounded a common theme, praising a life that combined "the profoundest *scientific researches*" with "the exercise of the best *social affections.*" Judge Samuel Putnam toasted Bowditch as "*First* of his Countrymen in the walks of science" and "*Second* to no man on earth for purity and honor." Henry Prince Jr., son of the captain Bowditch had sailed under, was less flowery but better captured the essence of his subject. He described Bowditch as "the eminent master of that *indisputable* science which contemplates whatever is capable of being numbered and measured."[68]

But far more toasts took Salem as their subject. Bowditch himself started the trend when he gave the first of the volunteer toasts to "SALEM— Distinguished for its commercial information, activity and enterprise— ornamented by its literary and scientific society—honoured by the general purity of the public morals—May this fair character of our town remain unimpaired to the latest time." A hint of uncertainty about the town's future haunted the evening's celebration. In part it found expression in nostalgia for Essex County's glorious past. Salemites lifted their glasses to Theophilus Parsons, George Cabot, and Elias Hasket Derby, all long since gone. Insecurity hung heavy in a salute to the "commercial prosperity of Salem" and no less so in a wry toast to "Our republican institutions and laws—To the injury of *this* class of our *domestic fabrics*, we never will permit any *foreign importations*."[69]

Perhaps most poignant was the acknowledgment of the larger meaning of Bowditch's move to Boston. One guest toasted "the good people of Boston," who "not content with their own capital . . . avail themselves of their neighbours' funds," adding sardonically, "this last *Draft* on our *stock* of Science, has been *duly honored*." Another feebly hoped that "the tide of intellectual wealth" flowing from Essex County into Boston might somehow "bring back increasing treasures to her own shores." However much Salemites "would rejoice" if Bowditch, "this luminary were a *fixed star*," they knew that few of the fixed truths of the world in which they had grown up could be counted on to hold. Toasting the "ancient town of Salem," one guest conceded that "stars of the first magnitude occasionally quit their orbit." No one at the dinner expressed that feeling that the world had gone topsy-turvy better than the Reverend Flint. "Boston, the *Sun*—Salem the *first satellite* of this Commonwealth," he began. "The law of the solar system reversed, the *Sun* borrowing light of the *Moon*."[70] But to Bowditch, who had quit the dinner early, the move to Boston was a predictable response to gravity.

CHAPTER SEVEN

The Clockwork Corporation

For the last fifteen years of his life, from 1823 to 1838, Bowditch headed the Massachusetts Hospital Life Insurance Company (MHL), a position that gave him prominence and prosperity. The move to Boston alone brought rewards. Bowditch became a leader in some of the city's most important institutions, including Harvard, the Boston Athenaeum, and the American Academy of Arts and Sciences. He and his family joined the metropolis's elite social circles. Among his friends could be found fellow émigrés from Salem, companions of old like Thomas Wren Ward and John Pickering, along with Bostonians like John Lowell and Edward Everett, whom he had known before but would now know better. As in Salem, Bowditch moved in two distinct but overlapping circles, one of men active in business affairs, and another consisting of the local literati. Now though, the circles took on a particular luster from their metropolitan base. These were men of greater wealth, growing economic power, and larger and more influential literary reputations.

Bowditch's position at the Life Office, as MHL was known, was also rewarding. His salary and the access to lucrative investments the company offered made the Bowditch family prosperous. Though never as rich as the industrial magnates of Boston, the Bowditches lived in a fine house in a fashionable neighborhood. The children received the best of educations. Bowditch added expensive European scientific works to his library and eventually underwrote the cost of publishing his four-volume translation and annotation of Laplace's *Mécanique Céleste*. But MHL also offered work that Bowditch found intellectually, emotionally, and even morally rewarding. "On the day before his death," his son Nat would write, he spoke of the company "as 'the child of his affections.'" He had indeed raised it from its infancy. "The business for which the corporation was created was novel in New England," reflected company officers, and on him, "more than any other individual, was devolved the arduous task of devising and organizing a system for conducting" its affairs. Inside of a decade, Bowditch led it to become the largest financial institution in New England.[1]

As head of the Essex Fire and Marine Insurance Company (EFM), Bowditch had carried on operations much like the heads of other marine insurance companies. Though he had run a corporation in Salem, his work involved the same personal interactions with well-known individuals that had long characterized business life in port communities. In some ways the Life Office was no different. Stockholders, officers, investors, borrowers— these were often one and the same, and all from the same closed community of social and economic familiars. But the Life Office was also different. Unlike marine insurance companies, it *did* deal with "outsiders"—the thousands of Massachusetts farmers living many miles from Boston who took out mortgage loans from the company. In his interactions with these kinds of people, Bowditch pioneered a new style of conducting business. He imagined the corporation as a "great machine"—the phrase was the company's—not unlike the Laplacean mechanism of the heavens that acts according to fixed and unvarying rules. He introduced innovative forms of office procedure and business conduct that realized that Laplacean vision. His approach was new to rural borrowers and only exacerbated their suspicion of the faceless and distant corporation that held so much economic power over them.

But Bowditch did something even more unprecedented. He was capable of turning the great machine on elite Bostonians, requiring that they too be subject to its rules. This business of having a mathematician run the Life Office created mixed responses, from praise to resentment, but ultimately the city's upper crust appreciated the advantages of Bowditch's methods. Those advantages were mainly political, ideological, and even psychological, not economic, but all the more valuable for it. Bowditch would lead Bostonians into a new kind of capitalist institution, one that folded an impersonal bureaucracy into an enterprise dedicated to serving the interests of a self-consciously interconnected community. What he had learned from the navigator's timepiece sky, from the Laplacean solar system, and from his efforts to bring some system and regularity to Salem's institutions, he now brought to the Life Office. If his scientific work lacked originality, the same cannot be said of his contributions to the world of affairs.

IN AUGUST 1823 Bowditch moved to Boston to take up his duties at MHL. He was a stranger in the city, quite alone—Mary and the children would follow him that fall—when, as the newspaper reported, he "was attacked by sudden illness while walking in the Main-street, and actually fell down as in a fit." The details were even more embarrassing. Struck by dizziness on his morning walk, he reported to Mary, he hoped to "retreat into one of the shops . . . but not seeing any one whom I knew,"—oh, for Salem!— he kept going, till he "fairly staggered down & was taken into an adjoining shop." There he "threw off the contents of his stomach" and then fainted. "They found my name in my hat," Bowditch wrote, perhaps taken aback by the unaccustomed experience of anonymity, "& I soon had Dr. Brown whom I know & several Salem friends around me." Having his private affairs publicly revealed, in a newspaper no less, could not have been more distasteful, but the proximity of Salem friends must have comforted him. What was even more gratifying, flattering really, was the concern shown him by the Bostonians. James Jackson, elite Boston's foremost physician, called on Bowditch three times that day. "Every thing goes on here as well as I could wish," Bowditch wrote Mary the next day. "The gentlemen are very attentive to me."[2] The "gentlemen" were the Life Office directors, as powerful a group of Bostonians as one could find in this era.

It was time to get down to business. Bowditch had two corporations to get up and running, MHL and the Commercial Insurance Company (CIC), though as was common in this era, the line separating them was something of a fiction. Ebenezer Francis was a dominant presence in both, as was merchant William Sturgis, whose Columbian Bank, on 70 State Street, gave both institutions their first home. The offices shared a messenger, as well as a secretary, the man who became Bowditch's trusted deputy for a decade and a half, Moses L. Hale.[3] But the corporations were not identical in their operations and aims. Like EFM, CIC issued marine insurance policies and loans using vessels and their cargoes as collateral, but under the terms of enabling legislation passed in 1818 it also invested capital in loans secured by land and stock holdings. These kinds of loans went to elite Bostonians—company incorporator William Appleton, for example—and they dwarfed the financial resources committed to and realized from marine-related enterprises.[4] In this way CIC resembled older marine insurance corporations, for though its investment vehicles were novel, it was always investment of the capital, not premiums or maritime loans, that made money for the stockholders.[5]

The Massachusetts Hospital Life Insurance Company was a new kind of enterprise altogether, though its name obscures the nature of its business. Let us start with the "Hospital." As we have seen, the origins of the company lie in an 1814 scheme to raise funds for the Massachusetts General Hospital through the sale of annuities, but by the time it received its corporate charter in 1818 it had added the goal of private profit for its stockholders, along with the sale of life insurance. Still, it was only in 1823, when it scaled down its generosity to the hospital and shored up shareholder profits, that it could attract stockholders.[6] "Life Insurance" is also misleading. Such policies accounted for only a small portion of company business, in part because life insurance was

W. H. Bartlett, "State Street, Boston." Engraving, ca. 1837. Boston's financial district as it appeared during Bowditch's tenure at the Massachusetts Hospital Life Insurance Company. Author's collection.

still a new enterprise in America—only gradually would middle-class men be convinced insurance was a way to protect their families and invest wisely— but also because the Life Office had little interest in selling policies. In 1837, the high point of insurance activity under Bowditch, insurance accounted for less than $10,000 of MHL's business, compared with tens of thousands in annuities and millions in its trust deposits. These numbers tell the real story.[7]

Trusts lay at the heart of MHL operations. Bowditch was familiar with them from his work with the Orne and Forrester trusts, and it was at his urging that the Life Office amended its corporate charter in the summer of 1823 so it could enter this line of business. He regarded trusts as the key to company profitability, but as we have seen, they served elite interests more broadly, maintaining dynastic fortunes over generations while providing capital for economic enterprises. What is more, as a trust and investments corporation pooling the wealth of an entire class, the Life Office could do what individual trusts could not: underpin the scope and longevity of Brahmin economic power as a whole. Small wonder the list of beneficiaries reads like a who's who of antebellum Boston, well stocked with Appletons, Cabots,

Eliots, Grays, Lawrences, Lees, Lowells, Perkinses, and Thorndikes. Huge sums poured into MHL trust accounts in the 1820s and 1830s, roughly the same amount of money that elite Bostonians invested in their new, signature source of wealth, textile manufacturing.[8]

Bowditch's role was to be the "prudent man" safeguarding the wealth deposited in trust accounts. The bulk of this money was therefore invested conservatively, in loans on the mortgage of farmland that yielded an unspectacular but steady 6 percent interest, the rate set by state law. Thousands of farmers from western Massachusetts, an area with few banks or private lenders, jumped at the opportunity. But there was a second kind of loan that outpaced the rural mortgages by the 1830s, so-called collateral loans made to local individuals, institutions, and companies. Though often backed by inadequate security, these loans were also regarded by company officers, including Bowditch, as safe. That was because they knew the borrowers personally. Most were elite Bostonians involved in Life Office affairs. Israel Thorndike, a company stockholder and vice president, borrowed $25,000. Bowditch's friend Josiah Quincy applied for a loan. Bowditch himself borrowed $3,250. The mercantile firms, banks, and textile mills that took out loans were owned and run by these same kinds of individuals. Ebenezer Francis borrowed $30,000 on behalf of his bank. Patrick T. Jackson and Nathan Appleton, both stockholders and directors, borrowed capital on behalf of the textile-producing Boston Manufacturing Company.[9] Boston's family trusts were preserving Boston family wealth even as they provided the capital for those same families' business enterprises.

All this lay in the future when Bowditch accepted the Life Office post. A major institution had to be created from scratch. Before officially assuming his duties, Bowditch had traveled to New York and Philadelphia to consult with the only companies engaged in anything like the same activities MHL would embark upon. New York's Mechanic Life Insurance and Coal Company gave him a chilly reception, but the city's Union Insurance Company and Philadelphia's Pennsylvania Company for Insurances on Lives and Granting Annuities proved more cooperative. Their actuaries were forthcoming with advice on life policies; one even provided Bowditch with the types of documents used in insurance offices. But neither company was in the trust business. There Bowditch would be on his own.[10]

In August 1823 the Life Office issued its *Proposals*, outlining the kinds of insurance, annuities, and trust accounts it offered. It was now open for business. Bowditch shared responsibility with a committee of directors for major decisions regarding loans and investments, but he alone was in charge of daily operations. He would run MHL far more systematically than he had run EFM, to such an unusual degree in fact that what might seem like the most trivial and prosaic office practices repeatedly drew laudatory notice. In 1826 the company's Board of Control, an internal auditing committee—itself an innovation—praised "the remarkably simple and perspicuous method in which the whole business of the office is conducted, and the regular order maintained in the books of accounts and records." In 1833 the board remarked on "the judicious, clear, and intelligible rules and methods of conducting the business, which that officer early adopted and has since uniformly adhered to," and the following year, on "the beautiful simplicity, order, exactitude and method with which the accounts and books of the Corporation are managed." In 1836 it commended the "wise and perspicuous method of conducting" the MHL's affairs, and "keeping their books and records."[11] Such lavish praise, for what seems like the most banal of business virtues, merits closer consideration.

In 1823 the modern office, with its hierarchy of managers and minions, its accounting departments and file clerks, and its systems of internal communications and controls, lay decades in the future. Counting houses, banks, and insurance offices were small operations. EFM and MHL fit this description; at both Bowditch worked with a handful of employees. In an era when face-to-face interactions still set the tone for business conduct, many business transactions—those that were not oral ones—were a matter of handwritten letters, invoices, receipts, and legal agreements executed on miscellaneous bits of paper. That had largely been the case at EFM. The typical office of Bowditch's era managed this paperwork in ways that strike us as quaint, if not haphazard. Copies of outgoing letters were recorded in bound letter books ordered chronologically, making subsequent retrieval reliant on a memory for dates. Incoming documents were sorted, if they were sorted, into desk pigeon-holes or simply impaled on a desk spindle. Eventually documents dating from the same time span might be tied into bundles and housed in boxes. Now familiar systems and technologies for organizing and storing documents—the file folder, the file cabinet, the stapler, the humble paper clip—did not appear until the last decades of the nineteenth century. Bookkeeping practices were also surprisingly unbusinesslike, rarely approaching the textbook ideal of double entry and regular balancing, let alone external auditing.[12] Systematic oversight was rare. The scandal of the Essex Bank was not just that the institution was run by a couple of thieves but that nobody noticed what they were up to. The secretary at Newburyport's Union Marine and Fire Insurance Company may not have been a crook, but his procedures were lax and his books were a mess, and the directors did not seem to care.

It would be different at the Life Office. For starters, Bowditch was intent on regularizing business documents; among his first acts at MHL was to have sets of various blank forms printed up. As we have seen, Bowditch had long been drawn to the use of blank forms, but in the 1820s their use in the business world was still rare.[13] When his mortgage agent in western Massachusetts, lawyer Elijah Alvord, forwarded him handwritten documents, Bowditch made clear how the new regime would work. The applicant's deed was so "very badly written . . . on a little nasty piece of paper," Bowditch wrote, that the Company was "almost tempted to decline" the loan. "All the notes & mortgages *must* be on the Office blanks." He refused to leave the final proofreading of business documents to his able secretary, subjecting them instead to his own "minute and careful scrutiny" in search of "some clerical error, which had escaped all who had preceded him." Your paperwork is usually "beautifully written, easy to read as printed papers & I will add with truth, wonderfully correct," he wrote Alvord on one occasion, but a recent batch had been uncharacteristically sloppy. Several documents lacked a signature, and dates were wrong on others. "I could not help thinking of the old saying 'aliquando domitat Homeri' when reading over your papers," he wrote, fracturing a quotation from Horace (remember, no classical education), roughly translated as "sometimes even the good Homer nods." Should the mistake mean a defective property title, Bowditch added, "it would have to be proclaimed to the Board of Control & all the Stockholders at their meeting which would be extremely unpleasant to the Directors as well as to yourself."[14]

What was unpleasant to Bowditch was admitting his own errors. In 1835 he picked up a letter at the post office, opened it to find a check, and then lost it on his walk to the office. But that is not how he told the story in a letter to the bank cashier who had signed and mailed the check on his depositor's behalf. Though his signature appears at the end, Bowditch wrote in the third person, as if he needed to dissociate himself from the sorry sort of man capable of such carelessness. "A letter directed to Nathl Bowditch Actuary &c. was taken out from the Boston Post Office the 19th & was opened by him"—here he penned "him" over the word "me"—"enough to see that it was a draft for interest." He continued in the passive voice, sidestepping the issue of responsibility. "Without looking at the signature or the amount it was placed aside & in carrying to the office was accidentally lost." Later that same day a boy found the check in the street and delivered it to the Life Office. Bowditch might have gotten away with hiding his shame had the check not become detached from the cover letter and the check alone

No. 3.

APPLICATION FOR A DEFERRED ANNUITY.

of   in the State of

on behalf of   of   n the State

of   desires to purchase an Annuity of

dollars, for the life of   of

to commence at   attaining the age of

years, to be paid   on the   day of

annually ; the first payment to be made on the   day

of   in the year one thousand eight hundred and

The said   having been born

at   on the   day of   in the

year one thousand   hundred and

THIS DECLARATION to be the basis of the agreement : and if any thing false or fraudulent is contained therein, all monies paid, or which shall be paid to the Company in consequence thereof, shall be forfeited.

Dated at   18

"No. 3. Application for a Deferred Annuity." In Massachusetts Hospital Life Insurance Company, *Proposals of the Massachusetts Hospital Life Insurance Company*. Boston: James Loring, 1823. Detail of page 42. As Life Office actuary, Bowditch worked to replace the nonstandardized, handwritten documents in common use with printed blank forms. Collection of the Massachusetts Historical Society.

recovered. Without the accompanying note there was no way of knowing on whose behalf the bank check had been drawn. He had no choice but to fess up to the bank cashier.[15]

But such mistakes were rare. Bowditch took unusual care in organizing documents, moving well beyond the desktop spindle and pigeonhole desk if not as far as the file cabinet. In the case of mortgages, he assigned each loan a number and soon began referring to them with that designation. To organize documents by number, he insisted that mortgage applications for different individuals be separate. "*We wish for all the papers for each loan to be distinct & separate from others, so that they may be folded up together,*" he wrote one of his agents. He even specified *how* he wanted the papers folded, so that the loan number could be penned on the outside of the document and all documents with the same number could be bundled together. He instructed his agents to refer to each loan separately, taking care to write on only one side of the paper, so that he could cut up the "letter & put the part relative to each loan in its proper bundle."[16] Compare this system of organizing large quantities of information with the one followed over a generation later at the New York Mercantile Agency, the pioneer in credit reporting. Often characterized by historians as a herald of a new capitalist order, the company kept records that were anything but systematic until well after the Civil War. Its bound ledgers were organized by location, not alphabetically or by any other uniform system of classification. As the space allotted each business in the volumes ran out, the tens of thousands of handwritten pages became a warren of multiple paginating and indexing systems, with cross-references indicated by images of pointing fingers.[17] No "proper bundles" marked with numbers here.

Bowditch also enforced a strict bookkeeping regimen. At MHL all transactions were recorded and rerecorded according to the system he had learned as an apprentice: first into daily, chronological records of transactions called waste books; then into journals, now organized into debits and credits; and finally into ledgers, with debits and credits grouped into separate accounts for each individual and branch of business. The account books themselves contained preruled columns and printed column headings, a practice sufficiently novel in this era as to merit notice in a biographical memoir published after his death, and like blank forms, a guarantor of the uniform, impersonal recording of data. Meanwhile, at the technologically advanced textile mills run by the Boston Associates, accounting information, though extensive, was often found not in columns of figures recorded in ledgers but as remarks made in letters, notebooks, and memoranda. Bowditch also insisted on a system of internal controls. He personally balanced the cash account every day at two o'clock. He never failed to record each loan interest payment "at the time it is received," and he then summarized these payments in monthly statements to the directors for comparison against the original records. Only after the directors, Hale, and Bowditch himself had each recalculated the monthly sums were the totals certified and entered into the company's general account books. As an additional check on their accuracy, Bowditch had Hale prepare "in a book kept for that purpose, a table or statement of all the interest that will fall due in each successive month," and as payments were received they were entered in this book as well. Yearly audits accounted for income and expenditures to the penny. Profits and losses were calculated annually.[18]

Bowditch had long brought his organizing, standardizing, systematizing instincts to paperwork procedures, both in and out of the business world. As the East India Marine Society Inspector of Journals he had followed his charge to "arrange & methodize" the log books by binding them in groups of ten, complete with annotated index. Later he organized, numbered, and cataloged the society's collection of artifacts. Then there was his affinity for the printed blank form, starting with the blank logbooks provided to the marine society's outbound members. Sometime later, he modified a printed form generated by the American Philosophical Society for use by the Salem society.[19] As trustee of the Forrester estate, one of his first acts had been to have blank receipts printed for beneficiaries to sign acknowledging payments.[20] Bowditch's personal scientific papers reveal the same penchant. His homemade commonplace notebook of 1797, for example, stands out not for its contents—scholars had long transcribed excerpts for later reference—but for its format. He paginated and indexed it alphabetically, and even cut away the edges of the index pages to make address-book-style tabs labeled A to Z.[21]

Science and the world of learning had long offered models for systematizing practices. In the early modern era scholars in all fields dealt with what they perceived as information overload by using such techniques as indexing, alphabetizing, paginating, and methodized note-taking. In an influential treatise John Locke explained how to use alphabetized headings, keyed to page number, to retrieve information from one's commonplace books efficiently. Gottfried Leibniz experimented with an ingenious multi-compartmented cabinet in which 3,000 metal hooks, bearing alphabetically sequenced subject headings, held slips of paper with entries corresponding to the headings. By the eighteenth century scientists in particular were complementing these paperwork systems with such conceptual systems of organization and classification as the Linnaean system, systems of chemical nomenclature, and the metric system. But regardless of the scholarly field in which they were applied, information systems increasingly drew on a new analytical conception of knowledge, ultimately derived from the abstract analysis associated with mathematics. Not just scientists but scholars of all types, along with government administrators and merchants, conceptualized their labors as the collection and interpretation of data.[22]

Many of these organizational techniques were consciously appropriated from the world of commerce. The merchant's waste book, journal, and ledger served as models for scientific data entry. Nor should we ignore the similarities between the natural historian's gridded and compartmentalized cabinet of specimens, Leibniz's "note closet," and the merchant's pigeon-hole desk. But the point is neither that trade was the ultimate source of scientific practices nor that science was the ultimate source of mercantile practices. Instead, mercantile and scholarly traditions overlapped, mingled, and borrowed from each other, even as both followed the same trajectory toward system and quantification. When we look at Bowditch's 1819 comet

"Dr. Bowditch's Study in Early Life." Frontispiece to Henry Ingersoll Bowditch, *Nat the Navigator. A Life of Nathaniel Bowditch. For Young Persons.* Boston: Lee and Shepard, 1870. At home Bowditch conducted his mathematical studies at a tall, sloping desk with high stool typical of a merchant's counting house. Author's collection.

notebook, for example, filled with thousands of astronomical observations and calculations, we should notice that it is a leather-bound and ruled 8″ × 13″ ledger book that could easily be mistaken for a counting house journal. When we look at his Life Office records, we should recognize that Bowditch was bringing his mathematician's eye to them as well. Such procedures as his insistence that all business transactions be recorded as they happened therefore echoed two parallel and interconnected traditions, related as much to Michael Faraday's instructions on the use of the laboratory notebook as the bookkeeper's prescribed use of the waste book.[23]

If the Life Office directors praised Bowditch for something so seemingly mundane as office paperwork and procedures, it was certainly because they appreciated both their novelty and their practical value. But there was more to it. To attract deposits MHL needed to inspire confidence in what was, after all, a new kind of enterprise. Shady financial schemes were not unknown in Boston. Not many years before, the seemingly respectable Andrew Dexter Jr. had scammed Boston on a grand scale with paper money sleights-of-hand.[24] How could the Life Office distinguish itself from such an operation? Nothing inspired trust in business enterprises in this era like double-entry bookkeeping, as much for its symbolic association with disinterested expertise as for the transparency and rational decision making it allegedly offered. In part this association derived from the growing prestige of numbers as the exemplar of objective truth. In part it derived from the larger *system* of waste books, journals, and ledgers in which these numbers were recorded, its very order and precision suggesting virtue.[25] If a well-kept set of books spoke of a merchant's prudence and probity, Bowditch's even fuller array of office procedures waxed yet more eloquent.

It was not Bowditch's long experience in the world of affairs that made him an exemplar of numbers and systems, prominent Bostonians believed, so much as his work as a mathematician and astronomer. Who in Boston did not know Bowditch as a man of precision and method? "As you have the reputation of being very accurate in every thing," began a letter from a prominent Bostonian to Bowditch in 1807. Bowditch was the man who found 8,000 errors in Moore, and yet others in Laplace and even the great Isaac Newton. He had brought these mathematical habits to Salem's institutions: the EFM, the East India Marine Society and Salem Athenaeum, even the church he attended. The congregation's ledger books bore the marks of his "minute labor," wrote Daniel White, its "accounts and pecuniary affairs. . . accurately and thoroughly attended to." MHL had recruited him for precisely these mathematical working habits and personal traits. If "simplicity, perspicuity, order, and system" distinguished the company's "accounts, books, [and] forms of proceedings," that is precisely what it had "expected from the well known character of the Actuary, Dr. Bowditch."[26]

But mathematical habits and traits meant more than tidy ledgers. They also underpinned the moral probity the Life Office prized so highly. "Dr. Bowditch was a man of great order and system," wrote his minister Alexander Young, "and he required it of all with whom he had to do, or over whom he exercised any control." For Bowditch "there was a sort of moral virtue" in these practices, so that he "could not tolerate any thing like negligence or irregularity." To Young the source of Bowditch's "habits of accurate calculation and rigid method" was clear—mathematical pursuits are "peculiarly suited to form habits of exactness and precision"—and their link to his "inflexible integrity" equally clear, encapsulated in the image of a "straight line" from which Bowditch never deviated. He was not the only one to seize on mathematical vocabulary to describe Bowditch's moral rectitude. When he needed a frank opinion, Boston physician Benjamin Waterhouse turned to Bowditch as a man he knew to be a true "homo *perpindiculariter* honestus." "All who knew him," wrote Daniel White, "would as soon have thought of the sun's turning back in its course, as of his deviating from the straight line of integrity and truth." He "as much believed, that if an action was *right, it must be done,"* remarked another, "as that if the earth and sun attracted each other, they must have a tendency to come together," noting that "whatever he saw in *right or wrong,* he saw as *clearly* as in *plus and minus.*"[27]

Quite apart from his mathematically inspired office procedures, then, Bowditch's reputation as a "perpendicular" man helped establish the Life Office as an economic cornerstone of the antebellum Boston elite. "Identified almost with himself"—it was often referred to simply as the "Bowditch Office"—MHL enjoyed an unprecedented degree of trust from its stockholders and depositors. That confidence was rooted in Bowditch's "financial skill, sound judgment, strict integrity, and watchful vigilance," but also in "the fearless and decided manner in which he always, checked, prevented, and guarded against, every possible abuse." As a mathematician he knew right from wrong as surely as he knew plus from minus, and woe to the man who blurred the two. His attacks on such mathematical lightweights as John Wood and William Lambert demonstrated just how "fearless and decided" he could be in taking on venality and ineptitude. "Order, method, punctuality, and exactness were, in his esteem, cardinal virtues," wrote Josiah Quincy, "the want of which, in men of official station, he regarded not so much a fault as a crime."[28] As we shall see, when he called out members of his own social circle for their shortcomings, he could invite social censure, but even those episodes added to his credibility as a man who would not, *could* not, compromise his standards.

Though Bowditch's standing as a mathematician was central to his appointment as MHL actuary, he did not need advanced mathematics or use it in his Life Office work. As practiced today, actuarial science is all about mathematics, of course, for the predictions it makes about life expectancies are anchored in the science of probability. But that field was new in 1823, and few Americans knew anything about it. Through his studies of Laplace, Bowditch was aware of it, but well into the nineteenth century, none of the American companies dealing in insurance and annuities, including MHL, made use of this new science, relying instead on an English mortality table published in 1783.[29] True, MHL director William Prescott reported that Bowditch would "devote a portion of his time to making calculations" before his move to Boston, but he was referring only to a set of tables that precalculated 6 percent interest payments. And yes, a Life Office committee voted to publish Bowditch's insurance and annuity tables, but these were not original actuarial calculations, only tables that gave the premiums and rates for different ages and contract periods.[30] This was not Laplacean probability. It was business arithmetic, plain and simple. Being a mathematician was relevant to Bowditch's appointment as actuary, but not in the way we usually think of it. Instead, it was the mathematician as arch systematizer and quantifier that insurance companies like the Life Office sought out. To them, mathematicians epitomized a set of practices and principles that would inspire trust in their fledgling institutions.

THE LIFE OFFICE got into the business of mortgages because of their reputation as safe investments. Agricultural land, it was believed, would hold its value come what may. But while political rhetoric celebrated farmers as the backbone of the republic, to the company's decision makers the western counties of Massachusetts where they made most of their mortgage loans was a frontier, with all the unruly behavior we associate with that term. This was, after all, the region that had produced Shays's Rebellion, a postrevolutionary protest of farmer-debtors against their Boston creditors. Western farmers were also strangers and social inferiors, unlike the known quantities and social equals eastern elites were used to dealing with. Under Bowditch MHL set out to minimize the risk by establishing stringent procedures and criteria for awarding mortgages. Its regional agents used their on-the-ground knowledge to screen applicants, assessing their work, spending, and drinking habits, all with an eye to what Bowditch repeatedly emphasized was the key consideration: punctual payment. Company loan policies also served to screen applicants. Debtors were required to pay off the principal in one lump sum, for example, though, as one agent pointed out, "poor farmers *cannot* ordinarily raise four, or five, or even *three* hundred dollars at a time without great difficulty." But MHL did not want "poor farmers" among its clientele. It was tough to do business with MHL; that was the idea.[31]

Despite this rigorous screening process, Bowditch was plagued by western debtors who did not pay on time. Borrowers offered all kinds of reasons for tardiness: "Influency," "forgetfulness," "absent on a Journey." The "delay has been caused by the unusual inclemency & backwardness of the season," explained Russell Gibbs, "which had prevented my sheep (as I am a grower of wool) being shorn at the usual period." Others barely offered any excuse. Three months in arrears, Cyrus Stearns wrote, "I send the money due my interest which ought to ben [*sic*] sent before if any thing wrong I will make it wright." Edmund Joyner discovered his local representative had neglected to deliver the money as promised when attending the next legislative session in Boston. Would it "make any difference with the co.," asked Joyner in a March letter, "if it should not be paid untill [*sic*] the Summer Session" of the General Court? Many borrowers probably did not know better. In rural areas debts among neighbors could be carried on the books for years, often paid off only at death or when the parties owed each other roughly equal amounts. Men of wealth who invested money in local mortgages expected to be paid, of course, but due dates were not hard and fast.[32]

Bowditch was not about to be flexible. Among the printed forms he ordered were ones that hammered home the message. Mortgage applications stated the terms: punctual payment or immediate lawsuit. Printed notices mailed to all borrowers reminded them when their payments fell due and warned that if they were at all late in paying, "it shall be the duty of the Actuary" to initiate legal action. Tardy borrowers received letters from company agents and solicitors warning them to pay up immediately or they would be sued. Adding insult to injury, they had to pay for the dunning notices. The usual fee was two dollars, but the cost could run higher. "Charge him enough to make him remember that he must be more punctual in [the] future," Bowditch instructed agent Elijah Alvord. "Give his memory *a jog* with one of your highest priced letters," he wrote of another debtor. Make him pay "smart money," he prescribed for a third, referring to the sting of such letters.[33] Clearly there was a part of Bowditch that enjoyed this kind of disciplinary measure. It was the part that was not so much mean as petty and self-righteous, the same part driven to distraction by a drunken first mate or a mathematically incompetent critic.

Every one of the procedures insisted upon by Bowditch increased the tension between the company and its western borrowers. There was the trouble of finding bills that would be accepted by Boston banks. There was the difficulty of getting the payments to faraway Boston. And then there were the annual notices informing debtors that their interest was soon due. "Sir, Yours of the 12th inst. is this moment rcd," wrote J. C. Bates. "I am not ignorant of the amt of my note, nor of the time of payt, and in the future will thank you to spare me the trouble of this form of notice in advance." More than feelings were involved, since it was the letter's recipient who had to pay the postage. Spare me "the expense of a letter," wrote Joseph Albee, "as I shall not forget the time." The two-dollar dunning letters ordered by Bowditch were even worse. "I should have bene punktual [*sic*] on the day notwithstanding my disappointments if I had known your rates before," wrote one recipient. Remember that the threats of lawsuits were triggered not by long-term delinquency but mere tardiness. With few exceptions, these men were not deadbeats skulking from their creditors and scorned by their neighbors. Almost all paid fairly quickly, as they probably had intended to all along— once the sheep were shorn, the illness had passed, or the legislator headed for Boston. They perceived themselves as respectable yeomen, like debtor John Billings, "able" and "punctable in sich bisness."[34]

Receipt for interest payment, E[lijah] Alvord to Henry W. Taft, 24 Apr. 1837.
Recognizing the difficulties that borrowers from western Massachusetts faced in
getting interest payments to Boston, Life Office agent Elijah Alvord allowed them
to pay him, for his later forwarding to the capital. In these transactions, far from
Bowditch's surveillance, Alvord issued handwritten receipts. Author's collection.

None of this would have mattered to Bowditch had it confined itself to
debtor correspondence with the Life Office. He may even have relished
the conflict, as he usually did when he was convinced he was in the right—
and when was he not? But individual grumbling turned to organized dissent. In 1826 a legislator (and MHL debtor) from westernmost Berkshire
County, perhaps figuring in the company agent's closing fees, alleged that
the company charged mortgage interest rates exceeding the legally man-
dated limit of 6 percent. Soon the "Berkshire people" were making a "*fuss
about notifications &c.*," those obnoxious COD reminder letters.[35] By 1828
Berkshire representative Henry Shaw called for the Commonwealth's House
of Representatives to review the Life Office's annual report, and then came
a move for the House Finance Committee to consider "the Expediency of
Imposing a Tax upon the Capital Stock of the Massachusetts Hospital Life
Insurance Company." The committee, chaired by merchant Stephen White
of Salem, sat on the matter for a full year, but Shaw pressed the issue, and
within days the committee issued its report. At some point Bowditch stepped
in to head off the legislation. He succeeded in "disarming all jealousy upon the
part of the legislature," wrote Nat, and in overcoming "much of that prejudice
which a republican form of government naturally tends to foster against all
large moneyed institutions." The committee recommended against taxing the
Life Office, and though Shaw soon gave his own report, the House accepted
the committee's "by the casting vote of the Speaker."[36] It had been close.

The House report was, at a minimum, misleading, stating that "excepting
the investing their funds," the company's "sole business" was insurance and

annuities. But that "exception" constituted *the* business of MHL, as even a cursory glance at the annual report must have shown. In 1829 the company had over $4 million to invest from its close to 800 trust accounts, while its seventy-six insurance policies and thirty-three annuity accounts represented only about $50,000. In an age when the privilege of incorporation was still contingent on serving the public welfare, the committee strategically focused on the arrangement whereby the Massachusetts General Hospital received a share of Life Office profits and held MHL stock. It concluded that because any tax on that stock would "operate with nearly as much severity on the Hospital as on the Insurance Company," no such "pecuniary demands" should be made. With Bowditch's guidance, the committee managed to spin the Life Office as more concerned with civic good than private gain.[37]

But political dissent did not disappear. Now it focused on the threat of foreclosure. The "Berkshire delegation in the Gen. Court complain that we are going to absorb all their estates," reported Bowditch in 1829. When English traveler Harriet Martineau visited the Massachusetts countryside, the farmers there must have given her an earful. "The great Insurance Company at Boston is the formidable creditor to many," she wrote in 1837. "This Company will not wait a day for the interest. If it is not ready, loss or ruin ensues." These resentments and suspicions reflected a broader political reaction against corporate power and privilege in this era. But the issue of farm foreclosures hit a particularly sensitive spot. Even a centrist leader like Governor Levi Lincoln warned in 1827 that as corporations accumulated real estate, the Commonwealth's "high minded and independent yeomanry" stood in danger of being replaced by "a humble and dependent tenantry," working the land as the "Lessees of Corporations."[38]

Opposition leaders went further. Identifying MHL by name, a Springfield newspaper warned against "the *grappling-irons* of this giant monopoly." A candidate for the Workingmen's Party singled out corporate mortgages as a special cause "of alarm . . . bringing the yeomanry of the country into a state of dependence and peril." Unlike local lenders, faceless corporate capital "belongs to no country." There "is no moral tie that binds it."[39] Abel Cushing included MHL in his tirade against "rich capitalists," "monied power," and "special privileges." In Boston "and among the rich" it is called the Life Office, he continued, "but in the country, among the poor farmers, it is called the *Death Office*; because its immense capital, which is more than five millions, being loaned upon real estate, devours their lands like a beast of prey." He warned that it would seize properties for nonpayment and "carry on the farming busines [*sic*] by its corporate power," and if the legal power to do so was not explicit, then "some cunning Bank lawyer, well skilled in constructive charter privileges, will devise that the powers are necessarily implied." Then, concluded Cushing, the "once hardy democracy" will be "forced to submit to the insolence of corporate agents, and like the operatives in our factories, go to their daily toil at the sound of the bell!"[40] His accusations resonated with many Massachusetts farmers as they faced the unprecedented scale and anonymity of corporate power and the erosion of their economic independence. In mortgaging their land, farmers risked the very property that gave them economic autonomy and their standing as citizens and as men. Every MHL mortgage meant appraisals of assets and habits, formal contracts, and postage-due letters with printed warnings. Many entailed two-dollar letters penned by a "cunning Bank lawyer." If they had not yet lost their autonomy, farmers could see what the future might hold.

Bowditch and his associates at the Life Office recognized that the company's public image mattered because suspicion could turn into political action. In order "to take the field, fearlessly, agt the enemy, & put him on the defensive," John Lowell drafted a pointed version of the company's annual Board of Control report in 1834. He knew the Life Office, though under no legal obligation to do so, regularly published these reports in Boston's newspapers, thereby making a public show of probity. But previous reports, he wrote Bowditch, looked "too much like *fac similes*, as if there was a stereotype, in the office, prepared for them"—in other words, as if they had been rubber stamped from year to year. In his report, he characterized the Life Office as "one of the most benevolent institutions existing in the world," pointed to its role in "the advancement of agriculture," and, referencing rural mortgages in particular, added that "the farmer . . . is sure of not being called upon in pressing times (as he would be) when he is a borrower of small institutions, or of individuals, upon whom, such temporary pressures often operate."[41] Bowditch had a different strategy. Rather than court the farmer with verbiage, he avoided damaging MHL's public image by minimizing legal action. He regularly reminded his agents that "the Company wish to avoid suits," or at least "suits carried on in the name of the Office." Company reports openly acknowledged that MHL adopted loan policies to avoid "the trouble and odium of dispossessing a poor debtor" and "the very appearance even of oppression and hardship . . . when the day of payment arrives." Occasionally the company name appeared in local newspapers under the headline "Sheriff's Sale," just the kind of bad publicity Bowditch dreaded, but lawsuits and foreclosure were actually quite rare.[42]

Nevertheless, Bowditch and his secretary kept telling borrowers that the company would sue if the interest was at all overdue. They wanted nothing to interfere with the *perception* of the due date as inviolable. When Rufus Gorham paid his interest one month late, Moses Hale informed him that the interest "must be punctually paid in future, or the usual course will be taken therewith—it was a mere accident that prevented a suit in the present instance." He was bluffing. The company took no action on late payments for at least three days, and most warning letters were not sent for weeks, sometimes months. "To be sure it may be imprudent to let the practice be known," MHL told Elijah Alvord regarding the unofficial grace period, "for fear that none would be paid punctually." The company had a point. Explaining one borrower's tardy payment, Alvord wrote Bowditch, "Tabor Jones says he has no excuse except it was more convenient to wait till this time, and that once before he did the same and you found no fault."[43]

Late payments meant lost profits of course, but in fact the policies Bowditch developed regarding late payments were not meant to shore up the company's bottom line. Agents and solicitors, not MHL, pocketed the fees imposed for dunning letters. The company levied no additional sums on payments made even years late. It could have compounded the interest to make up for the lost revenue, as was the practice with elite borrowers, but Bowditch explicitly rejected that course of action, even when some tardy debtors sought to do just that. He did not want debtors to simply add a few cents or dollars to late payments *in lieu of* punctuality. Rather than striving for profit maximization, Bowditch was looking to make his corporation function like the Laplacean solar system: predictably, regularly, eternally. He ran it accordingly, insisting on standardized forms, numbered loans, organized bundles of letters, and bookkeeping records as accurate as astronomical tables. He would present the Life Office as an impersonal and inflexible bureaucracy that could no more bend to the circumstances of individual debtors than the planets could choose to modify their orbits. When one borrower asked permission to send in his payment late, Moses Hale responded that "the officers of the Co. have no power to suspend the By-Law," as if it were a law of physics.[44] The rules of business conduct appeared as inviolable as the laws of Bowditch's beloved celestial mechanics.

IN EARLY 1827 the stockholders of the Commercial Insurance Company voted to dissolve the corporation, citing "the present state of the Company," the "low rate of premiums," and the "great number of competitors in the business of insurance." In its three years of operation marine losses had exceeded policy premiums half the time, but except for the first few months of its existence, the company's involvement in marine insurance was actually quite small.[45] Quite possibly the men in charge realized that the real business of the CIC, making profits for shareholders by making loans to elite Bostonians (often one and the same), was better accomplished at MHL. The transition was seamless: Bowditch wound up CIC affairs, with the Life Office now paying him the same salary once divided between the two corporations. At a meeting of five CIC directors, it was voted to assign the company's outstanding mortgage loans to the Life Office. Four of the directors held the same post at MHL, and the fifth was Bowditch. When MHL voted to buy new office furniture, CIC offered its own for sale, and the Life Office approved the deal. Thereafter the CIC directors met at MHL headquarters.[46] Behind the corporate facade lay the networks of personal and business relationships that had long made decision making in mercantile communities informal, flexible, and personal. This was no Laplacean mechanism.

In his business relations with urban elites Bowditch was used to this style of interaction. As we have seen, at EFM he had generally extended the due date of a loan at the borrower's request, and he had overseen loans to company directors and stockholders. In many ways these kinds of cozy relations were even cozier at the Life Office. When it came to making collateral loans to Boston's wealthy men, for example, MHL was anything but the impersonal bureaucracy it presented to its mortgage debtors. Picture the meetings where Bowditch and the Finance Committee reviewed loan applications: four people, all well known to one another socially and professionally, all more than willing to lend to their friends and business associates. To rural borrowers Bowditch insisted that company bylaws were inviolable, but when it came to elite borrowers, even the laws of the Commonwealth of Massachusetts could be bent, or even broken. Not only did Bowditch and the Finance Committee authorize loans with laughably inadequate assets as collateral, but they also accepted as collateral certain types of assets, such as textile factory shares, that were legally proscribed from being used in this manner.[47]

That practice raised at least one eyebrow. "There shd. be no manufacturing stock in the Life Office," wrote company stockholder Thomas Wren Ward in his diary. "The object shd. be security—not high interest—only the best kind of property shd. be taken.—no precedent shd. be established." But Bowditch saw things differently, even when the value of such stocks fell in the Panic of 1837 and he was obliged to call for additional assets as security. The value of one particular borrower's collateral had indeed plummeted, he reported to the Board of Control, "but even in this case, the promissor gives assurances that he shall be able finally to pay the whole amount when he can realize the value of his real estates & other property." No rush. We can wait. Several other borrowers paid off loans early so they could raise much-needed funds by cashing in the collateral, a favor, he noted, the borrowers found most "gratifying."[48]

It might seem as if Bowditch conducted business with wealthy Bostonians in the manner to which they were accustomed and that only rural debtors were subject to the forces of Bowditch's Laplacean mechanism. Stockholder Benjamin Guild would tell you otherwise. In August 1825 Bowditch contacted Guild about a late payment. Undeterred that Guild was on vacation, Bowditch sent the letter to Guild's seaside hotel, to the recipient's astonishment and irritation. "It is true that the day had been forgotten, but not the fact that the payment was to be made," Guild wrote, explaining that he planned to pay in a few months' time. "I spoke one day to [Company director] Mr. Francis on the subject," Guild continued, "& intended to have gone to you but some one called me away & I left town without thinking of it again. . . . I supposed like assessments in all other corporations, that as the payment was secure & interest from the time it was due would be acquired, that punctuality was not of much importance." This was the way elite Bostonians usually conducted business among themselves: informally, through personal contacts, as the need arose. Bowditch *did* extend payment due dates for men like Guild, charging interest accordingly, but it would not do to forget the day or to assume that prompt payment did not matter.[49]

Bowditch was introducing a new model of business operations: all matters should adhere to fixed rules, regardless of the persons involved. As we have seen, in practice there was often flexibility, but it is significant that the ideal of inflexibility found widespread support. The Life Office stood behind Bowditch, not despite his new approach but because of it. Its annual Board of Control reports, strategically published in Boston newspapers, made a point of praising its actuary's "rigid adherence to established rules."[50] Elite Boston in general came to understand and celebrate Bowditch's rigidity as the way a corporation should naturally run, as predictably as the laws of nature themselves. Here lay the deepest significance of having a mathematician running business affairs, not the calculation of actuarial tables, or the implementation of rigorous office procedures, or even the confidence in the enterprise's soundness such practices inspired. Let us take a closer look at what it was about this Laplacean vision that appealed to patrician Boston.

In a biographical memoir of his father, Nat provided anecdote after anecdote illustrating the rigor with which Bowditch had enforced company rules. Some read like parables—the parable of the faithless guardian, the parable of the greedy borrower—ending with Bowditch rebuffing any attempt to raid the moneys entrusted to the company on behalf of otherwise defenseless women. Others related occasions when Bowditch refused to make exceptions for those he knew and trusted. In one story, after he left Moses Hale alone in the office "for a few moments," he insisted on checking the contents of an unlocked trunk to see that nothing had been stolen. "Though he would have unhesitatingly left his own property uncounted," explained Bowditch, "and have felt that there was not the slightest risk from the exposure, he could not answer it to his conscience, as the responsible guardian of the property of others, knowingly to subject it even to a possibility of loss." Nat himself came in for this kind of treatment when he assumed the post of company solicitor. On one occasion he felt sorry for the messenger who tearfully confessed to having stolen money and begged for a day to repay. When the payment never came, Nat revealed all to his father. Bowditch told his son he would have to pay the sum out of his own pocket and that the directors would determine if "further action" would be taken. He would not protect his own son.[51]

The moral of Nat's stories was that Bowditch enforced the rules not only even but in fact *especially* in the cases of prominent men. "One of the wealthiest citizens of Boston, himself a member of the Board of Control," he related, wanted to deposit a check for $10,000 in a trust account on a Saturday, but his bank account contained only $9,700. The gentleman explained that he would deposit the additional $300 on Monday, but Bowditch insisted that to accept the check would violate company rules. "It is my duty," Bowditch asserted, "to enforce this rule against the most powerful and influential, as well as the most humble, individual who deals with the institution." The board member reportedly "was at first not a little astonished at such a novelty as the refusal to trust him for three hundred dollars for one day." But Bowditch replied, "I am happy, sir, that it has become necessary to enforce this rule in an extreme case. Having been once applied to yourself, no one else can ever object to a compliance with it."[52]

We need to recognize the realities of inequality lurking just below these claims of impartiality. For one, there is no doubt that class-dependent personal relationships formed the basis of many aspects of the company's functioning, such as evaluating loan applications. In Bowditch's youth lines of patronage cut through strata of wealth and status. Now they extended only horizontally, to others in the elite. There was nothing impartial or impersonal about this new state of affairs. Then too, even when MHL

stockholders and directors were held to the same procedural rules as everyone else, the rules that put them in positions of power in the first place were
anything but equitable. Not just anyone could buy shares in the corporation,
for example. They were initially offered to a select few, and the bylaws stipulated that these shares could not be resold on an open market but instead
must first be offered to the company. Another bylaw stipulated that directors were to be drawn from the ranks of the stockholders. Unwritten rules
funneled loans to individuals in the same circles of wealth and prominence.
Long before Bowditch insisted such men follow the company's rules in their
everyday business conduct, deeper "rules" of privilege established a much
more fundamental inequity.

But all this could remain unspoken and unacknowledged. Meanwhile,
there remained the spectacle of the millionaire forced to abide by the same
rules as the farmer. Bowditch's reply to the astonished board member points
to a prime reason elite Bostonians were drawn to his embrace of rule-bound
regularity as an abstract principle. For just who might the "humble" people
objecting to company rules *be*, if not those irksome western debtors and
people like them? Responding to the public hostility toward the "Death
Office" and the political challenges to company power, elite Bostonians
emphasized the impartiality with which Bowditch enforced the rules.
What rural borrowers and their political advocates interpreted as the cold-
blooded and menacing exercise of power, the company represented as the
dispassionate application of impersonal procedures. If Bowditch made it
clear to farmers that the interest would "not wait a day," well, hadn't he made
the same point to vacationing stockholder Benjamin Guild? If rules were
enforced "among the most powerful and influential," then those without
power and influence could hardly complain of harsh treatment. The image
of evenhandedness, what Nat described as his father's "exact and equal justice" in company affairs, answered the critics.[53]

Bowditch's scientific background reinforced that image, for by the nineteenth century quantification had become established as the exemplar and
guarantor of objectivity. We are used to thinking that mathematically established truths are free of personal bias and individual peculiarity. Numbers
are impartial. They do not lie. But historians of science have detailed a
centuries-long process whereby numbers acquired this reputation, shedding
associations with magic and mysticism, and have argued that establishing
quantification as a realm of objectivity served a variety of human goals.
Objectivity, they point out, is defined not so much as realism but as the
opposite of subjectivity, in other words, as impersonality. Removing bias,

idiosyncrasy, and arbitrariness from the picture, impersonality invites trust and establishes moral legitimacy.[54] Bowditch's tables and ledgers won the trust of Boston's patrician investors, but there was still the problem of a hostile public and their elected representatives. Having a mathematician administer the Life Office as a mathematician would—impersonally, impartially, with rich and poor subjected to the same rules—might just allay public resentment and forestall public protest.

There was a second reason elite Bostonians lined up behind the new approach to business. They had made their fortunes taking risks at sea, and now they were looking to maintain their wealth over generations, not wager it on bigger gains. A corporation pooling millions of dollars in trust accounts was new to America, and if it lost that money, the consequences for an entire class would be enormous. The man who ran it had to consider the good of this collective entity above all. He could not be partial to one person or corporation. Known for his temperamental adherence to system and rule, Bowditch was the man for them. Although he displayed "the utmost courtesy, and the most liberal spirit of accommodation towards other institutions and individuals who dealt with the company," wrote Nat, Bowditch's first priority was always "the permanent and ultimate good of the institution over which he presided." He "never compromised its interests or rights."[55] If Benjamin Guild had to be offended to protect the company's deposits, so be it.

Then too, antebellum businessmen throughout America operated within a highly unstable economic environment that was enough to disquiet anyone, whether pursuing a steady income or the main chance. Andrew Jackson's bank policies, for example, sent the economy reeling. Public confidence in paper currency depends "upon the regularity of the whole machine," stated Pennsylvania Congressman Horace Binney in an 1834 speech, but now "the gravitation of the system is disturbed," and "there is no political La Place, or Bowditch, that can foretell the extent or mischiefs of the derangement, or in what new contrivance a compensation may be found for the disturbing force." Panics were even more alarming. Wealthy individuals foundered, and institutions regarded as secure proved unstable. Boston was hardly immune. "We have twenty six machines running a race in the manufacture of money," wrote Boston businessman J. J. Dixwell of his city's banks in the throes of the Panic of 1837, "with no fly wheel or regulator to control their movements."[56]

The picture of Life Office operations during the Panic stood in stark contrast to Dixwell's image of mechanical and economic chaos. "Perfect order prevails," read the Board of Control's report, "and this great machine is moved with the regularity and harmony of clock-work." Given that the company's business was the long-term preservation of wealth, this Laplacean vision of reliability and predictability held strong appeal. And sure enough, during the Panic, when Boston banks suspended specie payments, Bowditch announced an 8 percent dividend and stated that the company would meet all its trust and annuity obligations. "In the regularity of the income, and in the certainty of its payments," commented the report, "they who are dependent on it for their annual support, are in a very great degree relieved from those fluctuations which are so common in all commercial communities." The source of "regularity" and "certainty" was as clear to the company board as the origin of the clockwork universe was to many contemporary scientists. Men like Bowditch and mathematician John Playfair regarded the physical creation as reflecting and revealing the qualities of the Deity. Similarly, the Life Office board members regarded their "great machine" as "one of those noble indexes that exhibits the mind of the distinguished Actuary."[57] Amidst the unnerving oscillations of a modernizing economy, the Laplacean mathematician as executive offered reassurance that the mighty mechanism of business, like the clockwork universe of Enlightenment science, was stable, predictable, and benign.

IN THE FALL OF 1823 the Bowditches moved into a brick townhouse at 8 Otis Place. Bowditch's business and social acquaintance, Beverly-turned-Boston merchant Israel Thorndike, had developed the fashionable neighborhood in the preceding decade. The spire of the New South Church, which the Bowditches joined, dominated the tree-lined streets. The Bowditch residence was elegant but architecturally restrained, ornamented only by stone lintels over the shuttered windows, slender Doric columns flanking the entryway, and iron fencing fronting the sidewalk. In his specifications to the builder, Thorndike had called for quality workmanship: "stone steps to the doors," bricks laid "in the best manner," interior plasterwork with materials "of the best kind," and "stucko Cornises." That did not prevent the house from being damp—water dripped from the banisters and the dining room wallpaper peeled off—or a bedroom fireplace from smoking. Mice scampered in the attic. Cockroaches scurried in the kitchen.[58]

The heart of the home was the library. With its enormous collection of books housed in mahogany-faced shelves, celestial and terrestrial globes, and bust of Laplace, it offered Bowditch a fit setting for his scholarly work. After hours of concentration he would sometimes remove his spectacles to bathe his eyes with a basin of water.[59] But the library was not just a study. Here Bowditch took his afternoon naps, with a silk bandanna over his head.

"Dr. Bowditch's Study in Later Years." In Henry Ingersoll Bowditch, *Nat the Navigator. A Life of Nathaniel Bowditch. For Young Persons*. Boston: Lee and Shepard, 1870. A bust of Laplace presided over the library where Bowditch pursued his scholarship, gathered with his family, and socialized with friends. Author's collection.

Here he locked up the keys to the Life Office safe in a secretary. Here he "read with his thumbs," as he called it, drawing his thumb diagonally down the page of the sort of volume that did not require "close study," such as the *North American Review*. And here he drank "boiling hot tea"—or something stronger. "Father carried his mathematics with him always," wrote William, recalling how Bowditch drank what he termed his "certain quantity" of wine every day. Occasionally, quipped William, Bowditch also imbibed an "uncertain quantity" of wine, and "brandy also when he felt the need of extra stimulus." The library was also the place the family gathered and entertained guests. "A rational and profitable evening," wrote Benjamin Silliman after taking tea at the Bowditches' fireside. "A charming family, and Dr. Bowditch a delightful man . . . with buoyant spirits and the kindest manners."[60]

The Bowditches' neighbors on Otis, Summer Street, and Winthrop Place included the prosperous and distinguished. Among these were Israel Thorndike and his two sons; merchants William Sturgis and Thomas Handasyd Perkins, both Life Office stockholders and directors; and the eminent physician James Jackson, Massachusetts chief justice Isaac Parker, and Daniel Webster. Doors away were merchant William Ropes and attorney William Prescott, Salem transplants, personal friends, and insurance company associates. Though he had moved from a dying town to a booming metropolis, Bowditch's life continued to play out amidst a dense network of associates and friends packed into a geographically small area. In an era before public transportation, people were used to living in tight quarters and walking everywhere, but the social boundaries in which elite families like the Bowditches operated made their world even more insular. From Otis Place it was steps to the family pew and the family doctor, a few blocks to the State Street office, and a short walk to an evening of socializing.[61]

Though the Bowditches had moved in Salem's best circles, the move to Boston upped the social ante, requiring new standards of polish and display. Only after the move did the family acquire silver forks, for example, in preparation for a dinner party. William recalled being sent to the silversmith with a request "to let us have them as soon as possible, because we wanted to practice with them before the party took place." Access to this social network afforded important opportunities to the Bowditch children.[62] For seven-year-old Mary and baby Elizabeth, Boston offered superior educational choices and marriage partners, but all that lay ahead. William was only four when the family left Salem, but Nat, Ingersoll, and Henry were all teenagers for whom career decisions loomed. In Boston Nat continued his legal training under William Prescott and then parlayed his fascination with old land records—Ralph Waldo Emerson described him as "the antiquarian in real estate titles"—into a post as the Life Office solicitor and a lucrative if unglamorous career in property conveyancing. Bowditch had already yielded to Ingersoll's rejection of a Harvard education for a mercantile career, setting him up as a clerk at Boston's Ropes and Ward. It proved a path to success: he would rise from clerk to supercargo and grow wealthy from his related investments in vessels and cargoes. Henry prepared for Harvard at the Boston Latin School, but he had little interest in his college studies. Far more distracting were the "very pretty girls" he caught sight of at the Boston Athenaeum and the meetings of the Decaphiloi club, where students discussed such topics as "the beneficial effects produced by playing cards." Yet while he complained of "the soporific effects of Astronomy" lessons, the subject stirred his deep spiritual impulses. "The thought of a comet's orbit excited in me the most sublime ideas of the power of the one who made all the worlds," he wrote. Eventually, those impulses left their impress on his career as a physician and an abolitionist.[63]

Bowditch too found his social opportunities expanded by the move to Boston. He was now in close contact with men who occupied levels of wealth and distinction no longer available in Salem. Ebenezer Francis was the richest man in the city. Josiah Quincy was its mayor, soon to be president of Harvard. Bowditch also valued friendships with "literary men," many of whom came from these same families. Luckily for Bowditch, John Pickering relocated to a residence just a few blocks from Otis Place, but there were new attachments of this sort to be made in Boston. Two men became especially close friends. One was Francis C. Gray, who lived right around the corner on Summer Street. Frank, as he was known, was the son of "Billy" Gray, the fabulously wealthy merchant forced out of Salem for his endorsement of Jefferson's embargo. Gray went to Harvard and read law with William Prescott, but when he turned twenty-one and came into $100,000, he settled into the life of a gentleman of leisure, cultivating his interests in shells, fossils, and the fine arts. The other close friend was George Ticknor. The son of a merchant, Ticknor had graduated from Dartmouth and then studied in Göttingen and traveled the Continent. An expert on Spanish literature, he served as Harvard's first professor of modern languages, but marriage to a wealthy merchant's daughter later allowed him to pursue his scholarly interests at his leisure. What Bowditch's private library was to science, Ticknor's was to literature. When it came to the standards and practices of modern scholarship and academic life, the two were kindred spirits.[64]

Intriguingly, many in the learned circle that Bowditch joined were considerably younger. Whereas Bowditch was born before the Revolution, these men were born in the 1790s: Frank Gray (1790), George Ticknor (1791), diplomat and literary editor Alexander Hill Everett (1792), Harvard classics professor Edward Everett (1794), and the future historian William H. Prescott, son of his longtime friend and associate (1796). The life of the mind, not parallel life experiences, forged bonds among Boston's learned men, and they formed a distinct community defined by lively intellectual interchange. More than anyone else, it was Ticknor who gathered around him a circle of the scholarly and cultivated at his elegant home, a short walk from Otis Place. On Sunday nights he hosted late suppers where literary friends "dropped in uninvited" for "conversation full of vivacity and variety." Topics of discussion included "books, or society, or reminiscences of foreign travel, or the news of the day." Bowditch participated fully. He was "was by no means a mere mathematician," Ticknor later remarked of his friend, for both his knowledge and interests were broad. Conversation "flowed freely," ran the account of one Sunday supper, "and as it naturally would among cultivated persons who led busy lives."[65]

That mix of cultivation and busyness was typical. Though Bowditch's activities and friendships as a man of letters and a man of affairs were in some sense distinct, they were not mutually exclusive. Ticknor, for example, served as a Life Office director. And while Bowditch rubbed shoulders with William Ellery Channing and Daniel Webster at literary soirees, he also handled the Unitarian divine's financial affairs and oversaw an MHL loan to the distinguished statesman. Elite Bostonians celebrated and encouraged this way of life, with its dual concerns. The degree to which their economic and literary activities partook of each other seemed to lend a moral and intellectual weight to both, and therefore to themselves as a class. Even as they made money, they claimed, their attentions turned to the higher pursuits of the mind, a sure indication that they were not driven by materialism and greed. In a poem delivered at Harvard in 1829, Bowditch was the perfect foil for the "miser," the latter a man "who never found what good from science grew, / Save the grand truth, that one and one are two, / And marvels Bowditch o'er a book should pore, / Unless to make those two turn into four." And on the other hand, the argument continued, their literary men avoided solipsistic abstraction by being grounded in the world of practical affairs. By itself, the Reverend Alexander Young argued, a talent for business is "a minute species of wisdom, narrow in its views, limited in its plans, and selfish in its aims." On the other hand, "merely speculative philosophers and theorists" accomplish nothing of lasting value to humanity. Combine the two talents, though, let them be "guided by humane and benevolent feelings," and you have "a species of moral greatness" that "becomes the instrument of advancing civilization" and "improving the condition of our race." For Young, nobody exemplified this ideal of balance, blending "philosophy and business," better than Bowditch.[66]

In practice, of course, life was more complicated. Bringing the mathematician's habits of rule-bound regularity to patrician business dealings had come as something of a shock to elite Bostonians. But if they thought they had seen Bowditch at his most punctilious when the actuary chased Benjamin Guild to his seaside hotel, they were sorely mistaken. The Life Office was only the first corporation Bowditch sought to remake in the Laplacean image. Other corporations were in need of reform, including Boston's major cultural institutions: the Boston Athenaeum, the American Academy of Arts and Sciences, and the most central and venerable of them all, Harvard University itself. In the late 1820s Bowditch would take them all on. Proper Bostonians needed to brace themselves.

CHAPTER EIGHT

Harvard and Other Imperfect Mechanisms

Bowditch had been a corporation man since 1804, when he assumed leadership of the Essex Fire and Marine Insurance Company. Then, as actuary of the Life Office, as the Massachusetts Hospital Life Insurance Company (MHL) was known, he directed the affairs of a much richer, more powerful, and more consequential corporation. But these were not the first or only corporations with which Bowditch was involved. There was the Essex Bank, of course, and he personally owned shares in a number of insurance companies and textile concerns. But the East India Marine Society was also a corporation, as was the Salem Marine Society, the Salem Athenaeum, and Salem's First Church. Earlier he had been of service to Massachusetts General Hospital, and now as a proper Bostonian he was a parishioner of the New South Church, an honorary member of the Massachusetts Charitable Mechanic Association, and sometime president of the Boston Mechanics Institution. From the late 1820s he would play major roles in three other Commonwealth-chartered corporations: the American Academy of Arts and Sciences, the Boston Athenaeum, and Harvard University.[1]

We recognize differences among these kinds of corporations, of course, distinguishing businesses like banks, insurance companies, and manufacturing concerns from charitable, educational, and cultural institutions. But the legal foundations were the same, and in the early republic all were understood to in some way benefit the public good, a goal seen as compatible with and even promoted by private profit. By the 1820s Bostonians were engaged in drawing ever tighter links between their business and nonbusiness corporations. The same web of connections we see in patrician neighborhoods like Boston's Otis Place was paralleled in the interlocking directorates of elite institutions, profit-making and nonprofit alike.[2]

At the same time, elite Bostonians were instrumental in establishing the legal equivalence of the two kinds of corporations. In *Trustees of Dartmouth College v. Woodward,* in which Daniel Webster argued for the college, the Supreme Court famously ruled in 1819 that as a corporation Dartmouth had an existence legally equivalent to personhood. Its property rights, like those of the individual, were beyond the reach of the state. In his concurring opinion, Justice Joseph Story extended the argumentation in Chief Justice

Marshall's opinion, building a bridge between nonprofit institutions like Dartmouth to business corporations. Story, you may recall, was the Salem lawyer so influential in establishing trusts in America, and a collaborator with Bowditch on bank affairs. His court opinion distinguished between private and public corporations not by their purpose, a criterion that led into the confusing overlap of public good and private gain, but solely by the source of their original capital stock. Municipal corporations—towns and cities—were public, and everything else was private. That definition, the one that soon took hold in legal treatises and judicial opinions, classified businesses like MHL and the Merrimack Manufacturing Company with institutions like the Boston Athenaeum and Harvard University. Together, these institutional and legal developments enabled patrician Boston to consolidate its economic and cultural influence, even as its political influence waned.[3]

As the Life Office actuary Bowditch played an important role in this consolidation. Under him MHL provided investment capital for Boston enterprises while assuring the continuity of Boston wealth. His vision of the corporation as a clockwork mechanism provided a critical ideological basis for the company's exertion of economic power. But we need to separate the impulse to create the mechanism from its subsequent uses. Much as Bowditch assimilated happily into patrician society and identified with its ways and goals, we should not imagine that his Laplacean approach to MHL was motivated by a desire to increase its profits and power, even if it did have that effect. He was an Enlightenment scientist, smitten with systems. Like Story, he would not distinguish between corporations designed to make money and those designed to make scholars. He now turned from the Life Office to cast his mathematical eye on Boston's literary institutions. If enforcing MHL bylaws among elite stockholders and borrowers had caused a stir, it was nothing like the reaction he encountered when he set out to repair Harvard's faulty mechanism. It was the style more than the substance of his reforms that provoked controversy, exposing internal divisions in the city's elite and raising questions of just what it took to be a true patrician in a republic.

WITH HIS PURCHASE OF a $300 share in 1824 Bowditch joined the Boston Athenaeum, a gentlemen's private library incorporated a generation earlier. Two years later he was elected a trustee, and soon he became head of the institution's Library Committee. There was much to do. Librarian Octavius Pickering (John's brother) had recently reported that 75 books were missing and another 100 or so mutilated, their maps, illustrations, and plates cut out.[4] Bowditch was a man on a mission: first to organize the library and then to expand its holdings.

Bowditch would not be the first man of science to impose order on a library. Since the early modern era, scholars had taken an interest in such work as part of their broader impulse to develop systems of information management. Gottfried Leibniz, for example, served as librarian of a nobleman's collection. In Bowditch's Massachusetts, William Croswell, a recent Harvard librarian, also taught navigation and mathematics, published *Tables, for Readily Computing Longitude, by the Lunar Observations* and a *Mercator Map of the Starry Heavens*, and submitted papers to the American Academy. Croswell's replacement, Göttingen-trained Joseph Green Cogswell, recalled as "a man of broad scholarship and minute accuracy," doubled as a professor of mineralogy. In Salem Bowditch engaged physician and naturalist Seth Bass to catalog and number the East India Marine Society's artifact collections. By this time, though, even men with no such background were catching onto a newly scientific approach to librarianship. The detail-oriented systematizer was replacing the scholar as the ideal of a librarian. New attention was focused on the cataloging of collections—by author? by subject?—on their physical arrangement in library spaces, and on the relationship, if any, between the two. There was as yet no such thing as a card catalog or the Dewey Decimal System, but systems were required for printed catalogs and shelving arrangements.[5]

Systematizing the Athenaeum's collections would take a librarian with this approach, so Bowditch brought in Seth Bass from Salem. But it would also require direction from above. Bowditch's coworkers on the library committee included his literary companions George Ticknor and Frank Gray; his old Salem friend and Life Office stockholder, merchant Thomas Wren Ward; and Francis J. Oliver, president of a marine insurance company. Ticknor especially could be counted on to have strong opinions regarding libraries. In Europe he had studied in Göttingen's exemplary library, and he had also visited an "abominably administered" library in Madrid. They have here "a lumber-room, where there is a great pile of books called useless," Ticknor had written from Spain, and though assured it was all "mere waste-paper . . . the second book I took up was Laplace's *Mécanique Céleste*."[6]

The Athenaeum was no lumber room, but it needed work. ("A Museum burlesque!!" wrote Bass upon first encountering the institution's jumbled cabinet of minerals and shells, neither "arranged nor catalogued.") By the following year the committee reported that every library shelf and box had been numbered, every book marked in pencil with its shelf number, and a collections catalog arranged by shelf, rather than subject, had been drawn up. These steps ensured that future annual examinations of the books would be made "much more easily & much more exactly," just as the Life Office's annual examinations of the "books" had been streamlined by the organizational innovations Bowditch had introduced there. That same year the Athenaeum published an updated catalog. It had been prepared "in some haste," so as to get something in print as soon as possible, and was therefore organized alphabetically by author rather than organized into subject areas in the manner of a cutting-edge "scientific Catalogue." What was novel was the inclusion of printed numbers—Bowditch's calling card—next to each entry indicating shelf placement, allowing the catalog to function not just as an inventory but as a finding aid.[7]

Simultaneously, in his capacity as a fellow of the Harvard Corporation, Bowditch took the lead in reforming the college library. He first arranged to bring Salemite Benjamin Peirce to organize the collections. Peirce was a Harvard graduate with literary tastes, but more important, as a former merchant he was expected to bring his "accurate business habits" to the task. Bowditch "is very desirous of your attending immediately to the Catalogue," wrote Benjamin Nichols to Peirce in 1826. Though it "would be very well to have a scientific arrangement at some future period," as at the Athenaeum, the first priority was to get something in print. By 1830 the new catalog was ready. Peirce had complied with the initial instructions to produce something "simply alphabetical," but a third volume, the "Systematic Index," responded to the "strong desire" felt since then to find some "expedient" answering the purposes of a more "scientific," subject-classified work. Meanwhile, orders came down to document new acquisitions with a formal system of records, to prepare monthly lists of newly received works, and to open packages of books within ten days of receipt, check the contents against the booksellers' lists, and insert the new entries in the catalog. Bowditch directed Peirce's successor to have the books "classified and arranged in the Library; and numbered with reference to their places on the shelves."[8]

Back at the Athenaeum, the library was now in order, and the way was clear to achieve a second goal, the expansion of the collections. The situation was urgent. In 1825 an Athenaeum committee had "lamented" the institution's inability to buy "even the works of literature and science which appear in our own country," not coincidentally, the same evaluation Bowditch had made of Harvard's library years earlier as an overseer. Bowditch seized the opportunity provided by a recent matching grant challenge, raising money well beyond the sum required with an eye to spending it on the library. Within a matter of months his committee had spent over $13,000 on books from England, France, Germany, Italy, Spain, and Portugal.[9] The buying spree raised concerns among at least some trustees, who demanded a detailed record of the purchases. They soon got it: yet another $12,000 spent on books, once again heavy on foreign-language and scientific titles. By 1830 the treasurer was reporting that expenditures had exceeded income by over $2,300, and most of the shortfall could be traced to the purchase and binding of books. The reports for the following two years were substantially the same. Alarmed, the trustees in 1832 "directed all orders for books to be countermanded, and voted that no orders for books be sent to Europe except through the Treasurer." The spree had ended, the hands of the book-buying trustees tied, even slapped. By 1834 the budget was back in balance. Perhaps it was coincidental, but that same year Bowditch and Ticknor declined reelection.[10]

IN THE SUMMER OF 1826 Bowditch was appointed to Harvard's supreme governing board, the Harvard Corporation. Unlike the very large body of overseers, dominated by public officials and Massachusetts clergymen, the corporation counted only seven members—the president, treasurer, and five additional fellows—and none was there to represent the interests of the Commonwealth at large. It set the course and made the final decisions for the institution. Because it was a self-perpetuating body—as fellows resigned, the remaining members replaced them with a choice made among themselves—it normally maintained a fair degree of continuity in its approach to Harvard governance. But now there was rapid turnover, with four new members: Frank Gray, Joseph Story, Charles Jackson, and Bowditch. They were there to clean house, for in 1826 Harvard was facing something of a crisis.[11]

In some respects all seemed well. Harvard had taken many strides forward since John Thornton Kirkland, a genteel and amiable if not especially scholarly minister, had assumed the presidency in 1810.[12] Many Boston patricians had contributed substantial sums to the college, fueling its rapid growth. Several major new buildings had been erected. The medical and divinity schools moved into new quarters, and a law school was established, with Story as professor. The faculty more than doubled in size, and four of these new professors, including George Ticknor and Edward Everett, had received advanced training in Germany and offered a level of sophistication in scholarship unprecedented in Harvard's history. Library holdings increased, and the college made investments in scientific apparatus. Given this progress, the Boston elite rewarded Kirkland with their confidence.

The president was equally popular among the students. A childless man, he treated his Harvard boys in the manner of an understanding father, and they responded with affection, if not always obedience. He recognized when students were running into financial difficulties and let their term bills slide or tapped into Harvard's funds to help them out. If they misbehaved, he offered paternal advice or, as with Nat Bowditch, sent them off with a kind word and anticipated their quick return. But Kirkland's genial laxity also created problems. In what became known as the Great Rebellion, most of the graduating class of 1823 was expelled for behavior that included off-campus carousing, an extended dining hall melee, and the vandalizing of Harvard Yard. The breakdown in discipline reinforced a growing public concern that something was rotten at Harvard, and given the state's financial support of the institution, public opinion mattered.[13]

Public suspicion dated to at least 1805, when for the first time a Unitarian was appointed to the Hollis Chair of Divinity, even as most Massachusetts taxpayers belonged to orthodox Congregational churches. Meanwhile, the college's ever-rising tuition, far heftier than that levied by Yale, Williams, or Bowdoin, excluded many boys. The elitism many perceived was also a matter of cultural style. For Kirkland a Harvard education was as much about elegant accomplishments and fine manners as it was about academics or preparation for a profession. For critics, that meant encouraging profligacy, frivolity, and immorality. "'Tis said that your Principal and Professors take a pride in the extravagance of the students and encourage it," Virginian John Randolph wrote Josiah Quincy. Boston periodicals published reports of free-spending and loose-living students, and even a committee of the overseers fretted over the students' "perpetual inclination to indulge in expensive pleasures, & in useless & unnecessary extravagances of dress." Meanwhile, Professor George Ticknor was uncovering sordid tales of student behavior that included billiards, cigars, liquor, and prostitutes.[14]

By 1821 Ticknor was proposing reforms, though as much to raise academic standards as to control student behavior. Some curricular innovations and new rules of student conduct were enacted by 1825, but the faculty opposed the changes, and with Kirkland's passive cooperation they found ways to stymie them. Ultimately it was neither Harvard's academic shortcomings nor its disciplinary woes but its money problems that precipitated real change. After the Great Rebellion, the state's legislators voted to let the General Court's funding of the college expire in 1824. The cutoff came just as enrollment was dropping and, with it, income from student fees. An 1825 report revealed that Harvard was operating at a deficit and there was no obvious way out of the financial hole. It was under these circumstances that the reconstituted Harvard Corporation decided that a major shake-up was in order.[15] Bowditch was the clear leader in pressing for change. Frank Gray and Joseph Story supported him, and though Charles Jackson balked at some of the more extreme measures pursued by the fellows, he did too. We can follow the two years of turmoil in astounding detail because Bowditch himself left a written record, his "College History" of 1828. The portrait of Bowditch that emerges from it is unflattering. He is petty, self-righteous, inflexible, relentless, and tactless, all traits that ring true to his character and therefore mark the document as accurate.[16]

Conflict began immediately. Convinced that Hollis professor John Farrar exaggerated the burdens of teaching, Bowditch sought to reduce the number of his assistants. When Kirkland argued that Farrar's preparation of lectures was a "great labour," Bowditch replied that Farrar recycled lectures written years ago. When Kirkland alluded to the time required to prepare recitations, Bowditch countered that he "should as soon as think of a school master's *wanting time to prepare himself to hear a boy repeat the multiplication table*" and suggested Farrar resign if he was not willing to put in a full day's work. Bowditch was offended by the easy circumstances of Farrar's professorship, calling it "almost a sinecure." In his spare time Farrar had time to translate elementary French mathematical treatises, receiving $20,000 for the copyrights, noted Bowditch. He did not add that his own Laplace had yet to be published and that he planned to underwrite the expense of doing so.[17]

The Farrar conflict was symptomatic of what Bowditch and his allies on the corporation regarded as the root of the problem: a failure to run Harvard in a businesslike manner. So the real assault began a few months later, when Bowditch moved to establish a committee to examine Harvard's income and expenses. To Kirkland's objection that the accounts had been examined only a few months earlier, Bowditch replied, "I would not give the snap of my finger for such an examination." The motion passed, and a committee consisting of Bowditch, Frank Gray, and Charles Jackson was appointed. Harvard's treasurer, John Davis, did his best to dither. After Bowditch refused to grant him a postponement in turning over the documents, Davis tried a softer target, Charles Jackson, and succeeded. No sooner did Bowditch hear of the delay then he "hastened to Judge Jackson's house," one street over from Otis Place, and threatened to resign unless the meeting went on as scheduled. Jackson quickly gave in, but the examination accomplished little. The accounts were in such disorder as to be incomprehensible.[18]

The more Bowditch and his allies examined Davis's records, the more they became convinced he could not manage Harvard's financial affairs. Davis was honest, Bowditch wrote, but "his habits of procrastination and indecision were so inveterate, that no hope of cure remained." It was time for him to go, and Bowditch, by his own admission, set about squeezing him out. At a December meeting of the corporation, with Davis present, Bowditch recommended that the treasurer's salary be cut. Davis took the hint and remarked that, given his advancing age and responsibilities as a district judge, he had been thinking of resigning his position for the last few years. He mentioned the end of the college year as a time when he might retire. Suspecting that Davis was playing for time to put the accounts in order, Bowditch casually mentioned to him that, should he retire, say next month, he was sure there would be no problem turning over the books at some later date. Davis seemed interested and thought he would talk the idea over with Jackson. That was all Bowditch needed to hear.[19]

At eight o'clock the next morning Bowditch called on Jackson and suggested they go right over to Davis's house to seal the deal. "Judge Jackson seemed a little surprised at this off hand process," related Bowditch, "but fully co-operated in the measure and went with me to Judge Davis.'" Davis agreed to resign "during that session of the Legislature," but again this was not soon enough for Bowditch. That very evening, Bowditch explained, Kirkland was scheduled to have dinner in Boston. Suppose Davis wrote a letter of resignation right now, to be presented to Kirkland? Davis must have seen it was useless to put off the inevitable. Within days the corporation accepted Davis's resignation and tendered its sentiments of respect and appreciation. In his place, it appointed Beverly-born merchant and Life Office founder Ebenezer Francis. By virtue of his office, Francis became a fellow, now the second Essex County businessman on the corporation without a college degree.[20]

Davis might have hesitated to resign had he known what was yet in store for him. The accounts dribbled in, "a few books or old useless bundles" at a time, and the committee put pressure on the former treasurer to bring matters to a final settlement. By March the corporation discovered that it had been over three years since entries had been made in the college ledgers and that there was therefore no way to assess the current state of finances until past transactions had been sorted out. Outside help was needed, someone, wrote Bowditch, "whose stand in society was such that Judge Davis could not put him off upon every frivolous pretense." The man selected was Benjamin R. Nichols, Nat's first legal mentor, now a Boston attorney and

Life Office director, and formerly the Salem lawyer with whom Bowditch had worked on the Essex Bank affair, what Bowditch now referred to as a "very intricate & troublesome" business.[21]

What Nichols encountered in Davis's records was "utter confusion" and "strange omissions and neglects." He would have to examine all the accounts dating back to 1810, when Davis first assumed the post. When it was done, a task that took almost six months of full-time labor, the audit implicated the treasurer as the responsible party in several species of financial mismanagement. Davis had no proper system for organizing documents; papers simply went missing. The mistakes in his accounts amounted to $120,000. Chaos reigned. Davis had paid for hundreds of textbooks that had never been delivered, neglected to collect rents on college-owned property, failed to press Harvard's claims on various estates, and lost thousands of acres in Maine by overlooking their peaceable possession by squatters. Bowditch got a taste of Davis's management style firsthand when a craftsman presented him with a bill. Convinced the college was being overcharged by a factor of four, Bowditch made some protest. "Judge Davis was never the man to dispute my bill," responded the man with "great indignation." "I used to call on him at his house, at 3 o'Clock, just after he had eaten his dinner, and was smoking his cigar, and he was always in his study, *and he was not the man to complain of my bills, but always looked at the bottom of the account, and gave me his check without saying a word.*"[22]

It is important to recognize that the bitterness of the relations between Davis and the Harvard Corporation came in the context of years of personal and professional interaction. Nichols rented his house from Davis; the two were next-door neighbors. Like Davis, corporation fellows Charles Jackson and Joseph Story were Harvard-trained lawyers and judges. They must have rubbed shoulders. Frank Gray, the fourth of the new fellows, knew Davis from years of close association at the Boston Athenaeum, the American Academy of Arts and Sciences, and the now defunct Linnaean Society, an organization of naturalists. Bowditch's links to Davis stretched back even further, because the two shared an interest in astronomy. They had been fellow members of the American Academy since Bowditch joined it. In other words, these men had known each other for decades, cooperated in developing Boston's cultural institutions, and participated in them as social equals.[23] They had raised many a glass of Madeira together. Yet here was Davis, forced out unceremoniously, hung out to dry.

There was another way to go about this sort of thing, a model of behavior with which Bowditch, the other members of the corporation, and the

Harvard administration were familiar. Only a few years earlier a parallel situation had occurred at the Athenaeum.[24] The problem in this case was the institution's secretary and librarian, William Smith Shaw. While no one could deny Shaw's devotion in developing the Athenaeum's collections, it appeared that, to quote Josiah Quincy's tactful rendering of the situation, he had been extended "a greater confidence in respect to his discharge of the formal and mechanical part of his duties, than the state of his general health and temperament justified."[25] In a word, Shaw was sloppy. He barely kept the records of the trustees' meetings. He made no effort to separate his own personal acquisitions from those he purchased for the Athenaeum. Nor, since he kept no receipts, was it possible to reconstruct who had paid for what and who owned what.

When this state of affairs first came to light in 1818, there was no move to fire Shaw. He was a Harvard graduate and clerk of the district court, serving under none other than Harvard treasurer and Athenaeum trustee John Davis. The trustees responded instead by establishing a new office of sub-librarian, a position inferior to Shaw's on paper but in fact his replacement. That did not solve the problem of separating the Athenaeum's collections from Shaw's personal acquisitions, but when the trustees asked him to do so, he "delayed to respond to all solicitations on the subject."[26] Loath to give offense, they pressed no further. In 1822 they created a new office of librarian, ostensibly at Shaw's request—his health was given as the reason—and appointed a new person to take charge of the library, though Shaw retained the title of secretary. The following year, when they appointed a new secretary, they softened the slight by commissioning Shaw's portrait, to be hung in the reading room in tribute to his services. But once Bowditch became an Athenaeum trustee, shortly after Shaw's death in 1826, things proceeded less gingerly. Shaw's executor claimed that the Athenaeum owed the librarian's estate over $10,000 for money Shaw had paid out of his own pocket for collections housed in the Athenaeum. That would not do. With Gray and Ticknor, Bowditch negotiated an agreement whereby in exchange for the donation of most of Shaw's collections, the Athenaeum would drop *its* claims against the estate. Bowditch could play rough. One month after strong-arming the Shaw estate to drop its claims against the Athenaeum, Bowditch forced Davis's Harvard resignation.

Of course, it didn't end with Davis. Benjamin Nichols's report also found fault with the college steward, Stephen Higginson. A member of one of Boston's most prominent families, Higginson had accepted the position at Harvard after failing in business. His chief qualification for the post seemed

to be that he was, as one alumnus fondly remembered him, a "finished gentleman," displaying "the courtliness and refinement which belonged to the
born aristocracy." Like Davis, he kept Harvard's records in a state of "wretched
order," on one occasion losing over $20,000 of receipts. More serious, he
treated Harvard's money as if it were his own, dispensing it seemingly without regard to standing policies or procedures. He routinely neglected to turn
over payments received by the college to the treasurer, made disbursements
without consulting either the president or the treasurer, and funneled college moneys through his own personal bank account.[27] Higginson was not
dishonest. Back when he was a merchant that kind of informality, including
the mixing of personal and business accounts, was commonplace. The secretary of Newburyport's Union Marine and Fire Insurance Company had
done the same thing. So too had Shaw, when he mixed his own collections
with the Athenaeum's. But for Bowditch such conduct was unacceptable.

Kirkland himself seemed to be behind many of Higginson's irregular
disbursals. "The Steward paid any bills or accounts which the President
authorized," noted Bowditch, "without examining whether the College laws
permitted it or not." Worse, "in some instances payments were made contrary
to the express vote of the Corporation." Instead of receiving his salary at
regular, quarterly intervals, for example, Kirkland simply had Higginson
withdraw money for him as he needed it, a problem given Kirkland's "habit
of overdrawing." He directed the steward to draw on the charity fund established for poor students, even though, claimed Bowditch, some of them
were anything but indigent, and the two drew down into the principal of the
charity fund, thus disposing of college property without the consent of the
corporation.[28] Just as he had determined to get rid of Davis, so now Bowditch
set about getting rid of Higginson.

Higginson was connected by marriage, friendship, and business to the
prominent Jackson family. Bowditch's plan was to get the three Jackson
brothers, all of whom he knew from the hospital, the Athenaeum, and the
Life Office, to convince their cousin to resign. After Patrick proved resistant, Bowditch moved on to James. It was a short stroll from Otis Place to
his family physician's residence. Dr. Jackson informed him that Patrick had
already told him what Bowditch had in mind, and that all three Jacksons
were opposed to it. Much as he would love to discuss the topic further, he
continued, he was expecting visitors in three or four minutes. Bowditch took
this as a challenge rather than a polite dismissal. "*I made therefore the most of
my time,*" he wrote, and turned quickly to a matter he suspected might trump
family loyalty. Higginson was certainly an honorable man, Bowditch stated,

but "careless and negligent" in conducting business. He then detailed one particular case in which over $21,000 of receipts could not be accounted for, making not just Higginson but his bondsmen liable. "This short speech settled the matter," he wrote, "as *Dr. Jackson was one of the bondsmen*."[29]

But, as Bowditch reported, "Mr. Higginson could not bear the idea of resignation." James and Charles Jackson softened and urged Bowditch to give Higginson another chance. To Charles Jackson, his colleague on the corporation, Bowditch pointed out that if he convinced his cousin to resign, then "he might afterwards boldly press down every other object which *came in his way* as the public would be fully satisfied that he *did not* hesitate to displace his friends and relations when it became necessary for the public service."[30] Seizing the moral high ground by proving even-handedness, in other words, was the way to greater power. It was the same strategy Bowditch and his associates at the Life Office used in facing political opposition.

Jackson gave in, and within a few days Higginson tendered his unconditional resignation. But the drama did not end there, for when the corporation next met Kirkland made no mention of the resignation. He was all set to call for the meeting to adjourn when Bowditch spoke up. Hadn't the president received Higginson's letter of resignation? Ah yes, replied Kirkland, but alas, I forgot to bring it with me. To be sure, continued Kirkland, Higginson was thinking of resigning in three or four years, when he turned sixty. Bowditch countered that it was his understanding that Higginson had resigned unconditionally. "The President," related Bowditch, "angrily and very improperly replied to me '*that he had no idea of an officer of the College being elbowed out in that way*,' moving his body round as if in the action of 'elbowing' as he uttered these words." Bowditch turned to Jackson and asked him whether he had seen the letter of resignation. Yes, replied Jackson, and it was unconditional resignation. Could we accept the letter of resignation on Jackson's word regarding its contents, asked Bowditch? Yes, replied Jackson, and so moved. Bowditch seconded the motion, the vote was taken, and the deed was done. Shortly thereafter, Higginson was replaced by Charles Sanders, Benjamin Nichols's brother-in-law, recommended by Bowditch's friend Dudley Pickman as "very correct and methodical in his accounts," a "penny-wise" man "of rare precision in manners and habits," and yet another Salem merchant.[31]

IT WAS KIRKLAND who was the ultimate target, of course. The corporation, with Bowditch in the lead, had been reining in the president's control of Harvard affairs for months. In response to Kirkland's penchant for calling corporation meetings on short notice, when potential opponents might be absent, the fellows passed a regulation stipulating that, except in cases of dire necessity, all corporation business be transacted in regular monthly meetings. They took away Kirkland's power of executing deeds and leases. Even more insulting, they relieved him of his duty to keep the official records of corporation proceedings. Bowditch had observed that Kirkland's notes were little more than "detached scraps" of shorthand "hieroglyphics," often mixed in with some "stray record" or "strange paper." Worse, he noticed that Kirkland had recorded several corporation votes as positive when in fact they had been negative. From now on Frank Gray would take notes.[32]

Meanwhile, the corporation wrested control of the college budget away from Kirkland. In December 1826 a committee on college expenses—Bowditch, Gray, and Jackson—reported that the college was spending $4,000 more than it took in every year, even as enrollment, and therefore income, was falling. The report put forward a retrenchment plan designed to save not $4,000 dollars but $9,000, the balance representing the income Harvard would forgo should it, as the plan vigorously endorsed, lower its tuition to a level on par with other colleges. Harvard was never meant to be "an establishment for the rich alone," it stated, "but rather as a place where persons with a moderate property might have their children educated upon equal terms with the rich without being under the necessity of soliciting pecuniary aid in a manner unpleasant to their feelings."[33] The fellows may have had an eye toward reviving political support for the college, but it is also possible that Bowditch, at least, saw the value in keeping Harvard's doors open. To be sure he was now a member of Boston's elite, but he had long experienced the social insecurity his lack of a classical education entailed.

Whatever the mix of motives behind it, the plan to reduce tuition meant that deep cuts would have to be made in expenditures associated with instruction. A particularly contentious fight ensued over the proposed firing of James Hayward, an instructor in mathematics. Kirkland proposed rehiring him into a vacant tutor position, arguing that Hayward was a "very good mathematician." He should have known that he was speaking to an individual who could distinguish a very good mathematician from a mediocre one and who would have no hesitation in characterizing Hayward as one or the other. "There is nothing very great in him," countered Bowditch, "for at the moment, [Benjamin] Peirce of the Sophomore Class knows more of pure mathematics than he does." Still, Kirkland would not let the matter drop, though the corporation members were clearly anxious to change the subject. Exasperated, Bowditch finally "alluded to" Hayward's involvement in some past scandal, "the affair of Miss Coolidge," and to the instructor's "want of veracity in some statements made at that time." Kirkland seemed nonplussed. That was old news, he stated, and "in his most smiling manner" suggested that Bowditch had been listening to student gossip. But Bowditch would have none of Kirkland's charm or the insulting insinuation that he relied upon teenagers for his information. His intelligence did not come from "young men," he noted, but from a letter written by an individual associated with the president himself in the administration of the college. Kirkland caught on and quickly dropped the business.[34]

There were many such moments of confrontation before matters finally came to a head. One such occurred right before the commencement ceremony in 1827. Four years after many in the Great Rebellion class of 1823 had been denied their degrees, Kirkland hoped to make it up to at least some of them by granting them honorary master's degrees. The corporation voted down the proposal, but on commencement day Ebenezer Francis discovered a diploma that Kirkland intended to give one such student. He turned it over to Bowditch. "*I defaced the diploma,*" wrote Bowditch, "*by cutting out the name.*"[35]

Then there was the matter of Kirkland's supervision of prayers. It was the president's duty to preside over twice-daily chapel services, but he often missed the second round in favor of extended three o'clock dinners with his patrician friends in Boston. When Kirkland was gone, chapel duty fell to a young tutor, and "scenes of riot" often ensued. Kirkland first proposed to move afternoon prayers to nine p.m., leaving unstated the corollary that by this hour he would have returned from Boston. Convening the student body at night seemed like a bad idea, since, as Bowditch commented, "in the dark . . . every kind of noise and disturbance might be made with impunity." Kirkland then suggested eliminating afternoon prayers altogether, but such a move, explained Bowditch, could only provoke "the enemies of the College to excite a prejudice in the public mind that the institution was becoming a mere school of Philosophy to the utter neglect of religious opinions." The matter might have ended there had Kirkland not been so foolish as to ask for reimbursement of his bridge tolls to and from Boston. At a February 1828 meeting, once Kirkland had left, Bowditch noted that the charges "proved conclusively that the President had been *absent from his duty four days in the week during the whole 17 years of his Presidency.*" He continued on to express his general dissatisfaction with Kirkland's leadership, making clear to the rest of the corporation just who his next target would be.[36]

A few days after that meeting, Charles Jackson approached Bowditch with a solution to the whole "*plaguy account.*" Kirkland "*was not the man he once was,*" he admitted, and it would be best for him to retire from presidential duties. He may have been referring to the mild stroke Kirkland had suffered the previous year, an affliction that had lasting effects, but not severe enough to prevent him from getting married the following month to Elizabeth Cabot, the daughter of a Federalist merchant. Jackson had come up with two plans that would avoid embarrassing the institution or humiliating Kirkland. The first was to appoint a vice president of the college who would do all the actual work. Kirkland would remain president in name only. This plan resembled the sub-librarian plan used to ease Shaw out of his Athenaeum responsibilities, and in fact Jackson had served a term as an Athenaeum trustee during the Shaw affair. The alternative plan was for Kirkland to resign but with the promise of a generous pension. Rarely disposed to see the uses of obfuscation or the virtue of tact, Bowditch rejected both plans out of hand. Who would possibly agree to do all the work of a college presidency at the lower salary of a vice president? How could an annual pension of $1,000 be approved in a time of austerity? Jackson must have felt frustrated by Bowditch's unwillingness to finesse a difficult situation. He made it clear that if neither of the two plans would be pursued, he simply could not advise Kirkland to relinquish his duties.[37]

Bowditch decided he would have to force the issue. He resolved that "every time the President threw obstacles in the way of the measures of the Corporation," no matter how minor the issue, he would let Kirkland "know that I perfectly understood his motions," with the full understanding that the confrontation might "produce his resignation."[38] Bowditch had long been prone to spontaneous eruptions of temper, but now he was planning a deliberate provocation. He had rarely found a transgression too slight to be overlooked, interpreting such small-mindedness as moral consistency, but now he was ready to challenge Kirkland on matters he admitted were of little consequence. And indeed, the final showdown came over just such a trivial matter, the remodeling of a student dormitory to accommodate classroom space.

Initially Kirkland raised no objection to the proposal, but when one student refused to cooperate, Kirkland sided with him. Just as he had determined to do, Bowditch called him on it. "I understand this business perfectly well," he said to the president, "and that the failure of this measure has arisen from your being wholly opposed to it." And who is this recalcitrant student, he asked rhetorically. "A thief, an idle fellow, who if he had his deserts would have been sent from College two years ago," he answered,

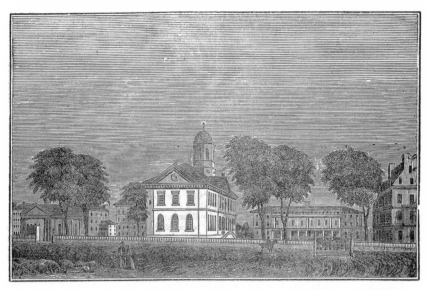

"Harvard University." An engraving in the *American Magazine of Useful and Entertaining Knowledge* 1 (Jan. 1835): 201. The college as it appeared not long after Bowditch and his allies instituted administrative reforms and forced the president's resignation. HUY 23 (17), Harvard University Archives.

referring to the boy's earlier theft of a library book and Kirkland's decision to forgo punishment. "And what did he say? *That he would be damned if he would remove.*" Kirkland interrupted, saying that there was no proof the boy had made any such statement, but Bowditch insisted that everyone in Cambridge knew it to be so. "If I had been President," Bowditch continued, ever more provocative, "and such an answer had been given even to one of the humblest officers or servants of the College, I would make him remove or would resign my station." He was on a roll now and began to dredge up points of conflict dating back years. Then, incomprehensibly, he concluded by seconding a suggestion that the renovations be postponed until summer. Perhaps he sensed he might lose this one. Certainly on some level Bowditch knew that he had crossed a line, for after the meeting he seemed to be looking for support. When Ebenezer Francis sought him out, it was Bowditch who immediately remarked that he had "spoken quite plainly" to Kirkland. The merchant agreed but felt that it was entirely in order. When Frank Gray joined them, Bowditch again raised his plain speaking. "Yes," replied the gentlemanly Gray, "perhaps too plain."[39]

Not long after the meeting, Francis contacted Kirkland's friends to broker a deal, promising a lump sum of $2,000 if the president resigned. Kirkland submitted a letter of resignation to Frank Gray, a fellow Harvard graduate and gentleman of letters, not the unlettered merchant Francis. When Bowditch came into the Life Office on Monday morning he found the two fellows on the stairs, discussing the letter. It was evidently the first Bowditch had heard of it. Gray reported that "there was a great excitement in Cambridge about the resignation" and "severe remarks were made about the language" Bowditch had used. Bowditch insisted he would stand by what he had said, and if the board did not back him on Kirkland's resignation, he would resign his own seat. If the corporation accepted the president's resignation, continued Bowditch, he would not oppose the usual expressions of gratitude and appreciation made on such occasions, though, he warned Gray, you "must take care not to have them too full." He was as good as his word. Unable to countenance the use of the word "faithful," Bowditch abstained from voting altogether.[40]

IF BOWDITCH IS TO BE believed, and there is no reason to doubt his honesty, the foregoing is a true record of events, but there was another account making the rounds. This one, according to Bowditch, was traceable to Elizabeth Cabot Kirkland. In this version Bowditch had so insulted the president at the March corporation meeting that both Kirkland and Jackson left the meeting forthwith and, more important, the president felt he had no choice but to resign. A corollary of this account was that the scathing criticism of the president did not represent the majority opinion of the corporation. Bowditch was the first to admit he had been critical of the president, but he steadfastly denied what the story that later circulated claimed, namely, that he had described Kirkland as an *"imbecile, unfit for his office,"* adding that *"if he had any regard to his own dignity he would resign."* But meanwhile the story gained credibility. In a farewell letter a committee of seniors expressed their affection for the president and their undisguised resentment of the circumstances under which he was leaving. "To seize the opportunity of physical weakness," they wrote, referring to Kirkland's stroke, "to choose this time, to sit in judgment upon inadvertent errors or improvident virtues; such malignity, we are grieved to say, has been reserved to be exhibited by individuals in our own community."[41]

It was Bowditch's opinion that Kirkland should never have accepted such a letter, or at least have insisted on changes in it, not just because it was "a libel on the doings of the Corporation" but because, if the letter were ever to be made public, its "expressions and allusions" to Kirkland's management of the college "might excite the curiosity of the public to know more particularly what was meant." (It was understood that transparency was out of the question.) Instead, Kirkland kept silent, as did his allies, even as the senior class voted to publish the letter in the newspapers. There was at least one dissenting voice, that of Salemite George Nichols, whose uncles were steward Charles Sanders and auditor Benjamin Nichols. He argued that not all the facts were known, and the corporation had its own side of the story. Henry Bowditch, also in the class of 1828, chose to keep silent. But the lead author of the letter won the day when he countered that several members of the corporation had heaped insults on the president and that he had it on good authority that "the President had not been altogether silent or else knocked down a certain individual of that Body." Within days the letter made the rounds of the local newspapers. It blew the cover provided by the many press reports that Kirkland had resigned for health reasons.[42]

Each newspaper felt called upon to offer commentary. "It is represented, we know not how justly," read the *Boston Bulletin*, that President Kirkland "has been treated with disrespect, bordering upon indignity, at which the whole community is electrified with resentment." The press demanded to know why an "accomplished, beloved, and venerated individual," an "accomplished and elegant Scholar," a "cultivated gentleman," and a "kind-hearted observer of the humanities of life" should be dismissed. The consensus seemed to be that Kirkland had been "harassed by obloquy" and "insult" and was the victim of "the tyrannous exertion of a 'brief authority,' or the expression of a disgraceful ingratitude." Kirkland became an object of even greater sympathy when the newspapers printed warm letters of appreciation to the president penned by Harvard instructors and distinguished alumni of years past. Bowditch had his defenders. A letter to the *Salem Gazette* branded the students who had gone public with their letter as mere "striplings," guilty of a "gross insult" to the corporation. A letter to the *Boston Patriot* argued that "however harsh the manner," the corporation may have done only what it needed to do.[43] But the bulk of newspaper coverage tilted against Bowditch.

In private correspondence, prominent Bostonians were abuzz with talk of the affair. "It is said that, at a meeting of the Corporation," financier Peter Chardon Brooks informed his son-in-law Edward Everett, Kirkland's "feelings were very much wounded by some remarks of Dr. Bowditch—so much so,—that he never could meet the Corporation again as President." His sudden resignation, continued Brooks, had precipitated "no small degree of excitement—and somewhat at the expense of Dr. B.—at this moment." Charlotte Brooks Everett was convinced her father had been "a little too *prudent*" in describing the "commotion." Her brother, on the other hand, "hopes the students will tar & feather &c. Bowd." Everett in turn informed his own brother that the resignation had caused a "great sensation" and attributed Kirkland's decision to "harsh language used by Mr. Bowditch." Sarah McKean Folsom, the daughter of a Harvard professor and wife of a Harvard librarian, wrote that there were reports that "Dr. B. insulted the President by hinting his personal incapacity now for office," giving vent to his "irritability" in a "*personal*" attack laced with "intemperate language." Ralph Waldo Emerson identified both Bowditch and Ebenezer Francis as the personae non grata of the day. "Our friend the Treasurer [Francis] is in as bad odour within the walls as a pot of onions," he wrote his brother William, "and Bowditch is sincere assafoetida," a reference to a bitter and foul-smelling gum.[44]

For at least a generation many citizens of Massachusetts had complained about the course of affairs at Harvard. Orthodox Congregationalists were aghast at the college's embrace of Unitarianism. Ordinary people and their legislators portrayed Harvard as the pleasure ground of the privileged classes. This criticism was different. It was not aimed at Harvard in general, or even the corporation as a whole, only at some fellows, really just Bowditch and Francis, with Bowditch taking most of the heat. And it came not from the citizenry but the elite itself. At issue were the set of values and the accompanying cultural style the Boston elite would represent as its own. Boston patricians liked to think there was more to their class than making money. Hence, they supported cultural and philanthropic institutions and embraced cultural ornaments like Kirkland and Harvard itself. They understood that Harvard's books had to be balanced, but they disapproved of the manner in which Bowditch and Francis set about it. One newspaper put its finger on the critical issue when it dissented from the majority view in the press that a full accounting of corporation proceedings was due the public. "We very much doubt the utility of any formal statement of the circumstances," it stated. "It would be difficult to give an account of them on paper that would show precisely what degree of delicacy has been observed towards the President: and this is the whole question." In his diary Charles Francis Adams pinpointed the same key issue: that "Mr. Bowditch insulted him [Kirkland] grossly at the Corporation board" is "a shameful business," he wrote. "But some men have no delicacy."[45]

The Athenaeum trustees had acted with just this kind of delicacy in dealing with William Smith Shaw. For Bowditch the genteel value placed on delicacy had no place in business affairs and was suspect altogether, since in his mind it ran counter to such virtues as honesty and integrity. His opponents, on the other hand, perceived Bowditch and Francis as men who lacked an intuitive grasp of how to act with delicacy or even to understand why

such behavior was desirable. Many identified their lack of a college education, a deficit that had long haunted Bowditch, as the crux of the matter.
The *Evening Gazette* pointed a finger at "some, who, either without classical
education, or not originally belonging to the Alumni of Harvard, have been
recently fomenting difficulties and encouraging opposition with regard
to the President." Regardless of "the literary and scientific achievements
of these gentlemen," wrote "A Graduate" in the *Boston Patriot*, obviously
referring only to Bowditch, they could never have a grasp of the affairs of
a college like "those who have served a regular apprenticeship within its
walls." The problem, then, was not so much the lack of learning as the lack
of those acquisitions—polish, gentility, *delicacy*—imparted by a four-year
stroll through the groves of academe.[46] Bowditch's mathematical sophistication could actually reinforce this assessment, for some continued to believe
that, as John Farrar explained, "the study of mathematics . . . contracts the
mind," rendering it "unsusceptible of that accurate perception of beauty
and truth, so requisite to quick and fair judgment in matters of taste and
morals." Bowditch's "mind [was] so abstracted from all softer sentiments, by
mathematical calculations," commented one newspaper, "as to have treated"
Kirkland "with harshness, or insult, or irreverence."[47]

It did not escape these critics' notice that the corporation was dominated
by men from Salem and the adjacent town of Beverly. Bowditch, Story, Gray,
and Francis, all Essex County men, constituted a majority. Add Salemites
Nichols and Sanders and you have something of a power bloc. Since the
late eighteenth century Salem had suffered a reputation among Bostonians
as a place where materialism trumped culture. The town was shorthand
for all that was about moneymaking pure and simple, about being a boorish
arriviste or an ignorant salt. Press reports alluded to Bowditch as "a Salem
sailor." It was the "Salem junta" that forced out Kirkland, wrote Emerson,
adding, "tis queer that little men should . . . spill the President out of the
window." Sarah Folsom wrote of the corporation that "some of their
number & some of their advisers . . . are not considered the most liberal,
nobler-minded people in the world, & the most capable of conducting
any interests of a literary institution but the money concerns." One alumnus recalled that "what was sometimes called the Salem administration—a
régime financial as well as literary,—had now come into power."[48] In truth,
prominent men from both cities blurred the line between the financial and
the literary. Harvard graduate John Lowell, for example, could live as a gentleman of leisure and letters because his family's commercial and manufacturing wealth, which originated in Newburyport, allowed him to do so.

The difference seemed to be less a matter of objective fact than subjective style. What really marked the corporation's reformers was not their birthplace or their careers but their advocacy of a set of values many associated with the business world. An insistence on keeping tidy books and following corporate bylaws to the letter seemed to belong more to the world of maximizing profits than grooming young gentlemen.

While it is true that men like Francis, later described as "a shrewd and close financier," epitomized the calculating, grasping businessman, Bowditch's reforms focused on regularity and precision for their own sake, not for the money that might be squeezed from them. Ironically, those priorities came from the world of learning—Laplacean science—not the traditionally informal and flexible style of profit-making enterprises. For Bowditch a well-running mechanism was an end in itself. Only weeks before Kirkland's resignation he had commented on just such a "beautiful machine," not MHL's clockwork operation but a model steam engine he had acquired for the Boston Mechanics Institution. "Those who have had an opportunity of examining it have been struck with admiration at the extraordinary delicacy and perfection of the workmanship," he wrote with an aesthetic appreciation limited to these kinds of phenomena, "and the great accuracy with which all the parts of this most complex machine are represented." Such models should be both useful and beautiful, he added, because "finely wrought instruments possess a value from the excellence of their workmanship, almost independent of their use."[49]

As the Life Office actuary, Bowditch proudly stood for these mathematical values, and Life Office directors like Lowell praised him for it. But in the context of Harvard's affairs Bowditch suddenly faced opposition and scorn. What then was he to do? Bowditch himself felt that denying the rumors in any public forum would violate his sense of integrity. "Of course Dr. Bowditch is not very anxious to defend himself," explained Sarah Folsom. "He feels as if he had done his duty—he does not wish that every one should approve his conduct—he only wishes them to know in truth *what* that conduct was." But he could hardly sit still. To quash the rumors, he informed the corporation that "if the President, or his friends, did not immediately put a stop to the circulation of such reports," he would "publish a full statement of all the College affairs." Even now, he let it be known, he "was writing scraps of College History, which would be published if occasion should require." That changed everything. The negative newspaper reports dried up. Mrs. Kirkland told some of Bowditch's acquaintances that perhaps *"she had said too much"* and *"wished the business to entirely subside."*

Bowditch never published his "scraps," which were, of course, anything but. It is a paginated, annotated, indexed 200-plus-page document in Bowditch's tidy hand, and it enumerates Kirkland's "slovenly" ways in true Bowditch fashion: methodically, meticulously, and exhaustively.[50]

SHORTLY AFTER HE resigned as president of Harvard, Kirkland resigned from another office, the vice presidency of the American Academy of Arts and Sciences. He had held the post for seventeen years. No doubt he had no further desire to attend meetings of an organization whose most prominent member was Nathaniel Bowditch. At its annual meeting in May 1828 the American Academy members unanimously resolved "that the thanks of the Academy be presented to the late Vice President, for the able and faithful manner in which he has so long presided at their meetings, together with their best wishes for his happiness." Then they elected Kirkland's replacement. It was none other than Bowditch. The following year he was elected president. Though elite Bostonians might question his style of action, they could not deny the positive outcomes of his initiatives.[51]

Much as he had at the Athenaeum and then at Harvard, Bowditch assumed the office with an agenda. In recent years the academy had become increasingly moribund. Meetings had been canceled for lack of a quorum. No *Memoirs* had been issued since 1820. As usual, Bowditch started with the library. He brought in Seth Bass, the man who had followed him from the East India Marine Society to the Athenaeum. Within months of his election to the academy presidency the library had been cataloged, incomplete sets identified, and the appropriate volumes acquired. The institution moved its collections and its meeting place from the Athenaeum and set up shop at a hall in the Life Office building. There Bowditch personally directed the installation of the academy's library, ensuring that it was "neatly and elegantly arranged." The move cut the rent in half, and it also firmly established the American Academy as Bowditch's domain.[52]

Raising the quality of scholarship and, with it, the academy's international reputation was also on Bowditch's mind. By the 1830s he oversaw a new wave of honorary memberships awarded to scientists from Britain, France, Germany, Russia, Italy, and Belgium. The usual procedure would be to send them all the back copies of the *Memoirs*, but Bowditch was not keen on letting them see just how marginal some of the institution's early publications had been. His solution was quite ingenious. The next volume of the *Memoirs* would be designated volume one of a new series.[53] Leave it to Bowditch to find the solution in a numbering system.

Expanding the academy's range of activities beyond monthly meetings and occasional publications would take more than verbal sleight of hand—it would take money. The institution had $4,000 to its name, but it had far more, untouched and so far untouchable, in its Rumford Premium Fund.[54] In 1796 Count Rumford (born Benjamin Thompson of New Hampshire) gave $5,000 to the academy, the interest on which would fund a biannual prize medal, worth $300 dollars in gold or silver. It was to reward an important discovery on heat or light made in the intervening period. But in 1829, when Bowditch assumed the academy presidency, the medal had never been awarded, even as the original bequest had ballooned to over $20,000, yielding a biannual income of $2,000. The problem, as an academy committee established that year reported, was that it was impossible to meet Rumford's terms. This was the New World, not the Old; major discoveries did not come along every two years, and if they did, their significance might not be apparent so quickly. Ironically, the rapid growth of the fund created additional problems, for, as the committee pointed out, "an invention may merit a premium of 300 dollars, which is altogether unworthy of one of 2000." Nor would it ever be a good idea to award such a huge sum, for fear that the premium would "lose the character of a prize, and be sought with mercenary views, rather than as an honorable distinction."[55] But the committee—Bowditch, Frank Gray, and the new Harvard president Josiah Quincy—saw an opportunity in these difficulties. The terms of the bequest must be loosened so as to fit the academy's new agenda. A portion of the Rumford Fund would be used to fund the premium, but the bulk of it could be used toward what could be construed as Rumford's larger priority, the advancement of science. That could mean buying books and scientific apparatus and underwriting lectures and experiments.

No one knew better than trustee Bowditch how difficult it was to reinterpret the terms of a charitable trust. Such alterations could be authorized only by a court of equity, and its involvement was contingent on two occurrences. First, the state legislature would have to pass a bill designating the state's Supreme Judicial Court a court of equity with jurisdiction over the matter. By March 1831 that bill had passed. Second, there had to be a legal conflict between two parties for the court to consider. Enter the *American Academy of Arts and Sciences v. the President and Fellows of Harvard College*, whereby the plaintiff disputed the defendant's claim to the academy's Rumford Fund, a claim based on Rumford's parallel bequest to Harvard to fund a science professorship. It was in fact a sham conflict, agreed to by both sides purely as a legal strategy to realize the academy's agenda. Why did Harvard go along with it? Consider the parties to the dispute. Bowditch, the academy's president, who presented the institution's case before the court, was also a Harvard fellow, while Harvard's president Quincy was also the vice president of the academy. The third member of the academy's Rumford committee, Frank Gray, was the academy's corresponding secretary, as well as a member of the Harvard Corporation. And the presiding judge? Lemuel Shaw, Harvard class of 1800, elected a fellow of the American Academy in 1823.

Given the legal status of Rumford's donation, the academy had little choice but to turn to the courts to modify the fund's terms. Still, the use of the judicial system appeared to place the decision in the scales of blind justice when what was really going on was a legal charade among close associates. As with the Life Office, personal ties were simultaneously vital to academy operations and invisible within them. As academy president, Bowditch once more represented corporate bylaws—not corporate officers—as the institution's prime mover. When one member asked to publish in an outside publication some tables he had earlier submitted to the academy, Bowditch turned him down, explaining that "he had no authority to permit them to be so published," since the "rules" of the organization declared those tables to be academy property. We don't know why Bowditch refused this member's request, but it hardly matters. He was making it clear that this institution was yet another impersonal mechanism, even as an unseen web of personal relationships shaped its every operation.[56]

Back at Harvard, Bowditch and his closest associates were optimistic they could put the college in order. The college had always been led by a minister, but after Kirkland's resignation, wrote President Quincy's son, the corporation "though it important that a man of the world, accustomed to business, should be placed at the head of the university." Bowditch spearheaded the appointment of his longtime friend, who had just completed five years as the city of Boston's chief executive, and would come to be heralded as "THE GREAT ORGANIZER OF THE UNIVERSITY." It did not take long for the new style of administration to take hold. Responding to "suspicions of partiality," an elaborate system of numerical grading, the so-called Scale of Comparative Merit, was implemented that reduced academic rank "to a matter of mathematical certainty." It was a claim for evenhandedness based on the objectivity of systems and numbers familiar to Bowditch. The corporation voted in and Quincy enforced another policy aimed at uniformity: the decision to subject law-breaking students to "the usual forms of proceedings . . . applicable to like crimes and offenses committed by other citizens," that is, the state's criminal courts. Just as Bowditch had once opposed executive pardons as undermining the rule of law, so now did he oppose a double standard of justice for Harvard's unruly youths.[57]

Meanwhile a new financial regime was also put in place, with monthly statements, annual audits, and investments, disbursements, and debt collection "under the watchful superintendence of Dr. Bowditch and Mr. Francis." Life Office secretary Moses Hale was brought in to keep the records. By 1830 matters had stabilized to the point that Francis felt he could resign as treasurer. The corporation responded with a resolution praising the "method and economy in his arrangements," "accuracy and promptness in the settlement of accounts," and "systematic" organization of college papers. Francis was replaced by Bowditch's old friend Thomas Wren Ward, another Salem merchant who had migrated to Boston. The Life Office actuary maintained his vigilance—"Mr. Bowditch frets me about the College," Ward wrote in his diary that winter—but the crisis, at least the financial one, appeared to have passed.[58]

Still, the effects of the Davis-Higginson-Kirkland putsch lingered. As Bowditch had predicted, press reports stimulated suspicion among the citizens of Massachusetts, especially those who had long resented Harvard as a Unitarian-run playground for wealthy boys. The Reverend Parsons Cooke, a Calvinist from the center of the state, suggested that the college finances might have been subject to something more than mere mismanagement and that the skullduggery might have extended all the way to the top. John Lowell vigorously defended Kirkland against Cooke's "malicious" charges of embezzlement, and Francis and Nichols signed statements to the effect that accounts had been squared, but suspicion remained. Bowditch did not involve himself in this war of words, but his name came up anyway. "The commentator of La Place" is a man capable of threading his way "through any mathematical tortuosities but those of an Egyptian labyrinth," wrote one observer, so if even *he* turned to an outside auditor to reconcile Harvard's books, it must have been because he "would rather have weighed the sixth satellite of Herschel, than have attempted to adjust and rectify" them himself.[59]

Elite Bostonians expected Harvard to take heat from the likes of the Reverend Cooke, but their own discomfort with what one newspaper commentator termed the "Essex influence" lingered into the 1830s. "We apprehend that *Suavitur* [*sic*] *in modo* [agreeable in manner] is not considered at Cambridge so pure Latin as *Fortiter in re* [resolute in action]," read one newspaper piece. (Those who had actually attended Cambridge, it would have been noted, would understand this Latin reference and know that it came from a popular handbook for gentlemanly behavior.)[60] The problem,

explained another contributor, was not so much Quincy as his "secret coun-
sellors," most of all Bowditch. "It is plainly obvious that one may command a
ship well, or manage well the complicated affairs of a Life Insurance Office,"
continued this commentator, "and yet not know how to control an Academy
or a College." Rather than gentlemanly tact, this "Atlantean astronomer,"
this "self-taught *La Place*" exhibited "that confidence," a kind of brassy push-
iness, "which so usually and so unpleasantly characterizes *self-taught* men."
Upon Kirkland's death in 1840, eulogist John Gorham Palfrey referred to
the widespread belief that Kirkland's resignation had been precipitated by
one lacking "delicacy"—that word again—who "for a moment so unhappily
[did] forget himself as to offer disrespect to that venerable excellence." As
late as 1861 John Langdon Sibley, who had been a student at Harvard in the
1820s, confided to his diary that Bowditch, "being only a man of dollars &
cents," had been "severe on Kirkland."[61]

But for the most part, Boston patricians put the incident behind them. In
1831 John Lowell wrote James Jackson that "those, who raised the College,
from its state of depression in 1810 . . . have been treated with the most abom-
inable, and outrageous injustice," but he remained one of Bowditch's closest
supporters at the Life Office. Charles Francis Adams had looked down his
nose at Bowditch for his lack of "delicacy," but he nonetheless relied on him
to invest his wife's money. It was this very interweaving of Bowditch into
the fabric of elite Boston—its business affairs, its cultural institutions, and
its social relations—that made it impossible for Bowditch to become an
outcast. As Peter Chardon Brooks privately commented, Kirkland's forced
resignation "caused a good deal of embarrassment and the more because the
friends of the college and of the President, and of Dr. Bowditch, are mainly
the same men."[62]

Elite Bostonians understood that Bowditch had both virtues and faults,
but also that the two were linked. "In the expression of his opinions," wrote
John Pickering, "he had an unmeasured frankness" rooted in his "reverence
for truth, and for probity of character." If he "was sometimes quick, warm,
and vehement in expressing his disapprobation of the character or conduct
of an individual," explained his minister, such expression only followed from
his otherwise admirable "rigid integrity" and "straight-forwardness and
frankness." Nat too admitted that his father did not possess "that guarded
demeanor, which, upon every occasion of life, prevents the utterance of
a word which it may be desirable to recall," but he also revealed that his
father had expressed a disinclination to imitate the sort of gentleman with
"courtly manners" who hides "profound contempt" behind a "mild and

conciliatory" politesse.[63] One of Bowditch's associates on the Harvard Corporation focused on the impartiality with which Bowditch passed judgment. Referring to the final meeting of the fellows with Kirkland, he stated that Bowditch had there "expressed himself, on the spur of the occasion, with that earnestness and vehemence of manner, . . . with which, in cases of strong interest, he was known to condemn what he deemed totally wrong, whatever might be the talents or station of those with whom he differed."[64] It was the same point made about Bowditch's conduct as Life Office actuary, and it reinforced the image of the mathematician as the evenhanded wielder of power.

Elite Bostonians needed Bowditch's take-no-prisoners approach to putting affairs in order. Under his leadership the Life Office was making money for them and preserving their wealth for future generations, and Harvard was back on track, yielding its own sort of dividends to current and future generations of Brahmins. The Athenaeum and the American Academy were thriving as never before. A more "delicate" man might have been less effective. Perhaps *fortiter in re* was precisely what was needed to run their enterprises. That was certainly the opinion of textile magnate Amos Lawrence as he reflected back on the Kirkland affair in a letter to Nat Bowditch. Where "a good-natured carelessness is apparent in the *head*, the subordinates are likely to become equally so, & no institution can sustain for a great length of time, such want of fidelity in the person who administers it." Even at the time of the Harvard brouhaha there were those who understood that the institution must function with machinelike efficiency and regularity. "The government of the College," wrote an "Observer" within days of Kirkland's resignation, "operated unequally, and with fits and starts, like machinery out of order. Some of the parts were screwed up too tight, others were loose and shackling, and the main-spring had lost all its elasticity." Literary men, the writer intimated, were not the ones with the expertise to repair this machine. It took "men of business" to "set the old wheel work in order."[65] No one was better suited to transform Boston's institutions into Laplacean mechanisms than Nathaniel Bowditch.

CHAPTER NINE

Apogee

In the last decade of his life Bowditch reached the height of his fame. The name "Bowditch" had long been synonymous with the maritime best seller. More recently, in Boston, it had attached itself to what was known simply as the "Bowditch Office." But by the 1830s Americans everywhere recognized Bowditch as their nation's very own mathematical genius. To establish the impossibility of one particular mathematical problem, a Washington newspaper explained that "Mr. Bowditch himself" would not be able to solve it. A short story in a New York paper featured a character who, knowing "no more about ciphering than the man in the moon," generates a problem "which would have puzzled Mr. Bowditch himself." Another story, this one written for children, had a similar character who "had conquered a sum in Mathematics, that would have puzzled Bowditch."[1] Why the rise in fame? Between 1829 and 1839 Bowditch published the four volumes of his magnum opus, his massive translation of Laplace's *Mécanique Céleste*. It seemed to solidify his reputation for all time.

It certainly was about time. Already partial English translations were appearing. Although these were incomplete, and the commentary was nowhere near as learned or detailed as his own, Bowditch may have worried about getting scooped. Meanwhile, Laplace published a fifth volume and then died soon after, in 1827. There would be no changes to the first four volumes as Bowditch had anticipated. So in 1828 Bowditch initiated the process of putting his manuscript into print. I waited "till I could afford to publish it at my own expense," he told his minister, and that time has "at last arrived; and if, instead of setting up my coach, as I might have done, I see fit to spend my money in this way, who has any right to complain?" When he told Mary the project would cost $10,000—it would actually cost $12,000 —she told him she would make any sacrifice necessary.[2]

As the four volumes were published, they made their way to readers in the United States and Europe, even as far away as India, through a personal network of booksellers, merchants, and fellow men of letters. The response was gratifying. Prominent British and Continental scientists sent letters full of praise, and yet more European learned societies honored Bowditch with membership. Henry reported from Paris and London that his surname was a passport to learned circles. A discerning eye would have noted that Europeans shied away from celebrating Bowditch as an original thinker and focused instead on the sheer size and utility of the task he had undertaken. How wonderful, they wrote, that an American of all people should have translated Laplace. If he was aware of the condescension that tinged the praise, Bowditch did not let on, and his countrymen were certainly deaf to it. As far as they were concerned, those haughty Europeans had been upstaged by their American Newton.

Bowditch had other reasons to feel a sense of accomplishment. As his children came of age, they prospered. Networks of family and friends smoothed their paths as they had his own, but there was a difference. In postrevolutionary Salem those networks had followed vertical lines of personal patronage—Derby had reached down to put Bowditch on board the *Henry*—whereas in antebellum Boston they followed horizontal lines of class. Even as Bowditch pioneered clockwork institutions, personal connections in the city's uppermost stratum shaped professional advancement and marital choices alike.

It was probably a day in 1832 or 1833 that marked the zenith of his life. Perhaps it was the day he received a letter from Charles Babbage in London. Perhaps it was the day he received a bust of Laplace from the great man's widow, or himself sat for a marble bust commissioned by the Boston Athenaeum. By 1834, though his standing as a man of affairs and a man of science would only rise, those halcyon days had passed. At 8 Otis Place, Mary died after a long illness. In the streets of Boston, rioters attacked Catholics and abolitionists. The New England nation had become irrecognizably lawless. The glory days of the republic seemed to belong more to his youth than his old age. Then, as he faced his own inevitable fate, he wondered what would remain of his memory when he was gone.

ALL TOLD, BOWDITCH'S four volumes came to some 3,000 pages, far longer than Laplace's *Mécanique Céleste*. Much of the extensive annotation had been added in the 1820s and 1830s, reflecting a change in Bowditch's goals. Originally his objective had been to instruct a mathematically unsophisticated audience, just the kind—though he did not state this explicitly—one would find in America. He would make Laplace accessible to those familiar with geometry, trigonometry, and the old-fashioned fluxions, but not with "the late important improvements in the analytical calculus."[3] He soon realized there was even more science his American students had to catch up with, even as he developed a new awareness of Laplace's shortcomings. No longer just an instructional work for an American audience, Bowditch's *Mécanique Céleste* was now designed to accomplish three more ambitious goals.

His primary objective was to fill in the frequent gaps in Laplace's presentation. He was often heard to remark that "whenever I meet in La Place with the words 'Thus it plainly appears,' I am sure that hours, and perhaps days, of hard study will alone enable me to discover *how* it plainly appears." In print Bowditch was more tactful, referring to "the abridged manner, in which the analytical calculations have been made" and the resulting "time and labour required, to insert the intermediate steps of the demonstrations." To make these steps more comprehensible to those with a weak mathematical background, Bowditch included a preliminary list of formulas and explained such basic concepts of analytical calculus as functions, the same instructional approach he had taken with his *Navigator*. Many of his annotations begin with phrases like "as an example of the application" or "for the purpose of illustration." But even those with advanced training appreciated the commentary that followed such phrases as "this follows from the known principle."[4]

A second objective was to incorporate the scholarship generated since Laplace first published his volumes. This, as we have seen, was the challenge Bowditch recognized only after his initial translation and annotation. In his third volume, for example, Bowditch added a 200-page appendix dedicated to "the improvements made by Gauss, Olbers, and others, in the calculation of the orbit of a planet or comet"—precisely the task where his own use of Laplace's technique had marked him as behind the times. So committed was Bowditch to maintaining the currency of his contributions that he made revisions up to the last possible moment, making liberal use of his "little black handled eraser" even as the volumes were in press. A third goal was not directly acknowledged by Bowditch: to give credit where credit was due. Bowditch felt it was a matter of "literary justice" to correct omissions, but there was at least some personal animus to this task. Years earlier Bowditch had pointed out an error in Laplace's work in both a published essay and a private communication to the author. Laplace fixed the error in a subsequent edition, but he did so, wrote Nat, betraying the memory of his father's resentment, "without even a private acknowledgement." Perhaps it gave Bowditch a certain sort of satisfaction to point out and correct further errors in his published translation.[5]

Given their mathematical figures, symbols, and shapes, getting the volumes into print was an exacting process that required three times the work of standard text. At one point Bowditch kept two compositors busy, but he could not keep up with their work without compromising his own time and health, and he was concerned that he would miss something. Better to leave it all to Robert Macnair, the man Bowditch admired for his particular "accuracy, neatness, and assiduity." Once the type was set, there was the matter of proofreading. William spent Sundays on the proof sheets, much to his pious mother's chagrin. Henry too lent a hand. Most important was Benjamin Peirce, Bowditch's mathematical protégé since the boy's schooldays in Salem. It was Peirce that Bowditch had been referring to when he told Kirkland that there was a sophomore who knew more mathematics than his math tutor. "You will be professor by and by," Bowditch once predicted, rubbing his hands with delight, and he was right.[6]

Inevitably a few mistakes made it into the printed volumes. Bowditch received unsolicited lists of errata, mostly from young men seeking to ingratiate themselves. A Buffalo physician relayed errors along with a request for a Life Office loan. A recent Harvard graduate sent several lists and then asked for advice on obtaining a university appointment. A young tutor at the University of Georgia provided similar information and later asked for a letter of recommendation for a permanent post at the college. Bowditch appreciated notice of errata. The man who had found 8,000 errors in Moore's *Navigator* wanted none in his own work.[7]

If the accuracy of his publication was a special point of pride for Bowditch, others took even greater notice of its physical appearance. Daniel White admired the "beauty of paper and typography" as "corresponding to the intrinsic dignity of the work." American periodicals took note of the volume's "new type" and "fine paper" and described it as "the finest specimen of typography that has ever issued from the American press," comparable in its "typographical execution" to the *Transactions* of London's Royal Society.[8] These comments may sound trivial, even trivializing, as if their authors were searching for something, *anything*, to praise, but such commentary was typical of the era. Paper and type were understood to carry meaning in and of themselves. White's reference to the "dignity" of the work came at a time when less dignified genres of print, such as the sensationalist penny newspaper, were beginning to flood the market. They were typeset with ordinary care at best, and printed on a new kind of cheap, and cheap-looking, paper made from wood pulp instead of the traditional cotton or linen rags. High-quality printing also reflected America's technological accomplishment and its level of taste. The reputations of nations were at stake. "Your work," wrote Sylvestre Lacroix from Paris, "by the beauty of its typographical execution, does honor to the country where it is published." His countryman Adrien-Marie Legendre admitted to being "particularly astonished at the magnificence of the typographical execution," adding that "in this regard France is very far from being able to compete." From London, Henry Beaufoy complimented "the beauty of the printing and paper of your national undertaking."[9]

Bowditch successfully produced a set of volumes that did him and his nation proud, but publication was followed by a second challenge— distribution of the 500 copies of each volume printed. It was possible to find copies at Carvill's bookstore in New York and Obadiah Rich's in London. But Bowditch understood from the first that selling his books was not the way to get them out there, and not just because of the hefty eight-dollar price.[10] For one, Europeans were hardly used to looking out for the newest scientific publication in the New World. Then too, the Republic of Letters was not driven by markets but by reciprocal exchange. Bowditch would have to give away copies of his work to the right individuals and institutions.

In the United States he sent copies to scientific colleagues, learned insti- tutions, and university libraries from Vermont to Philadelphia. Word spread as far away as Little Rock, Arkansas. Getting books to Europe presented a greater logistical challenge.[11] London bookman Obadiah Rich acted as a middleman for some of Bowditch's British recipients, but for other copies Bowditch sought help from American friends on their way abroad. The first volume, for example, went to France with Reuben Mussey, a professor of medicine at Dartmouth whom Bowditch had befriended in their Salem days. Once in Paris Mussey was assisted by David Bailie Warden, an Irish- born American citizen who served as something of an informal cultural attaché. "Mr. Warden was a great deal of high American feeling," Mussey wrote Bowditch, "and he was not a little gratified, in being able to present, to the Savans [*sic*] of France, such a work as yours."[12] Thereafter, Bowditch's couriers included Solomon Miles, the librarian of the American Academy of Arts and Sciences; Daniel Treadwell, a Harvard professor and American Academy officer; and George Ticknor, the learned host of Boston's Sunday evening literary circle. Merchant William Ropes and James Thal, an astron- omer in St. Petersburg, carried volumes to Russia. Without such personal agents, anything could happen. When Bowditch used the postal system to send eight copies of his first volume to various German institutions and scientists, none arrived.[13]

It was with an element of uncertainty, then, that he awaited word from abroad. He was hoping for kudos, of course. "Dr. Bowditch was well aware of that natural self-love," wrote Nat, "by which every one is gratified at finding his labors approved by others." By 1830 the letters began to arrive. Some were routine institutional acknowledgments of the receipt of publications, but others were fuller communications from individuals. From France came letters from Adrien-Marie Legendre, Sylvestre Lacroix, Louis Puissant, and Laplace's son Charles; and from Britain, correspondence arrived from Charles Babbage, Francis Baily, George Airy, John Herschel, and Mary Somerville. Once the German scholars received copies, they too wrote Bowditch: Heinrich Christian Schumacher, Friedrich Wilhelm Bessel, and Johann Franz Encke. We cannot overstate the gratification Bowditch felt upon receiving these letters. With the exception of Laplace himself, these men were the objects of his greatest intellectual admiration. He read the letters out loud to Mary, the better to savor their contents.[14]

What does a European scientist with a prominent place on the world's stage write to Nathaniel Bowditch of Boston? Probably the most complimentary Europeans were those that recognized the utility of Bowditch's annotations and the intellectual sophistication they required. Typical of these was Legendre, whose mock quibble with Bowditch's subtitle—"Your work is not merely a *Translation with a Commentary*"—continued with the assertion that he regarded "it as a new edition, augmented and improved, and such an one as might have come from the hands of the author himself . . . if he had been solicitously studious of being clear." In addition to the clarifying power of Bowditch's text, there was the matter of the updates to scholarship it provided. "Your work will embrace the actual state of science at the time of its publication," pointed out Lacroix, while Bessel noted that "through your labors . . . La Place's work is brought down to our own time." There were even scattered suggestions that Bowditch might have contributed some of his own ideas, as when Bessel added, "you yourself enrich this science by your own additions," but such hints at originality were counterbalanced by references to sheer labor. When he received the first volume, Lacroix praised Bowditch as an "able, patient, and conscientious geometer." After a subsequent volume, he confessed to being "more and more astonished at your continued perseverance in a task so laborious and extensive."[15]

The most prominent theme of these letters was the credit Bowditch's work reflected on his nation. Legendre noted "with great pleasure that the mathematical sciences, in their most elevated branches, are cultivated in the United States of America, with so marked a success," while Beaufoy characterized Bowditch's translation as testimony to the young republic's "rising character and interests." For Herschel, Bowditch's publications demonstrated that America's well-known "spirit of energy & enterprise" was now extending "into the regions of Science." But what Bowditch's work said about his American *readers* might not be as flattering. Beaufoy actually suggested that Bowditch had needed to dumb down Laplace for this audience. You have "laudably condescended to adapt your clear and elaborate commentary," he wrote, to the "requirements" of your "vigorous yet infant state."[16]

In a few cases, Bowditch's European correspondents went beyond formulaic, often patronizing sentiments and approached Bowditch as a fellow citizen of the Republic of Letters. The hallmark of that relationship was reciprocal exchange. Legendre sent Bowditch his own recent treatise, discussed its relationship to the work of two other mathematicians, and described his new scholarly project. Briton Mary Somerville, like Bowditch self-taught in the highest levels of contemporary mathematics, sent him a copy of her own *Mechanism of the Heavens*, a condensed translation of four of Laplace's volumes.[17]

But of all his correspondents, the one who most readily treated Bowditch as a peer was the Englishman Charles Babbage, the man Bowditch recommended in 1821 for honorary membership in the American Academy—with comical understatement—as "a very good mathem[aticia]n." No sooner had Babbage received Bowditch's first volume than he returned the favor with copies of his own publications. More important, he shared his current work on the calculating engine. That early computer, you may recall, was inspired by the formidable task Bowditch had once embraced with gusto: the production of error-free navigation tables. Colleague to colleague, Babbage discussed the mathematics of the machine. In a subsequent letter he presented the workings of his engine as a mechanical metaphor for the divine presence in nature. Bowditch was enthralled. "When you carried me from the simple machine made by a man to the grand machine of the Universe," Bowditch wrote, "I wish I could express to you one half of the enthusiasm I felt." That vision of a "grand machine" had inspired Bowditch in all his labors. How marvelous to have found a spiritual soulmate. Then in 1835 Babbage sent Bowditch a long, mathematically sophisticated description of his new analytical engine, addressing his letter not "to a stranger, but to a friend whose person I have not yet seen." After complaining about the British government's reluctance to fund the project, he added that "you who have yourself made great pecuniary sacrifices for the production of a great and important work will understand my feelings."[18] It was a remarkably intimate exchange.

By the mid-1830s Bowditch had achieved an impressive degree of international standing. From India came news from Ingersoll that "5 copies of the Mec. Cel. were subscribed for in Calcutta—*one* by a *Hindoo*." From Europe, George Ticknor wrote that though he had traveled thousands of miles, he was not "beyond the reach of your reputation." I "have been asked after you everywhere, and it has been a good passport to kindness that I could say I was known to you." During the 1830s Bowditch received notice of his election to honorary memberships in a second round of learned societies: the Royal Astronomical Society of London (1832), the British Association and the Royal Academy of Palermo (1835), and the Royal Academy of Berlin (1836). He suspected Ticknor had used his influence to bring about his Berlin election, but that hardly detracted from what he termed "the honor of being enrolled on the list of members of a society which has had for its presidents such men as Euler, La Grange, &c." Even better to be informed that, no, it was "the great man himself," Encke, who had put up Bowditch's name.[19] France, we might note—surely Bowditch did—dragged its feet. According to his friend John Pickering, Paris's Royal Academy had begun the process of honorary membership, but Bowditch died before it could finalize the matter. It was not quite the same thing, but the gift of Laplace's bust from his widow gratified Bowditch deeply. He set aside one of his globes in its favor, then determined that it deserved a finer piece of furniture for its display and bought a brand new secretary for his library.[20]

If European men of science praised Bowditch's work, it was in part because they hardly expected scientific contributions of *any* note to emerge from an American. They viewed Bowditch not unlike the way many viewed Mary Somerville: the wonder was that they produced any science at all.[21] But we need to acknowledge that, truth be told, Bowditch's translation did not rank as a major intellectual achievement. After his death the Astronomical Society of London, headquarters of England's cutting-edge mathematicians (including several of his correspondents), published what is probably the most astute analysis of his labors. Bowditch's commentary on Laplace, it noted, "bears the mark" of a mathematical neophyte encountering advanced analytical techniques for the first time. "We see in it," the society's council continued, "not the performance of a practised analyst, but the record of the steps by which the translator became one." Precisely because he had once been as ignorant as his readers, then, Bowditch's annotations were "invaluable" to a mathematically unsophisticated reader, but they were largely "needless" to an "expert mathematician," whose own commentary would have been filled "with difficulties of the same order" as those generated by Laplace. The project, it concluded by way of posthumous praise, "required sound knowledge, power of combining, brevity and clearness, an accurate remembrance of the nature of a beginner's difficulties, and determined perseverance."[22] Not a word about genius.

As far as Americans were concerned, though, Bowditch's work had forced Europeans to acknowledge their nation's cultural greatness at last. According to Philadelphia's *National Gazette*, Bowditch's *Mécanique Céleste* had "raised him in the estimation of the most eminent savans [*sic*] of Europe, to the highest rank in the intellectual world." There "is a fluttering among the stooled pigeons of Europe at this achievement of our countryman," reported the *Mathematical Diary*. They "begin to open their eyes at last to see what has been snatched from them." Several American newspapers republished a French review that had commended Bowditch's work as "evidence of the progress which the mathematics have made in the United States, a country which we have been accustomed to regard as barren in the purely specula-tive sciences." Also reprinted was the *London Quarterly Review*'s admission that it had hardly expected to find such a praiseworthy work emanating from "the opposite shores of the Atlantic." Even in distant India, it was reported, "mortification is expressed, that the work should have come from Boston, in North America, instead of Cambridge, in England."[23]

It felt especially good to have the British eat crow. Americans were still smarting over Sydney Smith's comments in an 1820 issue of the *Edinburgh Review*, in which he famously fired a series of damning questions, begin-ning with, "In the four quarters of the globe, who reads an American book?" and including "what have they done in the mathematics?" How delightful it must have been to suggest that "the Edinburgh critic should have had on his table the first volume of Bowditch's translation of La Place's *Mecanique Celeste*"! How delicious to add that "some of the most eminent astronomers and mathematicians of Europe" had sent letters to Bowditch expressing "the highest admiration for his science and labors"![24]

Of course, Bowditch's reputation as a mathematical wunderkind went back to the days when Henry Prince placed bets on his supercargo's com-putational abilities. In Salem Bowditch had been sought to solve mathe-matical conundrums on matters ranging from comets to textile machinery. In Boston he remained the go-to person for these kinds of problems. The state legislature asked him and John Farrar "to ascertain the present value of the reversionary interest of the Commonwealth in the several Bridges, &c." Mayor Josiah Quincy sought his advice on future population trends in the city. In 1830 he was asked to review the date for the celebration of Boston's bicentennial, in light of the intervening shift from the Gregorian to the Julian calendar. His imprimatur was also key on maritime matters. Matthew Fontaine Maury sought out his endorsement for his *New Theoretical and Practical Treatise on Navigation*. The United States Navy consulted him regarding their South Seas Exploring Expedition, and his praise for one of Lt. Charles Wilkes's oceanographic surveys influenced the navy's selection of Wilkes as the expedition's commander.[25]

But the new round of European plaudits boosted his fame even further. Edward Everett went so far as to claim that Bowditch stood "upon an equality with the most distinguished philosophers of Europe" and that his name could be added to "those of Newton and La Place, upon that list of great minds, to which scarcely one is added in a century." Bowditch became an ornament to Boston's vaunted cultural scene, the Pythagoras or the Euclid in the American Athens. Bostonians liked to show him off to distinguished foreign visitors. He was among the "brilliant and select company" introduced to the highly respected phrenologist Johann Gaspar Spurzheim. Harriet Martineau, the English social commentator, was another eminent foreign visitor who paid her respects to Bowditch. Mary Somerville had provided her with a letter of introduction, and Bowditch invited her for tea, along with a number of Harvard professors and their wives. Joseph Gauss, son of the German mathematician Carl Friedrich Gauss, also made it a point to visit Bowditch, as did the distinguished Russian astronomer James Thal. Bowditch now found himself included in, even at the head of, a select company featuring the intellectual cream of Harvard's graduates and faculty. If he had ever felt unworthy of Harvard, that moment was fading.[26]

Bowditch's position in the firmament of Boston culture took on concrete form in 1834, when the Athenaeum commissioned sculptor John Frazee to make a marble bust of him.[27] Bowditch had taken Frazee's name to mean he was a Frenchman or Italian, but when the sculptor arrived in Boston and Bowditch discovered he was from New Jersey, he grilled him on his qualifications. "I saw plainly that he was fearful of being caught in the hands of a Charlatan," wrote Frazee. But Thomas Wren Ward's assurance of Frazee's skill "seemed to reconcile the old gentleman," reported the sculptor, "and brighten up his countenance with a more cheering and confiding aspect," and the two soon got along famously. One afternoon Bowditch ran into Frazee's studio and asked him to accompany him on a carriage ride. The sculptor might have reconsidered had he known that Bowditch was known for his wild ways on the road—racing with carts and carriages till their wheels rubbed together—but instead he "hop'd [*sic*] into the gig," and off they went "like 'old scratch,'" in other words, like the Devil. None of that spirit survives in Frazee's bust of a square-jawed Bowditch in toga-like costume, but a classical presentation was precisely what was expected. The Athenaeum's trustees are "highly pleased with it," Nat wrote the sculptor, "as are also Mr. Bowditch [*sic*] family."[28]

Not to be outdone, Salem's East India Marine Society soon commissioned Charles Osgood, a local artist, to execute a portrait for their collection. The society was pleased with the result—"the *tout ensemble* reflects great credit upon the artist"—but Bowditch's son Henry did not agree. "His *face perhaps*," he later commented, "but *without his soul!*"[29] But we may beg to differ with Henry (see cover illustration). Osgood's portrait delineates a skinny and bald man of advanced years, not a Roman senator. It shows Bowditch in his library, backed by shelves of learned works, the first two volumes of his *Mécanique Céleste* translation on the table, his right arm resting on an open book and several papers. Bowditch holds his spectacles in his left hand, as if caught at work. He has just taken them off to look at us with a forthright gaze. Osgood has illuminated the dome of Bowditch's forehead, emphasizing the illuminating power of the brain within. Above, in shadow, is the bust of Laplace on a pedestal, his lips set in what appears to be a slight but approving smile.

IN 1830 THE household at 8 Otis Place was a full one, with eleven people under one roof. Besides Nathaniel, Mary, and their six children, there was another woman and a teenage boy—likely the cook Abigail and an Irish serving man—as well as Elizabeth Martin, Bowditch's unmarried niece, who had lived in the household since the death of her mother in 1808, tending to household tasks.[30] The Bowditch children fell into two distinct cohorts of three, with eight years separating the three oldest, Nat, Ingersoll, and Henry, from the youngest, Mary, William, and Elizabeth. (In between were an infant who had died soon after birth, and Charles, who had died at the age of ten.) To a very real extent the two groups had different upbringings. The eldest three had spent their formative years in Salem and retained powerful attachments to their native town. The younger Bowditches, on the other hand, had grown up in Boston. When, on one carriage drive to Salem, young William asked "how far it was to the village," his father replied, "'Village! Village! Salem is the second city in the Commonwealth!'" It could not have meant much to the Boston boy. But the two cohorts were separated by more than geography. Nat, Ingersoll, and Henry shared fond memories of their parents. William, on the other hand, described a father who would thrash the children if they disturbed his mathematical labors and a mother prone to spanking according to what he termed "the Ingersoll theory of education."[31] Chances are, all these memories are accurate. In Salem, Nathaniel and Mary had been young, energetic, and healthy. By the time the family moved to Boston, Nathaniel and Mary were older and, as we shall see, in a declining state of health.

For all six children, success in later life went hand in hand with immersion in Boston society and its networks of personal connections. The Bowditches provided Mary and Eliza with genteel schooling and then looked for their daughters to find good marriage matches. The transition into young adulthood, with all its social expectations, was not always easy. As a little girl Mary had been free to play with her brothers—"Mary with my knapsack I with sword belt & cap," wrote Henry of their make-believe militia—but as she got older that kind of life was no longer possible. As boys filed off into college and careers, their sisters remained at home. We "were concluding the other day that we should quite miss our *little brothers*," she wrote Henry of her sewing circle conversation, the emphasis indicating some inchoate sense of unfairness. Strenuously genteel education and chaperoned excursions were the order of the day. Mary may have felt stifled by the demands of Boston's social scene—oh to be visiting you in Vermont, she wrote her grandfather, where she "could run out of the front door, without *stopping to put on my gloves*"—but as a girl, participating in Boston society was of primary importance. Her future husband, Epes Dixwell, remembered Mary at the age of sixteen, "a little girl in muslin—a school girl—not out," though nonetheless at Miss Martha Ward's ball. Two years later she was making the rounds of the balls, attracting considerable attention ("unconsciously blooming—buxom—lovely," wrote Dixwell) and enjoying it. Her future dependent on the choice of a husband, romance soon absorbed her. "Mary B. has been in the depths of distress one night & the next night in the 7th heaven," wrote Jane Wigglesworth, describing Mary's responses to the alternating attentions and inattentions of one young man.[32]

Marriage was not irrelevant to the Bowditches' expectations for their sons either. For generations, after all, it had been something of a Bowditch tradition to make an advantageous choice of a wife, and elite Bostonians were well aware of the implications of a strategic alliance. Of the children, only two married during their father's lifetime, both with his hearty approval. Nat's marriage to Elizabeth Francis was nothing short of a coup. She was the granddaughter of the Beverly-turned-Boston merchant Israel Thorndike, and the daughter of Ebenezer Francis, Bowditch's Life Office and Harvard associate, one of Boston's richest men. "Mother often has said in my hearing that she should 'hold up both hands for the matter,'" Nat wrote Caroline Plummer. "Father and all our household are highly pleased with the engagement." Ingersoll also married into a prominent, if somewhat less prosperous, North Shore family. His wife was the daughter of Benjamin Nichols, Nat's first legal mentor in Salem and Bowditch's associate in the financial management of the Essex Bank and Harvard. Not long after his wedding, Ingersoll advised a friend that the best way to pick a wife was to forget about love, put the names of six young ladies into a hat, shake, and marry the one whose name falls out. What he did not say, what did not *need* to be said, was that the candidates must first be carefully vetted.[33]

The boys also had to meet expectations regarding their careers. The culturally acceptable alternatives for patrician sons were few—preferably the learned professions, with business a sound choice for perhaps one among them—but in each case personal relationships would smooth the way. After reading law with his father's associates Benjamin Nichols and William Prescott, Nat enjoyed a lucrative practice as the Life Office solicitor and did well in the real estate business it spawned. But because of his wife's wealth, he was able to engage in another approved pursuit, philanthropy. He contributed both time and money liberally to Massachusetts General Hospital, another institution with many links to the Bowditch and Francis families. Echoing his father's approach, he revised the hospital's rules and regulations and made it a national leader in mandating written records of patient care and their daily entry in a centralized case ledger.[34]

For a while it may not have been clear that the youngest Bowditch son would end up as successful as the eldest. Willy was a high-spirited boy who often ran afoul of the stern discipline of his parents and teachers. It was one thing to engage in fights with working-class boys from the North End, but when he and his friends broke into a neighbor's vacant house and vandalized its adjacent woodshed, he was "rudely awakened" by his father, bent on "suddenly and effectively" disturbing his son's slumbers. At preparatory school Willy endured corporal punishment at the hands of its arch-disciplinarian headmaster, a man he later nicknamed "Magister Thrashandi." (The school's many "Prohibitions" included "to nick-name any person.") Then at Harvard he was admonished "for excessive absences from prayers and recitations" and ordered to spend his summer vacation studying navigation and nautical astronomy, a pointed directive if ever there was one. But William got the Harvard degree, followed Nat into a legal career, and eventually married a Boston Higginson.[35]

Ingersoll began his career in commerce clerking for Thomas Wren Ward, Bowditch's longtime friend and his ally in Life Office, Athenaeum, and Harvard affairs. When the young man set sail for Calcutta on his first voyage as supercargo, his father's contacts were there to ensure his success. "Several of the shippers," wrote Bowditch, "have taken an interest in this voyage for the purpose of giving him employment." Ebenezer Francis was one such.

Bowditch even went so far as to ask the captain and supercargo of another Calcutta-bound vessel to offer his son "advice and assistance" in his Indian business dealings, "as his future prospects in life will depend very much on a judicious investment of the property." Ironically, though he had rejected Bowditch's dream of a Harvard education, Ingersoll turned out the most like his father. Not only did he become the head of an insurance company, but he also shared his father's mathematical interests and, at least to some extent, aptitude. He tackled algebra at the age of ten and at thirteen wrote his brother, "I have got into Geometry and I like it very much, and Father says I get along very well." While still active in trade, he erected an observatory at his summer residence in Canton. Later he contributed solutions to problems posed in the *Mathematical Diary*, published actuarial tables in the American Academy's *Memoirs*, pressed for a Harvard observatory, contributed new tables to the 1837 *Navigator*, and eventually took over the work of new editions.[36]

As for Henry, we last saw him as a dreamy and distracted youth at Harvard. "I never awoke to the dignity & beauty of work in life till *I left College*," he wrote many years later. "The moment I graduated I felt like a fool that *somehow*, I had wasted (nearly) my time at Cambridge." Henry did not feel up to the law or ministry, and as his son later wrote, "the life of a business man was most uncongenial to him." There was only one option left for a Harvard graduate: medicine. So Henry became a physician, training at Harvard and Massachusetts General Hospital under the Bowditches' doctor and neighbor, James Jackson. After receiving his M.D. in 1832, he set sail for Europe, planning a year in Paris and another in London, determined to receive the kind of up-to-date medical studies only a sojourn abroad could provide. Familiar with the superiority of European science, Bowditch gave the plan his full support, instructing him to "spend what you find necessary for the advancement in knowledge of your profession." If he had been self-taught, he saw no reason why his son should have to be. Along with a small coterie of other Americans, Henry studied in Paris's hospitals under Pierre-Charles-Alexandre Louis, whose "numerical method" of collating empirical clinical observations represented the cutting edge of Western medical science. Testing the waters in London, Henry soon realized that English medicine was far behind its French counterpart and decided he had much more to learn from a second year in Paris. He worried that his father might not approve the change in plan, but he need not have. Even at the height of Federalist Francophobia, Bowditch had recognized the superiority of French science. Back to Paris went Henry.[37]

What must have given Bowditch special pleasure was his son's admission into the world of European science, an entrée assured by his own international reputation. "Your name, my dear father," wrote Henry, "carries me anywhere, and introduces to the best and most learned as well (I may add) as the most fashionable circles." To his Ingersoll grandparents he wrote, "In truth I loved my father much before I left America, but I felt *proud of him* in Europe." His fellow medical student, Oliver Wendell Holmes, wrote of Henry that "there are not probably a dozen young men in the country whose name is so powerful an introduction in Europe." Within a few weeks of his arrival, Siméon Denis Poisson called on him, and Laplace's widow invited him to visit her at her château. "She received me very cordially," reported Henry, "made me sit on the sofa with her, and we talked French for a long time." He noted that the second volume of his father's translation, along with Bowditch's letter, "was the only book to be seen lying on the grand table in the Salon at Madame's." He hinted that Madame Laplace had a surprise gift in store for her husband's translator—it was the marble bust of Laplace. In a reply, Bowditch asked Henry to relay his gratitude to Madame Laplace but admitted to a less high-minded interest in Parisian scientific circles. "I have much curiosity to know the ages and habits of the savants, Poisson, Arago, etc.," he confessed. "Are they married or single, big or little, pleasant or taciturn, children or childless, etc., etc. You may pick up much gossip which will be interesting to us."[38]

Quite certain that his father was his calling card and that no letter of introduction was needed, Henry took the initiative to call on Mary Somerville, then in Paris. Somerville was most courteous and spoke "very highly" of the Laplace translation, a copy of which Bowditch had recently sent her. "You have every reason to be proud of him," Somerville wrote Bowditch of his son. "When he visits London we shall be happy to renew our acquaintance with him, and if he goes to Edinburgh, our native place, it may lie in our power to introduce him to some of the professors." She was as good as her word. In Britain she introduced Henry to mathematician John Herschel, the son of William; George Airy, professor of mathematics at Cambridge; and Charles Babbage. At a dinner party hosted by businessman-astronomer Francis Baily, he was seated between Babbage and Mary Somerville's husband, William. "Do tell me," Henry reported William Somerville as inquiring, "can your father laugh with the world?" To which Baily added: "Can he laugh *at* it?" Perhaps it seemed impossible to think of this human computer as entirely human. But Henry responded, "Why, gentlemen, there is no person who can laugh more loudly or rub his hands with more glee than

Louis-Léopold Boilly (1761–1845), *Jean Antoine Houdon (1741–1828) Sculpting the Bust of Pierre Simon (1749–1827) Marquis de Laplace in the Presence of His Wife and Daughters,* 1804. Oil on canvas. Madame Laplace, seated, later presented Bowditch with a copy of her husband's bust. Musée des Arts Decoratifs, Paris, France. Bridgeman Images.

my father," and to Baily's delight, Henry proceeded to imitate his father's signature idiosyncrasy. As for Babbage, he and Henry struck up a continuing friendship. On subsequent visits, wrote Henry, the two "let out our hearts toward each other," speaking of love, death, and God.[39] Perhaps the intimacy Babbage developed with the young man explains the freedom with which he wrote Bowditch.

Even as Henry studied to become America's first pulmonologist, his mother was dying of tuberculosis in Boston. The symptoms of her fatal disease had long been present, but because they periodically disappeared her family and friends alternated between renewed hope and an unspoken fatalism. Mary's many doctors, all Harvard graduates, had done what they could. "Poor mother was dreadfully dosed," recalled William. "The mantel-piece in her chamber at No. 8 Otis Place, was crowded with bottles of various sizes and colors, and filled with all sorts of nauseous stuff given to cure or alleviate" consumption. The drugs may have precipitated some degree of mental confusion in Mary. On one occasion she could not recognize a miniature of her daughter, though both her husband and other daughter "knew it at once." Bowditch hired nurses for her, and after the move to Boston Mary spent many summers outside the city in search of health. The last such sojourn was in 1833, and while she was gone Bowditch undertook some remodeling of 8 Otis Place he thought would please her. But when she returned, a "melancholy feeling" seemed to come over her as she took in the improvements. "She saw every thing around her exactly as she could have wished," wrote Nat, but she barely noticed "all the comforts & conveniences which had been collected for her gratification," because "she probably realized that it was soon to be her grave."[40]

Protestant Americans of this era had distinct ideas of how one should die: resigned to one's fate and cheerful in it, and so Mary was, but also conscious, surrounded by all one's loved ones, and able to convey last messages of familial love and religious faith. Here Mary's death in April 1834 fell short, adding disquiet to the family's grief. Never suspecting she would not live through the night, neither Bowditch nor the children were present when she died. By the time a nurse summoned them to her bedside, she was already "wholly insensible, her eyes closed." Bowditch said to the nurse, "She is dying," and the nurse replied, "She is dead." It had happened too fast. "The whole passed in a moment," wrote Nat to Henry. As he continued the letter, his story seemed to change almost immediately, as if he were looking for some way to rewrite such a disturbing ending. "The nurse says that when Father came in & took mother's hand," he wrote, "she said in a low tone, 'You have come to bid me Good Bye.'" But Bowditch was "so discomposed at finding her thus far gone, that he did not hear it." Several years later, in a published memoir, the story softened even further. Now it was Mary who "extended her hand," and gently pressed her husband's, "a proof of consciousness and of love." Her last words—"My dear, you have come to bid me farewell"—were "murmured so feebly that they did not reach his ear," but the nurse "distinctly heard" them.[41]

The funeral took place early the following day, a cold and cloudless April Saturday. Bowditch wanted only family to be present. Mary was buried in a tomb under Trinity Church, an Episcopalian congregation, with the family's Unitarian minister conducting the service. Husband and wife had never quite seen eye to eye on matters of religion. That afternoon, both Bowditch and Nat went to their offices. "We have returned [to] the discharge of the duties of life," explained Nat to Henry, "being satisfied that occupation in our respective pursuits is more conducive to our own happiness & more proper in itself than the indulgence of unavailing regrets." In his grief, Bowditch became anxious that the family tomb would at some point in the future be sold or seized by creditors. It was a far-fetched scenario, but one akin to those he dealt with professionally every day, and therefore perhaps offered him the comfort of being able to achieve a solution. That same day he drew up papers conveying the tomb in trust to his four sons, guaranteeing that it would never be sold or conveyed. "There is not perhaps one chance in a million that such a paper will ever prove necessary," Nat wrote Henry, "but it was Father's wish that nothing should be left to accident." In an actuarial universe, what Nat termed "the change"—death—was the fundamental fact of life. Law, like mathematics, gave Bowditch a way of maintaining stability and predictability as even deeper realities.[42]

Henry returned home later that year, but not because he had completed his studies. In Paris he had become engaged to an English woman, and his father, fearing that his son was about to make the mistake of a lifetime, ordered him home. To Bowditch, Olivia Yardley was, as Henry's son would later write, "a perfect stranger"—not from Salem, not from Boston or New England, not even from America. Back home, Henry launched his medical practice. His father marked the occasion with a gift that could not have been more in character—printed blank forms for patient referrals to the Boston Medical Dispensary. But with one year apart, and the two lovers still pining for each other, Henry pleaded his case to his father, insisting that he would never marry anyone but Olivia while she lived. Meanwhile, one of Henry's acquaintances visiting Paris provided a flattering portrait of Miss Yardley. She "speaks French, is learning Italian, draws beautifully, plays on the pianoforte and harp delightfully, and sings divinely," he wrote, continuing on to praise Olivia's liveliness, modesty, "deep moral and religious feelings," and good sense balanced with a loving and compassionate heart. Bowditch gave in. Until his medical practice got off the ground, Henry could not afford to get married, but while Olivia waited for him in London, he sent her a portion of Laplace's fifth volume, and she worked on its translation. It was a stroke of genius. She sent Bowditch her work in December 1837 and in his reply to her, he now called her "My dear daughter Olivia" and signed his letter "Your Father."[43]

SOMETIME IN THE early 1830s Bowditch reflected on the state of the nation to his friend George Ticknor. "We are living in the best days of the republic," he began, but his tone was somber, not celebratory. "That the worst will follow soon does not seem to me very likely," he continued. "But nations advance, and thrive, and die, like men; and can no more have a second youth than their inhabitants can."[44] His nation was on the cusp of change—he could feel it—and that change gave him a sense of foreboding. His mood may well have been influenced by his dying wife and his own advancing age, but his assessment was not just an artifact of his personal life. The United States *was* changing, and changing fast. For an old New England Federalist whose beliefs in harmony and order died hard, the upswelling of ideological and social conflict was alarming, especially as it found expression in lawlessness.

The 1830s saw an unprecedented rash of riots based in these conflicts in northern cities—riots against immigrants, Catholics, African Americans, and abolitionists. Boston was no exception. In 1834 a mob of working-class Protestants burned down a convent in nearby Charlestown. Bowditch responded with shock and dismay. As we saw in his reactions to life in Réunion, Portugal, and the Philippines, he regarded Catholicism as riddled with superstition, but he had little patience for religious intolerance, and even less when it turned violent. So incensed was he by the events in Charlestown that he called on the bishop of Boston to express his solidarity. "Though our forms of worship are the most opposite and widely separated of all the creeds by which the Christian church has ever been divided," Nat reported him as having stated, "upon this ground I make common cause with you." The riot had "awakened" him "from a pleasant dream of security," Bowditch continued, revealing the "fanaticism" in "this our orderly community."[45]

For Bowditch the "orderly community" he had in mind was not so much the United States but New England or, even more narrowly, Massachusetts and its capital city. He was patriotic to be sure, but he had also been raised with a powerful identity as a Yankee. In his youth, even his manhood, Massachusetts girls stitched samplers with the formulaic text: "_____ is my name / New England is my Nation. / Salem is my Dwelling Place, / and Christ is my Salvation." Yankee schoolchildren were taught to sing "Rule, New England! New England rules and saves," to the tune of "Rule Britannia." Bowditch regarded his region as exceptional in its history, principles, and habits of life and thought. The Yankee town was the embodiment of community harmony, and the Bay State, home to Lexington, Concord, and Bunker Hill, was the crucible of freedom. It was this perception that he now saw as a "pleasant dream." He felt that "the fair fame of the state had received a deep, if not an indelible stain." How could it be that the same town that had witnessed "the first of freedom's battles in modern times" now would "exhibit a monument of the most ruthless violation of private rights"?[46]

The convent riot was not the only species of "fanaticism" that threatened the "orderly community" of Boston. So too, in Bowditch's way of thinking, was abolitionism—*and* anti-abolitionism. His feelings regarding race and slavery were complex. Recall his disgust with the slave ships he encountered at sea and his sympathy for the slaves of the Indian Ocean. On the other hand, he also believed that, as his son reported, black people were "a race of men naturally less intelligent than the whites." It was not as if Bowditch did not know any people of African descent. During his childhood Salem's population included dozens of African Americans, both enslaved and free. There were several black sailors on the *Astrea*. In the early nineteenth century African American Salemites John and Nancy Remond were the caterers of choice for events held at tony Hamilton Hall, across the street from the Bowditches. When the Essex Fire and Marine Insurance Company leased out commercial space, Bowditch was the Remonds' landlord. York Morris was the "stout colored waiter" who served guests at parties the couple attended. Lemon Shillaber, described by the *Salem Gazette* as "a highly respectable black man," cleaned the East India Marine Society's museum. Boston too had a significant black population, close to 2,000 in 1830, and their presence was no abstraction. "Black Peter" played the fiddle at Judge Jackson's Thanksgiving parties, a black servant lived with an Otis Place family, and an African American bootblack plied his trade in the neighborhood.[47] But moral disgust at slavery and a belief in white superiority were not incompatible.

Bowditch strongly opposed the extension of slavery into America's West. Father "often said," wrote Nat, "that he never wished to shake hands with, or even to see, a northern man who, surrounded by free institutions at home"—the harmonious community, the schoolroom, the church, the press—"had voted for any extension of the evils of slavery." In 1820 he urged Congressman Nathaniel Silsbee, the same man who as a shipmaster in Réunion in 1795 had sent two black stowaways back to shore, to vote against the Missouri Compromise. "May the Almighty give" Congress "firmness to go in the straightforward path [of] duty," he wrote, "to prevent the extension of slavery, and laws which authorize the burning of a human being alive!" He was referring to articles that had just appeared in the *Salem Gazette*, describing the fate of a Georgia slave found guilty of murdering his master. On the other hand, Bowditch recoiled from the immediate abolition of slavery advocated by the likes of William Lloyd Garrison as dangerously extremist. Ever the defender of the rights of property, he could not see how slave owners could legally be deprived of theirs, at least without compensation, and he believed that black people were incapable of self-government and could only make a go of it if they had a helping hand from their former masters. That hand, he reasoned, would only be extended if slave owners were compensated financially for the loss of their slave property.[48]

Bowditch was by no means the most conservative in his social circle. Epes Dixwell, the man who would marry his daughter Mary, was far more hostile to African Americans, to abolitionism, and to its sister movement, feminism. Commenting on an antislavery meeting, for example, he alluded to the unspeakable results when women and blacks stepped out of their proper places. One "Amazonian abolitionist," he declared, had "made herself quite conspicuous . . . walking up Chestnut Street with two blackies, one on each hand, & with arms endearingly entwined with hers." George Ticknor likewise shrank from abolitionism. From Dresden he reported that, with the rare exception of a few "sensible individuals," Europeans simply point to the contradiction of slavery in a republic dedicated to equal rights and, with little understanding of the complexities of the situation, condemn America. Somewhere between Ticknor and Garrison were men like William Ellery Channing, who opposed slavery on moral grounds but insisted that, given their racial inferiority, freed slaves would need "overseers" to make certain they would not lapse into laziness. His antislavery views were of the politest sort. A man prized by Unitarians for his elegance, he found Garrison's radical, evangelical fire "tasteless." But within Boston's elite social circles there were some individuals, especially among the younger generation, who took up the Garrisonian cause. Wendell Phillips, son of Boston's first mayor, was one, as was Edmund Quincy, son of Harvard president Josiah.[49] And so too was Henry Bowditch.

Henry's very public, very active participation in the abolitionist movement alienated many of his class. Epes Dixwell kept his mouth shut but privately suggested that Henry lacked "the balast [*sic*] of good common sense." Henry's medical practice fell off. He was no longer welcome at Ticknor's literary evenings. He became estranged from one of his closest companions at Harvard, because he sought to introduce antislavery teachings into the Sunday school the friend had established. One of his father's old shipmaster friends "would stare and scowl without speaking" when he encountered Henry. Bowditch felt caught in between. "Once," recalled Henry many years later, "my father said to me when I was rather notorious for my antislavery view, 'Henry, I agree with you. I do not deny my sentiments but I feel I can do more good by being quietly a worker than by talking openly.'"[50]

Bowditch read Lydia Maria Child's *An Appeal in Favor of That Class of Americans Called Africans* and a work by English abolitionist William Wilberforce, the only topical books he borrowed from the Boston Athenaeum. When he encountered George Ticknor's disgusted appraisal of European opinion on American slavery, he tried to explain that the "southern interest" was engaged in rapaciously aggressive efforts to make slavery a national institution. On some level he recognized a need for those on the right side of history to match the intemperance of those on the wrong side. Though Bowditch opposed Garrisonian abolitionism, wrote Nat in 1839, he "admitted that no great moral or religious revolution had ever been accomplished except through the agency of a few excited and enthusiastic spirits"—Henry among them—"whose apparently excessive and over-zealous efforts at last aroused *the many* to a sound, moderate, and successful reformation of abuses." When Harvard professor Charles Follen was attacked for his abolitionist views, Bowditch made a point of encouraging him to "go on, courageously," adding, "It is the cause of humanity, of truth, of God that you are maintaining." Yet when all is said and done, Bowditch did not move beyond private reflection and conversation to any sort of public position. Though he "felt keenly the greatness of this wrong," wrote Channing of his friend, and "lamented that public opinion among us on this subject was so low and faint," yet his own sentiments were "not so generally known."[51]

Bowditch was not one to hold his tongue for fear of alienating his social set. If he kept a low profile on the issue of abolition, it was because deeper than his convictions on either race or slavery was his commitment to order. He could no more look upon social turbulence with equanimity than he could contemplate cosmic confusion. The social disruption brought on by extremist views, especially his era's rising tide of violence, filled him with horror. "We are at present fallen upon excitable times," he wrote Ticknor in 1836. "The spirit of agitation, and a lawless propensity to *mobbing & lynching* has increased considerably since you left us . . . and we are not wholly free from this contagious fever in this vicinity." He pointed to the burning of the convent in 1834 and to the anti-abolitionist mob that had inspired Henry to the cause in 1835. For him the issue was not so much the blood shed as the laws broken. So he also pointed to an incident that had occurred in 1836, at a Boston court hearing involving two black women claiming to be free who were about to be shipped south into slavery. The judge was about to release them, but the African American spectators, misunderstanding the hearing's outcome, believed the women were going to be seized again and made a rush for the women and spirited them away. It bothered Bowditch that, though legally free, they had not yet been formally discharged.[52] As with natural laws, so with human laws—there cannot be the slightest deviation from them.

IN THE FALL OF 1837 Bowditch began to experience pain in his belly. When he mentioned it to Henry at the end of the year, his son urged him to consult Dr. Jackson, but Bowditch insisted that, until he took care of the Life Office's January payments, he did not have "leisure to be ill." But he *was* ill, fatally so. Jackson recognized the disease as stomach cancer. Leeches, blisters, opium, and mercury did nothing to arrest its course. Surgical interference was ruled as futile and, in this age before anesthesia, inhumane. Slowly he wasted away. He suffered from bouts of severe pain, relieved only by Henry's application of hot towels. For the most part Bowditch bore the suffering with fortitude, but in his moments of greatest agony he could not help but buckle, once crying out "why was I born!" It is not clear when he knew his disease was fatal. In mid-February Nat informed his grandfather Ingersoll that Bowditch was "hopelessly unwell," but he asked him to keep that knowledge to himself as his father was "perhaps the happier for still having hope." In early March Bowditch sent a letter to the Life Office, indicating that the directors must look for his replacement. "I showed it to Dr. Jackson to know if I had expressed myself too strongly," he related, "& he said I had not." Bowditch himself was reluctant to say recovery was impossible, instead playing the actuary, putting the odds now at one in a thousand, then at one in a million.[53]

In the days leading up to his death, Bowditch bid his closest friends farewell. Above all others, he wanted to see George Ticknor and Frank Gray, but they were in Europe. With old friends from Salem he waxed fondly on his birthplace, speaking "of the kindness he had experienced in his native place, especially in his early life, when he was enabled to get access to such scientific books, by the aid of several enlightened gentlemen." He gave free vent to his emotions. Josiah Quincy related that Bowditch kissed his hand. Edward Everett recalled an even more intimate encounter: "We knew each other a good many years ago," Bowditch said, "& (after some expressions which I cannot repeat) he added, I loved you. In saying these words his countenance was flushed; he pressed my hand affectionately and his eyes were filled with tears."[54]

In light of the era's understanding of what constituted a good death, Bowditch's visitors often left inspired and uplifted by his "cheerful & happy... frame of mind," his resignation "to the will of Providence," and his "serenity" and "pious submission" in the face of death. Given his aversion to the public declaration of faith required for church membership, his minister in particular was gladdened to hear of Bowditch's religious conviction. In my youth, "my companions were filled with Tom Paine notions," Bowditch recollected, referring to the *Age of Reason*'s scathing critique of Christianity as superstition, but such ideas were "perfectly abhorrent to me." I challenged my friends not with any learned philosophical arguments, he continued, placing his hand over his heart, but "with arguments from within." But on other occasions he grew irritated, sensing an invasive, almost prurient, interest in the state of mind of one facing eternity. "Of what importance are *my* opinions to any one?" he snapped. "I do not wish to be made a show of."[55]

He put his personal affairs in order, winding up his financial concerns, paying debts, and in what Henry later termed a "general conflagration," burning all the letters he had exchanged with Mary, along with a manuscript oral history of his youth that Nat had taken down over the years. He drew up a will. Bowditch had wealth, but not enormous wealth. All told—house, furnishings, books, scientific instruments, and stocks—the estate amounted to about $57,000. By comparison, Dr. Jackson was said to be worth $100,000, George Ticknor twice that, Frank Gray and Josiah Quincy both $300,000, merchant and Life Office director William Appleton $1 million, and marine insurer Peter Chardon Brooks $4 million. In disposing of his estate, Bowditch left sums to three Salem institutions: $5,000 to the Salem Athenaeum, recalling the "inestimable advantage" his access to the Philosophical Library had given him; $1,000 to the Salem Marine Society in recognition of the assistance it had provided to several of his family members; and another $1,000 to the East India Marine Society. With regret, he noted that he did not have the pecuniary means to support Boston institutions, but he left his *Mécanique Céleste* manuscripts and his bust of Laplace to Harvard. Except for small amounts to a few individuals, he left the rest of his estate to his children. He rejoiced that his two prosperous sons, Nat and Ingersoll, suggested that the house be held as common property among the six, so that it would not have to be sold, displacing Henry, Willy, and the girls. Their selfless act showed that he was leaving "*a family of love*," he said repeatedly, and nothing gave him greater comfort or joy.[56]

Bowditch kept on working. In the last month of his life Moses Hale came to his house every day with papers for his signature and books for him to examine. Above all, he was racing to finish the fourth volume of the *Mécanique Céleste*. "There are only about ten pages wanting," he said to Josiah Quincy. "Perhaps I may live to finish them." He methodically examined each proof sheet, sending the corrected work to Benjamin Peirce in bundles of 120 pages. Peirce then returned them with a list of typographical errata for Bowditch's final review. Bowditch only made it two-thirds of the way through the manuscript for this last step, but he made it further in his initial review. "The last page upon which his eye was ever to rest," wrote Nat, aware of the special significance of numbers, "was *the thousandth*." Ill as he was, Bowditch had also been able to attend to corrections of a substantive nature. A week before he died he was working on some particularly diffi-cult revisions, a demonstration that Poisson had not, as that mathematician claimed, invented a method that improved upon Laplace but only one that could be deduced from Laplace. "I feel that I am Nathaniel Bowditch still," he stated, certain of the core of his identity, "only a little weaker." [57]

Bowditch was sizing up his life as only a dying person could. He evaluated his moral conduct and concluded that, although he had made errors, by and large "my life has been somewhat blameless." He evaluated his work as a mathematician far more unsparingly. To Henry, his constant attendant, he expressed regret at having left his Laplace manuscript to Harvard. "It is a mere bagatelle," he said, soon to become "obsolete . . . nobody will look at it." Henry replied that all work becomes obsolete, but "still we honor talent." That got Bowditch thinking. Archimedes was "of the same order of talent" as Newton and Leibniz, and though superseded by both of them, it was true that, as Henry had pointed out, he was still honored. But Bowditch recog-nized he was no Archimedes. He was, he said, more on a par with Euclid, "a second-rate mathematician." My "order of talent is very different from that of La Place [*sic*]," he confided to Henry. "La Place originates things which it would have been impossible for me to have originated." Then, setting up his conclusion as the equality of two ratios (A:B=C:D), he said: "La Place was of the Newton class; and there is the same difference between La Place and myself as between Archimedes and Euclid." [58]

His last days were intimate ones with his children. Moved by their tender care, he was, Henry later wrote, "inexpressibly affectionate." "Come, my dears," Bowditch said, "I fear you will think me very foolish, but I cannot help telling you all how much I love you; for whenever any of you approach me, I feel as if I had a fountain of love which gushes out upon you." He praised Mary as his "ministering angel" and nicknamed her his "Jessamina" for the blossom that, in the Victorian language of flowers, denoted amia-bility. "My first-born, my beloved," he called Nat, using the language of the Bible. "When I come in he kisses me," wrote Willy in his diary, a week before his father's death, "and when I go away he kisses me again." [59]

The fifteenth of March was the last full day of Bowditch's life. For the first time he was unable to get out of bed. When Mary brought him a jessamine flower, he asked her to "put it in front of Laplace & tomorrow if I'm alive let me see it." In the middle of the night Henry told Bowditch that it was time. Soon all six children were there. Even now in search of mathematical order, he arranged them around his bed in order of their birth. He addressed each by name—Willy he called his "little mopstick"—and gave each his blessing, and they kissed his hand. "Now lettest thou thy servant depart in peace," he said "for mine eyes have seen thy salvation." It would have been the perfect death had it come at that moment, but there was more to come: three hours of terrible suffering. "Henry dear," he said a half hour before he died, hands clenched in pain. After he was gone, the children gathered and kissed their father one last time. There was a smile upon his face.[60]

Bowditch's death was a public event. Among those institutions passing resolutions "appropriate to the occasion" were the City of Salem, the East India Marine Society, the Salem Marine Society, the Salem Athenaeum, the American Academy, Harvard, the Boston Athenaeum, the Life Office, the Boston Marine Society, and the Shipmasters, Supercargoes, Officers, and Seamen of Boston. Even Yale's faculty joined in. The Reverend Alexander Young, John Pickering, and Daniel White composed eulogies cum biographical sketches that soon went into print. Meanwhile, the news spread through the nation's newspapers, from Belfast, Maine, to Charleston, South Carolina. In Salem, Boston, and Baltimore, vessels flew their colors at half mast, as did much of the shipping in the Russian port of Kronstadt. In Norfolk, Virginia, the navy's midshipmen wore black armbands for thirty days.[61]

It was the Bowditch children who understood what their father would have found to be the most meaningful memorial. Though Henry and Olivia now headed the household at 8 Otis Place, the siblings decided to grant free access to their father's scientific library of scientific works. "It was very perfect to the time of his death," the sons wrote of the collection, and "one of *the* best, if not actually the best of the kind" in the United States. As a physical space, the library held memories the children hoped to hold for all time, and they were reluctant to break the spell. It "will remain as it was left by our father," Nat wrote of the room. His chair, the desk as he last worked at it, the table where he gathered with family and friends "will all long remain undisturbed." But aware of their father's engagement with research, the children understood that a static collection would pay imperfect homage to him. They wrote to Bowditch's correspondents overseas, asking them to help them keep pace with the rapid "progress of science" by donating the many works "constantly published in Europe."[62] Bowditch's presence was there in the ever-growing collection, far more than in the room frozen in time.

CHAPTER TEN

Final Reckonings

As Bowditch lay dying he made one thing perfectly clear: he did not want to be eulogized. "I do not wish to have Mr. Bowditch's feelings & views held up to people who know & care nothing about him," he told his daughter. "I do not want to be set up as a show like a wild animal at sixpence a sight."[1] He must have known his wish would not be granted, for in his day he was a famous man. He could probably have guessed how his contemporaries would remember him; he knew the kinds of stories elite Bostonians liked to tell about themselves and what they wanted others to hear. To some extent he had participated in creating those story lines, even where, as in the story of Bowditch as a self-made man, the narrative was most at odds with reality. Within the space of a few decades, though, his life story was out of both his hands and those of his contemporaries. Entire aspects of his earthly career, including the ones in which he took the most pride, disappeared from the biographical record, and his biography narrowed to an inspirational tale aimed largely at juvenile audiences. Yet it is precisely where Bowditch is least remembered—as a man of science and of practical affairs—that he exerted the most transformative and enduring influence on American life.

Soon after his death those closest to Bowditch published eulogies and memoirs that documented his careers in business, science, and public affairs and described him at work and in the company of family and friends. In presenting so comprehensive a portrait, they were praising his character as epitomizing their ideal of the balanced self. Bowditch, reflected the Reverend Alexander Young in a eulogy titled *The Varieties of Human Greatness*, engaged in both "the higher pursuits of intellectual culture" and "the practical details of common life," blending "contemplation" with "action" to "make up the full, complete man." He was also ever the warm family man and companion. "Follow him to his fireside, or into the social circle" exclaimed his friend Daniel White, and "you would see nothing to remind you of the profound philosopher, or the grave man of business."[2]

There was a second narrative of Bowditch's life, the story of what Young termed the "self-taught and self-made man." We first see a hint of it in 1818, when William Bentley classed Bowditch with Benjamin Franklin as "a happy instance of well directed ambition," noting that the Salem boy had lacked "the means for a public education," that is, the ability to go to Harvard. The narrative soon gained steam and laid ever greater emphasis on the obstacles Bowditch had overcome through his own efforts. By 1823 Joseph Story was insisting that without the "means to avail himself of an education" Bowditch "had been obliged to depend upon his own personal exertions." When Bowditch published his first volume of Laplace the American press celebrated the event in a much reprinted article titled "A Self-Made Man." By the time of his death the emplotment of Bowditch's life as an up-by-the-bootstraps story was firmly in place.[3]

Bowditch was undoubtedly self-taught, but he was not self-made. Though Story might claim his friend had lacked the "patronage of powerful friends," the *Salem Gazette* was more accurate when it alluded to "the privilege of a respectable ancestry."[4] The young Bowditch's connections made him a fit candidate for sponsored mobility, affording him opportunities, from access to the Philosophical Library to a clerkship on a Derby vessel, which would otherwise not have existed. Merit mattered, of course. Had Bentley not been impressed by the youth's mathematical talents, had Derby not heard good reports of the boy's work, they would not have assisted Bowditch, but nor would they have lent this kind of aid to a boy from a less than respectable family.

No one could have known this better than Bowditch himself, yet he related this version of his life story to his children. Nat, who had taken down his father's oral history, described his father as "the son of a poor mechanic, with no expectations from family or friends," whose "energy of purpose" allowed him to "surmount all obstacles."[5] It would seem as if at some point Bowditch himself had come to see himself from this perspective. If so, he was only reinterpreting his life in the terms of the day. The antebellum era's culture hero was the self-made man, a model championed by a burgeoning middle class. As a formula for success it touted industry, thrift, and sobriety, values that made for productive workers in a developing economy while offering answers to the anxieties and temptations of a rapidly changing society. The pace of economic growth was dizzying, political life was raucous, and America's expanding cities teemed with saloons, gambling dens, and brothels, but as long as boys subscribed to the virtues of the self-made man, the threats of materialism, corrupt ambition, and sin would be turned aside. By the time Bowditch moved to Boston there was no escaping this narrative.

He may also have been drawn to this account of his life as a way to contend with how members of his social set evaluated him. Much as Bowditch was lauded by the Salem and Boston elites, he was also intermittently subjected to social disdain. The issue was not that his father had been a cooper. The

Reverend John Prince was also the son of an artisan. It was the lack of a collegiate education that was the problem. In fact, Bowditch had attained a much higher level of intellectual accomplishment than the Harvard graduates of his acquaintance, but scholarly sophistication could not compensate for what others thought was imparted by a classical education—social polish, refinement, delicacy. That left him open to being classified as a rough-and-ready sea captain like his first father-in-law, Francis Boardman, or a parvenu merchant like Ebenezer Francis. The self-made narrative did not refute this image of Bowditch as a "Salem sailor," but it did offer a different standard of achievement and identity.

It was only in private that elite Bostonians equated the self-made man with the boorish arriviste. Publicly they celebrated the self-made man, as in their eulogies to Bowditch, because they could not ignore the increasing power of the middle class. If that class did not own the factories and run the banks, it did set the cultural agenda of the nation through its sermons and schoolbooks. The families that would soon be titled "the Brahmin caste of New England" therefore found reason to stress their own "self-made" origins, even if doing so was a stretch. By claiming Bowditch as their own, elite Bostonians established their bona fides in a republican nation. His life story showed that theirs was a class based on merit and open to merit. It was also a class, they hastened to add, that for all its wealth was unselfishly devoted to the public welfare and therefore deserving of their place in society. Bowditch's eulogists therefore represented him as a scientific genius who had harnessed his talents in service of the practical needs of his brother sailors. Not only had the *Navigator's* accurate tables saved lives, but the instruction it offered allowed men of the sea to rise in the nautical world.[6]

In the decades after Bowditch's death the themes of the self-made man and benefactor of humankind resonated powerfully in American popular culture. Along with Benjamin Franklin, Bowditch was a staple of collective juvenile biographies with titles like *Lives of Benefactors; Famous Boys; and How They Became Great Men; Biography of Self-Taught Men*; and *Uncrowned Kings, or, Sketches of Some Men of Mark Who Rose from Obscurity to Renown.* Such books provided models of self-development for middle-class youths, but Bowditch's story held even broader appeal. His life was featured in *Biographical Sketches of Distinguished Mechanics*, while the *Colored American* hoped to inspire its readers with a "sketch of the early struggles of the boy BOWDITCH with the disadvantages of fortune."[7]

Increasingly, the story of the methodical man of business, the brilliant translator of Laplace, the public citizen, and the family man yielded to a

Robert Ball Hughes (1806–1868), statue of Nathaniel Bowditch, 1847. "The Bronze Statue," a poem of 1847, depicted Bowditch as a "brother of the toiling poor" and a "man of uses," while the statue itself portrays him as a navigator, not a mathematician or businessman. Mount Auburn Cemetery, Cambridge, Mass. Author's photograph.

narrow portrait of the poor boy who gave the world the "seaman's Bible." Henry's 1841 *Memoir of Nathaniel Bowditch, Prepared for the Young* gave about equal time to the pre- and post-*Navigator* years. In 1870 it was republished as *Nat the Navigator*. Or compare the 1835 portrait by Charles Osgood of the elderly scientist in his library, *Mécanique Céleste* on the table before him and bust of Laplace on the mantle (see cover illustration), with the statue erected above Bowditch's grave in 1847, which depicts Bowditch in the breeches and stockings of his Salem days, an unidentified book balanced on his knee and a globe and sextant at his feet.[8] By the twentieth century many accounts of Bowditch's life were not only incomplete but inaccurate. Now Bowditch became the inventor of the lunar method of navigation. "For the first time in history men could accurately establish positions east or west of the prime meridian," read one popular biographical article. There is an asterisk—maybe all the other reliable lunar methods available before Bowditch's?—but no, it only informs the reader of the existence of chronometers.[9]

The self-made man, the scientific sailor, and the boy who never grows old came together in 1955 in a juvenile biography titled *Carry On, Mr. Bowditch*. It won the prestigious Newbery Medal for children's literature, assuring it a place on librarians' lists of recommended works and a shot at immortality. At least as influential in keeping the book alive is the Christian home-schooling movement. The evangelical organization Focus on the Family recommends the book for its themes of hard work, persistence, and self-improvement and points out its Christian content. ("Nat learns several languages, including Latin, Spanish and French, by using the Bible [and specifically, the first chapter of John] as a translation tool.") A Christian study guide asks students, "What helped Nat persevere through the difficult times of his indenture?," with the answer key providing Bible verses on themes of trust and reliance on God.[10]

Imagine what Bowditch's reaction would be to all this. As a Unitarian resistant to evangelical Protestantism, he would have bristled at the way his life has become an object lesson for evangelical values. As a man dedicated to telling the truth, even to the point of tactlessness, he would have been horrified to see himself set up as having invented the lunar method of navigation. As a Laplacean intent on introducing system and regularity into the Life Office, he would have regretted the amnesia surrounding his business career. And he would surely have been distressed by the almost exclusive focus on his *Navigator*. What about his Laplace?

Today's historians of science recommend Bowditch's volumes as the best way to approach the *Céleste Mécanique*, but Bowditch remains a footnote in their discussions of scientific research in his era. To the extent they have addressed his work, it has been to illustrate how difficult it was to become a professional scientist in early America, or to point to Bowditch as opening a door through which his successors "might enter into full participation" in the scientific enterprise.[11] If he had little chance to be remembered as a mathematician, it was both because Laplacean science soon became outdated and because everything about the practice of science was changing. The Republic of Letters may have accommodated a self-trained mathematician like Bowditch, but that regime of scientific endeavor was disappearing. The new world of university laboratories, advanced research facilities, and specialized professional journals had little room for amateurs and their efforts at observing and collecting, and even translating and annotating. To achieve lasting renown a man of science had to make original discoveries, especially now that the romantic cult of genius required sudden inspiration followed by a grand idea.[12]

Ironically, our memory of Bowditch's influence on practical affairs is lost not because his innovations were soon made obsolete but because they became the norm. Filling out forms, classifying and filing documents, separating business from personal records, meeting rigid deadlines—these are so much a part of our existence that we hardly understand they have a history. We take for granted that much of what we call modern life consists of dealings with impersonal institutions. Precisely where his impact was the greatest, Bowditch is a historical cypher. But in a final reckoning of his life we need to number him among those who transformed our world.

For in the 1820s and 1830s it would have been impossible to be a patrician in Boston's world of interlocking institutions and not be aware of Bowditch's clockwork mechanisms or to absorb their logic and practices as advantageous, ultimately a matter of simple common sense. The novelty and ideological utility of these innovations generated considerable publicity. The annual reports of the Life Office's Board of Control provided stockholders and investors—everyone who was anyone in the Boston business establishment—with the details of how these mechanisms functioned. Even ordinary Bostonians could read those reports in the local newspaper. Nat Bowditch's biographical memoir piled on anecdote after anecdote exemplifying his father's rigid adherence to business procedures and reported the minutiae of Life Office clerical work as worthy of perpetual memory. Anyone connected with Harvard—and who in that elite was not?—knew that Bowditch's clockwork approach had effected a permanent reform of Harvard's administrative conduct. "Great as were his [Bowditch's] literary and scientific attainments," wrote Josiah Quincy, "the influence he exercised in Boston and its vicinity" was far more a matter of "his disinterestedness, his independence of spirit," and his devotion to "order, method, punctuality, and exactness." That influence was broad and deep. "Almost every important literary and charitable institution of which he was a member contains durable monuments of his efficiency and fidelity" to those "cardinal virtues," wrote Quincy.[13]

Much work remains to be done on the precise vectors of Bowditch's influence, but we can detect the outlines of at least some of them. The burgeoning financial sector is one such vector. In Boston Bowditch's mathematically talented son Ingersoll assumed the helm of the American Insurance Company in 1835. Moses Hale, Bowditch's able secretary, retained his Life Office position for decades after Bowditch's death, providing a continuity of procedural expertise. "A more careful, methodical, upright, and conscientious business man never stood in State Street," it was said of him.

No doubt Hale brought his systematic ways to his work as manager of the Massachusetts Sabbath School Society, treasurer and vice president of the Boston City Missionary Society, and auditor of the Academy of Music and the American Board of Commissioners for Foreign Missions. Intriguingly, two of Hale's brothers played major roles in several insurance companies in Boston and New York.[14] We know for certain that, when investors set about establishing the New York Life Insurance and Trust Company in 1829, they began by requesting information from "Dr. Bowditch," a man as "highly distinguished" for his business acumen as for his "deep scientific attainments." The "simplicity of arrangement in the business of his office," read the letter appended to a bill for a corporate charter, "merit every commendation." And appended to this letter was that year's Board of Control report, detailing the Life Office's "strict and minute" clerical practices and operating procedures.[15]

Another direction of influence ran through Harvard. As we have seen, under President Quincy reforms proceeded apace, complete with methodical record keeping, monthly financial statements, and a numerical Scale of Comparative Merit. But in the long run it may have been Bowditch's impact on the library that had the most effect. Already as a Harvard overseer Bowditch had taken a particular interest in the library, and once he became a fellow of the Harvard Corporation he took the lead on library affairs. It was Bowditch, we have seen, who pushed librarian Benjamin Peirce to produce a new catalog and who led the drive for shelf-correlated call numbers and systematic paperwork. When Peirce died in 1831 he was replaced by the "methodical and accurate" entomologist William Thaddeus Harris, whom Bowditch knew as a fellow member of Boston's American Academy of Arts and Sciences. From that date the library's borrowing records are indexed in an alphabetically tabbed volume reminiscent of Bowditch's scientific commonplace book. In the early 1830s Harris produced catalogs of insects compiled "upon uniform pieces of paper, three or four inches square, which he afterwards tied in bundles, and carefully labelled," procedures reminiscent of those at the Life Office. He cataloged the Harvard library in the same manner, thereby producing one of the earliest card (as opposed to printed and bound) catalogs in America.[16] After midcentury, Harris's techniques were taken up by American library professionals. By the end of the century governments and businesses appropriated them from the library world, so we can draw a direct line from the modern file cabinet back to Harris's catalogs and Bowditch's cataloging impulses.[17]

IN THE EARLY twenty-first century many historians have focused on precisely the kinds of banal procedures and bureaucratic policies we associate with Bowditch as essential to the transformation of capitalism in the nineteenth century. Their work is less concerned with the displacement of artisans and exploitation of industrial workers than with the daily duties and emotional travails of clerks. These scholars examine processes of financialization and commodification, whereby the assignment of value migrates from real things to bits of paper. Instead of a world of farm, factory, and trading vessel, yielding wheat, cloth, and pepper, we have mortgage documents, stock certificates, insurance policies, bookkeeping ledgers, and, yes, blank forms. Even the power of slavery is said to lie not just in the lash but also in the account book. It is "a flatland of ordinary material practices" that interests such historians, comments Jean-Christophe Agnew, practices "that habituated Americans to the new, systemic rules of capitalism as a market form of life and that did so in ways of which most Americans at the time were only dimly and bemusedly aware." Noting that this approach seems to omit the "*action* of capitalism" and, implicitly, its actors, Agnew titles his essay "Anonymous History."[18] But there *were* actors in this transformation, of course, and they were not nameless. One of them was surely Nathaniel Bowditch. What does his life add to our understanding of this process of transformation?

First, it points to the role of the quantitative sciences in shaping the ways capitalist institutions operated and legitimated their operations. Bowditch's perspective as an Enlightenment astronomer and mathematician was anything but incidental to his approach to practical affairs. Its influence went beyond the broad-brush Enlightenment parallel drawn between the self-regulating solar system and the self-regulating market to something more specific, a vision of institutions, business and nonbusiness alike, as Laplacean mechanisms. Unlike the abstraction of Adam Smith's economy ruled by an invisible hand, the Laplacean corporation was a concrete model that could be implemented by a man like Bowditch. And so he did, instituting paperwork procedures and institutional policies to guarantee that his corporations—whether the Life Office or Harvard—would function with precision and regularity. Critically, Bowditch was not entirely exceptional in his mathematical approach to practical affairs. There were others like him in this era. They made up a small but nonetheless recognizably coherent cohort of mathematician-administrators. Their existence suggests that the transformational influence of the quantitative sciences ran broader and deeper than we have recognized.

Historian of science William J. Ashworth has drawn our attention to just such a group of "business astronomers" active in England in the 1820s and 1830s. Stockbroker Francis Baily sought to produce more accurate annuity and astronomical tables alike, while mathematician Charles Babbage served as actuary of the Protector Life Assurance Society of London. (Recall that both corresponded with Bowditch and made Henry's acquaintance in London.) In what Ashworth terms "the reciprocal relationship of accountancy and astronomy," these men drew on the values and practices of Regency-era astronomy—vigilance, calculation, precision, and the "disciplined numerical technique[s]" of meticulous data collection and record keeping—to reform the British scientific establishment, as well as to order the world of financial management and factory production. "Inspired by the French analytical system of institutional administration," writes Ashworth, "the business astronomers saw calculation and analysis as a set of value-free technocratic techniques, in which, natural, moral and economic philosophy could be founded on a mathematically based system."[19]

In America such hybrid characters are far more obscure. A number combined science with the practical work of systematizing Harvard's library. We have just met the entomologist-librarian William Thaddeus Harris, and earlier the mathematical practitioner and collections cataloger William Croswell, and his successor, mineralogist-librarian Joseph Green Cogswell. We should also include the physician and naturalist Seth Bass, who systematized collections under Bowditch at the East India Marine Society, the Boston Athenaeum, and the American Academy.[20] Outside of Boston, other hybrids can be found in insurance circles: actuary James Renwick, Bowditch's contact in New York, subsequently professor of natural philosophy at Columbia, and one of the few Americans to whom Bowditch sent his *Mécanique Céleste*; Robert M. Patterson, M.D., Bowditch's insurance contact in Philadelphia, a member of the American Philosophical Society (APS), and a professor of natural philosophy and mathematics at the University of Pennsylvania; and Eugenius Nulty, another Philadelphia actuary, mathematics professor, APS member, and *Mécanique Céleste* recipient, honored in 1832 with membership in Bowditch's American Academy. Bowditch was in touch with a third Philadelphia actuary, Joseph Roberts Jr., an APS member who left behind a portrait in which he is shown with a telescope, celestial globe, and a volume of Bowditch's Laplace.[21] Just how these men conducted business is a subject for future research, but we know that none made use of actuarial mathematics in their work. As with Bowditch, the links between science and business were conceptual and procedural, not substantive.

Those links are far more clear when we look at a government enterprise run by another such hybrid character, Colonel George Bomford, a member of West Point's U.S. Military Philosophical Society and the supervisor of the United States Army's ordnance production and storage facilities. Like Bowditch, Bomford drew inspiration from French Enlightenment mathematics, not Laplace's *Mécanique Céleste* but Louis de Tousard's *American Artillerist's Companion*, which called for "a system of uniformity and regularity" in arms manufacture. The interchangeable part was therefore to Bomford what the blank form was to Bowditch, a guarantor of just such uniformity and regularity. But since, like Bowditch, he conceptualized the institution he ran as *itself* a mechanism, he made liberal use of blank forms as well. His 1834 *Regulations for the Government of the Ordnance Department* included no fewer than fifty-eight of them, dedicated to accounting and manufacturing alike, along with an entire chapter enumerating Bowditch-like instructions for folding and bundling documents. And just as the Massachusetts Hospital Life Insurance Company invoked the image of the mathematician-administered "great machine" to represent the even-handedness of it operations, so too did Bomford. When the replacement of the Harpers Ferry armory's civilian supervisor with an army appointee sparked fears of a military dictatorship, Bomford replied that impartiality would be ensured by bureaucratic impersonality. "The authority of the officer is not more extensive or despotic than that of the citizen," he stated. "Both are equally bound by the laws and regulations provided for the government of the armories."[22]

Early nineteenth-century armory operations have long been on historians' radar screens, and not just for the technological advances they forwarded. Alfred Chandler remarked that the officers in charge of armory operations in this era "had an awareness of organizational and bureaucratic procedures that was still totally foreign to the American merchants," while Richard R. John has pointed to armories as evidence of the critical role of state institutions in instigating economic change.[23] The parallels between Bowditch and Bomford invite us to shift our focus away from the public versus private sector issue to what these innovators held in common: a mathematical background and worldview. Quantitative science underpinned the conceptualization of institutions in general as impersonal mechanisms. We therefore need to decouple our analytical exploration of the origins of these mechanisms from both the state and the business corporation.

Many historians examining the development of bureaucratic machinery in Europe have focused on the state, with paperwork procedures and numerical data emerging as technologies of government surveillance and control. The similarities with what Bowditch was up to at the Life Office suggest that the state may not have been the prime, or at least the sole, mover in the emergence of impersonal bureaucracies. In 1831, for example, a House of Commons report recommended the British government imitate "the French system" to create "harmony and order" and to enforce "uniformity" in all public accounts. That system called for double-entry bookkeeping, such "as the best regulated commercial establishment offers of its own trans-actions," as well as liberal use of printed blank forms, "since it is only by the presentation of Tables, resembling one another, and in fact emanating all from a common original model, that the completeness and efficiency of the machine can be shown." Here we see the influence of both mercantile practice and French Enlightenment philosophy and science, just as we did at the Life Office, but now in reforming a state bureaucracy.[24]

Just as we should not focus solely on the state, neither should we focus solely on the business corporation. Though the public-private divide was a real one in antebellum America, a man like Bowditch did not approach his work with an eye to this boundary. As a Laplacean scientist he brought his methodizing ways to every institution he ran, the Life Office to be sure but also the East India Marine Society, Harvard University, and the Boston Athenaeum. If a scientific perspective was as relevant to Bowditch's work at a gentlemen's library as at a financial corporation, does this mean that it was ultimately not a force in shaping nineteenth-century capitalism? Hardly. Bowditch's life underscores a second point, namely, that if we are to under-stand the ways in which capitalist elites exerted and experienced their power, we should look for new perspectives on their entire range of enterprises.

Bowditch played a major role in two kinds of institutions that contrib-uted to the strength, reach, and longevity of elite influence: the trust and the corporation. Though ostensibly private, both relied on the apparatus of the state—the legislature and the courts—for their creation and contin-uing operation. Both could be used to maintain and generate wealth, plain and simple, as in the cases of the Forrester trust, the Essex Fire and Marine Insurance Company, the trust accounts of the Massachusetts Hospital Life Insurance Company (MHL), and MHL itself. But trusts and corporations could also be used to generate a soft power for these same capitalist elites. In endowing Salem's First Church, the Orne trust established that family's commitment to public piety and morals. The charitable, cultural, and educational corporations established by the Salem and Boston elites cast them as civic-minded benefactors and polished gentlemen, countering the association of wealth with single-minded wealth seeking. Bowditch's dual life as a businessman and a scientist made the same point. Life Office affairs kept this mathematician's head out of the clouds so he could benefit humankind, while his pursuit of Laplacean science proved he valued undertakings that brought no pecuniary rewards and in fact demanded pecuniary sacrifice.

If this panoply of corporations provided the means to exert power, they also constituted a seamless world of opportunity and experience for the powerful. Consider, for example, the Massachusetts General Hospital. Raising funds for the hospital gave Bowditch a simultaneous entrée into Boston philanthropy and business even before his move to the capital. The hospital's prime mover, Ebenezer Francis, would be the individual above all others responsible for luring Bowditch to the Life Office, a corporation spawned by the hospital. The two soon worked together as fellows of the Harvard Corporation. Meanwhile, MHL was providing employment for Bowditch's eldest son, though once he married Francis's daughter, Nat Bowditch could devote much of his energy elsewhere. Elsewhere proved to be the Massachusetts General Hospital. This was, of course, the same corporation that provided Henry Bowditch with his medical training. For the elite men of Boston—but not the city's elite women—much of life took place in this corporate environment: the Harvard college campus, the insurance and bank office, the Athenaeum library, the charitable or cultural organization meeting room, the church.[25] Even when men engaged in private socializing, as at George Ticknor's literary soirees, it was with men known to them in multiple corporate contexts. And when they died, many were buried in the Mount Auburn Cemetery, incorporated in 1835.

Finally, Bowditch's life warns us against casting the narrative of capitalist transformation as a straightforward transition from a personal to an impersonal world. The temptation is certainly there, especially given Bowditch's strenuous efforts to make every institution he ever encountered into a Laplacean mechanism and the MHL's endorsement of the vision of a "great machine." But there are problems with this schema. First, even the personal world of Salem commerce had elements of, if not impersonality, then certainly unfamiliarity. True, at home Bowditch and his fellow merchants were used to dealing with a well-known cast of characters, according to notably flexible, informal, often individualized rules of business conduct. But once they rounded the Cape of Good Hope they were forced to engage in trade with unknowns. Dealings might be face-to-face, but the faces were those of strangers. When we characterize life in postrevolutionary port cities as personal, we leave out a key aspect of port dwellers' experience, the toggling back and forth between the exhaustively known and the utterly unknown, social claustrophobia and cultural disorientation.

We need to attach even more caveats to the idea that, as it developed over the nineteenth century, capitalism created a newly impersonal world. Our skepticism should not be taken too far. Bowditch's use of standardized data-gathering and classification systems, his strict segregation of personal from corporate paperwork, his insistence on contractually stipulated due dates and rigid adherence to company procedures—all these took as their watchword the impersonal operation of practical affairs. Berkshire County farmers certainly felt the sting of an impersonal bureaucracy. But in dealings with elite Bostonians impersonal procedures and policies were more rhetoric than reality, though not the less powerful and useful for it. Yes, Bowditch chased stockholder Benjamin Guild to his seashore hotel to inform him of a late payment, but Guild would only need to pay compound interest on his debt, an option the Life Office's rural debtors were never offered. The true value of refusing to accept a wealthy man's check until he backed it with a deposit was in telling that story very publicly, as Nat Bowditch did. Then MHL operations could be touted as impartial, precisely what one would expect when a man of numbers was running them. Representations of impartiality reassured those who deposited their wealth in trust accounts that company operations would not favor the interests of one beneficiary over another. More important, they conveyed the politically potent message that the company treated rich and poor alike.

Meanwhile, the world of Boston capitalists continued to operate as a highly personal world. The MHL stockholders, directors, borrowers, and depositors were often one and the same. Loans were made to members of this stratum with only the flimsiest of excuses for collateral. The company violated the terms of its corporate charter—Laplacean Bowditch *broke the law*—when it accepted manufacturing stock as security for loans. When the Panic of 1837 hit, Bowditch granted some elite borrowers the favor of terminating their loans early so they could regain access to their collateral. Still, the company lauded its actuary for overseeing a "great machine."

In one critical way, though, this personal world had changed. It now constituted a horizontal stratum of privilege rather than a more generalized mode of social relations. When Bowditch was a young man Salemites of greater means and higher status regularly favored those beneath them as customers, employers, and patrons. Sometimes they did so in recognition of their social inferiors' deference and loyalty; at other times, especially if they were sponsoring mobility, it was because of connections of kinship and friendship. Always it was in the context of a community in which their dominance was an accepted fact of life. By the antebellum era elite Bostonians reserved their favor for members of their own class. Others did not belong to their community; they might even be a threat to it. If the teenage Nathaniel had advanced with the help of his superiors, his sons advanced with the assistance—apprenticeship in a law office, clerkship in a counting house, investment in a cargo, training in a hospital, marriage into a family— provided by older members of their social set. As favor morphed into privilege, an intimate network of social and economic relations did not yield to an impersonal world of clockwork corporations so much as it was incorporated into the new mechanisms' workings.

When he first introduced them, Bowditch's clockwork corporations were novel. It took his social equals time to get used to the values of system, precision, uniformity, and regularity they represented. Shipmasters proved reluctant to fill out printed logbooks. Elite Bostonians took exception to following strict bookkeeping procedures. Harvard administrators resented being elbowed out for their less than businesslike handling of college affairs. But they soon embraced these institutions, recognizing the advantages of associating themselves with mechanisms represented as impartial in their operations and productive of economic stability and social harmony.

The ordinary people of Massachusetts saw things differently. When Jacksonian newspaperman Abel Cushing identified the Life Office as a "beast of prey," devouring the farmers' lands, he summoned an age-old metaphor of overt aggression. But recognizing the novelty and subtlety of the means by which this corporation exerted control, he soon moved from the language of blood and soil to the language of paper, warning that the Life Office would use its corporate "charter privileges" to "carry on the farming business."[26] Though Cushing did not grasp MHL's true aims, his dim awareness of the new direction to American life it heralded may have been greater than our own, steeped as we are in its values and practices. The Laplacean vision continues to suffuse our world with the power of numbers.

Notes

Abbreviations

PROPER NAMES

AAAS	American Academy of Arts and Sciences
APS	American Philosophical Society
CP	Caroline Plummer
EBIBD	Eliza Boardman Ingersoll Bowditch Dixwell
EE	Edward Everett
EIMS	East India Marine Society
EO/EOW/EOWW	Eliza Orne/Eliza Orne Wetmore/Eliza Orne Wetmore White
HIB	Henry Ingersoll Bowditch
JI	Jonathan Ingersoll
JIB	Jonathan Ingersoll Bowditch
NB	Nathaniel Bowditch
MGH	Massachusetts General Hospital
MHL	Massachusetts Hospital Life Insurance Company
MI/MIB	Mary Ingersoll Bowditch (b. 1781)
MIB2	Mary Ingersoll Bowditch Dixwell (b. 1816)
NIB	Nathaniel Ingersoll Bowditch
TJ	Thomas Jefferson
WIB	William Ingersoll Bowditch

PERIODICALS

BDA	*Boston Daily Advertiser*
CC	*Boston Columbian Centinel*
CorrAst	*Correspondance Astronomique, Géographique, Hydrographique et Statistique du Baron de Zach*
EG	*Salem Essex Gazette*
ER	*Salem Essex Register*
MAAAS	*Memoirs of the American Academy of Arts and Sciences*
NAR	*North American Review*
NH	*Newburyport Herald*
SG	*Salem Gazette*
SIR	*Salem Impartial Register*
SR	*Salem Register*

ARCHIVES

BPL	Boston Public Library
HUA	Harvard University Archives
MHS	Massachusetts Historical Society
PEM	Phillips Library, Peabody Essex Museum

ARCHIVAL COLLECTIONS

BF-PEM	Bowditch Family Papers, 1726–1942, 1961, 1975, undated, PEM
EE Papers	Edward Everett Papers, 1675–1910, MHS
EFMR	Essex Fire and Marine Insurance Company Records, 1776–1887, PEM
EIMSR	East India Marine Society Records, 1799–1972, PEM
HIB Papers, Countway	Papers of Henry Ingersoll Bowditch, 1827–88, Francis A. Countway Library of Medicine, Harvard Medical School
HIB Papers, MHS	Henry Ingersoll Bowditch Papers, 1822–1903, MHS
MHLC	Massachusetts Hospital Life Insurance Company Collection, Baker Library, Harvard Business School
MIB Papers	Mary Ingersoll Bowditch Papers, 1779–1887, MHS
NBC	Nathaniel Bowditch Collection, BPL
NBLW	Nathaniel Bowditch's Life and Works, 1939–56, PEM

Introduction

1. TJ to NB, 2 May 1815, Ms.E.210.19 v.1 (29), NBC; James Madison to NB, 16 May 1818, Stagg, *Papers of James Madison*; *Baltimore Patriot*, 27 Sept. 1823; *SG*, 20 Mar. 1838; Quincy, *History of Harvard*, 2: 438; "Sullivan's Island," 13.

2. NB, "College History," 56 [quotation], UA 120.828.9, HUA.

3. Pickering, *Eulogy*, 12. Updated and revised editions of the *Navigator* continued to be published during Bowditch's lifetime and after, even after 1868, when the U.S. government took over the copyright. The most recent edition, published in 2013 with Bowditch's name on the cover, differs entirely in content.

4. For an entrée into the new literature on capitalism, see Zakim and Kornblith, *Capitalism Takes Command*. On these particular practices, see Rosenthal, "From Memory to Mastery," chaps. 1, 2; Lauer, "From Rumor to Written Record"; and Levy, *Freaks of Fortune*, chap. 5. Much of the literature on the bureaucratic state focuses on Europe, often influenced by Michel Foucault's understanding of the technologies of knowledge and power. See, e.g., Hacking, "Biopower and the Avalanche of Printed Numbers"; Caplan and Torpey, *Documenting Individual Identity*; and Dandeker, *Surveillance, Power and Modernity*. Historians addressing these issues as they relate to the American state in the early nineteenth century often introduce alternative or additional analytical frameworks. See, e.g., Cohen, *Calculating People*, 150–226; and Robertson, *Passport in America*. Earlier, important treatments of bureaucracy

include those by business historian Alfred Chandler, who focused on technological imperatives, large-scale enterprises, and the era between 1840 and 1920; and by Max Weber, who characterized the legal-administrative authority of bureaucracy, with its impartially executed rules, as the form compatible with rationalized capitalism. See Chandler, *Visible Hand*; and Weber, *Economy and Society*, 3: 956–1005.

5. [William Bentley], *ER*, 29 Apr. 1818 [italics mine]; White, *Nathaniel Bowditch*, 57; Benjamin Waterhouse to NB, 19 Oct. 1833, H MS c16.1, Harvard Medical Library, HIB Papers, Countway.

6. White, *Nathaniel Bowditch*, 57; Young, *Nathaniel Bowditch*, 79n; NIB, "Memoir," 164.

Chapter 1

1. *EG*, 30 Mar. 1773.

2. Vickers, *Young Men and the Sea*, 61–77.

3. Bentley, *Diary*, 18 June 1792, 29 Dec. 1790; *Elephant . . . Salem, August 29, 1797*.

4. Hunter, *Purchasing Identity*, 117–18; Johnston, "Global Knowledge in the Early Republic"; Johnston, "Depicting Geographic Knowledge"; Vickers, *Young Men and the Sea*, 77–80, 128–29. On the Atlantic context of geographical knowledge, see Ogborn and Withers, "Travel, Trade, and Empire." On the place of scientific and mercantile communities in the development of cosmopolitanism, see Jacob, *Strangers Nowhere in the World*.

5. Tagney, *World Turned Upside Down*, 17, 19.

6. Ibid., 19; Felt, *Annals of Salem*, 2: 410–11.

7. William Pynchon to unknown correspondent, 16 Apr. 1775, in Pynchon, *Diary*, 42n; Diary of John Adams, 5 Nov. 1776, in Dow, *Two Centuries of Travel in Essex County*, 90. On class hierarchy in colonial America, see Wood, *Radicalism*, 11–56. For the Salem case, on land and sea, see Vickers, *Young Men and the Sea*, 86–94, 126–28, 221–24.

8. Wood, *Radicalism*, 57–77; Morris, "Redefining the Economic Elite"; Vickers, *Young Men and the Sea*, 77–80, 128–29, 132–36.

9. Habakkuk Bowditch: WIB, "Our Family Story from 1639 to 1838 told by William I. Bowditch 1896," MSS 3, ser. II, B6, 1: 54–69, BF-PEM; *Early Coastwise and Foreign Shipping*, 180. Nathaniel Ingersoll and family: Avery, *Ingersoll Family*, 4, 8, 16, 26; Perley, *History of Salem*, 1: 132; Phillips, *Salem in the Eighteenth Century*, 181, 190–91; Inventory of the Estate of Capt. Nathaniel Ingersoll, 6 Dec. 1773, B22, F3, BF-PEM [quotations].

10. Gardner/Bowditch connections: WIB, "Our Family Story," 21–35; Gardner, *Thomas Gardner*, 107, 111. John Turner and family: Goodwin, *Archaeology of Manners*, 68–80, 117–25, 131–34, 141–43; Moriarty, "Turner Family," 274–75; Inventory of the Estate of John Turner, 25 June 1743, B4, F9, BF-PEM; Vickers, *Young Men and the Sea*, 48–50; White, *Nathaniel Bowditch*, 68. On the ideal of refinement among America's colonial gentry, see Bushman, *Refinement of America*. See also Hunter, *Purchasing Identity*, chap. 4; and Phillips, *Salem in the Eighteenth Century*, 179–88, 253–57.

11. WIB, "Our Family Story," 36–53; [Bowditch], *Bowditch Family*, 5; land transfer and probate documents regarding Ebenezer Bowditch, B4, F7, BF-PEM.

12. For typical Salem voyages, see Vickers, *Young Men and the Sea*, 72–77, 287n; and Cary, "Sea Logs of Francis Boardman," 3–26. Just such peripatetic activity is documented in Habakkuk's voyages. For a 1770–71 example, see *Early Coastwise and Foreign Shipping*, 46, 180; *Georgia Gazette*, 7, 14 Feb. 1770; and *EG*, 28 Aug., 18 Dec. 1770, 9 July 1771. On mariners' wives, see Vickers, *Young Men and the Sea*, 145–49.

13. Marine Society at Salem, *Laws of the Marine Society*; Smith, "Salem Marine Society," 272–76; Jenkins, "Marine Society," 199–220. The gravestones can be found at Saint Peter's Church Cemetery, Salem [Nathaniel Ingersoll], and Burying Point Cemetery, Salem [Habakkuk Bowditch].

14. Smallpox: Clarfield, "Salem's Great Inoculation Controversy." Anti-imperial sentiment and activity in Salem and Essex County: John Adams to Elbridge Gerry, 14 Nov. 1772, in Cushing, *Writings of Samuel Adams*, 2: 209; Tagney, *World Turned Upside Down*, chaps. 3–15 [quotations, 91, 129]; Hoffer, *Prelude to Revolution*; Phillips, *Salem in the Eighteenth Century*, chaps. 23–27.

15. Edward Holyoke to Mary Vial Holyoke, 18, 20 June 1775, in Dow, *Holyoke Diaries*, 90n; Tagney, *World Turned Upside Down*, 194–96, 213–15; Vice Admiral Samuel Graves to Lieutenant Henry Mowat, 6 Oct. 1775, in Clark, *Naval Documents*, 2: 234, 236; Elizabeth Smith to Rev. Isaac Smith Jr., 28 Oct. 1775, in "Some Letters of 1775," 132. For similar accounts, see James Winthrop to John Adams, 21 June 1775, in Taylor, *Adams Papers Digital Edition*; "Extracts from . . . William Wetmore," 116; Love Rawlins Pickman to Benjamin Pickman, Apr. 1775, in Dow, *Diary and Letters of Benjamin Pickman*, 58–60; and "Extracts from . . . Deacon Joseph Seccombe," 115.

16. Pynchon, Diary, 28 April, 16 May 1777, in Pynchon, *Diary*, 29, 31; Tagney, *World Turned Upside Down*, 238–39, 336–37, 342–44.

17. [HIB], *Memoir*, 2, 7; Salem, Mass., Valuations and Directories, 1761–1850, microfilm 55, PEM [hereafter Salem Tax Records], records for 1779; Morris, "Social Change, Republican Rhetoric," 420. Danvers, originally known as Salem Village, was the site of Nathaniel Ingersoll's tavern, which played a role in the Salem witch trials. This Nathaniel Ingersoll (1632–1719) was Mary Ingersoll Bowditch's great-great-uncle [Avery, *Ingersoll Family*, 5].

18. [HIB], *Memoir*, 4–5 [quotation, 4]; HIB, *Sketch*, 6–7; Young, *Nathaniel Bowditch*, 20.

19. "Compilations by Mary Ingersoll Bowditch about her Father Nathaniel Bowditch," 15 Mar. 1838, B23, Wigglesworth Family Papers, 1682–1966, MHS; NIB, "Memoir," in NB, *Mécanique Céleste*, 14–15; Bentley, *Diary*, 5 Jan. 1800. All Bowditch's siblings succumbed to an early death, from accidents, drowning, death at sea (probably from disease), and tuberculosis [(Bowditch), *Bowditch Family*, 6; NIB, "Memoir," 14–16; *Vital Records of Salem*].

20. Young, *Nathaniel Bowditch*, 20–22 [quotations, 21, 22]. See also White, *Nathaniel Bowditch*, 8; and NIB, "Memoir," 13, 17–18.

21. NIB, "Memoir," 16–17. For other stories of poverty, see HIB, *Sketch*, 8; and [HIB], *Memoir*, 7.

22. [HIB], *Memoir*, 5–6; NIB, "Memoir," 12–14; St. Peter's Church Cemetery; *Vital Records of Salem*; Tagney, *World Turned Upside Down*, 256–57, 262. The children born after the demise of St. Peter's were baptized at the North Church in Salem [*Vital Records of Salem*].

23. Son William was born in May 1776, placing Habakkuk in Salem the previous summer. When precisely the capture occurred is not known, but American prisoners were held in Halifax from early 1776 [Bowman, *Captive Americans*, 8–9; "Records of the Vice-Admiralty Court at Halifax"].

24. Viscount Barrington to Lord George Germain, 5 Nov. 1778, quoted in Cogliano, *Maritime Prisoners*, 39; *Independent Chronicle*, 13 Feb. 1777, in Clark, *Naval Documents*, 7: 1187; *Independent Chronicle*, 5 Feb. 1778, in Clark, *Naval Documents*, 11: 288–91 [quotations, 288, 289, 290]; Blatchford, *Narrative of Remarkable Occurrences*, 3–5 [quotation, 3]; Allen, *Narrative*, 23–26 [quotation, 25]. On Revolutionary War POWs: Cogliano, *Maritime Prisoners*; Gilje, *Liberty on the Waterfront*, 116–27; Burrows, *Forgotten Patriots*; Knight, "Prisoner Exchange and Parole."

25. Committee of Correspondence, Inspection, and Safety of Salem to the Massachusetts General Court, 30 June 1777, in Clark, *Naval Documents*, 9: 189 [quotation]; Petition of Richard Valpey to the Council of the State of Massachusetts-Bay, 3 Oct. 1776, and Council of the State of Massachusetts-Bay, Response to Petitions of Ebenezer Porter, Richard Valpey, et al., 4 Oct. 1776, in Poole, *Annals of Yarmouth*, 9; "Resolve on the Petition of Samuel Tufts," 12 June 1777, in Ames, *Acts and Resolves*, 20: 23. The captain's grandmother was the sister of Mary's grandfather Ingersoll [Cutter, *Genealogical and Personal Memoirs*, 3: 1407; Avery, *Ingersoll Family*, 15–16].

26. Ingersoll privateering: Allen, *Massachusetts Privateers*, 76, 94, 117, 124, 161, 183–84, 193, 204, 223–25, 231, 260, 263, 271, 283–84, 298; Paine, *Ships and Sailors of Old Salem*, App. D, 671, 673, 674; "Auction Sales," 109, 115. The Salem Tax Records illustrate the wealth to be made in privateering, documenting, for example, Jonathan Ingersoll's rapid acquisition of real property, shares in vessels, and goods in the late 1770s.

27. "Auction Sales," 109, 119, 120; Allen, *Massachusetts Privateers*, 94; Habakkuk Bowditch, Salem Tax Records. The *Monmouth* was commanded by Samuel Ingersoll and owned mainly by Elias Hasket Derby, but also in part by Jonathan Ingersoll [Allen, *Massachusetts Privateers*, 223; JI, Salem Tax Records, 1779].

28. Morris, "Social Change, Republican Rhetoric"; Goodwin, *Archaeology of Manners*, 76–79; Avery, *Ingersoll Family*, 26; Ellery and Bowditch, *Pickering Genealogy*, 1: 44–45, 86–87, 171–73; Farber, *Guardians of Virtue*, 122–23.

29. Habakkuk Bowditch, Salem Tax Records; Mary Turner Bowditch, Will, 8 Feb. 1783; Habakkuk Bowditch, property transaction documents, 20 June, 1 Dec. 1785, 3 July 1787, B4, F8, BF-PEM; NIB, "Memoir," 12; Jenkins, "Marine Society," 220; Hab[k] Bowditch to Capt. Jon[a] Gardner, Esq., 11 Dec. 1790, in WIB, "Our Family Story," interleaved with p. 66; Estate inventory, List of Debts, Statement of Insolvency, 5 Feb. 1799, in B4, F8, BF-PEM; WIB, "Our Family Story," 54–58, 68–69. Descendant Harold Bowditch suggested another cause of decline when he argued that Ebenezer "is said to have borrowed and lost his [son's] savings," but the debt ran to only a little

over eleven pounds and was contracted during years when Habakkuk was an active shipmaster [(Bowditch), *Bowditch Family*, 6; WIB, "Our Family Story," 49–50].

30. NIB, "Memoir," 12, 14, 15; *Vital Records of Salem*; Bentley, *Diary*, 25 July 1798.

31. WIB, "Our Family Story," 62. See also NIB, "Memoir," 12.

32. NIB, "Memoir," 12; Bentley, *Record of the Parish List of Deaths*, 42.

33. Nathaniel's sons differed somewhat in their dating of their father's apprenticeship, but given his genealogical interests, and the fact that Bowditch related his life history to him, NIB's account is probably the most reliable [NIB, "Memoir," 19; Family Record in NIB's 1857 Bible, in Harold Bowditch, "A Collection of Data Made for the Possible Future Use of a Biographer," 1: 283, MH 42, NBLW; [HIB], *Memoir*, 10; WIB, "Our Family Story," 74]. See also White, *Nathaniel Bowditch*, 10; D. A. White to Nathan Reed [*sic*], 8 May 1838, and Nathan Read to D. A. White, 16 May 1838, MSS 148, B1, F8, Nathan Read Papers, 1709–1914, PEM.

34. The family relationship was sealed only in 1788 when Jonathan married John's sister Elizabeth. On family partnerships, see Lamoreaux, "Partnership Form of Organization"; Hall, *Organization of American Culture*, 37–38, 63–68; and Van, "Free Trade and Family Values."

35. *Salem Mercury* [hereafter *SM*], 15 Dec. 1789; E. S. W., "Ropes Family," 153, 199–200; Perley, *History of Salem*, 1: 343–46; Hodges, *Hodges Family*, 40–41; Farber, *Guardians of Virtue*, 118, and fig. 4-1; *Christian Register*, 26 July 1828, 119 [quotation], 5 July 1845, 107; NIB [per NB's request] to Mrs. John Ropes, 2 Apr. 1838, Quincy, Wendell, Holmes, and Upham Family Papers, 1633–1910, MHS [quotation]. NB may have lived under the roof of first one and then the other partner. Two of Nathaniel's sons stated that their father had lived with the Hodges in the house of Judge Ropes [NIB, "Memoir," 21; WIB, "Our Family Story," 71], but he may eventually have gone to live with John Ropes when that partner married his [John's] cousin Abigail Ropes in 1784. Nathaniel himself doodled "Mrs. Ropes" on the cover of a notebook in 1784. He might have been referring to the judge's widow or to Abigail [NB, Bookkeeping Notebook, 1784, BI, F6, BF-PEM]. At the end of his life Bowditch identified "Mrs. John Ropes," still alive, as the head of the household in which he had lived for at least some of his apprenticeship. That would have been Ropes's second wife, Hannah Haraden Ropes [NIB to Mrs. John Ropes, 2 Apr. 1838].

36. NB, Diary, 15 Jan., 18 Apr., 25 Aug., 12, 15 Sept., 1, 3, 24 Oct., 3, 26 Dec. 1789, private collection of Nate and Susan Bowditch.

37. *SM*, 1 Dec. 1789; NB, Diary, 23 Apr. [quotation], 8 June, 8 Sept. [quotation], 2 Dec. 1789. Bowditch may have gone on the New England journey for his health, since upon his return he reported: "my health much better than when I left home" [8 June 1789].

38. Bentley, *Diary*, 2 Apr. 1786. See Bruegel, "Evolution of Time," 547–64; and McCrossen, "Sound and Look of Time."

39. The 1784 location was "opposite Mr. Woodbridge's" [*SG*, 3 Aug. 1784]. When Ward took over, he advertised his business as "at the Store lately occupied by Messrs. Ropes & Hodges, near Gen. Fisk's Dwelling-House" [*SM*, 22 Dec. 1789], so he must

have taken over the premises. Fisk's house was located near Phippen's Wharf, and Woodbridge's property bordered that same wharf [*SM*, 15 Apr. 1788; *SG*, 6 Nov. 1800; Felt, *Annals of Salem*, 2: 373].

40. Account of Elias H. Derby with Samuel C. Ward, 28 Mar.–29 Aug. 1791, MSS 37, B1, F9, Derby Family Papers, 1716–1921, PEM.

41. Account of Elias H. Derby, 20 May 1791; NIB, "Memoir," 20. See also WIB, "Our Family Story," 74–75.

42. NB, Bookkeeping Notebook; Dowling, *Complete System*. The source text was identified by comparing the Dowling text with Bowditch's notebook. There was no American edition of Dowling. It is likely that Bowditch's teacher, Michael Walsh, a graduate of Dublin's Trinity College, brought the book with him from Ireland [Currier, *History of Newburyport*, 1: 316–17; Booth, "Salem as Enterprise Zone," 78]. On bookkeeping manuals, see Rosenthal, "From Memory to Mastery," 151–57.

43. Dowling, *Complete System*, "Waste Book of Domestic Proper Accounts," 1–12 [separately paginated; quotation, 1].

44. [HIB], "Memoir," 13; Young, *Nathaniel Bowditch*, 24; White, *Nathaniel Bowditch*, 20.

45. HIB, *Sketch*, 12; [HIB], *Memoir*, 24–25; HIB, handwritten comments in Tacet, *German Flute*, copy in Bowditch Collection, MHS; Young, *Nathaniel Bowditch*, 31n; NB, Diary, 21 Sept. 1789; *SM*, 29 Sept. 1789.

46. HIB, *Sketch*, 7–8; NIB, *Memoir*, 19; [HIB], *Memoir*, 16–17; NB, Algebra Notebook, Ms.E.5127.44, NBC. Patricia Cline Cohen points out that arithmetic was generally considered too difficult to teach to boys under the age of ten or twelve [Cohen, *Calculating People*, 118, 120, 125].

47. Felt, *Annals of Salem*, 1: 490–95; Winterer, *Culture of Classicism*, chap. 1; Cajori, *Mathematics*, 60; James, "Engineering an Environment for Change," 56.

48. Cajori, *Mathematics*, 23–28, 57–59; Stearns, *Science in the British Colonies*, 446–55, 642–70; Harvard University, *Mathematical Theses*; P[alfrey], "John Farrar," 126–27 [quotation, 126]; Kerber, "Science in the Early Republic," 271.

49. Genuth, "From Heaven's Alarm to Public Appeal."

50. *SM*, 24 July, 11 Sept. 1787, 19 Feb., 5 Aug. 1788, 6 Jan. 1789; *SG*, 1 Jan. 1784.

51. On gentlemen of science in the colonial era and early republic, see Parrish, *American Curiosity*, esp. chaps. 3–4; Lewis, *Democracy of Facts*, esp. 1–45; Stearns, *Science in the British Colonies*, 533–35; and Greene, *American Science*. On the Republic of Letters, see Daston, "Ideal and Reality of the Republic of Letters"; and Grafton, "Sketch Map of a Lost Continent."

52. Bell, "Holyoke"; Upham, "John Prince" [quotation, 208]; Brown, *Knowledge Is Power*, 187–217; Bentley, *Diary*, 29 Sept. 1807. Bentley's "Dolland" refers to Peter and John Dollond, celebrated makers of optical instruments in London.

53. The place of American scientists in the world of European science is explored in Stearns, *Science in the British Colonies*; Parrish, *American Curiosity*; Lewis, *Democracy of Facts*; and Greene, *American Science*. On Franklin's mathematical background, see Chaplin, *First Scientific American*, 19–21, 30, 60–61. Paul C. Pasles makes the case

in *Benjamin Franklin's Numbers* that Franklin was a mathematical thinker, in both his analytical approach to social issues and his love for magic squares, but Pasles does not argue that Franklin had mastered advanced mathematics.

54. Bedini, *Thinkers and Tinkers*; Warner, "What Is a Scientific Instrument." For London's world of mathematical practitioners as an alternative to the Royal Society, and their links with the world of commerce, see Stewart, "Other Centres of Calculation."

55. Greene, *American Science*, 41–42, 134–35; Hindle, *Pursuit of Science*, chaps. 7–9, 11, 15 passim; Bedini, "Rittenhouse, David."

56. Bosse, "Osgood Carleton"; *Massachusetts Centinel*, 5 Jan., 16 Feb. 1788; *SM*, 17 Nov. 1789; *BG*, 21 Mar. 1791; Bedini, *With Compass and Chain*, 256–64; *Boston Evening-Post*, 26 Oct. 1747 [quotation]; Bentley, *Diary*, 27 June 1790. On electrical demonstrations, see Delbourgo, *Most Amazing Scene of Wonders*, 87–128.

57. *EG*, 21–28 July 1772; Cohen, *Calculating People*, chap. 4; Thornton, *Handwriting in America*, 4–12; Seybolt, *Evening School*.

58. The identification of Smith as Bowditch's instructor and as a former sailing master (eligible for half pay) is based on descriptions given in NIB, "Memoir," 20–21 [quotation, 21]; HIB, *Sketch*, 10; and Bentley, *Diary*, 1 Mar. 1791, 2 Apr. 1802 [quotation].

59. NB, Navigation Notebooks, Ms.E.5092.91, NBC. The title page of the first dates to Nov. 1786. By the time Bowditch got to the model of a nautical journal, he began the hypothetical London to Madeira voyage on 1 May 1787. The title page for "Astronomy," marking the beginning of the second notebook, is dated 29 Jan. 1787. Toward the end of the third notebook, the celestial positions of stars are those for 1789.

60. NB, Navigation Notebook 1, unpaginated cover, and Notebook 3, 253; NB, Algebra Notebook; NB, Surveying Notebooks, 1787, Ms.E.5092.92, NBC.

61. NIB, "Memoir," 19–20; Bowditch and Archibald, *Catalogue*, 22; [NB], "An Almanac for the Year of the Christian Aera 1790, being the Second after Bissextile or Leap Year, And the Fourteenth of the Independence of America which began July 4th 1776 by Isaac Bickerstaff," Bowditch Collection 16, MHS. The handwritten pamphlet bears the name of Isaac Bickerstaff, a common pseudonym for almanac makers. HIB's handwritten comments, dated 1889, in the flyleaf identify the almanac as made by his father "before he was fifteen years old."

62. "A full Church," he recorded in his diary on 25 Dec. 1789, even as most of his townsmen rejected Christmas as an undesirable remnant of Roman Catholicism and went about their usual Friday business [NB, Diary, 25 Dec. 1789].

63. *SG*, 19 Apr. 1785; *SM*, 23 Sept. 1788.

64. NIB, "Memoir," 21.

65. HIB, handwritten comments in flyleaf of Tacet, *German Flute*.

66. NIB, "Memoir," 22 [quotation]; [HIB], *Memoir*, 14–15; White, *Nathaniel Bowditch*, 12–14; Yeo, *Encyclopaedic Visions*. The encyclopedia held an almost talismanic value for him for the rest of his life. As an old man he purchased "a rare copy of it" and gave it to his son Henry "as an affectionate memorial of his boyhood"

[HIB, *Sketch*, 9]. For the contents of a similar library, that of Salem lawyer William Pynchon, see Tapley, *Salem Imprints*, 285–87.

67. Read to White, 16 May 1838; NB, [1789] Notebook [transcription of Ferguson], Ms.E.5092.90 (2), NBC. On Read, whose name is often spelled "Reed," see Williamson, "Autobiography of Hon. Nathan Read," and "Nathan Reed." Robert Simson was a Scottish mathematician whose widely translated edition of Euclid's *Elements* offered an introduction to ancient Greek geometry. William Enfield, an English Unitarian minister, published mainly on such topics as history and elocution, but following a summer's worth of mathematical study he published his *Institutes of Natural Philosophy, Theoretical and Experimental* in 1783. James Ferguson was a self-taught mathematical practitioner from Scotland whose popular lectures on the workings of the solar system featured orreries of his own making. The title of his 1756 work exemplified his approach: *Astronomy Explained upon Sir Isaac Newton's Principles and Made Easy for Those Who Have Not Studied Mathematics* [Carlyle, "Simson, Robert (1687–1768)"; Webb, "Enfield, William (1741–1797)"; Rothman, "Ferguson, James (1710–1776)"].

68. Wheatland, "Historical Sketch"; Burstyn, "Salem Philosophical Library"; Wiggin, "Kirwan Collection"; Wiggin, *Salem Athenaeum*, 7–9; Tapley, *Salem Imprints*, 248–54; Scott, "Kirwan, Richard (1733–1812)." The library stands in contrast to the many private libraries established at the same time that required payment of only a minimal fee [Raven, "Social Libraries and Library Societies"; Green, "Subscription Libraries and Commercial Circulating Libraries"].

69. Read to White, 16 May 1838; [HIB], *Memoir*, 18 [quotation]; NIB, "Memoir," 22–23, 26 [quotation, 26]; White, *Nathaniel Bowditch*, 16 [quotation]; Vote of 1 June 1791, Record Book, 1781–1810, MSS 56, B2, Vol. 1, Salem Athenaeum Records, 1760–1889, PEM. Until he purchased his own share in 1797, Nathaniel's borrowing privileges at the Philosophical Library were renewed annually, except when he was at sea [Votes of 5 June 1792, 12 June 1793, 4 June 1794, Record Book, 1781–1810].

70. Catalogue and Charge Book, 1781–1809, B2, vol. 2, Salem Athenaeum Records, 1760–1889, PEM: NB, Commonplace Books, 1791–181–, NBC. Until he became a formal member of the Philosophical Library in 1797, Bowditch's borrowings were not recorded in the Charge Book.

71. The book was purchased at an auction of the Reverend Mather Byles's three-thousand-volume library of "ancient and modern Authors in Divinity, Physick, History, Philosophy, Geography, &c. &c." On the flyleaf of the book Nathaniel wrote, "Began to study Latin." Alexander Young contended that Bowditch dated the flyleaf comment January 1790, but since the auction did not take place until November 1790, either the date is wrong or Bowditch began to study Latin even before he owned the book. HIB stated that his father began the study of Latin in June 1790 [Young, *Nathaniel Bowditch*, 39; CC, 3 Nov., 8 Dec. 1790; *Boston Independent Chronicle*, 4 Nov. 1791; [HIB], "Memoir," 21–22].

72. White, *Nathaniel Bowditch*, 17–18; Pickering, *Eulogy*, 88–89; WIB, Bowditch Library Catalog, 1837, E.166.17–18, NBC. Read claimed to have seen "incontestable proof" of Nathaniel's "persevering industry" with his own eyes, when Bowditch, then

a clerk to S. C. Ward, showed Read his own translation of the *Principia*. No such manuscript has ever come to light [Read to White, 16 May 1838; NIB, "Memoir," 25].

73. [Bentley], *ER*, 29 Apr. 1818; [HIB], *Memoir*, 21–23; HIB, *Sketch*, 11–12; NIB, "Memoir," 25. Eulogist Daniel White claimed the boy borrowed a Latin grammar and dictionary [White, *Nathaniel Bowditch*, 17].

74. Jaffee, "Village Enlightenment"; Appleby, *Inheriting the Revolution*; Gross and Kelley, *Extensive Republic*.

75. *SM*, 8 Dec. 1789; Dabney, *Catalogue of Books*; Tapley, *Salem Imprints*, 172–73.

76. [Bentley], *ER*, 29 Apr. 1818 [italics mine].

77. George Washington to Nicolas Pike, 20 June 1788, in Appleton, *Catalogue of the Washington Collection*, 165; Cohen, *Calculating People*, 112–14; Dowling, *Complete System*, ix; MacLaurin, *Fluxions*, 1: 1–2. See also Grabiner, "Newton, Maclaurin, and the Authority of Mathematics." [I am using the spelling of MacLaurin's name as it appeared on the title page of his *Fluxions*, rather than following historian Grabiner's example.] The borrowing records of the Philosophical Library cover Bowditch's borrowing activity only after he became a member, in 1797. He likely borrowed MacLaurin's book at an earlier date [Catalogue and Charge Book, 1781–1809].

Chapter 2

1. On risk and trust in early mercantile communities, see Mathias, "Risk, Credit and Kinship"; Ditz, "Secret Selves, Credible Personas"; and Sleeswijk, "Social Ties and Commercial Transactions."

2. There is a large literature on Salem's Golden Age, its East Indies trade, and its neutral carrying trade, much of it more or less celebratory in tone: Morison, *Maritime History*, chap. 7; Peabody, *Merchant Venturers*; Phillips, *Salem and the Indies*; U.S. National Park Service, *Salem*; and Booth, "Salem as Enterprise Zone." For more recent and complex perspectives, see Fichter, *So Great a Profitt*; Bean, *Yankee India*; and Vickers, *Young Men and the Sea*, 166–74.

3. For the global profile of the so-called neutral carrying trade, see Fichter, *So Great a Profitt*. For the sailor's perspective, see Vickers, *Young Men and the Sea*, 170–72, 178–81; and Gilje, *Liberty on the Waterfront*, chap. 6.

4. Vickers, *Young Men and the Sea*, 169–70; Osgood and Batchelder, *Historical Sketch*, 205.

5. Bentley, Diary, 15 Apr. 1796. Derby: Murphy, "'To Keep Our Trading for Our Livelihood'"; McKey, "Elias Hasket Derby"; Peabody, *Log of the Grand Turks*; Peabody, *Merchant Venturers*; U.S. National Park Service, *Salem*, 46–47, 51; Fichter, *So Great a Profitt*, 132–35; Morrison, "Derby."

6. Habakkuk Bowditch, property transaction documents, 3 July 1787, MSS 3, B4, F8, BF-PEM; Account of Elias H. Derby with Samuel C. Ward, 28 Mar.–29 Aug. 1791, MSS 37, B1, F9, Derby Family Papers, 1716–1921, PEM [hereafter Derby Papers]; Peabody, *Log of the Grand Turks*, 42–60. Derby's mother, Mary Hodges Derby, was sister to Gamaliel Hodges, whose daughter, also named Mary Hodges, married Nathaniel's maternal uncle Jonathan Ingersoll.

7. Gibaut: Peabody, *Log of the Grand Turks*, 130–33; Bentley, *Diary*, 12 Mar., 18 Oct. 1786, 20 May 1787, 8 Oct. 1793, 1–3 May, 13, 29 Aug. 1794, 30 Apr. 1802, 11 Aug. 1805, 27 Apr. 1818. Survey announcement: *SG*, 22 July 1794. One of Bowditch's eulogists noted that Gibaut's "mathematical taste and sympathies" formed the basis of his friendship with Bowditch [White, *Nathaniel Bowditch*, 23].

8. Bentley, *Diary*, 11 Aug. 1805; [Bentley], *ER*, 29 Apr. 1818. The later assessment is consistent with Bentley's diary entries at the time of the survey. "Capt Gibaut managed the Theodolite," wrote Bentley, referring to the surveying instrument, and "Mr Bowditch the offsets, & kept the book" [Bentley, *Diary*, 4 Sept. 1794]. Offsets are survey lines calculated to be at ninety-degree angles to the survey baseline. For Bowditch's field books, see NB, Field Book for Land Survey of Salem, undated [1794], MSS 3, BI, F7, BF-PEM; and NB, Record Book, 1794 Survey, B34, vol. 1, BF-PEM.

9. Receipt, 7 Jan. 1795, pasted inside flyleaf, [HIB], *Memoir*, copy in Bowditch Collection, MHS; Bentley, *Diary*, 5 Dec. 1794; White, *Nathaniel Bowditch*, 23.

10. Vickers, *Young Men and the Sea*, 199–201; Fichter, *So Great a Profitt*, 129–31.

11. Mathias, "Risk, Credit and Kinship," 16–21; Morison, *Maritime History*, 45n; Cleveland, *In the Forecastle*, 25–27.

12. Hitchings, *Ship Registers*, 83; Vickers, *Young Men and the Sea*, 74–76, 169–70. The exception proved the rule when the 820-ton *Massachusetts*, modeled on an Indiaman for an abortive American East India Company, proved a disaster. Poorly built, its gigantic cargo rotted, and the owners sold it off in Canton [Fichter, *So Great a Profitt*, 43–45].

13. Small, *Derby House*, 66–71; *Vital Records of Ipswich*; *Vital Records of Salem*; Phillips, *Salem and the Indies*, 149, 239, 330; Hitchings, *Ship Registers*, 19.

14. Delano, *Narrative*, 36–37. On the determination of longitude, see Stimson, "Longitude Problem," and Howse, "Lunar-Distance Method." On the lunar method in America, see Thornton, "'Intelligent Mariner,'" 613–17. See also chapter 3 in this volume.

15. NB, "Journal of a Voyage from Salem to the East Indies in the Ship Henry, Henry Prince Master," 11 Jan. 1795–11 Jan. 1796, NBC [hereafter *Henry* Log], 5, 26 Apr., 5 Oct. [quotation] 1795. For other negative references to Batton, again in French, see *Henry* Log, Harbour Journal [hereafter *Henry* Harbour] 5, 8, 9 June 1795. On Batton, the son of a Hugenaut sea captain who had immigrated to Salem, see Bentley, *Diary*, 17, 18 Dec. 1801.

16. "Ship Henry's Portage Bill" (in Bowditch's hand), 23 Mar. 1796, B4, F2, Derby Papers. Beadle: *Vital Records of Salem*; *ER*, 7 Sept. 1826; *SG*, 14 Oct. 1836; *Salem Directory*, n.p.; Downes: *Vital Records of Salem*; *Vital Records of Marblehead*; U.S. Navy, *General Register*, 510. Hulen (sometimes spelled Heulen or Eulen): Bentley, *Diary*, 20 Mar. 1791, 7 Jan. 1792, 18 Dec. 1801; Commonwealth of Massachusetts, *Report of the Committee . . . on the Subject of Impressed Seamen*, 27; Higginson, *Travellers and Outlaws*, 50–52; *Columbian Courier*, 27 Nov. 1801; *CC*, 9 Dec. 1801; *Boston Commercial Gazette*, 29 Apr. 1802; *Vital Records of Salem* [quotation]. On the changing composition of crews and maritime career trajectories, see Vickers, *Young Men and the Sea*, chaps. 4, 6.

17. *Henry* Log, 12 Jan., 20 Feb., 10 Apr. 1795.

18. Ibid., 9 [quotation], 24 Feb. 1795; Vickers, *Young Men and the Sea*, 92, 195–96; Rediker, *Between the Devil and the Deep Blue Sea*, 186–89. For an account of crossing the line written by one of Bowditch's future scientific correspondents, see Baily, *Journal of a Tour*, 84–85.

19. On trade with the Mascarene Islands (Mauritius and Réunion), see Fichter, *So Great a Profitt*, 155–56, 158–60.

20. *Henry* Harbour, 10, 11 May 1795.

21. Ibid., 10 May, 4 June 1795.

22. Ibid., 17 May 1795; *Henry* Log, 7 Feb. 1795.

23. *Henry* Harbour, 11 May [quotations], 5 [quotation], 14 [quotation], 22, 23 June 1795.

24. *Henry* Harbour, 9–16, 29 May, 10–13, 20–30 June, 3, 9–13, 23, 25 July, 19, 24, 28 Sept. 1795; "Account sales of the Cargo of the Ship Henry," 28 Sept. 1795, B4, F1, Derby Papers; "Invoice of Sundry Merchandize shipped on board the Ship Henry," 28 Sept. 1795, B4, F1, Derby Papers; Account of Ship *Henry* Disbursements, 20 July–28 Sept. 1795, B4, F1, Derby Papers; Henry Prince to Elias Hasket Derby, 8 May, 22 July 1795, B4, F5, Derby Papers.

25. *Henry* Harbour, 10 [quotation], 11, 16, 21 [quotations] May, 3 [quotation], 29 June 1795. For Bowditch's almost constant social contact with creoles, see *Henry* Harbour, 9 May–27 Sept. 1795, passim.

26. *Henry* Harbour, 21 May 1795. Bowditch recorded this anecdote in French.

27. Ibid., 5, 10 [quotation], 11 June 1795.

28. Ibid., 28, 31 May, 10, 18, 28 June, 6, 8, 14, 19, 20, 29 July, 17 Aug., 26 Sept. 1795.

29. Henry Prince to Elias Hasket Derby, 8 May, 22 July 1795; *Henry* Harbour, 25 July, 28 September 1795; *Henry* Log, 10, 25, 26 Dec. 1795, 11 Jan. 1796.

30. NB, "Journal of a Voyage from Salem to the East Indies via Lisbon & Madeira in the Ship Astrea Henry Prince Master," 26 Mar 1796–22 May 1797, Ms.E.5092.93, NBC [hereafter *Astrea* Log 1796–97]. Sometime after 1801 Bowditch submitted an "official" log of the voyage to the EIMS, with much material from the original expurgated [NB, "Journal in the Ship Astrea, Henry Prince, Master, March 27, 1796 to October 3, 1797, from Salem to Lisbon, Manilla (*sic*) and back," Bound EIMS Journals, vol. 1, no. 3, MH 88, EIMSR]. Bowditch's original Harbour Journal in Manila was transcribed in McHale and McHale, *Early American-Philippine Trade*, 26–62. On the *Astrea*, see Hitchings, *Ship Registers*, 14. On Western trade with the Philippines, see McHale and McHale, *Early American-Philippine Trade*, 8–15, 19–24; and Fichter, *So Great a Profitt*, 156–59, 162–66.

31. *Astrea* Log 1796–97, 28 June, 6 July 1796.

32. Ibid., 6–17 Sept. 1796 [quotation, 10 Sept.].

33. Ibid., Harbour Journal at Manila [hereafter *Astrea* Manila], 2 Oct.–9/10 Dec. 1796, passim. Beginning on 15/16 October 1796 often Bowditch provides two dates for each entry, the first according to the local Manila calendar and the second according to that used elsewhere.

34. Fichter, *So Great a Profitt*, 158–59, 168.

35. *Astrea* Manila, 4, 15/16 [quotation], 23/24, 30 Oct., 2 [quotations], 20/21, 27/28 Nov., 12 Dec. 1796.

36. Ibid., 6, 23/24 Oct., 9/10 Dec. [quotations] 1796.

37. Ibid., 2, 6, 23/24 Oct., 9/10 Dec. [quotations] 1796.

38. Ibid., 4, 6 [quotation], 30 Oct. [quotation], 2 Nov. 1796.

39. Ibid., 6 Oct. 1796 [quotation]; NB, "Remarks at Lisbon," Bound EIMS Journals, vol. 1, no. 3, MH 88, EIMSR.

40. *Astrea* Manila, 4, 5, 6 Oct., 9/10 Dec. 1796. On the Filipino sugar trade in its global context, see Fichter, *So Great a Profitt*, 156–59, 162–66.

41. *Astrea* Manila, 6 Oct. [quotation], 9/10 Dec. 1796.

42. Ibid., 23/24 Oct. [quotations], 20/21 Nov.[quotations], 4/5 Dec. 1796.

43. Ibid., 20/21 Nov., 9/10 Dec. 1796. Bowditch spelled the name "Dobel," but the name consistently appears as "Doble" in the shipping news columns of American newspapers. In 1798 Doble carried Monsieur Vergoz and his family to the United States in the *Three Sisters*, as they fled from Réunion in fear of what might happen when the French emancipated the island's slaves. In 1804 Felix Vergoz advertised his services as a Bourbon commission merchant in the *Salem Gazette* [Theal, *Records of the Cape Colony*, 248–49; SG, 1 May 1798, 20 Jan. 1804].

44. *Grammatica de la Lengua Castellana Compuesta a Por la Reala Academia Espanola* (Manila, 1793), copy in Bowditch Collection, MHS; *Astrea* Log 1796–97, 31 Jan., 18, 19, 20 Feb. 1797; McHale and McHale, *Early American-Philippine Trade*, 63; Bentley, *Diary*, 6 June 1797.

45. Bentley, *Diary*, 10 July 1797.

46. Henry Prince, Log of the *Astrea*, 1798–99, Log 1301, PEM [hereafter Prince, *Astrea* Log, 1798–99], 27 Aug., 7, 8, 12, 17, 18, 19, 20, –21 Sept. 1798; NB, "Journal of a Voyage from Salem to Europe & India [*sic*] in the Ship Astrea of Salem, Henry Prince Master," Log for 1798–99 [hereafter NB, *Astrea* Log, 1798–99], 20 Sept. 1798 [quotation], Ms.E.5092.94 [call number refers to journal containing logs for two voyages], NBC; NB, *Astrea* Log, 1798–99, Harbour Journal, Cádiz, 12 Nov. 1798.

47. Prince, *Astrea* Log, 1798–99, 14, 16, 18 Nov. 1798; NB, *Astrea* Log, 1798–99, 18 Nov. 1798.

48. [HIB], *Memoir*, 52 [quotation]; Young, *Nathaniel Bowditch*, 27–28 [quotation, 27]. For contemporary accounts of the incident, which make no mention of Bowditch's role in it, see Prince, *Astrea* Log, 1798–99, 19 Nov. 1798, and NB, *Astrea* Log, 1798–99, 19 Nov. 1798.

49. Prince, *Astrea* Log, 1798–99, Harbor Journal, Alicante, 24 Nov. 1798.

50. Ibid., 14–25, 27–28 Feb., 1 [quotation], 2–4, 6, 10 [quotation] Mar. 1799; NB, *Astrea* Log, 1798–99, 10 Mar. 1799 [quotation]; CC, 30 Mar. 1799.

51. Henry Prince to [Thomas] Amory, 10 July 1799, B1, F9, Derby Papers; NB to MI, 22 July 1799, B1, F5, BF-PEM. On the changes in crew composition and the increase in desertion, see Vickers, *Young Men and the Sea*, chap. 4.

52. NB to MI, 22 July 1799.

53. NB, "Journal of a Voyage from Boston to India [*sic*] in the Ship Astrea. Henry Prince master," Log for 1799–1800 [hereafter *Astrea* Log, 1799–1800], 15 Sept. 1799, 7 Feb., 25 Apr., 9, 11 Sept. 1800 [quotations], Ms.E.5092.94 [call number refers to journal containing logs for two voyages], NBC; NB, *Astrea* Log, 1799–1800, Harbour Journal, Batavia, 17–18 Dec. 1799, Harbour Journal, Manila, 13–14 Feb. 1800; *SG*, 19 Sept. 1800 [quotations]. In a 1798 document, Samuel Cook is listed as "an American seaman," age nineteen, five foot eight inches, and "of a dark complexion." Thomas Gardner of Salem and Lucina Lovett of Beverly announced their intention to marry in June 1798 [citizenship certificate, 6 Sept. 1798, B1, F10, BF-PEM; *Vital Records of Salem*].

54. Salem, Mass., Valuations and Directories, 1761–1850, microfilm 55, PEM [hereafter Salem Tax Records], records for 1795–1800; Philosophical Library, Record Book, 1781–1810, MSS 56, B2, vol. 1, 6 June 1797, Salem Athenaeum Records, 1760–1889, PEM. On officers' privilege, see Vickers, *Young Men and the Sea*, 83–86.

55. NIB, "Memoir," 39; Cary, "'A Contrary Wind at Sea,'" 3–26; Bentley, *Diary*, 16 Mar. 1792; Tapley, *Salem Imprints*, 88 [quotation]. Elizabeth's maternal grandfather, John Hodges, was brother to Gamaliel Hodges, Bowditch's maternal grandfather [Farber, *Guardians of Virtue*, 122–23; Hodges, *Hodges Family*, 35, 36, 39, 41]. At the time of their marriage, Boardman's estate was valued at $6,300, a mix of real estate, money gathering interest, and five shares in the Essex Bridge, a private venture linking Salem and nearby Beverly [Salem Tax Records, 1798].

56. *Vital Records of Salem.*

57. *SG*, 31 Oct. 1800; Ernest William Bowditch, "Traditions Concerning the Older Generations, 1909," in Harold Bowditch, "A Collection of Data Made for the Possible Future Use of a Biographer," 1: 403 [quotation], MH 42, NBLW; NIB, "Memoir," 119 [quotation]. No doubt the marriage had been agreed upon before Nathaniel left for Batavia. He had addressed his Boston letter of 22 July 1799 to "my dearest friend." The required public declaration of intention to marry had been filed less than two weeks after his return. [In *Vital Records of Salem*, "Mary Ingersoll is listed as "Polly," a common alternate name.]

58. NB to MIB, 5 May 1803, B1, F5, BF-PEM; NIB, "Memoir," 39. Accordingly, Salem tax records show Bowditch as part owner of a house in 1798 but not in 1797 or 1799 [Salem Tax Records, 1797–99].

59. *SG*, 21 May 1793 [quotation]; Phillips, *Salem in the Eighteenth Century*, 345; H[enry] Ingersoll to MI, 20 Sept. 1799, B22, F1, BF-PEM; MIB to EOW, 14 May 1817, B1, F1, BF-PEM; D[aniel] A. White, "A Brief Memoir of the Plummer Family," in *Proceedings upon the Dedication of Plummer Hall*, 61 [quotation]; Silsbee, *Half Century in Salem*, 48–52; Bentley, *Diary*, 20 Jan. 1818; *SG*, 21 July 1846.

60. Mary Ingersoll, undated Cypher Notebook, and Notebook, dated 4 Mar. 1794, MIB Papers.

61. MIB, Notebook, 1800–20, and HIB to EBIBD, 10 Nov. 1887, bound in "Mementos of Mary Bowditch," MIB Papers. On sensibility, see Kelley, *Learning to Stand and Speak*, 17–19; Bushman, *Refinement of America*, 80–83; and Knott, *Sensibility and the American Revolution*, 4–15.

62. HIB to EBIBD, 10 Nov. 1887; "To the Author of the Latitudinarian," *CC*, 14 Feb. 1801; Barnard, *Sermon*, 14; "Subscribers Names," MSS 359, B2, F9, Salem Female Charitable Society Records, 1801–2001, PEM.

63. MIB to NB, 15 Dec. 1802, B1, F2, BF-PEM; MIB, "Journey 1813," B22, F1, BF-PEM; NB to MIB, 20 Apr. 1823, B1, F5, BF-PEM.

64. NB, *Astrea* Log, 1798–99, Harbour Journal, Cádiz, 12 Nov. 1798; Prince, *Astrea* Log, 1798–99, 21 Sept. 1798. On Mallevault, see Cormack, "Legitimate Authority in Revolution and War," 15–17; and Stephens, *History of the French Revolution*, 2: 481, 482. The first observatory in Cádiz dates from 1753, but in 1798 it moved to the Isla de León (now San Fernando), some eight kilometers from the city. The original building still stands.

65. NB, *Astrea* Log, 1798–99, Harbour Journal, Cádiz, 12 Nov. 1798. The almanac in question was Churruca's Spanish version, identical to the English one, Bowditch later informed Bentley, "excepting the accomodation [*sic*] merely to the Longitude of Cadiz" [Bentley, *Diary*, 10 Apr. 1799]. Churruca: "Extracts from the Grenada Handbook," 62; Harbron, *Trafalgar and the Spanish Navy*, 143–45.

66. *NH*, 24 Sept. 1799; Moore, *New Practical Navigator*, 1st Am. Ed., title page, vii.

Chapter 3

1. NB, "Lettre XIII" (dated 22 Nov. 1823), 224–25; Melville, *Moby-Dick*, 174–75. For a critique of the *Navigator* as oriented toward rote learning suitable for merchant sailors vs. the theoretical understanding appropriate for naval officers, see Maury, "Scraps from the Lucky Bag," 315–20 and Jones, *Sketches of Naval Life*, 2: 263–64.

2. Three dollars was the price advertised in 1802, compared with Blunt's 1799 American edition of Englishman John Hamilton Moore's *New Practical Navigator*, at $2.50 [*Gazette of the United States* (Philadelphia), 9 July 1802; *Constitutional Diary* (Philadelphia), 2 Jan. 1800].

3. [Zach], "Notes," *CorrAst* 4 (1820): 62–64 [quotation, 64, as translated in *SG*, 30 Aug. 1822]; "A Colored Navigator," *Christian Reflector* 1 (5 Oct. 1838): 4. Among the numerous reprints of this anecdote, see, e.g., *American Repertory* (Burlington, Vt.), 17 Sept. 1822; *City Gazette* (Charleston, S.C.), 10 Sept. 1822; Young, *Nathaniel Bowditch*, 28n; "A Colored Navigator," *Colored American*, 27 Oct. 1838; and *Western Messenger* 6 (Nov. 1838): 65. In the journal of the yacht's owner, George Crowninshield, the cook is identified as William Chapman, but this incident is not recorded. Crowninshield did record that Baron von Zach made an appearance in Genoa and asked whether Americans were familiar with working lunars. Zach had indicated that the English were convinced Americans were not familiar with this technique but that he had placed a bet with an Englishman that Americans were indeed familiar with it. The yacht's navigator, Benjamin Crowninshield, was married to the sister of Bowditch's first wife, and the yacht's clerk was Bowditch's former master, Samuel Curwen Ward [Crowninshield, *Cleopatra's Barge*, 44–45, 169–70; Ferguson, *Cleopatra's Barge*, 108–9].

4. For a recent example of this view, see Kalkstein, "World According to Bowditch," 43–44. The term "seaman's Bible" seems to have made its appearance only in the

twentieth century, forwarded not by mariners but by Bowditch's biographers. On "seaman's Bible," full-text word searches were conducted in the following databases: American Periodical Series, 1741–1900 (Proquest), America's Historical Newspapers, ser. 1–3, 1690–1922 (Readex), and 19th-Century U.S. Newspapers (Gale-Cengage).

5. Young, *Nathaniel Bowditch*, 27 [quotation]; White, *Nathaniel Bowditch*, 27–28 [quotations, 28]. White was quoting the account provided by an unnamed individual who had sailed with Bowditch as both a common sailor and subordinate officer [27]. Bowditch's son Henry clarified that it was not until his later voyages, now a supercargo relieved of many shipboard duties, that Bowditch had sufficient time to engage in this extent of study [(HIB), *Memoir*, 78–79].

6. Young, *Nathaniel Bowditch*, 32–33.

7. Costa, "Ladies' Diary"; Ozanam, *Recreations Mathematical and Physical*; Pasles, *Benjamin Franklin's Numbers*, 45–46, 61–78, 82–91. For American examples, see "Questions in Arithmetic," *Boston Royal American Magazine* 1 (July 1774): 260; *Falmouth (Me.) Gazette*, 12 Feb. 1785; *New York Columbian Gazetteer*, 10 Feb. 1794; and "New Mathematical Questions," *Monthly Magazine, and American Review* 2 (Apr. 1800): 242–43.

8. Pickering, *Eulogy*, 7; [HIB], *Memoir*, 36–37 [quoting Prince's account]; Young, *Nathaniel Bowditch*, 26–27 [quotation, 27]; [HIB], "Memoir," 288 [quoting Prince's account].

9. Daston, "Enlightenment Calculations," 184–86; NB to Theophilus Parsons, 23 Nov. 1797, Ms.Ch.A.9.1, NBC; White, *Nathaniel Bowditch*, 32 [quotation]. On Parsons and his mathematical interests, see Ross, "Parsons," and Parsons, *Memoir of Theophilus Parsons*, 273–82, 295–97, 304–5. It may well have been John Prince, Bowditch's intellectual benefactor, who introduced Bowditch to Parsons, for the minister and attorney shared a close friendship based on a common interest in natural philosophy [(Parsons), *Memoir of Theophilus Parsons*, 273]. The borrowing records of the Philosophical Library show that Bowditch borrowed all four volumes of Newton's *Principia* between 11 and 26 Sept. 1797 [Catalogue and Charge Book, 1781–1809, MSS 56, B2, vol. 2, Salem Athenaeum Records, 1760–1889, PEM]. He is the only member recorded as having borrowed the *Principia* in these years. On the AAAS, see Greene, *American Science*, 64–70; Stone, "Scientific Boston," chaps. 2, 3; and Whitehill, "Early Learned Societies in Boston," 151–62.

10. [HIB], *Memoir*, 82. On Blunt and his nautical publications, see Burstyn, *At the Sign of the Quadrant*, chaps. 1–3; and Campbell, *History and Bibliography*.

11. Campbell, *History and Bibliography*, 13–15, 43–44; McGill, "Copyright."

12. The following discussion of navigation is based on Stimson, "Longitude Problem"; Howse, "Lunar-Distance Method"; and McKenzie, "Vocational Science," 38–41, 155–77. See also Thornton, "'Intelligent Mariner,'" 613–17.

13. NB, *New American Practical Navigator* (Newburyport, 1802) [hereafter *1802 Navigator*], 179. Though not conceptually new, the lunar method was made possible only in this era by the invention of a new nautical instrument, Hadley's quadrant (soon improved into a sextant), and a literally astronomical research program that resulted in an accurate star catalog and equally accurate predictions of celestial positions.

14. Ebenezer Bowditch Jr., Navigation Notebook of 1749–51, MSS 399, B11, F8, American and Canadian Ciphering Books, 1727–1864, PEM.

15. Moore, *New Practical Navigator*, 13th ed.; TJ to James Madison, 21 June 1791, Stagg, *Papers of James Madison*.

16. Moore, *New Practical Navigator*, 1st Am. ed. [hereafter *1799 Moore*], title page [quotation], vii–viii [quotation, vii], note to table XIV (unpaginated). William Bowditch's correction was required only during the days surrounding the vernal and autumnal equinoxes. See also William Bowditch's original annotations in his own copy of Moore (12th London ed.), which he bought in Sept. 1796, in Harold Bowditch, "A Collection of Data Made for the Possible Future Use of a Biographer," 2: 47–59, MH 42, NBLW. On Pike and his contributions, see NB to Nicholas [*sic*] Pike, 7 Apr. 1798, Nicolas Pike Papers, 1783–98, MHS; and Cohen, *Calculating People*, 132. In 1794, Pike had collaborated with Blunt on a new edition of a *Ready Reckoner*, a common kind of cheat sheet used for calculating figures in the era's bewildering variety of nondecimal currencies, weights, and measures. In May 1798 Blunt registered a federal copyright for a *New Theoretic and Practical Navigator* with Pike's name on the title page. This book was never printed. Instead, almost exactly a year later, Blunt registered a second copyright for the book that did come out in 1799 [Gilreath and Wills, *Federal Copyright Records*, 93, 96; Campbell, *History and Bibliography*, 73].

17. NB, "Journal of a Voyage from Salem to the East Indies in the Ship Henry, Henry Prince Master," 11 Jan. 1795–11 Jan. 1796, 25 Dec. 1795, and "Problem," "Solution," "Remarks" appended at end of the log, 267–68, Ms.E.5092.95, NBC; NB, "New Method"; NB, "Journal of a Voyage from Salem to Europe & India [*sic*] in the Ship Astrea of Salem, Henry Prince Master," Log for 1798–99, Harbour Journal, Cádiz, 12 Nov. 1798, Ms.E.5092.94 [call number refers to journal containing logs for two voyages], NBC.

18. *1799 Moore*, vii; NB to Pike, 7 Apr. 1798. Of the errors, over three hundred were corrected in the published text, and over a hundred fifty more "not discovered in season," that is, submitted after type had been set, were then listed in a separate "Errata" [ibid., n.p.]. Given the timing of the publication, these errata are almost certainly ones Bowditch detected on his third voyage, perhaps the very ones he was working on during the French privateer alarm. Leap year: As the *Salem Gazette* reported, Moore's volume presented two separate sets of solar declination tables, one for 1800 as a leap year and the other in which that year's February had only twenty-eight days. This writer speculated that, though aware of the parliamentary act, Moore "felt an uncertainty whether the year 1800 would be accounted a leap year or not, as far as it respects other countries." Moore's section titled "To find the Leap-Year" simply indicated that any year divisible by four is a leap year, an error neither Blunt's 1799 nor his 1800 edition corrected. American almanacs got it right, although some almanac titles and contents indicate that their writers recognized there might be confusion ["Chronology," *SG*, 3 Sept. 1799; Moore, *New Practical Navigator*, 13th ed., table XVII, n.p., and 135–36; *Columbian Almanac*; *Virginia Almanac*; Bickerstaff, *Astronomical Repository*; *Citizen and Farmer's Almanac*; *Greenleaf's . . . Almanack*].

19. Moore, *New Practical Navigator*, 2nd Am. ed., vii–viii.

20. Young, *Nathaniel Bowditch*, 34–36 [quotations, 34, 35]. On the front flyleaf of Bowditch's copy of Moore, the one Bowditch took on his fourth voyage, son Henry wrote in 1887 that the volume was "of inestimable value," since here "in his own handwriting" was "virtually the germ of Bowditch's Navigator i.e. Blunts corrected" [*1799 Moore*, copy in Bowditch Collection, MHS].

21. *1802 Navigator*, v–vii, "Advertisement."

22. Ibid., vi–xii [quotations, viii, x, xii].

23. Ibid., xii. On the strength of his 1787 treatise on navigation, Mendoza y Rios had been made a Fellow of the Royal Society in 1793, and he counted among his correspondents and patrons some of the leading luminaries of British and French science. Indeed, the essay in question took the form of a communication, dated November 1796, addressed to the head of the Royal Society, Sir Joseph Banks, and commented upon by renowned English scientist Henry Cavendish [Mendoza y Rios, Banks, and Cavendish, "Recherches sur les Principaux Problèmes de l'Astronomie Nautique"; Ortiz, "Mendoza y Ríos"]. The Philosophical Library's records do not show Bowditch borrowing this volume at any time between its publication and the 1802 publication of the *Navigator* [Salem Athenaeum Records, 1760–1889, PEM].

24. NB to Nathan Read, 28 June 1799, MSS 148, B1, F2, Nathan Read Papers, 1709–1914, PEM. The next volume of *MAAAS*, published in 1804, carried Bowditch's "New Method of Working a Lunar Observation" but with no reference to Mendoza y Rios's method appended. Too much time had passed. Verification of a letter from NB to the AAAS on 28 Aug. 1797 can be found in "Records of Meetings," *Proceedings of the AAAS* 45 (Sept. 1910): 564. An AAAS online finding aid places the document at Jan. 1797 [Entry for "A New Method of working a Lunar Observation—By Nathaniel Bowditch AAS," Jan. 1797, in AAAS, *Academy Archives*, ser. I-C-1, 42], but Bowditch was then on an ocean voyage. The original communication is no longer available to scholars.

25. Howse, "Lunar-Distance Method," 154–56.

26. The common representation of the *Navigator* as offering common sailors the opportunity to advance in the maritime world is premised on this alleged accessibility. On the *Navigator*'s purported links to upward social mobility, see Thornton, "'Intelligent Mariner.'"

27. *1802 Navigator*, 17, 19, 64. I have compared Bowditch's *1802 Navigator* with the last edition of Moore published before Bowditch began his revisions of that text, the 13th edition of 1798.

28. Ibid., 59, 545–89.

29. Ibid., *1802 Navigator*, [iii] [quotation]; *Columbian Courier* (New Bedford, Mass.), 16 Apr. 1802; *SR*, 6 Sept. [quotation], 24 May 1802.

30. "Report," *1802 Navigator*, [iii].

31. NB to Pike, 7 Apr. 1798; Edmund Blunt to NB, 9 June 1817, MSS 3, B1, F3, BF-PEM; NB to Blunt, 18 Sept. 1817, Washburn Papers, vol. 11, Autographs and Prints, MHS. Among several lawsuits in which Blunt was involved are *Edmund M. Blunt v.*

John Melcher, George F. Williams v. Edmund M. Blunt, Sarjeant [*sic*] *v. Blunt,* and *Blunt v. Little.* Only when Blunt left Newburyport for New York in 1810 or 1811 and New-buryporter Edmund Little briefly took over the copyright did Bowditch work with a different publisher [see chapter 6 in this volume].

32. "Animadversions on the Present State of Literature and Taste in the United States," *Monthly Magazine* 14 (Jan. 1803): 624–27 [quotation, 626]; "M.," "For the Repertory," *New-England Repertory,* 10 Sept. 1803.

33. On Baron, see Hogan, "George Baron"; Zitarelli, "American Mathematics Journals"; Rickey and Shell-Gellasch, "Mathematics Education at West Point"; *Memoirs of Gen. Joseph Gardner Swift,* 27–28, 31; George Baron to TJ, 21 Dec. 1801, and note, Oberg and Looney, *Papers of Thomas Jefferson;* entry for Baron to AAAS, 2 May 1798, AAAS, *Academy Archives,* ser. I-B-1, 2: 21; *New-York Herald,* 25 Sept. 1802; *Local Collections . . . Borough of Gateshead,* 137. For Baron's subsequent descent into "mental derangement," including allegations of "deep laid snares of a wicked man," and a mathematical discovery that drew on ancient accounts of "*cubical* altars and *seven* candlesticks all of gold," see "E.," Letter to the Editor, *Daily National Intelligencer* (Washington, D.C.), 29 Sept. 1815 [quotation]; "A Card," *New York Commercial Advertiser,* 27 June 1810; "A Card," *New York Commercial Advertiser,* 29 June 1810 [quotation], 2 Apr., 8 Aug [quotation] 1811, 18 June 1812; *New York Mercantile Advertiser,* 5 Mar. 1811; *New-York Gazette,* 6 June 1812.

34. Baron, *Exhibition of the Genuine Principles,* 3, 26–28, 32–33 [quotations, 26, 32, 33].

35. *New York People's Friend,* 25 Nov. 1806.

36. Though Bowditch pointed out the "gross improprieties" in Baron's behavior to John Davis of the AAAS's publications committee, Baron's essay was published, albeit with a note at the end stating that several AAAS members, "skilled in mathematical science," believed that Baron "had not demonstrated his theorem" [Davis to John Adams, 9 Apr. 1804, Bound Letterbook, vol. 3, AAAS, http://www.amacad.org/archive/images/V03p010.001.jpg, and http://www.amacad.org/archive/images/V03p010.002.jpg; Baron, "Remarks on Mr. Winthrop's Paper on the Duplication of the Cube in Part 1st of This Volume," *MAAAS* 2 (1804): 40–42 (quotation, 42)].

37. Rubenstein, "James Akin"; Little, "Cartoons of James Akin"; Currier, *History of Newburyport,* 2: 371–75.

38. *NH,* 5 Apr. 1803 (republished in *SG,* 7 Apr. 1803); "Five Hundred Dollars Reward," *New York Mercantile Advertiser,* 22 Apr. 1803; *New York Evening Post,* 25 Apr. 1803.

39. Gavine, "Mackay"; Mackay, *Complete Navigator* (London, 1804), vii, x–xv [quotations, xiv]; *United States' Gazette* (Philadelphia), 9 Feb. 1807; *NH,* 26 May 1807.

40. NB, *New American Practical Navigator,* 2nd ed., v–x [quotations, vi, ix–x]; Campbell, *History and Bibliography,* 19–21.

41. Norie, *New and Complete Epitome,* vii. For examples of advertisements for multiple manuals, see *National Intelligencer* (Washington, D.C.), 15 Sept. 1806; *Baltimore Patriot,* 7 Dec. 1813; *Poulson's American Daily Advertiser* (Philadelphia), 2 Feb. 1809; *New York Commercial Advertiser,* 11 Jan. 1808; *NH,* 15 Sept. 1807. The timing of

Bowditch's dominance is based on a search in booksellers' advertisements through 1840, America's Historical Newspapers. For the use of Norie on non-U.S. vessels, see U.S. Department of State, *Report of the Commercial Relations*, 3: 504, 521, 561, 612, 619, 625, 662, 714, 727. For a contrary view, see Review of "A Discourse on the Life and Character of the Hon. Nathaniel Bowditch," *Athenaeum* [London] (28 Apr. 1838): 452.

42. Brady, *Kedge-Anchor*, 208; Chase, *Whaleship Essex*, 32.

43. NB, *New American Practical Navigator*, 5th ed., 148 [quotation], 167–69 [quotation, 167]; NB, *New American Practical Navigator*, 6th ed., 162 [quotation], 182–85; NB, *New American Practical Navigator*, 7th ed., 182–85, advertisement (n.p.) [quotation]. The 1807, 1811, and 1817 editions included a single mention of the use of a chronometer in a footnote [NB, *New American Practical Navigator*, 2nd ed., footnote to table XXXVII, n.p.; NB, *New American Practical Navigator*, 3rd ed., footnote to table XLVI, n.p.; NB, *New American Practical Navigator*, 4th ed., footnote to table XLVI, 272].

44. On computers and their work, see Grier, *When Computers Were Human*, 16–33; Croarken, "Tabulating the Heavens"; Croarken, "Mary Edwards"; Croarken, "Astronomical Labourers."

45. "Qualities to be required for an Assistant May 19, 1787," Maskelyne Memorandum Book, 2, 1782–88, and John Evans, *Juvenile Tourist* (London, 1810), 333–35, quoted in Croarken, "Astronomical Labourers," 292, 285.

46. Francis Baily, "On Mr. Babbage's New Machine for Calculating and Printing Mathematical and Astronomical Tables," in Babbage, *Babbage's Calculating Engines*, 225–26 [quotations, 226]; Buxton, *Memoir . . . Charles Babbage*, 6; See also Schaffer, "Babbage's Intelligence."

47. Charles Babbage to [NB], 2 Aug. 1835, in Williams, "Babbage and Bowditch," 289; NB, Algebra Notebook, 1787–88, 241, Ms.E.5137.44, NBC; [Peirce], "Nathaniel Bowditch," 319. According to Benjamin Peirce, Samuel Webber was said "to have sneered at the audacity of the youth," and it was several years before Bowditch presented his work to the AAAS and published it in its *Memoirs*. According to John Pickering, the correspondent was not Webber but Harvard president James Willard. A still extant letter of Webber to NB from 1799 refers to a critique of James Winthrop's essay in the AAAS *Memoirs*. No such letter regarding Newton is extant. However, the borrowing records of the Philosophical Library do show Bowditch as having borrowed the *Principia* earlier that year [Pickering, *Eulogy*, 26–27; Webber to NB, 4 July 1799, Ms.E.210.19 v.1 (2), NBC; Catalogue and Charge Book].

48. NB to Pike, 7 Apr. 1798; NB, *1802 Navigator*, vi.

49. Cohen, *Calculating People*, 114–15; Swift, *Gulliver's Travels*, 179, 182.

50. [Peirce], "Nathaniel Bowditch," 316–20 [quotations, 316, 318, 320].

51. Montgomery and Kellam, "Mathematical Backwoodsman"; Young, "Memoir of... Nathaniel Bowditch," 36–37 [quotation, 37]; Webber to NB, 4 July 1799. George Baron critiqued Winthrop's essay in his own *MAAAS* essay, the same publication that Bowditch had opposed. For more on the Winthrop incident, see Davis to Adams,

9 Apr. 1804; Hindle, *Pursuit of Science in Revolutionary America*, 331; and Kaminski et al., *Documentary History*, note for "*Massachusetts Gazette*, 9 October."

52. NB to [Robert Patterson], 11 June 1802, Ms.E.210.19 v.1 (4–5), NBC.

53. NB to Sylvestre Lacroix, 18 Sept. 1805, Ms.E.210.19 v.1 (10), NBC; Hopkins, *Address*, 16–17.

54. Harvard University, Corporation, Corporation records: minutes, 1643–1989, 3 May 1802, ser. III, 4: 621, 630, UAI 5.30.2, HUA; Harvard University, Board of Overseers, Records of the Board of Overseers: formal meeting minutes, 1707–1932, 4 May, 22 July 1802, 4: 351, 352, UAII 5.5.2, HUA; *CC*, 25, 28 Aug. 1802; NIB, "Memoir," 37.

55. *CC*, 25 Aug. 1802; Harvard University, *Mathematical Theses*.

56. Daston, "Enlightenment Calculations," 186; Schaffer, "Genius in Romantic Natural Philosophy"; Holmes, *Age of Wonder*.

57. Daston, "Enlightenment Calculations," 186; Alexander, *Duel at Dawn*. In "Fear and Loathing of the Imagination in Science," Daston argues that, by the beginning of the nineteenth century, the very objectivity and communicability of mathematical and scientific truths placed them in opposition to the subjectivity and originality associated with artistic genius. Americans may have persisted in the notion that mathematical eminence is revealed in lightning quick computations, as when one antebellum writer characterized both Isaac Newton and Bowditch in these terms ["The Art of Teaching," *Massachusetts Teacher* 4 (Jan. 1851): 38].

58. Pickering, *Eulogy*, 12.

Chapter 4

1. *By-laws and Regulations of the East India Marine Society*, 3–4 [quotation, 3]; *NH*, 13 Jan. 1801; *SG*, 6 Jan. 1804 [quotations]. On the EIMS and cosmopolitan knowledge, see Johnston, "Global Knowledge in the Early Republic"; Lindgren, "East India Marine Society"; Dodge, "Contributions to Exploration"; and Dodge, "Captain Collectors." On Salem and global awareness more generally, see Bean, *Yankee India*, and Morrison, "Salem as Citizen of the World." On cosmopolitan knowledge and mercantile identity, see Holdsworth, "Counting-House Library"; Ogborn and Withers, "Travel, Trade, and Empire"; and Hancock, *Citizens of the World*, 31–36.

2. Umbrella: *SG*, 19 Oct. 1804.

3. [HIB], *Memoir*, 64, 66; Hitchings, *Ship Registers*, 98, 151; illegible to JIB, 6 June 1836, F1, B3, Bowditch-Loring Family Papers, 1762–1940, MHS; Hurd, *History of Essex County*, 1: 83; *SIR*, 19 Oct. 1801; *SR*, 22 Nov. 1802; Invoice, 18 Nov. 1802, Ms. Am. 1442, BPL [quotation]. On the pepper trade, see Fichter, *So Great a Profitt*, 83–88; Trowbridge, *Old Shipmasters of Salem*, 135–39; and Putnam, *Salem Vessels and Their Voyages*. Bowditch was also one of the *Putnam*'s four owners.

4. NIB, "Memoir," 35 [quotation]; [HIB], *Memoir*, 66–68; NB to MIB, 5 May 1803, MSS 3, B1, F5, BF-PEM; NB, "Remarks on the N.W. Coast of Sumatra," in "Journal, in the Ship Putnam, Nathaniel Bowditch, Master, November 21, 1802 to December 25, 1803, to Sumatra, Isle of France & back," Bound EIMS Journals, vol. 2, no. 20, MH 88,

EIMSR [quotation]; NB, "Journal in the Ship Putnam from Beverly to Sumatra," 21 Nov. 1802–25 Dec. 1803, 2, 3, 4, 7, 9, 10, 25, 30, 31 May, 20 June, 18, 25 Aug.–1 Sept. 1804, Ms.E.5092.96, NBC; Account, NB to Booyang Etam (sp?), 9 May to 10 July 1803, B1, F11, BF-PEM; "Disbursement of the Ship Putnam, Nathaniel Bowditch Master, on the coast of Sumatra and at the Isle of France," 30 Aug. 1803, B1, F11, BF-PEM.

5. NIB, "Memoir," 30–31; [HIB], *Memoir*, 74–77 [quotations]; "Memoranda by Dr. Henry Ingersoll Bowditch," in Harold Bowditch, "A Collection of Data Made for the Possible Future Use of a Biographer," 1: 312 [quotation], MH 42, NBLW; *SR*, 29 Dec. 1803; Edward A. Holyoke and Enoch Hale, "A Meteorological Journal from the Year 1768 to the Year 1829," *MAAAS*, n.s. 1 (1 July 1833): 154; NB, "Journal, in the Ship Putnam, Nathaniel Bowditch, Master, November 21, 1802 to December 25, 1803, to Sumatra, Isle of France & back," 25 Dec. 1803, Bound EIMS Journals, vol. 2, no. 20, MH 88, EIMSR; NB, "Journal in the Ship Putnam from Beverly to Sumatra," 21 Nov. 1802–25 Dec. 1803, 25 Dec. 1803, Ms.E.5092.96, NBC. Compare Holyoke's entry to those some two months later, when a real nor'easter, reported in the newspaper, jumps out from Holyoke's records as two rows of subfreezing temperatures and accompanying "S"s. In addition, compulsive diarist William Bentley made no comment regarding the weather on 25 December but recorded weather-related difficulties for vessels in the February storm [Holyoke and Hale, "Meteorological Journal," 155; *SG*, 28 Feb. 1804; Bentley, *Diary*, 23 Feb. 1804].

6. MIB to NB, 15 Dec. 1802, B1, F2, BF-PEM; NB to MIB, 5 May 1803. Henry Ingersoll's death: *SR*, 24 May 1802; "Family Records," ser. II, B7, 2: 46, BF-PEM. Bowditch was entitled to a quarter of the profits from the sale of 3,325 pecules—almost half a million pounds—of pepper and 260 bales of coffee. Although we don't know how much the owners got for their cargo, we do know that they paid close to $28,000 in customs duties. In addition, as captain of the *Putnam*, his private venture had consisted of 113 pecules of pepper and 139 bales of coffee [Hurd, *History of Essex County*, 1: 76; "Disbursement of the Ship Putnam"; Bowditch and Archibald, *Catalogue*, 26].

7. White, *Nathaniel Bowditch*, 35; NB, *Directions for Sailing*, iv–vi [quotation, v–vi]; "Review of 'Chart of the Harbours,'" 493.

8. Minutes of Directors' Meeting, 4 Dec. 1804, MH 88, B1, F1, EFMR; [HIB], *Memoir*, 91–92. See also NIB, "Memoir," 32, for the suggestion of "a powerful competitor" for the post. The minutes of the Essex Fire and Marine Insurance Company directors' meetings are maddeningly opaque, but the outlines of some sort of conflict are apparent. In October 1804 James King, the first president, resigned, perhaps over a long-standing salary dispute. When the directors, according to King, dithered in appointing his successor, King resigned for a second time. Two weeks later, the directors elected Bowditch [Minutes of Directors' Meetings, 9 July 1803, 20 Nov., 4 Dec. 1804; King to the Essex Fire and Marine Directors, 20 Nov. 1804, B1, F3, EFMR].

9. *Putnam* insurance: Bowditch and Archibald, *Catalogue*, 26. Ashton: Essex Institute, *Fifth Half Century*, 200; Hurd, *History of Essex County*, 1: 72, 86; Hitchings, *Ship Registers*, 45, 63, 87, 115, 120, 135, 162, 168, 187; *SG*, 19 Mar. 1802. Peele: Essex Institute, *Fifth Half Century*, 203; Hitchings, *Ship Registers*, 12, 15, 66, 95, 152, 144, 181; *SG*, 14

Oct. 1794. Possibly a legal, and even a classical, education may have seemed of some substantive importance. Among the books Bowditch ordered within a few months of his appointment were John Weskett's *Complete Digest of the Theory, Laws, and Practice of Insurance* and Charles Molloy's *De Jure Maritimo et Navali, or, A Treatise of Affairs Maritime and of Commerce* [White Burdett & Co. to NB, 30 May 1805, B1, F3, EFMR]. See Goebel and Smith, *Practice and Procedure*, 427–33, on the marine insurance literature of Bowditch's day.

10. *Massachusetts Register ... 1807*, 56–60. On fire and marine insurance, see Baranoff, "Shaped by Risk," 29–52; Farber, "Underwritten States"; Ruwell, *Eighteenth-Century Capitalism*; Kingston, "Marine Insurance in Britain and America"; Kingston, "Marine Insurance in Philadelphia"; Crothers, "Commercial Risk and Capital Formation"; Fowler, "Marine Insurance in Boston"; and Levy, *Freaks of Fortune*, chap. 2.

11. On early corporations and anticorporate sentiment, see Maier, "Revolutionary Origins of the American Corporation"; Maier, "Debate over Incorporations"; Handlin and Handlin, *Commonwealth*; Schocket, *Founding Corporate Power*; and Wright, *Corporation Nation*.

12. *Act for Incorporating the Essex Fire and Marine*, 10.

13. One anecdote has Bowditch denying insurance to a certain captain because the shipmaster was "unlucky." When the captain complained that Bowditch was placing blame where mere misfortune had occurred, Bowditch replied: "If you do not know that, when you got your vessel on shore on Cape Cod, in a moon-light [*sic*] night, with a fair wind, you forfeited your reputation as an intelligent and careful ship-master, I must now tell you so; and THIS IS WHAT I MEAN BY BEING UNLUCKY." Repeated instances of bad luck surely "indicated incapacity," as any believer in a law-abiding universe knew [NIB, "Memoir," 84].

14. NB to N[athaniel] Ingersoll, 27 Nov. 1812, B1, F5, EFMR. On the workings of the Atlantic mercantile community, see Mathias, "Risk, Credit and Kinship"; Hancock, *Citizens of the World*, 83–84, 139–41; Van, "Free Trade and Family Values"; Sleeswijk, "Social Ties and Commercial Transactions"; Goloboy, "Business Friendships"; Lamoreaux, "Rethinking the Transition to Capitalism," 446–49; Ditz, "Shipwrecked," 56–57; and Porter, *Jacksons and the Lees*, 1: 88–98. Hannah Atlee Farber argues that the corporate form regularized but did not depersonalize marine insurance, which continued to function in the context of a mercantile community with a collective identity ["Underwritten States," 30–32].

15. Leonard Kimball to J. and T. H. Perkins, 8 Nov. 1810 [quotation], B1, F4, EFMR; "Names of the Subscribers," B1, F2, EFMR; JIB, Undated Memorandum Book [quotation], B1, F21, Bowditch-Loring Family Papers.

16. Lamoreaux, *Insider Lending*; Mathias, "Risk, Credit and Kinship"; Olegario, *Culture of Credit*, 97–100, which also notes that expectations of reciprocity and flexibility persisted well into the nineteenth century.

17. NB to Israel Thorndike, 29, 31 May 1811, and Thorndike to NB, 31 May 1811 [quotation], B1, F4, EFMR; "Names of the Subscribers"; Prescott, receipts for legal services, 3 Apr. 1807, 14 July 1810, B4, F1, EFMR; Forbes, *Israel Thorndike*.

18. Thomas C. Amory to Jacob Ashton, 21 Apr. 1813, B1, F5, EFMR; Dudley Pickman to NB, 16 or 18 Mar. 1809, B1, F4, EFMR. See also Farber, "Underwritten States," 120–22.

19. Hurd, *History of Essex County*, 1: 104, 105, 114, 121; Hodgson, *Letters from North America*, 2: 7; *SG*, 26 June 1804, 7 June, 1 July 1814; White Burdett & Co. to NB; Account with Cushing & Appleton, 31 May to 13 Sept. 1809, B3, F8, EFMR; Bills and Receipts, 1804–10, B4, F1, EFMR; Kendall, *Travels*, 3: 27 (quotation); [NB], "Marine Notes." On mercantile districts as centers of information, see McCusker, "Demise of Distance"; Holdsworth, "Counting-House Library"; Kingston, "Marine Insurance in Britain and America," 381–90; Hancock, *Citizens of the World*, 88–90; and Farber, "Underwritten States."

20. Sarah Hodges to Richard M. Hodges, 9 Sept. 1822, in Harriet Hodges, "Nathaniel Bowditch, 1904–5, a Ms. Account," in Bowditch, "Collection of Data," 1: 384; Silsbee, *Half Century in Salem*, 107–8.

21. Leonard Kimball was a twenty-three-year-old Harvard graduate when he took up his duties as secretary. He did not marry until after his removal from Salem. His replacement, James Mansfield Jr., was a teenager when he began work. He died in 1815, at the age of twenty. His successor, Benjamin Pitman, assumed his duties at the age of twenty-two and did not marry for another ten years [Morrison and Sharples, *History of the Kimball Family*, 1: 353–55; *SG*, 9 June 1815, 7 Feb. 1823; Leavitt, "Essex Lodge," 215].

22. Hurd, *History of Essex County*, 1: 114; *SG*, 11 Jan., 28 May 1805, 22 May 1807, 22 Aug. 1809, 20 Apr. 1810, 3 May 1815; Kendall, *Travels*, 3: 24.

23. In 1805 his salary increased to $1,300, and by the middle of 1806 to $1,500, where it remained until his resignation in 1823 [receipts, 30 May 1805, 29 May 1806, 29 Nov. 1806, B4, F1, EFMR].

24. *By-laws and Regulations of the East India Marine Society*, 8; *SG*, 6 Nov. 1807. A possible parallel may be found in the poor response to printer James Aitken's 1772 publication of a daily planner, with its printed grid for recording moneys and comments. Perhaps because potential customers "appeared reluctant to submit themselves to a calculated regimen a printer imposed," the planner found no ready market [McCarthy, *Accidental Diarist*, chap. 2 (quotation, 56)]. On the mercantile decision to share and publicize information, see McCusker, "Demise of Distance," 298–307, and Goloboy, "Business Friendships," 116–19.

25. EIMS Minutes, 4 Nov. 1801, B1, F1, and 4 Jan. 1804, vol. 1, B1, EIMSR; printed directions, EIMS Journals, vol. 1, EIMSR; *By-laws and Regulations of the East India Marine Society*, 8; Whitehill, *East India Marine Society*, 9, 135n; Pickering, *Eulogy*, 13–14. Knowing his protégé's temperament, Bentley referred to Bowditch's 1804 appointment as "a most happy arrangement" [Bentley, *Diary*, 4 Jan. 1804]. The office of "Inspector of the Journals" first appears in the 1808 bylaws [*Bye-laws and Regulations of the Salem East-India Marine Society*, Articles 3, 7, pp. 8–10], but Bowditch already referred to himself with that title in 1804, in the first bound volume of journals. Bowditch did not serve in 1814, perhaps because of political tensions in the

society. Between March 1813 and January 1815 he did not attend EIMS meetings. On 4 Jan. 1815 he was again unanimously elected inspector [EIMS Minutes, vol. 1, B1,4 Jan. 1804–2 Jan. 1820].

26. Logs and journals: García-Herrera et al., "Ships' Logbooks," 22–28. Advertisements for blank "Seaman's Journals" first appear in 1786 but become more numerous after 1800 [America's Historical Newspapers, ser. 1–3, 1690–1922 (Readex), "Seaman's Journals" search; Early American Imprints (Readex), ser. I, II, "Blank Forms"/"seaman" search]. Invoices and Receipts: B4, F1–5 [bills and receipts], B3, F6 [powers of attorney], B5, F2, 3 [proposals for marine insurance], EFMR. Bookkeeping: Lamoreaux, "Rethinking the Transition to Capitalism"; Baxter, "Accounting in Colonial America," 272–87. Baxter notes that "'colonial accounting' in fact out-lasted the colonial period by many years," with "the modern look" only "beginning to creep in" by 1820 [286–87]. Census: https://www.census.gov/history/www/through_the_decades/overview/1830.html [accessed 28 Oct. 2014]. Passport: Robertson, *Passport in America*, chap. 6. Blank forms: Wroth, *Colonial Printer*, 181, 218–26; Rickards, *Encyclopedia of Ephemera*, 31–32, 47–48, 49–52, 150–52, 267–68; Agar, *Government Machine*, 2, 84. Though understudied, a sense of the uses and chronology of blank forms can be gleaned from digital collections in America's Historical Imprints (ser. I, II, and "Broadsides and Ephemera," "blank forms") and the Library of Congress's American Time Capsule: Three Centuries of Broadsides and Other Printed Ephemera ("blank forms"). Rickards notes that the rise of the blank form coincided "with the need for authorities of all kinds to gather information and exercise control" [150]. See also chapter 7 in this volume, note 13.

27. Croarken, "Tabulating the Heavens," 56.

28. Report of the EIMS committee to procure a new catalogue of the museum, 5 Feb. 1820, ser. VII, Scrapbook no. 2 [quotations], EIMSR. The report is signed by Bowditch and is in his hand. For the contrast between the first and second catalogs and the process of reorganization, see also "Original First Manuscript Catalogue of the Specimens in the Museum of the East India Marine Society," ser. VII, Scrapbook no. 2, EIMSR; collections list, B18, F5, EIMSR; East-India Marine Society of Salem, *Act of Incorporation, Bylaws and Catalogue*, 30–80.

29. Bentley, *Diary*, 13 Apr. 1804; Salem Athenaeum, *Catalogue*, 9. On the Athenaeum in Bowditch's era, see Ashton, *Salem Athenaeum*, 9–16; and Wiggin, *Salem Athenaeum*, 4–11.

30. Harold Bowditch conjectured that the couple first lived in the home of NB's first wife, Elizabeth Boardman, but provided no evidence [Bowditch, "Buildings Associated with Nathaniel Bowditch," 213–14]. Several documents place the Bowditches at the Market Street house from at least the autumn of 1803 and confirm the move as taking place in June 1805. The Bowditches first divided the Market Street house with merchant William Appleton, and later with William R. Lee, Collector of the Port [Daniel White to NIB, 24 Mar. 1838, MSS 445, B3, F7, White Family Papers, 1746–1906, PEM; "Notes in Cash Book of Essex Bank, 1804"; SG, 27 July 1804 (quotation), 29 Oct. 1824]. Chestnut Street/Hodges: Bowditch, "Buildings Associated

with Nathaniel Bowditch," 217–18; NB, "Observations on the Total Eclipse of the Sun . . . 1806," 19; Tolles, *Architecture in Salem*, 189–90, 192; Phillips, "Hamilton Hall"; Hodges, *Hodges Family*, 40–41.

31. Sale of Property, William Ward to NB, 6 May 1811, B4, F10, BF-PEM; Bowditch, "Buildings Associated with Nathaniel Bowditch," 218–19; NB to N[athaniel] Ingersoll [quotation]; Bowditch, *Henry Ingersoll Bowditch*, 1: 1–2; JIB to NIB, 30 Apr. 1820, Bowditch, "Collection of Data," 1: 97; EOWW to Margaret Emory, 15 Feb. 1820, B8, F9, White Family Papers; NB to George Bancroft, 21 Feb. 1821, George Bancroft Papers, 1816–90, MHS.

32. NB to Elizabeth Clarke, 9 Feb. 1814, and MIB to Clarke, 28 Aug. 1814 [quotation], PV, N1, F1, Forbes Family Papers, 1732–1931, MHS [hereafter Forbes]; "Family Records," ser. II, B7, 2: 12–13, BF-PEM; Felt, *Annals of Salem*, 1: 461. A sixth son died the day after he was born, in 1813.

33. MIB to Elizabeth Clarke, 28 Sept. 1813, 28 Aug. 1814, PV, N1, F1, Forbes; NIB, "Memoir," 132; NIB, Navigation Notebook, 1816, MSS 399, B10A, F4, American and Canadian Ciphering Books, 1727–1864, PEM [a comparison of its content with the 1811 *Navigator* confirms the source]; "Christmas in 1857" (typescript), unpaginated, Bowditch Family Christmas Collection, 1843–1936, MHS.

34. Silsbee, *Half Century in Salem*, 22.

35. NB to Elizabeth Clarke, 3 Aug. 1813, PV, N1, F1, Forbes.

36. NIB, "Memoir," 131; Walker, *Memoir*, 13–20, 30–33 [quotations, 19, 30].

37. Ellery and Bowditch, *Pickering Genealogy*, 1: 263–64 [quotations, 264]; SG, 15 May 1838 [quotations]; *Cyclopedia of American Literature*, "Henry Pickering"; HIB, "Memoir of Visit to Salem, 1889," 34, HIB Papers, MHS.

38. Pickering, *Life of John Pickering*; Ellery and Bowditch, *Pickering Genealogy*, 1: 258–62 [quotations, 258, 260]; Prescott, *Memoir of Hon. John Pickering*, 204–24; White, *John Pickering*; Pickering, "Problematum Solutiones Fluxionarie," 1796, in Harvard University, *Mathematical Theses*; White to NIB, 24 Mar. 1838 [quotation]; HIB, "Memoir of Visit," 34 [quotation]. Bowditch's aunt had married Timothy Pickering's cousin.

39. D[aniel] A. White, "A Brief Memoir of the Plummer Family," in *Proceedings upon the Dedication of Plummer Hall*, 51–63 [quotations, 55, 61, 62]; Perley, *Plumer* [sic] *Genealogy*, 131; NB to MI, 22 July 1799, B1, F5, BF-PEM; Daniel White to Mrs. Foote, 5 Mar. 1838, B3, F7, White Family Papers; Judith Sargent Murray to Mrs. Plummer, 4 Oct. 1788, in Smith, *Letters of Loss and Love*, 247. A survey of correspondence from her brothers and from Eliza Orne Wetmore reveals that letters were addressed to Caroline Plummer care of Bowditch between 1807 and 1813 [Letters of Ernestus and Theodore Plummer to CP, 1802–16, ser. V, B25, F5–6, 12, BF-PEM; EOW to CP, 29 Apr., 23 Oct. 1811, 1 July 1812, Papers of Professor Henry William Wilder Foote and Family, Andover-Harvard Theological Library, Harvard Divinity School]. Another letter reveals the Bowditches proposing to Ernestus Plummer that Caroline come live in their household [NB and MIB to Ernestus A. Plummer, "Wednesday evening," B1, F1, BF-PEM].

40. MIB to Clarke, 9 Feb. 1814 [quotations]; NB to Elizabeth Clarke, 13 Feb. 1814, PV, N1, F1, Forbes [quotation]. See also EOW to CP, 1 Jan. 1813, ser. II, B7, vol. 1, BF-PEM, for a description of the "Turkish turban" festooned with a "bird of paradise" worn by Mary to a New Year's Eve ball.

41. Silsbee, *Half Century in Salem*, 20–23 [quotations, 21, 22].

42. NIB, "Memoir," 96; [HIB], "Notes by Henry Ingersoll Bowditch," 188 [quotation]; White, *Nathaniel Bowditch*, 33, 64, Young, *Nathaniel Bowditch*, 78, 79n. See also Francis C. Gray's poetic tribute to his friend Bowditch's "simplicity" and "playfulness," excerpted in "Gray's 'Phi Beta Kappa Poem,'" *NAR* 52 (Jan. 1841): 265.

43. Alexander, *Duel at Dawn*; Shapin, "Image of the Man of Science," 172–74; Young, *Nathaniel Bowditch*, 78. For a similar, implicit contrast with pedantry, see Eliza Susan Quincy, Diary, 6 Feb. 1816, Quincy, Wendell, Holmes, and Upham Family Papers, 1633–1910, MHS.

44. White, *Nathaniel Bowditch*, 70; EOWW to CP, 11 Dec. 1819, Papers of Professor Henry William Wilder Foote and Family. See also NIB, "Memoir," 130.

45. White, *Nathaniel Bowditch*, 58; Young, *Nathaniel Bowditch*, 79.

46. NIB, "Memoir," 149–52 [quotation, 152]; Young, *Nathaniel Bowditch*, 91–92; White, *Nathaniel Bowditch*, 64–65; WIB, "Our Family Story from 1639 to 1838 told by William I. Bowditch 1896," MSS 3, ser. II, B6, 1: 117, BF-PEM; NB, Travel Journal, 10 Sept. 1808, Bowditch Family Papers, 1800–94, MHS. On Bentley's Unitarianism, see Ruffin, *Paradise of Reason*.

47. WIB, "Our Family Story," 1: 86, 90–91, 93–94 [quotation, 1: 93]; HIB, description of contents of compartment 7, in "Descriptive Catalogue," bk. 1, Bowditch Memorial Cabinet Catalogue, 1877, Nathaniel Bowditch Memorial Collection, 1851–86, MHS; HIB, "Memoir of Visit," 20–22. In 1813 the Bowditch family celebrated Christmas with the Ingersolls, a year in which Bentley reported that only the Catholic, Universalist, and Episcopalian congregations recognized the holiday [EOW to CP, 1 Jan. 1813; Bentley, *Diary*, 26 Dec. 1813].

48. Bowditch, *Henry Ingersoll Bowditch*, 2: 340–42 [quotations, 341]; HIB, "Memoir of Visit," 15–17 [quotations 16, 17]; HIB, *Sketch*, 15; NIB, "Memoir," 126n; NB to MIB, 20 Sept. 1808, B1, F5, BF-PEM; MIB to NB, 5 June [1811], B1, F2, BF-PEM.

49. Bentley, *Diary*, 13 Apr. 1804; Ruffin, *Paradise of Reason*, 10–15, 26–28, 38–39, 45–47, 142–43.

50. For these events from the perspective of New England Federalists like Bowditch, see Banner, *Hartford Convention*.

51. Bentley, *Diary*, 18 Mar. 1802; MIB to NB, 15 Dec. 1802. On Salem partisanship, see Geib, "Landscape and Faction"; Robbins, "Impact of the First American Party System"; Phillips, "Political Fights and Local Squabbles"; and Robotti, *Chronicles of Old Salem*, 49–55.

52. Bentley, *Diary*, 12 Jan. 1802; *SR*, 11 Jan. 1802; EIMS Minutes, 5 May, 7 July, 3 Nov. 1802, B1, F1; EIMS Minutes, 3 Nov. 1802, vol. 1, B1 [quotation]; Whitehill, *East India Marine Society*, 17–18. A year earlier Salem's Jeffersonian newspaper praised the EIMS for its "liberal and philanthropic principles," designed to "promote a friendly

intercourse among the members." The new bylaws seemed to do the job. In 1804 Bentley reported that "the toasts were of the moment, & without any offence," and in 1806 the toasts were led off with one to the society itself: "*Improvement* 'ahead,' *Harmony* 'in the beam,' and *Party Spirit* 'astern,' *hull-down*" [*SIR*, 12 Jan. 1801; Bentley, *Diary*, 4 Jan. 1804; *SR*, 6 Nov. 1806].

53. Bowditch was a member of the school committee in 1802 and 1806 but lost when he ran in 1807 [*SR*, 25 Mar. 1802, 10 Apr. 1806, 6 Apr. 1807; *Federal Meeting*]. For an example of partisan politics in school elections, see the reference in the Federalist *Gazette* to one committeeman as "the learned bombardier of the *Register*" [*SG*, 11 May 1802].

54. NIB, "Memoir," 163n; *SG*, 30 Mar. 1804; *SR*, 17 May 1804.

55. *SG*, 7, 11 April, 4 Dec. 1812, 16, 19 Nov. 1813; *ER*, 1, 8, 15, 18 Apr. 1812; *BDA*, 17 Nov. 1813; Bentley, *Diary*, 8 Dec. 1812, 18 Nov. 1813. Bowditch may have been called to testify at the initial trial, but Bentley's reference to Bowditch was in connection to a defamation suit pressed by one of the men found guilty of "rioting." According to Bentley, Bowditch's role in this trial had to do with placing the litigant at the scene.

56. "Salem Town Meeting," *SG*, 23, 26 June 1812. Bowditch's name had inadvertently been omitted from the list of committee members [*SG*, 26 June 1812].

57. [HIB], *Memoir*, 96–97; *Boston Repertory*, 31 July 1812; HIB, description of contents of compartment 2, in "Descriptive Catalogue."

58. "A Proclamation," *Federal Republican*, 30 July 1813; NB to Elizabeth Clarke, 21 Sept. 1813, PV, N1, F1, Forbes; MIB, "Journey 1813," [9] Sept. 1813, BF-PEM; NB to Clarke, 13 Feb. 1814. Bowditch was not entirely aloof from public affairs. A month earlier he responded to Timothy Pickering's request for information regarding the nationality of the sailors aboard the USS *Chesapeake*, defeated by the HMS *Shannon* in June 1813. The sailors' nativity was relevant to the contentious issue of impressment [NB to Pickering, 18 Jan. 1814, Timothy Pickering Papers, 1731–1927, MHS].

59. Bentley, *Diary*, 18 July, 5, 10, 12, 17, 24 Sept., 18 Oct. 1814; HIB, description of contents of compartment 7; *SG*, 13 Sept. 1814. See also EOW to Samuel Orne, 12 Sept. 1814, B9, F8, White Family Papers.

60. NB to Elizabeth Clarke, 14 Oct. 1814, PV, N1, F1, Forbes; MIB to Clarke, 23 Oct. 1814, PV, N1, F1, Forbes.

61. Young, *Nathaniel Bowditch*, 68; NIB, "Memoir," 76 [quotation], 163n.

Chapter 5

1. White, *Nathaniel Bowditch*, 32 [quotation]; NB to Samuel Webber, 8 July 1806, Harvard University, Board of Overseers, Records of the Board of Overseers: formal meeting minutes, 1707–1932, 5: 52–53, UAII 5.5.2, HUA; John Pickering to Timothy Pickering, 28 Mar. 1806 [quotation], in MSS 400, B19, F3, Pickering Family Papers, 1662–1887, PEM; Pickering, *Eulogy*, 16; [HIB], *Memoir*, 103. Apparently, Pickering was unofficially first offered his pick of either the Hollis chair or a professorship in Hebrew and Oriental Languages. He ultimately rejected Harvard's formal offer of the

latter [Daniel A. White to John Pickering, 19 Mar. 1806, John Pickering to Timothy Pickering, 28 Mar. 1806, Timothy Pickering to John Pickering, 6 Apr. 1806, and John Pickering to Samuel Webber, 23 Aug. 1806, in Pickering, *Life of John Pickering*, 228–29, 230–33].

2. NB to Samuel Webber; [HIB], *Memoir*, 103–4 [quotation, 104]; Henry A. S. Dearborn to TJ, 14 Oct. 1811, in Oberg and Looney, *Papers of Thomas Jefferson*; Bentley, *Diary*, 19 Apr. 1807; NIB, "Memoir," 78n.

3. NB to CP, 30 Jan. 1805, MSS 3, B1, F1, BF-PEM. The link between a salary and security becomes even clearer when we look at the Salem Marine Insurance Company's early secretaries. Its first was Jonathan Hodges, Bowditch's kinsman and former master, now fallen on hard times after a failed commercial investment. The second was Samuel Curwen Ward, again Bowditch's former master, and again fallen on hard times. Salaries could give young company secretaries a start in their mercantile careers, but they could just as easily provide a safety net for the socially connected on their way down [Hodges, *Hodges Family*, 41; *SIR*, 14 July 1800; Bentley, *Diary*, 27 Nov. 1797; *SG*, 31 May 1803].

4. NB to TJ, 4 Nov. 1818, Ms.E.210.19 v.1 (55), NBC; [HIB], *Memoir*, 92–93 [quotations, 93]; Deposition of Benjamin Pitman, 3 May 1822, and Deposition of NB, 15 May 1822, *Shepard et al v. EFM*, in Konefsky and King, *Boston Practice*, 450, 467. See also, Pickering, *Eulogy*, 16; and Young, *Nathaniel Bowditch*, 77.

5. NB to TJ, 4 Nov. 1818; TJ to NB, 26 Oct. 1818, John C. Calhoun to NB, 7 Oct. 1820, and NB to Calhoun, 13 Oct. 1820, Ms.E.210.19 v.1 (54, 67, 68), NBC.

6. NB to Sylvestre Lacroix, 18 Sept. 1805, Ms.E.210.19 v.1 (10), NBC; Lacroix to NB, 1 Sept. 1806, Ms.E.210.19 v.1 (13), NBC [my thanks to my colleague Liana Vardi for her translation]; Lacroix, *Connaissance des Tems* [*sic*], 437–43 [quotations, 440]. Bowditch's demonstration had been printed as an appendix to the *Navigator* in 1804.

7. Brinkley, "Investigations," 70; Zach, "Übersicht," 411–14 [quotation, 411]. In 1803 NB had informed Zach of tabular errors in one of his publications [Zach, "Vermischte Nachrichten," 449].

8. See, e.g., NB, "Solution of Mr. Patterson's Prize Question."

9. NB, "On the Motion of a Pendulum." One specialist source notes only that the curves "are sometimes known as Bowditch curves" [Weisstein, "Lissajous Curve"].

10. NB, "Observations on the Total Eclipse of the Sun . . . 1806" [garden/theodolite: 19]; NB, "Addition to the Memoir on the Solar Eclipse . . . 1806"; NB to David Leslie, 29 Aug. 1808 [quotation], B1 F1, BF-PEM.

11. [NB], "The Comet," *SG*, 10 Nov. 1807 [identified by NB as his: NB, "Observations of the Comet of 1807," 3]; NB, "Elements of the Orbit of the Comet of 1811," 314 [quotation]; NB, "The Comet. Elements of the Orbit of the Comet, now Visible. Calculated by Nathaniel Bowditch," *SG*, 11 Oct. 1811; NB, "Additional Observations on the Comet," *SG*, 1 Nov. 1811; *Analyst* 1 (Jan. 1808): 71; Samuel L. Mitchill to Henry A. S. Dearborn, 21 Oct. 1811, Ms.Ch.A.7.59, NBC.

12. Wood, *Richmond Enquirer*, 1 Nov. 1811; NB, "The Comet," *SG*, 15 Nov. 1811; "From the Paris Moniteur," *ER*, 14 Dec. 1811. See also Bentley, *Diary*, 13 Dec. 1811.

13. A British periodical had critiqued Wood's *Elements of Perspective* as superficial and scattered, with a show of learning "perhaps rather too sedulously displayed." The story circulated that he had sailed for America in disgrace after he was discovered to have obtained a position at the Edinburgh Drawing Academy by falsifying his credentials. His Republican Party activities probably salvaged his career. By 1810 Wood was teaching at a Richmond academy and had published a treatise that claimed that the earth's two hemispheres move at different velocities. He later won a state contract to map Virginia's counties [Review of "Wood's *Elements of Perspective*," *Monthly Review* (London) 35 (May 1801): 49; Campbell, *Journey from Edinburgh*, 256; "To the Public," *Petersburg Daily Courier*, 24 Nov. 1814; Wood, *New Theory*; *Richmond Enquirer*, 12 June 1810, 17 May 1822; Durey, *Transatlantic Radicals*, 160–63].

14. Compare, e.g., [NB], "The Comet," *SG*, 10 Nov. 1807, with NB, "The Comet," *SG*, 11 Oct. 1811. For the geographic reach of press attention to Bowditch's 1811 calculations, see, e.g., *Eastern Argus* (Portland, Me.), 17 Oct. 1811; *Hagers-Town [Md.] Gazette*, 22 Oct. 1811; *Balance and State Journal* (Albany, N.Y.) 1 (22 Oct. 1811): 43; and "History of the Comet," *Niles' Weekly Register* 2 (7 Mar. 1812): 10–12. On the delays in the publication of the *MAAAS*, note that Bowditch's essay on meteors was published in England before it was published in America.

15. On efforts to construct a Harvard observatory, see Bond, "History and Description of the Observatory" [NB's role, ii, lxxxiii]; Quincy, *History of Harvard*, 2: 566–67; [NB], "Encke's Comet," 33; and NB to Jared Sparks, 3 Jan. 1824, Carl A. Kroch Library, Division of Rare and Manuscript Collections, Cornell University.

16. "Presents Received by the Royal Society"; *Jenaische Allgemeine Literatur Zeitung* 3 (17 July 1812): 100; *Monatliche Correspondenz* 25 (Feb. 1812): 143.

17. Lindenau, "Einleitung," 44–45.

18. NB, "Estimate of the Height, Direction, Velocity" [quotations, 214, 236]. Benjamin Silliman, a young chemistry professor at Yale, established his scientific reputation by publishing a chemical analysis of the meteor fragments [Brown, *Benjamin Silliman*, 221–29].

19. NB, "Estimate of the Height, Velocity, and Magnitude," 89n; *Zeitschrift für Astronomie* 1 (Jan./Feb. 1816): 137–44 [reprint/partial translation]; Lindenau, "Einleitung," 37–38 [quotation, 37]; *Annales de Chimie et de Physique* 3 (1816): 206–12; Chladni, *Über Feuer-Meteoren*, 148–49; NB, "On the Meteor Which Passed over Wilmington"; Dutrochet, "Observation de la hauteur du Météore," 228; Chladni, "Neue Beiträge," 235, 240; Argelander, *Untersuchungen*, 2; "Feuerkugel." When the Royal Society of Edinburgh honored NB with membership in 1818, it cited him as "author of several Memoirs on Astronomy, Meteorology &c.," presumably referring to the study of meteors, not the weather [Applications and Lists of Members: "Candidates for admission," Bound volume containing applications for admission to the Royal Society of Edinburgh, 1815–19, entry for 26 Jan. 1818. By permission of the Royal Society of Edinburgh and NLS Trustees, from "Papers of the Royal Society of Edinburgh," NLS Acc. 10000/42, held on deposit at the National Library of Scotland].

20. Joseph Cogswell to John Farrar, 11 June 1817, Harvard College Papers, 1st ser., 1: 50, UAI 5.131 mf, HUA; George Ticknor to NB, 23 Oct. 1836, Ms.Am.2346 (3), NBC; NIB, "Memoir," 49n; Chladni, "Neue Beiträge," 240 [quotation]; Lindenau, "Einleitung," 76, 89; Lindenau, "Nordamerikanischen Beobachten," 225.

21. [HIB], *Memoir*, 68–69. A fifth volume of the *Mécanique Céleste* appeared in installments between 1823 and 1825, and although Bowditch read it and made some preliminary notes on it, he did not present it in any way to the public.

22. [Playfair], Review of "Traité de Méchanique [*sic*] Céleste" [quotations, 277, 278]; Hahn, *Laplace*, 1 [quotation], 44; Gillispie, "Pierre Simon Laplace," 273 [quotation]. The following discussion of Laplace's work is based on Hahn, *Laplace*; Gillispie, "Pierre Simon Laplace"; Gillispie, *Pierre-Simon Laplace*; and [Playfair], Review of "Traité de Méchanique [*sic*] Céleste."

23. Denoting irregularities that spanned long periods of time, the term "secular" found its root in the Latin term for "century." It did not refer to a realm of phenomena separate from divine presence or religious considerations.

24. [Playfair], Review of "Traité de Méchanique [*sic*] Céleste," 277–79 [quotations, 277, 279].

25. [Farrar], "Ferguson's *Astronomy*," 208–9; [Renwick], "Astronomy of Laplace," 258. See also "Poetical Astronomy," *Boston Repertory*, 14 Sept. 1810.

26. Weatherwise, *Town and Country Almanack*, copy in Bowditch Collection, MHS; NB, "Modern Astronomy," 339.

27. Laplace, *Exposition du Système du Monde*; NB, "Modern Astronomy," 339–40. Such speculations did not necessarily call into question the divine imprint on the universe. Benjamin Peirce, Bowditch's protégé, would also subscribe to the notion that "there is a force in operation, which is directly opposed to the eternal duration of the solar system," namely, "the constant resistance of the ether or light which pervades all space" and must eventually cause all the planets to "fall into the sun." For Peirce this story pointed to God just as the opposite story had for Playfair. "That there is such a sure principle of destruction in our world," Peirce wrote in 1839, "affords an irresistible proof, that the system cannot have existed in its present form beyond a certain time; but it must have had a beginning, a creation, a Creator" [(Peirce), "Bowditch's Translation of the Mécanique Céleste," 171–72].

28. NB, "Remarks on the Usual Demonstration of the Permanency of the Solar System," 74, 75.

29. TJ to NB, 11 Apr. 1818, Ms.E.210.19 v.1 (42), NBC. Commenting on one of Bowditch's mathematical essays to John Adams the following year, TJ expressed similar concerns, noting that the essay "impairs the confidence I had reposed in La Place's demonstration that the excentricities of the planets of our system could oscillate only within narrow limits, and therefore could authorise no inference that the system must, by it's [*sic*] own laws, come one day to an end. This would have left the question of infinitude, at both ends of the line of time, clear of physical authority" [TJ to Adams, 21 Mar. 1819, in Cappon, *Adams-Jefferson Letters*, 2: 536]. Although TJ did not have the mathematical expertise to read the *Mécanique Céleste*, he had read

Laplace's popular exposition of his work, the *Exposition du Système du Monde* of 1796. He ordered this work, as yet untranslated into English, in 1802, though he did not receive a copy until 1809 [Entry for *Exposition du Systeme* [*sic*] *du Monde*, in Sowerby, *Catalogue of the Library of Thomas Jefferson*, 4: 73].

30. For Peirce's refutation of Bowditch's objections, see [Peirce], "Bowditch's Translation," 170–71.

31. Hahn, "Laplace and the Mechanistic Universe," 259–60; NB to Benjamin Vaughan [hereafter BV], 15 June 1818, Benjamin Vaughan Papers, APS. On Laplace as the most influential purveyor of the power of mathematization for science and human intellect more generally, see Hahn, "Laplacean View of Calculation."

32. On the slow acceptance of Leibnizian calculus in America in the 1820s and 1830s, see Timmons, *Mathematics in Nineteenth-Century America*, chaps. 5, 6.

33. [Playfair], Review of "Traité de Méchanique [*sic*] Céleste," 281. See also Topham, "Science, Print, and Crossing Borders," 324–28.

34. Richards, "Geometrical Tradition," 460–62.

35. NB, "Remarks on Doctor Stewart's Formula," 118–19; Rosenstein, "American Calculus Textbooks," 77–80; Ackerberg-Hastings, "Mathematics Is a Gentleman's Art," 155–214; NB, *Mécanique Céleste*, "Introduction by the Translator," 1: v.

36. On Federalist views of science, see Kerber, *Federalists in Dissent*, chap. 3. For an example of the Boston Federalist perception of French (and Philadelphia) science as quixotic and impious, see [Josiah Quincy], "Climenole. A Review Political and Literary. No. 11," *Port-Folio* 4 (13 Oct. 1804): 322.

37. For references to Laplace in Massachusetts newspapers, see, e.g., *NH*, 28 Jan. 1800, 19 July 1803; *Boston Repertory*, 17 May 1805; *BDA*, 24 May 1813; and "The Secret History of the Court and Cabinet of St. Cloud . . .," *Massachusetts Spy*, 27 May 1807 [quotation]. Conservative Britons and Americans fingered Laplace as "an eminent astronomer and atheist" guilty of "impiety" even before he forwarded some of these ideas, and at any rate, independent of them [Richards, "God, Truth, and Mathematics," 60–62; Kippis, *New Annual Register*, 474 (quotation); "W.," *Daily National Intelligencer* (Washington, D.C.), 12 Apr. 1817 (quotation)]. For the persistence of this reputation in America and Britain, see Norton, *Statement of Reasons*, xxiv; [Peirce], "Bowditch's Translation," 175; and Whewell, *Astronomy and General Physics*, esp. 323–42. Nebular hypothesis: Bowditch was familiar with the hypothesis, but he was among a very few Americans aware of it until well into the 1820s. By then there were those who cited it as proof of Laplace's atheism, but that charge preceded American familiarity with these speculations [Numbers, *Creation by Natural Law*, 8–27; Orr, "On the Formation of the Universe"; "Astronomy of Laplace," *American Quarterly Review* 7 (June 1830): 279]. Probability theory: Bowditch owned both Laplace's *Analytical Theory of Probabilities*, published in 1812, and a popular treatment of the subject, his *Philosophical Essay on Probabilities*, published two years later [(WIB), Bowditch Library Catalog, E.166.17–18, NBC].

38. On the suspicion aroused by Laplace's omission, see, e.g., [Playfair], Review of "Traité de Méchanique [*sic*] Céleste," 279. Laplace may or may not have believed

in God, but he certainly believed that scientific knowledge neither relies on nor provides knowledge of a Deity. When Napoleon asked Laplace in 1802 where God fit into his system of the world, the scientist replied, "Sire, I have no need of that hypothesis." The anecdote was first recorded in an 1872 publication, but it is substantially confirmed in the diary of William Herschel, an eyewitness to the interchange. For an evaluation of this anecdote and, more generally, Laplace's views on God and the place of religious ideas in science, see Hahn, "Laplace and the Vanishing Role of God," and Hahn, "Laplace and the Mechanistic Universe."

39. NB to BV, 10 Apr. 1818, Benjamin Vaughan Papers; [NB], "Modern Astronomy," *NAR* 20 (Apr. 1825): 309, 316, 363 [quotations, 309, 363]; NIB, "Memoir," 76. On Bowditch's resistance to public shows of piety, see WIB, "Our Family Story from 1639 to 1838 told by William I. Bowditch 1896," MSS 3, ser. II, B6, 1: 117, BF-PEM; Young, *Nathaniel Bowditch*, 92n; NIB, "Memoir," 150–51; MIB2, "Compilations by Mary Ingersoll Bowditch about Her Father Nathaniel Bowditch" (diary), 2 Mar. 1838, B23, Wigglesworth Family Papers, 1682–1966, MHS. For the standard Federalist assessment of d'Alembert, see, e.g., "Extract from President Dwight's Discourse on the 4th of July 1798," *Berkshire [Mass.] Gazette*, 5 Sept. 1798; "An Abridgement of Barruel's Memoirs of Jacobinism No. V," *Connecticut Journal*, 7 Aug. 1799; CC, 8 Aug. 1810; "Retrospect of French Literature," *Monthly Anthology and Boston Review* (June 1808): 296–97; and "French Philosophers," *Port-Folio* 2 (Nov. 1809): 437–39.

40. Crosland, "Relationships"; De Beer, "Relations between Fellows." Similar relations existed between the Americans and the British during the Revolution [Greene, *American Science, 145–46*].

41. "Members of the Academy," *MAAAS*, n.s. 11 (1882): 55–59; EE to NB [16 May 1821], and NB to EE [20 May 1821], Ms.E.210.19 v.1 (78–80), NBC. A few of the men elected only in the 1830s—Charles Babbage, for example—had been suggested over a decade earlier by Bowditch.

42. Lambert, *To the Critical Reviewers of Boston*, 2 [quotation]. The fullest selection of documents related to this proposal can be found in Lambert and Monroe, *Message from the President*. On Lambert, see his letters to TJ, 8 June 1793 (and note), 23 May 1801 (and note), 14 Mar. 1809 (and note), 13 June, 23 July, 17 Sept. 1809, 5 Dec. 1809 (and note), and 19 Feb. 1810, in Oberg and Looney, *Papers of Thomas Jefferson*. See also Edney, "Cartographic Culture."

43. [NB], Review of "Memorial of William Lambert," 249–53 [quotation, 252].

44. Ibid., 257–66 [quotations, 257, 262]; Lambert, *To the Critical Reviewers of Boston*, 1 [quotation], 2; [NB], "Defence [sic] of the Review." See also NB to William S. Shaw, 11, 14 Jan. [1811], in Harold Bowditch, "A Collection of Data Made for the Possible Future Use of a Biographer," 1: 33–36, MH 42, NBLW. Opinion on Lambert's proposal did not in fact fall along regional or partisan lines. Timothy Pitkin, Federalist congressman from Connecticut, chaired the committee that supported the proposal.

45. Lambert, *To the Critical Reviewers of Boston*, 1; [NB], "Defence of the Review," 48; *ER*, 7 Sept. 1811.

46. The navigation teacher was James M. Elford: NB, "Lettre XXV" (dated 22 Nov. 1822). On Elford, see *Charleston City Gazette,* 21 June 1803, 12 Apr. 1820, 20 Sept. 1822; Zach, "Lettre XIV," dated 1 Feb. 1822, in *CorrAst* 6 (1822): 217; Elford, *Second Edition of Longitude Tables.* The mathematics professor was James Wallace: NB, "Remarks on Several Papers"; NB, "Remarks on Mr. Wallace's Reply." On Wallace, see "Death of Professor Wallace," *Daily Globe* (Washington, D.C.), 7 Feb. 1851. See also NB to Benjamin Silliman, 17 May 1825, Simon Gratz Autograph Collection, Historical Society of Pennsylvania.

47. NB to Jedidiah Morse, 12 Dec. 1808, Gratz Collection; Bentley, *Diary,* 19 Sept. 1806, 24 Jan. 1810, 13 Dec. 1811, 28 Mar. 1817; "Eclipse of the Sun," *SG,* 3 Sept. 1811; *Alexandria Daily Gazette,* 11 Sept. 1811.

48. Henry A. S. Dearborn to TJ, 14 Oct. 1811, and TJ to Dearborn, 15 Nov. 1811, in Oberg and Looney, *Papers of Thomas Jefferson.* Bowditch maintained a similar relationship with James Madison [Madison to NB, 16 May 1818, in Stagg, *Papers of James Madison;* NB to Madison, 18 May 1827, Ms.E.210.19 v.1 (100), NBC].

49. TJ to NB, 2 May 1815, Ms.E.210.19 v.1 (29), NBC. A year earlier, in a letter to TJ, John Adams had praised David Rittenhouse as "a virtuous and amiable Man; an exquisite Mechanician; Master of the Astronomy known in his time; an expert Mathematician, a patient calculator of Numbers," but insisted that Bowditch was "his Superior in all these Particulars, except the Mechanism" [Adams to TJ, Feb. 1814, in Looney et al., *Papers of Thomas Jefferson, Retirement Series,* 7: 217].

50. TJ to NB, 26 Oct. 1818, and NB to TJ, 4 Nov. 1818; TJ to James Madison, 7 July 1819, in Stagg, *Papers of James Madison.*

51. *BDA,* 5 Jan. 1818; EE to R[obert] Walsh, 28 Dec. 1817, EE Papers, MHS.

52. Ellis, *After the Revolution,* chaps. 1, 2; Simpson, *Man of Letters,* 32–40. See also Kaplan, *Men of Letters in the Early Republic,* esp. chaps. 5, 6.

53. BV to NB, 13 Aug. 1817, Ms.E.210.19 v.1 (40), NBC; EE to Walsh, 28 Dec. 1817. On the post-1800 decline of the AAAS, see Stone, "Scientific Boston," 158–67. See also John Pickering's complaints of the Boston-centered provinciality of the AAAS in Pickering to Timothy Pickering, 5 Apr. 1816, B19, F3, Pickering Family Papers. On Vaughan, see Murray, *Benjamin Vaughan.*

54. BV to NB, 13 Aug. 1817. With respect to the AAAS's standing in New England, Vaughan was concerned about competition from Benjamin Silliman's Connecticut Academy.

55. NB to BV, 7 Jan. 1818, Benjamin Vaughan Papers. Besides the essay concerning solar tables, the critical articles include "On the Calculation of the Oblateness of the Earth," "On the Method of Computing the Dip of the Magnetic Needle," "On a Mistake Which Exists in the Calculation of Mr. Poisson," "Remarks on Doctor Stewart's Formula," "Remarks on the Usual Demonstration of the Permanency of the Solar System," and "Remarks on the Methods . . . in Newton's 'Principia' and in Laplace's 'Mécanique Céleste.'"

56. EE to Walsh, 28 Dec. 1817; Adams, Diary, 28 Feb. 1811, in Adams, *Memoirs of John Quincy Adams,* 2: 220. Lindenau confirmed the rarity of the journal ("so seldom

in Germany") and confirmed its provenance. Jeremias David Reuss, professor and library director at Göttingen, had provided Lindenau with "the sole [copy] now to be found on the continent" [*Zeitschrift* 1: (1816): 137n]. EE's contact with Reuss is discussed in Eck, "Die Amerikanische Kolonie in Göttingen," 234.

57. John A. Vaughan to EE, 12 Apr. 1817, EE Papers; William Vaughan [hereafter WV] to EE, 13 May 1838, EE Papers; WV to NB, 5 May 1818, and BV to NB, 11 Aug. 1818, Ms.E.210.19 v.1 (45, 51), NBC; Journal Book of the Royal Society, entry for 15 May 1817, XLI, and entry for 12 Mar. 1818, XLII, Archives of the Royal Society, London. See also BV to NB, 13 Aug. 1817. The French fellows included Gaspard Riche de Prony, François Arago, René Just Haüy, and Siméon Denis Poisson.

58. WV to EE, 13 May 1838; Dugald Stewart to Thomas Thompson, 8 Dec. 1817, quoted in MacIntyre, *Dugald Stewart*, 192. On the Edinburgh and Dublin honors, see also WV to NB, 16 Apr. 1818, BV to NB, 9 June 1818, Nathaniel Silsbee to NB and John Pickering, 7 Feb. 1820, Silsbee to NB, 24 Feb. 1820, WV to NB, 9 Mar. 1820 [quotation], Ms.E.210.19 v.1 (43, 48, 59, 60, 62), NBC; and NB to BV, 7 Jan., 1, 15 June, 25 Sept. 1818, and BV to Parker Cleaveland, 22 May 1818, Benjamin Vaughan Papers. For Bowditch's election to the Royal Society of Edinburgh, see "Candidates for admission" and Minutes of Statutory and Special General Meetings and notes of extraordinary business conducted at Ordinary Meetings, Nov. 1812 to Oct. 1926, entry for 15 Dec. 1817, By permission of the Royal Society of Edinburgh and NLS Trustees, from "Papers of the Royal Society of Edinburgh," NLS Acc. 10000/11, held on deposit at the National Library of Scotland. For Dublin, see Minutes of the Royal Irish Academy, 22 June 1818, 16 Mar. 1819, 1: 293, 300, Royal Irish Academy Papers.

59. "Von der Unterrichtsweise," 444; NB, "Lettre XIII" (dated 22 Nov. 1822), 223n [editor's note]; NB to Thomas Young, 20 Aug. 1818, Ms.E.210.19 v.1 (52), NBC; Quincy, *Extracts from Journals*, 2.

60. SG, 2 June 1818; *Boston Repertory*, 4 June 1818; *New-York Evening Post*, 5 June 1818; *ER*, 6 June 1818; *City of Washington Gazette*, 10 June 1818. Almost certainly the *Essex Register* mistook the relatively unknown John Herschel for his celebrated father, William.

61. NB to BV, 15 June 1818; election certificates, 12 Mar. 1818, Journal Book of the Royal Society, XLII. A comparison of certificates indicates that the reference to solicitation of the honor in Bowditch's certificate was not standard, though the rest of the wording was. It may be significant that Bowditch's name was presented eighteen times before his nomination was approved; the usual number was ten [Heindel, "Americans and the Royal Society," 269].

62. "For the Port Folio—Literary Intelligence," *Port-Folio* 5 (Mar. 1818): 225; John Adams to NB, 4 Apr. 1818, Ms.E.210.19 v.1 (41), NBC; Young, *Nathaniel Bowditch*, 51–53 [quotation, 52]; J. Blunt to NB, 21 Nov. 1818, B1, F3, BF-PEM; NIB, "Memoir," 69–70; BV to NB, 9 June 1818. Robert Adrain was the only other American of his day to rank with Bowditch in mathematical sophistication. Even before he had met Bowditch, Adrain named his son after the man whose work he so admired. The two men became warm friends [NB to MIB, 20 Apr. 1823, B1, F5, BF-PEM; Adrain to NB,

9 Aug. 1830, and 12 May 1832, Ms.E.210.19 v.2 (50, 67), NBC; and Hogan, "Adrain, Robert"].

63. NB to BV, 15 June 1818; NIB, "Memoir," 70.

64. Bowditch pointed to improvements made by Poisson and James Ivory in particular [NB, *Mécanique Céleste*, 1: vi–vii; Royal Astronomical Society of London, "Necrological Notice of the Late Dr. Bowditch, from the Report of the Council . . . 1839," 2, Misc. Mss., APS].

65. NIB, JIB, HIB, WIB, cover letter of *Mécanique Céleste* Ms., 29 Jan. 1859, first folio volume, *Mécanique Céleste*, Ms.E.210.11 (v.1), NBC. Bowditch's son noted that, although in the preface to the *Mécanique Céleste* his father had stated the translation took place between 1815 and 1817, the correct dates were 1814 to 1817. Those dates are verified by a note in Bowditch's handwriting on the title page of the original manuscript, vol. 1 [NIB, "Memoir," 60; *Mécanique Céleste* ms., BPL].

66. Some of these German-surnamed and German-speaking individuals lived elsewhere, including Russia (Theodor von Schubert) and Italy (Zach). Some of those scientists working in Germany originated from elsewhere (Chladni). Yet others, like the Swiss Leonhard Euler, were German speakers.

67. NB listed a publication by Zach on light and one by Euler on the solar parallax in his Index to Commonplace Book, 18 Nov. 1797, Ms.E.5092.87 (2), NBC.

68. NB to BV, 15 June 1818; NB, "Lettre XIII," 228.

69. Bentley, *Diary*, 22 June 1818; George Bancroft to NB, 31 Mar. 1819, George Bancroft Collection, Special Collections and Archives, Knox College Library; NB to Bancroft, 21 Feb. 1821, George Bancroft Papers, 1816–90, MHS.

70. [NB], "Works of the German Astronomers," 269–70 [quotation, 270]; NB to Edward Eulenkamp, 13 Dec. 1819, ser. II, B7, vol. 1, BF-PEM. On NB's progress with German, see also NB to George Bancroft, and NB to Friedrich Theodor von Schubert, 25 Mar. 1820, Ms.E.210.19 v.1 (63), NBC. In the latter, Bowditch was responding to Schubert's earlier letter to him, in which the astronomer stated that though "I doubt whether You read german [*sic*] books," he enclosed a copy "of a *popular astronomy*, which I have written for general use" [Schubert to NB, 25 July 1819, Ms.E.210.19 v.1 (57), NBC]. As catalogued in 1837, Bowditch's library contained Crabb's *German Exercises* (1811), Nöhden's *German Exercise* (1818), Nöhden's *Grammar* (1818), *Life of Washington* in German (1817), and *Amerikanischen Kriegs* (1817) [(WIB), Bowditch Library Catalogue]. See also his English-German Vocabulary Book, Charles Edward French Autograph Collection, 1337–1897, MHS.

71. [NB], "Works of the German Astronomers," 260–63, 270–72 [quotations, 260, 270, 272].

72. Ibid., 272.

Chapter 6

1. Hodgson, *Letters from North America*, 2: 6–7.

2. Pickering, *Report of the Committee*; Kornblith, "Rise of the Mechanic Interest."

3. Gibson, "Population of the 100 Largest Cities," tables 2, 6; *Massachusetts Register... 1801*, 44–45; *Massachusetts Register . . . 1829*, 171–78. On the decline of Salem vis-à-vis Boston, see also Labaree, "Making of an Empire," and Booth, *Death of an Empire*.

4. Hodgson, *Letters from North America*, 2: 146–47.

5. Holmes used the term to describe Boston's State House, but the sense of the phrase was that Boston was the center of everything important ["Autocrat of the Breakfast-Table," 734].

6. John Pickering to Alexander von Humboldt, 27 Nov. 1827, in Pickering, *Life of John Pickering*, 351–52.

7. NB to EOW, 14 May 1817, B1, F1, and 25 June 1817, B1, F5, BF-PEM.

8. *SG*, 8, 11, 18 July 1817 [quotations, 8, 11]; *ER*, 12, 16 July 1817 [quotation, 16]; *Boston Commercial Gazette*, 14 July 1817 [quotation]; Bentley, *Diary*, 7, 8, 9, 10, 11, 12 July 1817. On the "Era of Good Feelings" in Massachusetts, see *CC*, 12 July 1817; Moats, "Limits of 'Good Feelings.'"

9. Moats, "Limits of 'Good Feelings,'"; *ER*, 12 July 1817 [quotations]. James Monroe soon reconsidered even this double-talk as insufficiently noncommittal, directing "a small alteration" in it for the record [Monroe to unknown, 15 July 1817, in Preston and DeLong, *Papers of James Monroe*, 1: 412]. In private letters to Timothy Pickering, Bowditch had opposed these tariffs on precisely these grounds [NB to Pickering, 24 Dec. 1815, 29 Feb. 1816, Timothy Pickering Papers, 1731–1927, MHS].

10. Hartford, *Money, Morals, and Politics*, 43–64; Sheidley, "Politics of Honor," 298–300.

11. *SG*, 27 Dec. 1816, 21 Feb. 1817; Bentley, *Diary*, 27 Dec. 1816; Loring, *Nathaniel Bowditch*, 17–18; "Sketch of First Church," 34; George Richards Minot, "Noteworthy Union of 'Boston Trustees,'" *Boston Evening Transcript*, 5 Jan. 1935. Historians have dated the trust legislation to 1817 [Curran, "Struggle for Equity Jurisdiction," 275; Hall and Marcus, "Class, Dynasty, and Inheritance," 145; Johnson, "No Adequate Remedy at Law," 5, 33–35], but in fact, while the bill was first considered by the state legislature in June 1817, it was not passed and signed into law until February 1818 [*Boston Intelligencer*, 7 June 1817; *Boston Repertory*, 10 June 1817 and 30, 31 Jan. 1818; *Boston Commercial Gazette*, 16 June 1817; *BDA*, 16 June 1817; *Boston Weekly Messenger*, 12 Feb. 1818; *Boston Commercial Gazette*, 26 Feb. 1818; *Laws of the Commonwealth . . . 1818*, 486].

12. The following discussion of trusts and equity powers is based on Blackmar, "Inheriting Property and Debt," 102–13; Hall, *Organization of American Culture*, 114–24; Hall and Marcus, "Class, Dynasty, and Inheritance"; Friedman, "Dynastic Trust," 551–55; and Shammas, Salmon, and Dahlin, *Inheritance in America*, 56–57, 75–76, 107–8. For Massachusetts trusts in particular, see Hall, "What the Merchants Did with Their Money"; Curran, "Struggle for Equity Jurisdiction"; Johnson, "No Adequate Remedy at Law"; Story, *Life and Letters of Joseph Story*, vol. 1: 138–39, 371–81; and [Story], "Chancery Jurisdiction." On the general workings of trusts, see Hall and Clark, *Oxford Companion to American Law*, s.v. "Trust."

13. Newmyer, *Joseph Story*; Howe, *What Hath God Wrought*, 120–24; Bentley, *Diary*, 2 Apr. 1803 [quotation], 7 Nov. 1808.

14. [Story], "Chancery Jurisdiction," 147, 156, 157. According to William J. Curran, this unsigned article was an expanded version of Joseph Story's 1808 committee report, which Story in fact excerpts in the essay ("Struggle for Equity Jurisdiction," 274, 280). On Theophilus Parsons, see Newmyer, *Joseph Story*, 68, 120.

15. "Juridicus," "Communication," *Boston Patriot*, 23 Feb. 1818; "Communication," *BDA* 26 Feb. 1818; "Justice," "Communication," *Boston Patriot*, 26 Feb. 1818; "Juridicus," "Communication," *Boston Patriot*, 5 Mar. 1818; "Communication," *Boston Yankee*, 6, Mar. 1818. For other contributions to this debate and the unsuccessful legislative attempts to water down the enacted bill, see *BDA*, 11 June 1817; *Boston Repertory*, 14, 17, 21 Feb. 1818; *CC*, 14 Feb. 1818; and *Boston Intelligencer*, 21 Feb. 1818.

16. Belknap, "Simon Forrester," 29–64 [quotation, 55]; Loring, *Nathaniel Bowditch*, 18–19; Bentley, *Diary*, 11, 14 Apr. 1816, and 5 July 1817 [quotations]. Bowditch's lead role in the trust is inferred from the consistent use of his name as the first among the three in trust-related legal documents, and from the use of "Bowditch, Nathl. And Trustees" in a congressional document regarding Bank of the United States stockholders [Forrester, Codicil to Will, 21 Jan. 1817, in Belknap, "Simon Forrester," 30; Dudley Leavitt Pickman Papers, 1721–1938 (hereafter DLP Papers), PEM, ser. I, B1, F5–8, and B2, F1–2 passim; "List of Stockholders," in U.S. Congress, *Report of the Committee*, 339].

17. For the probate documents, see Belknap, "Simon Forrester," 29–42. For the investment activity, as conducted over several decades, see the large cache of Forrester trust papers in ser. I, B1, F5–9, B2, F1–2, DLP Papers; and Rice, "Worcester Town Records," 201.

18. For trustees' neglect and pillaging of trusts and their slipshod administrative practices, see [Story], "Chancery Jurisdiction," 163; Blackmar, "Inheriting Property and Debt," 102–4; and James King to State Chancellor, 2 Oct. 1832, and 15 Aug. 1835, quoted in Blackmar, "Inheriting Property and Debt," 103. The Forrester trustees' careful practices emerge from an examination of trust documents in DLP Papers; NB to Leverett Saltonstall, 20 Aug. 1835, B8, vol. XI, no. 107, Saltonstall Family Papers, 1524–1999, MHS; and Memorandum of Property Transferred to Surviving Trustees, Apr. 1838, Estate of NB, B22, F1, BF-PEM. For Bowditch's order of blank forms, see Invoice, Cushing & Appleton, 28 Nov. 1817, DLP Papers. See also Loring, *Nathaniel Bowditch*, 17–18.

19. NB to TJ, 4 Nov. 1818, Ms.E.210.19 v.1 (55), NBC. Forrester's will stipulated that the trustees receive "reasonable compensation" for their services [Forrester will, Codicil, 21 Jan. 1817, in Belknap, "Simon Forrester, 30].

20. *Harvard College and Massachusetts General Hospital v. Francis Amory* (quotation, 461); Hall and Marcus, "Class, Dynasty, and Inheritance," 146–51; Friedman, "Dynastic Trust," 551–55; Holbrook, *Boston Trustee*; Curtis, "Manners and Customs of the Boston Trustee"; Allen, *Investment Management in Boston*, chap. 3. Judge Samuel Putnam was an incorporator and member of the Salem Athenaeum and, with Bowditch, a delegate to the 1812 antiwar Essex Convention [Baird, *Samuel Putnam*; *SG*, 17 Apr. 1810; *Boston Repertory*, 31 July 1812].

21. Bentley, *Diary*, 24 Aug., 5 Sept., 6 Nov. [quotation] 1818; Dow, *Diary and Letters of Benjamin Pickman*, 212 (entry for 19 July 1818); *SG*, 1 Sept. 1818; *ER*, 2 Sept., 7 Nov. 1818, 2; *Niles Weekly Register*, 19 Sept. 1818, 59; *New-York Columbian*, 11 Sept. 1818; *Foster v. Essex Bank*. The bank directors included Joseph White, the bank president, with whom Bowditch had served on the Monroe Committee of Arrangements; Abel Lawrence, one of Bowditch's partners in the *Putnam*; merchant Samuel Orne, one of the organizers of the Orne Trust; and Bowditch's friend Dudley Pickman [*SG*, 22 May 1818].

22. Dow, *Diary and Letters of Benjamin Pickman*, 213 (entry for 30 Nov. 1818).

23. [Benjamin Pickman], Diary, 13 Mar. 1818, ser. II, B4, DLP Papers; Bentley, *Diary*, 24 Aug. [quotations], 11 Sept., 6 Nov. 1818, 8 Jan. 1819; HIB, "Memoir of Visit to Salem, 1889," 33, HIB Papers, MHS. Gray: *Federal Meeting*; Ashton, *Salem Athenaeum*, 49; Gray, "William Grays in Salem in 1797," 146–47. Henry Ingersoll Bowditch reported that, many years later, Gray returned "a poor, broken down man" but that he was not prosecuted. "He was so great a criminal that the people *allowed him to die without notice!*" ["Memoir of a Visit to Salem," 33].

24. *SG*, 7 Aug. 1792, 5 Jan. 1816; *ER*, 14 May 1817; Bentley, *Diary*, 24 Aug. 1818; Whipple, *History of the Salem Light Infantry*, 11 [quotation].

25. Halttunen, *Confidence Men and Painted Women*; Mihm, *Nation of Counterfeiters*; Kamensky, *Exchange Artist*; Anthony, *Paper Money Men*. Jordy: Bentley, *Diary*, 8 Oct. 1793, and 29 Aug. 1794 [quotation].

26. *Foster v. Essex Bank*; Bentley, *Diary*, 22 June 1819; *SG*, 2, 6 July 1819; Rental Receipts, B4, F1, EFMR; Bank Account Book, B2, F9, EFMR; Statement of Profit and Loss, Dec. 1810, B2, F6, EFMR; Minutes of Directors Meetings, 30 Apr. 1803, B1, F1, EFMR; "Names of the Subscribers and the times they paid their first Installment," [1802], B1, F2, EFMR; Farber, "Underwritten States," 97–107.

27. Bentley, *Diary*, 7 Jan., 10 Nov. [quotation] 1819; *SG*, 12 Jan. 1819; *New-Bedford Mercury*, 5 May 1820.

28. The first of many newspaper notices appeared in *SG*, 4 May 1819, even before the legislature extended the life of the Essex Bank to settle its affairs. See also Printed Circular, "Essex Bank," 21 May 1822, E S1 B1 E1 1822, PEM.

29. Bentley, *Diary*, 8 Jan. 1819; *Act to Incorporate the . . . Commercial Bank*; *Massachusetts Register . . . 1820*, 170; Dennis, *Merchants National Bank*, 7–23. The new bank's act of incorporation even referenced (and reprinted) the Merchants Bank act of incorporation as an explicit template.

30. *Foster v. Essex Bank* [quotation, 506].

31. *Report of the Auditors . . . of the Union Marine and Fire Insurance Company* [quotations, 4–6]. See also Bentley, *Diary*, 5 Nov. 1816.

32. Fowler, "Marine Insurance in Boston," 178–79; Vote of the Board, 11 Feb. 1805, quoted in Fowler, "Marine Insurance," 179.

33. *Act for Incorporating the Essex Fire and Marine*, 9–10; receipt [Essex Fire and Marine Insurance Company] to J. Waters and W. Peele [June 1819], B4, F1, and Accounts, ser. II, B3, F8, EFMR.

34. NB to CP, 2 June 1811, B1, F5, BF-PEM. Little: Chapman, *Sketches*, 88–89; Currier, *History of Newburyport*, 1: 520, 680; *NH*, 26 May, 13 June 1809. Blunt/Little arrangement: *NH*, 1 May 1810; New York *Mercantile Advertiser*, 5 June 1811; Campbell, *History and Bibliography*, 80–82.

35. The following account has been reconstructed from the following scattered correspondence: Edward Little to NB, 1 Apr., 24 May, 22 July 1817, 18 Apr., 6 July 1818, 15 Mar. 1819, B1, F2, BF-PEM; NB to Edmund Blunt, 18 Sept. 1817, 19 Mar. 1818, vol. 11, Alexander Calvin and Ellen Morton Washburn Autograph Collection, 1600–1895, MHS; NB to Blunt, 6 June 1819, Simon Gratz Autograph Collection, Historical Society of Pennsylvania, and B1, F1, BF-PEM (two copies of the same letter); NB to Blunt, 21 May, 6 June 1819, B1, F3 and F1, BF-PEM; Blunt to NB, 25 May, 25 Jan. 1818, 27 Mar., 18, 22 May, 5 Aug. 1819, B1, F3, BF-PEM; John Blunt, memorandum, 16 July 1819, B1, F3, BF-PEM.

36. Quotations: Little to NB, 24 May, 22 July 1817, 18 Apr. 1818; Blunt to NB, 25 May 1818; Little to NB, 15 Mar. 1819; NB to Blunt, 6 June 1819; Blunt to NB, 5 Aug. 1819. Given that legal wrangling between Blunt and Edward Little's father Josiah continued into the 1830s, it seems unlikely that Bowditch was ever paid [*Josiah Little v. Edmund M. Blunt*].

37. *NH*, 23 Apr. 1811, 26 Sept. 1809 [quotation]; Bentley, *Diary*, 3 June 1811; *Account of the Great Fire*, 3–4; *N.H. Patriot*, 7 Feb. 1815; *Hallowell [Me.] Gazette*, 15 Feb. 1815; *Conn. Courant*, 15 Feb. 1840; *Eastern Argus* (Portland, Me.), 26 June 1827. No doubt, the fact that Little was a fellow attorney and judge, the son of a prominent landowner, and therefore what the newspaper termed one of the "*great* folks" was also a factor in the judge's decision. In 1849, in recognition of Little's philanthropic contributions to the Lewiston Falls Academy in Auburn, Maine, the name of the institution was changed to the Edward Little Institute, today Edward Little High School. Reportedly, the text for his funeral sermon was "whatsoever thy hand findest to do, do with all thy might" [Edith Labbie, "Who Was Edward Little?" *Lewiston (Me.) Journal*, 19 Sept. 1981, 2A].

38. JI to NB, 17 Apr., 18 Aug. 1818, B1, F2, BF-PEM; Bowditch, *Henry Ingersoll Bowditch*, 1: 3; NB to Benjamin Vaughan, 15 June 1818, Benjamin Vaughan Papers, APS; MIB to Sally Endicott, 16 Apr. 1819, PV, F1, N1, Forbes Family Papers, 1732–1931, MHS [hereafter Forbes]; EOWW to Mrs. [Sophia D.] Orne, 5 Aug. 1819, B8, F9, White Family Papers, 1746–1906, PEM [hereafter White]; EOWW to Sophia D. Orne, 27 Dec. 1819, B26, F45, Papers of Professor Henry William Wilder Foote and Family, Andover-Harvard Theological Library, Harvard Divinity School [quotation]. For earlier expressions of concern regarding Mary's health, see EO to CP, 11 Aug. 1801, 21 Apr., 16 Dec. 1802, B9, F6, White, and EOW to Lucinda D Orne, 21 Nov. 1811, B9, F8, White.

39. NB to NIB, 4, 19 Nov. 1819 [quotation, 19], 28 June [quotation], 21 July 1821, and MIB to NIB, 2 July 1820, PV, N1, F1, Forbes.

40. Morison, "Great Rebellion"; Lothrop, *Memoir of Nathaniel Ingersoll Bowditch*, 5; MIB and NB to EOW, 18 Nov. 1818, B1, F2, BF-PEM. When the students, unaware of

Bowditch's identity, reacted with further impudence, the dean asked them, "Do you know you are talking to the Hon N.B. of Salem, one of the overseers of Hd. College"? The teenagers straightened up, and Bowditch heard one whisper to another that the stranger on the stage must be "*Little Bowditch's father*" [NB to EOW, 18 Nov. 1818].

41. MIB and NB to Sally Endicott, 16 Apr. 1819; Harvard University, Votes of the Faculty Relating to Academic and Administrative Affairs, 1636–1870, 6 Apr. 1819, IX: 9, UAIII 5.5.2, HUA.

42. MIB to NIB, 30 Apr., 12 June 1820, in Harold Bowditch, "A Collection of Data Made for the Possible Future Use of a Biographer," 1: 98, 100, MH 42, NBLW; NB to NIB, 4 Nov. 1819 [quotation]; Diary of Pickering Dodge, 2 Nov. 1820, in Morison, "Great Rebellion," 70; Harvard University, Votes of the Faculty, 4 Nov. 1820, 30 Apr., 7 May 1821, IX: 242, 253, 255; EE to NB, 16 May 1821, Ms.E.210.19 v.1 (78–80), NBC.

43. NB to NIB, n.d., and MIB to NIB, 4 Nov. 1819, 7 Aug. 1820, in Bowditch, "Collection of Data," 1: 85, 87–88, 105–6; MIB to NIB, 2 July 1820; NB to NIB, 9 Nov. 1819 [quotation]; HIB, "Memoir of Visit to Salem, 1889," 34, HIB Papers, MHS. The emotional effect seems to have been lasting. Sometime in the mid-1850s Nat brought several "test" questions with him to a spiritual medium, the answers to which only the person on the "other side"—Nathaniel Bowditch—would know. Among the questions: "Was I censured in College?" (yes); the cause? (fire); censured again? (yes); cause? (cannon ball) [Luther V. Bell, "Two Dissertations on what are termed the 'Spiritual Phenomena,'" c. 1855, p. 111, B MS b45. 1, Boston Medical Library, HIB Papers, Countway].

44. NIB, "Projection of the Solar Eclipse, Feb. 21, 1822," Harvard University, *Mathematical Theses*.

45. NB to NIB, 21 Feb. 1820, PV, N1, F1, Forbes; "Your sister N H Ingersoll" to MIB, 8 and 9 May 1817, ser. II, B7, vol. 1, BF-PEM. For examples of his affectionate letters home, see his postscript to the letter of 8 and 9 May, and Charles Ingersoll Bowditch to NB, undated, ser. II, B7, vol. 1, BF-PEM.

46. EOWW to Margaret Emory, 15 Feb. 1820, B8, F9, White [quotation]; NB to NIB, 20 Feb. 1820, in Bowditch, "Collection of Data," 1: 89–90; NB to CP, Monday morning [27 Feb. 1820], ser. II, B7, vol. 1, BF-PEM; SG, 22 Feb. 1820.

47. NB to CP [27 Feb. 1820]; gravestone, Old Burying Point or the Charter Street Cemetery, Salem, Mass.; Charles Ingersoll Bowditch, Notebook, 29 Dec. 1816–7 Feb. 1820, ser. II, B7, vol. 1, BF-PEM.

48. SG, 8 June 1821; NB to John Lathrop, 30 May 1810, Harvard University, College Papers, 1st ser., 6: 51, UAI 5.131 mf, HUA [quotation]; Harvard University, Board of Overseers, Records of the Board of Overseers: formal meeting minutes, 1707–1932, vol. 5 from 24 May 1810, vol. 6, vol. 7 to 15 June 1826, passim [quotation, 27 Oct. 1818, 6: 294], UAII 5.5.2, HUA; [NB], "Encke's Comet," 33.

49. Foletta, *Coming to Terms with Democracy*.

50. Records of the Massachusetts Executive Council [hereafter RMEC], 29 May, 4 July, 28 Aug. 1816, Massachusetts State Archives. The records note attendance by name for each meeting.

51. RMEC, 9, 12 June, 28 Aug. 1815, 8 Feb., 30 May 1816.

52. NIB, "Memoir," 77; RMEC, 22 Nov., 14 Dec. 1816, 6 Mar. 1817; *BDA*, 3 June 1816; *Boston Commercial Gazette*, 20 June 1816; Chase, *Wiscasset*, 218–19.

53. NIB, "Memoir," 77. In his advocacy of granting equity powers to Commonwealth courts, Joseph Story had made similar arguments regarding the need for "determinate principles" and "exactness and regularity" [(Story), "Chancery Jurisdiction," 156, 157].

54. *Report of the Trial of Henry Phillips*; *Boston Commercial Gazette*, 3 Feb. 1817; RMEC, 14, 15 Jan., 6, 7 Feb., 5 Mar. 1817; "Legum Vindex," "A Government of Laws and Not of Men," *BDA*, 6 Feb. 1817 [quotation]; "On the Right and Expediency of Circulating Petitions for Pardons," *BDA*, 15, 18 [quotation] Feb. 1817; Rogers, *Murder and the Death Penalty*, 72–76.

55. HIB to George C. Mason, 2 Sept. 1878, B1, MSS 7412, George Champlin Mason Papers, Rhode Island Historical Society; Drake, *Old Landmarks*, 307; Eliza Susan Quincy, Diary, 17 Jan., 6 Feb. 1816, and added, undated commentary, Quincy, Wendell, Holmes, and Upham Family Papers, 1633–1910, MHS.

56. MGH, Board of Trustees, Minutes, 6 Feb., 10, 17 [quotation] Mar. 1816, 16 Feb 1817, Massachusetts General Hospital Archives and Special Collections NIB, *Massachusetts General Hospital*, 10, 20, 26; Coburn, *History of Lowell*, 1: 141; Peter Chardon Brooks to NB, 4 Aug. 1807, NB to Brooks, 5 Aug. 1807, EFMR.

57. NIB, *Massachusetts General Hospital*, 27; MGH, Board of Trustees, Minutes, 9 Mar. 1817.

58. NIB, *Massachusetts General Hospital*, 23–26; MGH, Board of Trustees, Minutes, 20 Dec. 1816; *SG*, 14 [quotation], 21 Jan. 1817; *ER*, 29 Jan. 1817.

59. EE, *Memoir of John Lowell*, 21; Coburn, *History of Lowell*, 1: 141; Appleton, *Introduction of the Power Loom*, 10; John A. Lowell, "Mercantile Biography. The Late Patrick Tracy Jackson," *Merchants' Magazine* 18 (Apr. 1848): 359. The case was *Paul Moody v. Jonathan Fiske et al.* See also NB to George Sullivan, 29 Sept. 1821, ser. II, B7, vol. 1, BF-PEM.

60. Appleton, *Introduction of the Power Loom*, 21–22; Dalzell, *Enterprising Elite*, 47–48.

61. "Report of Mr. Lowell Feb 15 1818 on the subject of application to legislature respecting annuities & life ins," Massachusetts General Hospital Archives and Special Collections; Act of Incorporation, 24 Feb. 1818, in MHL, *Proposals*, 29–33 [quotation, 32]; White, *Massachusetts Hospital Life*, 8–10.

62. White, *Massachusetts Hospital* Life, 10–19.

63. NIB, "Memoir," 79–80 [quotations, 80]; White, *Massachusetts Hospital Life*, 13; MHL, Directors' Records, 3, 10, 12, 20 Mar., 8 Apr. 1823, A-2–3, MHLC. The MHL records confirm Nat's story of an increased salary offer, but in a letter to his father dated March 4 son Ingersoll cited $5,000 as the combined offer expected to become official, in contrast to $4,500 recorded in the MHL minutes of 10 March [JIB to NB, 4 Mar. 1823, B4, F1, Joseph Bowditch Papers, 1699–1941, PEM].

64. TJ to NB, 26 Oct. 1818, Thomas Jefferson Papers, 1606–1827, Library of Congress, *http://hdl.loc.gov/loc.mss/mtj.mtjbib023300*; NB to TJ, 4 Nov. 1818.

65. JIB to NB, 4 Mar. 1823.

66. NB to CP, 27 Nov. 1821, B1, F1, BF-PEM; NB, Travel Journal, 14 Sept. 1816, Bowditch Family Papers, 1800–94, MHS; MIB to Eliza Babcock Ingersoll Wetmore, 1 Mar. 1817, B1, F5, BF-PEM; "Valuable Farm for Sale," *Conn. Courant*, 25 Jan. 1840.

67. JIB to NB, 4 Mar. 1823; Lothrop, *Memoir of Nathaniel Ingersoll Bowditch*, 6–7 [quotation, 7]; *SG*, 6 Jan. 1824; Pulsifer, *Witch's Breed*, 115–16.

68. *SG*, 12 Aug. 1823; Daniel A. White to Samuel Orne, 3 Aug. 1823, B6, F60, Papers of Professor Henry William Wilder Foote and Family.

69. *SG*, 12 Aug. 1823.

70. Ibid.

Chapter 7

1. NIB to the MHL, 19 Mar. 1838, AA-1, MHLC; Resolution of the Board of Control, 19 Mar. 1838, CAA-1, MHLC; White, *Massachusetts Hospital Life*, 3.

2. NB and JIB to MIB, 13 Aug. 1823, MSS 3, ser. II, B7, vol. 1, BF-PEM; *Boston Independent Chronicle*, 13 Aug. 1823; NB to MIB, 14 Aug. 1823, B1, F5, BF-PEM.

3. *Boston Directory*, 273, 276; *Massachusetts Register . . . 1824*, 190; Records of Stockholders' Meeting, 10 Mar. 1823, and Records of Directors' Meeting, 11 Mar. 1823, "Records of the Commercial Insurance Company in Boston, Incorporated February 10, 1823," vol. 6, Commercial Insurance Co. Collection [hereafter CIC Records], Baker Library; Directors' Records, 11 Feb., 3 Mar., 18 Aug., 2, 3 Sept. 1823, A-2–3, MHLC.

4. "Act of Incorporation" and "An Act to Define the Powers, Duties and Restrictions of Insurance Companies" [1818], transcribed in CIC Records. In April 1826, for example, the Commercial Insurance Company balance sheet shows (in rounded numbers) $21,000 in policy premiums—and $28,000 paid for losses; $55,000 on loans on bottomry and respondentia (vessels and cargoes); $72,000 on notes secured by stock as collateral; and $146,000 on notes secured by mortgages as collateral [balance sheets, 13 Apr., 12 Oct. 1824, 12 Apr., 11 Oct. 1825, 11 Apr., 10 Oct. 1826, CIC Records].

5. Farber, "Underwritten States," 92, 96n.

6. The MHL scrapped the agreement to give MGH one-third of the net profits from the life insurance business for one whereby MGH would receive a share of profits from *all* company operations, but calculated only after stockholders had received a generous dividend on their shares. Soon afterward it hammered out a further agreement that postponed any profit-sharing until 1829 [White, *Massachusetts Hospital Life*, 7–10, 20–22].

7. White, *Massachusetts Hospital Life*, 28–32, 192; Murphy, *Investing in Life*, chaps. 5, 6. If life policies constituted only a small part of MHL business, it was because, Bowditch noted, prosperous Bostonians maintained a "suspicion that the Insurance part of the business of the Company was too hazardous for the safety of the Trusts" [Report of the Actuary, 8 Jan. 1827, A-5, MHLC].

8. NIB, "Memoir," 84; White, *Massachusetts Hospital Life*, 32–41; Dalzell, *Enterprising Elite*, 100–104, 107–8; Hall, "What the Merchants Did with Their Money." For MHL as the pioneer in corporate trust companies, and these companies elsewhere

in the antebellum era, see Smith, *Development of Trust Companies*, 238–82; Blackmar, "Inheriting Property and Debt," 108–13; and Haeger, "Eastern Financiers and Institutional Change."

9. White, *Massachusetts Hospital Life*, 41–54, 190; Dalzell, *Enterprising Elite*, 105–7; Israel Thorndike to NB, 23 July 1830, LB-1, case 5, MHLC [hereafter LB-1]; Quincy to NB, 7 July 1826, Bowditch Family Business Letters, 1826–61, MHS; Loan 112, Ledger, B-1, MHLC; Proprietors of the Mill Pond Wharf, 15 Nov. 1831, AB-4, case 10, MHLC; Journal, vol. 1, C-1, MHLC.

10. NB to MIB, 20 Apr. 1823, B1, F1, BF-PEM; "Notes on the Pennsylvania Life Assurance Company," "Notes on the Union Insurance Company New York," "Notes on the Mechanic Life Insurance and Coal Company New York," AB-1, MHLC; Murphy, *Investing in Life*, 155; Bartlett, "Nathaniel Ingersoll Bowditch" [author's error in title]. Companies: Morris, *Sketch of the Pennsylvania Company*, 27–29; *Prospectus of the Union Insurance Company*; *New York Columbian*, 17 Jan., 8 Mar. 1821; *New-York Spectator*, 13 Mar. 1821; *Laws of the State of New-York*, 54. The Mechanic, which changed its name in 1823 to the Life and Fire Insurance Company, was less an insurance company and more a shadow bank engaging in shady operations [Hilt, "Rogue Finance"].

11. MHL, *Proposals*; Board of Control Reports, 16 Jan. 1826, 4 Jan. 1833, 31 Dec. 1834, 31 Dec. 1836, A-7, MHLC.

12. On early business offices, see Yates, *Control through Communication*, 25–39, 206; Yates, "From Press Book and Pigeonhole," 7–11; Hancock, *Citizens of the World*, 101–2; Zakim, "Business Clerk as Social Revolutionary," 576–85, 593; Chandler, *Visible Hand*, 36–48; Lamoreaux, "Rethinking the Transition to Capitalism," 442–45; and Rosenthal, "Storybook-keepers." For another typical example of the small size of an office staff, see Gras, *Massachusetts First National Bank*, 27, 77–78, 531–32, 535–36. For the development of office technologies in the nineteenth century, see esp. Yates, *Control through Communication*; Gardey, *Écrire, Calculer, Classer*; Tenner, "From Slip to Chip"; and Rhodes and Streeter, *Before Photocopying*. For a consideration of new scholarship that seeks "to put the *bureau* back in bureaucracy," see Kafka, "Paperwork" [quotation, 341].

13. Directors' Records, 18 Aug., 1 Dec. 1823, A-2–3, MHLC; Minutes of Directors' Meeting, 18 Aug. 1823, AA-1, MHLC; NIB, "Memoir," 94. Technological changes in printing made the mass production of blanks cheaper, but such advances do not fully explain their spread from government-citizen interactions, such as bills of lading filed with customs officials, to businesses and other private institutions. A comprehensive 1829 inventory of a stationer catering to merchants lists blanks of this first sort. As an example of their slow adoption in business, only in the 1870s did the New York Mercantile Agency, the pioneer in credit reporting, begin to distribute preprinted financial statement forms [Saxe, "Job Printing in Lower Manhattan," 7–12; Scarry, "Robert Bowne and His Company," 31; Lauer, "From Rumor to Written Record," 315].

14. NB to Elijah Alvord [hereafter EA], 12, 14 Jan. 1826, LA-1, MHLC; NIB, "Memoir," 94–95. The correct quotation is, "aliquando bonus dormitat Homerus" [Macdonnel, *Dictionary of Quotations*, 12].

15. NB to E. Burrill, 21 July 1835, LA-2, MHLC.

16. NB to EA, 18, 29 Mar. 1824, 15 Mar. 1831, LA-1; NB to Frederick A. Packard, 11 Dec. 1824, LA-1 [quotation]; NB to EA, 14 Sept. 1829, LA-1 [quotation].

17. Lauer, "From Rumor to Written Record," 310–13; Sandage, *Born Losers*, chap. 4. Lauer links credit reporting with "the invention of disembodied financial identity" in the 1840s ["From Rumor to Written Record," 302]. As he documents, however, the signature mark of this development, the shift from narrative credit reports to a quantitative credit rating, did not occur until the 1860s. With the numerical rating, he argues, the "socially determined markers of trustworthiness and economic legitimacy" are "obscured behind the veil of quantification and technical neutrality" [ibid., 305]. I am arguing that Bowditch's MHL represents not just an earlier emergence of the impersonal bureaucracy—represented in part by information systems and office procedures adopted in the 1820s—but that this early emergence is causally linked with Bowditch's persona as the Enlightenment mathematician, for whom systematization and quantification are characteristic modus operandi.

18. NIB, "Memoir," 94–95; Board of Control Report, 11 Jan. 1830, A-7, MHLC; White, *Massachusetts Hospital Life*, 24–25. For "ad hoc" Lowell mill practices, see Lubar, "Managerial Structure," 24.

19. EIMS Records, 4 Jan. 1804, vol. 1, B1 9 [quotation], and 4 Nov. 1801, MH 88, B1, F1, EIMSR; Report of the EIMS committee to procure a new catalogue of the museum, 5 Feb. 1820, ser. VII, Scrapbook no. 2, EIMSR; American Philosophical Society, undated printed form, signed R. M. Patterson, with manuscript alterations in NB's hand, Ms. E.210.19 v.3 (105), NBC. Bowditch may possibly be associated with an even earlier use of the printed blank form, when Salem's Philosophical Library first voted to procure printed book labels in 1798, at the first meeting in which Bowditch participated [Vote of 5 June 1798, Record Book, 1781–1810, MSS 56, B2, vol. 1, Salem Athenaeum Records, 1760–1889, PEM].

20. The very first trust payment was acknowledged with a handwritten receipt. Just weeks later, the second payment was acknowledged with a printed receipt that referenced the Forrester Trust [receipts, 7, 24 Oct. 1817, MSS 360, B2, F10, Dudley Leavitt Pickman Papers, 1721–1938, PEMDLP; invoice/receipt, Cushing & Appleton, 28 Nov. 1817, B1, F7, Dudley Leavitt Pickman Papers].

21. NB, Index to Commonplace Book, vol. 2, 18 Nov. 1797, stored with NB, Surveying Notebook, 7 Mar. 1787, NBC. Edward Tenner claims that alphabetical tabs did not come into use until the end of the nineteenth century ["From Slip to Chip," 126].

22. On scholarly systems for organizing knowledge, see Blair, *Too Much to Know*; Headrick, *When Information Came of Age*; Hobart and Schiffman, *Information Ages*; Soll, "From Note-Taking to Data Banks"; Yeo, "John Locke's 'New Method' of Common-Placing"; and Malcolm, "Thomas Harrison and His 'Ark of Studies.'" Headrick argues that in the eighteenth and early nineteenth centuries the major contribution of science was the production of data and the development of systems to organize it [*When Information Came of Age*, chap. 2].

23. NB, Comet Notebook, 1819, Ms.E.5092.88, NBC. On the links between scientific note-taking and mercantile records, and the place of numbers in both, see Soll, "From Note-Taking to Data Banks"; te Heesen, "Accounting for the Natural World"; and Sibum, "Narrating by Numbers." Sibum discusses Faraday's 1827 instructions, as well as Charles Babbage's use of a ledger book to record electrical experiments. Conversely, Edward Tenner argues that in the late nineteenth century "businesses looked to scholarship for information-handling techniques," citing the adoption of the card catalog from the world of academic libraries ["From Slip to Chip," 126].

24. Kamensky, *Exchange Artist*.

25. Carruthers and Espeland, "Accounting for Rationality"; Poovey, *History of the Modern Fact*; Porter, "Quantification and the Accounting Ideal in Science"; Zakim, "Bookkeeping as Ideology"; Hobart and Schiffman, *Information Ages*.

26. P. C. Brooks to NB, 22 Apr. 1807, MSS 134, B1, F3, EFMR; Daniel White to NIB, 24 Mar. 1838, MSS 445, B3, F7, White Family Papers, 1746–1906, PEM; Board of Control Report, 19 Jan. 1825, A-7, MHLC.

27. Young, *Nathaniel Bowditch*, 43–44, 67–68; Benjamin Waterhouse to NB, 19 Oct. 1833, H MS c16.1, Harvard Medical Library, HIB Papers, Countway; White, *Nathaniel Bowditch*, 57; "Life and Character of Hon. Nathaniel Bowditch," *Christian Review* 3 (Sept. 1838): 330.

28. NIB, "Memoir," 85–86; Quincy, *History of Harvard*, 2: 439.

29. Murphy, *Investing in Life*, 16–22; White, *Massachusetts Hospital Life*, 29.

30. William Prescott, Report of Committee Assigned to Engage Nathaniel Bowditch [1823], and Minutes of Directors' Meeting, 18 Aug. 1823, AA-1, MHLC; MHL, *Proposals*, 9, 12, 18, 20–23, 27; NIB, "Memoir," 85; White, *Massachusetts Hospital Life*, 24–25.

31. NB to EA, 19 Feb., 23 Mar. 1824, LA-1; NB to Abijah Bigelow, 4 Mar. 1824, LA-1; NB to Joseph G. Kendall, 15 Mar. 1824, LA-1; NB to Lewis Strong, 27 Mar., 24 Apr. 1824, LA-1; NB to Rejoice Newton, 6 May 1824, LA-1; NB to Frederick Packard, 11 Dec. 1824, LA-1; EA to NB, 24 Mar. 1824, Box 2 (AB-2), MHLC; Packard to NB, 3 Mar. 1825, LB-1 [quotation]. For a fuller discussion of the Life Office and its relations with rural debtors, see Thornton, "Great Machine."

32. Elijah Brigham to Mr. Hale, 13 Jan. 1832, LB-1; Sylvester Allen to "Sir," 9 May 1834, LB-1; Liberty Bartlett to M. L. Hale, 19 July 1835, LB-1; Russell Gibbs to Hale, 25 June 1832, LB-1; Cyrus Stearns to Hale, 18 Apr. 1830, LB-1; Edmund Joyner to MHL, 17 Mar. 1829, LB-1. On rural practices and sense of time, see Clark, *Roots of Rural Capitalism*, 28–38; Whitney, "'An art that requires capital,'" 180–220; and Bruegel, "'Time That Can Be Relied Upon.'"

33. Printed mortgage application form, AB-2, MHLC; MHL to EE (printed form letter), 26 Oct. 1830, LB-1; NB to EA, 7 Oct. 1826, LA-1; NB to Rejoice Newton, 3 Nov. 1826, LA-1; NB to EA, 30 Sept. 1829, LA-1.

34. J. C. Bates to Moses Hale, 16 Apr. 1825, LB-1; Joseph Albee to NB, 31 Aug. 1831, LB-1; John Brisco to the Secy. of MHL, 16 Jan. 1836, LB-1; John Billings to Hale, 10 Apr. 1829, LB-1. On the cultural meanings of business failure, see Balleisen, *Navigating*

Failure; Mann, *Republic of Debtors*; and Sandage, *Born Losers*. Among farmers, failure held a somewhat different significance, compromising traditional notions of household independence and competency [Clark, *Roots of Rural Capitalism*; Vickers, "Competency and Competition"].

35. NB to EA, 26, 30 June 1826, LA-1. In 1824, NB chided Alvord for assessing closing fees as a percentage of the loan amount, rather than a flat sum, noting that such a practice might lead to charges of usury [NB to EA, 12 Apr. 1824, LA-1].

36. Commonwealth of Massachusetts, *Report of the Committee . . . Massachusetts Hospital Life Insurance Company*; *Pittsfield Sun*, 24 Jan. 1828, 29 Jan. 1829; *NH*, 15, 27 Jan. 1828, 10 Feb. 1829 [quotation, 10 Feb.]; *SG*, 20, 30 Jan. 1829; NIB, "Memoir," 85–86.

37. Commonwealth of Massachusetts, *Report of the Committee . . . Massachusetts Hospital Life Insurance Company*, 1–3; Report of the Actuary, 12 Jan. 1829, A-5, MHLC; White, *Massachusetts Hospital Life*, 20–21, 192. This reasoning had some basis, since the hospital owned 10 percent of the company's stock, but the report was silent on the other 90 percent, which in 1829 yielded its owners a healthy 8 percent dividend. Even before the Life Office opened, Bowditch was of the explicit opinion that, given hostility to institutions of wealth, the profit-sharing arrangement would offer political benefits "in coming times" [NIB, *Massachusetts General Hospital*, 77].

38. NB to EA, 6 May 1829, LA-1; Martineau, *Society in America*, 1: 294; Levi Lincoln, veto message, 16 Feb. 1827, in *Resolves of the General Court of Massachusetts*, 475–76.

39. *NH*, 24 May 1833 (reprinted from the *Hampden Whig*); Allen, *Address*, 27–28. Elsewhere Samuel C. Allen described MHL as "an anti-republican, mischievous institution" [*EG*, 16 Nov. 1833]. See also the opposition to "private entails in life annuities and life Insurance offices" as "the favorite means by which the federal party has built up an Aristocracy, and sought to establish its permanency" expressed in an endorsement of the Democratic candidates for governor and lieutenant governor, the latter an MHL debtor from Berkshire County ["To the Electors of the Commonwealth," *Pittsfield Sun*, 18 Feb. 1830; Smith, *History of Pittsfield*, 2: 410–11; deeds, 26 June 1826, 14 Mar. 1827, Berkshire County Registry of Deeds]. On Democratic Party opposition to monopoly privilege in Massachusetts, see Formisano, *Transformation of Political Culture*, 272–76.

40. Cushing, *Oration*, 10, 11, 12. On the Workingmen's movement in Massachusetts, see Clark, *Roots of Rural Capitalism*, 204–9; and Formisano, *Transformation of Political Culture*, 222–44. For further evidence of suspicion, see "Hospital Insurance Company," in Attwood, *Reminiscences of Old Boston*, 38. Massachusetts Democrat David Henshaw opposed the accumulation of wealth "in trust companies and in life insurance offices" as contributing to the inequitable distribution of wealth [*Address*, 28–29 (quotation, 28)].

41. John Lowell to NB, 23 Dec. 1834, and Lowell, draft of Board of Control Report, 23 Dec. 1834, AA-1, MHLC. For these reports at they appeared in newspapers, see, e.g., *Boston Weekly Messenger*, 3 Feb. 1825, 22 Jan. 1829. For reasons we cannot know, the 1834 annual report was nothing like the one Lowell had drafted. Only at the end, when it alluded to "its importance to society at large, to the helpless part of it in

particular," and to itself as "an eminently Christian establishment" did it make use of Lowell's language [Board of Control Report, 31 Dec. 1834, A-7, MHLC]. Lowell was not new to the task of managing the company's image. It was probably he who, as "the Friend of the Fatherless," penned a newspaper essay in 1823 explaining how MHL contributed to the "protection, and comfort, and ease of mind of great classes of our society." Back then he had not disguised who these classes were and even stated that the wealthy suffer more than others when impoverished because they are used to physical comfort and are humiliated by "the degradation from the rank once enjoyed." Attribution is based on Lowell's known description of MHL as "*eminently* the *Savings bank of the wealthy*" and "Friend's" description of MHL as "the 'Savings Banks' of the middling and more opulent classes" ["The Friend of the Fatherless," "The Hospital Life Insurance Company," *BDA* 6, 10 Dec. 1823; Lowell to Samuel Appleton, 26 Dec. 1834, quoted in White, *Massachusetts Hospital Life*, 200n].

42. NB to EA, 21 Apr. 1828, LA-1 [quotation]; NB to Lewis Strong, 23 June [quotation], 23 Nov. 1829, LA-1; Board of Control Reports, 31 Dec. 1836, 9 Jan. 1838 [quotations], A-7, MHLC; *Berkshire Star*, 11 Dec. 1828; *Berkshire Journal*, 22 July 1830, 7 Apr. 1831.

43. Moses L. Hale to Rufus Gorham, 24 Nov. 1830, LA-1; Joseph Tilden to EA, 26 May 1838, LA-2; EA to NB, 11 May 1832, LB-1.

44. Moses Hale, reply to Edmund Joyner, recorded at the bottom of Joyner to MHL, 17 Mar. 1829, LB-1. Company policy stipulated that warning letters sent to tardy debtors should cost more than compounded interest would have cost but that the agents and the solicitor should pocket those fees. "The only object of our making the parties pay the Solic. Fees," explained Bowditch, "is to make them punctual in their payments" [NB to EA, 14 May 1835, LA-2].

45. Records of Stockholders' Meeting, 12 Mar. 1827, CIC Records [quotations]; balance sheets, 13 Apr., 12 Oct. 1824, 12 Apr., 11 Oct. 1825, 11 Apr. 10, Oct. 1826, CIC Records.

46. NIB, "Memoir," 83; Records of Directors' Meetings, 19 Mar., 25 Sept. 1827, 10 Mar. 1828, 9 Mar. 1829, 10 Mar. 1830, 14 Mar. 1831, CIC Records; Directors' Records, 8 Feb., 2 July, 3 Sept. 1827, A-2–3, MHLC.

47. White, *Massachusetts Hospital Life*, 47–54, 204n; Dalzell, *Enterprising Elite*, 105–6. Only when the company amended its corporate charter in 1839 did this practice become legal.

48. Ward, Diary, May 1829, case 1, Thomas Wren Ward Papers, 1717–1943, MHS; Report of the Actuary, 26 Dec. 1837, A-5, MHLC.

49. Benjamin Guild to NB, 20 Aug. 1825, LB-1. For examples of loan extensions/extended interest payments, see Daybook, CA-1, MHLC.

50. Board of Control Report, 31 Dec. 1838, A-7, MHLC.

51. NIB, "Memoir," 87–93 [quotations, 91, 92, 93].

52. Ibid., 86–87.

53. Ibid., 92.

54. See esp. Porter, *Trust in Numbers*; Porter, "Objectivity as Standardization"; Daston and Galison, "Image of Objectivity," 82; Daston, "Objectivity and the Escape

from Perspective"; Poovey, *History of the Modern Fact*; and Porter, "Quantification and the Accounting Ideal in Science." Patricia Cline Cohen's imaginative work *Calculating People* remains the only monograph to consider the broad diffusion of numeracy skills and quantitative frame of mind in America before the mid-nineteenth century. Like historians of European science, she linked the growing prestige of numbers to their associations with objectivity and precision. Her focus was largely on *counting* as a cultural and social practice and the generation of political and social *data* and *statistics*. Here I focus on the overtones of *calculation* and *pure number*, abstracted from the phenomena of human life and associated with not only objectivity and precision but also the mathematical perfection and regularity of the Laplacean solar system.

55. Dalzell, *Enterprising Elite*; NIB, "Memoir," 85.

56. Binney, *Speech*, 4–5; J. J. Dixwell to Joshua Bates, 6 Mar. 1839, quoted in Gras, *Massachusetts First National Bank*, 101.

57. Board of Control Report, 9 Jan. 1838; Report of the Actuary, 26 Dec. 1837.

58. Memorandum of Agreement between Israel Thorndike and Thomas Tilden, 12 Mar. 1818, in Konefsky and King, *Boston Practice*, 383 [quotations]; Forbes, *Israel Thorndike*, 144–46; Lodge, *Early Memories*, 14–15; WIB, "The Home of Nathaniel Bowditch in Boston, 1823–38," in Harold Bowditch, "A Collection of Data Made for the Possible Future Use of a Biographer," 1: 126, 129, MH 42, NBLW.

59. WIB, "Home of Nathaniel Bowditch," 1: 123–28. We catch a glimpse of Bowditch spurring himself on from the jottings he penned inside a leather folder kept on his desk. On the left side he copied mathematical formulas, and on the right quotations in English, German, French, and Latin. At the very top was "Ne tentes aut perfice," roughly, "do not attempt what you cannot accomplish." Below, we find "Ohne hast, ohne rast"—without haste, but without rest—a verse Goethe used to describe the stars [folder, identified by Eliza Bowditch Dixwell in 1885, as "in daily use by my father Nathaniel Bowditch on his writing desk," B35, F1, BF-PEM].

60. WIB, "Our Family Story from 1639 to 1838 told by William I. Bowditch 1896," MSS 3, ser. II, B6, 1: 76–77, 132–33 [quotations, 76, 77, 132], BF-PEM; WIB, "Home of Nathaniel Bowditch," 1: 128; Silliman, Diary, 14 Mar. 1835, in Fisher, *Life of Benjamin Silliman*, 1: 349.

61. *Boston Directory*, 136, 177, 182, 188, 197, 218, 223; *Stimpson's Boston Directory*, 198, 260, 269, 306, 313; Forbes, *Israel Thorndike*, 144–46.

62. WIB, "Our Family Story," 1: 131–32 [quotation, 132].

63. NIB: Lothrop, *Memoir of Nathaniel Ingersoll Bowditch*, 6–7; Emerson, *Journals and Miscellaneous Notebooks*, 15: 122; Harvard University, "Class Book of 1822," 7, HUD 222 714f., HUA. NIB's predecessor at the Life Office, Samuel Hubbard, may have been forced out to make room for him. The company directors had imposed new limits on the solicitor's company-related earnings, and when Hubbard objected and asked for a raise, the company decided it was "not expedient" to do so. The very same day that Hubbard turned down the salary offer, the company elected NIB [Directors' Records, 5 Feb., 5, 10 (quotation), 14 Mar. 1827, A-2-3, MHLC]. JIB: "Jonathan Ingersoll Bowditch." HIB: [HIB], "A Retrospective Glimpse in 1888 upon

the Life & Work of the Class of 1828, Harv. University," (1888), 11, HUD 228.809, HUA; HIB, Journal, 9 Jan., 23 June, 18 Sept., 4 Nov. 1827, Harvard Medical Library, HIB Papers, Countway (quotations).

64. Pickering, *Life of John Pickering*, 346; Cohn, *Francis Calley Gray*; Tyack, *George Ticknor*; Stimpson's *Boston Directory*, 166.

65. Ticknor, *George Ticknor*, 1: 316, 391–92 [quotations, 391–92]; WIB, "Our Family Story," 1: 76 [quotation]. For sketches of Ticknor's circle, see Ticknor, *George Ticknor*, 1: 315–19. For further glimpses of Bowditch's intellectual and social network in Boston, see Silliman, Diary, 24 Mar. 1835, in Fisher, *Life of Benjamin Silliman*, 1: 354; and NB to William H. Prescott, 5 Aug. 1827, William Hickling Prescott Papers, 1665–1959, MHS.

66. NB to William Marchant, 23 Feb., 24 Mar., 16, 26 July, illegible Sep., 1, 29 Oct. 1827, 19, 28, Jan., 1 Sept. 1828, Marchant Family Papers, MSS 552, Rhode Island Historical Society; NB to William Ellery Channing, May 1826, vol. 48, scrapbook 30, p. 51, Channing Autograph Collection, MSS 9009, Rhode Island Historical Society; Webster loan entry, Schedule of Notes and Mortgages, GA-1, MHLC; Sprague, *Curiosity: A Poem*, 16; Young, *Nathaniel Bowditch*, 13–15, 66 [quotations]. On the ideal of balance, which involved the superiority of moral and rational faculties over lower impulses, as well as the proper equipoise among all components of the self, see Howe, *Making the American Self*. On the Boston elite's mix of cultivation and business, see Story, "Class and Culture"; Dalzell, *Enterprising Elite*; and Thornton, *Cultivating Gentlemen*.

Chapter 8

1. Inventory of NB's Estate, 24 Mar. 1838, Probate 275: 78, Massachusetts State Archives; Massachusetts Charitable Mechanic Association, *Annals*, 588; Boston Mechanics Institution, *First Annual Report*, 3–8.

2. Story, *Forging of an Aristocracy*; Dalzell, *Enterprising Elite*.

3. Newmyer, "Justice Joseph Story's Doctrine."

4. Records of the Proprietors of the Boston Athenaeum, vol. 2 [hereafter RPBA], 5 Jan. 1824, Archives of the Boston Athenaeum [hereafter ABA]; Records of the Trustees of the Boston Athenaeum, vol. 1, 14 Oct. 1822, 13 Oct. 1823, 12 Apr. 1824, ABA. On the Athenaeum, see Quincy, *Athenaeum*; Story, "Class and Culture"; Wolff, *Culture Club*; and Field, *Crisis of the Standing Order*, 103–10.

5. Krajewski, *Paper Machines*, 22, 69–79; Soll, "From Note-Taking to Data Banks," 365–66; Walton, *Harvard College Library*, 27–31; Lovett, "William Croswell"; *Boston Independent Chronicle*, 12 May 1795; CC, 22 Sept. 1793; [Croswell], *Mercator Map of the Starry Heavens*; Croswell, *Tables*; entry for William Croswell to Samuel Webber, 28 Oct. 1790, in AAAS, *Academy Archives*, ser. I-C-1, 33; entry for NB, Report on William Croswell's solution of a problem of Diophantus, 25 Dec. 1815, in AAAS, *Academy Archives*, ser. I-C-2, 3; Report of the EIMS committee to procure a new catalogue of the museum, 5 Feb. 1820, ser. VII, Scrapbook no. 2, EIMSR; Gould, "Shells of Massachusetts," 484, 486; Minter, "Academic Library Reform"; Ticknor, *Cogswell*, 53–78 passim, 130–35; Potter and Bolton, *Librarians of Harvard College*, 37 [quotation].

6. Quincy, *Athenaeum*, 93, 173; Ticknor, Journal, 1818, in Ticknor, *George Ticknor*, 1: 197.

7. Seth Bass to Trustees of the Boston Athenaeum, "Schedule of the Books and Other Property Belonging to the Boston Athenaeum," 11 July 1825, ABA; RPBA, 7 Jan. 1827; Boston Athenaeum, *Catalogue of Books*, "Advertisement."

8. Peabody, *Harvard Reminiscences*, 68 [quotation]; typed transcription of Benjamin Nichols to Benjamin Peirce, 23 Aug. 1826, in Harold Bowditch, "A Collection of Data Made for the Possible Future Use of a Biographer," 2: 213, MH 42, NBLW; Harvard University, Corporation, Corporation records: minutes, 1643–1989 [hereafter Corporation minutes], 10 Feb. 1827, 6: 320, 19 Nov. 1829, 7: 152, 22, 29 Apr. 1830, 7: 173, 174, 15 Nov. 1832 [quotation], 7: 306–7, 19 Feb. 1835, 7: 387, UA 5.30.2, HUA; Peirce, "Preface," and "Advertisement," *Catalogue of the Library of Harvard University*, 3: v–vi [quotation, v]; Carpenter, *First 350 Years*, 27, 44. On new "scientific" approaches to cataloging, see Minter, "Academic Library Reform," 21–22, 25–26; Ranz, *Printed Book Catalogue*, chap. 2; Tenner, "From Slip to Chip"; and Taylor and Joudrey, *Organization of Information*, 71–75.

9. Quincy, *Athenaeum*, 92–93 [quotations, 93], 111–12; Harvard University, Board of Overseers, Records of the Board of Overseers: formal meeting minutes, 1707–1932, 27 Oct. 1818, 6: 294–95, UAII 5.5.2, HUA; RPBA, 7 Jan. 1827; Records of the Trustees of the Boston Athenaeum, vol. 1, 8 Jan., 11 Dec. 1827, 14 Apr. 1828, 12 May 1829. See also George Ticknor to Daniel Webster, 2 Feb. 1826, in Ticknor, *George Ticknor*, 1: 371. The critical contact was Obadiah Rich, a Cape-Cod-born merchant who yielded to his yen for antiquarian books and manuscripts and set up the Red Lion Bookshop in London. He became an indispensable conduit for many of America's learned men in pursuing their own research, including Bowditch, Ticknor, and William H. Prescott, who called Rich "a prince of Genii in the Bibliopolical way"[Hollinger, "Rich, Obadiah"; Allen, "Rich Family in Britain"; Ticknor, *George Ticknor*, 2: 245; Prescott to Rich, 9 May 1834, in Wolcott, *Correspondence*, 1–8 (quotation, 3)].

10. RPBA, 5 Jan. 1830, 3 Jan. 1831, 2 Jan. 1832, 7 Jan. 1833, 6 Jan. 1834; Quincy, *Athenaeum*, 121, 131–32 [quotation, 132], 135. Under Bowditch the library's holdings increased from fifteen thousand volumes in 1825 to over twenty-five thousand in 1831 [Quincy, *Athenaeum*, 93, 126].

11. My account of the background to the Harvard reforms led by Bowditch draws on Story, *Forging of an Aristocracy*; Morison, "Great Rebellion"; Tyack, *George Ticknor*, 85–128; and Bailyn, "Kirkland."

12. Young, *John Thornton Kirkland*; Peabody, *Harvard Reminiscences*, 9–17.

13. Morison, *Three Centuries of Harvard*, 160–61, 217–18, 294–96.

14. Bailyn, "Kirkland," 19; John Randolph to Josiah Quincy, 11 Dec. 1813, quoted in McCaughey, *Josiah Quincy*, 137; McCaughey, *Josiah Quincy*, 136–37; Overseers Report, 27 Apr. 1819, Overseers Reports, vol. 1, HUA, quoted in Story, *Forging of an Aristocracy*, 93; Tyack, *Ticknor*, 95–96.

15. On the immediate background to the Harvard Corporation shakeup, see Tyack, *Ticknor*, 96–123; McCaughey, *Josiah Quincy*, 140–42; Bailyn, "Kirkland," 35–40; and Quincy, *History of Harvard*, 2: 353–61.

16. NB, "College History," 12 May 1828, UA 120.828.9, HUA. Unless otherwise noted, the following account is based on this source.

17. NB, "College History," 72, 82–84 [quotations, 72, 84]; Kirkland, memorandum book titled "Votes of the Corporation, 1823–1827," notes on meetings of 23 Aug., 10 Sept. 1826, B5, Papers of John Thornton Kirkland, 1788–1837, UAI 15.880, HUA. On John Farrar's mathematical work, see Timmons, *Mathematics in Nineteenth-Century America*, 195–212.

18. NB, "College History," 10–16 [quotations, 10, 12].

19. Ibid., 14–18 [quotation, 16].

20. Ibid., 18–19 [quotation, 18]. On Francis, see "Mercantile Biography: Ebenezer Francis."

21. NB, "College History," 19–21 [quotations, 19, 21].

22. Ibid., 21–31, 40 [quotations, 22, 29, 30].

23. Ibid., 21; Kerber, "Science in the Early Republic"; Brown, "Natural History of the Gloucester Sea Serpent."

24. This account is based on Quincy, *Athenaeum*, 59–65, 73, 91–92; RTBA-1, 3 Feb., 20, 27 Apr., 5, 18 May, 6 July 1818, 1 Nov. 1819, 6 Feb. 1822, 9 May, 9 Oct. 1826; RPBA, 7 Jan. 1827; and NB to the Rev. J. B. Felt, 21 Oct. 1826, ABA. For a white-washed version, see Felt, *Memorials*, 327–31. See also Wolff, *Culture Club*, chap. 1.

25. Quincy, *Athenaeum*, 60.

26. Ibid., 64.

27. Peabody, *Harvard Reminiscences*, 17–19 [quotations, 19]; NB, "College History," 31, 42–49 [quotation, 48].

28. NB, "College History," 22–23, 31, 48–49 [quotations, 22, 23].

29. Ibid., 49–51 [quotations, 50].

30. Ibid., 51–52.

31. Ibid. [quotation, 52]; Dudley Pickman to Ebenezer Francis, 10 Oct. 1827, Harvard University, College Papers, 2nd ser., 2: 90, UAI 5.131.10 mf, HUA; Peabody, *Harvard Reminiscences*, 68–70.

32. NB, "College History," 36–38, 56–62 [quotations, 56, 62].

33. Ibid., 68–69; Quincy, *History of Harvard*, 2: 364–66; Harvard University, Committee appointed to inquire into the income and expenses of the College, Report on College Deficit, 26 Dec. 1826, UAI 10.85, HUA [quotation].

34. NB, "College History," 70–71, 74–77 [quotations, 75, 76, 77].

35. Ibid., 94–95 [quotation, 95].

36. Ibid., 6–8, 114–18 [quotations, 6, 8, 116]; Corporation minutes, 18 Oct. 1827, 7: 30 [quotation].

37. NB, "College History," 118.

38. Ibid., 119.

39. Ibid., 102–3, 119–26 [quotations, 123, 124, 126].

40. Ibid., 126–28 [quotations, 127].

41. Ibid., 128–29 [quotation, 129]; Senior Class Address, 2 Apr. 1828, ser. IB3, B1, F46, Papers of John Thornton Kirkland, 1788–1837, UAI 15.880, HUA.

42. NB, "College History," 129; Proceedings of the Class of 1828, meeting of 2 Apr. 1828, Class Book of 1828, 13, HUD 228.714f, HUA; *Massachusetts Journal*, 3 Apr. 1828; *New England Palladium*, 8 Apr. 1828; *SG*, 8 Apr. 1828. See also an unsigned letter in *SG*, 8 Apr. 1828, which referred mysteriously to "the provocation which is not at present before the public" and "the mismanagement of the government and funds of the college." For reports that Kirkland resigned for health reasons, see *SG*, 3 Apr. 1828; *Newport Mercury*, 5 Apr. 1828; and *Baltimore Patriot*, 7 Apr. 1828.

43. *Boston Bulletin*, 9 April 1828 [quotation]; *Boston Evening Gazette*, 5 Apr. 1828 [quotation]; *Boston Gazette*, 7 Apr. 1828 [quotations]; *Boston Courier*, 10 April 1828; *BDA*, 23 Apr. 1828; unsigned letter, *SG*, 8 Apr. 1828 [quotation]; "Observer," "Harvard College," *Boston Patriot*, 9 Apr. 1828 [quotation].

44. Peter Chardon Brooks to EE, 3 Apr. 1828, EE Papers; Charlotte Brooks Everett to EE, 3 Apr. 1828, EE Papers; EE to Alexander Everett, 11 June 1828, EE Papers; Sarah McKean Folsom to Catharine D. Haven, 21 Apr. 1828, HUA 828.29, B18, HUA; Ralph Waldo Emerson to William Emerson, 3 Apr. 1828, in Rusk, *Letters of Ralph Waldo Emerson*, 1: 230. See also Charlotte Brooks Everett to EE, 8 Apr. 1828, and Peter Chardon Brooks to EE, 14 Apr. 1828, EE Papers.

45. *Boston Bulletin*, 9 Apr. 1828; Adams, Diary, 3 Apr. 1828, in Adams, *Diary of Charles Francis Adams*, 2: 226.

46. *Boston Evening Gazette*, 5 Apr. 1828; *Boston Patriot*, 17 May 1828. The *Gazette* inserted the word "originally" in light of NB's honorary degrees.

47. [Farrar], Review of "An Elementary Treatise on Arithmetic," *NAR* 8 (Oct. 1821): 364; *Boston Gazette*, 7 Apr. 1828.

48. NIB, JIB, HIB, and WIB, "Letter Annexed to the Second Edition of the Memoir of Nathaniel Bowditch," Oct. 1840, in Palfrey et al., *Remarks Concerning the Late Dr. Bowditch*, 4; Emerson to Emerson, 3 Apr. 1828; Folsom to Haven, 21 Apr. 1828; Peabody, *Harvard Reminiscences*, 24. See also Hale, *New England Boyhood*, 357–58. For examples of Salem's reputation, see Morse, *American Universal Geography*, 1: 374; and Dwight, *Travels in New England*, 1: 448–49. When a writer for Boston's *Monthly Anthology* criticized the cheap paper on which Blunt had issued Bowditch's Salem harbor *Sailing Directions*, he smelled "a little of the odour of what has heretofore been called *Salem* economy, but what, in this instance"—for the blame lay with Blunt—"must be denomined [*sic*] *Newburyport* economy" [Review of "Chart of the Harbours," 493].

49. [Wilson], *Aristocracy of Boston*, 16; NB, "Report," in Boston Mechanics Institution, *First Annual Report*, 5–6. In remarking upon his father's lack of aesthetic sensibility, HIB wrote, "I love beauty of nature or art & delight in lingering near it. With Father it seemed not to be so. To say one had visited the spot was to him all that was necessary. He never felt the Divinity there is in the thousand objects along an oceans shore & in a leaping muscular ocean [HIB, "Pilgrimage to Appledore," 8 Aug. 1858, B MS b248. 11, Boston Medical Library, HIB Papers, Countway].

50. Folsom to Haven, 21 Apr. 1828; NB, "College History," 130–31, 37. After a European sojourn, the Kirklands returned to Boston in 1834. "Father has not called,"

reported Nat to his brother, "But the President met both him & me in the Street at different times & was as pleasant as 'May morning'" [NIB to HIB, 16 Dec. 1832, PV, N1, F4, Forbes Family Papers, 1732–1931, MHS].

51. *SG*, 30 May 1828. Bruce Winchester Stone characterizes the 1829 election, in which Bowditch replaced John Quincy Adams, as a coup and notes that there had been an earlier attempt to remove Adams from the AAAS post in 1827, led by the institution's "Essex men." The AAAS sources on which Stone relied are no longer available to researchers, but other sources verify his account. These years saw internal conflicts in the Boston elite, focused in part on long-standing political divisions and grudges, and Adams was a primary target [Stone, "Scientific Boston," 282–87; Sheidley, "Politics of Honor"; EE to Josiah Quincy, 4 Apr. 1829, Letter Books, LXV, 51–52, EE Papers; Adams, Diary, 7 Nov. 1830, 2 June 1831, in Adams, *Memoirs of John Quincy Adams*, 8: 247, 365–66].

52. Stone, "Scientific Boston," 281, 288–89; *Massachusetts Register . . . 1829*, 140, 162; NIB, "Memoir," 105 [quotation]. The AAAS's natural history collection was soon donated to the newly formed Boston Society for Natural History, where Bass served as librarian and cabinet keeper. Bass also served as cabinet keeper for the Boston Mechanics Institution under Bowditch, its president [Stone, "Scientific Boston," 289; Gould, "Boston Society," 237; *Massachusetts Register . . . 1829*, 160].

53. Stone, "Scientific Boston," 292–93; "Members of the Academy," *MAAAS*, n.s. 11 (1882): 57–59; James Thal to NB, 26 Jan. 1834, Ms.E.210.19 v.2 (101), NBC.

54. *American Academy of Arts and Sciences v. President and Fellows of Harvard College*; Stone, "Scientific Boston," 289–91; [Brown], "Rumford Fund Record," 99–101.

55. NB, Josiah Quincy, and Francis C. Gray, Report of the Committee to consider the subject of the Rumford Premium, 21 Dec. 1829, in *American Academy of Arts and Sciences v. President and Fellows of Harvard College*, 589.

56. NIB, *Ether Controversy*, 28.

57. Quincy, *Life of Josiah Quincy*, 430–31, 440–42, 482 [quotations, 43, 44, 482]; McCaughey, *Josiah Quincy*, 143–62; Peabody, *Harvard Reminiscences*, 29–31; Corporation minutes, 29 Sept. 1829, 7: 149. Even when the judicial policy accelerated into the so-called Rebellion of 1834, Bowditch held firm to the notion of criminal prosecution, though his son Nat had been punished for just such infractions with a temporary suspension [Adams, *Memoirs of John Quincy Adams*, 9: 160–86]. In detailing this era of "systematic measures," Ronald Story refers to the work of the "Quincy-Bowditch administration" [*Forging of an Aristocracy*, 62].

58. Quincy, *History of Harvard*, 2: 367–69 [quotation, 369]; Harvard University, *Third Annual Report*, 54; Harvard University, *Fourth Annual Report*, xlii; Harvard University, *Fifth Annual Report*, xlii; "Vote of the Corporation on the Resignation of the Office of Treasurer by Ebenezer Francis," 3 June 1830, in Quincy, *History of Harvard*, 2: 566; Ward, Diary, 11 Dec. 1830, B13, F3, Thomas Wren Ward Papers, 1717–1943; 1778–1858, MHS. On Quincy's administration, see Story, *Forging of an Aristocracy*, chaps. 3–8; and McCaughey, *Josiah Quincy*, chaps. 8, 9.

59. Statement of Benjamin R. Nichols, 10 Nov. 1827, Statement of Ebenezer Francis, 13 Nov. 1827, and John Lowell to John Davis, 2 Apr. 1829, reprinted in Review of "A Reply to a Letter in the Christian Examiner, Addressed to the Rev. Parsons Cooke," *Spirit of the Pilgrims* 3 (Jan. 1830): 25–26 [quotation, Lowell, 26]; Review of "A Reply," 27 [quotation].

60. "Students' Circular," unidentified newspaper clipping in [NB], comp., Scrapbook, 1828–1834, HUA 828.3, B17, HUA. The Latin quotation is from Lord Chesterfield's *Letters to His Son.* On the place of this book in the culture of American gentility, see Bushman, *Refinement of America,* 36–38. Given the use of the same Latin phrases in another piece about Bowditch, the Bowditch sons suspected the author of this piece was John Gorham Palfrey. Palfrey acknowledged authorship of this second piece [the final section (177–80) of Review of "Traite de Mecanique Celeste," *NAR* 48 (Jan. 1839): 143–80] but denied he was the author of the newspaper piece [NIB, JIB, HIB, and WIB, "Letter Annexed," and Palfrey, "Appendix to the Second Edition of the Rev. Dr. Palfrey's Eulogy on President Kirkland," in Palfrey et al., *Remarks Concerning the Late Dr. Bowditch,* 8–9, 17].

61. "To the Honorable President Quincy, D.D." [quoting Robert Southey's *The Doctor,* published in 1834], unidentified newspaper clipping in [NB], comp., Scrapbook, 1828–1834; Palfrey, *Discourse,* 47; John Langdon Sibley, Diary, 12 Mar. 1861, HUG 1791.72, HUA. It would appear that Palfrey's publication led the Bowditch sons to consider releasing their father's tell-all "College History." William H. Prescott wrote: "Palfrey and the four Bowditches have had some skirmishing. . . . It is now over just as the black book or red book which Dr. Bowditch left was about to be unclasped" [Prescott to Jared Sparks, 1 Jan. 1841, in Wolcott, *Correspondence,* 191].

62. John Lowell to James Jackson, 22 Nov. 1831, Corporation Papers, HUA, in Story, *Forging of an Aristocracy,* 51; Adams, Diary, 4, 6 May 1831, in Donald and Donald, *Diary of Charles Francis Adams,* 1: 41, 42; Brooks to EE, 14 Apr. 1828.

63. Pickering, *Eulogy,* 80; Young, *Nathaniel Bowditch,* 82–86 [quotations, 82, 85, 86]; NIB, "Memoir," 121–22. See also White, *Nathaniel Bowditch,* 58–60.

64. Palfrey, "Appendix to the Second Edition," in Palfrey et al., *Remarks Concerning the Late Dr. Bowditch,* 13–14. Palfrey was quoting a letter from "a gentleman, present at that meeting of the Corporation" (13), probably Frank Gray or Charles Jackson.

65. Amos Lawrence to NIB, 11 Dec. 1840, inserted in NB, "College History"; "Observer," "Harvard College," *Boston Patriot,* 9 Apr. 1828.

Chapter 9

1. NIB, "Memoir," 86; *United States' Telegraph,* 20 Aug. 1834; J. K. Paulding, "The History of Uncle Sam and His Womankind," *New-York Mirror* 10 (7 July 1832): 3; "Sullivan's Island," 13. See also "R.," Letter to the Editor, *Boston Courier,* 1 Jan. 1835.

2. Grattan-Guinness, "Before Bowditch"; Pickering, *Eulogy,* 58–59; Young, *Nathaniel Bowditch,* 46, 52–53 [quotation, 52–53]; Eliab Metcalf to NB, 8 May 1828, Ms.E.210.19 v.1 (5), NBC; NIB, "Memoir," 110–11.

3. NIB, "Memoir," 60–61; Young, *Nathaniel Bowditch*, 48; NB, "Introduction by the Translator," handwritten document, c. 1817, on the reverse of title page, original manuscript of NB, "Mécanique Céleste, by S. P. La Place, Member of the National Institute of France, and of the Board of Longitude, First Volume, Translated/with notes/by Nathaniel Bowditch," Ms.E.210.11 (v.1), NBC.

4. NIB, "Memoir," 62 [quotation]; NB, *Mécanique Céleste*, 1: v, viii–xi, 2, 39, 75, 78 [quotations, v, 39, 75, 78]. What Bowditch perceived as omission leading to confusion may have instead reflected what historian of science Joan Richards has argued was a characteristically French understanding of the nature and foundations of mathematical truth, one deeply at odds with even the most advanced English views. Hence, when in 1816 Charles Babbage and John Herschel, the champions of French infinitesimal calculus at Cambridge, translated a mathematical work by Sylvestre Lacroix, they included substantial endnotes that critiqued the original as insufficiently grounded. Similarly, Englishman Augustus De Morgan's introduction to the concept of limits as developed by Augustin-Louis Cauchy "abandoned all the crisp specificity of Cauchy's work for his conceptual elaborations" [Richards, "Rigor and Clarity" (quotation, 315)].

5. NB, *Mécanique Céleste*, "Appendix, by the Translator," 3: 761; WIB, "Our Family Story from 1639 to 1838 told by William I. Bowditch 1896," MSS 3, ser. II, B6, 1: 82, BF-PEM [quotation]; NIB, "Memoir," 63–67 [quotations, 65, 66]. See also Young, *Nathaniel Bowditch*, 51, on Laplace's lack of "grace." For NB's corrections, see NB, *Mécanique Céleste*, 2: 394, 412–16, 447, 459, 471, 4: 176–85.

6. Metcalf to NB, 8 May 1828; Young, *Nathaniel Bowditch*, 54; NIB, "Memoir," 61, 110n [quotation, 110n]; NB to Benjamin Vaughan, 3 Sept. 1830, Benjamin Vaughan Papers, APS; NB to Obadiah Rich, 22 July 1831, ser. II, B7, vol. 1, BF-PEM; WIB, "Our Family Story," 1: 83, 93 [quotation, 1: 83]; NIB to HIB, 29 July 1833, PV, N1, F4, Forbes Family Papers, 1732–1931, MHS [hereafter Forbes]; Hogan, *Of the Human Heart*, 28, 40–47, 52; Benjamin Peirce to NB, 23 Sept. 1833, Ms.E.210.19 v.2 (95), NBC. After Peirce had been scolded for failing to follow his Harvard instructor's explanation of a physics problem, Bowditch replied that "the pretended explanation was utterly false & the most unintelligible nonsense ever written by one who had crossed over the Pons Asinorum." Literally the "Bridge of Asses," the phrase referred to one of Euclid's geometrical propositions, but because that proposition acted as a test of who could successfully cross this intellectual bridge, the phrase was also a metaphor for any problem that separated out the incompetent from the capable [Peirce to Josiah Quincy, 14 Feb. 1835, quoted in Hogan, *Of the Human Heart*, 43].

7. James Jackson to NB, 2 Dec. 1833, Ms.E.210.19 v.2 (99), NBC; Lucien Caryl to NB, 10 Apr. 1835, 10 Aug. 1836, Ms.E.210.19 v.3 (17), Ms.E.210.19 v.3 (47), NBC; Frederick Furber to NB, 27 Aug., 8 Oct. 1833, 15 Feb. 1834, 3 July 1835, Ms.E.210.19 v.2 (94), Ms.E.210.19 v.2 (96), Ms.E.210.19 v.2 (104), Ms.E.210.19 v.3 (31), NBC; Charles Francis McCay to A. S. Clayton, 5 Jan. 1835, Ms.E.210.19 v.3 (5–6), NBC; Clayton to NB, 14 Jan. 1835, Ms.E.210.19 v.3 (4), NBC; NB to McCay, 19 Jan. 1835, and McCay to NB, 17 May 1835, Ms.E.210.19 v.3 (7), Ms.E.210.19 v.3 (23–25), NBC. On

the three correspondents, see Sellstedt, "Roswell Willson Haskins," 271–72 [Caryl]; Palmer, *Necrology of Harvard Alumni*, 20 [Furber]; and Montgomery and Kellam, "Mathematical Backwoodsman."

8. White, *Nathaniel Bowditch*, 49; "Bowditch's La Place," *Christian Register* 7 (4 Oct. 1828): 159; "Astronomy of La Place," *American Quarterly Review* 7 (June 1830): 256; "The Mecanique Celeste of La Place," *Virginia Literary Museum* 1 (21 Apr. 1830): 706. For NB's pride in these features, see NB to Obadiah Rich, and NB postscript to NIB to HIB, 9 July 1832, PV, N1, F4, Forbes.

9. Sylvestre Lacroix to NB, 5 Apr. 1830, Ms.E.210.19 v.2 (43), NBC; Adrien-Marie Legendre to David Bailie Warden, 2 Feb. 1830 [as translated in Reingold, *Science in Nineteenth Century America*, 24], Ms.E.210.19 v.2 (27), NBC; Henry Beaufoy to NB, 24 Aug. 1835, HUG 1231.7, HUA.

10. *New-York Morning Herald*, 22 Feb. 1830; NIB to HIB, 2 Sept. 1832 (second portion dated 9 Sept. 1832), PV, N1, F4, Forbes; Obadiah Rich to NB, 4 May 1835, Ms.E.210.19 v.3 (21), NBC; Metcalf to NB, 8 May 1828; *Journal of Belles Lettres* 20 (11 Nov. 1834): 3. By way of comparison, each volume of the *MAAAS* cost $2.50 [Oliver Everett to Daniel Appleton White, 23 Apr. 1822, Papers of Professor Henry William Wilder Foote and Family, Andover-Harvard Theological Library, Harvard Divinity School].

11. NIB, "Memoir," 166–68; George C. Shattuck Jr. to Benjamin Shattuck, 7 Dec. 1829, vol. 8, George Cheyne Shattuck Papers, 1797–1912, MHS. The full list of recipients recorded by NIB includes individuals and organizations in England, Scotland, Ireland, France, Germany, Belgium, Sweden, Denmark, Italy, Russia, and India.

12. William Vaughan to NB, 16 Feb. 1830, Ms.E.210.19 v.2 (33), NBC; John Herschel to NB, 8 Mar. 1830, Ms.E.210.19 v.2, NBC; Obadiah Rich to NB, 4 May 1835; NB to Marie Charles Fournier, 12 Nov. 1829, Ms.E.210.19 v.2 (12), NBC; NB to Reuben Mussey, 13 Nov. 1829, Mussey to NB, 4 Feb. [quotation], 6 Apr. 1830, Ms.E.210.19 v.2 (9), Ms.E.210.19 v.2 (30), Ms.E.210.19 v.2 (45), NBC; Legendre to Warden, 2 Feb. 1830; David Bailie Warden to NB, 5 May 1831, Ms.E.210.19 v.2 (55), NBC. On Warden, see Maryland Historical Society, "David Bailie Warden Papers." Warden performed similar services for TJ [TJ to Warden, 15 July 1810, in Oberg and Looney, *Papers of Thomas Jefferson*.]

13. NB to Sylvestre Lacroix, 10 April 1835, B1, F1, BF-PEM; Beaufoy to NB, 24 Aug. 1835; George Ticknor to NB, 19 Dec. 1835, Ms.Am.2346 (2), NBC; James Thal to NB, 26 Jan. 1834, Ms.E.210.19 v.2 (101), NBC; William Ropes to NB, 27 Aug. 1833, Ms.E.210.19 v.2 (92), NBC; NIB, "Memoir," 66n.

14. NIB, "Memoir," 65 [quotation], 111.

15. Adrien-Marie Legendre to NB, 2 July 1832, Ms.E.210.19 v.2 (69), NBC, as quoted and translated in Pickering, *Eulogy*, 98; Sylvestre Lacroix to NB, 1 July 1835, quoted and translated in Pickering, *Eulogy*, 98; Friedrich Wilhelm Bessel to NB, 18 Feb. 1836, Ms.E.210.19 v.3 (40, 21), NBC, as quoted and translated in Pickering, *Eulogy*, 99; Louis Puissant to D. B. Warden, 31 May 1835, as quoted and translated in Pickering, *Eulogy*, 99; Lacroix to NB, 5 Apr. 1830, as quoted and translated in Pickering, *Eulogy*, 97.

16. Legendre to Warden, 2 Feb. 1830; Beaufoy to NB, 24 Aug. 1835; Herschel to NB, 8 Mar. 1830. For other commentary on American readers, see John Brinkley to NB, 7 May 1830, Ms.E.210.19 v.2 (47), NBC; and *Memoirs of the Astronomical Society of London* 5 (1833): 389–90.

17. Adrien-Marie Legendre to NB, 4 Feb. 1830, Ms.E.210.19 v.2 (29), NBC [as translated in Reingold, *Science in Nineteenth Century America*, 24–25]; Mary Somerville to NB, 15 Dec. 1831, Ms.E.210.19 v.2 (59), NBC.

18. NB to EE, [20 May] 1821, Ms.E.210.19 v.1 (80), NBC; John Lewis Tiarks to NB, 24 Feb. 1830, Ms.E.210.19 v.2 (36), NBC; William Vaughan to NB, 24 Sept. 1830, Ms.E.210.19 v.2 (54), NBC; Charles Babbage to NB, 20 Mar. 1830, 5 Aug. 1832, Ms.E.210.19 v.2 (42), Ms.E.210.19 v.2 (74), NBC; NIB to HIB, 2 Sept. 1832; NB to Babbage, 15 Nov. 1829, copy from the British Museum in APS; NB to Babbage, 21 Feb. 1835 [quotation], British Library Mss., quoted in Schaffer, "Apotheosis of Machine Intelligence"; Babbage to NB, 2 Aug. 1835, Dibner Library, National Museum of American History, excerpted in Williams, "Babbage and Bowditch," 286–89 [quotations, 286–87, 289]. Williams, citing internal evidence, offers definitive proof that this letter to an unidentified recipient was addressed to NB.

19. NB postscript to NIB to HIB, 24 Feb. 1833, B2, F1, BF-PEM; Ticknor to NB, 19 Dec. 1835; NIB, "Memoir," 70; NB to George Ticknor, 5 Aug. 1836, Ticknor Autograph Collection, Rauner Special Collections Library, Dartmouth College; Ticknor to NB, 23 Oct. 1836, Ms.Am.2346 (3), NBC. From Calcutta, John Curnin, identifying himself as a fellow member of the Astronomical Society, actuary, and soon to be professor at a "Hindoo College," corresponded with Bowditch about his *Mécanique Céleste* [Curnin to NB, 9 Mar. 1835, B2, F1, Bowditch-Loring Family Papers, 1762–1940, MHS (hereafter BLF Papers)]. On Curnin, see Schaffer, "Bombay Case."

20. Pickering, *Eulogy*, 101; NIB to HIB, 2 Sept. 1832 (second portion dated 9 Sept. 1832).

21. One American newspaper reported that this "English lady" had studied Laplace so thoroughly that "she used his analytical methods *like one* perfectly versed" in these arcane techniques [italics mine]. Another praised her "little volume." "Petticoat government," noted a third, is surely on its way [*Southern Patriot*, 17 Apr. 1832; *Newport Mercury*, 14 Apr. 1832; "Female Supremacy," *Providence Patriot*, 5 Apr. 1834].

22. *Monthly Notices of the Astronomical Society of London* 4 (8 Feb. 1839): 174–75.

23. *National Gazette*, republished in the *Boston Courier*, 7 May 1832; "Sigma," "Horae Decerptae. From a Mathematician's Diary," *Mathematical Diary* 2 (Mar. 1832): 298; *SG*, 26 Nov. 1830, 4 Sept. 1832; *Baltimore Patriot*, 10 Nov. 1830; *Rhode Island American*, 10 Jan. 1832; *Southern Patriot*, 19 Jan. 1832.

24. Smith, "Statistical Annals of the United States" 79–80; *National Gazette*, quoted in *SG*, 23 July 1830.

25. *ER*, 23 Feb. 1824 [quotation]; Josiah Quincy to NB [October 1829], Quincy, Wendell, Holmes, and Upham Family Papers, 1633–1910, MHS [hereafter QWHU Papers]; *From the Mechanicks Magazine*, Bdses 1830 Mar. 12, MHS; Maury, *Treatise on Navigation*, 337; NB to Mahlon Dickerson, 29 Sept. 1836, and Robert Treat Paine to

Dickerson, 14 Apr. 1837, in U.S. Congress, *"Message from the President,"* 105, 281–82; NB to Dickerson, 11 Oct. 1837, Alexander Calvin and Ellen Morton Washburn Autograph Collection, 1600–1895, MHS; Erskine, *Twenty Years before the Mast*, 10, 198; Philbrick, *Sea of Glory*, 36–37. In 1841 Charles Wilkes named one of the South Pacific islands his expedition explored Bowditch Island. It is now known as Fakaofo.

26. EE, "Address Delivered as the Introduction to the Franklin Lectures, in Boston, Nov. 14, 1831," *United States Catholic Miscellany* 12 (22 Dec. 1832): 200; NIB to HIB, 2 Sept. (second portion dated 9 Sept. 1832), 23 Oct. 1832, PV, N1, N4, Forbes; NIB to HIB, 16 Nov. 1832, excerpted in Warren, "Phrenological Society," 3n; Somerville to NB, 8 July 1834, Ms.E.210.19 v.2 (111), NBC; Martineau to HIB, 10 Dec. 1838, in Bowditch, *Henry Ingersoll Bowditch*, 1: 108; [Jane Norton Wigglesworth] to Anna Wigglesworth, 3 Sept. 1835, B2, Wigglesworth Family Papers, 1682–1966, MHS [hereafter Wigglesworth]; Dunnington, *Carl Friedrich Gauss*, 281–82; Joseph Gauss to Carl Friedrich Gauss, 18 July 1830, in *Carl Friedrich Gauss und die Seinen, Festschrift zu seinem 150 Geburtstag, herausgegeben von Heinrich Mack* (Braunschweig: E. Appelhans, 1927), 84–85, as translated by Dirk Struik, in Harold Bowditch, "A Collection of Data Made for the Possible Future Use of a Biographer," 2: 265, MH 42, NBLW; Thal to NB, 26 Jan. 1834 [quotation]; Saul, *Distant Friends*, 156.

27. Spearheading the commission was Bowditch's longtime friend and associate Thomas Wren Ward, who had recently collaborated with Bowditch on disposing of Johann Spurzheim's effects when the lecturer unexpectedly died during his Boston visit. A good part of the estate had consisted of human skulls, casts, and masks, for the phrenologist had advocated that the heads of especially distinguished men be cast for scientific study. When he visited Frazee's studio in New York, Ward may have determined that Boston should have its intellectual giants celebrated in this manner ["Expenses of Procuring a Marble Bust of Dr. Bowditch executed by Mr. John Frazee," Thomas Wren Ward Papers, 1717–1943; 1778–1858, MHS; Warren, "Phrenological Society"; Walsh, "American Tour of Dr. Spurzheim"; Colbert, *Measure of Perfection*, 14–18].

28. "Autobiography of Frazee," 22–23 [quotations, 23]; Charles Turrell to NB, 14 Oct. 1833, Ms.E.210.19 v.2 (98), NBC; John Frazee to Family, 24 Oct. 1833, John Frazee Papers, Archives of American Art, Smithsonian Institution http://www.aaa.si.edu/collections/container/viewer/John-Frazee-Letters-to-Family—280100; WIB, "Our Family Story," 1: 122–23, 129; NIB to Frazee, 12 Apr. 1836, John Frazee Papers, http://www.aaa.si.edu/collections/container/viewer/General-Letters—280101 [quotation]. Bowditch's initial unease may have had its roots in an earlier attempt to render his likeness when, in 1826, he sat for a portrait by Gilbert Stuart, who died before he could finish it. Mary thought the sketch made her husband look sick. Friends suggested another artist should "colour the face and paint the body." Unwilling for it to fall into others' hands, Bowditch quickly bought it and hung it in an unheated second floor hall [George Ticknor to NB, 31 May 1826, Ms.Am.2346 (1), NBC; EIMS Committee to NB, 6 Nov. 1834, MH 88, ser. VII, Scrapbook 3, EIMSR; HIB to George C. Mason, 2 Sept. 1878, B1, George Champlin Mason Papers, MSS 742, Rhode Island Historical

Society; WIB, "The Home of Nathaniel Bowditch in Boston, 1823–38," in Bowditch, "Collection of Data," 1: 128 (quotation)].

29. EIMS Committee Report, 6 May 1835, ser. VII, Scrapbook 3, EIMSR; HIB, "Memoir of Visit to Salem, 1889," 36, HIB Papers, MHS.

30. Servants: The 1830 U.S. Census shows a woman in her thirties (Abigail the cook) and an older teenage boy, perhaps the "Patrick" referred to by Nat in one of his letters, or the John Hurley or an unnamed "Irishman" recalled by William [U.S. Bureau of the Census, *Fifth Census . . . 1830*, 276; NIB to HIB, 2 Sept. 1832; WIB, "Home of Nathaniel Bowditch," 128; WIB to HIB, 2 Feb. 1834, ser. II, B2, F1, BF-PEM]. Elizabeth Martin: *Vital Records of Salem*; Bowditch, *Henry Ingersoll Bowditch*, 1: 11; WIB, "Home of Nathaniel Bowditch," 1: 126, 129; WIB, "Our Family Story," 1: 161; NIB, "Memoir," 14.

31. "WIB, "Our Family Story," 94, 125, 156 [quotations, 94, 156]. Grandson Ernest came to a similar conclusion regarding two cohorts of children based on a distinct divide in the stories relayed by the grandchildren [Ernest William Bowditch, "Impressions concerning Nathaniel Bowditch and his wife Mary (Ingersoll) Bowditch, 1909," in Bowditch, "Collection of Data," 1: 405–13].

32. HIB to NIB, 12 June 1820, in Bowditch, "Collection of Data," 1: 102; MIB2, postscript to NIB to HIB, 23 Oct. 1832 [quotation]; essay signed by M.I.B. [MIB2], c. 1830–35, B2, Wigglesworth; NIB to HIB, 9 July 1832; MIB2 to JI, 17 Oct., no year, MSS 159, B2, F6, Endicott Family Papers, 1638–1936, PEM; Dixwell, annotated document of 6 Dec. 1832, B2, and annotated diary entry of 7 Jan. 1834, B17, Wigglesworth [quotations]; WIB to HIB, 2 Feb. 1834; NIB to HIB, 15 Feb. 1834, PV, N1, F4, Forbes; Jane Norton Wigglesworth to Anna Wigglesworth, 30 March, 3 Sept. 1835, Wigglesworth. On the whirl of soirees and balls attended by the Bowditch children, see, e.g., NIB to HIB, 16 Dec. 1832, PV, N1, F4, Forbes; WIB to HIB, 2 Feb. 1834; Anna Cabot Lowell Quincy Waterston, Diary, 22 Mar. 1833, QWHU Papers.

33. NIB to CP, 19 Dec. 1834, PV1, N7, F6, Forbes, MHS; NIB to JI, 13 Dec. 1834, B2, F6, Endicott Family Papers; Edward Austen to JIB, 21 Jan. 1837, B1, F4, BLF Papers.

34. Lothrop, *Memoir of Nathaniel Ingersoll Bowditch*, 6–11; NIB to HIB, 2 Sept. 1832 (second portion dated 9 Sept. 1832); Harvard University, "Class Book of 1822," 7, HUD 222 714f., HUA; NIB, *Massachusetts General Hospital*, 131–32; MGH, *Acts, Resolves, By-laws, and Rules and Regulations*, chap. 5, art. 7; Reiser, "Creating Form out of Mass," 303–4.

35. WIB, "Our Family Story," 148–50; WIB, "Home of Nathaniel Bowditch," 128; Harvard University, "Class Book of 1838," 53–55, HUD 238 714f., HUA; Cushing, *Historical Sketch of Chauncy-Hall School*, 208; Harvard University, Votes of the Faculty Relating to Academic and Administrative Affairs, 1636–1870, 30 Nov. 1835, 12, 21 Mar., 24 Apr. 1836, XI: 254, 265, 267, UAIII 5.5.2, HUA.

36. "Jonathan Ingersoll Bowditch," 435–37; Charles Pickering Bowditch, "Reminiscences," "Father," n.d., MSS 156, B3, F6, Joseph Bowditch Papers, 1699–1941, PEM; NB to Augustine Heard, 24 June 1828, B1, F4, BF-PEM [quotation]; JIB to Ebenezer Francis, 28 Apr. 1831, B1, F1, BLF Papers; NB to George Ticknor, 5 Aug. 1836; JIB to NIB, 30 April 1820, in Bowditch, "Collection of Data," 1: 97 [quotation];

Mathematical Diary 2 (1828): 17, 18, 20, 21–22; NB to Nathaniel Silsbee, 12 Dec. 1831, Grenville H. Norcross Autograph Collection, 1489–1937, MHS; NB, *New American Practical Navigator*, 9th ed., preface, x; Campbell, *History and Bibliography*, 69–70, 86–98.

37. [HIB], "A Retrospective Glimpse in 1888 upon the Life & Work of the Class of 1828, Harv. University," (1888), 11, HUD 228.809, HUA; Bowditch, *Henry Ingersoll Bowditch*, 1: 14 [quotation]; HIB to NB, 8 Aug. 1833, in Bowditch, *Henry Ingersoll Bowditch*, 1: 56; HIB to James Jackson Jr., January 1834?, B2, Putnam-Jackson-Lowell Family Papers, 1769–1922, MHS; WIB to HIB, 24 Feb. 1833, 2 Feb. 1834, ser. II, B2, F1, BF-PEM. On HIB's medical education, see Warner, *Against the Spirit of System*; Jones, "American Doctors and the Parisian Medical World," and HIB, *Brief Memories of Louis*.

38. HIB to NB and MIB, 29 June 1832, NB to HIB, 16 Sept. 1832, and HIB to MIB2, 17 Dec. 1832, in Bowditch, *Henry Ingersoll Bowditch*, 1: 19–21, 23, 33–34 [quotations, 1: 19, 21, 23]; HIB to JI, 23 Dec. 1834, B2, F6, Endicott Family Papers; Holmes to his parents, 13 Jan. 1834, in Morse, *Life and Letters of Oliver Wendell Holmes*, 1: 126.

39. HIB to NB and MIB, 17 Nov. 1832, HIB to NB, 8 Aug., 13 Dec. 1833, and HIB to his daughter, 26 Nov. 1871, in Bowditch, *Henry Ingersoll Bowditch*, 1: 30–32, 52–54, 68, 2: 265–69 [quotations, 1: 32, 53, 2: 268]; Mary Somerville to NB, 29 Nov. 1832, Ms.E.210.19 v.2 (80), NBC. After his father died, HIB asked Somerville to "write an elaborate review" of his father's Laplace. "Though highly sensible of the honour," she declined, "fearing that I should not do justice to the memory of so great a man" [Somerville, *Personal Recollections*, 223–24].

40. EO to CP, 21 Apr., 16 Dec. 1802, MSS 445, B9, F6, White Family Papers, 1746–1906, PEM [hereafter White]; EOW to Lucinda D Orne, 21 Nov. 1811, B9, F8, White; EOWW to Mrs. Orne, 5 Aug. 1819, B8, F9, White; HIB, Journal, vol. 1, 10 Feb., 19 Dec. 1827, GA 9.20, Harvard Medical Library, HIB Papers, Countway; NB to HIB, 3 Jan. 1833, vol. 1, R. C. Waterston Autograph Collection, 1542–1886, MHS; HIB to NIB, 5 June 1834, in Bowditch, *Henry Ingersoll Bowditch*, 1: 81; NIB to HIB, 25 July, 2 Sept. [quotation], 23 Oct., 1832, 18 Apr. 1834 [quotation], PV, N1, F4, Forbes; WIB, "Our Family Story," 141–43 [quotation, 142]; NB to Miss A. Ropes, 6 Sept. 1826, QWHU Papers; NIB, "Memoir," 112.

41. NIB to HIB, 18 Apr. 1834 [quotations]; NIB, "Memoir," 112 [quotations]. On the "Good Death," see Faust, *This Republic of Suffering*, 6–11.

42. NIB to HIB, 18 Apr 1834 (second and third portions dated 19, 20 Apr. 1832); NIB, "Memoir," 113.

43. Bowditch, *Henry Ingersoll Bowditch*, 1: 82–96 [quotations, 85, 92, 93]; NB to Olivia Yardley, 10 Mar. 1838, in Bowditch, *Henry Ingersoll Bowditch*, 1: 95–96 [quotations]; HIB to Francis Henry Brown, 9 Nov. 1873, and attached blank form, 1830s, "To the Physician of the Boston Dispensary . . . 183_," B MS c75.9, Boston Medical Library, HIB Papers, Countway; NIB, "Memoir," 60n. After Bowditch's death, Ingersoll's contact in London responded to his earlier request for a candid assessment of Yardley and reported that she was a "sterling coin with no fake gilding,"

possessing the "simplicity & ease of a lady," much superior in cultivation to her friends and family [J. J. Dixwell to JIB, 23 May 1838, B1, F7, BLF Papers].

44. George Ticknor, quoting NB, in Ticknor to Robert H. Gardner, 11 Nov. 1863, in Ticknor, *George Ticknor*, 2: 464.

45. NIB, "Memoir," 114–15 [quotations, 115]; Tager, *Boston Riots*, chaps. 4, 5.

46. Fischer, *Albion's Seed*, 845; Conforti, *Imagining New England*, chaps. 3, 4; Solis-Cohen, *Maine Antique Digest*, 318 [Salemite Prisce (*sic*) Gill's 1782 sampler]; NIB, "Memoir," 115 [quotation]. See also Nissenbaum, "New England as Region and Nation."

47. NIB, "Memoir," 116 [quotation]; Porter, "Remonds of Salem"; Silsbee, *Half Century in Salem*, 21 [quotation], 88, 94; Rental Ledger, 1814–26, MSS 134, B3, F1, EFMR; receipts, B4, F24, EIMSR; *SG*, 30 Sept. 1825; WIB, "Our Family Story," 119, 150, 162.

48. NIB, "Memoir," 116–17 [quotation, 117]; NB to Nathaniel Silsbee, 19 Feb. 1820, case 5, B38, Simon Gratz Autograph Collection, Historical Society of Pennsylvania; "BURNING ALIVE!" and "HORRID EXECUTION," *SG*, 18 Feb. 1820.

49. Epes Dixwell to John James Dixwell, 28 May 1838, B2, Wigglesworth; George Ticknor to William Prescott, 8 Feb. 1836, in Ticknor, *George Ticknor*, 1: 479; Howe, "Channing, William Ellery" [quotation].

50. Epes Dixwell to George Basil Dixwell, 16 Jan. 1842, B2, Wigglesworth; Bowditch, *Henry Ingersoll Bowditch*, 1: 101–2, 112–32 [quotation, 101]; [HIB], "Retrospective Glimpse," 9; HIB, Journal, 1880, in Bowditch, "Collection of Data," 2: 255 [quotation].

51. Books Borrowed, vol. 1 (1827–34), vol. 2 (1835–43), Archives of the Boston Athenaeum; NB to George and Anna Ticknor, 5 Aug. 1836, Ticknor Autograph Collection; NIB, "Memoir," 117; W[illiam] E[llery] C[hanning], Letter, *Christian Register and Boston Observer* 17 (21 Apr. 1838): 62; Follen, *Life of Charles Follen*, 266.

52. NB to George and Anna Ticknor, 5 Aug. 1836; "Rescue of the Slaves," *Liberator*, 6 Aug. 1836.

53. NIB, "Memoir," 137–39, 146–47, 152 [quotations, 138, 147]; NIB to JI, 18 Feb. 1838, PV, N1, F2, Forbes [quotations]; NIB to Mr. [John] Brazer, 4 Mar. 1838, PV, N1. F2, Forbes; MIB2, "Compilations by Mary Ingersoll Bowditch about her Father Nathaniel Bowditch," 4 Mar. 1838, B23, Wigglesworth; Daniel A. White to Eliza Dwight, 26 Feb. 1838, B3, F7, White; EE, "Memorandum," 7 Mar. 1838, attached to EE to NIB, 11 May 1839, 68: 174–75 [quotation, 175], EE Papers; William Appleton, Diary, 8 Mar. 1838, William Appleton and Company Records, Baker Library, Harvard Business School.

54. NIB, "Memoir," 149–53; MIB2, "Compilations," 2 Mar. 1838; Appleton, Diary, 8 Mar. 1838; George Cleveland, "Interview with Nathaniel Bowditch," 9 Mar. 1838, interleaved with NIB, *Memoir of Nathaniel Bowditch*, copy in MHS [quotation]; Daniel White to NIB, 24 Mar. 1838, MSS 445, B3, F7, White; EE, "Memorandum," 68: 177.

55. Cleveland, "Interview with Nathaniel Bowditch"; NIB, "Memoir," 149–52 [quotation, 152]; EE, "Memorandum," 68: 174–75 [quotations]; MIB2, "Compilations," 2, 4, 11 Mar. 1838 [quotation, 11 Mar.]; White, *Nathaniel Bowditch*, 53–54 [quotations, 54].

56. NIB, "Memoir," 142n, 143–44, 153–54; MIB2, "Compilations," 2, 11, 15 Mar. 1838; NB, Will, 28 Feb. 1838 [quotation], and Estate Inventory, 24 Mar. 1838, Suffolk County

Probate Records, Massachusetts State Archives; [Hildreth], *"Our First Men,"* 11, 15, 24, 27, 37–38, 44; HIB to EBIBD, 10 Nov. 1887, MIB Papers; NIB to Brazer, 4 Mar. 1838, 4 Mar. 1838 [quotation]; Cleveland, "Interview with Nathaniel Bowditch."

57. NIB, "Memoir," 139–41, 150 [quotations, 140, 150]; Moses L. Hale to Elijah Alvord, 10 Mar. 1838, LA-2, MHLC.

58. [HIB], *Memoir*, 153 [quotations]; HIB, Diary, 4 Mar. 1838, excerpted in NIB, "Memoir," 147–48 [quotations]. See also Young, *Nathaniel Bowditch*, 82–83n. Bowditch may have been getting his ideas from a book he purchased in 1796, an English translation of the Abbé Claude François Xavier Millot's *Elements of General History*. In it, Millot stated that "had Archimedes lived in our days, he would have been another Newton" and was "a prodigy of genius" [1: 294. Bowditch's name appears in the "Subscribers' Names," unpaginated].

59. [HIB], *Memoir*, 153; NIB, "Memoir," 143 [quotation]; MIB2, "Compilations," 10, 11 Mar. 1838 [quotations]; WIB, Diary, 1838–39, 8, 15 Mar. 1838, B3, F2, BF-PEM [quotation, 8 Mar.].

60. MIB2, "Compilations," 15, 18 Mar. 1838 [quotation, 15 Mar.]; [HIB], *Memoir*, 157; WIB, Diary, 15, 16 Mar. 1838 [quotation, 16 Mar.]; NIB, "Memoir," 157–58.

61. White, *Nathaniel Bowditch*, 67–68; *Waldo Patriot*, 23 Mar. 1838; *Southern Patriot*, 24 Mar. 1838; *SG*, 27, 30 Mar., 3, 20 Apr. 1838; *Baltimore Sun*, 23 Mar. 1838; NIB, "Memoir," 44–45.

62. "Children of the late Nath' Bowditch," [NIB, JIB, HIB, WIB] to Sir J. W. Herschel, 27 Sept. 1838, HS.4.201, John W. Herschel Letters, Royal Society, London [quotation]; NIB, "Memoir," 159–61 [quotations, 160].

Chapter 10

1. MIB2, "Compilations by Mary Ingersoll Bowditch about her Father Nathaniel Bowditch," 14 Mar. 1838, B23, Wigglesworth Family Papers, 1682–1966, MHS.

2. Young, *Nathaniel Bowditch*, 66; White, *Nathaniel Bowditch*, 63. See also the Boston Athenaeum eulogy quoted in NIB, "Memoir," 104.

3. Young, *Nathaniel Bowditch*, 56–58, 101 [quotation, 56]; [William Bentley], *ER*, 29 Apr. 1818 [quotation]; "Dinner to Dr. Bowditch," *SG*, 12 Aug. 1823 [quotation]; *New-York Morning Herald*, 29 Mar. 1830; *Alexandria Gazette*, 6 Mar. 1830; *SG*, 18 May 1830; White, *Nathaniel Bowditch*, 5–6, 11–12, 19–21 [quotation, 6]; *BDA*, reprinted in *SG*, 20 Mar. 1838; EE to the Duke of Sussex, 27 July 1838, 68: 64–67, EE Papers.

4. "Dinner to Dr. Bowditch," *SG*, 12 Aug. 1823; *SG*, 20 Mar. 1838.

5. NIB, "Memoir," 17. See also [HIB], *Memoir*, 1.

6. On Bowditch as instructor of the "hardy mariner," see, e.g., Young, *Nathaniel Bowditch*, 15; and Sigourney, *Pocahontas*, 217.

7. [Goodrich], *Lives of Benefactors*, 288–304; *Famous Boys*, 116–23; Edwards, *Biography of Self-Taught Men*, 325–70; Wise, *Uncrowned Kings*, 218–44; Connell, *Biographical Sketches*, 36–39; "An Example for Young Men," *Colored American*, 21 July 1838.

8. An exception to the focus on NB's youth is Robert Elton Berry's *Yankee Stargazer* of 1941, though not his later juvenile biography of Bowditch, *Sextant and Sails*.

9. Rink, "Nathaniel Bowditch," 85. See also Kalkstein, "World According to Bowditch."

10. Latham, *Carry On, Mr. Bowditch*; Focus on the Family, "Carry On, Mr. Bowditch"; Pelttari, *Carry On, Mr. Bowditch Study Guide*, 25, 60.

11. Gillispie, *Pierre-Simon Laplace*, 283; Hahn, *Laplace*, 143–44; Greene, *American Science*, 157 [quotation]; Reingold, *Science in Nineteenth Century America*, 11–14; Struik, *Yankee Science*, 108–14, 229–32.

12. The professionalization and institutionalization of American science during the antebellum period is a major theme explored by an older generation of historians of American science. See, e.g., Daniels, "Professionalization in American Science," and Reingold, "Definitions and Speculations." For more recent perspectives, see Lucier, *Scientists and Swindlers*, and Spanagel, *DeWitt Clinton and Amos Eaton*.

13. Quincy, *History of Harvard*, 2: 439.

14. "Congregational Necrology," *Congregational Quarterly* 16 (Oct. 1874): 613–14 [quotation, 613]; "Boston Department," *New York Evangelist* 16 (21 Aug. 1845): 134; Phillips Library, Finding Aid for "Hale Family Papers"; "Mr. Josiah L. Hale," *New York Observer and Chronicle* 53 (18 Mar. 1875): 83.

15. "Report of the Committee on the Incorporation and Alteration of the Charters of Banking and Insurance Companies," 3 Feb. 1830, and "Extracts of a Letter of the Hon. James Lloyd to William Bard, Esq.," 7 Sept. 1829, in *Legislative Documents of the Senate and Assembly of the State of New-York*, 1–8, 9–13 [quotations, 11, 13]; Board of Control Report, 13 Jan. 1829, A-7, MHLC.

16. Elliott, *Thaddeus William Harris* [relationship with NB, 42, 177]; Higginson, "Memoir" [quotations, xvi, xxiv]; Carpenter, *First 350 Years*, 70–73; Harvard College Library, *Records of the Harvard College Library*. Even Harris's private reading notes were "systematized with French method." He recorded information in standardized data fields ("genus, species, locality, and even measurements, to the fraction of an inch"), rearranged entries alphabetically, and generated "elaborate indices." Intriguingly, one of Harris's entomological correspondents was Thomas Affleck, better known for the plantation account books, featuring data entry forms, that figure prominently in recent historiography on capitalism and the cotton plantation [Higginson, "Memoir," xviii–xix (quotations); Elliott, *Thaddeus William Harris*, 66–67, 161–62; Rosenthal, "From Memory to Mastery," chap. 1; Beckert, *Empire of Cotton*, 116].

17. Yates, *Control through Communication*, 56–63; Krajewski, *Paper Machines*, chaps. 5, 6; Tenner, "From Slip to Chip."

18. Agnew, "Afterword: Anonymous History," 279. For additional reflections on this historiographical trend, see Sklansky, "Elusive Sovereign," and Rockman, "What Makes the History of Capitalism Newsworthy?"

19. Ashworth, "Calculating Eye," 409, 410, 414.

20. For William Croswell, Joseph Green Cogswell, and Seth Bass, see chapter 8 in this volume. The librarian of the American Antiquarian Society, Christopher

Columbus Baldwin, a lawyer and antiquarian, did not grasp how the systematizing practices of the scientist carried over into libraries. Noting that Harris had "a prodigious fondness for bugs," and Bass "more love for shells and objects of Natural History than for Black Letter," he fulminated: "What right has a librarian to have any affection but for books and MSS.?" [Baldwin, *Diary*, entry for 20 Jan. 1834, 264].

21. On these actuaries and their connections to Bowditch, see *Prospectus of the Union Insurance Company*, 16; "Professor James Renwick," *Scientific American* 8 (24 Jan. 1863): 58; NB to MIB, 20 Apr. 1823, MSS 3, B1, F5, BF-PEM; "Notes on the Union Insurance Company," and "Notes on the Pennsylvania Life Assurance Company," AB-1, MHLC; Renwick to NB, 18 Dec. 1827, LB-1, MHLC; Renwick to NB, 12 Dec. 1829, Ms.E.210.19 v.2 (20), BPL; NIB, "Memoir," 166; Eugenius Nulty to NB, 14 Dec. 1829, Ms.E.210.19 v.2 (21), NBC; Morris, *Sketch of the Pennsylvania Company*, 27–29; Moorhead, "Sketches of Early North American Actuaries," 355–56; Cajori, Mathematics, 95–96; "Notes and Queries," *Pennsylvania Magazine of History and Biography* 13 (July 1889): 253; MAAAS, n.s. S1 (1833): 589; Nulty, "Solution of a General Case"; Nulty, *Elements of Geometry*; *Philadelphia Inquirer*, 4 July 1871; American Philosophical Society, "Joseph Roberts Philosophical and Mathematical Papers"; Albert Newsam after Manuel Joachim de Franca, *Joseph Roberts, Jr.*, lithograph, https://www.pafa.org/collection/joseph-roberts-jr. Both Bowditch and Nulty contributed solutions to mathematical problems posed in the *Mathematical Diary*. See, e.g., *Mathematical Diary* 2 (Jan. 1828): 3, 17, 19–20, 31–35, 37, 38, 76, 81, 91–92, 94, 102.

22. Smith, *Harpers Ferry Armory*; Smith, "Military Entrepreneurship"; Smith, "Army Ordnance"; O'Connell, "Corps of Engineers"; Chandler, *Visible Hand*, 72–75; Mahon, "Bomford, George"; Forman, "United States Military Philosophical Society," 274–75, 279; Wade, "Military Offspring"; Tousard, *American Artillerist's Companion*, 1: vi [quotation]; U.S. Army, *Regulations*; George Bomford to James Bell, 6 Apr. 1841, quoted in Smith, *Harpers Ferry Armory*, 267. Keith Hoskin and Richard Macve in "Genesis of Accountability" argue that it was the disciplinary pedagogical regime at West Point, rather than its mathematical content, that shaped its graduates' emphasis on accountability in large enterprises. On the French Enlightenment underpinnings of the ideal of interchangeability, see Hounshell, *From the American System to Mass Production*, 25–27.

23. Chandler, *Visible Hand*, 73; John, "Governmental Institutions as Agents of Change," 370–71.

24. Bowring, "Report on the Public Accounts of France" [quotations, 3, 4]. On bureaucracy, quantification, and the surveillance state, see, e.g., Agar, *Government Machine*, and Hacking, "Biopower and the Avalanche of Printed Numbers." On the French and British reforms, see Nikitin, "Birth of a Modern Public Sector Accounting," and Soll, *Reckoning*, 166–68. Earlier references to French public administration as a machine can be found in Bosher, *French Finances*, 133–36, 249–50, 296–97.

25. Elite women would have participated in a corporate environment in their churches and, in some cases, the female benevolent societies to which some belonged. The three female benevolent organizations in Boston with the heaviest Unitarian

(elite) memberships did incorporate, though only after their establishment: the Female Asylum (established 1800, incorporated 1803), the Fatherless and Widows' Society (1816, 1837), and the Seamen's Aid Society (1833, 1845). The organization to which Mary Bowditch belonged, the Salem Female Charitable Society, was established in 1801 and incorporated in 1804, though the enabling legislation stipulated that the treasurer be a single woman at least twenty-one years of age and that the husbands of members were liable for money received by their wives in connection with the society [Boylan, *Origins of Women's Activism*, 20–21, and table A.1; "An Act to Incorporate the Boston Fatherless and Widows' Society," 1837, chap. 23, in *Private and Special Statutes of the Commonwealth . . . 1837*, 733; "An Act to Incorporate the Seamen's Aid Society," 1845, chap. 51, in *Private and Special Statutes of the Commonwealth . . . 1848*, 423; Salem Female Charitable Society, *Constitution*; "An Act to Incorporate Lucretia Osgood and Others into a Society by the Name of the Salem Female Charitable Society," 1804, chap. 23, in *Acts and Laws . . . 1804*, 517–19].

26. Cushing, *Oration*, 12. See chapter 7 of this volume.

Bibliography

Primary Sources

ARCHIVES AND MANUSCRIPT COLLECTIONS

Adams, Great Barrington, and Pittsfield, Mass.
  Berkshire County Registry of Deeds
Boston, Mass.
  Baker Library, Harvard Business School
    Commercial Insurance Company Collection
    Massachusetts Hospital Life Insurance Company Collection
    William Appleton and Company Records
  Boston Athenaeum
    Archives of the Boston Athenaeum
  Boston Public Library
    Nathaniel Bowditch Collection
  Francis A. Countway Library of Medicine, Harvard Medical School
    Papers of Henry Ingersoll Bowditch, 1827–88
  Massachusetts General Hospital
    Archives of the Massachusetts General Hospital
  Massachusetts Historical Society
    Alexander Calvin and Ellen Morton Washburn Autograph Collection,
      1600–1895
    Bowditch Family Business Letters, 1826–61
    Bowditch Family Christmas Collection, 1843–1936
    Bowditch Family Papers, 1800–94
    Bowditch Family Papers, 1834–82
    Bowditch-Loring Family Papers, 1762–1940
    Bowditch Memorial Cabinet Catalogue, 1877
    Charles Edward French Autograph Collection, 1337–1897
    Edward Everett Papers, 1675–1910
    Forbes Family Papers, 1732–1931
    George Bancroft Papers, 1816–90
    George Cheyne Shattuck Papers, 1797–1912
    Grenville H. Norcross Autograph Collection, 1489–1937
    Henry Ingersoll Bowditch Papers, 1822–1903
    Jonathan Ingersoll Bowditch Papers, 1836–62
    Mary Ingersoll Bowditch Papers, 1779–1887
    Massachusetts Charitable Mechanic Association Papers, 1791–1995

Nathaniel Bowditch Memorial Collection, 1851–86
Nicolas Pike Papers, 1783–98
Putnam-Jackson-Lowell Family Papers, 1769–1922
Quincy, Wendell, Holmes, and Upham Family Papers, 1633–1910
R. C. Waterston Autograph Collection, 1542–1886
Saltonstall Family Papers, 1524–1999
Thomas Wren Ward Papers, 1717–1943; 1778–1858
Timothy Pickering Papers, 1731–1927
Wigglesworth Family Papers, 1682–1966
William Hickling Prescott Papers, 1665–1959
Massachusetts State Archives
Records of the Massachusetts Executive Council
Suffolk County Probate Records
Massachusetts Supreme Judicial Court Archives
Records of the Supreme Judicial Court
State Library of Massachusetts
Massachusetts General Court, Journal of House of Representatives
Cambridge, Mass.
Andover-Harvard Theological Library, Harvard Divinity School
Papers of Professor Henry William Wilder Foote and Family
Harvard University Archives
Chronological miscellany: Harvard University Corporation
Harvard University, Board of Overseers, Records of the Board of Overseers:
formal meeting minutes, 1707–1932
Harvard University, "Class Book of 1822"
Harvard University, "Class Book of 1838"
Harvard University, College Papers
Harvard University, Corporation, Corporation records: minutes,
1643–1989
Harvard University, Votes of the Faculty Relating to Academic and
Administrative Affairs, 1636–1870
Harvard University Biographical files
Papers of John Thornton Kirkland, 1788–1837
Scrapbook, 1828–34
Dublin, Ireland
Royal Irish Academy
Royal Irish Academy Papers
Edinburgh, Scotland
National Library of Scotland
Papers of the Royal Society of Edinburgh
Galesburg, Ill.
Knox College Library, Special Collections and Archives
George Bancroft Collection

Hanover, N.H.
  Rauner Special Collections Library, Dartmouth College
    Ticknor Autograph Collection
Ithaca, N.Y.
  Cornell University
    Carl A. Kroch Library, Division of Rare and Manuscript Collections
London, England
  Royal Society
    Archives of the Royal Society
    John W. Herschel Letters
    Joseph Banks Letters
Philadelphia, Pa.
  American Philosophical Society
    American Philosophical Society Archives
    Benjamin Vaughan Papers
    Charles Babbage selected correspondence, 1827–71 (British Museum microfilm)
    Madeira-Vaughan Collection
    Miscellaneous Manuscript Collection
  Historical Society of Pennsylvania
    Simon Gratz Autograph Collection
Providence, R.I.
  Rhode Island Historical Society
    Channing Autograph Collection
    George Champlin Mason Papers
    Marchant Family Papers
Salem, Mass.
  Phillips Library, Peabody Essex Museum
    American and Canadian Ciphering Books, 1727–1864
    Bowditch Family Papers, 1726–1942, 1961, 1975, undated
    Derby Family Papers, 1716–1921
    Dudley Leavitt Pickman Papers, 1721–1938
    East India Marine Society Records, 1799–1972
    Endicott Family Papers, 1638–1936
    Essex Fire and Marine Insurance Company Records, 1776–1887
    Forrester Family Papers, 1664–1835
    Joseph Bowditch Papers, 1699–1941
    Nathaniel Bowditch's Life and Works, 1939–56
    Nathan Read Papers, 1709–1914
    Pickering Family Papers, 1662–1887
    Salem Athenaeum Records, 1760–1889
    Salem Female Charitable Society Records, 1801–2001
    Salem, Mass., Valuations and Directories, 1761–1850
    White Family Papers, 1746–1906

Washington, D.C.
  Archives of American Art, Smithsonian Institution
    John Frazee Papers

BOOKS

An Account of the Great Fire, Which Destroyed about 250 Buildings in Newburyport, on the Night of the 31st of May, 1811. 2nd. ed. Newburyport, Mass.: W. and J. Gilman, 1811.

An Act for Incorporating the Essex Fire and Marine Insurance Company. Salem, Mass.: Thomas C. Cushing, 1803.

An Act to Incorporate the President, Directors, and Company of the Commercial Bank. Salem, Mass.: W. Palfray Jr., 1819.

Adams, Charles Francis. *Diary of Charles Francis Adams.* 8 vols. Edited by Aida DiPace Donald and David Donald. Cambridge, Mass.: Harvard University Press, 1964.

————, ed. *Memoirs of John Quincy Adams, Comprising Portions of His Diary from 1795 to 1848.* 12 vols. Philadelphia: J. B. Lippincott, 1874–77.

Allen, Ethan. *A Narrative of Colonel Ethan Allen's Captivity.* Philadelphia: Robert Bell, 1779.

Allen, Samuel C. *An Address, Delivered at Northampton, before the Hampshire, Franklin, and Hampden Agricultural Society, October 27, 1830.* Northampton, Mass.: T. Watson Shepard, 1830.

American Academy of Arts and Sciences. *Catalogue of Books, in the Library of the American Academy of Arts and Sciences.* Boston: n.p., 1802.

Appleton, Nathan. *Introduction of the Power Loom; and, Origin of Lowell.* Lowell, Mass.: B. H. Penhallow, 1858.

Argelander, Friedrich. *Untersuchungen über die Bahn des Grossen Cometen vom Jahre 1811.* Königsberg: Gebrüder Bornträger, 1823.

Articles of the Amity Fire-Club, Associated in Salem, February 10, 1796. Salem, Mass.: William Carlton, 1796.

Articles of the Washington Fire Club, Associated in Salem, October 10, 1803. Salem, Mass.: Joshua Cushing, 1803.

Babbage, Henry Prevost, ed. *Babbage's Calculating Engines: Being a Collection of Papers Relating to Them; Their History and Construction.* London: E. and F. N. Spon, 1889.

Baily, Francis, *Journal of a Tour in Unsettled Parts of North America in 1796 and 1797.* London: Baily Bros., 1856.

Baird, Cyrus Augustus. *A Discourse on the Life and Character of Samuel Putnam.* Boston: Crosby, Nichols, 1853.

Baldwin, Christopher Columbus. *Diary of Christopher Columbus Baldwin, Librarian of the American Antiquarian Society, 1829–1835.* Worcester, Mass.: American Antiquarian Society, 1901.

Barnard, Thomas. *A Sermon, Preached before the Salem Female Charitable Society.* Salem, Mass.: William Carlton, 1803.

Baron, George. *Exhibition of the Genuine Principles of Common Navigation, with a Complete Refutation of the False and Spurious Principles Ignorantly Imposed on the Public in the "New American Practical Navigator"*. . . . New York: Sage and Clough, 1803.

Bentley, William. *The Diary of William Bentley, D.D.* 4 vols. Gloucester, Mass.: Peter Smith, 1962.

———. *Record of the Parish List of Deaths, 1785–1819*. Salem, Mass.: Essex Institute, 1882.

Berry, Robert Elton. *Sextant and Sails; the Story of Nathaniel Bowditch*. New York: Dodd, Mead, 1943.

———. *Yankee Stargazer; the Life of Nathaniel Bowditch*. New York: Whittlesey House, 1941.

Bickerstaff, Isaac. *Astronomical Repository*. Boston: Benjamin Edes, 1799.

Binney, Horace. *Speech of the Hon. Horace Binney, on the Question of the Removal of the Deposites [sic]*. Washington, D.C.: Gales and Seaton, 1834.

Blatchford, John. *Narrative of Remarkable Occurrences in the Life of John Blatchford*. New London, Conn.: T. Green, 1788.

Boston Athenaeum. *Catalogue of Books in the Boston Atheneum [sic]*. Boston: W. L. Lewis, 1827.

Boston Directory. Boston: John H. A. Frost and Charles Stimpson Jr., 1823.

Boston Mechanics Institution. *The First Annual Report of the Board of Managers of the Boston Mechanics Institution; Made to the Institution at the Annual Meeting Held on the Evening of Jan. 7, 1828*. Boston: John Cotton, 1828.

———. *The Third Annual Report of the Board of Managers of the Boston Mechanics Institution; with the Constitution; By-laws, and a List of the Members of the Institution*. Boston: Samuel N. Dickinson, 1830.

Bowditch, Henry I[ngersoll]. *Brief Memories of Louis and Some of His Contemporaries in the Parisian School of Medicine Forty Years Ago*. Boston: J. Wilson, 1872.

[———]. *Memoir of Nathaniel Bowditch, Prepared for the Young*. Boston: J. Munroe, 1841.

———. *Nat the Navigator. A Life of Nathaniel Bowditch*. Boston: Lee and Shepard, 1870.

———. *Sketch of the Life and Character of Nathaniel Bowditch, LL.D., Made at the Dedication of the Bowditch School, January 7, 1862*. Boston: J. E. Farwell, 1863.

Bowditch, Nathaniel. *Directions for Sailing into the Harbours of Salem, Marblehead, Beverly and Manchester*. Newburyport, Mass.: Edmund M. Blunt, 1806.

———. *Mécanique Céleste by the Marquis de la Place, Translated with a Commentary, by Nathaniel Bowditch, LL.D.* 4 vols. Boston: Hilliard, Gray, Little, and Wilkins, 1829–39.

———. *The New American Practical Navigator*. Newburyport, Mass.: Edmund M. Blunt, 1802.

———. *The New American Practical Navigator*, 2nd ed. Newburyport, Mass.: Edmund M. Blunt, 1807.

———. *The New American Practical Navigator*, 3rd ed. Newburyport, Mass.: Edward Little, 1811.

———. *The New American Practical Navigator*, 4th ed. New York: E. M. Blunt and Samuel Burtus, 1817.

———. *The New American Practical Navigator*, 5th ed. New York: Edmund M. Blunt, 1821.

———. *The New American Practical Navigator*, 6th ed. New York: E. M. Blunt, 1826.

———. *The New American Practical Navigator*, 7th ed., 2nd printing. New York: E. and G. W. Blunt, 1833.

———. *The New American Practical Navigator*, 8th. ed. New York: E. and G. W. Blunt, 1836.

———. *The New American Practical Navigator*, 9th. ed. New York: E. and G. W. Blunt, 1837.

Bowditch, N[athaniel] I[ngersoll]. *The Ether Controversy: Vindication of the Hospital Report of 1848*. Boston: John Wilson, 1848.

———. *A History of the Massachusetts General Hospital*. Boston: J. Wilson and Son, 1851.

Bowditch, Vincent Y. *Life and Correspondence of Henry Ingersoll Bowditch*. 2 vols. Boston: Houghton, Mifflin, 1902.

Brady, William N. *The Kedge-Anchor, or, Young Sailor's Assistant*. 6th ed. New York: Brady, 1847.

Bye-laws and Regulations of the Salem East-India Marine Society, Massachusetts. Salem, Mass.: Pool and Palfray, 1808.

By-laws and Regulations of the East India Marine Society, Massachusetts. Salem, Mass.: Thomas C. Cushing, 1800.

Campbell, Alexander. *A Journey from Edinburgh through Parts of North Britain*. London: T. Longman and O. Rees, 1802.

Capen, Nahum. *Reminiscences, of Dr. Spurzheim and George Combe*. New York: Fowler and Wells, 1881.

Cappon, Lester. J., ed. *The Adams-Jefferson Letters: The Complete Correspondence between Thomas Jefferson and Abigail and John Adams*. 2 vols. Chapel Hill: University of North Carolina Press, 1988.

Chapman, George T. *Sketches of the Alumni of Dartmouth College*. Cambridge, Mass.: Riverside Press, 1867.

Chase, Owen. *Narrative of the Most Extraordinary and Distressing Shipwreck of the Whaleship Essex*. New York: W. B. Gilley, 1821.

Chladni, Ernst Florens Friedrich. *Über Feuer-Meteoren*. Vienna: J. G. Heubner, 1819.

Citizen and Farmer's Almanac, for the Year 1800. Philadelphia: John M'Culloch, 1799.

Cleveland, Richard J. *In the Forecastle, or, Twenty-Five Years a Sailor*. New York: Hurst, 1899.

Coburn, Frederick W. *History of Lowell and Its People*. 3 vols. New York: Lewis Historical Publishing, 1920.

Columbian Almanac . . . for the Year of Our Lord 1800; Being One of the Centurial Years, Not Bissextile. Wilmington, Del.: Peter Brynberg, 1799.

Connell, John. *Biographical Sketches of Distinguished Mechanics*. Wilmington, Del.: Porter and Eckel, 1852.

[Croswell, William]. *Description and Explanation of the Mercator Map of the Starry Heavens*. Boston: John Eliot, 1810.

———. *Tables, for Readily Computing Longitude, by the Lunar Observation*. Boston: I. Thomas and E. T. Andrews, 1791.

Cushing, Abel. *Oration Delivered at the Celebration of the Democratic Working-Men, in Milford, Mass., July 4, 1834*. Providence, R.I.: n.p., 1834.

Cushing, Harry Alonzo, ed. *The Writings of Samuel Adams*. 4 vols. New York: G. P. Putnam's Sons, 1904–8.

Cutter, William Richard. *Genealogical and Personal Memoirs . . . Massachusetts*. 4 vols. New York: Lewis Historical Publishing.

Dabney, John. *Catalogue of Books, for Sale or Circulation*. [Salem, Mass.]: J. Dabney, 1791.

Dana, Richard Henry, Jr. *Two Years before the Mast: A Personal Narrative of Life at Sea*. 1840; New York: Penguin, 1981.

Delano, Amasa. *A Narrative of the Voyages and Travels, in the Northern and Southern Hemispheres*. Boston: E. G. House, 1817.

Dow, Francis George, ed. *The Diary and Letters of Benjamin Pickman, 1740–1819, of Salem, Massachusetts*. Newport, R.I.: Wayside Press, 1928.

———, ed. *The Holyoke Diaries, 1709–1865*. Salem, Mass.: Essex Institute, 1911.

———, comp. *Two Centuries of Travel in Essex County, Massachusetts, a Collection of Narratives and Observations Made by Travelers, 1605–1790*. Topsfield, Mass: Topsfield Historical Society, 1921.

Dowling, Daniel. *A Complete System of Italian Book-keeping, according to the Modern Method, Practised by Merchants and Others*. 4th ed. Dublin: P. Wogan, 1781.

Dwight, Timothy. *Travels in New England and New-York*. 4 vols. New Haven, Conn.: T. Dwight, 1821–22.

East-India Marine Society of Salem. *Act of Incorporation, Bylaws and Catalogue*. Salem, Mass.: n.p., 1821.

Edwards, B. B. *Biography of Self-Taught Men*. Boston: J. E. Tilton, [1859].

Elford, James M. *Second Edition of Longitude Tables for Correcting the Distance of the Sun and Moon . . . . Improved by James M. Elford*. Charleston, S.C.: J. Hoff, 1818.

Emerson, Ralph Waldo. *The Journals and Miscellaneous Notebooks of Ralph Waldo Emerson*. 16 vols. Edited by Linda Allardt, David W. Hill, and Ruth H. Bennett. Cambridge, Mass.: Harvard University Press, 1960–1982.

Erskine, Charles. *Twenty Years before the Mast*. Philadelphia: George W. Jacobs, 1896.

Everett, Edward. *Memoir of John Lowell, Jr*. Boston: n.p., 1840.

———. *Orations and Speeches on Various Occasions*. 8th ed. 4 vols. Boston: Little, Brown, 1870.

Fairburn, William Armstrong, and Ethel M. Ritchie. *Merchant Sail*. Vol. 2. Lovell, Me.: Fairburn Marine Educational Foundation, [1945–55].

Famous Boys and Famous Men. New York: Worthington, 1887.

Famous Boys: And How They Became Great Men. Dedicated to Youths and Young Men, as a Stimulus to Earnest Living. New York: J. G. Gregory, 1864.

Federal Meeting. At a Meeting of the Federalists of Salem, at Concert-Hall, on Friday Evening, March 6th, 1807. . . Salem, Mass.: n.p. 1807.

Felt, Joseph B., *Annals of Salem.* 2 vols. Salem, Mass.: W. and S. B. Ives, 1845–49.

———. *History of Ipswich, Essex, and Hamilton.* Cambridge, Mass.: C. Folsom, 1834.

———. *Memorials of William Smith Shaw.* Boston: S. K. Whipple, 1852.

Fenning, Daniel. *The Young Algebraist's Companion.* 5th ed. London: S. Crowder, 1787.

Fisher, George Parker. *The Life of Benjamin Silliman, M.D., LL.D.* 2 vols. New York: C. Scribner, 1866.

Follen, E[liza] L[ee]. *The Life of Charles Follen.* Boston: Thomas H. Webb, 1844.

Forbes, A[bner], and J. W. Greene, *The Rich Men of Massachusetts.* Boston: W. V. Spencer, 1851.

From the Mechanicks Magazine, for April 1830. Boston: n.p., 1830.

Goebel, Julius, and Joseph Henry Smith. *Practice and Procedure.* Vol. 2 of *The Law Practice of Alexander Hamilton: Documents and Commentary.* New York: Columbia University Press, 1964.

[Goodrich, Samuel Griswold]. *Lives of Benefactors: By the Author of Peter Parley's Tales.* New York: J. M. Allen, 1844.

Greenleaf's New-York, Connecticut, and New Jersey Almanack . . . 1800. Brooklyn, N.Y.: Printed by T. Kirk, for Benjamin Gomez, 1799.

Hale, Edward Everett. *A New England Boyhood and Other Bits of Autobiography.* Boston: Little, Brown, 1900.

Harvard University. *Fifth Annual Report of the President of Harvard University to the Overseers, on the State of the Institution, for the Academical Year 1828–9.* Cambridge, Mass.: E. W. Metcalf, 1831.

———. *Fourth Annual Report of the President of Harvard University to the Overseers, on the State of the Institution, for the Academical Year 1828–9.* Cambridge, Mass.: E. W. Metcalf, 1830.

———. *Third Annual Report of the President of Harvard University to the Overseers, on the State of the Institution, for the Academical Year 1827–8.* Cambridge, Mass.: Hilliard, Metcalf, 1829.

Henshaw, David. *An Address, Delivered before an Assembly of Citizens . . . July 4, 1836.* Boston: Beals and Greene, 1836.

Higginson, Thomas Wentworth. *Travellers and Outlaws: Episodes in American History.* Boston: Lee and Shepard, 1889.

[Hildreth, Richard]. *"Our First Men": A Calendar of Wealth, Fashion and Gentility.* Boston: n.p., 1846.

Hodgson, Adam. *Letters from North America Written during a Tour in the United States and Canada.* 2 vols. London: Hurst, Robinson, 1824.

Hopkins, Albert. *An Address, Delivered at the Opening of the Observatory of Williams College, June 12, 1838.* Pittsfield, Mass.: Phinehas Allen, [1838].

Hunt, Freeman, ed. *Lives of American Merchants.* 2 vols. New York: A. M. Kelley, 1856.

Jones, George. *Sketches of Naval Life: With Notices of Men, Manners and Scenery on the Shores of the Mediterranean.* 2 vols. New Haven, Conn.: Hezekiah Howe, 1829.

Kendall, Edward Augustus. *Travels through the Northern Parts of the United States, in the Years 1807 and 1808.* 3 vols. New York: I. Riley, 1809.

Kippis, Andrew. *The New Annual Register, or, General Repository of History, Politics, and Literature for the Year 1799.* London: G. G. and J. Robinson, 1800.

Konefsky, Alfred S., and Andrew J. King, eds. *The Boston Practice.* Vol. 2 of *The Papers of Daniel Webster,* ser. 2, *Legal Papers.* Hanover, N.H.: Published for Dartmouth College by the University Press of New England, 1982.

Buruau des Longitudes. *Connaissance des Tems* [*sic*] *... Pour L'An 1808.* Paris: L'Imprimerie Impériale, 1806.

Lambert, William. *To the Critical Reviewers of Boston, in the State of Massachusetts.* Washington, D.C.: n.p., 1815.

Lambert, William, and James Monroe. *Message from the President of the United States, Transmitting a Supplemental Report of William Lambert, Explanatory of His Astronomical Calculations, with a View to Establish the Longitude of the Capitol of the United States.* Washington, D.C.: n.p., 1824.

Laplace, P[ierre]. S[imon]. *Exposition du Système du Monde.* Paris: Cercle-Social, 1796.

———. *The System of the World.* Translated by J. Pond. 2 vols. London: Richard Phillips, 1809.

———. *Traité de Mécanique Céleste.* 5 vols. Paris: J .B. M. Duprat, 1798–1825.

Latham, Jean Lee. *Carry On, Mr. Bowditch.* Boston: Houghton, Mifflin, 1955.

Local Collections; or, Records of Remarkable Events Connected with the Borough of Gateshead, 1852. Gateshead-on-Tyne, U.K.: William Douglas, 1852.

Lodge, Henry Cabot. *Early Memories.* New York: C. Scribner's Sons, 1913.

Looney, J. Jefferson, ed. *The Papers of Thomas Jefferson, Retirement Series.* 11 vols. Princeton, N.J.: Princeton University Press, 2004–15.

Lord, Nathan. *A Discourse Commemorative of Abiel Chandler.* Boston: J. Wilson, 1852.

Loring, Augustus Peabody. *Nathaniel Bowditch, 1173–1838, of Salem and Boston.* New York: Newcomen Society of North America, 1950.

Lothrop, S. K. *Memoir of Nathaniel Ingersoll Bowditch.* Boston: J. Wilson, 1862.

Macdonnel, D. E. *Dictionary of Quotations from the Latin, French, Greek, Spanish, and Italian Languages.* London: E. T. Gover, 1858.

Mackay, Andrew. *The Complete Navigator, or, An Easy and Familiar Guide to the Theory and Practice of Navigation.* London: T. N. Longman, and O. Rees, 1804.

———. *The Complete Navigator, or, An Easy and Familiar Guide to the Theory and Practice of Navigation.* Philadelphia: B. B. Hopkins, 1807.

MacLaurin, Colin. *A Treatise of Fluxions. In Two Books.* 2 vols. Edinburgh: T. W. and T. Ruddimans, 1742.

Marine Society at Salem. *Laws of the Marine Society, at Salem, in the Commonwealth of Massachusetts as Amended ... November 4, 1790.* Salem, Mass.: T. C. Cushing, 1801.

Martineau, Harriet. *Society in America.* 3rd ed. 2 vols. New York: Saunders and Otley, 1837.

Massachusetts Charitable Mechanic Association. *Annals of the Massachusetts Charitable Mechanic Association, 1795–1892.* Boston: Rockwell and Churchill, 1892.

———. *Order of Services on the Occasion of the Eulogy Pronounced before the Massachusetts Charitable Mechanic Association, on the Life and Character of the Hon. Nathaniel Bowditch, L.L.D., F.R.S.* Boston: n.p., 1838.

Massachusetts General Hospital. *Acts, Resolves, By-laws, and Rules and Regulations.* Boston: James Loring, 1837.

Massachusetts Hospital Life Insurance Company. *Proposals of the Massachusetts Hospital Life Insurance Company.* Boston: James Loring, 1823.

Massachusetts Register and United States Calendar; for the Year of Our Lord 1801. Boston: Manning and Loring, 1800.

Massachusetts Register and United States Calendar; for the Year of Our Lord, 1807. Boston: John West and Manning and Loring, 1806.

Massachusetts Register and United States Calendar; for the Year of Our Lord 1820. Boston: James Loring, and West, Richardson, and Lord, 1819.

Massachusetts Register and United States Calendar; for the Year of Our Lord 1824. Boston: Richard and Lord, and James Loring, 1823.

Massachusetts Register and United States Calendar; for the Year of Our Lord 1829. Boston: Richardson and Lord, and James Loring, 1828.

Massachusetts Soldiers and Sailors of the Revolutionary War. 17 vols. Boston: Wright and Potter, 1896–1908.

Maury, Matthew Fontaine. *A New Theoretical and Practical Treatise on Navigation.* Philadelphia: Key and Biddle, 1836.

Melville, Herman. *Moby-Dick; or, The Whale.* New York: Harper, 1851.

Millot, François Xavier. *Elements of General History.* 2nd Am. ed. 8 vols. Salem, Mass.: Thomas C. Cushing, 1796.

Moore, John Hamilton. *The New Practical Navigator.* 13th ed. London: B. Law, 1798.

———. *The New Practical Navigator.* 1st Am. ed. Newburyport, Mass.: Edmund M. Blunt, 1799.

———. *The New Practical Navigator.* 14th ed. London: J. Crowder, 1800.

———. *The New Practical Navigator.* 2nd Am. ed. Newburyport, Mass.: Edmund M. Blunt, 1800.

Morse, Jedidiah. *The American Universal Geography.* 2 vols. Boston: Isaiah Thomas and Ebenezer T. Andrews, 1793.

Morse, John T., Jr., ed. *Life and Letters of Oliver Wendell Holmes.* 2 vols. Boston: Houghton, Mifflin, 1896.

Norie, J. W. *A New and Complete Epitome of Practical Navigation.* London: William Heather, 1805.

Norton, Andrews. *A Statement of Reasons for Not Believing the Doctrine of Trinitarians.* Cambridge, Mass.: Brown, Shattuck, and Hilliard, Gray, 1833.

Nulty, Eugenius. *Elements of Geometry, Theoretical and Practical.* Philadelphia: J. Whetham, 1836.

Order of Exercises Accompanying the Discourse on the Life and Character of the Late Nathaniel Bowditch, LL.D., Delivered at Salem, By Request of the City Authorities, Thursday, May 24, 1838. [Salem, Mass.]: Salem Gazette Press, 1838.

Ozanam, [Jacques]. *Recreations Mathematical and Physical.* London: R. Bonwick et al., 1708.

Palfrey, John Gorham. *A Discourse on the Life and Character of the Reverend John Thornton Kirkland, D.D., LL.D., Late President of Harvard College.* Cambridge, Mass.: John Owen, 1840.

Palfrey, John Gorham, N. I. Bowditch, et al. *Remarks Concerning the Late Dr. Bowditch, by the Rev. Dr. Palfrey, with the Replies of Dr. Bowditch's Children.* Boston: Charles C. Little, 1840.

Palmer, Joseph. *Necrology of Harvard Alumni, 1851–52 to 1862–63.* Boston: John Wilson, 1864.

Parsons, Theophilus, [Jr.]. *Memoir of Theophilus Parsons, Chief Justice of the Supreme Judicial Court of Massachusetts.* Boston: Ticknor and Fields, 1859.

Peabody, Andrew P. *Harvard Reminiscences.* Boston: Ticknor, 1888.

Peirce, Benjamin. *A Catalogue of the Library of Harvard University in Cambridge, Massachusetts.* 3 vols. Cambridge, Mass.: E. W. Metcalfe, 1830–31.

Pickering, John. *Eulogy on Nathaniel Bowditch, LL. D., President of the American Academy of Arts and Sciences; Including an Analysis of His Scientific Publications. Delivered before the Academy, May 29, 1838.* Boston: C. C. Little and J. Brown, 1838.

———. *Report of the Committee Appointed to Enquire into the Practicability and Expediency of Establishing Manufactures in Salem.* Salem, Mass.: W. Palfray Jr., 1826.

Pickering, Mary Orne. *Life of John Pickering.* Boston: n.p., 1887.

Pickering, Octavius. *The Life of Timothy Pickering.* 4 vols. Boston: Little, Brown, 1867–73.

Poole, Edmund Duval, ed. *Annals of Yarmouth and Barrington (Nova Scotia) in the Revolutionary War.* Yarmouth, N.S.: J. M. Lawson, 1899.

Prescott, William Hickling. *Memoir of Hon. John Pickering, LL.D.* Cambridge, Mass.: Metcalf, 1848.

Preston, Daniel, and Marlena C. DeLong, eds. *The Papers of James Monroe.* 5 vols. Westport, Conn.: Greenwood Press, 2003–14.

Proceedings in the City of Lowell at the Semi-centennial Celebration. Lowell, Mass.: Penhallow Print, 1876.

Proceedings upon the Dedication of Plummer Hall . . . and Judge White's Memoir of the Plummer Family. Salem, Mass.: W. Ives and G. W. Pease, 1858.

Prospectus of the Union Insurance Company, Incorporated by the Legislature of the State of New-York, for Making Insurance on Lives, and Granting Annuities. New York: J. Seymour, 1818.

Pynchon, William. *The Diary of William Pynchon of Salem.* Edited by Edward Fitch Oliver. Boston: Houghton, Mifflin, 1890.

Quincy, Edmund. *Life of Josiah Quincy of Massachusetts.* Boston: Fields, Osgood, 1869.

Quincy, Eliza Susan. *Extracts from Journals, 1816–1838.* Quincy, Mass.: n.p., 1880.

Quincy, Josiah. *The History of Harvard University.* 2 vols. Cambridge, Mass.:
J. Owen, 1840.

———. *The History of the Boston Athenaeum, with Biographical Notices of the Deceased Founders.* Cambridge, Mass.: Metcalf, 1851.

Report of the Auditors Appointed by the Justices of the Supreme Court to Examine the Accounts of the Union Marine and Fire Insurance Company in Newburyport [Newburyport, Mass.: n.p., 1816].

Report of the Trial of Henry Phillips. Boston: Russell, Cutler, 1817.

Rink, Paul. *To Steer by the Stars: The Story of Nathaniel Bowditch.* Garden City, N.Y.: Doubleday, 1969.

Robb, James B. *A Collection of Patent Cases: Decided in the Supreme and Circuit Courts of the United States, from Their Organization to the Year 1850.* 2 vols. Boston: Little, Brown, 1854.

Rusk, R[alph], and Eleanor M. Tilton, eds. *The Letters of Ralph Waldo Emerson.* 10 vols. New York: Columbia University Press, 1939–95.

Salem Athenaeum. *Catalogue of the Books belonging to the Salem Athenaeum, with the By-laws and Regulations.* Salem, Mass.: Thomas C. Cushing, 1811.

Salem Directory, and City Register. Salem, Mass.: Henry Whipple, 1837.

Salem Female Charitable Society. *The Constitution of the Salem Female Charitable Society.* Salem, Mass.: William Carlton, 1801.

Sigourney, L[ydia] H[oward]. *Pocahontas and Other Poems.* New York: Harper and Brothers, 1841.

Silsbee, M. C. D. *A Half Century in Salem.* Boston: Houghton, Mifflin, 1887.

Smith, Bonnie Hurd, ed. *Letters of Loss and Love: Judith Sargent Murray Papers, Letter Book 3.* n.p.: Hurd Smith Communications, 2009.

Somerville, Mary. *Personal Recollections, from Early Life to Old Age, of Mary Somerville.* Boston: Roberts Brothers, 1874.

Sowerby, E. Millicent, comp. *Catalogue of the Library of Thomas Jefferson.* 5 vols. Washington, D.C.: Library of Congress, 1952–59.

Sprague, Charles. *Curiosity: A Poem, Delivered at Cambridge, before the Phi Beta Kappa Society.* Boston: J. T. Buckingham, 1829.

Stanford, Alfred. *Navigator; the Story of Nathaniel Bowditch.* New York: W. Morrow, 1927.

Stimpson's Boston Directory. Boston: Stimpson and Clapp, 1832.

Story, William W., ed. *Life and Letters of Joseph Story.* 2 vols. Boston: Charles C. Little and James Brown, 1851.

Swift, Jonathan. *Gulliver's Travels.* 1726; Chicago: Rand, McNally, 1912.

Tacet, [Joseph]. *New Instructions for the German Flute.* London: Longman and Broderip, [178?].

Tharp, Louise Hall. *Down to the Sea; a Young People's Life of Nathaniel Bowditch, the Great American Navigator.* New York: R. M. McBride, 1942.

Theal, George McCall. *Records of the Cape Colony, from December 1796 to December 1799*. Vol. 2 of *Records of the Cape Colony, from February 1793 to April 1831*. London: Printed for the Government of the Cape Colony, 1898.

Ticknor, Anna, ed. *Life, Letters, and Journals of George Ticknor*. 5th ed. 2 vols. Boston: J. R. Osgood, 1876.

———, ed. *Life of Joseph Green Cogswell, as Sketched in His Letters*. Cambridge, Mass.: Riverside Press, 1874.

Tousard, Louis de, *American Artillerist's Companion*. 3 vols. Philadelphia: C. and A. Conrad, 1809.

Virginia Almanac, for the Year of Our Lord 1800. Fredericksburg, Va.: Printed by T. Green, for the Rev. Mason L. Weems, [1799].

Walker, James. *Memoir of Hon. Daniel Appleton White*. Boston: J. Wilson, 1863.

Ward, John. *The Young Mathematician's Guide*. 11th ed. Dublin: Thomas Ewing and William Smith, 1769.

Weatherwise, Abraham. *The Town and Country Almanack for the Year of Our Lord 1790*. Cambridge, Mass.: J. H. White, [1789].

Whewell, William. *Astronomy and General Physics Considered with Reference to Natural Theology*. London: William Pickering, 1833.

White, Daniel Appleton. *Eulogy on John Pickering, LL.D.* Cambridge, Mass.: Metcalf, 1847.

———. *An Eulogy on the Life and Character of Nathaniel Bowditch, LL.D. F.R.S., Delivered at the Request of the Corporation of the City of Salem, May 24, 1838*. Salem, Mass.: Office of the Gazette, 1838.

[Wilson, Thomas L. V.]. *The Aristocracy of Boston; Who They Are, and What They Were*. Boston: [T. L. V. Wilson], 1848.

Wise, Daniel. *Uncrowned Kings, or, Sketches of Some Men of Mark Who Rose from Obscurity to Renown, Especially Illustrative of the Means by Which They Achieved Success*. Cincinnati: Hitchcock and Walden, 1875; New York: Nelson and Phillips, 1875.

Wolcott, Roger, ed. *The Correspondence of William Hickling Prescott, 1833–1847*. Boston: Houghton Mifflin, 1925

Wood, John. *A New Theory of the Diurnal Rotation of the Earth*. Richmond, Va.: Office of the [Richmond] Enquirer, 1809.

Young, Alexander. *A Discourse on the Life and Character of the Reverend John Thornton Kirkland*. Boston: C. Little and J. Brown, 1840.

———. *The Varieties of Human Greatness. A Discourse on the Life and Character of the Hon. Nathaniel Bowditch, LL.D., F.R.S., Delivered in the Church on Church Green, March 25, 1838*. Boston: Charles C. Little and James Brown, 1838.

DIGITAL EDITIONS AND ONLINE SOURCES

Attwood, Lydia B., comp. *Reminiscences of Old Boston; or, The Old Exchange Coffee House No. 2: Scrapbook*. https://archive.org/details/reminiscencesofoo2attw. 23 May 2015.

Focus on the Family. "Carry On, Mr. Bowditch: A Book Review for Parents." http://www.focusonthefamily.com/parenting/protecting_your_family/book-reviews/c/carry-on-mr-bowditch.aspx. 6 June 2013.

Harvard College Library. *Records of the Harvard College Library: Library Charging Records: An Inventory.* http://oasis.lib.harvard.edu/oasis/deliver/deepLink?_collection=oasis&uniqueId=hua12009. 23 May 2015.

Harvard University. *Mathematical Theses, 1782–1839: An Inventory.* http://oasis.lib.harvard.edu/oasis/deliver/~hua17004. 23 May 2015.

Kaminski, John P., Gaspare J. Saladino, Richard Leffler, Charles H. Schoenleber, and Margaret A. Hogan, eds. *Documentary History of the Ratification of the Constitution Digital Edition.* Charlottesville, Va.: University of Virginia Press, 2009. http://rotunda.upress.virginia.edu/founders/RNCN.html. 23 May 2015.

Oberg, Barbara B., and J. Jefferson Looney, eds. *The Papers of Thomas Jefferson, Digital Edition.* Charlottesville: University of Virginia Press, 2009. http://rotunda.upress.virginia.edu/founders/TSJN.html. 23 May 2015.

Stagg, J. C. A., ed. *The Papers of James Madison, Digital Edition.* Charlottesville: University of Virginia Press, 2010. http://rotunda.upress.virginia.edu/founders/JSMN.html. 23 May 2015.

Taylor, C. James, ed. *Adams Papers Digital Editions.* Charlottesville: University of Virginia Press, 2008. http://rotunda.upress.virginia.edu/founders/ADMS.html. 23 May 2015.

Thomas Jefferson Papers, 1606–1827. http://memory.loc.gov/ammem/collections/jefferson_papers/index.html. 23 May 2015.

Vital Records of Danvers, Ma., to the End of the Year 1849. http://ma-vitalrecords.org/MA/Essex/Danvers/. 23 May 2015.

Vital Records of Ipswich, Ma., to the End of the Year 1849. http://ma-vitalrecords.org/MA/Essex/Ipswich/. 23 May 2015.

Vital Records of Marblehead, Ma., to the End of the Year 1849. http://ma-vitalrecords.org/MA/Essex/Marblehead/. 23 May 2015.

Vital Records of Salem, Ma., to the End of the Year 1849. http://ma-vitalrecords.org/MA/Essex/Salem/. 23 May 2015.

ARTICLES, ESSAYS, AND BOOK CHAPTERS

"Auction Sales in Salem, of Shipping and Merchandise, during the Revolution." *Essex Institute Historical Collections* 49 (Apr. 1913): 97–124.

"The Autobiography of Frazee, the Sculptor." *North American Quarterly Magazine* 6 (July 1835): 1–26.

"Beobachtungen des Kometen von 1807 . . . vom Herrn Bowditch." *Astronomisches Jahrbuch* (1811): 148–51.

Berman, Mildred. "Salem's Stellar Scientist: Nathaniel Bowditch, an Appreciation." *Sextant: The Journal of Salem State College* 7 (1996): 0–14, 26–27.

Bolton, Charles Knowles. "Memoir of Francis Calley Gray." *Proceedings of the Massachusetts Historical Society* 47 (June 1914): 529–34.

Bowditch, Harold. "Nathaniel Bowditch." *American Neptune* 5 (Apr. 1945): 99–110.

[Bowditch, Henry Ingersoll]. "Memoir of Dr. Nathaniel Bowditch." *Common School Journal* 2 (15 Aug., 1, 15 Sept., 1, 15 Oct., 1, 16 Nov., 1 Dec. 1840): 256–59, 272–77, 287–91, 305–9, 318–23, 333–37, 348–60, 361–65.

———. "Notes by Henry Ingersoll Bowditch." *Essex Institute Historical Collections* 83 (Apr. 1947): 185-88.

[Bowditch, Nathaniel]. "Additional Observations on the Comet." *SG*, 1 Nov. 1811.

———. "Addition to the Memoir on the Solar Eclipse . . . 1806." *Memoirs of the American Academy of Arts and Sciences* 3 (1809): 23–32.

———. "Application of Napier's Rules for Solving the Cases of Right-Angled Spherical Trigonometry to Several Cases of Oblique-Angled Trigonometry." *Memoirs of the American Academy of Arts and Sciences* 3 (1809): 33–38.

———. "Astronomy." *Monthly Anthology and Boston Review* 4 (Dec. 1807): 653–54.

[———]. "Defence [*sic*] of the Review of Mr. Lambert's Memorial." *Monthly Anthology and Boston Review* 10 (Jan. 1811): 40–49.

———. "Demonstration of the Rule for Finding the Place of a Meteor." *Memoirs of the American Academy of Arts and Sciences* 3 (1815): 437–39.

———. "Elements of the Comet of 1819." *Memoirs of the American Academy of Arts and Sciences* 4 (1818): 17–19.

———. "Elements of the Orbit of the Comet of 1811." *Memoirs of the American Academy of Arts and Sciences* 3 (1815): 313–26.

[———]. "Encke's Comet." *North American Review* 14 (Jan. 1822): 26–34.

———. "An Estimate of the Height, Direction, Velocity and Magnitude of the Meteor that Exploded over Weston, Connecticut, December 14, 1807." *Memoirs of the American Academy of Arts and Sciences* 2 (1815): 213–37.

———. "An Estimate of the Height of the White Hills in New Hampshire." *Memoirs of the American Academy of Arts and Sciences* 3 (1815): 326–28.

———. "An Estimate of the Height, Velocity, and Magnitude of the Meteor That Exploded over Weston, Connecticut, December 14, 1807." *Journal of Natural Philosophy, Chemistry and the Arts* [London] 28 (Feb, Mar. 1811): 89–98, 206–19.

———. "Lettre XIII. de M. Nathaniel Bowditch." *Correspondance Astronomique, Géographique, Hydrographique et Statistique du Baron de Zach* 10 (1824): 223–30.

———. "Lettre XXV. de M. Nathaniel Bowditch." *Correspondance Astronomique, Géographique, Hydrographique et Statistique du Baron de Zach* 10 (1824): 449–53.

[———]. "Marine Notes. From a News Book Kept in Salem, Mass., 1812–15, at the Office of the Essex Insurance Company, Nathaniel Bowditch, President." *Essex Institute Historical Collections* 36–39 (1900–1903), passim.

———. "Method of Correcting the Apparent Distance of the Moon from the Sun, or a Star, for the Effects of Parallax and Refraction." *Memoirs of the American Academy of Arts and Sciences* 4 (1818): 24–31.

[———]. "Modern Astronomy." *North American Review* 20 (Apr. 1825): 309–66.

———. "New Method of Working a Lunar Observation." *Memoirs of the American Academy of Arts and Sciences* 2 (1804): 1–11.

————. "Observations of the Comet of 1807." *Memoirs of the American Academy of Arts and Sciences* 3 (1809): 1–18.

————. "Observations on the Total Eclipse of the Sun . . . 1806." *Memoirs of the American Academy of Arts and Sciences* 3 (1809): 18–22.

————. "Occulation of Spica by the Moon, Observed at Salem." *Memoirs of the American Academy of Arts and Sciences* 4 (1818): 14.

————. "On a Mistake Which Exists in the Calculation of Mr. Poisson Relative to the Distribution of the Electrical Matter upon the Surface of Two Globes. . . ." *Memoirs of the American Academy of Arts and Sciences* 4 (1818): 15–17.

————. "On a Mistake Which Exists in the Solar Tables of Mayer, Lalande, and Zach." *Memoirs of the American Academy of Arts and Sciences* 4 (1818): 2–3.

————. "On the Calculation of the Oblateness of the Earth . . . according to the Method Given by Laplace. . . ." *Memoirs of the American Academy of Arts and Sciences* 4 (1818): 3–24.

————. "On the Eclipse of the Sun of Sept. 17, 1811." *Memoirs of the American Academy of Arts and Sciences* 3 (1815): 255–305.

————. "On the Meteor Which Passed over Wilmington, in the State of Delaware, Nov. 21, 1819." *Memoirs of the American Academy of Arts and Sciences* 4 (1818): 3–14.

————. "On the Method of Computing the Dip of the Magnetic Needle in Different Latitudes, according to the Theory of Mr. Biot." *Memoirs of the American Academy of Arts and Sciences* 4 (1818): 31–36.

————. "On the Motion of a Pendulum Suspended from Two Points." *Memoirs of the American Academy of Arts and Sciences* 3 (1815): 413–27.

————. "On the Variation of the Magnetic Needle." *Memoirs of the American Academy of Arts and Sciences* 3 (1815): 337–44.

————. "Remarks on Doctor Stewart's Formula, for Computing the Motion of the Moon's Apsides." *Memoirs of the American Academy of Arts and Sciences* 4 (1818): 51–61.

————. "Remarks on Mr. Wallace's Reply." *American Journal of Science* 9 (1825): 293–304.

————. "Remarks on Several Papers Published in Former Volumes of This Journal." *American Journal of Science* 8 (1824): 131–39.

————. "Remarks on the Methods of Correcting the Elements of the Orbit of a Comet, in Newton's 'Principia' and in Laplace's 'Mécanique Céleste.'" *Memoirs of the American Academy of Arts and Sciences* 4 (1818): 36–48.

————. "Remarks on the Usual Demonstration of the Permanency of the Solar System, with Respect to the Eccentricities and Inclinations of the Orbits of the Planets." *Memoirs of the American Academy of Arts and Sciences* 4 (1818): 74–76.

[————]. Review of "Report of the Committee to Whom Was Referred . . . the Memorial of William Lambert." *Monthly Anthology and Boston Review* 9 (Oct. 1810): 245–65.

————. "Solution of Mr. Patterson's Prize Question for Correcting a Survey." *Analyst* 1 (Jan. 1808): 88–109.

————. "Sur la Hauteur, la Direction, la Vitesse et la Grandeur du Météore. . . ." *Annales de Chimie et de Physique* 3 (1816): 206–12.

[————]. "Works of the German Astronomers." *North American Review* 10 (April 1820): 260–72.

Bowditch, Nathaniel Ingersoll. "Memoir." In Nathaniel Bowditch, *Mécanique Céleste by the Marquis de la Place, Translated with a Commentary, by Nathaniel Bowditch, LL.D*, vol. 4, 9–168. Boston: Hilliard, 1839.

Brinkley, J[ohn]. "Investigations Relative to the Problem for Clearing the Apparent Distance of the Moon from the Sun, or a Star, from the Effects of Parallax and Refraction, and an Easy and Concise Method Pointed Out." *Transactions of the Royal Irish Academy* 11 (1810): 69–85.

Browne, B. F. "An Account of Salem Common and the Levelling of the Same in 1802, with Short Notices of the Subscribers." *Essex Institute Historical Collections* 4 (Feb., Apr., June 1862): 2–13, 76–88, 129–40.

Cary, John. "'A Contrary Wind at Sea and Contrary Times at Home': The Sea Logs of Francis Boardman." *Essex Institute Historical Collections* 101 (Jan. 1965): 3–26.

Chladni, E. F. F. "Neue Beiträge zur Kenntnis der Feuermeteore . . . von Chladni." *Annalen der Physik* 75, no. 11 (1823): 229–57.

Cleaveland, [Parker]. "Observations of the Eclipse of the Sun . . . Communicated in a Letter to Nathaniel Bowditch." *Memoirs of the American Academy of Arts and Sciences* 3 (1815): 247–48.

Dean, James. "Observations on the Eclipse . . . Extracted from Letters to Nathaniel Bowditch." *Memoirs of the American Academy of Arts and Sciences* 3 (1815): 249–51.

Dutrochet, M. H. "Observation de la hauteur du Météore." *Journal de Physique* 90 (1820): 227–28.

"Ebenezer Francis." *Historical Magazine* 2 (Nov. 1858): 347–48.

Elephant . . . Salem, August 29, 1797. Broadside. [Salem, Mass.: Thomas C. Cushing, 1797].

"Ensign Williams' Visit to Essex County in 1776." *Essex Institute Historical Collections* 83 (Apr. 1947): 144.

E. S. W., comp. "Materials for a History of the Ropes Family." *Essex Institute Historical Collections* 7 (Feb., Apr., June, Aug., Oct., Dec. 1865): 25–34, 91–94, 133–40, 150–67, 198–205, 248–55, 8 (Mar. 1866): 49–62.

"Extracts from 'Text Books' of Deacon Joseph Seccombe, 1762–1777." *Historical Collections of the Danvers Historical Society* 9 (1921): 112–15.

"Extracts from the Interleaved Almanacs of William Wetmore of Salem, 1774–1778." *Essex Institute Historical Collections* 43 (1907): 115–20.

[Farrar, John]. Review of "Ferguson's *Astronomy*." *North American Review* 8 (Jan. 1818): 205–24.

"Feuerkugel," s.v. *Johann Samuel Traugott Gehler's Physikalisches Wörterbuch* 4:209–30. Leipzig: E. B. Schwickert, 1827.

Fisher, Alexander M. "On the Orbit of the Comet of 1810. Communicated in a Letter to the Hon. Nathaniel Bowditch." *Memoirs of the American Academy of Arts and Sciences* 4 (1818): 309–16.

Folger, Walter. "Observations of the Solar Eclipse . . . Communicated in a Letter to Nathaniel Bowditch." *Memoirs of the American Academy of Arts and Sciences* 3 (1815): 252–54.

Gould, Augustus A. "Notice of the Origin, Progress and Present Condition of the Boston Society of Natural History." *American Quarterly Register* 14 (Feb. 1842): 236–41.

———. "Results of an Examination of the Shells of Massachusetts, and Their Geographical Distribution." *Boston Journal of Natural History* 3 (Nov. 1840): 483–94.

Hewes, Edwin B. "Nathaniel Bowditch, Supercargo and Mariner." *Essex Institute Historical Collections* 70 (July 1934): 209–26.

Higginson, Thomas Wentworth. "Memoir of Thaddeus William Harris." In *Entomological Correspondence of Thaddeus William Harris, M.D.*, edited by Samuel H. Scudder, xi–xxxvii. Boston: Boston Society of Natural History, 1869.

[Holmes, Oliver Wendell]. "The Autocrat of the Breakfast-Table." *Atlantic Monthly* 1 (Apr. 1858): 734–43.

"Jonathan Ingersoll Bowditch." *Proceedings of the American Academy of Arts and Sciences* 24 (May 1888–May 1889): 435–37.

Kalkstein, Molly E. "The World According to Bowditch." *Naval History* 17 (Apr. 2003): 42–45.

Lindenau, Bernhard von. "Einleitung." *Zeitschrift für Astronomie* 1 (Jan./Feb. 1816): 3–123.

———. "Nordamerikanische Beobachten der Sonnenfinsterniss vom 17 Sept. 1811." *Zeitschrift für Astronomie* 3 (Mar./Apr. 1817): 224–26.

Loring, George B. "Some Account of Houses and Other Buildings in Salem, from a Manuscript of the Late Col. Benj. Pickman." *Essex Institute Historical Collections* 6 (June 1864): 93–109.

"Mathematik." *Jenaische Allgemeine Literatur-Zeitung* 3 (17 July 1812): 97–104.

Maury, Matthew. "Scraps from the Lucky Bag." *Southern Literary Messenger* 6 (May 1840): 306–20.

Mendoza y Rios, Josef de, Joseph Banks, and H. Cavendish. "Recherches sur les Principaux Problèmes de l'Astronomie Nautique. Par Don Josef de Mendoza y Rios, F. R. S. Communicated by Sir Joseph Banks, Bart. K. B. P. R. S." *Philosophical Transactions of the Royal Society of London* 87 (1797): 43–122.

"Mercantile Biography: Ebenezer Francis." *Merchants' Magazine and Commercial Review* 40 (Apr. 1859): 436–46.

Moody, Robert E., ed. "Leverett Saltonstall: A Diary Beginning Jany. A.D. 1806." *Proceedings of the Massachusetts Historical Society*, 3rd ser., 89 (1977): 127–77.

Morison, Samuel Eliot. "The Great Rebellion in Harvard College, and the Resignation of President Kirkland." *Publications of the Colonial Society of Mass.* 27 (Apr. 1928): 55–113.

"Nathan Reed." *Essex Institute Historical Collections* 1 (Nov. 1859): 184.

"Nathaniel Bowditch." *Merchants' Magazine and Commercial Review* 1 (July 1839): 33–44.

Nichols, Ichabod. "Observations of the Eclipse of the Sun . . . Extracted from a Letter to Nathaniel Bowditch." *Memoirs of the American Academy of Arts and Sciences* 3 (1815): 246.

"Notes in Cash Book of Essex Bank, 1804," *Essex Institute Historical Collections* 68 (July 1932): 240.

Nulty, Eugenius. "Solution of a General Case of the Simple Pendulum." *Transactions of the American Philosophical Society*, n.s., 2 (1825): 466–77.

Ocko, Stephanie. "Nathaniel Bowditch." *Early American Life* 10 (Dec. 1979): 38–39, 70–74.

Orr, Isaac. "An Essay on the Formation of the Universe." *American Journal of Science and Arts* 6 (1823): 128–49.

P[alfrey], J[ohn] G. "John Farrar." *Christian Examiner* 55 (July 1853): 121–36.

[Peirce, Benjamin]. "Bowditch's Translation of the Mécanique Céleste." *North American Review* 48 (Jan. 1839): 143–80.

———. "Nathaniel Bowditch." *New York Review* 4 (Apr. 1839): 308–23.

Pierce, John. "Some Notes on the Commencements at Harvard University, 1803–1848." *Proceedings of the Massachusetts Historical Society*, 2nd. ser., 5 (1889–90): 167–263.

[Playfair, John]. "Laplace's 'System of the World.'" *Edinburgh Review* 15 (Jan. 1810): 396–417.

———. Review of "Traité de Méchanique [*sic*] Céleste." *Edinburgh Review* 11 (Jan. 1808): 249–83.

"Presents Received by the Royal Society, from November 1810 to July 1811, with the Names of the Donors." *Philosophical Transactions of the Royal Society of London* 101, pt. II (1811): 394–95.

[Renwick, James]. "Astronomy of Laplace." *American Quarterly Review* 7 (June 1830): 255–79.

Review of "A Discourse on the Life and Character of the Hon. Nathaniel Bowditch." *London Athenaeum*, 28 Apr. 1838: 451–53.

Review of "Chart of the Harbours of Salem, Marblehead, Beverly, and Manchester." *Monthly Anthology and Boston Review* 3 (Sept. 1806): 490–94.

Review of "Traité de Mecanique Celeste, par M. Le Marquis De Laplace, Pair de France." *American Quarterly Review* 5 (June 1829): 310–43.

Rink, Paul E. "Nathaniel Bowditch, the Practical Navigator." *American Heritage* 11 (Aug. 1960): 56–60, 85–90.

[Silliman, Benjamin]. "Obituary—the Hon. Nathaniel Bowditch." *American Journal of Science* 34 (July 1838): 220–24.

Silliman, Benjamin, and James J. Kinglsey. "Memoir on the Meteoric Stones Which Fell from the Atmosphere, in the State of Connecticut, on the 14th of December 1807." *Transactions of the American Philosophical Society* 6 (Jan. 1809): 323–45.

Smith, Sydney, "Rev. of Statistical Annals of the United States, by Adam Seybert."
    Edinburgh Review 33 (Jan. 1820):69–80.

"The Solar Eclipse." *Medical Repository* 3 (Nov. 1811–Jan. 1812): 295–99.

"Some Letters of 1775." *Proceedings of the Massachusetts Historical Society*, 3rd. ser., 59
    (Dec. 1925): 106–38.

[Story, Joseph]. "On Chancery Jurisdiction." *North American Review* 11 (July 1820):
    140–66.

"Sullivan's Island." *Rose Bud, or Youth's Gazette*, 22 Sept. 1832, 13–14.

Upham, Charles W. "Memoir of Rev. John Prince, LL.D." *American Journal of Science
    and Arts* 31 (Jan. 1837): 201–22.

"Von der Unterrichtsweise und dem Zustande der Gelehrsamkeit in den
    Vereinigten Staaten." *Kieler Blätter* 7 (1819): 395–450.

Young, Alexander. "Memoir of the Life and Character of Nathaniel Bowditch."
    American Journal of Science 35 (Jan. 1839): 1–47.

Zach, Franz Xaver von. "XXVI. Übersicht der Neuesten Astronomischen
    Ephemeriden." *Monatliche Correspondenz* 17 (May 1808): 387–417.

———. "LIII. Vermischte Nachrichten." *Monatliche Correspondenz* 8 (Nov. 1803):
    444–52.

GOVERNMENT DOCUMENTS, RECORDS, AND LEGAL CASES

*Acts and Laws, Passed by the General Court of Massachusetts, at the Session Begun and
    Held at Boston, in the County of Suffolk, on Wednesday, the Thirtieth Day of May,
    Anno Domini, 1804.* Boston: Young and Minns, [1804].

American Academy of Arts and Sciences v. President and Fellows of Harvard College,
    78 Mass. 582 (1832).

Ames, Ellis, et al., eds. *The Acts and Resolves, Public and Private, of the Province of the
    Massachusetts Bay.* 21 vols. Boston: Wright and Potter, 1869–1922.

Blunt v. Little, 3 Mason 102 (New York, 1822).

Bowring, John. "Report on the Public Accounts of France" (1831). *Selection of
    Reports and Papers of the House of Commons* 26 (1836): 3–161.

Clark, William Bell, ed. *Naval Documents of the American Revolution.* 12 vols.
    Washington, D.C.: Naval History Division, U.S. Navy, 1964–.

Commonwealth of Massachusetts, General Court, House of Representatives. *Report
    and Bill to Cause the Several Insurance Companies to Make Annual Returns.* House
    no. 46. [March 1837].

Commonwealth of Massachusetts, General Court, House of Representatives,
    Committee on Finance. *Report of the Committee on Finance Who Were Instructed
    to Enquire into the Expediency of Imposing a Tax upon the Capital Stock of the
    Massachusetts Hospital Life Insurance Company.* Boston: True and Greene, 1829.

Commonwealth of Massachusetts, General Court, House of Representatives,
    Committee on the Subject of Impressed Seamen. *Report of the Committee of the
    House of Representatives on the Subject of Impressed Seamen.* Boston: Russell and
    Cutler, 1813.

Dow, George Francis, and Mary G. Thresher, eds. *Records and Files of the Quarterly Courts of Essex County.* 9 vols. Salem, Mass: Essex Institute, 1911–75.

Edmund M. Blunt v. John Melcher, 2 Mass. 228 (1806).

Expediency of Imposing a Tax upon the Capital Stock of the Massachusetts Hospital Life Insurance Company. Boston: True and Greene, 1829.

Foster v. Essex Bank, 17 Mass. 479 (1821).

George F. Williams v. Edmund M. Blunt, 2 Mass. 207 (1806).

Gilreath, James, ed., and Elizabeth Carter Wills, comp. *Federal Copyright Records, 1790–1800.* Washington, D.C.: Library of Congress, 1987.

Harvard College and Massachusetts General Hospital v. Francis Amory, 26 Mass. 446 (1830).

Josiah Little v. Edmund M. Blunt, 9 Pickering 488 (Mass., 1830), 13 Pickering 463 (Mass., 1833), 16 Pickering 359 (Mass., 1835).

Laws of the Commonwealth of Massachusetts Passed at the Several Sessions of the General Court, Beginning May 31st, 1815, and Ending on the 24th February, 1818. Boston: Russell, Cutler, 1818.

Laws of the State of New-York. Albany, N.Y.: Cantine and Leake, 1822.

Legislative Documents of the Senate and Assembly of the State of New-York, Fifty-Third Session, 1830. Vol. 2. Albany, N.Y.: E. Croswell, 1830.

Paul Moody v. Jonathan Fiske et al., 2 Mason 112 (Mass., 1820).

Private and Special Statutes of the Commonwealth of Massachusetts, from January 1838, to May 1848. Boston: Dutton and Wentworth, 1848.

Private and Special Statutes of the Commonwealth of Massachusetts, from May 1830, to April 1837. Boston: Dutton and Wentworth, 1837.

"Records of the Vice-Admiralty Court at Halifax, Nova Scotia: The Condemnation of Prizes and Recaptures of the Revolution and the War of 1812." *Essex Institute Historical Collections* 45 (Jan., Apr., July, Oct., 1909): 28–48, 161–84, 221–44, 309–32; 46 (Jan. 1910): 69–71.

Resolves of the General Court of Massachusetts. Boston: Dutton and Wentworth, 1828.

Rice, Franklin P. "Worcester Town Records, 1817–1832." *Collections of the Worcester Society of Antiquity* 11 (1893): 1–363.

Sarjeant [*sic*] *v. Blunt,* 16 Johns. 74 (New York, 1819).

U.S. Army, Ordnance Department. *Regulations for the Government of the Ordnance Department.* Washington, D.C.: F. P. Blair, 1834.

U.S. Bureau of the Census. *Fifth Census of the United States, 1830.* Boston, Ward 8, Suffolk, Massachusetts. National Archives and Records Administration Series M19.

U.S. Congress, House of Representatives. "Message from the President of the United States, Transmitting the Information . . . Exploring Expedition." 25th Cong., 2nd sess., 1838. H. Doc. 147.

———. *Report of the Committee Appointed on the 30th of November, 1818, to Inspect the Books and Examine into the Proceedings of the Bank of the United States.* 15th Cong., 2nd sess., 1819. H. Doc. 92.

U.S. Department of State. *Report of the Commercial Relations of the United States with All Foreign Nations*. 3 vols. Washington, D.C.: O. P. Nicholson, 1857.

U.S. Navy. *A General Register of the Navy and Marine Corps*. Washington, D.C.: C. Alexander, 1848.

Secondary Sources

BOOKS

Adams, Charles Francis, *Richard Henry Dana: A Biography*. Boston: Houghton, Mifflin, 1890.

Agar, Jon. *The Government Machine: A Revolutionary History of the Computer*. Cambridge, Mass.: Massachusetts Institute of Technology Press, 2003.

Alborn, Timothy. *Regulated Lives: Life Insurance and British Society, 1800–1914*. Toronto: University of Toronto Press, 2009.

Alexander, Amir. *Duel at Dawn: Heroes, Martyrs, and the Rise of Modern Mathematics*. Cambridge, Mass.: Harvard University Press, 2011.

Allen, David Grayson. *Investment Management in Boston: A History*. Amherst: University of Massachusetts Press, 2015.

Allen, Gardner Weld. *Massachusetts Privateers of the Revolution*. Boston: Massachusetts Historical Society, 1927.

Amory, Hugh, and David D. Hall, eds. *The Colonial Book in the Atlantic World*. Vol. 1 of *A History of the Book in America*. Cambridge: Cambridge University Press, 2000.

Anthony, David. *Paper Money Men: Commerce, Manhood, and the Sensational Public Sphere in Antebellum America*. Columbus: Ohio State University Press, 2009.

Appleby, Joyce. *Inheriting the Revolution: The First Generation of Americans*. Cambridge, Mass.: Belknap Press of Harvard University Press, 2001.

Appleton, P. C. Griffin, comp. *A Catalogue of the Washington Collection at the Boston Athenaeum*. Boston: Boston Athenaeum, 1897.

Ashton, Joseph. N. *The Salem Athenaeum, 1810–1910*. Salem, Mass.: Salem Athenaeum, 1917.

Avery, Lillian Drake. *A Genealogy of the Ingersoll Family in America, 1629–1925*. New York: Frederick H. Hitchcock, 1926.

Balleisen, Edward J. *Navigating Failure: Bankruptcy and Commercial Society in Antebellum America*. Chapel Hill: University of North Carolina Press, 2001.

Banner, James M. *To the Hartford Convention: The Federalists and the Origins of Party Politics in Massachusetts, 1789–1815*. New York: Knopf, 1970.

Bean, Susan S. *Yankee India: American Commercial and Cultural Encounters with India in the Age of Sail, 1784–1860*. Salem, Mass.: Peabody Essex Museum, 2001.

Beckert, Sven. *Empire of Cotton: A Global History*. New York: Knopf, 2014.

Bedini, Silvio A. *Thinkers and Tinkers: The Early American Men of Science*. New York: Scribner, 1975.

———. *Thomas Jefferson and His Copying Machines*. Charlottesville: University Press of Virginia, 1984.

————. *With Compass and Chain: Early American Surveyors and Their Instruments*. Frederick, Md.: Professional Surveyors Publishing Company, 2001.

Blair, Ann M. *Too Much to Know: Managing Scholarly Information before the Modern Age*. New Haven, Conn.: Yale University Press, 2010.

Bolton, Charles Knowles. *The Athenaeum Centenary*. [Boston]: Boston Athenaeum, 1907.

Booth, Robert, *Death of an Empire: The Rise and Murderous Fall of Salem, America's Richest City*. New York: Thomas Dunne, 2011.

Bosher, J. F. *French Finances, 1770–1795: From Business to Bureaucracy*. Cambridge: Cambridge University Press, 1970.

[Bowditch, Harold]. *The Bowditch Family of Salem, Massachusetts*. n.p, 1936.

Bowditch, Harold, and Raymond Clare Archibald. *A Catalogue of a Special Exhibition of the Manuscripts, Books, Portraits, and Personal Relics of Nathaniel Bowditch . . . with a Sketch of the Life of Nathaniel Bowditch by Dr. Harold Bowditch and an Essay, with a Bibliography of His Publications*. Salem, Mass.: Peabody Museum, 1937.

Bowman, Larry G. *Captive Americans: Prisoners during the American Revolution*. Athens: Ohio University Press, 1976.

Boylan, Anne M. *The Origins of Women's Activism: New York and Boston, 1797–1840*. Chapel Hill: University of North Carolina Press, 2002.

Brown, Chandos Michael. *Benjamin Silliman: A Life in the Young Republic*. Princeton, N.J.: Princeton University Press, 1989.

Brown, Richard D. *Knowledge Is Power: The Diffusion of Information in Early America, 1700–1865*. New York: Oxford University Press, 1989.

Burrows, Edwin G. *Forgotten Patriots: The Untold Story of American Prisoners during the Revolutionary War*. New York: Basic, 2008.

Burstyn, Harold L. *At the Sign of the Quadrant: An Account of the Contributions of American Hydrography Made by Edmund March Blunt and His Sons*. Mystic, Conn.: Marine Historical Association, 1957.

Bushman, Richard L. *The Refinement of America: Persons, Houses, Cities*. New York: Vintage, 1993.

Buxton, H. Harry Wilmot. *Memoir of the Life and Labours of the Late Charles Babbage, F.R.S.* Cambridge, Mass.: Massachusetts Institute of Technology Press, 1987.

Cajori, Florian. *The Teaching and History of Mathematics in the United States*. Bureau of Education, Circular no. 3. Washington, D.C.: Government Printing Office, 1890.

Campbell, John F. *History and Bibliography of the New American Practical Navigator and the American Coast Pilot*. Salem, Mass.: Peabody Museum, 1964.

Caplan, Jane, and John Torpey, eds. *Documenting Individual Identity: The Development of State Practices in the Modern World*. Princeton, N.J.: Princeton University Press, 2001.

Carpenter, Kenneth E. *The First 350 Years of the Harvard University Library: Description of an Exhibition*. Cambridge, Mass.: Harvard University Library, 1986.

Chandler, Alfred D., Jr. *The Visible Hand: The Managerial Revolution in American Business.* Cambridge, Mass.: Belknap Press of Harvard University Press, 1977.

Chandler, Alfred D., Jr., and James W. Cortada, eds. *A Nation Transformed by Information: How Information Has Shaped the United States from Colonial Times to the Present.* Oxford: Oxford University Press, 2000.

Chaplin, Joyce E. *The First Scientific American: Benjamin Franklin and the Pursuit of Genius.* New York: Basic, 2006.

Chase, Fannie S. *Wiscasset in Pownalborough.* Wiscasset, Me.: n.p., 1941.

Clark, Christopher. *The Roots of Rural Capitalism: Western Massachusetts, 1780–1860.* Ithaca, N.Y.: Cornell University Press, 1990.

Clarke, Julius. *History of the Massachusetts Insurance Department: Including a Sketch of the Origin and Progress of Insurance and of the Insurance Legislation of the State, from 1780 to 1876.* Boston: Wright and Potter, 1876.

Cogliano, Francis D. *American Maritime Prisoners in the Revolutionary War: The Captivity of William Russell.* Annapolis, Md.: Naval Institute Press, 2001.

Cohen, Patricia Cline. *A Calculating People: The Spread of Numeracy in Early America.* Chicago: University of Chicago Press, 1982.

Cohn, Marjorie B. *Francis Calley Gray and Art Collecting for America.* Cambridge, Mass.: Harvard University Press, 1986.

Colbert, Charles. *A Measure of Perfection: Phrenology and the Fine Arts in America.* Chapel Hill: University of North Carolina Press, 1997.

Conforti, Joseph. *Imagining New England: Explorations of Identity from the Pilgrims to the Mid-Twentieth Century.* Chapel Hill: University of North Carolina Press, 2001.

Cox, Richard J. *Closing an Era: Historical Perspectives on Modern Archives and Management.* Westport, Conn.: Greenwood Press, 2000.

Crocker, Matthew H. *The Magic of the Many: Josiah Quincy and the Rise of Mass Politics in Boston, 1800–1830.* Amherst: University of Massachusetts Press, 1999.

Crowninshield, Francis B. *The Story of George Crowninshield's Yacht, Cleopatra's Barge.* Boston: Private print, 1913.

Currier, John J. *History of Newburyport, Mass: 1764–1905.* 2 vols. Newburyport, Mass.: John J. Currier, 1906–9.

Cushing, Thomas. *Historical Sketch of Chauncy-Hall School.* Boston: D. Clapp, 1895.

Dalzell, Robert F., Jr. *Enterprising Elite: The Boston Associates and the World They Made.* Cambridge, Mass.: Harvard University Press, 1987.

Dandeker, Christopher. *Surveillance, Power and Modernity: Bureaucracy and Discipline from 1700 to the Present Day,* Cambridge: Polity, 1990.

Daniels, George H. *American Science in the Age of Jackson.* Reprint ed. Tuscaloosa: University of Alabama Press, 1994.

Delbourgo, James. *A Most Amazing Scene of Wonders: Electricity and Enlightenment in Early America.* Cambridge, Mass.: Harvard University Press, 2006.

Dennis, Albert W. *The Merchants National Bank of Salem, Massachusetts: An Historical Sketch.* Salem, Mass.: Salem Press, 1908.

Doerflinger, Thomas M. *A Vigorous Spirit of Enterprise: Merchants and Economic Development in Revolutionary Philadelphia*. Chapel Hill: University of North Carolina Press, 1986.

Drake, Samuel Adams. *Old Landmarks and Historic Personages of Boston*. Boston: James R. Osgood, 1873.

Dunnington, G. Waldo. *Carl Friedrich Gauss: Titan of Science*. New York: Exposition Press, 1955.

Durey, Michael. *Transatlantic Radicals and the Early American Republic*. Lawrence: University Press of Kansas, 1997.

Early Coastwise and Foreign Shipping of Salem: A Record of the Entrances and Clearances of the Port of Salem, 1750–1769. Salem, Mass.: Essex Institute, 1934.

Ellery, Harrison, and Charles Pickering Bowditch. *The Pickering Genealogy: Being an Account of the First Three Generations of the Pickering Family of Salem, Mass.* 3 vols. Cambridge, Mass.: Harvard University Press, 1897.

Elliott, Clark A. *Thaddeus William Harris (1795–1856): Nature, Science, and Society in the Life of an American Naturalist*. Bethlehem, Pa.: Lehigh University Press, 2008.

Ellis, Joseph J. *After the Revolution: Profiles of Early American Culture*. New York: Norton, 1979.

Essex Institute. *The Fifth Half Century of the Landing of John Endicott at Salem, Massachusetts*. Salem, Mass.: Essex Institute, 1879.

Farber, Bernard. *Guardians of Virtue: Salem Families in 1800*. New York: Basic, 1972.

Farrell, Betty G. *Elite Families: Class and Power in Nineteenth-Century Boston*. Albany: State University of New York Press, 1993.

Faust, Drew Gilpin. *This Republic of Suffering: Death and the American Civil War*. New York: Knopf, 2008.

Ferguson, David L. *Cleopatra's Barge: The Crowninshield Story*. Boston: Little, Brown, 1976.

Fichter, James R. *So Great a Profitt: How the East Indies Trade Transformed Anglo-American Capitalism*. Cambridge, Mass.: Harvard University Press, 2010.

Field, Peter S. *The Crisis of the Standing Order: Clerical Intellectuals and Cultural Authority in Massachusetts, 1780–1833*. Amherst: University of Massachusetts Press, 1998.

First Centenary of the North Church and Society in Salem, Massachusetts. Salem, Mass.: Printed for the Society, 1873.

Fischer, David Hackett. *Albion's Seed: Four British Folkways in America*. New York: Oxford University Press, 1989.

Fisher, George Park. *Life of Benjamin Silliman, M.D., LL.D.* 2 vols. New York: C. Scribner, 1866.

Foletta, Marshall. *Coming to Terms with Democracy: Federalist Intellectuals and the Shaping of an American Culture*. Charlottesville: University Press of Virginia, 2001.

Forbes, John Douglas. *Israel Thorndike, Federalist Financier*. New York: Published for the Beverly Historical Society by Exposition Press, 1953.

Formisano, Ronald P. *The Transformation of Political Culture: Massachusetts Parties, 1790s–1840s.* New York: Oxford University Press, 1983.

Frängsmyr, Tore, J. L. Heilbron, and Robin E. Rider, eds. *The Quantifying Spirit in the Eighteenth Century.* Berkeley: University of California Press, 1990.

Gardey, Delphine. *Écrire, Calculer, Classer: Comment une Révolution de Papier A Transformé les Sociétés Contemporaines (1800–1940).* Paris: Découverte, 2008.

Gardner, Frank A. *Thomas Gardner, Planter.* Salem, Mass.: Essex Institute, 1907.

Gilje, Paul A. *Liberty on the Waterfront: American Maritime Culture in the Age of Revolution.* Philadelphia: University of Pennsylvania Press, 2004.

Gillispie, Charles Coulton. *Pierre-Simon Laplace, 1749–1827: A Life in Exact Science.* With Robert Fox and Ivor Grattan-Guinness. Princeton, N.J.: Princeton University Press, 1997.

Goodwin, Lorinda B. R. *An Archaeology of Manners: The Polite World of the Merchant Elite of Colonial Massachusetts.* New York: Kluwer, 1999.

Gras, N. S. B. *The Massachusetts First National Bank of Boston, 1784–1934.* Cambridge, Mass.: Harvard University Press, 1937.

Gray, Edward. *William Gray of Salem, Merchant.* Boston: Houghton Mifflin, 1914.

Greene, John C. *American Science in the Age of Jefferson.* Ames: University of Iowa Press, 1984.

Grier, David Alan. *When Computers Were Human.* Princeton, N.J.: Princeton University Press, 2005.

Gross, Robert A., and Mary Kelley, eds. *An Extensive Republic: Print, Culture, and Society in the New Nation, 1790–1840.* Vol. 2 of *A History of the Book in America.* Chapel Hill: University of North Carolina Press, 2010.

Hahn, Roger. *Pierre Simon Laplace, 1749–1827: A Determined Scientist.* Cambridge, Mass.: Harvard University Press, 2005.

Hall, Kermit L., and David Scott Clark, eds. *The Oxford Companion to American Law.* New York: Oxford University Press, 2002.

Hall, Peter Dobkin. *The Organization of American Culture, 1700–1900: Private Institutions, Elites, and the Origins of American Nationality.* New York: New York University Press, 1982.

Halttunen, Karen. *Confidence Men and Painted Women: A Study of Middle-Class Culture in America, 1830–1870.* New Haven, Conn.: Yale University Press, 1986.

Hancock, David. *Citizens of the World: London Merchants and the Integration of the British Atlantic Community, 1735–1785.* Cambridge: Cambridge University Press, 1995.

Handlin, Oscar, and Mary Flug Handlin. *Commonwealth: A Study of the Role of Government in the American Economy: Massachusetts, 1774–1861.* New York: New York University Press, 1947.

Hanson, John Wesley. *History of the Town of Danvers, from Its First Settlement to 1848.* Danvers, Mass.: John Wesley Hanson, 1848.

Harbron, John D. *Trafalgar and the Spanish Navy.* Annapolis, Md.: Naval Institute Press, 1988.

Hartford, William F. *Money, Morals, and Politics: Massachusetts in the Age of the Boston Associates*. Boston: Northeastern University Press, 2001.

Headrick, Daniel R. *When Information Came of Age: Technologies of Knowledge in the Age of Reason and Revolution, 1700–1850*. Oxford: Oxford University Press, 2000.

Hindle, Brooke. *The Pursuit of Science in Revolutionary America 1735–1789*. Chapel Hill: University of North Carolina Press, 1956.

Hitchings, A. Frank. *Ship Registers of the District of Salem and Beverly, Massachusetts, 1789–1900*. Salem, Mass.: Essex Institute, 1906.

Hobart, Michael E., and Zachary S. Schiffman. *Information Ages: Literacy, Numeracy, and the Computer Revolution*. Baltimore: Johns Hopkins University Press, 1998.

Hodges, Almon D., Jr., comp. *Genealogical Record of the Hodges Family of New England, Ending December 31, 1894*. Boston: F. H. Hodges, 1896.

Hoffer, Peter Charles. *Prelude to Revolution: The Salem Gunpowder Raid of 1775*. Baltimore: Johns Hopkins University Press, 2013.

Hogan, Edward R. *Of the Human Heart: A Biography of Benjamin Peirce*. Bethlehem, Pa.: Lehigh University Press, 2008.

Holbrook, Donald. *The Boston Trustee*. Boston: Marshall Jones, 1937.

Holmes, Richard. *The Age of Wonder: How the Romantic Generation Discovered the Beauty and Terror of Science*. New York: Pantheon, 2008.

Hounshell, David A. *From the American System to Mass Production, 1800–1932: The Development of Manufacturing Technology in the United States*. Baltimore: Johns Hopkins University Press, 1984.

Howe, Daniel Walker, *Making the American Self: Jonathan Edwards to Abraham Lincoln*. Cambridge, Mass.: Harvard University Press, 1997.

———. *The Political Culture of the American Whigs*. Chicago: University of Chicago Press, 1979.

———. *The Unitarian Conscience: Harvard Moral Philosophy, 1805–1861*. Cambridge, Mass.: Harvard University Press, 1970.

———. *What Hath God Wrought: The Transformation of America, 1815–1848*. New York: Oxford University Press, 2009.

Howe, Octavius T. *Beverly Privateers in the American Revolution*. Cambridge, Mass.: Harvard University Press, 1922.

Hunter, Phyllis Whitman. *Purchasing Identity in the Atlantic World: Massachusetts Merchants, 1670–1780*. Ithaca, N.Y.: Cornell University Press, 2001.

Hurd, D. Hamilton, comp. *History of Essex County, Massachusetts*. 2 vols. Philadelphia: J. W. Lewis, 1888.

Jacob, Margaret C. *Strangers Nowhere in the World: The Rise of Cosmopolitanism in Early Modern Europe*. Philadelphia: University of Pennsylvania Press, 2006.

Jaher, Frederick Cople. *The Urban Establishment: Upper Strata in Boston, New York, Charleston, Chicago, and Los Angeles*. Urbana: University of Illinois Press, 1982.

Kafka, Ben. *The Demon of Writing: Powers and Failures of Paperwork*. New York: Zone, 2012.

Kamensky, Jane. *The Exchange Artist: A Tale of High-Flying Speculation and America's First Banking Collapse.* New York: Viking, 2008.

Kaplan, Catherine O'Donnell. *Men of Letters in the Early Republic: Cultivating Forums of Citizenship.* Chapel Hill: University of North Carolina Press, 2008.

Kelley, Mary, *Learning to Stand and Speak: Women, Education, and Public Life in America's Republic.* Chapel Hill: University of North Carolina Press, 2006.

Kerber, Linda K. *Federalists in Dissent: Imagery and Ideology in Jeffersonian America.* Ithaca, N.Y.: Cornell University Press, 1970.

———. *Women of the Republic: Intellect and Ideology in Revolutionary America.* Chapel Hill: University of North Carolina Press, 1980.

Knott, Sarah. *Sensibility and the American Revolution.* Chapel Hill: University of North Carolina Press, 2009.

Kohl, Lawrence Frederick. *The Politics of Individualism: Parties and the American Character in the Jacksonian Era.* New York: Oxford University Press, 1989.

Krajewski, Markus. *Paper Machines: About Cards and Catalogs, 1548–1929.* Cambridge, Mass.: Massachusetts Institute of Technology Press, 2011.

Lamoreaux, Naomi R. *Insider Lending: Banks, Personal Connections, and Economic Development in Industrial New England.* Cambridge: Cambridge University Press, 1994.

Lepler, Jessica M. *The Many Panics of 1837: People, Politics, and the Creation of a Transatlantic Financial Crisis.* New York: Cambridge University Press, 2013.

Levy, Jonathan. *Freaks of Fortune: The Emerging World of Capitalism and Risk in America.* Cambridge, Mass.: Harvard University Press, 2012.

Lewis, Andrew J. *A Democracy of Facts: Natural History in the Early Republic.* Philadelphia: University of Pennsylvania Press, 2011.

Lucier, Paul. *Scientists and Swindlers: Consulting on Coal and Oil in America, 1820–1890.* Baltimore: Johns Hopkins University Press, 2008.

MacIntyre, Gordon. *Dugald Stewart: The Pride and Ornament of Scotland.* Brighton, U.K.: Sussex Academic Press, 2003.

Mann, Bruce H. *Republic of Debtors: Bankruptcy in the Age of American Independence.* Cambridge, Mass.: Harvard University Press, 2002.

Marshall, Megan. *The Peabody Sisters: Three Women Who Ignited American Romanticism.* Boston: Houghton Mifflin, 2005.

Matson, Cathy. *Merchants and Empire: Trading in Colonial New York.* Baltimore: Johns Hopkins University Press, 1998.

McCarthy, Molly. *The Accidental Diarist: A History of the Daily Planner in America.* Chicago: University of Chicago Press, 2013.

McCaughey, Robert A. *Josiah Quincy, 1772–1864: The Last Federalist.* Cambridge, Mass.: Harvard University Press, 1974.

McHale, Thomas R., and Mary C. McHale, eds. *Early American-Philippine Trade: The Journal of Nathaniel Bowditch in Manila, 1796.* New Haven, Conn.: Yale University Press, 1962.

Memoirs of Gen. Joseph Gardner Swift, LL.D., U.S.A. Worcester, Mass.: F. L. Blanchard, 1890.

Mihm, Stephen. *A Nation of Counterfeiters: Capitalists, Con Men, and the Making of the United States*. Cambridge, Mass.: Harvard University Press, 2007.

Montgomery, James W., Jr., and Laura V. Monti. *The Papers of Nathaniel Bowditch in the Boston Public Library: Guide to the Microfilm Edition*. Boston: Boston Public Library, 1963.

Morison, Samuel Eliot. *The Maritime History of Massachusetts, 1783–1860*. 1921; Boston: Northeastern University Press, 1979.

———. *Three Centuries of Harvard, 1636–1936*. Cambridge, Mass.: Harvard University Press, 1936.

Morris, Harrison S. *A Sketch of the Pennsylvania Company for Insurances on Lives and Granting Annuities*. Philadelphia: Lippincott, 1896.

Morrison, Dane Anthony, and Nancy Lusignan Schultz, eds. *Salem: Place, Myth, and Memory*. Boston: Northeastern University Press, 2004.

Morrison, Leonard Allison, and Stephen Paschall Sharples. *History of the Kimball Family in America, from 1634 to 1897*. 2 vols. Boston: Damrell and Upham, 1897.

Murphy, Sharon Ann. *Investing in Life: Insurance in Antebellum America*. Baltimore: Johns Hopkins University Press, 2010.

Murray, Craig C. *Benjamin Vaughan (1751–1835): The Life of an Anglo-American Intellectual*. New York: Arno Press, 1982.

Nadis, Steven, and Shing-Tung Yau. *A History in Sum: 150 Years of Mathematics at Harvard (1825–1975)*. Cambridge, Mass.: Harvard University Press, 2013.

Newmyer, R. Kent. *Supreme Court Justice Joseph Story: Statesman of the Old Republic*. Chapel Hill: University of North Carolina Press, 1985.

Norton, Mary Beth. *Liberty's Daughters: The Revolutionary Experience of American Women, 1750–1800*. 1980; Ithaca, N.Y.: Cornell University Press, 1996.

Numbers, Ronald. *Creation by Natural Law: Laplace's Nebular Hypothesis in American Thought*. Seattle: University of Washington Press, 1977.

Olegario, Rowena. *A Culture of Credit: Embedding Trust and Transparency in American Business*. Cambridge, Mass.: Harvard University Press, 2006.

Osgood, Charles S., and Batchelder, H. M. *Historical Sketch of Salem, 1626–1879*. Salem, Mass.: Essex Institute, 1879.

Paine, Ralph Delahaye. *The Ships and Sailors of Old Salem: The Record of a Brilliant Era of American Achievement*. New York: Outing, 1909.

Parrish, Susan Scott. *American Curiosity: Cultures of Natural History in the Colonial British Atlantic World*. Chapel Hill: University of North Carolina Press, 2006.

Pasles, Paul C. *Benjamin Franklin's Numbers: An Unsung Mathematical Odyssey*. Princeton, N.J.: Princeton University Press, 2008.

Peabody, Robert E. *The Log of the Grand Turks*. Boston: Houghton Mifflin, 1926.

———. *Merchant Venturers of Old Salem*. Boston: Houghton Mifflin, 1912.

Pelttari, Carole. *Carry On, Mr. Bowditch Study Guide*. Fall Creek, Wisc.: Progeny Press, 1995.

Perley, Sidney. *The History of Salem, Massachusetts*. 3 vols. Salem, Mass.: S. Perley, 1924–28.

————. *The Plumer* [*sic*] *Genealogy*. Salem, Mass.: Essex Institute, 1917.

Philbrick, Nathaniel. *Sea of Glory: America's Voyage of Discovery, the U.S. Exploring Expedition, 1838–1842*. New York: Viking, 2003.

Phillips, James Duncan. *Salem and the Indies: The Story of the Great Commercial Era of the City*. Boston: Houghton Mifflin, 1947.

————. *Salem in the Eighteenth Century*. Boston: Houghton Mifflin, 1937.

————. *Salem in the Seventeenth Century*. Boston: Houghton Mifflin, 1933.

Poovey, Mary. *A History of the Modern Fact: Problems of Knowledge in the Sciences of Wealth and Society*. Chicago: University of Chicago Press, 1998.

Porter, Kenneth Wiggins. *The Jacksons and the Lees: Two Generations of Massachusetts Merchants, 1765–1844*. 2 vols. Cambridge, Mass.: Harvard University Press, 1937.

Porter, Theodore. *Trust in Numbers: The Pursuit of Objectivity in Science and Public Life*. Princeton, N.J.: Princeton University Press, 1995.

Potter, Alfred Claghorn, and Charles Knowles Bolton. *The Librarians of Harvard College, 1667–1877*. Cambridge, Mass.: Library of Harvard University, 1897.

Power, Michael, ed. *Accounting and Science: Natural Inquiry and Commercial Reason*. Cambridge: Cambridge University Press, 1996.

Pulsifer, Susan Nichols. *Witch's Breed: The Peirce-Nichols Family of Salem*. Cambridge, Mass.: Dresser, Chapman and Grimes, 1967.

Putnam, George Granville. *Salem Vessels and Their Voyages: A History of the Pepper Trade with the Island of Sumatra*. Salem, Mass.: Essex Institute, 1922.

Ranz, Jim. *The Printed Book Catalogue in American Libraries, 1723–1900*. Chicago: American Library Association, 1964.

Rediker, Marcus. *Between the Devil and the Deep Blue Sea: Merchant Seamen, Pirates, and the Anglo-American Maritime World, 1700–1750*. Cambridge: Cambridge University Press, 1989.

Reingold, Nathan. *Science in Nineteenth Century America: A Documentary History*. New York: Hill and Wang, 1964.

Rhodes, Barbara, and William Wells Streeter. *Before Photocopying: The Art and History of Mechanical Copying, 1780–1938*. New Castle, Del.: Oak Knoll Press, 1999.

Rickards, Maurice. *Encyclopedia of Ephemera*. New York: Routledge, 2000.

Robertson, Craig. *The Passport in America: The History of a Document*. New York: Oxford University Press, 2010.

Robotti, Frances Diane. *Chronicles of Old Salem: A History in Miniature*. New York: Bonanza, 1948.

Rogers, Alan. *Murder and the Death Penalty in Massachusetts*. Amherst: University of Massachusetts Press, 2008.

Ruffin, J. Rixey. *A Paradise of Reason: William Bentley and Enlightenment Christianity in the Early Republic*. New York: Oxford University Press, 2008.

Ruwell, Mary Elizabeth. *Eighteenth-Century Capitalism and the Formation of American Marine Insurance Companies*. New York: Garland, 1993.

Sandage, Scott A. *Born Losers: A History of Failure in America.* Cambridge, Mass.: Harvard University Press, 2005.

Saul, Norman E. *Distant Friends: The United States and Russia, 1765–1867.* Lawrence: University Press of Kansas, 1991.

Schocket, Andrew M. *Founding Corporate Power in Early National Philadelphia.* DeKalb: Northern Illinois University Press, 2007.

Seaburg, Carl, and Stanley Patterson. *Merchant Prince of Boston: Col. T. H. Perkins, 1764–1854.* Cambridge, Mass.: Harvard University Press, 1971.

Seavoy, Ronald E. *The Origins of the American Business Corporation, 1784–1855.* Westport, Conn.: Greenwood Press, 1982.

Seybolt, Robert Francis. *The Evening School in Colonial America.* Urbana: University of Illinois Press, 1925.

———. *Source Studies in American Colonial Education: The Private School.* Urbana: University of Illinois Press, 1925.

Shammas, Carole, Marylynn Salmon, and Michel Dahlin. *Inheritance in America from Colonial Times to the Present.* New Brunswick, N.J.: Rutgers University Press, 1987.

Sheidley, Harlow W. *Sectional Nationalism: Massachusetts Conservative Leaders and the Transformation of America, 1815–1836.* Boston: Northeastern University Press, 1998.

Simpson, Lewis P. *The Man of Letters in New England and the South.* Baton Rouge: Louisiana State University Press, 1973.

Small, Edwin W. *Notes on the Derby House, Part of Salem Maritime National Historic Site, Derby Street, Salem, Massachusetts.* n.p.: [U.S. National Park Service?] 1954.

Smith, Baxter Perry. *History of Dartmouth College.* Boston: Houghton, Osgood and Company, 1878.

Smith, David Eugene, and Jekuthiel Ginsburg. *A History of Mathematics in America before 1900.* Chicago: Mathematical Association of America, 1934.

Smith, James G. *The Development of Trust Companies in the United States.* New York: H. Holt, 1928.

Smith, Joseph Edward Adams. *The History of Pittsfield (Berkshire County) Massachusetts.* 2 vols. Boston: Lee and Shepard, 1869–76.

Smith, Merritt Roe. *Harpers Ferry Armory and the New Technology: The Challenge of Change.* Ithaca, N.Y.: Cornell University Press, 1977.

Sobel, Dava. *Longitude: The True Story of a Lone Genius Who Solved the Greatest Scientific Problem of His Time.* New York: Walker, 1995.

Solis-Cohen, Lita. *Maine Antique Digest: The Americana Chronicles.* Philadelphia: Running Press, 2004.

Soll, Jacob. *The Reckoning: Financial Accountability and the Rise and Fall of Nations.* New York: Basic Books, 2014.

Spanagel, David I. *DeWitt Clinton and Amos Eaton: Geology and Power in Early New York.* Baltimore: Johns Hopkins University Press, 2014.

Stearns, Raymond Phineas. *Science in the British Colonies of America*. Urbana: University of Illinois, 1970.

Stephens, H. Morse. *A History of the French Revolution*. 3 vols. New York: Charles Scribner's Sons, 1891.

Story, Ronald. *The Forging of an Aristocracy: Harvard and the Boston Upper Class, 1800–1870*. Middletown, Conn.: Wesleyan University Press, 1980.

Struik, Dirk J. *Yankee Science in the Making: Science and Engineering in New England from Colonial Times to the Civil War*. Boston: Little, Brown, 1948.

Swade, Doron. *The Cogwheel Brain: Charles Babbage and the Quest to Build the First Computer*. London: Little, Brown, 2000.

Tager, Jack. *Boston Riots: Three Centuries of Social Violence*. Boston: Northeastern University Press, 2001.

Tagney, Ronald N. *The World Turned Upside Down: Essex County during America's Turbulent Years, 1763–1790*. West Newbury, Mass.: Essex County History, 1989.

Tapley, Harriet. *Salem Imprints, 1768–1825*. Salem, Mass.: Essex Institute, 1927.

Taylor, Adrene G., and Daniel N. Joudrey. *The Organization of Information*. 3rd ed. Westport, Conn.: Libraries Unlimited, 2009.

Taylor, E. G. R. *The Mathematical Practitioners of Hanoverian England, 1714–1840*. London: Cambridge University Press for the Institute of Navigation, 1966.

Thornton, Tamara Plakins. *Cultivating Gentlemen: The Meaning of Country Life among the Boston Elite, 1785–1860*. New Haven, Conn.: Yale University Press, 1989.

———. *Handwriting in America: A Cultural History*. New Haven, Conn.: Yale University Press, 1996.

Timmons, Todd. *Mathematics in Nineteenth-Century America: The Bowditch Generation*. Boston: Docent Press, 2013.

Tolles, Bryant Franklin. *Architecture in Salem: An Illustrated Guide*. Salem, Mass.: Essex Institute, 1983.

Trowbridge, Charles Edward. *Old Shipmasters of Salem*. New York: G. P. Putnam's Sons, 1905.

Tyack, David B. *George Ticknor and the Boston Brahmins*. Cambridge, Mass.: Harvard University Press, 1967.

U.S. National Park Service. *Salem: Maritime Salem in the Age of Sail*. Washington, D.C.: National Park Service, 1987.

Vickers, Daniel, *Young Men and the Sea: Yankee Seafarers in the Age of Sail*. New Haven, Conn.: Yale University Press, 2005.

Walton, Clarence E. *The Three-Hundredth Anniversary of the Harvard College Library*. Cambridge, Mass.: Harvard College Library, 1939.

Warner, John Harley. *Against the Spirit of System: The French Impulse in Nineteenth-Century American Medicine*. Princeton, N.J.: Princeton University Press, 1998.

Weber, Max. *Economy and Society: An Outline of Interpretive Sociology*. Edited by Guenther Roth and Claus Wittich. 2 vols. 1922; Berkeley: University of California Press, 1978.

Whipple, George M. *History of the Salem Light Infantry from 1805 to 1890.*
Salem, Mass.: Essex Institute, 1890.

White, Gerald T. *A History of the Massachusetts Hospital Life Insurance Company.*
Cambridge, Mass.: Harvard University Press, 1955.

Whitehill, Walter Muir. *Boston: A Topographical History.* 2nd ed. Cambridge,
Mass.: Belknap Press of Harvard University Press, 1968.

———. *The East India Marine Society and the Peabody Museum of Salem:
A Sesquicentennial History.* Salem, Mass.: Peabody Museum, 1949.

Wiggin, Cynthia B. *Salem Athenaeum: A Short History.* Salem, Mass.: Forest
River Press, 1971.

Winsor, Justin, ed. *The Memorial History of Boston.* 4 vols. Boston: J. R. Osgood,
1880–81.

Winterer, Caroline. *The Culture of Classicism: Ancient Greece and Rome in American
Intellectual Life, 1780–1910.* Baltimore: Johns Hopkins University Press, 2002.

Wise, M. Norton, ed. *The Values of Precision.* Princeton, N.J.: Princeton University
Press, 1995.

Wolff, Katherine. *Culture Club: The Curious History of the Boston Athenaeum.*
Amherst: University of Massachusetts Press, 2009.

Wood, Gordon S. *Empire of Liberty: A History of the Early Republic, 1789–1815.*
New York: Oxford University Press, 2009.

———. *The Radicalism of the American Revolution.* New York: Knopf, 1992.

Wright, Robert E. *Corporation Nation.* Philadelphia: University of Pennsylvania
Press, 2014.

Wroth, Lawrence C. *The Colonial Printer.* Charlottesville: University of Press of
Virginia, 1964.

Yates, JoAnne. *Control through Communication: The Rise of System in American
Management.* Baltimore: Johns Hopkins University Press, 1989.

Yeo, Richard. *Encyclopaedic Visions: Scientific Dictionaries and Enlightenment Culture.*
Cambridge: Cambridge University Press, 2001.

Zabin, Serena R. *Dangerous Economies: Status and Commerce in Imperial New York.*
Philadelphia: University of Pennsylvania Press, 2009.

Zakim, Michael, and Gary J. Kornblith, eds. *Capitalism Takes Command: The Social
Transformation of Nineteenth-Century America.* Chicago: University of Chicago
Press, 2012.

DIGITAL SOURCES

American Academy of Arts and Sciences. *Academy Archives—Processed Collections
with Online Finding Aids.* https://www.amacad.org/contentu.aspx?i=316. 23 May
2015.

American Philosophical Society. Finding aid for "Joseph Roberts Philosophical and
Mathematical Papers, 1812–1814." http://amphilsoc.org/mole/view?docId=ead/
Mss.510.R54-ead.xml;query=%22joseph%20roberts%22;brand=default. 23 May
2015.

Gibson, Campbell. "Population of the 100 Largest Cities and Other Urban Places in the United States: 1790 to 1990." Population Division Working Paper no. 27. U.S. Bureau of the Census, June 1998. https://www.census.gov/population/www/ documentation/twps0027/twps0027.html. 23 May 2015.

Grafton, Anthony. "A Sketch Map of a Lost Continent: The Republic of Letters." *Republics of Letters* 1 (1 May 2009). http://rofl.stanford.edu/node/34. 6 June 2013.

Johnson, Phyllis Maloney. "No Adequate Remedy at Law: Equity in Massachusetts 1692–1877." Student Legal History Papers no. 2, 2012. http://digitalcommons.law .yale.edu/student_legal_history_papers/2. 23 May 2015.

Maryland Historical Society. "Guide to the Microfilm Edition of the David Bailie Warden Papers." http://www.mdhs.org/findingaid/warden-papers-1797- 1851-ms-871. 23 May 2015.

Massachusetts Historical Society. "Thomas Wren Ward Papers, Guide to the Collection. Biographical Sketch." http://www.masshist.org/findingaids/doc .cfm?fa=fa0013. 23 May 2015.

McCrossen, Alexis. "The Sound and Look of Time." *Common-place* 13 (Oct. 2012). http://www.common-place.org/vol-13/no-01/mccrossen/. 23 May 2015.

Phillips Library, Peabody Essex Museum. Finding aid for "Hale Family Papers, 1784–1915." http://phillipslibrarycollections.pem.org/cdm/ref/collection/ p15928coll1/id/2399. 23 May 2015.

Rickey, V. Frederick, and Amy Shell-Gellasch. "Mathematics Education at West Point: The First Hundred Years." *MathDL: The MAA Mathematical Sciences Digital Library*. http://web.archive.org/web/20080803041608/http://mathdl .maa.org/mathDL/46/?pa=content&sa=viewDocument&nodeId=2590. 23 May 2015.

Rosenthal, Caitlin. "Storybook-keepers: Narratives and Numbers in Nineteenth-Century America." *Common-place* 12 (Apr. 2012). http://www.common-place .org/vol-12/no-03/rosenthal/. 23 May 2015.

Schaffer, Simon. "The Apotheosis of Machine Intelligence." http://www.hrc.wmin .ac.uk/theory-babbagesintelligence11.html. 23 May 2015.

Stagg, Allison. "'All in My Eye!' James Akin and His Newburyport Social Caricatures." *Common-place* 10 (Jan. 2010). http://www.common-place.org/ vol-10/no-02/lessons/. 23 May 2015.

Weisstein, Eric. W. "Lissajous Curve." *Wolfram MathWorld*. http://mathworld .wolfram.com/LissajousCurve.html. 23 May 2015.

Zakim, Michael. "Bookkeeping as Ideology: Capitalist Knowledge in Nineteenth-Century America." *Common-place* 6 (Apr. 2006). http://www.common-place .org/vol-06/no-03/zakim/. 23 May 2015.

DISSERTATIONS

Ackerberg-Hastings, Amy K. "Mathematics Is a Gentleman's Art: Analysis and Synthesis in American College Geometry Teaching, 1790–1840." Ph.D. diss., Iowa State University, 2000.

Baranoff, Dalit. "Shaped by Risk: Fire Insurance in America 1790–1920." Ph.D. diss., Johns Hopkins University, 2003.

Cunsolo, Ronald Charles. "Nathaniel Bowditch: A Biographical Study of the Social Uses of Mathematics." Ph.D. diss., State University of New York, Stony Brook, 2001.

Farber, Hannah Atlee. "Underwritten States: Marine Insurance and the Making of Bodies Politic in America, 1622–1815." Ph.D. diss., University of California, Berkeley, 2014.

McKenzie, Matthew Gaston. "Vocational Science and the Politics of Independence: The Boston Marine Society, 1754–1812." Ph.D. diss., University of New Hampshire, 2003.

McKey, Richard H. "Elias Hasket Derby, Merchant of Salem, Massachusetts, 1739–1799." Ph.D. diss., Clark University, 1961.

Murphy, Emily Axford. "'To Keep Our Trading for Our Livelihood': The Derby Family of Salem, Massachusetts, and Their Rise to Power in the British Atlantic World." Ph.D. diss., Boston University, 2008.

Rosenthal, Caitlin Clare. "From Memory to Mastery: Accounting for Control in America, 1750–1880." Ph.D. diss., Harvard University, 2012.

Stone, Bruce Winchester. "The Role of the Learned Societies in the Growth of Scientific Boston, 1780–1848." Ph.D. diss., Boston University, 1974.

Van, Rachel Tamar. "Free Trade and Family Values: Kinship Networks and the Culture of Early American Capitalism." Ph.D. diss., Columbia University, 2011.

Whitney, Jeanne Ellen. "'An art that requires capital': Agriculture and mortgages in Worcester County, Massachusetts, 1790–1850." Ph.D. diss., University of Delaware, 1991.

BIOGRAPHICAL DICTIONARIES AND ENCYCLOPEDIAS

Ackerberg, Amy. "Peirce, Benjamin." *American National Biography Online*, Feb. 2000. http://www.anb.org/articles/13/13-01291.html. 23 May 2015.

Bedini, Silvio A. "Rittenhouse, David." *American National Biography Online*, Feb. 2000. http://www.anb.org/articles/13/13-01396.html. 23 May 2015.

Bell, Whitfield J. "Holyoke, Edward Augustus." *American National Biography Online*, Feb. 2000. http://www.anb.org/articles/12/12-00408.html. 23 May 2015.

"Bowditch, Nathaniel," s.v. *Dictionary of Scientific Biography*. 18 vols. New York: Scribner, 1981.

Nugent, Jim. "Bowditch, Nathaniel," *Dictionary of Unitarian and Universalist Biography*. http://uudb.org/articles/nathanielbowditch.html. 23 May 2015.

Brown, Richard D. "Bentley, William." *American National Biography Online*, Feb. 2000. http://www.anb.org/articles/08/08-00123.html. 23 May 2015.

Carlyle, E. I. "Simson, Robert (1687–1768)." Revised by Ian Tweddle. *Oxford Dictionary of National Biography*, Oxford University Press, 2004. http://www.oxforddnb.com.gate.lib.buffalo.edu/view/article/25606. 23 May 2015.

Fara, Patricia. "Desaguliers, John Theophilus (1683–1744)." *Oxford Dictionary of National Biography*, Oxford University Press, 2004. http://www.oxforddnb.com .gate.lib.buffalo.edu/view/article/7539. 23 May 2015.

Gale, Robert L. "Lowell, Francis Cabot." *American National Biography Online*, Feb. 2000. http://www.anb.org/articles/10/10-01023.html. 23 May 2015.

Gavine, David. "Mackay, Andrew (1758–1809)." *Oxford Dictionary of National Biography*, Oxford University Press, 2004. http://www.oxforddnb.com.gate.lib .buffalo.edu/view/article/17552. 23 May 2015.

Gillispie, Charles Coulton. "Pierre Simon Laplace." *Complete Dictionary of Scientific Biography* 15: 273–403. Gale Virtual Reference Library. http:// go.galegroup.com/ps/i.do?id=GALE%7CCX2830904079&v=2.1&u=sunybuff_ main&it=r&p=GVRL&sw=w&asid=bb974d8b31ee7fc1f3ec5203c21fe856. 23 May 2015.

Hogan, Edward R. "Adrain, Robert." *American National Biography Online*, Feb. 2000. http://www.anb.org/articles/13/13-00013.html. 23 May 2015.

Hollinger, Richard. "Rich, Obadiah." *American National Biography Online*, Feb. 2000. http://www.anb.org/articles/20/20-00855.html . 23 May 2015.

Hoogenboom, Olive. "Mussey, Reuben Diamond." *American National Biography Online*, Feb. 2000. http://www.anb.org/articles/12/12-00656.html. 23 May 2015.

Howe, Daniel Walker Howe. "Channing, William Ellery." *American National Biography Online*, Feb. 2000. http://www.anb.org/articles/08/08-00251.html. 23 May 2015.

Killick, J. R. "Ward, Thomas Wren." *American National Biography Online*, Feb. 2000. http://www.anb.org/articles/10/10-01715.html. 23 May 2015.

Mahon, John K. "Bomford, George." *American National Biography Online*, Feb. 2000. http://www.anb.org/articles/03/03-00045.html. 23 May 2015.

Morrison, Dane A. "Derby, Elias Hasket." *American National Biography Online*, Feb 2000. http://www.anb.org/articles/10/10-00407.html. 23 May 2015.

Ortiz, Eduardo L. "Mendoza y Ríos, Joseph de (1761–1816)." *Oxford Dictionary of National Biography*, Oxford University Press, 2004. http://www.oxforddnb.com .gate.lib.buffalo.edu/view/article/18557. 23 May 2015.

Patterson, Elizabeth C. "Somerville, Mary Fairfax Greig." *Complete Dictionary of Scientific Biography* 12: 251–55. Gale Virtual Reference Library. http:// go.galegroup.com/ps/i.do?id=GALE%7CCX2830904079&v=2.1&u=sunybuff_ main&it=r&p=GVRL&sw=w&asid=bb974d8b31ee7fc1f3ec5203c21fe85. 23 May 2015.

"Pickering, Henry," s.v. *Cyclopedia of American Literature.* 2 vols. Philadelphia: W. Rutter, 1875.

Ross, William G. "Parsons, Theophilus." *American National Biography Online*, Feb. 2000. http://www.anb.org/articles/11/11-00663.html. 23 May 2015.

Rothenberg, Mark. "Nathaniel Bowditch." *American National Biography Online*, Feb. 2000. http://www.anb.org/articles/13/13-00173.html. 23 May 2015.

Rothman, Patricia. "Ferguson, James (1710–1776)." *Oxford Dictionary of National Biography*, Oxford University Press, 2004. http://www.oxforddnb.com.gate.lib .buffalo.edu/view/article/9320. 23 May 2015.

Scott, E. L. "Kirwan, Richard (1733–1812)." *Oxford Dictionary of National Biography*, Oxford University Press, 2004. http://www.oxforddnb.com.gate.lib.buffalo.edu/view/article/15686. 23 May 2015.

Webb, R. K. "Enfield, William (1741–1797)." *Oxford Dictionary of National Biography*, Oxford University Press, 2004. http://www.oxforddnb.com.gate.lib.buffalo.edu/view/article/8804. 23 May 2015.

ARTICLES AND BOOK CHAPTERS

Agnew, Jean-Christophe. "Afterword: Anonymous History." In *Capitalism Takes Command: The Social Transformation of Nineteenth-Century America*, edited by Michael Zakim and Gary J. Kornblith, 277–84. Chicago: University of Chicago Press, 2012.

Alborn, Timothy L. "A Calculating Profession: Victorian Actuaries among the Statisticians." *Science in Context* 7 (Autumn 1994): 433–68.

Allen, D. E. "The Rich Family in Britain: An Appendix to Hispano-American Biography." *Archives of Natural History* 18 (Oct. 1991): 375–78.

Ashworth, William J. "The Calculating Eye: Baily, Herschel, Babbage and the Business of Astronomy." *British Journal of the History of Science* 27 (Dec. 1994): 409–41.

———. "England and the Machinery of Reason, 1780–1830." *Canadian Journal of History* 35 (Apr. 2000): 1–36.

———. "Memory, Efficiency, and Symbolic Analysis: Charles Babbage, John Herschel, and the Industrial Mind." *Isis* 87 (Dec. 1996): 629–53.

Bailyn, Bernard. "Why Kirkland Failed." In *Glimpses of the Harvard Past*, by Bernard Bailyn, Donald Fleming, Oscar Handlin, and Stephan Thernstrom, 19–44. Cambridge, Mass.: Harvard University Press, 1986.

Bartlett, Dwight K., III. "Nathaniel Ingersoll Bowditch." *Actuary* 13 (June 1979): 1, 4–5, 8.

Baxter, W. T. "Accounting in Colonial America." In *Studies in the History of Accounting*, edited by A. C. Littleton and D. S. Yamey, 272–87. Homewood, Ill.: Richard D. Irwin, 1956.

Belknap, Henry Wyckoff. "Simon Forrester of Salem and His Descendants." *Essex Institute Historical Collections* 71 (Jan. 1935): 17–64.

Blackmar, Elizabeth. "Inheriting Property and Debt: From Family Security to Corporate Accumulation." In *Capitalism Takes Command: The Social Transformation of Nineteenth-Century America*, edited by Michael Zakim and Gary J. Kornblith, 93–117. Chicago: University of Chicago Press, 2012.

Bond, William Cranch. "History and Description of the Observatory." *Annals of the Astronomical Observatory at Harvard* 1 (1856), i–cxci.

Booth, Robert. "Salem as Enterprise Zone." In *Salem: Place, Myth, and Memory*, edited by Dane Anthony Morrison and Nancy Lusignan Schultz, 63–90. Boston: Northeastern University Press, 2004.

Bosse, David. "Osgood Carleton, Mathematical Practitioner of Boston." *Proceedings of the Massachusetts Historical Society*, 3rd ser., 107 (1995): 141–64.

Bowditch, Harold. "The Buildings Associated with Nathaniel Bowditch (1773–1838)." *Essex Institute Historical Collections* 79 (July 1943): 205–21.

Brooke, John Headley. "Science and Religion." In *The Cambridge History of Science,* Vol. 4, *Eighteenth-Century Science,* edited by Roy Porter, 741–61. Cambridge: Cambridge University Press, 2003.

Brown, Chandos Michael. "A Natural History of the Gloucester Sea Serpent: Knowledge, Power, and the Culture of Science in Antebellum America." *American Quarterly* 42 (Sept. 1990): 402–36.

[Brown, Sanborn C.] "The Rumford Fund Record" *Proceedings of the American Academy of Arts and Sciences* 78 (Feb. 1950): 96–132.

Bruegel, Martin. "'Time That Can Be Relied Upon': The Evolution of Time Consciousness in the Mid-Hudson Valley." *Journal of Social History* 28 (Spring 1995): 547–64.

Burstyn, Harold L. "The Salem Philosophical Library: Its History and Importance for American Science." *Essex Institute Historical Collections* 96 (July 1960): 169–206.

Carruthers, Bruce G., and Wendy Nelson Espeland. "Accounting for Rationality: Double-Entry Bookkeeping and the Rhetoric of Economic Rationality." *American Journal of Sociology* 97 (July 1991): 31–69.

Chipley, Louise. "The Enlightened Library of William Bentley." *Essex Institute Historical Collections* 122 (Jan. 1986): 2–29.

Clarfield, Gerard H. "Salem's Great Inoculation Controversy, 1773–74." *Essex Institute Historical Collections* 106 (Oct. 1970): 277–96.

Coolidge, J. L. "Robert Adrain and the Beginnings of American Mathematics." *American Mathematical Monthly* 33 (Feb. 1926): 61–76.

———. "Three Hundred Years of Mathematics at Harvard." *American Mathematical Monthly* 90 (Feb. 1943): 347–56.

Cormack, William S. "Legitimate Authority in Revolution and War: The French Navy in the West Indies, 1789–1793." *International History Review* 18 (Feb. 1996): 15–17.

Costa, Shelley. "The 'Ladies' Diary': Gender, Mathematics, and Civil Society in Early-Eighteenth-Century England." *Osiris,* 2nd ser., 17 (2002): 49–73.

Craik, Alex D. "James Ivory's Last Papers on the 'Figure of the Earth' (with Biographical Additions)." *Notes and Records of the Royal Society of London* 56 (May 2002): 187–204.

Croarken, Mary. "Astronomical Labourers: Maskelyne's Assistants at the Royal Observatory, Greenwich, 1765–1811." *Notes and Records of the Royal Society of London* 57 (Sept. 2003): 285–98.

———. "Mary Edwards: Computing for a Living in 18th-Century England." *IEEE Annals of the History of Computing* 25 (Oct.–Dec. 2003): 9–15.

———. "Tabulating the Heavens: Computing the *Nautical Almanac* in 18th-Century England." *IEEE Annals of the History of Computing* 25 (July 2003): 48–61.

Crosland, Maurice. "Relationships between the Royal Society and the Académie des Sciences in the Late Eighteenth Century." *Notes and Records of the Royal Society* 59 (22 Jan. 2005): 25–34.

Crothers, A. Glenn. "Commercial Risk and Capital Formation in Early America: Virginia Merchants and the Rise of American Marine Insurance, 1750–1815." *Business History Review* 78 (2004): 607–34.

Curran, William J. "The Struggle for Equity Jurisdiction in Massachusetts." *Boston University Law Review* 31 (June 1951): 269–96.

Curtis, Charles P. "Manners and Customs of the Boston Trustee." *Trusts and Estates Bar Proceedings* 97 (Oct. 1958): 902–4.

Daniels, George H. "The Process of Professionalization in American Science: The Emergent Period, 1820–1860." *Isis* 58 (Summer 1967): 151–66.

Daston, Lorraine. "Enlightenment Calculations." *Critical Inquiry* 21 (Autumn 1994): 182–202.

———. "Fear and Loathing of the Imagination in Science." *Daedalus* 127 (Winter 1998): 73–95.

———. "The Ideal and Reality of the Republic of Letters in the Enlightenment." *Science in Context* 4 (Autumn 1991): 367–86.

———. "Objectivity and the Escape from Perspective." *Social Studies of Science* 22 (Nov. 1992): 597–618.

———. "Taking Note(s)." *Isis* 95 (Sept. 2004): 443–48.

Daston, Lorraine, and Peter Galison. "The Image of Objectivity." *Representations* (Autumn 1992): 81–128.

Davis, Lance E. "Stock Ownership in the Early New England Textile Industry." *Business History Review* 32 (Summer 1958): 204–22.

De Beer, G. R. "The Relations between Fellows of the Royal Society and French Men of Science When France and Britain Were at War." *Notes and Records of the Royal Society* 9 (May 1952): 244–99.

Ditz, Toby L. "Secret Selves, Credible Personas: The Problematics of Trust and Public Display in the Writing of Eighteenth-Century Philadelphia Merchants." In *Possible Pasts: Becoming Colonial in Early America*, edited by Robert Blair St. George, 219–42. Ithaca, N.Y.: Cornell University Press, 2000.

———. "Shipwrecked; or, Masculinity Imperiled: Mercantile Representations of Failure and the Gendered Self in Eighteenth-Century Philadelphia." *Journal of American History* 81 (June 1994): 51–80.

Dodd, E. Merrick. "The Evolution of Limited Liability in Massachusetts." *Proceedings of the Massachusetts Historical Society*, 3rd ser., 68 (Oct. 1944–May 1947): 228–56.

Dodge, Ernest S. "Captain Collectors: The Influence of New England Shipping on the Study of Polynesian Material Culture." *Essex Institute Historical Collections* 81 (Jan. 1945): 27–34.

———. "The Contributions to Exploration of the Salem East India Marine Society." *American Neptune* 25 (July 1965): 176–88.

Dupree, Hunter A. "The Measuring Behavior of Americans." In *Nineteenth-Century American Science: A Reappraisal*, edited by George H. Daniels, 22–37. Evanston, Ill.: Northwestern University Press, 1972.

Eck, Reimer. "Die Amerikanische Kolonie in Göttingen." In *Amerika und Deutschland: Ambivalente Begegnungen*, edited by Frank Kelleter and Wolfgang Knöbl, 224–41. Göttingen: Wallstein, 2006.

Edney, Matthew H. "Cartographic Culture and Nationalism in the Early United States." *Journal of Historical Geography* 20 (Oct. 1994): 384–95.

"Extracts from the Grenada Handbook." *Caribbean Quarterly* 20 (Mar. 1974): 60–68.

Field, Peter S. "The Birth of Secular High Culture: The *Monthly Anthology and Boston Review* and Its Critics." *Journal of the Early Republic* 17 (Winter 1997): 575–609.

Forman, Sidney. "The United States Military Philosophical Society, 1802–1813: Scientia in Bello Pax." *William and Mary Quarterly* 2 (July 1945): 273–85.

Fowler, William M., Jr. "Marine Insurance in Boston: The Early Years of the Boston Marine Insurance Company, 1799–1807." In *Entrepreneurs: The Boston Business Community, 1700–1850*, edited by Conrad Edick Wright and Katheryn P. Viens, 151–79. Boston: Massachusetts Historical Society, 1997.

Fox, Robert. "Laplacian Physics." In *Companion to the History of Modern Science*, edited by R. C. Olby, G. N. Cantor, J. R. R. Christie, and M. J. S. Hodge, 278–94. London: Routledge, 1990.

Fraser, Craig. "Mathematics." In *The Cambridge History of Science*, Vol. 4, *Eighteenth-Century Science*, edited by Roy Porter, 305–27. Cambridge: Cambridge University Press, 2003.

Friedman, Lawrence. "The Dynastic Trust." *Yale Law Journal* 73 (Mar. 1964): 547–92.

García-Herrera, R., C. Wilkinson, F. B. Koek, M. R. Prieto, N. Calvo, and E. Hernández. "Description and General Background to Ships' Logbooks as a Source of Climatic Data." *Climatic Change* 73 (2005): 13–36.

Geib, Susan. "Landscape and Faction: Spatial Transformation in William Bentley's Salem." *Essex Institute Historical Collections* 113 (July 1977): 163–80.

Genuth, Sara Schechner. "From Heaven's Alarm to Public Appeal: Comets and the Rise of Astronomy at Harvard." In *Science at Harvard University: Historical Perspectives*, edited by Clark A. Elliott and Margaret W. Rossiter, 28–54. Bethlehem, Pa.: Lehigh University Press, 1992.

Goloboy, Jennifer L. "Business Friendships and Individualism in a Mercantile Class of Citizens in Charleston." In *Class Matters: Early North America and the Atlantic World*, edited by Simon Middleton and Billy G. Smith, 109–22. Philadelphia: University of Pennsylvania Press, 2008.

Grabiner, Judith V. "Newton, Maclaurin, and the Authority of Mathematics." *Mathematical Association of America Monthly* 111 (Dec 2004): 841–51.

Grattan-Guinness, I[vor]. "Before Bowditch: Henry Harte's Translation of Books 1 and 2 of Laplace's 'Mécanique Céleste.'" *NTM Schriftenreihe für Geschichte der Naturwissenschaften, Technik und Medizin* 24 (1987): 53–55.

———. "The Computation Factory: de Prony's Project for Making Tables in the 1790s." In *The History of Mathematical Tables: From Sumer to Spreadsheets*, edited by M. Campbell-Kelly, M. Croarken, R. Flood, and E. Robson, 105–22. Oxford: Oxford University Press, 2003.

Gray, Edward. "The William Grays in Salem in 1797." *Essex Institute Historical Collections* 56 (Apr. 1920): 145–47.

Green, James. "Subscription Libraries and Commercial Circulating Libraries in Colonial Philadelphia and New York." In *Institutions of Reading: The Social Life of Libraries in the United States*, edited by Thomas Augst and Kenneth Carpenter, 53–71. Amherst: University of Massachusetts Press, 2007.

Greene, John C. "Science, Learning, and Utility: Patterns of Organization in the Early Republic." In *The Pursuit of Knowledge in the Early American Republic: American Scientific and Learned Societies from Colonial Times to the Civil War*, edited by Alexandra Oleson and Sanborn C. Brown, 1–20. Baltimore: Johns Hopkins University Press, 1976.

Guinnane, Timothy W., Naomi Lamoreaux, and Jean-Laurent Rosenthal. "Putting the Corporation in Its Place." *Enterprise and Society* 8 (Sept. 2007): 687–729.

Hacking, Ian. "Biopower and the Avalanche of Printed Numbers." *Humanities in Society* 5 (Summer/Fall 1982): 279–95.

Haeger, John Denis. "Eastern Financiers and Institutional Change: The Origins of the New York Life Insurance and Trust Company and the Ohio Life Insurance and Trust Company." *Journal of Economic History* 39 (Mar. 1979): 259–73.

Hahn, Roger. "Laplace and the Mechanistic Universe." In *God and Nature: Historical Essays on the Encounter between Christianity and Science*, edited by David C. Linberg and Ronald L. Numbers, 256–76. Berkeley: University of California Press, 1986.

———. "Laplace and the Vanishing Role of God in the Physical Universe." In *The Analytic Spirit: Essays in the History of Science in Honor of Henry Guerlac*, edited by Henry Guerlac and Harry Woolf, 85–95. Ithaca, N.Y.: Cornell University Press, 1981.

———. "The Laplacean View of Calculation." In *The Quantifying Spirit in the Eighteenth Century*, edited by Tore J. Frängsmyr, J. L. Heilbron, and Robin E. Rider, 363–80. Berkeley: University of California Press, 1990.

Hall, Peter Dobkin. "What the Merchants Did with Their Money: Charitable and Testamentary Trusts in Massachusetts, 1780–1880." In *Entrepreneurs: The Boston Business Community, 1700–1850*, edited by Conrad Edick Wright and Katheryn P. Viens, 365–421. Boston: Massachusetts Historical Society, 1997.

Hall, Peter Dobkin, and George E. Marcus. "Why Should Men Leave Great Fortunes to Their Children? Class, Dynasty, and Inheritance in America." In *Inheritance and Wealth in America*, edited by Robert K. Miller Jr. and Stephen J. McNamee, 139–71. New York: Plenum, 1998.

Heindel, R. Heathcote. "Americans and the Royal Astronomical Society." *Science*, n.s., 87 (24 June 1938): 575–76.

Hilt, Eric. "Rogue Finance: The Life and Fire Insurance Company and the Panic of 1826." *Business History Review* 83 (Spring 2009): 87–112.

Hogan, Edward R. "George Baron and the *Mathematical Correspondent*." *Historia Mathematica* 3 (Nov. 1976): 403–15.

Holdsworth, Deryck W. "The Counting-House Library: Creating Mercantile Knowledge in the Age of Sail." In *Geographies of the Book*, edited by Miles Ogborn and Charles W. J. Withers, 133–56. London: Ashgate, 2010.

Hoskin, Keith W., and Richard H. Macve. "The Genesis of Accountability: The West Point Connections." *Accounting, Organizations and Society* 13 (Jan. 1988): 37–73.

Howse, Derek. "The Lunar-Distance Method of Measuring Longitude." In *The Quest for Longitude*, 2nd ed., edited by William J. H. Andrewes, 150–61. Cambridge, Mass.: Collection of Historical Scientific Instruments, Harvard University, 1998.

Jaffee, David. "The Village Enlightenment in New England, 1760–1820." *William and Mary Quarterly* 47 (July 1990): 327–46.

James, Mary Ann. "Engineering an Environment for Change: Bigelow, Peirce, and Early Nineteenth-Century Practical Change at Harvard." In *Science at Harvard University: Historical Perspectives*, edited by Clark A. Elliott and Margaret W. Rossiter, 66–75. Bethlehem, Pa.: Lehigh University Press, 1992.

Jenkins, Lawrence Waters. "The Marine Society at Salem in New England." *Essex Institute Historical Collections* 86 (July 1940): 199–220.

John, Richard R. "Governmental Institutions as Agents of Change: Rethinking American Political Development in the Early Republic, 1787–1835." *Studies in Political Development* 11 (Fall 1997): 347–80.

Johnston, Patricia. "Depicting Geographic Knowledge: Mariners' Drawings from Salem, Massachusetts." In *New Views of New England: Studies in Material and Visual Culture, 1680–1830*, edited by Georgia B. Barnhill and Martha J. McNamara, 17–46. Boston: Colonial Society of Massachusetts, 2012.

———. "Global Knowledge in the Early Republic: The East India Marine Society's 'Curiosities' Museum." In *East-West Interchanges in American Art: "A Long and Tumultuous Relationship*," edited by Cynthia Mills, Lee Glazer, and Amelia Goerlitz, 68–79. Washington, D.C.: Smithsonian Institution Scholarly Press, 2012.

Jones, Russell M. "American Doctors and the Parisian Medical World, 1830–1840." *Bulletin of the History of Medicine* 47 (Jan. 1973): 40–65.

Kafka, Ben. "Paperwork: The State of the Discipline." *Book History* 12 (2009): 340–53.

Katznelson, Ira. "Flexible Capacity: The Military and Early American Statebuilding." In *Shaped by War and Trade: International Influences on American Political Development*, edited by Ira Katznelson and Martin Shefter, 82–110. Princeton, N.J.: Princeton University Press, 2002.

Kerber, Linda K. "Science in the Early Republic: The Society for the Study of Natural Philosophy." *William and Mary Quarterly*, 3rd. ser., 29 (Apr. 1972): 263–80.

Kingston, Christopher. "Marine Insurance in Britain and America, 1720–1844: A Comparative Institutional Analysis." *Journal of Economic History* 67 (June 2007): 379–409.

———. "Marine Insurance in Philadelphia during the Quasi-War with France, 1795–1801." *Journal of Economic History* 71 (Mar. 2011): 162–84.

Knight, Betsy. "Prisoner Exchange and Parole in the American Revolution." *William and Mary Quarterly* 48 (Apr. 1991): 201–22.

Knight, D. M. "The Scientist as Sage." *Studies in Romanticism* 6 (Winter 1967): 65–88.

Kornblith, Gary J. "The Rise of the Mechanic Interest and the Campaign to Develop Manufacturing in Salem, 1815–1830." *Essex Institute Historical Collections* 121 (Jan. 1985): 44–65.

Labaree, Benjamin W. "The Making of an Empire: Boston and Essex County, 1790–1850." In *Entrepreneurs: The Boston Business Community, 1700–1850*, edited by Conrad Edick Wright and Katheryn P. Viens, 343–63. Boston: Massachusetts Historical Society, 1997.

Labbie, Edith. "Who Was Edward Little?" *Lewiston Journal*, 19 Sept. 1981.

Lamoreaux, Naomi R. "The Partnership Form of Organization: Its Popularity in Nineteenth-Century Boston." In *Entrepreneurs: The Boston Business Community, 1700–1850*, edited by Conrad Edick Wright and Katheryn P. Viens, 269–95. Boston: Massachusetts Historical Society, 1997.

———. "Rethinking the Transition to Capitalism in the Early American Northeast." *Journal of American History* 90 (Sept. 2003): 437–61.

Lauer, Josh. "From Rumor to Written Record: Credit Reporting and the Invention of Financial Identity in Nineteenth-Century America." *Technology and Culture* 49 (Apr. 2008): 301–24.

Leavitt, William. "History of the Essex Lodge of Freemasons." *Essex Institute Historical Collections* 3 (Feb., Apr., June, Aug., Oct., Dec. 1861): 37–47, 84–95, 121–33, 174–86, 207–18, 253–72.

Lewin, Christopher, and Margaet de Valois. "History of Actuarial Tables." In *The History of Mathematical Tables: From Sumer to Spreadsheets*, edited by M. Campbell-Kelly, M. Croarken, R. Flood, and E. Robson, 79–104. Oxford: Oxford University Press, 2003.

Lindgren, James M. "'That Every Mariner May Possess the History of the World': A Cabinet from the East India Marine Society of Salem." *New England Quarterly* 68 (June 1995): 179–205.

Lipartito, Kenneth. "Introduction: Crossing Corporate Boundaries." In *Constructing Corporate America: History, Politics, Culture*, edited by Kenneth Lipartito and David B. Sicilia, 1–26. Oxford: Oxford University Press, 2004.

———. "The Utopian Corporation." In *Constructing Corporate America: History, Politics, Culture*, edited by Kenneth Lipartito and David B. Sicilia, 94–119. Oxford: Oxford University Press, 2004.

Little, Nina Fletcher. "The Cartoons of James Akin upon Liverpool Ware." *Old Time New England* (Jan. 1938): 103–8.

Livermore, Seward W. "Early Commercial and Consular Relations with the East Indies." *Pacific Historical Review* 15 (March 1946): 31–58.

Lovering, Joseph. "The Mécanique Céleste of Laplace, and Its Translation, with a Commentary by Bowditch." *Proceedings of the American Academy of Arts and Sciences* 24 (May 1888–May 1889): 185–201.

Lovett, Robert W. "William Croswell: Eccentric Scholar." *New England Quarterly* 38 (Mar. 1965): 35–53.

Lubar, Steven. "Managerial Structure and Technological Style: The Textile Mills of Lowell, Massachusetts." *Business and Economic History*, 2nd ser., 13 (1984): 20–30.

Lucier, Paul. "The Professional and the Scientist in Nineteenth-Century America." *Isis* 100 (Dec. 2009): 699–732.

Luskey, Brian P. "'What Is My Prospects?': The Contours of Mercantile Apprenticeship, Ambition, and Advancement in the Early American Economy." *Business History Review* 78 (Winter 2004): 665–702.

Maier, Pauline. "The Debate over Incorporations: Massachusetts in the Early Republic." In *Massachusetts and the New Nation*, edited by Conrad Edick Wright, 73–111. Boston: Massachusetts Historical Society, 1992.

———. "The Revolutionary Origins of the American Corporation." *William and Mary Quarterly*, 3rd ser. 50 (Jan. 1993): 51–84.

Malcolm, Noel. "Thomas Harrison and His 'Ark of Studies': An Episode in the History of the Organization of Knowledge." *Seventeenth Century* 19 (Oct. 2004): 196–232.

Marché, Jordan D., II. "Restoring a 'Public Standard' to Accuracy: Authority, Social Class, and Utility in the American Almanac Controversy, 1814–1818." *Journal of the Early Republic* 18 (Winter 1998): 693–710.

Mathias, Peter. "Risk, Credit and Kinship in Early Modern Enterprise." In *The Early Modern Atlantic Economy*, edited by John H. McCusker and Kenneth Morgan, 15–35. Cambridge: Cambridge University Press, 2001.

McClellan, James, III. "Scientific Institutions and the Organization of Science." In *The Cambridge History of Science*, Vol. 4, *Eighteenth-Century Science*, edited by Roy Porter, 87–106. Cambridge: Cambridge University Press, 2003.

McCusker, John J. "The Demise of Distance: The Business Press and the Origins of the Information Revolution in the Early Modern Atlantic World." *American Historical Review* 110 (Apr. 2005): 295–321.

McGill, Meredith L. "Copyright." In *A History of the Book in America*, edited by David D. Hall, Vol. 2, *An Extensive Republic: Print, Culture, and Society in the New Nation, 1790–1840*, edited by Robert A. Gross and Mary Kelley, 198–210. Chapel Hill: University of North Carolina Press, 2010.

Minter, Catherine. "Academic Library Reform and the Ideal of the Librarian in England, France, and Germany in the Long Nineteenth Century." *Library and Information History* 29 (Mar. 2013): 19–37.

Moats, Sandy. "The Limits of 'Good Feelings': Partisan Healing and Political Futures during James Monroe's Boston Visit of 1817." *Proceedings of the American Antiquarian Society* 118 (Apr. 2008): 155–91.

Montgomery, James W., Jr., and W. Porter Kellam. "Mathematical Backwoodsman of the West: Charles Francis McCay." *Georgia Historical Quarterly* 67 (Summer 1983): 206–14.

Moorhead, E. J. "Sketches of Early North American Actuaries." *Transactions of the Society of Actuaries* 36 (1984): 351–97.

Moriarty, G. Andrews. "Additional Records Relating to the English Ancestry of the Bowditch Family of Salem, Mass." *New England Historical and Genealogical Register* 82 (July 1928): 303–12.

———. "Genealogical Research in England: Bowditch." *New England Historical and Genealogical Register* 72 (July 1918): 223–40.

———. "Genealogical Research in England II: Bowditch." *New England Historical and Genealogical Register* 78 (Apr.1924): 144–46.

———. "The Turner Family of Salem." *Essex Institute Historical Collections* 48 (July 1912): 263–74.

Morris, Richard J. "Redefining the Economic Elite in Salem, Massachusetts, 1759–99: A Tale of Evolution, Not Revolution." *New England Quarterly* 73 (Dec. 2000): 603–24.

———. "Social Change, Republican Rhetoric, and the American Revolution: The Case of Salem, Massachusetts." *Journal of Social History* 31 (Winter 1997): 419–33.

Morrison, Dane Anthony. "Salem as Citizen of the World." In *Salem: Place, Myth, and Memory*, edited by Dane Anthony Morrison and Nancy Lusignan Schultz, 106–28. Boston: Northeastern University Press, 2004.

Munsterberg, Margaret. "The Bowditch Collection in the Boston Public Library." *Isis* 34 (Autumn 1942): 140–42.

Newmyer, R. Kent. "Justice Joseph Story's Doctrine of 'Public and Private Corporations' and the Rise of the American Business Corporation." *Depaul Law Review* 25 (Summer 1976): 825–41.

Nikitin, Marc. "The Birth of a Modern Public Sector Accounting System in France and Britain and the Influence of Count Mollien." *Accounting History* 6 (May 2001): 75–101.

Nissenbaum, Stephen. "New England as Region and Nation." In *All over the Map: Rethinking American Regions*, edited by Edward L. Ayers, Patricia Nelson Limerick, Stephen Nissenbaum, and Peter S. Onuf, 38–61. Baltimore: Johns Hopkins University Press, 1995.

O'Connell, Charles F., Jr. "The Corps of Engineers and the Rise of Modern Management, 1827–1856." In *Military Enterprise and Technological Change*, edited by Merritt Roe Smith, 87–116. Cambridge, Mass.: Massachusetts Institute of Technology Press, 1985.

Ogborn, Miles, and Charles W. J. Withers. "Travel, Trade, and Empire: Knowing Other Places, 1680–1800." In *A Concise Companion to the Restoration and Eighteenth Century*, edited by Cynthia Wall, 14–36. Malden, Mass.: Blackwell, 2005.

Perley, Sidney. "Salem in 1700: No. 27." *Essex Antiquarian* 11 (Apr. 1907): 66–75.

Phillips, James Duncan. "East India Voyages of Salem Vessels before 1800." *Essex Institute Historical Collections* 79 (Apr., July, Oct. 1943): 117–32; 222–45, 331–65.

———. "Hamilton Hall, the Home of the Federalists." *Essex Institute Historical Collections* 83 (Oct. 1947): 295–307.

———. "Political Fights and Local Squabbles in Salem, 1800–1806." *Essex Institute Historical Collections* 82 (Jan. 1946): 1–11.

Porter, Dorothy Burnet. "The Remonds of Salem, Massachusetts: A Nineteenth-Century Family Revisited." *Proceedings of the American Antiquarian Society* 95 (Oct. 1985): 259–95.

Porter, Theodore M. "The Culture of Quantification and the History of Public Reason." *Journal of the History of Economic Thought* 26 (June 2004): 165–77.

———. "Objectivity and Authority: How French Engineers Reduced Public Utility to Numbers." *Poetics Today* 12 (Summer 1991): 245–65.

———. "Objectivity as Standardization: The Rhetoric of Impersonality in Measurement, Statistics, and Cost-Benefit Analysis." *Annals of Scholarship* 9 (1992): 19–59.

———. "Precision and Trust: Early Victorian Insurance and the Politics of Calculation." In *The Values of Precision*, edited by Norton M. Wise, 173–97. Princeton, N.J.: Princeton University Press, 1995.

———. "Quantification and the Accounting Ideal in Science." *Social Studies of Science* 22 (Nov. 1992): 633–65.

Pycior, Helena M. "British Synthetic vs. French Analytic Styles of Algebra in the Early American Republic." In *Ideas and Their Reception*. Vol. 1 of *The History of Modern Mathematics*, edited by David E. Rowe and John McCleary, 125–54. Boston: Academic Press, 1989–94.

Raven, James. "Social Libraries and Library Societies in Eighteenth-Century North America." In *Institutions of Reading: The Social Life of Libraries in the United States*, edited by Thomas Augst and Kenneth Carpenter, 24–52. Amherst: University of Massachusetts Press, 2007.

Reiser, Stanley Joel. "Creating Form out of Mass: The Development of the Medical Record." In *Transformation and Tradition in the Sciences: Essays in Honour of I. Bernard Cohen*, edited by Everett Mendelsohn, 303–16. Cambridge: Cambridge University Press, 2003.

Reingold, Nathan. "Definitions and Speculations: The Professionalization of Science in America in the Nineteenth Century." In *The Pursuit of Knowledge in the Early American Republic: American Scientific and Learned Societies from Colonial Times to the Civil War*, edited by Alexandra Oleson and Sanborn C. Brown, 33–69. Baltimore: Johns Hopkins University Press, 1976.

Richards, Joan L. "The Geometrical Tradition: Mathematics, Space, and Reason in the Nineteenth Century." In *The Cambridge History of Science*, Vol. 5, *The Modern Physical and Mathematical Sciences*, edited by Mary Jo Nye, 449–67. Cambridge: Cambridge University Press, 2002.

———. "God, Truth, and Mathematics in Nineteenth Century England." In *The Invention of Physical Science: Intersections of Mathematics, Theology, and Natural Philosophy since the Seventeenth Century: Essays in Honor of Erwin N. Hiebert*, edited by Mary Jo Nye et al., 51–78. Dordrecht: Kluwer, 1992.

———. "Rigor and Clarity: Foundations of Mathematics in France and England, 1800–1840." *Science in Context* 4 (Autumn 1991): 297–319.

Robbins, James H. "The Impact of the First American Party System on Salem Politics." *Essex Institute Historical Collections* 107 (July 1971): 254–67.

Rockman, Seth. "What Makes the History of Capitalism Newsworthy?" *Journal of the Early Republic* 34 (Fall 2014): 439–66.

Rosenstein, George M., Jr. "The Best Method. American Calculus Textbooks of the Nineteenth Century." In *A Century of Mathematics in America*, Part 3, edited by Peter Duren, 77–109. Providence, R.I.: American Mathematical Society, 1988.

Rothenberg, Winifred Barr. "The Invention of American Capitalism: The Economy of New England in the Federal Period." In *Engines of Enterprise: An Economic History of New England*, edited by Peter Temin, 69–108. Cambridge, Mass.: Harvard University Press, 2000.

Rubenstein, Lewis C. "James Akin in Newburyport." *Essex Institute Historical Collections* 102, no. 4 (Oct. 1966): 285–98.

Saxe, Stephen O. "Job Printing in Lower Manhattan." In *Billheads and Broadsides: Job Printing in the 19th-Century Seaport*, 7–14. New York: South Street Seaport Museum, 1985.

Scarry, Ginna Johnson. "Robert Bowne and His Company: The Evolution of a Seaport Printer." In *Billheads and Broadsides: Job Printing in the 19th-Century Seaport*, 29–36. New York: South Street Seaport Museum, 1985.

Schaffer, Simon. "Astronomers Mark Time: Discipline and the Personal Equation." *Science in Context* 2 (Mar. 1988): 115–45.

———. "Babbage's Intelligence: Calculating Engines and the Factory System." *Critical Inquiry* 21 (Autumn 1994): 203–27.

———. "The Bombay Case: Astronomers, Instrument Makers and the East India Company." *Journal for the History of Astronomy* 43 (May 2012): 151–80.

———. "Genius in Romantic Natural Philosophy." In *Romanticism and the Sciences*, edited by Andrew Cunningham and Nicholas Jardine, 82–98. Cambridge: Cambridge University Press, 1990.

———. "Newtonianism." In *Companion to the History of Modern Science*, edited by R. C. Olby, G. N. Cantor, J. R. R. Christie, and M. J. S. Hodge, 610–26. London: Routledge, 1990.

Sellstedt, Laurentius G. "Roswell Willson Haskins." *Publications of the Buffalo Historical Society* 4 (1896): 257–84.

Shapin, Steven. "The Image of the Man of Science." In *The Cambridge History of Science*, Vol. 4, *Eighteenth-Century Science*, edited by Roy Porter, 159–83. Cambridge: Cambridge University Press, 2003.

Sheidley, Harlow W. "'The Old Fabrick': The Massachusetts Conservative Elite and the Constitutional Convention of 1820–1821." *Proceedings of the Massachusetts Historical Society*, 3rd ser., 103 (1991): 114–37.

———. "The Politics of Honor: The Massachusetts Conservative Elite and the Trials of Amalgamation, 1824–1829." In *Entrepreneurs: The Boston Business Community, 1700–1850*, edited by Conrad Edick Wright and Katheryn P. Viens, 297–323. Boston: Massachusetts Historical Society, 1997.

Sibum, H. Otto. "Narrating by Numbers: Keeping an Account of Early 19th Century Laboratory Experiences." In *Reworking the Bench: Research Notebooks in the History of Science*, edited by Frederic L. Holmes, Jürgen Renn, and Hans-Jörg Rheinberger, 141–58. Dordrecht: Kluwer, 2003.

Simons, Lao G. "The Adoption of the Method of Fluxions in American Schools." *Scripta Mathematica* 4 (1936): 207–19.

———. "The Influence of French Mathematicians at the End of the Eighteenth Century upon the Teaching of Mathematics in American Colleges." *Isis* 15 (Feb. 1931): 104–23.

Sinclair, Bruce. "Americans Abroad: Science and Cultural Nationalism in the Early Nineteenth Century." In *The Sciences in the American Context: New Perspectives*, edited by Nathan Reingold, 33–53. Washington, D.C.: Smithsonian Institution Press, 1979.

"A Sketch of the First Church in Salem, Mass., and Its Ministers." *Magazine of New England History* 1 (Jan. 1891): 28–37.

Sklansky, Jeffrey. "The Elusive Sovereign: New Intellectual and Social Histories of Capitalism." *Modern Intellectual History* 9 (Apr. 2012): 233–48.

Sleeswijk, Ann Wegener. "Social Ties and Commercial Transactions of an Eighteenth-Century French Merchant." In *Entrepreneurs and Entrepreneurship in Early Modern Times: Merchants and Industrialists within the Orbit of the Dutch Staple Market*, edited by Clé Lesger and Leo Noordegraaf, 203–12. Den Haag, Neth.: Stichting Hollandse Historische Reeks, 1995.

Smith, Merritt Roe. "Army Ordnance and the 'American System' of Manufacturing." In *Military Enterprise and Technological Change*, edited by Merritt Roe Smith, 39–86. Cambridge, Mass.: Massachusetts Institute of Technology Press, 1985.

———. "Military Entrepreneurship." In *Yankee Enterprise: The Rise of the American System of Manufactures*, edited by Otto Mayr and Robert C. Post, 63–102. Washington, D.C.: Smithsonian Institution, 1981.

Smith, Philip C. F. "The Salem Marine Society, 1766–1966." *American Neptune* 26 (Oct. 1966): 272–79.

Soll, Jacob. "From Note-Taking to Data Banks: Personal and Institutional Information Management in Early Modern Europe." *Intellectual History Review* 20 (Aug. 2010): 355–75.

Stewart, Larry. "Other Centres of Calculation, or, Where the Royal Society Didn't Count: Commerce, Coffee-houses and Natural Philosophy in Early Modern London." *British Journal for the History of Science* 32 (June 1999): 133–53.

Stimson, Alan. "The Longitude Problem: The Navigator's Story." In *The Quest for Longitude*, edited by William J. H. Andrewes, 72–84. Cambridge, Mass.: Collection of Historical Scientific Instruments, Harvard University, 1996.

Story, Ronald. "Class and Culture in Boston: The Athenaeum, 1807–1860." *American Quarterly* 27 (May 1975): 178–99.

Swade, Doron. "The 'Unerring Certainty of Mechanical Agency': Machines and Table Making in the Nineteenth Century." In *The History of Mathematical Tables: From Sumer to Spreadsheets*, edited by M. Campbell-Kelly, M. Croarken, R. Flood, and E. Robson, 154–76. Oxford: Oxford University Press, 2003.

te Heesen, Anke. "Accounting for the Natural World." In *Colonial Botany: Science, Commerce and Politics in the Early Modern World*, edited by Londa L. Schiebinger and Claudia Swan, 237–51. Philadelphia: University of Pennsylvania Press, 2005.

Tenner, Edward. "From Slip to Chip: How Evolving Techniques of Information Gathering, Storage, and Retrieval Have Shaped the Way We Do Mental Work." *Microform Review* 21 (Jan. 1992): 123–27.

Thomas, Keith. "Numeracy in Early Modern England." *Transactions of the Royal Historical Society*, 5th ser., 37 (1987): 103–32.

Thornton, Tamara Plakins "'A Great Machine' or a 'Beast of Prey': A Boston Corporation and Its Rural Debtors in an Age of Capitalist Transformation." *Journal of the Early Republic* 27 (Winter 2007): 567–97.

———. "The 'Intelligent Mariner': Nathaniel Bowditch, the Science of Navigation, and the Art of Upward Mobility in the Maritime World." *New England Quarterly* 79 (Dec. 2006): 609–35.

Topham, Jonathan R. "Science, Print, and Crossing Borders: Importing French Science Books into Britain, 1789–1815." In *Geographies of Nineteenth-Century Science*, edited by David N. Livingstone and Charles W. J. Withers, 311–44. Chicago: University of Chicago Press, 2011.

Vickers, Daniel. "Competency and Competition: Economic Culture in Early America." *William and Mary Quarterly* 47 (Jan. 1990): 3–29.

Wach, Howard M. "'Expansive Intellect and Moral Agency': Public Culture in Antebellum Boston." *Proceedings of the Massachusetts Historical Society*, 3rd ser., 107 (1995): 30–56.

Wade, Arthur P. "A Military Offspring of the American Philosophical Society." *Military Affairs* 38 (Oct. 1974): 103–7.

Walsh, Anthony A. "The American Tour of Dr. Spurzheim." *Journal of the History of Medicine and Allied Sciences* 27 (Apr. 1972): 187–205.

Warner, Deborah Jean. "Astronomers, Artisans, and Longitude." In *Transport Technology and Social Change: Symposium 1979*, 131–40. Stockholm: Tekniska Museum, 1980.

———. "Astronomy in Antebellum America." In *The Sciences in the American Context: New Perspectives*, edited by Nathan Reingold, 55–75. Washington, D.C.: Smithsonian Institution Press, 1979.

———. "At the Sign of the Quadrant—the Navigational Instrument Business in America to the Civil War." *American Neptune* 46 (Sept. 1986): 258–63.

———. "Davis Quadrants in America." *Rittenhouse* 3 (Nov. 1988): 23–40.

———. "What Is a Scientific Instrument, When Did It Become One, and Why?" *British Journal for the History of Science* 23 (Mar. 1990): 83–93.

Warren, J. Collins. "The Collection of the Boston Phrenological Society—a Retrospect." *Annals of Medical History* 3 (Spring 1921): 1–11.

Weil, François. "Capitalism and Industrialization in New England, 1815–1845." *Journal of American History* 84 (Mar. 1998): 1334–54.

Wheatland, Henry. "Historical Sketch of the Philosophical Library at Salem, with Notes." *Essex Institute Historical Collections* 4 (Aug., Oct. 1862): 175–81, 271–82.

Whitehill, Walter Muir. "Early Learned Societies in Boston and Vicinity." In *The Pursuit of Knowledge in the Early American Republic: American Scientific and Learned Societies from Colonial Times to the Civil War*, edited by Alexandra Oleson and Sanborn C. Brown, 151–73. Baltimore: Johns Hopkins University Press, 1976.

Wiggin, Cynthia B. "The Kirwan Collection at the Salem Athenaeum, with a Biographical Sketch of Richard Kirwan and History of the Acquisition of the Collection." *Essex Institute Historical Collections* 102 (Jan. 1966): 26–36.

———. "Vignettes of Library History: No. 6. Salem Athenaeum." *Journal of Library History* 3 (July 1968): 257–60.

Williams, Michael R. "Babbage and Bowditch: A Transatlantic Connection." *Annals of the History of Computing* 9 (July–Sept. 1987): 283–90.

Williamson, Joseph, comp. "Autobiography of Hon. Nathan Read." *New England Historical and Genealogical Register* 50 (Oct. 1896): 434–36.

———. "Record of the Bowditch Family." *New England Historical and Genealogical Register* 50 (Oct. 1896): 436–48.

Wilson, Curtis. "Astronomy and Cosmology." In *The Cambridge History of Science*, Vol. 4, *Eighteenth-Century Science*, edited by Roy Porter, 328–53. Cambridge: Cambridge University Press, 2003.

Wise, M. Norton. Introduction to *The Values of Precision*, edited by Norton M. Wise, 3–13. Princeton, N.J.: Princeton University Press, 1995.

Woodruff, Edwin H. "Chancery in Massachusetts." *Law Quarterly Review* 5 (1889): 370–86.

Wright, Robert E., and Christopher Kingston. "Corporate Insurers in Antebellum America." *Business History Review* 86 (Autumn 2012): 447–76.

Wyatt-Brown, Bertram. "God and Dun & Bradstreet, 1841–1851." *Business History Review* 40 (Winter 1966): 432–50.

Yates, JoAnne. "From Press Book and Pigeonhole to Vertical Filing: Revolution in Storage and Access Systems for Correspondence." *Journal of Business Communication* 19 (July 1982): 5–26.

Yeo, Richard. "John Locke's 'New Method' of Common-Placing: Managing Memory and Information." *Eighteenth-Century Thought* 2 (2004): 1–38.

Zakim, Michael. "The Business Clerk as Social Revolutionary; or, a Labor History of the Nonproducing Classes." *Journal of the Early Republic* 26 (Winter 2006): 563–603.

Zakim, Michael, and Gary J. Kornblith. "Introduction: An American Revolutionary Tradition." In *Capitalism Takes Command: The Social Transformation of Nineteenth-Century America*, edited by Michael Zakim and Gary J. Kornblith, 1–12. Chicago: University of Chicago Press, 2012.

Zitarelli, David E. "The Bicentennial of American Mathematics Journals." *College Mathematics Journal* 36 (Jan. 2005): 2–15.

Index

Note: the initials "NB" refer to Nathaniel Bowditch.